D0035943

NICARAGUA

ELIZABETH PERKINS

HONDURAS

Catacamas

Siguatepeque
Comayagua
Campamento
Juticalpa

TEGUCIGALPA
Danlí
Jalapa
Rio Coca

EL SALVADOR

Santa María
NUEVA SEGOVIA

Ocotal
Wiwilí
San José de Bocay

Nacaome
Somoto
MADRIZ

San Miguel
El Espino
ESTELÍ

Cordillera

Choluteca
San Francisco del Norte
La Concordia

Golfo de Fonseca
Reserva Biológica Río Negro
Estelí
Jinotega
Lago de Apanás

Potosí
Guasaule
Somotillo
Cordillera Dariense

Reserva Natural Volcán Cosigüina
Estero Real
El Sauce
Matagalpa

El Cacao
24
Sébaco

Reserva Natural Padre Ramos
Estero Padre Ramos
CHINANDEGA
50
Cordillera los Maribios
26
LEÓN
CA1

Chinandega
12
Boaco
Sierra

Corinto
León
Lago Xolotlán
7

Poneloya
26
El Tamagás

PACIFIC OCEAN
MANAGUA
Tipitapa

12
MASAYA
Puerto Díaz

El Tránsito
Masaya
Granada

MANAGUA
GRANADA

Masachapa
Jinotepe
Nandaime
Isla de Zapatera

Casares
CARAZO
CA1

Rivas
Isla de Ometepe

RIVAS
16

San Juan del Sur
Peñas Blancas

La Cruz

0   50 mi
0   50 km

© AVALON TRAVEL

NICARAGUA

Río Coco

Reserva Natural
Cabo-Viejo-Tela Sulamas

Laguna
Bismuna

Waspam

Bismuna
Tara

Reserva Natural
Bosawas

REGIÓN
AUTÓNOMA
DEL ATLÁNTICO
NORTE

Santa Marta

Miskitos
Cays

Auastara

Laguna
Pahra

Reserva Natural
Cerro Cola Blanca

Tuapí

JINOTEGA

Bonanza

Susun

Kukalaya

Yulú

Puerto Cabezas
(Bilwi)

Isabella

Rosita

Laguna
Karatá

Siuna

COSTA DE MISKITOS

Laguna
Wouhnta

El Empalme

Prinzapolka

Makantaka

Río Grande de Matagalpa

Guerrera Cays

Río Tuma

MATAGALPA

Barra de Río Grande

Bela Vista

Reserva

Natural

Tyara
Cays

REGIÓN AUTÓNOMA
DEL ATLÁNTICO SUR

Cerro Wawashan

Bahía de
Perlas

Tasbapauni

BOACO

Pearl Cays

Amerrisque

CHONTALES

Pearl Lagoon

Little Corn
Island

Juigalpa

La
Gateada

7

Rama

Escondido

Tierra
Dorada

Big Corn
Island

Bluefields

El Guasimo

Talolinga

Reserva

Bahía de
Bluefields

25

El Almendra

Verdun

Natural

José Benito Escobar
Cerro Silva

Palos Ralos

Reserva
Natural
Punta Gorda

Caribbean

Lago
Cocibolca

Bahía de
Punta Gorda

Sea

Solentiname
Archipelago

RÍO
SAN JUAN

San
Carlos

Río

Upala

Los Chiles

San

Reserva Biológica
Indio Maíz

Bahía de
San Juan del Norte

San Juan
de Nicaragua

COSTA RICA

Juan

Contents

DISCOVER
Nicaragua

At first glance, Nicaragua is brilliant green trees and brightly colored flowers, birdcalls and rich coffee, colonial architecture, and monkeys swinging from branches. Spend some time here, and you'll hear the rhythmic pounding of hands forming wet cornmeal into tortillas and notice the scent of plantains frying in hot oil. Take a closer look, and you'll find community. Families sit in front of their houses after a hard day's work, chatting with their neighbors while children play in the street. Strangers look out for each other on public buses. Folks organize to change problems in their neighborhoods.

For travelers, Nicaragua is a gem hidden in the rough. Tropical rainforests and soaring volcanoes offer endless opportunities for hiking and exploring. Sandy beaches with shimmering waters allow for languid beachcombing and swimming, while surfers flock to the shores for some of the best waves in the region. Charming cities have thriving dining and nightlife scenes and flourishing café cultures set amidst grand cathedrals and centuries-old Spanish colonial architecture.

A culture of collectivism has emerged in response to centuries of injustice.

Clockwise from top left: exotic fruit from the Caribbean coast; road in Estelí; chilies in a market; fishing boats on the Pacific coast; colorful bottles; street in Granada.

Nicaragua has a tumultuous and battered past, but the Nicaraguan people have learned to depend on their own resourcefulness to get by. Today, you will see this spirit of self-reliance in agricultural cooperatives, artisan collectives, and community organizations—including a burgeoning industry of community tourism—across the country.

Nicaragua is a place to slow down and step into a more relaxed rhythm. Pack a little flexibility, good humor, and, ideally, some basic Spanish. Whether soaking up some sun while sipping rum on the beach, sharing coffee with a rural family, or speeding down a river on a motorboat, you'll find Nicaragua to be just as its Ministry of Tourism describes it: "unspoiled, uncommon, and unforgettable."

Clockwise from top left: swimmers in Gigante Bay; building in Granada; hand-rolled cigars; blooming tree in San Juan del Sur.

Planning Your Trip

Where to Go

Managua

Although you won't find the capital at the top of any tourist destination lists, the city is **full of history.** Managua is also the country's **transportation hub.** If you find yourself passing through on a weekend, make sure to check out the vibrant **nightlife.**

Granada and Masaya

Less than an hour south of Managua are the **colonial cities** of Granada and Masaya. Granada is the country's tourist hub, while smaller Masaya offers a more laid-back vibe. Both have developed international **café cultures** and **nightlife.** Between the two lies the **Laguna de Apoyo,** the perfect spot for a relaxing respite of swimming, kayaking, and sharing a beer with fellow travelers. Outside Masaya is one of the country's many active volcanoes, **Volcán Masaya. Volcán Mombacho,** a coffee farm and cloud forest, appeals to hikers and coffee enthusiasts.

La Isla de Ometepe and San Juan del Sur

One of Nicaragua's most sought-after destinations, Ometepe Island offers a little bit of everything, with options for every kind of traveler. Its **twin volcanoes** offer **hiking treks** full of howler monkeys, tropical plants, and waterfalls. There are **beaches** and lagoons for swimming, and plenty of **restaurants** that cater to tourists. San Juan del Sur on the Pacific coast is popular with foreigners. In addition to jaw-dropping sunsets, it offers a raging **nightlife.**

La Catedral de León

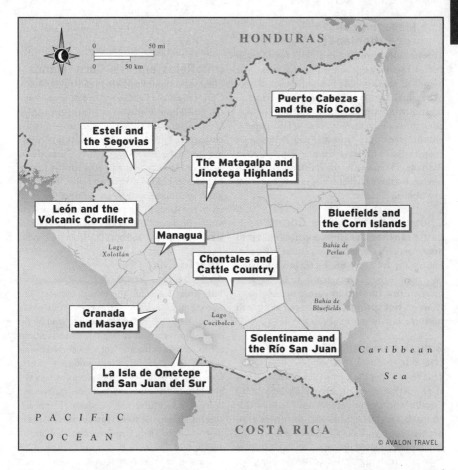

Tola is generally calmer and less full of tourists. Try **surfing, fishing,** or **sailing** on one of the region's many beaches.

León and the Volcanic Cordillera

León and Chinandega are **historical colonial cities** with vibrant urban life. Lots of bars and restaurants offer international food and serve clientele from all over the world. This is also the **hottest region of the country.** Escape the heat on the nearby Pacific coast where you can **surf** and observe **sea turtles.** This is the region that made **volcano boarding** a sport (on **Cerro Negro**). There are many **remote protected areas** throughout the Cosigüina peninsula.

Estelí and the Segovias

This **mountainous northern region** boasts an impressive landscape. Try **locally grown coffee, tobacco,** and **corn products.** Take a dip in the Estanzuela waterfall in the **Tisey Nature Reserve.** Meet other travelers and shop for mementos in the historical city of Estelí. From there you can head north towards the Honduran border and rock climb in the **Somoto Canyon,** or take a guided swimming tour.

The Matagalpa and Jinotega Highlands

This **heavily forested region** is full of small **coffee farming communities** that open their homes to visitors. The hilly, laid-back city of Matagalpa has impressive views of the surrounding **mountains,** and makes a great base for traveling through the area. It's easy to find popular **woven products** from the nearby women's cooperative in **El Chile.** Head north to **Peñas Blancas,** the mouth of the enormous biological reserve, **Bosawás,** where you can hike and swim in a tropical paradise.

Chontales and Cattle Country

Cattle ranches and farms populate this **rural area.** You can sample delicious cheese in **Boaco,** known for its dairy products. Most tourists pass right through on their way to El Rama, so there are **few foreign travelers** in this region. However, **hot springs, horseback riding,** and **hiking** await the more curious traveler.

Solentiname and the Río San Juan

This river along the Costa Rican border starts at the Atlantic coast, emptying into **Lake Cocibolca.** It's not easy to move around this **remote** area. The beautiful **Solentiname archipelago** in Lake Cocibolca is worth the trip for impressive landscapes and an up-close look at a thriving **artist colony.** Along the river, you'll come across **biological reserves,** lagoons, and the four-centuries-old fort at **El Castillo.**

Bluefields and the Corn Islands

The Autonomous Region of the South Caribbean Coast (RACCS) might as well be a different country. You'll hear **English** and a variety of **native languages** spoken here. Experience **Creole culture** and cuisine in Bluefields before checking out the nearby **Pearl Cays** or **Greenfields reserve.** The Corn Islands offer **diving** and, of course, clear blue **Caribbean** water. There's no highway connecting the Pacific side of the country to the Atlantic. You can take a plane straight to Bluefields or Corn Island from Managua, or take a 10-hour bus and boat trip from the capital.

Puerto Cabezas and the Río Coco

This area is not for the casual traveler. The Autonomous Region of the North Caribbean Coast (RACCN) is heavily marginalized by the central government in Managua. Inhabitants are mostly **Miskito** and not accustomed to foreigners. However, **Bilwi** (also known as Puerto Cabezas) has basic oceanfront services where you hire **tour guides** to take you to nearby rivers and beaches. Adventurers can wander to their hearts content among the **riverside communities** of the **Río Coco.** There is no road directly connecting the RACCN to the Pacific nor to the RACCS to the south. From Managua, the region is accessed by plane or by a very arduous bus journey.

Know Before You Go

When to Go

December-February is generally the coolest, least rainy time to visit. **August-October** is cool as well, but it's more likely to rain. You'll also find more Europeans and fewer North Americans during these months. During **March-May,** the hottest, driest months, dust is inescapable. **June** and **July** are hot and rainy, followed by hurricane season **September-November,** when you're likely to encounter torrential downpours most afternoons.

Invierno (winter) refers to Nicaragua's rainy season (May-November). *Verano* (summer) refers to the dry season (December-April). Due to global warming, it's now unlikely to encounter rain that lasts for days on the Pacific side of the

Public transportation is frequent and consistent.

Monkeys populate the forests of Nicaragua.

country, but it still may rain heavily for hours (or just briefly shower) every afternoon.

There are some events worth planning your time around. Anywhere you go during **Semana Santa** (the week leading up to Easter), expect big crowds and higher prices. Spanish-speakers (and learners) should make a point to attend Granada's **Poetry Festival** at the end of February. If you're looking for a party, San Juan del Sur's **Earthship Pitaya Festival** in early March is a must. Catch the **Palo de Mayo** festival on the Atlantic coast throughout May, and the **Crab Soup Festival** on the Corn Islands August 27-28. Masaya's **Agüisotes** festival on the penultimate Friday in October draws large crowds. In early December, Nicaragua celebrates **La Purísima.**

Passports and Visas

Every traveler to Nicaragua must have a **passport**

valid for at least six months following the date of entry. A **visa** is required only for citizens of the following countries: Afghanistan, Albania, Bosnia-Herzegovina, Colombia, Cuba, Haiti, India, Iran, Iraq, Jordan, Lebanon, Libya, Nepal, Pakistan, People's Republic of China, People's Republic of Korea, Somalia, Sri Lanka, Vietnam, and Yugoslavia. Everyone else is automatically given a tourist visa good for three months.

Vaccinations

A certificate of vaccination against **yellow fever** is **required** for all travelers over one year of age and arriving from affected areas.

Be sure your **tetanus, diphtheria, measles, mumps, rubella,** and **polio** vaccines are up-to-date. Protection against **hepatitis A** and **typhoid fever** is also recommended for all travelers.

The Best of Nicaragua

Nicaragua has a popular, carved-out tourist route based on its principal, most developed attractions. The beaten path is made up of the Granada-Ometepe-San Juan del Sur circuit, which can be done in about a week. Save another week for volcano-boarding near León, wildlife-viewing in Estelí, and relaxing on remote Big Corn Island. Wherever you head, Granada is a good place to ease into things, with colorful surroundings, wonderful cuisine, and a central location.

Day 1

Arrive in **Managua** in the early afternoon, and settle into your hotel. Visit **La Loma de Tiscapa** and have dinner in the city. Spend the evening listening to live music at a local bar or concert venue.

Day 2

In the morning, hop a bus to **Granada.** Choose a day trip to **Volcán Masaya, Mombacho,** or the **Laguna de Apoyo,** then head back to your hotel in Granada.

Day 3

Head south for **San Jorge** and catch a late morning ferry to **La Isla de Ometepe.** Spend the afternoon lounging on Playa Santo Domingo, or hiking trails in Charco Verde. Sleep on La Isla de Ometepe.

Day 4

Get up early for an all-day climb up a **volcano,** or visit **Finca Magdalena** for a coffee tour before heading south for a tour of the **Río Istián** or a shorter hike up to the **Cascada San Ramón.** Spend another night on La Isla de Ometepe.

Day 5

Catch a morning ferry to the mainland and make

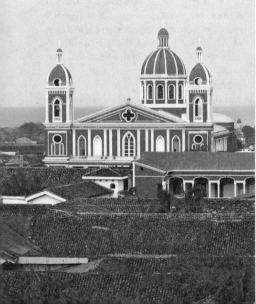

Granada's cathedral

Catedral de León

panga fishing boats, Brig Bay, Big Corn Island

your way to the Pacific coast. Head for **San Juan del Sur** for an international ambience, or if you prefer peace and quiet, choose a **Tola** beach. Spend your afternoon **surfing** or **sunbathing.** If the **turtles** are nesting, plan a trip for the next day. Sleep in a hotel in San Juan del Sur or one of the Tola beaches.

Day 6
Keep on enjoying the sun and surf, or make your way north to **León.** Spend the afternoon exploring the city and the evening enjoying the **nightlife.** Check into a hotel in León for the night.

Day 7
Try out **volcano boarding** on Cerro Negro or hike **Volcán Telica.** If you still have energy in

the afternoon, catch a bus to **Estelí** and stay the night in the city.

Days 8-9
In the morning, head to **La Garnacha** or **Miraflor Nature Reserve.** Take a wildlife tour and get to know your hosts who will house you for the next couple of days. Visit a nearby waterfall.

Day 10
Catch a bus back to Managua for your afternoon flight to **Big Corn Island.** Spend the evening relaxing under the stars.

Days 11-14
Spend languid days beachcombing, diving, or snorkeling on either **Big Corn** or **Little Corn.**

Hiking the Ring of Fire

No trip to Nicaragua is complete without visiting at least one volcano. Dormant and active peaks are scattered up and down the Pacific half of the country. The **Léon region** is the easiest base for volcano enthusiasts who want to hike. With a couple exceptions, most of these hikes are long and challenging, requiring an **experienced guide.** Using local guides is a great way to contribute to the local economy. From north to south:

Volcán Concepción

- **Cosigüina:** The southern shore of the Fonseca Gulf, Cosigüina's vegetation-carpeted crater lip boasts crazy views. Rest at the edge of the crater, or continue on, descending to the crater lake within (page 180).

- **San Cristóbal:** As the highest peak in the country (1,745 m), this is the granddaddy of volcano hikes. It's long but the grade is moderate (page 180).

- **Telica:** Rising out of a beautiful valley, this volcano makes for a moderate hike with impressive views. If you're lucky, or the light is low, you may get a glimpse of lava simmering within the smoking crater (page 180).

- **Cerro Negro:** The climb up is short, but the hot, rugged descent is even shorter careening down black sands on a modified snowboard (page 180).

- **Momotombo:** This peak rises up from the shores of Lago Xolotlán. It's climbable, but not easy, especially when you hit the loose volcanic gravel that comprises the upper half of the cone (page 180).

- **Masaya:** This is one of the most visibly active volcanoes in the country. From one of its craters, you may glimpse incandescent rock and magma. The park contains several short hiking trails through lava formations and scrubby vegetation (page 89).

- **Mombacho:** Every bit of cool, misty, cloud forest higher than 850 meters above sea level is officially protected as a nature reserve comprising a rich, concentrated island of flora and fauna. The longest trail (3 hours) is a loop with several difficult climbs that lead to a breathtaking viewpoint (page 80).

- **Concepción:** Large parts of the hike are treeless, rocky scrambles. As you reach the volcanic cone, the wind buffets you until you reach the crater lip, where the volcano's hot, sulphurous gas pours out—a stark contrast to its dormant neighbor on Ometepe (page 114).

- **Maderas:** Ometepe's more accessible option is still no easy feat. You'll be rewarded at the top with a forested lagoon within the crater (page 114).

The Great Green North

Nicaragua north of Managua is offbeat and less visited, giving the creative traveler lots of opportunities. If you're into hiking and mountains, you have a plethora of options in the northern part of the country. **Pueblo-hopping** through the Segovia mountains and Jinotega highlands, and visiting sites along the **Ruta de Café** will immerse you in an authentic and sublime world you won't soon forget. Each town has a swimming hole, local hike, or archaeological site that will beckon you farther. Alternate legs include passing through San Juan de Limay and the back roads to León; or from Ocotal, going east to Jalapa. This sample itinerary will give you a taste for what to expect.

Day 1

Arrive in Managua and head straight to **Matagalpa.** Enjoy your evening in the city.

Days 2-3

Relocate to a coffee farm. Choose from a chalet-style property at **Selva Negra,** a rustic retreat at **La Fundadora,** or a homestay near **San Ramón.**

Days 4-5

Make your way east to **El Macizo de Peñas Blancas** and explore the forest and waterfalls in the nature reserve. Book a room and meals through the local co-op GARBO (Guardianes del Bosque) or the Centro de Entendimiento con la Naturaleza (CEN) to spend these two nights at the base of the massif.

Day 6

Go west to the misty mountain city of **Jinotega** or a nearby farm. Hike to **La Peña de la Cruz** or take a **wildlife tour.** Spend the night in Jinotega or at a nearby eco-lodge.

horses grazing in Somoto Canyon

river in Somoto Canyon

Day 7

Head back to Managua from Jinotega.

Extend Your Stay

If you have more time to explore, hop a bus to **Estelí** instead of returning to Managua on Day 7. Spend your afternoon exploring the city's murals and spend the night in town.

DAY 8

Day trip north to **Somoto** where you'll tour the canyon from the water. Catch the last bus back to Estelí, where you'll spend the night.

DAY 9

Get on a bus bound for **El Tisey.** Swim all afternoon in the Estanzuela waterfall and visit Don Alberto's rock carving museum. Stay in **La Garnacha.**

DAYS 10-11

Back to Estelí, where you'll transfer to the cloud-covered **Miraflor Nature Reserve** for the next couple of nights. Or, head north to check into a hotel in **Ocotal** for some easy day trips to coffee farms and communities known for their crafts.

DAY 12

Back to the Managua heat.

Down the Río San Juan

The watery **"Golden Route"** through southern Lake Cocibolca and down the Río San Juan is unquestionably worth a visit, especially the photogenic fort and river town at El Castillo. Once you reach San Carlos, public boat transportation is regular and cheap. To explore this region, plan on spending about a week, though choosing just one of these places for a three-day trip is feasible.

Day 1

Fly from Managua to **San Carlos.** Catch a boat taxi to **Solentiname,** where you can find a place to sleep for the next few nights. If you go by bus, stay the night in San Carlos and leave the next morning.

Days 2-3

This archipelago is best explored by **kayak.** Don't miss **San Fernando's sunset** or the **artist colony on Mancarrón.** Sleep in Solentiname.

Day 4

Charter a boat direct to **Papaturro,** or get an early *panga* back to **San Carlos,** and another to **Los Guatuzos.** Settle in to your lodgings in Los Guatuzos and pull on some boots for a night tour.

Day 5

Explore Los Guatuzos in the daylight, or get up early and make your way back to San Carlos to get a boat upstream to **Boca de Sábalos,** where you can find a bed for the night.

Day 6

Take a **chocolate tour** at **Buena Vista** in the morning and catch an afternoon boat east to **El Castillo,** where you'll spend the next two nights.

Day 7 and Beyond

Visit the **old Spanish fort** and **Mariposario El Castillo,** a nearby butterfly reserve.

The next day, get a boat back to **San Carlos** for a flight to **Managua,** or with an extra couple of days, head out to the historic Creole, indigenous, and mestizo settlement of **San Juan de Nicaragua,** then fly back to Managua from there.

Spanish defensive fort in El Castillo

sunset in Solentiname

Adrenaline Rush

Athletes and extreme sports fanatics can easily meet their needs in Nicaragua.

Biking

Rent a bike in **Granada** or **Masaya** and take a back road to the **Laguna de Apoyo** (1.5-2 hours). The dirt roads are steady uphill treks that become steep towards the top of the dormant volcano. Once you're over the rounded crater lip, coast all the way down to the lake where you can jump in and cool off.

Kayaking

Kayaking through the sometimes smooth, sometimes choppy water to **Las Isletas,** off the coast of Granada, can be as languid or as vigorous as you like. Rent directly from the boat owners at the Marina Cocibolca, or set up a kayak tour. The enormous **Laguna de Apoyo,** just outside Masaya, is another excellent spot for kayaking. Kayaks are included for guest use in most hotels and hostels.

Scuba Diving, Snorkeling, and Paddle Boarding

Scuba dive and snorkel on the **Corn Islands,** and don't miss **Blowing Rock,** a reef formation home to a stunning variety of underwater life. Try a guided paddleboarding trip to Blowing Rock for snorkeling.

Rock Climbing

Spend a day rock climbing, rappelling, swimming, and hiking in the **Somoto Canyon**. The climbing route established by Namancambre Tours is accessible for all skill levels.

Volcano Boarding

Near the northern city of León, get your afternoon adrenaline rush volcano boarding over the black ash of **Cerro Negro.**

White-Water Rafting

Enjoy northern Nicaragua's natural beauty

rock climbing in the Somoto Canynon

kayaks at Laguna de Apoyo

surfer near Popoyo

The secret is out: Nicaragua is the new frontier for world-class waves. Swells from South Pacific storms pound Central America from June through September. The shape of Nicaragua's long, isolated shoreline helps form these pushes of water into perfect overhead barrels. Most surfers head straight to San Juan del Sur, where lake-generated offshore breezes blow year-round, and many surf shops offer shuttles to nearby beaches, as well as lessons for beginners. There are plenty of breaks to explore up and down the Pacific coastline. Do your research at **Nicaragua Surf Report** (www.nicaraguasurfreport.com) and **NicaSurfing** (www.nicasurfing.com).

BEST SURF SPOTS

- **Popoyo:** You can't come to Nicaragua without hitting the Popoyo break on Playa Sardinas. It's great for all skill levels but can get crowded. Near Popoyo is the Outer Reef break, which has huge waves dependent on the swell coming in. Base yourself in Guasacate for easy access (page 157).

- **Santana:** Find consistent but crowded waves at Playa Santana. Stay in Jiquilite (page 156).

- **Colorado:** Get barreled at this private beach near San Juan del Sur. Be warned: it gets crowded. The Panga Drops break is at the north end of the beach. Stay at Hacienda Iguana (page 156).

- **San Diego:** This surf spot is in front of the Gran Pacifica Resort complex, one hour from Managua. You can park in the community outside of the resort, and walk five minutes to the beach (page 55).

- **El Astillero:** The beach in this small fishing village isn't frequently visited. Stay in El Astillero or drive up from Guasacate and park your 4WD right in front of the wave (page 160).

- **Hermosa:** This mile-long beach south of San Juan del Sur doesn't get too crowded. Rent a boat to access the best waves (page 148).

SURF CAMPS

If you're looking to explore the north coast, **Rise Up Surf** (www.riseupsurf.com) in Chinandega offers fully guided surf tour packages to Nicaragua's central and northwest Pacific coast. Women surfers check out **ChicaBrava** (www.chicabrava.com) based in San Juan del Sur, the first all-girls surf camp in the country. The second is pro-surfer Holly Beck's **Surf With Amigas** (www.surfwithamigas.com) on the northern coast.

The best way to get to know Nicaragua is to spend time with Nicaraguans, and small farming communities across the country have created local tourism options for foreigners who want a deeper experience. You'll feel right at home sharing hot tortillas and beans over freshly roasted coffee. Supporting these tourism cooperatives keeps money in the local economy and promotes sustainable socio-economic growth, allowing communities to maintain their identities and allowing people to stay with their families instead of migrating to a city or to another country for jobs. Here are a few top-notch co-ops that have mastered the tourism trade:

- **Finca Magdalena:** This coffee farm on Volcán Maderas on Ometepe Island was once a wealthy hacienda. Now it's shared between a couple dozen families who offer lodging in the century-old plantation house and surrounding cabins. Learn about coffee and hike to the lagoon at the volcano's peak (page 121).

- **La Fundadora:** The Eco Albergue is nestled in the mountains between Matagalpa and Jinotega on the edge of the Datanlí el Diablo Nature Reserve. Hike to the nearby reserve and take a tour of the co-op's coffee crop. At night, snuggle around a bonfire under the stars (page 255).

- **La Garnacha:** This small rural community is located in Reserva El Tisey in the mountains of Estelí. Barring rain, you'll have some of the most impressive mountain views in the country, and may even get a good, long look at the Milky Way. Sleep in rustic wood cabins. Tour the agricultural cooperative, visit local artisans, and consult a natural medicine specialist. It's well worth the trip for the fantastic sunsets, cool air, and smell of pine (page 212).

coffee ready for roasting at a cooperative

- **Telica-Rota Tourism Cooperative:** Spend the night at the base of the smoldering Volcán Telica near León. Take a tour by foot or on horseback to the impressive crater where you can sometimes catch a glimpse of lava. Hike to the surrounding nature reserve and tour a bat cave (page 177).

- **UCA-San Ramón:** How better to learn about coffee than from the folks who grow it? Families in participating cooperatives offer lodging in their homes and tours of the coffee process. The nature in these highlands makes for beautiful hikes (page 247).

between paddling through class III rapids on the **Río Tuma** with Matagalpa Tours.

Zip Lining

Take in jaw-dropping views of the Pacific coast and La Isla de Ometepe while zip lining through the trees outside of **San Juan del Sur.** On Ometepe, try a canopy tour through the trees between the island's two volcanoes at **Reserva Charco Verde.** In Managua, zip line over open water at **Laguna de Tiscapa.**

Managua

Look for ★ to find recommended
sights, activities, dining, and lodging.

Highlights

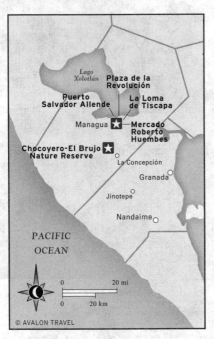

★ **Puerto Salvador Allende:** This port on Lake Xolotlán's waterfront is a popular gathering spot for locals and tourists alike (page 30).

★ **Plaza de la Revolución:** Most of Managua's historical sights are clustered in this four-block area, which is still the cultural heart of Nicaragua's capital (page 32).

★ **La Loma de Tiscapa:** Zip line over one of the area's many volcanic lakes—or just enjoy the spectacular view (page 35).

★ **Mercado Roberto Huembes:** This popular market is a great place to try Nicaraguan food while you shop for artisan souvenirs (page 41).

★ **Chocoyero-El Brujo Nature Reserve:** Located just south of Managua in a gorgeous patch of protected hillsides and ravines, this community-based tourism venture offers some wonderful day hikes (page 52).

By the late 1960s, Managua had earned the nickname "the Paris of Central America" as the most modern capital in the region, but the city has seen more than its fair share of ups and downs since then.

Home to a third of the country's population, Managua is not a favorite for most visitors. However, if you can see past what looks like chaos, you'll be surprised with glimpses of beautiful Lake Xolotlán and its dormant volcanoes, the most varied selection of restaurants in the nation, and a raging nightlife and music scene. This is the place to get your gear repaired and dance 'til you drop.

The stories of Managua and Nicaragua are largely parallel, from earthquake to revolution to economic revival and onward. An earthquake in 1972 laid waste to the city, killing 10,000 people and destroying the city's infrastructure. The last Somoza dictator ignored the tragedy, using the relief aid to swell his bank accounts. Seven years later, Managua bore the brunt of the final battles of the Sandinista Revolution. Fighting the Contras in the 1980s left no money to rebuild, but Managuans shoveled themselves out of the rubble, and the city began to grow organically, forming the twisting neighborhoods that make it so difficult to navigate today.

Since the end of the Contra War in 1990, Managua has grown quickly. Fear of another big earthquake has kept most developers from building structures taller than a few floors and from rebuilding in the seismic zone near the lake. Instead, new, upscale establishments stretch south through the city in the direction of Masaya.

You likely won't plan your trip around a visit to Managua, but neither should you necessarily avoid it. The city's charm will become apparent once you've spent a little time here. Managuans are full of stories (and opinions) about their history; the best way to learn is to strike up a conversation. The better you understand this city, the better you will understand Nicaragua itself.

Previous: view from La Loma de Tiscapa; bus at the Huembes terminal. **Above:** entrance to the Palacio Nacional de Cultura.

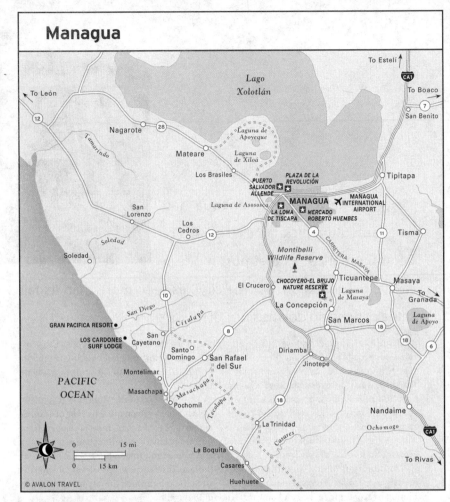

Managua

PLANNING YOUR TIME

You can easily visit all of Managua's main attractions, which are scattered along the Avenida Bolívar, in half a day. The city's biggest attraction is its nightlife, which brings folks together from all walks of life. Just outside the city, a few usually overlooked outdoor activities can provide a respite from the chaos of the capital. If you're just passing through, consider a stop at La Loma de Tiscapa for an amazing view.

Managua was not made for walking. Organize your day into trips to different regions of interest, and plan to get around by taxi, as the buses are slow and confusing. If you'd rather not walk between sights, negotiate a rate with a taxi driver to take you around (2 hours is enough and should cost you about $12). Any middle or upper range hotel can organize a guide and/or taxi to help you tour Managua. A taxi will cost around $25 per half day and a guide a similar amount.

ORIENTATION

Staying oriented in Managua is a challenge. The 1972 earthquake flattened the city, and

Following Directions in Managua

Addresses in Managua are unlike any system you've ever seen, but with a few tips, some basic vocabulary, and a couple of examples, you'll master Managua in no time. Street names and house numbers are few and far between, and where they do exist, they are universally ignored. Addresses begin with a landmark (either existing or historical), which is followed by the number of *cuadras* (blocks) and a direction. Remember this: **North** is *al lago* (toward the lake); **east** is *arriba* (up, referring to the sunrise); **south** is *al sur* (to the south); and **west** is *abajo* (down, where the sun sets).

Some other key phrases to know are ***contiguo a*** (next door to), ***frente a*** (across from), ***casa esquinera*** (corner house), and ***a mano derecha/izquierda*** (on the right-/left-hand side). Also note that *varas* are often used to measure distances of less than one block; this is an old colonial measurement just shy of a meter.

Directions throughout this chapter are given in English for consistency's sake, but always begin with the landmark exactly as it is referred to in Spanish. By studying the following examples, you should be able to find your way around with few hassles:

De la Plaza España, tres cuadras abajo, tres c. al lago, casa esquinera.
From Plaza España, three blocks west, three blocks north, corner house.

De los Semáforos El Dorado, dos cuadras al sur, una c. arriba, casa lila.
From the El Dorado traffic light, two blocks south, one block east, purple house.

Reparto San Juan, de la UNIVAL, 50 varitas al lago, edificio de cinco pisos.
In the San Juan neighborhood, just 50 meters north of the UNIVAL, five-story building.

it was never rebuilt with any kind of attention to city planning. There is no downtown, and its unnamed streets follow no grid pattern and are anything but pedestrian friendly. The city sprawls in every direction from Lake Xolotlán, its northernmost point. Focus on the following specific zones of interest: Near the **Malecón** and along **Avenida Bolívar** you'll find most of the city's tourist attractions, as well as a few restaurants and bars at Puerto Salvador Allende, but few options for lodging. The various neighborhoods that flank the length of **Carretera Masaya** south of Metrocentro are where you'll find most of the bars, clubs, and restaurants that make Managua fun for visitors, as well as an increasing number of charming guesthouses and boutique hotels. Lastly, Barrio Martha Quezada in **Bolonia** has historically been a backpacker and budget traveler center, and still houses international bus companies for those making overland connections.

SAFETY

Managua gets a bad rap, but compared to other Central American capitals (and even some U.S. cities) it's relatively safe. Exercise caution to avoid minor crimes like pickpocketing and purse snatching. Don't carry more than you have to. Keep valuables (like cell phones and cameras) stowed until you get to your destination. The best way to stay out of trouble is to avoid areas where you'll find it. The safest neighborhoods are Los Robles, Altamira along Carretera Masaya, plus Reparto San Juan (near the University of Central America), Las Colinas, and Villa Fontana, all of which offer more upscale accommodations and bed-and-breakfasts.

Dangerous neighborhoods include Reparto Schick, Dimitrov, La Fuente, San Judas, Las Américas, Bello Amanecer, Vida Nueva, Los Pescadores, Domitila Lugo, Santana, Hilaleah, and Barrio 3-80. You should be safe enough in and around the major shopping centers and

City of Managua

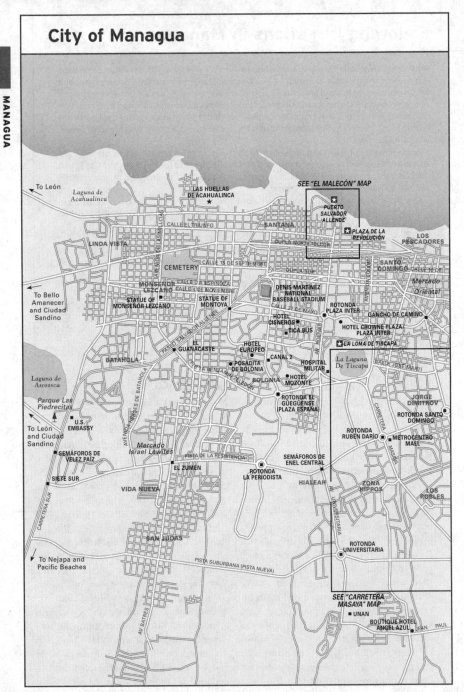

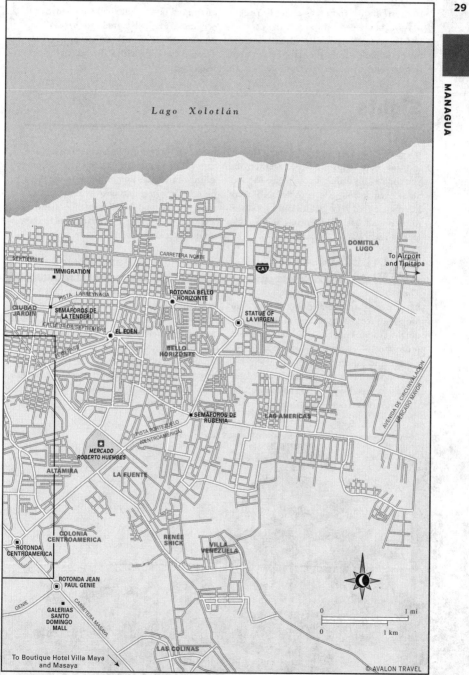

Lago Xolotlán

DOMITILA LUGO

To Airport and Tipitapa

CARRETERA NORTE

IMMIGRATION

CAT

ROTONDA BELLO HORIZONTE

PISTA LARREYNAGA

STATUE OF LA VIRGEN

SEMÁFOROS DE LA TENDERÍ

CIUDAD JARDÍN

EL EDÉN

CALLE 14 DE SEPTIEMBRE

BELLO HORIZONTE

SEMÁFOROS DE RUBENIA

LAS AMÉRICAS

AVENIDA DE CIRCUNVALACIÓN

MERCADO MAYOR

PISTA PORTEZUELO (CENTROAMÉRICA)

MERCADO ROBERTO HUEMBES

ALTAMIRA

LA FUENTE

COLONIA CENTROAMÉRICA

RENÉE SHICK

VILLA VENEZUELA

ROTONDA CENTROAMÉRICA

ROTONDA JEAN PAUL GENIE

GENIE

CARRETERA MASAYA

GALERIAS SANTO DOMINGO MALL

LAS COLINAS

To Boutique Hotel Villa Maya and Masaya

0   1 mi
0   1 km

© AVALON TRAVEL

the restaurants and clubs along Carretera Masaya, but in general you're better off staying in groups, especially when traveling by a taxi hailed from the street. Pay attention to your surroundings. Don't get into an unmarked taxi or a taxi where the driver is keeping his face obscured by a baseball cap (this is actually against the law) or where the driver is traveling with a "friend" in the passenger seat.

Sights

It's easiest to move around by taxi, though most of these sights are close together, and you could easily walk between them. The area along Avenida Bolívar is more patrolled by police than it used to be, but it's still a good idea to take some basic precautions and be alert for thieves.

EL MALECÓN AND AVENIDA BOLÍVAR

The backsides of Simón Bolívar, hero of the Latin American liberation movement, and his horse greet you upon arrival (he's peering northward for impending Yanqui invasions, probably). It's an inauspicious welcome to one of Managua's more interesting quarters. The government has been investing money lately in this area, making it safer and more attractive to tourists. There's no shade here, but the breeze off the lake provides a nice respite from the stifling heat of the city. Since the demolishing of the large amphitheater in the Plaza de la Fé (now solely occupied by a small monument to Pope John Paul II, who the amphitheater was built for) the breeze can travel farther up the Avenida Bolívar.

★ Puerto Salvador Allende

It was a loudly decried pity that rather than capitalizing on Lake Xolotlán's windswept lakefront, Managuan mayors had instead chosen for decades to defile it. However, the Malecón benefitted from a facelift in 2007 and **Puerto Salvador Allende** (at the end of Avenida Bolívar, tel. 505/2222-2745, $0.20, parking $1.15) opened for business not long after. Currently it offers plenty of dining and snacking options. There are several sit-down

Enjoy the breeze and the view of the lake at Puerto Salvador Allende.

El Malecón

restaurants and bars, and even more small kiosks and stands offering everything from local food like *raspados* and *quesillos* to seafood and steak to coffee. (For strong northern coffee, visit La Diosa del Café, in a kiosk across from the park.) There's also a recreation area for kids. You could easily spend a lazy few hours here.

The port offers **tourist cruises** (tel. 505/2222-3543 or 505/2222-2756, 1 hour round-trip) into the lake and around the

Isla de Amor, an islet at Managua's western side once used by the dictator for trysts. The lake is still polluted, but conditions have improved, and the pleasant cruise is certainly one of the better ways to spend a late afternoon in the capital. The **Novia de Xolotlán** (adults $4.60 upper deck, $3 lower deck with a/c) was the first to start running tours on the lake. Enjoy the view while a guide tells you about the history of the lake. Cruises on the newer **Meyer's Momotobito** (tel.

505/2276-2864, Tues.-Sun. noon-8pm, adults $4.60) depart five times a day and offer meals and drinks from their on-board kitchen. Both run a 7pm weekend night tour, where you can see the city lights from the water while enjoying the bar service.

Paseo de Xolotlán

Follow the yellow *árboles de la vida* (trees of life) along the lake and you'll find the newest addition to the Malecón, **Paseo de Xolotlán** (Mon.-Fri. 2pm-9pm, Sat.-Sun. 9am-10pm, $0.20, parking $0.75). It mostly holds playground equipment for children, but you'll also find a replica of old Managua before the 1972 earthquake.

Parque Rubén Darío

Dominated by a stark, white marble statue, the park is adjacent to the Parque Central and honors Nicaragua's most-beloved poet. Built in 1933, it was restored in 1998 with the help of the Texaco Corporation. Between the park and the Paseo de Xolotlán is the marble and brass **El Teatro Nacional Rubén Darío** (tel. 505/2228-4021 x113, www.tnrubendario.gob. ni), designed by the same architects that created New York's Metropolitan Opera House. It was one of a few surviving buildings in the 1972 earthquake and remains to this day a classy place to enjoy dance, theater, or musical presentations. Check the newspaper for performances or call for upcoming events.

★ Plaza de la Revolución

The **Plaza de la Revolución,** ostensibly just an open area, has become a living monument to the incessant bickering of Nicaragua's political elite. Under Somoza, it was known as Plaza de la República. The rebel Sandinista movement assembled huge crowds there to manifest their outrage against the dictator, and upon overthrowing him, the Sandinista government renamed it Plaza de la Revolución. Renowned Sandinista-hater President Alemán, upon taking power, was thus thrilled to punch a hole in the symbolic Sandinista chakra by building an audiovisual

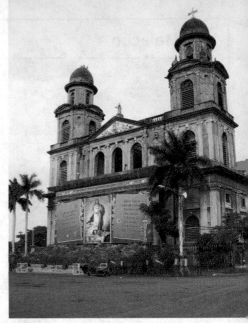

Catedral Santiago de los Caballeros

fountain in its center. So naturally when President Ortega returned to power in 2006 he wasted no time in demolishing Alemán's fountain and holding political rallies and celebrations here. Visit in the morning, when the breeze off the lake is cool, the trees are full of birds, and the traffic is momentarily silent.

On the north side of the plaza, in the direction of the lake, is the brightly painted **Casa Presidencial** (not open to visitors). It was built in 1999 by Alemán, despite popular outrage over the unjustifiable expense in Hurricane Mitch's aftermath. The list of countries on the facade recognizes those governments that financially contributed to its construction. President Ortega doesn't live there but has instead turned it into "the people's house."

CATEDRAL SANTIAGO DE LOS CABALLEROS

Managua's most iconic and evocative landmark, the **Catedral Santiago de los Caballeros** dominates the Plaza. It had

The Sandinista Tree of Life

As part of its attempt at rebranding, the Sandinista party has been moving away from the black and red of the revolution in favor of bold, bright blues, pinks, purples, yellows, and greens. As part of this effort, they've adopted the yellow *árbol de la vida* (tree of life) as a new party symbol. These metallic structures popped up all over Managua in 2013 and 2014. Made of solid steel and covered in dozens of small yellow light bulbs, it's estimated that each tree costs upwards of $20,000. Most folks credit First Lady Rosario Murillo (often referred to as *la chayo*) with this massive project. They've been installed in rotundas throughout the city as well as along the Avenida Bolívar, the Malecón, and Carretera Norte around the airport. Every Managuan has an opinion about these, good or bad, so it's a great conversation topic with city folks.

the Sandinista tree of life

barely been completed when the earthquake of 1931 struck. It survived relatively unscathed that time, but was all but destroyed by the 1972 earthquake that leveled Managua. During one of the aftershocks, the clock on the right tower stopped and hasn't been altered since. Still standing but structurally unsound, the **Ruinas de la Catedral Vieja** (as it is now known) are a poignant testimonial to the destruction caused by the quake. Until the late 1990s, the ruins of the cathedral were open to visitors, but due to continued structural degradation, it is no longer safe. You can still peer in, however, to appreciate its ravaged, sunlit interior.

PALACIO NACIONAL DE CULTURA

On the south side of the plaza, the **Palacio Nacional de Cultura** houses **El Museo Nacional de Nicaragua** (tel. 505/2222-2905, Tues.- Fri. 8am-5pm, Sat.-Sun. 9am-4pm, foreigners $3, nationals $0.75) but at various times has also housed the Ministry of Housing, the treasury, the comptroller-general, and the National Congress. Sandinista commandos raided the building

in 1978 and held the entire Congress hostage, winning international recognition and the liberation of several political prisoners. In addition to the national library, several murals and the Institute of Culture can be found here.

Once the prestigious Gran Hotel (severely damaged by the quake in 1972), the first two floors are now Managua's official **cultural museum**—look for the murals around the outside. The building hosts art exhibits, concerts, puppet shows, and dances. The second floor holds studios of prominent Nicaraguan artists. The hallways are lined with striking black-and-white photographs of old Managua, pre- and post-earthquake. Sneak up to the roof to see how the upper floors of the old hotel were never replaced, yet another monument to the earthquake.

PARQUE CENTRAL

Set in the small green space of the **Parque Central** (Avenida Bolívar, west of the Plaza de la Revolución) are several monuments of historical significance. An eternal flame guards the **Tomb of Comandante Carlos**

Revolutionary Driving Tour

Historical trivia buffs, take note! A lot of Managua's most historically salient points are close to invisible, in stark contrast to the role they played in the lead-up to the 1979 revolution. None of these destinations have gotten the granite monument they deserve, but their importance is no less diminished, even as life goes on around them. If you have a rainy afternoon in Managua, hop in a taxi and revisit history on this 30-minute driving tour. From your hotel go first to the **Plaza de la Revolución.**

One block south of the Guerrillero sin Nombre, the southwest corner with a lone wooden telephone pole marks the site of journalist **Pedro Joaquin Chamorro's assassination** as he drove to his office on January 10, 1978. Whether the drive-by was paid for by Tachito or his business partner in the infamous blood-bank business was never determined, but Chamorro's death helped spark the Revolution. Look for a concrete monument directly behind the telephone pole.

Turn south onto Avenida Bolívar. You'll pass some government buildings and Parque Luis Alfonso Velásquez Flores before coming to the **National Arboretum** (tel. 505/2222-2558, Mon.-Fri. 8am-5pm, free) on your left, home to more than 200 species of trees found in Nicaragua. It is practically unvisited except by local school groups but is especially attractive in March, when the fragrant *sacuanjoche* (Nicaragua's national flower) blooms brightly. The scarlet flowers of the *malinche* tree blossom May-August. The trees are planted atop the remnants of Somoza's *Hormiguero* (Anthill), a military base belonging to the National Guard and destroyed in 1972 by the earthquake. Popular legend has it that this was the site where, on February 21, 1934, General Sandino was ambushed and assassinated after meeting with President Sacasa at his home on the Loma de Tiscapa.

Turn left at Plaza Inter and head in the direction of the El Dorado neighborhood. The **monument to Bill Stewart** is one block west and two blocks south of the Semáforo El Dorado. Bill Stewart was a U.S. journalist for ABC in the 1970s. While reporting on the early days of the Sandinista insurrection he was brutally attacked and killed by members of Somoza's National Guard. Stewart's cameraman filmed and published the whole thing, forcing the U.S. government to stop turning a blind eye to the excesses of Nicaragua's dictator.

Finally, and in the opposite direction, just west of the petroleum refinery on the road leading west out of town is **La Cuesta del Plomo,** the ravine where Somoza was allegedly fond of making folks "disappear." Families whose loved ones didn't come home after a few days would go to this hillside to search for their bodies.

Fonseca, father of the Sandinista Revolution. Also buried here is another father of the Revolution, Tomás Borge (one of the political prisoners liberated as a result the 1978 raid of Congress). Across from the Fonseca tomb is Santos López, a member of General Sandino's "crazy little army" in the 1930s, who helped train latter-day Sandinistas in the general's ideology and the art of guerrilla warfare. The historical frieze that circles the **Templo de la Música,** a brightly painted gazebo, highlights the arrival of Columbus, Rafael Herrera fighting pirates, independence from Spain, Andrés Castro fighting William Walker, and more, but it's just as interesting for the antics of the sparrows in its arches.

Monumento de la Paz

Hugely representative of the peacemaking initiatives of former president Violeta Chamorro, the **Monumento de la Paz** (in the Parque de la Paz, north of Parque Luis Alfonso) celebrated a new era of peace. Beneath the concrete are buried the destroyed remains of thousands and thousands of weapons from the Contra War, many of which—including a tank—can be seen protruding through the cement. Almost directly across the street (just a bit west) is the unmistakable statue of the Guerrillero sin Nombre. There's continuous police presence now, but even so, play it safe and visit only during daylight hours.

El Guerrillero sin Nombre

You can't miss this guy. The Nameless Guerrilla Soldier grasps a pickax in one hand and an AK-47 in the disproportionately muscular other. This hulkish symbol of the Revolution's aspirations is inscribed with one of Sandino's most treasured quotations: "Only the laborers and farmers will go to the end." Arnoldo Alemán's administration countered with a different statue just across the road, honoring the working class with two cowed and undernourished looking figures, one representing a construction worker and the other a domestic servant, both representative of Nicaragua's growing laborer community in neighboring Costa Rica.

Earthquake Monument

Across from the *cancillería* (foreign affairs) building, where the old Iglesia de San Antonio used to stand, is the monument to victims of the earthquake of 1972. This touching statue, constructed in 1994, was the initiative of journalist Aldo Palacios and portrays a man standing amidst the wreckage of his home. It is inscribed with the poem, "Requiem a una Ciudad Muerta," by Pedro Rafael Gutierrez.

Parque Luis Alfonso Velásquez Flores

Parque Luis Alfonso (as it's commonly referred to) holds the remains of its namesake, a 10-year-old child killed nearby by Somoza's National Guard before the Revolution in 1979. In 2012, 146 families were relocated to allow for the park's expansion. It now holds a baseball stadium, multiple soccer fields and basketball courts, and several children's recreational parks. There are several refreshment stands dispersed throughout the park. It's a great space for an evening walk, attracting many Managuan families and youth.

★ La Loma de Tiscapa

If you only have time to make one tourist stop in Managua, this is it. The **Parque Histórica** ($4.60 for vehicles, $2 for foreigners on foot), which sits on the **Loma de Tiscapa,** offers

the best views of Managua. It holds the city's most recognized landmark, an enormous silhouette of Sandino, which now stands next to a Sandinista tree of life. To reach the park, follow the road south of the Crown Plaza Hotel up to the entrance. From far above, Managua's chaotic, unorganized streets seem almost tranquil. Here you can observe the stark contrast between the historical former downtown along Lake Xolotlán and the more developed southern half of the city. You can see everything from the city dump (now a brown patch along the lake) to the north to the new National Cathedral (the roof looks like many domes stacked next to each other) in the south.

After entering the park, the twin-towered monument halfway up the road is the **Monumento Roosevelt,** which was the southernmost point of the city pre-earthquake. Twenty meters farther up the hill is the statue of justice, sardonically decapitated ages ago. The park sits on the site of the former Presidential Palace and National Guard headquarters, which were destroyed in the 1972 earthquake. In Tiscapa's prisons (at the top of the hill, but closed to the public), Somoza tortured many resistance leaders, including current President Daniel Ortega. Revolutionary martyr Augusto C. Sandino ate his last meal here, lured under the pretense of a peace treaty. Follow the blue sign that says "Exposición" down the stairs to a historical revolutionary museum located in what remains of the palace. In theory there's always an attendant, who'll give you a brief tour in exchange for a tip ($1.50-4, depending on the number of people).

La Loma de Tiscapa sits above a lagoon of the same name, which fills in a dormant volcano. Once a popular swimming hole, the lagoon is now being cleaned up after decades of contamination. If you're feeling adventurous, zip line over it with **Tiscapa Canopy Tours** (tel. 505/8872-2555 or 505/8471-5516, Tues.-Sun. 9am-5:30pm, foreigners $17.25, Nicas $13.80). Wear your sunscreen, there's not a lot of shade!

CATEDRAL METROPOLITANA DE LA INMACULADA CONCEPCIÓN DE MARÍA

A short walk from the Metrocentro mall, at the center of an immense field of young coconut trees along the Carretera Masaya, is the **new cathedral** (mass: Tues.-Sat. noon and 6pm, Sun. 11am and 6pm), as it's commonly called. Constructed just two years after the conclusion of the civil war, it was commissioned by Thomas Monahan (founder of Domino's Pizza) and designed by Mexican architect Ricardo Legorreta. This dynamic and open cathedral houses the Dutch bells of the old cathedral. Its design plays on the soaring forms of Spanish colonial architecture, and its exterior roof has given rise to some interesting nicknames. It was once the pulpit of Nicaragua's famous and controversial Cardinal Miguel Obando Bravo. Cardinal Leopoldo Brene now presides over mass.

LAS HUELLAS DE ACAHUALINCA

Modest but intriguing, the site is a simple **museum** (tel. 505/2266-5774, Mon.-Fri. 8am-4pm, Sat. 8:30am-1:30pm, foreigners $4, $2 with student ID, Nicas $1, $1 charge for photos) built over the fossilized footprints of Managua's earliest known inhabitants who fished Lake Managua in 4,000 BC. The prehistoric footprints were found in the last century, four meters below the ground surface. Once thought to be the prints of people fleeing a volcanic eruption, forensic analysis now shows the walkers were unhurried. The women's prints are deeper, as they were carrying a heavier load, perhaps the children. The museum's exhibits on Nahuatl life and the volcanoes of Central America make clear that living in the shadow of imminent volcanic destruction is nothing new in town. The musem is a bit out of the way at the northwest end of the city, so call before going, and find a taxi to take you there and back ($5 an hour; 1 hour should be enough), as the surrounding neighborhood isn't safe for walking. The taxi will inevitably drive you through some of Managua's marginalized lakefront neighborhoods populated with folks who lived off of the nearby municipal dump until a recent investment by the Spanish government converted it into a private enterprise.

Zip line over la Laguna de Tiscapa with Tiscapa Canopy Tours.

Entertainment and Events

NIGHTLIFE

Nightlife is a central part of the Managua experience. Many Managuans are from other parts of the country, but come to the city to work or study. So, when the weekend rolls around they're ready to cut loose. The club scene trends more towards the hip-hop-influenced reggaeton, but there's plenty of salsa, merengue, bachata, and cumbia as well. Managua also has a couple of places to learn salsa and merengue if you are in town for a longer period of time.

If you prefer something more low-key, there are lots of bars and clubs with atmospheres that range from sultry to suspect, but they change on an annual basis, as Managuans flock inexorably to the newest scene. For classical music, dance, and theater, there is usually something happening at the Rubén Darío theater. For party and event listing, check www.hechomagazine.com or clickmanagua.com.

Bars

Zona Hippos, west of Carretera Masaya on the edge of Los Robles, is an area of tightly clustered fun spots where the bars serve food and the restaurants have a good bar scene. Their names change a lot, but regardless, you're sure to find something interesting. **Ron Kon Rolas** (2 blocks south of Piratas, tel. 505/8847-0842) provides a venue for local rock musicians. There's a concert happening in the back almost every weekend, otherwise rock music is always blaring (in English and Spanish).

Nearby is a popular karaoke bar, **Claps** (in Los Robles from Farma Descuento, half a block west, tel. 505/8448-5894), which invites the timid singer with its dim lighting and sofas you can sink into. Karaoke is an important part of the Managua experience. Often there is no stage, instead the DJ will bring the microphone to your table, so you don't even have to stand up.

El Panal (from the entrance of la UNI, 50 meters west, no tel.) serves good Nica food along with its liters of beer. This attracts a university crowd, but there're always at least a couple of plastic tables filled by the after-work crowd. **Santera Bar** (east side of the Pellas building, tel. 505/2278-8585) is similar but slightly more intentional in creating its laid-back atmosphere.

Near Plaza España in Boloña is **La Otra Embajada** (from the Rotonda el Güegüense, half a block west, tel. 505/2268-0732, Tues.-Wed. 4pm-midnight, Thurs.-Sat. 4pm-2am), a lively little bar that often has karaoke as well as movie nights.

If you're not pinching pennies and are looking for a chic scene, head down Carretera Masaya to Galerías Santo Domingo Mall. **Altabar** (tel. 505/2276-5276) in the mall's Zona Viva cultivates an intentionally trendy ambiance (complete with discotheque music and decorative lights). Sip a beer while you smoke a hookah.

Clubs and Dancing

BB Lounge (in Bolonia from the Óptica Pereira de Plaza España, 1 block west, 2 north, and 1 west, tel. 505/2266-8515 or 505/2268-2443) is a quality option for travelers staying nearby. The building is divided into three areas: a sports bar, a karaoke bar, and a club upstairs ($4 cover for men) playing a variety of popular music from salsa, merengue, and bachata to reggaeton. If you're with a group, ask about buying a promo package of drinks and food.

If you're looking to dance salsa (or just watch the pros), **Fandango** (from TipTop Chicken on Carretera Masaya, 400 meters south, tel. 505/8984-0494, Wed.-Sat. 7:30pm-2am) or **Fusión** (from Pool 8, 50 meters west, tel. 505/2252-4232 or 8529-7008, fusionnicaragua@gmail.com, Mon.-Sat. from 3pm) are more your speed. Fandango offers a free class before the party gets started on Wednesdays at 10pm. Fusión has classes throughout the week; email or call for walk-in information.

Tabú (east side of the Hotel Mansión Teodolinda, tel. 505/8420-2141) is Managua's most popular gay bar. They often host big parties and events that keep the dance floor full. All are welcome, and it's conveniently just around the corner from gay-friendly Caramanchel.

El Caramanchel (2 blocks south and 15 meters west of the Crowne Plaza Hotel, tel. 505/8931-4199, Wed.-Sat. from 7pm) often hosts live bands and attracts Managua's late-night crowd for after hours dancing (they normally close around 4am). It's a favorite bohemian haunt, with an inviting, casual atmosphere and a soundtrack that includes reggae and cumbia. The cozy, open-air dance floor doubles as a stage and has hosted some fantastic bands from as far away as Brazil. This is a relaxed and comfortable atmosphere in which to dance or enjoy live music.

Aché Bar (in east Altamira, tel. 505/2277-3644, Mon.-Fri. 1pm-3am, Sat. noon-3pm) brings a variety of crowds together on the dance floor with merengue, salsa, reggaeton, and more, but don't plan on having a conversation amongst the din. Aché Bar is located *donde fue La Vicky* (where la Vicky used to be). Across the street and one block west is **Havana Vieja** (no tel.), which has a small covered patio out front for salsa dancing, sometimes with live music. They attract an older, more mellow crowd that knows how to dance.

Mirador Tiscapa (on Paseo Tiscapa next to Radio Sandino, tel. 505/8209-3575, Fri.-Sun. from 8pm, no cover), an open-air venue on a balcony overlooking the crater, is an old Managua favorite, with a somewhat older crowd. It is largely spurned by the trendy crowd, making it unpretentious, inexpensive, and still a great place to dance.

Managua's *costeño* crowd still loves **Queen's** (in the Rotunda Bello Horizonte, no tel., $2 cover), somewhat far from the rest

of town and a bit run down these days, but well-loved (and packed!). Dancehall, soca, and reggae are what's playing. Go on a Thursday, when there's more elbowroom. Next door, and along the same lines is **Dancehall House** (tel. 505/2293-6267).

Live Music

Managua's music scene, both intimate and refined, shows a lot of local talent and energy. Without a doubt, the single best show in town is **Casa de los Mejía Godoy** (in front of the Hotel Crowne Plaza, in Plaza Inter, tel. 505/2222-6110 or 505/2254-5168, fmejiago@cablenet.com.ni, restaurant Mon.-Fri., shows Wed.-Fri. and some Sat., $5-20). The Mejía Godoy family has been a powerhouse of Nicaraguan songwriters and musicians for generations. Brothers Carlos and Luis Enrique essentially composed the soundtrack of the Revolution in the 1970s. They are born showmen and present a theatrical mix of stories, bawdy jokes, and famous songs. Both perform here, though less often now than in previous years. The restaurant features other Nicaraguan and international performers, including their nephew, popular *salsero* Luis Enrique. The club is expensive by Nica standards, but well worth it. Buy tickets the afternoon of the performance.

The breezy, open-air patio of **La Ruta Maya** (150 meters east of the Estatua de Montoya, tel. 505/2268-0698, www.rutamaya.com.ni, Sat.-Sun. only, $4-6) is a pleasant place to appreciate a wide variety of performers from singer-songwriters to reggae, jazz, and everything in between. This restaurant generally attracts a more mature, sit-down crowd (depending on the artist), though they sometimes make room for a small dance floor.

Cultura Quilombo (from the Busto of José Martí, 50 meters east, $2-5 cover) is an open outdoor space with trees and recycled tables, chairs, and light fixtures. They often hold workshops and community events (everything from drum circles and capoeira classes to discussion panels and poetry readings) but are most noteworthy for their ability to bring together musicians and a variety of other artists. It's a great place to discover a new local band. Check their Facebook page for upcoming concerts and events.

THE ARTS
Performing Arts

Managua's finest theater, **El Teatro Nacional Rubén Darío** (at the Malecón, tel. 505/2228-4021 x113, www.tnrubendario.gob.ni) hosts top-name international acts. Call or check the newspaper for performances. **La Escuela Nacional de Teatro** (Palacio Nacional de Cultura, tel. 505/2222-4100, office hours Mon.-Fri. 8am-noon) is primarily a teaching facility that presents performances on weekends by students and small professional troupes from all over Latin America; call for a list of events, as they're not always published. The **Sala de Teatro Justo Rufino Garay** (from Montoya, 3 blocks west, 20 meters north, next to Parque Las Palmas, tel. 505/2266-3714, www.rufinos.org) is better frequented and offers similar fare on weekends only. A calendar of events is often available at supermarkets and Texaco stations as well as in the arts magazine *Patadeperro*

if you're lucky enough to find a copy. Their Facebook page is your best bet.

Located across from the UCA, **La Academia de Danza** (Avenida Universitaria, in front of the UNI, tel. 505/2277-5557) has frequent dance performances and concerts. The students deliver professional and talented renditions of traditional, folk, modern jazz, Brazilian, and ballet; call or drop by for a schedule of events, or if you're in town for the long haul, consider taking one of their dance classes to prepare you for the club scene.

Galleries

Managua's art galleries showcase Nicaragua's creative artists. The **Galería de Los Tres Mundos** (Los Robles, 2 blocks north of the French restaurant La Marseillaise, tel. 505/2267-0304, Mon.-Fri. 9am-4pm) was Ernesto Cardenal's home base and showcases a variety of Solentiname artwork, from paintings to balsa work. More a cultural center than a museum, **Códice** (in Los Robles, from the Hotel Colón, 1 block south, 2.5 blocks east, tel. 505/2267-2635 or 505/2270-0740, www.galeriacodice.com, Mon.-Sat. 9am-7pm, sometimes open later) displays changing exhibitions of sculpture, paintings, and ceramics, all set around a lovely courtyard. There

gordita figures for sale

are frequent evening musical performances here set in a lovely outdoor patio. **Alianza Francesa** (Planes de Altamira, from the Embajada de México half a block north, tel. 505/2267-2811, www.alianzafrancesa.org.ni) and the **Centro Cultural de España** (from the first entrance of Las Colinas, 7 blocks east, tel. 505/2276-0733, www.ccenicaragua.org) have art showings, as well as frequent events including movie screenings, theater presentations, and concerts.

FESTIVALS AND EVENTS

Las Fiestas Patronales (Aug.) are when Managua celebrates its patron saint Santo Domingo and are the highlight of the calendar year. On the first of the month, the saint (a diminutive little figure under a glass dome) is brought down from a small church in the hilly neighborhood of Santo Domingo and on August 10 he is returned. On both those dates, and for much of the time in between, Managua celebrates. Expect parades,

horse shows, unlimited quantities of beer and rum, and a lot of fun and colors. INTUR sponsors a series of events during this time, like Las Noches Agostinas, featuring cultural presentations and live music throughout the capital.

Every **July 19th** since 1979, Nicaraguans have celebrated the final victory against Somoza during the Sandinista Revolution. July 19th celebrations bring out the Sandinista party faithful, many of whom are bused in by the government from all over the country. There's a rally and presentations in Plaza de la Fé and a show choreographed by the First Lady Rosario Murillo. The truly devout even stay through Ortega's predictable and lengthy speech at the end. The celebration can get crazy and a little sketchy as the sun goes down, so if you are planning to go, it's not a bad idea to leave early.

If you are in Managua in December, be sure to stroll down Avenida Bolívar and see the enormous altars to the Virgin Mary set up for the **Purísima,** a Nicaraguan tradition.

Shopping

In Los Robles the **Fábrica de Chocolate Momotombo** (from Pastelería Sampson 1 block south, tel. 505/2278-4918, www.chocolatemomotombo.com) has a mouth-watering array of locally made cacao products. Find unique souvenir tees at **Jincho** (second entrance to Las Colinas, Centro Comercial Plaza Mayor, 2nd Fl., tel. 505/2276-1285, www.soyjincho.com, Mon.-Fri. 10am-6pm, Sat. 1:30pm-6pm), a Nicaraguan brand that creates modern urban designs with a local Nica flare.

ARTS AND CRAFTS

Esperanza en Acción (from Km 8 on Carretera Sur, 4 blocks east, inside the Centro Kairos, tel. 505/2265-2634, www.esperanzaenaccion.org, Mon.-Fri. 9am-5pm)

sells fair trade crafts from all over the country including jewelry, clay pottery, woven bags, and coffee, among other items. The nonprofit teaches artisans (most are women) how to determine a fair price for their work and provides a venue for its sale. The small store located off Carretera Sur is worth the trip for the guaranteed great finds. They have regular hours, but it doesn't hurt to call ahead before you go to make sure someone's in the store.

BOOKS

The best bilingual selection of local and international books is **Frontera Books** (200 meters north of the Enitel Villa Fontana intersection, tel. 550/2270-2345). They've got a great children's section, plus the latest maps and magazines. **Hispamer** (Reparto Tiscapa, just east of the UCA, tel. 505/2278-1210) is the largest and oldest bookstore in the city. Read your new book in the attached air-conditioned coffee shop.

In the Centro Comercial de Managua, several small but interesting bookstores compete for your attention, including **Librería Rigoberto López Pérez** (tel. 505/2277-2240), named for the poet who, for love of his country, assassinated Anastasio Somoza García. (There's a monument in his honor in one of the rotundas.) It has a wide selection and a friendly atmosphere.

MARKETS
★ Mercado Roberto Huembes
Mercado Roberto Huembes (daily 7:30am-5pm, some vendors close on Sun.) is the best place to find local arts and crafts. It's a fun market full of the exuberance, color, and life that so typifies Nicaragua, and is tourist friendly and easily accessible. That's what makes it such a pleasant way to spend an afternoon in Managua. You will be perfectly safe while you shop. Although Managuans rely on Huembes for lots of day-to-day stuff (chicken cutlets, toothpaste, socks), the market also has a splendid selection of pottery, paintings, hammocks, leatherwork, and other Nicaraguan artisan specialties. Only Masaya is a better place to shop. Be sure to specify to your taxi driver that you're going to the section of *artesenía,* not the bus terminal.

Mercado Oriental
The largest market in Central America, **Mercado Oriental**, is huge, with winding passages full of shoppers and shouting vendors, and can be overwhelming for a newcomer. It's worth checking out, but only with someone who knows their way around, as it's easy to get lost and is notorious for pickpockets.

Shop for *artesanía* at Mercado Roberto Huembes.

Accommodations

Where to spend the night in Managua depends a lot on your reason for spending the night here. If all you need is the cheapest possible bed before boarding an international bus to a neighboring country, the *hospedaje* scene in **Bolonia** is probably your best bet. If you're overnighting in order to make an early morning flight, there are nicer options elsewhere, especially if you're willing to spend a few extra dollars. You can catch an early-morning taxi to the airport from anywhere in the city, or you can roll out of bed at the Best Western La Mercedes and walk across the street to check in. If you are planning to be in Managua more than one night, the most central location in the city (and most convenient for those traveling south) is anywhere along **Carretera Masaya.** You have to spend more in Managua to get comfort, safety, and peace of mind, and travelers are increasingly willing to do so. You can expect rooms over $40 to have air-conditioning and hot water, but it doesn't hurt to confirm before you check in.

CARRETERA MASAYA AND VICINITY

Carretera Masaya is a straight shot south from the Laguna de Tiscapa out of Managua towards Masaya and Granada. As a main highway, there are bus terminals located close by at the UCA and Mercado Roberto Huembes. Neighborhoods **Los Robles** and **Altamira** are relatively secure and well-serviced middle-class neighborhoods along Carretera Masaya. They're located along the highway in the heart of the city, reducing taxi fares significantly. **Villa Fontana** and **Las Colinas** are a bit farther south towards the quieter, more exclusive edge of town.

Los Robles and Altamira
UNDER $25

Located in the shadow of the grand Hotel Intercontinental in central Managua,

★ **Managua Backpacker's Inn** (Monte los Olivos, 1 block north, 1 block west, 1 block north, #56, tel. 505/2267-0006, www.managuahostel.com, $10 shared dorm, $24 private room) offers clean rooms, a laid-back friendly atmosphere, a pool, and small café. It's a great value in a safe neighborhood within walking distance to Metrocentro and Zona Hippos. It is very popular, so reserve (and even pre-pay) online.

★ **Hotel Maracuyá** (Reparto San Juan, from La Marseillaise, half a block north and 2.5 blocks west, tel. 505/2277-3336, www.maracuyahotels.com, $12 dorm, $35 private) opened its Managua location in August 2014 (the other location is in San Juan del Sur). Rooms are comfortable and clean and communal areas are cozy (especially if you make friends with the house pets). Its relaxed vibe and family atmosphere sets it apart. Ask about planning a BBQ night.

$25-50
Hotel Dulce Hogar (from the Banco BDF 50 meters south, tel. 505/2277-0865, www.hotelenmanagua.com, from $40, includes breakfast) is lauded for its great value. Its central location places it near to shopping and food, but the area remains quiet at night. The comfortable and clean rooms have hot water and air-conditioning.

$50-100
Casa San Juan (Reparto San Juan Calle Esperanza 560, tel. 505/2278-3220, www.casasanjuan.net, from $50) is quiet and centrally located. It offers wireless Internet throughout the hotel, air-conditioning, and hot-water showers.

★ **Hotel Pyramide** (Reparto San Juan, from Gimnasio Hercules 1 block south, 1 east, 2.5 blocks south, tel. 505/2278-0687, www.lapyramidehotel.com, from $57) is known for the attentiveness of the owner,

Carretera Masaya

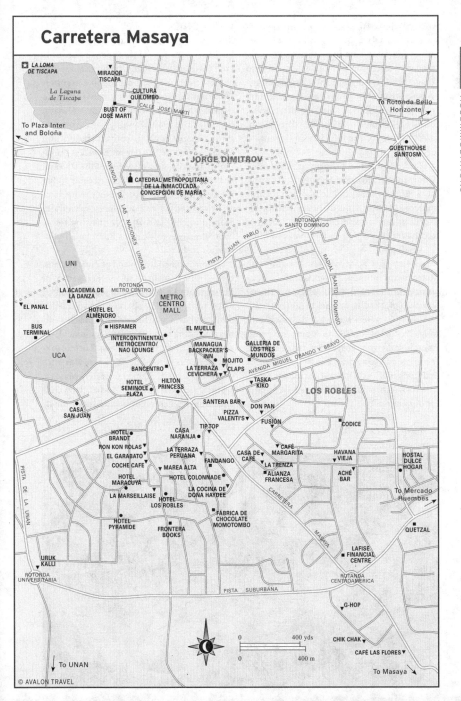

© AVALON TRAVEL

who will make sure you are comfortable as soon as you arrive. It is a good value for the money, but plan on a five-block walk to get to nearby restaurants. The owner will help you get taxis if you prefer. In the same neighborhood, **Hotel Brandt** (Reparto San Juan, from Zona Hippos, 1 block south, 1 west, tel. 505/2270-2114, $65 s, $75 d) is clean, safe, and pretty, and has been in business a long time.

Family-run **Hotel Colonnade** (Planes de Altamira, next to Doña Haydeé Restaurant, tel. 505/2277-4838, hotelcolonnadenicaragua.com, $90 s, $100 d) is known for its excellent service and convenient location. Rooms are clean and comfortable, and there is a small pool.

Hotel El Almendro (from the Metrocentro rotunda, 1 block south, 3 blocks west, tel. 505/2270-1260, www.hotelelalmendro.com, $80 s, includes breakfast) is accessible to Carretera Masaya and an easy walk to Metrocentro Mall. The rooms are great, though somewhat geared towards business travelers and long-stay guests (with suites and kitchenettes). Guarded parking is available for your rental car. There's a little pool for dipping.

OVER $100

Managua's premium chain hotels cater to business travelers with expense accounts (and travelers who want to splurge at the end of their trip). Your best bet in this category is ★ **Intercontinental Metrocentro** (next to the Plaza Metrocentro and Carretera Masaya, tel. 505/2276-8989, www.ihg.com, from $99 on weekends), with its convenient location and good service. It's one of the tallest buildings in the city, offering views of the lake and rush hour traffic. It has standard rooms (club level are the nicest), a pool, event center, and an overpriced bar and steakhouse restaurant. Stop in at **Nao Lounge** (on the first floor) on a Monday evening (6pm-8pm) for all-you-can-eat sushi rolls.

Towards the southern end of Zona Hippos, **Hotel Los Robles** (30 meters south of Restaurante La Marseillaise, tel. 505/2267-3008, www.hotellosrobles.com, $95) blends colonial charm with business-minded amenities (including some basic gym equipment), in addition to a beautiful pool area. Their breakfast buffet is splendid. ★ **Casa Naranja** (from Tip Top Chicken on Carretera Masaya, 1 block west, tel. 505/2277-3403, www.hotelcasanaranja.com, $100) stands out for its

Chill out in a hammock at Hotel Maracuyá.

understated colonial style and green backyard patio with dipping pool.

A short stroll from a dozen excellent restaurants, the **Hotel Seminole Plaza** (from Bancentro on Carretera Masaya 1 block west, 1 south, tel. 505/2270-0061, www.seminoleplaza.com, Mon.-Fri. $120, Sat.-Sun. $65 s, $75 d) is owned by the Seminole Indian tribe of Florida; the hotel is typically a bit less expensive than the competition.

Villa Fontana and Las Colinas
$50-100

In Las Colinas, **Boutique Hotel Villa Maya** (Las Colinas, second entrance, on Calle Los Laureles, House #105, tel. 505/2276-2175, $60 d) has pretty grounds and uses solar panels for energy, and rainwater irrigation for its garden. In Villa Fontana, a bit farther into the city, off of Carretera Masaya, **Boutique Hotel Angel Azúl** (from Club Terraza 1 block east, 75 meters north, #17, tel. 505/2270-5520, www.simedianet.com/hotelangelazul, $70) has great service and a calm atmosphere.

OVER $100

Down Carretera Masaya, past Las Colinas, is **Hotel Contempo** (Km 11 on Carretera Masaya, 400 meters west, Residencial Las Praderas, tel. 505/2264-9160, www.hotelcontempo.com, $120 d). This beautiful (but far away) boutique hotel is for folks who are looking to be pampered and do not need to be in the city proper.

BOLONIA

The Barrio Maria Quezada is a small neighborhood in Bolonia that has hosted international budget travelers since the *sandalistas* (referring to foreigners who came to support the Revolution) poured south to support the Revolution. It's especially convenient to overnighters bound for an international bus line (Tica Bus is in walking distance to most of these listings). However, since the **Hotel Tica Bus** (tel. 505/2298-5500, www.ticabus.com, $14 s, $23 d with fan, $29 s, $39 d with a/c) opened at their Bolonia station business has

declined for local businesses, as many travelers with early morning departures prefer to roll directly out of bed and onto the bus. Neighbors advise not to walk east of the Tica Bus station due to increased robberies in that area. Outside of this neighborhood in the Bolonia area, there are plenty of pleasant, upscale options.

Under $25

The family-run **Hostal Dulce Sueño** (50 meters east of Tica Bus, tel. 505/2228-4125 or 505/8424-0272, www.hostaldulcesueno. com, $10 s) is clean and safe, with private bathrooms, Wi-Fi, and laundry service. **Guesthouse Santos** (from Tica Bus, 1 block north, 1.5 blocks west, tel. 505/2222-3713, $7) has been around since 1979, and may not have changed a thing since. It remains quirky, gaudy, and well-liked by an ever-revolving international crowd.

Hotel Santa María (1.5 blocks west of Tica Bus, tel. 505/2222-7050, $15 s with fan, $30 with a/c) offers Internet, parking, a pool, a shady patio area under a thatched roof, laundry service, and private baths. **Hotel Cisneros** (from Tica Bus, 1 block north, 1.5 blocks west, tel. 505/2222-7273 or 8768 5183, hotelloscisneros.com, $21 with fan, $36 with a/c) offers similar comforts but is not quite as pretty.

$25-50

Posadita de Bolonia (3 blocks west of Canal 2, then 75 meters south, tel. 505/2268-6692, www.posaditadebolonia.com, $35 s, $47 d, includes breakfast) is a comfortable and quiet place offering cable TV, Internet, hot water, and private showers. Lunch and dinner can be provided by arrangement. The hotel offers a full range of tour and guide services.

$50-100

In a quiet Bolonia neighborhood, **Hotel Europeo** (75 meters west of Canal 2, tel. 505/2268-2130, www.hoteleuropeo.com.ni, $60 s) has a nice pool in an attractive garden patio. **Hotel Mozonte** (from the entrance to PriceSmart, 1.5 blocks north, across from the old French Embassy, tel. 505/2266-0686 or 505/8965-0855, www.hotelmozonte.com, info@hotelmozonte.com, $60) has attractive, clean rooms, pleasant common and sitting areas, and a gorgeous pool. Have them pick you up at the airport.

Over $100

Another option is the old pyramidal Hotel Inter at the base of the Tiscapa Crater, now the ★ **Hotel Crowne Plaza** (located in Plaza Inter, tel. 800/226-0109 or 505/2228-3530, from $102), a landmark since the Somoza days. Its rooms afford supreme views of the lake.

NEAR THE AIRPORT

A convenient place to stay if you have an early flight is the **Best Western Las Mercedes** (directly across from the airport, tel. 505/2255-9900, lasmercedes.com.ni, $85). The **Camino Real** (Km 9.5 on Carretera Norte, tel. 505/2255-5888, caminoreal.com.ni, $105 d) is very close to the airport (they have a free shuttle), just minutes away on Carretera Norte.

LONG-TERM ACCOMMODATIONS

Visiting students tend to gravitate to **Hospedaje Familia Horbaty** (Barrio Los

Robles, tel. 505/2278-0905, thorbaty@hotmail.com, $9/night), also known as Arcoiris. It's a clean, comfortable, family-run guesthouse in a safe neighborhood. Internet is available, and laundry and other meals can be arranged. **Hostal Dulce Sueño** (50 meters east of Tica Bus, tel. 505/2228-4125 or 505/8424-0272, www.hostaldulcesueno.com, $280/month s, $400/month d) offers similar services. **Belinda's House** (Canal 2, 2 blocks north and 75 meters west, tel. 505/2266-3856, $300/month) is a cozy, family-run, long-term guesthouse. Next to Las Cazuelas restaurant and across from Guesthouse Santos, **Hotel/Apartamentos Los Cisneros** (from Tica Bus, 1 block north, 1.5 blocks west, tel. 505/2222-3535, $30 d) rents small, fully furnished apartments that include refrigerator, private phone, and parking facilities.

At the higher end, several boutique hotels can accommodate long-stay visitors in luxury with full cable TV, Internet, and laundry service. **Hotel El Almendro** (from the Metrocentro rotunda, 2 blocks west, half a block south, tel. 505/2270-1260, www.hotelelalmendro.com, $40/night) specializes in long-term accommodations, offering studio suites with kitchenettes and parking; pricing depends on the length of your stay. Being able to cook your own meals is a huge advantage.

Food

Keeping up with restaurants is a challenge in a city where most restaurants thrive for a year or two and then vanish. Dining out is the mainstay of Managua's elite and they tend to abandon a place as soon as something newer and trendier comes along. But a few classics help hold the whole scene together. ¡Buen provecho!

La Colonia and **La Unión** are your go-to supermarkets, with produce and products varying based on the neighborhood. The

many branches of La Colonia and La Unión not only stock their modern aisles with national and imported foodstuffs, they also sell clothing, sandals, books, CDs, cosmetics, and more. The easiest to reach from Barrio Martha Quezada is just up the road at Plaza España. If you're in the Carretera Masaya area, you're closest to the Unión that is caddy corner to the Hilton Princess, or one of the Colonias in Metrocentro or Galerías. There are several other supermarkets around the city, but most travelers will find what they need at one of the many smaller "mini-supers" and *pulperías* (corner stores) that populate the neighborhoods.

Managua's coffee shop chain, **Casa de Café,** features a selection of pastries, smoothies, and Nicaraguan coffee. In the Los Robles location, food is served on an airy second-story open terrace overlooking the street. There are branches around the city and in many commercial centers as well. At most locations, solid breakfasts are served in addition to other meals, including delicious salads.

CARRETERA MASAYA AND VICINITY
Los Robles and Altamira

For home-cooked Nicaraguan cuisine in an upscale atmosphere, **La Cocina de Doña Haydee** (Carretera a Masaya Km 4.5, from Optica Matamoros 1 block west, No. 71, tel. 505/2270-6100, www.lacocina.com.ni, daily 7:30am-10:30pm, $3-7) has been around for ages and is popular among locals and foreigners alike. ★ **La Trenza** (in Altamira, next to Claro Altamira, tel. 505/2277-4001, daily 7am-8pm, $3-6) is a new option for local fare. This is a great place to give *quesillo* a try, as it's usually a street food not found in restaurants. Their fresh cheese comes straight from Boaco. They serve a different soup every day, and have great typical Nica breakfasts and *fritanga* (Nicaraguan fried food) at night. They have another location on Carretera Sur. **Café Margarita** (del Hotel Colón, 1 block south, half a block west, tel. 505/2277-1723 or 505/2278-1167, daily 8am-10pm, $2-5) is known for its cakes, but serves quality crepes and coffee as well.

La Terraza Cevichera (from Monte de los Olivos, 1 block north, 1 block west, tel. 505/2252-4240, Wed.-Sat. noon-10pm, Sun. noon-8 pm, $3-15) is a great place to have a cold beer (or margarita) and sample ceviche at a reasonable price. It's a popular place for the after-work crowd. **Mojitos** (from Monte de los Olivos, 1 block north, Mon.-Sat. from 3pm, $5-12) serves both Cuban and Nicaraguan

food on a grill set up inside the front end of an old car. Don't skip one of their fruit-infused mojitos!

Specializing in seafood, **Taska Kiko** (100 yards east of Monte de los Olivos, tel. 505/2270-1569, Mon.-Sat. noon-10:30pm, Sun. noon-9pm, $10) is a popular restaurant serving traditional Spanish food. Plates offer small portions, but you can get your money's worth by splitting a large platter or paella dish. There are no menus, instead food is listed on hard-to-read chalkboards, leaving waiters to promote pricey (but delicious) specials. This is relaxed fine dining.

Don Pan (2 blocks east of Lacmiel, across from Pizza Valenti) serves sandwiches, smoothies, coffee, and baked goods.

For tasty Peruvian-Asian fusion, ★ **La Terraza Peruana** (de Pastelería Sampson, 1 block north, Casa #14, Planes de Altamira, tel. 505/2278-0031, $5-10) has exquisite ceviches and other seafood dishes, and also a huge array of appetizers, chicken, and beef entrées served under romantically dim lighting. **El Muelle** (1 block east of the Hotel Intercontinental Metrocentro, $6-8) offers excellent seafood cocktails and main courses.

La Muralla China (from the stoplight at Plaza el Sol, 3.5 blocks south, in front of Telerepuestos, $7-10) is the best bang for your buck for Chinese food in Managua. Large portions of lo mein and fried rice with chicken, seafood, or pork are popular items.

Zona Hippos

Zona Hippos lies just off the Carretera Masaya and is thickly clustered with competing restaurants and lively sports bars with open-air seating. **El Garabato** (2 blocks south of the Hotel Seminole Plaza, tel. 505/2278-3156, daily noon-11pm, $2-12) is a great choice for their variety of Nicaraguan classic foods and internationally inspired chicken and beef dishes. The ambiance is pleasant, but it gets noisy later at night. Portions are small, but good quality.

Half a block south, you'll find ★ **Coche Café** (tel. 505/7734-5843, daily). Keep an eye out for their faded purple sign. This is a quiet place to grab panini and sip some of the best coffee in town (while enjoying the free Wi-Fi). For every pound of coffee they buy, 35 percent of the retail price goes straight to the local producer.

One of Managua's fanciest and oldest dining options, **La Marseillaise** (Calle Principal Los Robles, tel. 505/2277-0224, Mon.-Sat. noon-3pm and 6pm-11pm, $20-30) is a city classic since before the Revolution, serving traditional French cuisine and stunning desserts, all in a classy building adorned with works of art. It's also one of the city's most expensive, so be prepared.

One of the best seafood places in town, with an ample patio for outdoor seating, and air-conditioning indoors, is **Marea Alta** (across from La Marseillaise, tel. 505/2270-7959, $6-12).

Villa Fontana and Las Colinas

In this expat-populated area, there are plenty of pricey but delicious restaurants. ★ **Ola Verde** (Carretera Masaya, Km 8, first entrance to Las Colinas 1 block east, tel. 505/2276-2652, Mon.-Sat. 7am-11pm, Sun. 8am-9pm, breakfast from $5, lunch and dinner $7-12) features fresh juices, salads, soups, hummus, and baba ghanoush on a fresh menu of changing vegetarian and chicken dishes. Ola Verde has a small shop of natural products and is a popular meeting spot for foreigners.

On your way to Granada, **Sushi Itto** (tel. 505/2278-4886, Mon.-Thurs. 11:30am-11pm, Fri.-Sat. 11:30am-midnight, Sun. 11:30am-10pm, from $8), a Mesoamerican chain of good-quality sushi restaurants, has three branches in Managua, one in the Galerías Santo Domingo, with reasonably-priced rolls and meals. They get creative, mixing local fare with traditional Japanese cuisine (the Nica Roll features *gallo pinto* and fried chicken). ★ **Café Las Flores** (Km 6.5 Carretera Masaya, tel. 505/2252-6083, Mon.-Thurs. 7am-9pm, Fri. 7am-10pm, Sat. 8am-10pm, Sun. 8am-8pm) sells delicious coffee from the farm of the same name on Volcán

Mombacho. This contemporary café showcases their Rainforest Alliance-certified coffee in addition to offering a delicious food menu and a selection of coffee-related gifts. It's often full around mealtimes, creating a lively atmosphere.

In the Zona Rosa, **Chick Chak** (in Camino del Oriente complex on Carretera Masaya, tel. 505/2277-0167, daily, $5-10) is an Italian restaurant serving freshly made pizzas, calzones and pastas. This location offers both indoor and patio seating. (There's another location at Km 9 on Carretera Sur.) Come for their daily two-for-one happy hour, 5pm-7:30pm. This is one of the few places in the country that serves red wine at room temperature. **G-HOP** (Camino del Oriente complex on Carretera Masaya, Mon.-Sat. 7am-9pm, Sun. 8am-2pm, $3-10), which stands for George's House of Pancakes, has superb pancakes and French toast. They also serve hamburgers and fried ice cream, and have a respectable number of vegetarian options.

BOLONIA

The budget backpacker stronghold specializes in low-cost eating as well: it's nothing fancy, but the price is right. If you prefer a pastry for breakfast, try **Cafetín Tonalli** (from Tica Bus, 3 blocks east, half a block south, tel. 505/2222-2675, $2-5), a unique women's cooperative that produces extraordinarily good breads and cakes, and sells juices, cheese, coffee, and more (Swiss training!). Take out or eat in their enclosed outdoor patio.

The neighborhood's favorite *fritanga* has satisfied decades of backpack travelers and remains a great option for low-cost dining. **Fritanga Doña Pilar** (1 block west, half a block north of Tica Bus, daily 6pm-9pm) only serves dinner: chicken, *gallo pinto, tostones,* fried cheese, and an icy glass of fruit juice. The food will fill you up for a price that can't be beat, if you're comfortable eating at a plastic table, roadside. For a similar atmosphere, but higher quality eats, head to ★ **Comida's Sara** (from Tica Bus, 1 block north, 1.5 blocks west, across from Hospedaje

Santos, Mon.-Sat. 4pm-11pm, $4), where you'll find a surprising variety, including fried eggplant, grilled beef, pasta, and even curry. It's a rare treat for vegetarians.

★ **Restaurante Palace of Korea** (from the entrance of the Hospital Militar 1 block west, next to Western Union, tel. 505/2266-8968, $10-15), owned by a Korean family, serves tasty, high-quality authentic Korean and Japanese dishes listed on a long menu. The waiters are happy to explain dishes (and how to eat them). These are big portions, which make them great for sharing.

CARRETERA SUR

On your way out Carretera Sur towards the Pacific coast, you'll find a cluster of restaurants that expats flock to, and for good reason—they're some of the best in Managua.

★ **ImBiss** (Km 8.5 Carretera Sur, Plaza La Liga, tel. 505/2265-3613 daily noon-8pm, $4-6) is one of the few places in town for genuine gyros and falafel. Sip a cold German beer on the covered patio while you wait for your sandwich or salad. **The Diner** (Km 8.5 Carretera Sur, Plaza La Liga, tel. 505/2265-1837, Wed.-Mon., $4-10) has the best burger in town (made from quality Nicaraguan beef). Wash it down with one of their delicious milkshakes. On Sundays (from 8am), they serve North American breakfast food (pancakes, waffles, French toast).

The thin-crust brick-oven pizza at **Casa Mia** (Km 12.7 Carretera Sur, tel. 505/2271-7054 or 505/7809-2880, daily noon-11pm, $7-20) is worth the schlep to the southern edge of the city (or a stop on your way out of town). The dim lighting along with Italian music in the background creates a romantic atmosphere. If you're not up for going out, call to order delivery service.

At ★ **La Cueva del Buzo** (Km 13 Carretera Sur, 100 meters south, 100 meters east, tel. 505/2265-8336, Mon. and Wed. 6pm-11pm, Sat.-Sun. noon-11pm, $10-18) the passionate Italian chef-owner serves some of the classiest seafood in town, and makes each plate into a work of art. This is a truly culinary excellence, with delicate flavor combinations that take food to a whole other level.

La Casserole (Km 13.5, $6-15, open daily at noon) serves a sit-down meal of sushi, steak, duck, seafood, salad, or crepes on an open-air patio surrounded by plants and flowers.

If you're on a budget, get in line for the buffet at ★ **Comedor Xiomara Nuñez Hernandez** (Km 7.5 Carretera Sur, from Tip-Top Nejapa 20 meters south, tel. 505/2265-3494, $3) at 12pm on the dot to beat the lunch rush and have your pick of some of the best home-cooked food in Managua. Buffets in Nicaragua are not all-you-can-eat, so the price will depend on how heavy your plate is. There's no sign out front, but it's easy to spot at lunchtime by the long line of people coming out the door and the cluster of parked cars on the highway.

Information and Services

BANKS

Banking hours in Managua are Monday-Friday 8am-4:30pm and Saturday 8am-noon. Along Carretera Masaya, you'll find the **Banco de América Central (BAC), Bancentro** (in the LAFISE financial center), **Banco de Finanzas (BDF), Banpro,** and **Citi Bank. HSBC** is in the Discovery building in Villa Fontana. For travelers staying in Bolonia, the nearest bank is the Citi Bank or BAC in Plaza España. Most banks have branches in or near the main malls.

Bancentro will change euros directly to local currency without first changing them to U.S. dollars (and taking another commission). If you're looking to avoid ATM fees, BAC will swipe your card for no charge (except the exchange rate if you want *córdobas*).

You can also use the *coyotes* (money changers) on the streets or in the markets. Most offer reasonable rates, but to be sure, check the exchange rate before you go so you don't get swindled.

EMERGENCY SERVICES

There are several hospitals in Managua. The most modern are the private **Hospital Vivian Pellas** (outside of Managua on the highway to Masaya, tel. 505/2255-6900, www.metropolitano.com.ni) and **Salud Integral** (from the Montoya statue, 1 block north, 1 west, tel. 505/2251-2030, www.hospitalsaludintegral.com.ni). For less serious ailments and stomach disorders, **Hospital Bautista** (Barrio Largaespada, near the main fire station, tel. 505/2264-9020) is accustomed to dealing with foreigners. Salud Integral attends less serious ailments as well, but expect to pay $100 deposit to be seen there. You'll be seen for free at any public facility, but expect a long wait.

LAUNDRY

If you're roughing it, you'll have noticed most *hospedajes* have a *lavandero* (cement-ridged washboard). Buy a slug of bar soap ($0.30) at the local corner store, roll up your sleeves, and scrub away like everybody else. Most *hospedajes* have someone who will wash and iron for a reasonable fee as well. Otherwise, try one of the many **Dryclean USA** locations, such as behind the Tip-Top Chicken on Carretera Masaya. Another branch is located in La Colonia in Plaza España, but their prices will make you wish you'd bought the bar soap.

TRAVEL AGENTS AND TOUR OPERATORS

Many travel agents operate just southeast of the Plaza España and are a short cab ride from Barrio Martha Quezada. **Viajes Atlántida** (1 block east and half a block north of the Rotunda El Güegüense, tel. 505/266-8720) is a renowned agency and the official representative for American Express in Nicaragua. Close to Barrio Martha Quezada, **Viajes MTOM** (in Plaza Bolonia, tel. 505/2266-0017) is quite professional. For local tour operators based in the city, try **Solentiname Tours** (tel. 505/8852-3380, www.solentinametours.com) or **Güegüense Tours** (Km 5 Carretera Masaya, Plaza King Palace, tel. 505/2277-2280, www.gueguensetours.com).

OPPORTUNITIES FOR STUDY

You can join classes in Latin dancing any time at **La Academia Nicaragüense de Danza** (50 meters north of the UCA gates, tel. 505/2277-5557), **Cultura Salsera** (next to hotel Holiday Inn in Plaza Eclipse, tel. 505/8990-9577), or **Fusión** (from Pool 8, 50 meters west, tel. 505/2252-4232 or 505/8529-7008).

Viva Spanish School (in Barrio La Luz, from the Banco Produzcamos Building, 2 blocks south, tel. 505/2270-2339) offers Spanish classes for all levels and even has homestay opportunities with Nicaraguan families.

Transportation

GETTING THERE AND AWAY
Air

The **Augusto C. Sandino Airport** (Carretera Norte, www.eaai.com.ni) receives direct flights from Miami, Houston, Atlanta, Fort Lauderdale, Mexico City, San José, Panama City, Tegucigalpa, and San Salvador. Airline **La Costeña** (lacostena.online.com.ni) operates nationally between the RAAN and the RAAS, Ometepe, and Río San Juan. They have one international flight to Tegucigalpa.

A **taxi** from the airport to Carretera Masaya generally costs $12-15. A cab ride to and from the airport might cost you as much as $25 if you don't bargain well. If you're on a budget and traveling light, you can catch a bus along the highway in front of the airport heading towards the Mercado Mayoreo. From the terminal, ask someone to point you in the direction of the bus stop. You can take *ruta* 110 or 120 to Carretera Masaya (get off at Metrocentro) or the 102 to Bolonia (get off at Panadera Norma). If you arrive after dark, it's much safer to take a taxi.

Adelante Express (tel. 505/8850-6070 or 505/8325-9074, www.adelanteexpress.com, reservations@adelanteexpress.com) offers fast, direct ground transportation in private vehicles between the Managua airport and Peñas Blancas at the Costa Rican border for people looking to bypass Managua entirely. They stop in Granada, San Juan del Sur, and San Jorge. Prices vary, and you need to reserve ahead on their website. They don't operate during off-season (Sept. 15-Oct. 31).

Bus

Four main bus terminals link Managua to the towns and cities of Nicaragua's farthest corners.

TO POINTS NORTH AND EAST

Buses to and from Estelí, Matagalpa, Ocotal, Jinotega, Boaco, Juigalpa, El Rama, and San Carlos operate out of the **Mercado Mayoreo** bus terminal on the eastern edge of town. It's far from everything, except the airport. To get from the market to the other end of Managua on public transport, ask someone to point you to the parada de buses (bus stop). You can take the 102 *ruta* bus to get to Bolonia (get off in front of the Panadera Norma) or the 110 or 120 to get to Metrocentro (near Los Robles), but plan up to an additional hour's travel through Managua's heart (more during rush hour); a taxi is quicker and should cost no more than $8 for a solo traveler. If you're going with an unknown driver, it's best to fill your cab with other travelers.

TO POINTS WEST AND NORTHWEST

Buses to and from León, Chinandega, and the Pacific coast arrive and depart in the **Israel Lewites** market. The terminal is surrounded on all sides by a chaotic fruit market by the same name; watch your belongings and expect a slightly more aggressive crowd of *buseros* (bus drivers). *Microbuses* to León and

unloading cargo in the Huembes bus terminal

Chinandega are slightly more expensive, but faster, and can be found in front of the **UCA.** Both Mercado Israel and the UCA are on the same road. Cross the street to take a 110, 114, 120, or 210 bus to Metrocentro. A taxi should charge you $2 to get to Los Robles. To get to Bolonia, cross the street and take the 118 from Israel to the Panadera Norma stop. Expect a taxi to charge $3.

TO POINTS SOUTH

Fast, express minibuses, known as *interlocales,* are the best option for Jinotepe, Diriamba, Masaya, and Granada, and depart from a lot across the street from the **UCA.** Service runs 6am-9pm.

The terminal for buses from Carazo, Masaya, Granada, Rivas, Ometepe, the border at Peñas Blancas, and San Juan del Sur is at **Mercado Roberto Huembes** in south-central Managua. The taxi ride between the market and Bolonia or Los Robles should cost no more than $2-3 per person. The 110 *ruta* will take you to Metrocentro from here. This is a busy terminal, serving thousands of commuters from points south. Expect taxi drivers to swarm you as you leave the bus.

GETTING AROUND

Given the lack of landmarks and the confusing public transportation, Managua is easiest to deal with by taxi. The addresses given in this book are written with that in mind. Watch your step walking around Managua. Thousands of uncovered, ankle-breaking manholes abound, sometimes up to three meters deep.

Taxi

If you even approach the edge of the street, Managua's 14,000 taxis will circle you like vultures, beeping for your attention. *Taxistas* in the city work in weekly shifts, which change at 2pm daily (except Sundays when everyone's free to work all day). All drivers have a small sign on their dashboard. If they're on shift (*de turno*) the sign says "TAXI" and they have a tower on top of the car. Otherwise the sign will say, *"Fuera de turno."*

Taxis will take you most places for $1-7. Managua taxis have no meters, so settle on a price before getting in! (Drivers are used to haggling.) Hotel and guesthouse owners can usually arrange a reliable taxi driver if you feel insecure about taking a cab on the street. This is generally the safest option.

Near Managua

★ CHOCOYERO-EL BRUJO NATURE RESERVE

Less than 28 kilometers away from downtown Managua is a little pocket of wilderness so vibrant with wildlife you'll forget the capital is literally just over the horizon. The **Chocoyero-El Brujo Nature Reserve** (tel. 505/2276-7810, foreigners $3.50) is a 41-square-kilometer protected hardwood forest that provides nearly 20 percent of Managua's water supply. In the midst of moist hardwood forest and pineapple farms are two 25-meter waterfalls separated by a rocky knife-edge. El Brujo was named The Warlock

because to the locals the fact that no river flows out from the waterfall meant it must be enchanted. The other fall, Chocoyero, was named for the incredible number of *chocoyos* (parakeets) that inhabit the adjacent cliff walls.

In fact, this protected area is a naturalist's paradise, with five kinds of *chocoyo* and 113 other bird species (including several owls), plus 49 species of mammals, and 21 species of reptiles and amphibians. Sharp-eyed travelers may even spot small cat species, like *tigrillos* and *gatos de monte,* and you'll likely hear both howler and capuchin monkeys in the treetops. In addition to having well-kept hiking trails,

Chocoyero-El Brujo is one of the few places in Nicaragua that encourages tent camping, making it a great place to spend an evening in the wild. Conditions are simple: a rustic, wooden base camp where guides will meet you and walk you the remaining way to the falls. The two best times to see the *chocoyos* are at 5:30am, when they leave their nests, and at 4pm, when the flock returns. To catch the morning commute, you'll obviously have to spend the previous night there.

Guides, available on weekends, charge a nominal fee ($5-10 for a group of 12). You can rent two-person tents on the premises for $11 each, or set up your own. This is a safe, pretty, and easily accessible area in which to camp for a night. If you call ahead and make a reservation, they'll even cook simple, traditional Nica fare for you for about $3 per meal. The reserve is actively promoting low-ropes courses, enviro-camps, and more to local schools and church groups.

Unless you have rented a vehicle, you'll need to charter a sturdy taxi from Managua with a group to take you all the way to the reserve. In a vehicle the trip takes 45 minutes. Otherwise, take any bus leaving Managua's Huembes terminal bound for La Concepción (called La Concha for short); buses leave Managua every 15 minutes. Get off at Km 21.5, where you'll see a wooden sign for the park entrance, then stretch out for a long walk. The dirt road that travels seven kilometers southwest to the reserve leads down a series of volcanic ridges and across a broad valley to the falls. It's an easy two-hour walk, passing through fields of pineapples, bananas, and coffee. Halfway down the road, you'll find a small community where you can rent bikes or horses to take you the rest of the way (horse $1 per hour, guide $1 per hour, bicycle $0.50 per hour). There also may be some buses from Ticuantepe that take you all the way in—ask around.

MONTIBELLI WILDLIFE RESERVE

This 162-hectare private **reserve** (tel. 505/2220-9801, info@montibelli.com) and award-winning sustainable tourism project is set within the biological corridor between Chocoyero-El Brujo and Volcán Masaya National Park. In the family's eco-lodge **Oropéndola** (tel. 505/2220-9801), you'll find comfortable accommodations with private bathrooms and an ample deck perched on the edge of a valley—great for armchair birding. There are three trails to hike, with views of the Volcán Masaya and surrounding forest. The restaurant features family recipes and Sunday barbecues. Over 155 bird species have been spotted here, including manakins, motmots, oropendolas, trogons, tanagers, toucans, woodpeckers, and hummingbirds. You're also likely to spot howler monkeys. This is one of the most accessible wildlife reserves in the country, making it really easy to escape from the city.

To reach the reserve, **drive** south on Carretera Masaya, taking the turnoff through the town of Ticuantepe. Turn right at the only stoplight in town and drive until you reach the last street of Parque Juan Ramón Padilla, where you'll turn right. Go a block and turn left onto pavestone. When you hit the dirt road turn right. When the road ends turn left. When you get to the Enacal water well you'll find the entrance to Montibelli on your right-hand side. Go 700 meters until you arrive at the entrance. It should take you about a half hour. By **bus,** find a *micro* at Huembes, or stop one heading south on Carretera Masaya, going to La Concha and tell the *busero* to let you off at Parque Juan Ramón Padilla, where you can take a moto-taxi all the way to the reserve. Expect the trip to take 1.5 hours. Better yet, contact **Ileana Hernández** (tel. 505/2220-9801, info@montibelli.com) at the reserve to organize transport from Managua. **Va Pues Tours** (tel. 505/2315-4099, www.vapues.com) organizes transportation to and from your hotel in Managua and provides a guide for about $40 a person.

THE LAGUNA OF XILOÁ

Less than a half hour from the capital on the highway to León, the Peninsula de Chiltepe protrudes into the southwestern shore of Lake Xolotlán, cradling two ancient volcanic cones drowned in clean rainwater. Part of the Maribios chain, the twin crater lagoons of Xiloá and Apoyeque are a fun day trip if you find yourself in Managua for more than a weekend and eager for some greenery. Broader and more easily accessed, **Xiloá** has restaurants and a tourist center and is a nice area for swimming (you may see the occasional marine biologist scuba diving to study the lake's endemic species). There are great views from the surrounding hills, but no hiking trails. You can find a guide to take you on a hike at one of the lagoon restaurants.

Buses leave Managua's Mercado Israel Lewites infrequently and go directly to the water at Xiloá. It's easier to take any León-bound bus from the same market, get off at the top of the road to Xiloá, and walk (30 minutes). Pay $0.50 per person ($1 per vehicle) to enter the park facilities at the water's edge.

You can find fresh fish from the Pacific just a couple of hours from Managua.

PACIFIC BEACHES

Roughly 65 kilometers due west of the capital are a handful of easy-to-reach beaches, with facilities ranging from low-key, grungy *hospedajes* to all-out, all-inclusive resorts. In fact, the diversity along the coastline couldn't be greater. Pochomíl attracts the casual day-tripper and increasingly surfers, while Montelimar is a pricey but pleasurable all-inclusive resort. Los Cardones is an eco-friendly offbeat lodge popular with surfers and families that's harder to get to but worth the effort. When you hear about all the foreign real estate investment in Nicaragua, much of it is happening right here, so watch for big changes.

Pochomíl and Masachapa

Pochomíl is a sleepy beach town in the midst of an economic revival, while wealthy investors build beachfront estates and hotel complexes around it. Hotel and restaurant rates fluctuate wildly according to the calendar. Semana Santa and Christmas are the most expensive (and most crowded) times of year to visit. In the wet season, prices become significantly more flexible, but at any month of the year, traveling with a group gives you significant leverage to bargain for a good deal. Travelers driving their own vehicles will pay a $1 entrance fee to enter the tourist area.

Competition among hotel and restaurant owners is particularly fierce. As you get off the bus expect to be assaulted by employees of a dozen restaurants all trying to drag you into their establishments. No one place is any better than another; you can expect beachfront palm-thatch huts, fried fish, and cold beer no matter where you go. One of the longest-established places on the beach, **Hotel Vistamar** (505/2265-8099, vistamarhotel.com) has 43 rooms, one suite, and a pleasant restaurant overlooking the water.

Hostal Real Masachapa (from Petronic 1 block west and 75 meters south, tel. 505/2269-6772, $55) boasts room views of the sea and a beachfront pool. **Masachapa Escuela de Hotelería Hotel** (150 meters toward the beach after entering Masachapa, tel. 505/8988-9098, www.mhotelmasachapa.com, $55 d) is a

Pochomíl is an easy day trip from Managua.

88 double guest rooms with queen-size beds and 205 bungalows with king-size beds, private bath, air-conditioning, TV, strongbox, and minibar (but no free Internet access). The price includes 24 hours of unlimited feasting, drinking, swimming, and playing. Often crowded during weekends with visitors from Managua, it is more peaceful on weekdays when you can swim in one of the largest pools in Central America by yourself. Any bus to Pochomíl will also get you to Montelimar. There are various tour operators that arrange for transfers from the Managua airport or hotels. Ask about deep off-season discounts.

San Diego
LOS CARDONES SURF LODGE
Farther north of Pochomíl and Masachapa, ★ **Los Cardones** (tel. 505/8618-7314 or 505/8364-5925, www.loscardones.com, loscardonesecolodge@gmail.com, $70 plus tax pp) is a unique, peaceful, highly recommended beach escape with direct access to consistent surf breaks nearly year-round. Set on five acres of organically managed land, Los Cardones rents half a dozen simple but elegant bungalows made from wood and thatch. All have soft beds, no electricity, and composting toilets; all are also waterfront. Their inspired and creative menu involves lots of fresh fish, and their commitment to both the local community and the ecosystem is admirable. The energy use is solar-powered, and they work to promote conservation of sea turtles. (You may even see some lounging on the beach.) Rent surf or boogie boards for the waves, take a surf lesson or yoga class, collect shells on the beach, or hike to nearby pre-Columbian petroglyphs. Rates are all-inclusive. The managers started **Arte Acción,** which promotes social change through art classes, in a neighboring community. Many guests often join in and help the class.

hotel school famed for its service, but it's not right on the beach. The restaurant is closed on Mondays. Fifty-year-old **Hotel Summer** (next to the police station, tel. 505/2269-7754 or 505/8608-3283, hotelsummermasachapa. jimdo.com, $51) is right on the beach and popular with visiting Nicaraguans. They serve enormous fried fish, and if you're just there for the day, buying food will give you access to their pool.

Buses leave Managua's Israel Lewites for the two-hour trip to Pochomíl every 30 minutes all day until 5pm. The last bus from Pochomíl back to Managua departs at 5:30pm from the cul-de-sac.

Barceló Montelimar Beach
Somoza's former personal summer palace was converted into a resort in the 1980s and since being purchased by Barceló Resorts is now **Barceló Montelimar Beach** (tel. 505/2264-9310, U.S. and Canada tel. 800/227-2356, www.barcelomontelimarbeach.com, $90-150 pp), an all-inclusive five-star resort. It offers

They'll send a car to Managua for you, or you can take the bus to San Cayetano from Mercado Israel Lewites in Managua (leaves every 45 minutes 4am-9pm daily) and get off at "California." Then walk, or hitch, 15 kilometers toward the ocean and follow the signs. You could also pay $4 for a moto taxi. To drive, take the Carretera Masachapa to Km 49, then drive 15 kilometers on the Playa San Diego Road until you hit the beach.

GRAN PACIFICA RESORT

Milagro del Mar (tel. 505/8850-3061 or from the U.S. 832/886-0004, www.milagrodelmar.com, non-inclusive rates from $140 pp) is the resort at Gran Pacifica, a gringo residential development project complete with country club. The all-inclusive resort boasts a golf course, horseback riding, a spa, yoga classes, and access to word-class surf breaks. They can also arrange a tour of a nearby coffee plantation. If you want to come just for the day, expect to pay $5 at the gate and $5 to use the pool. If you have a reservation, ask about arranging an airport shuttle. Gran Pacifica is close to Los Cardones. To get there, instead of turning into Los Cardones, go right and continue until you get to the beach.

Granada and Masaya

Look for ★ to find recommended
sights, activities, dining, and lodging.

Highlights

© AVALON TRAVEL

★ **Iglesia La Merced:** Climb the bell tower for the best view in all of Granada (page 65).

★ **Las Isletas:** Spend a lazy day swimming, picnicking, and relaxing among hundreds of gorgeous islands (page 78).

★ **Zapatera Archipelago National Park:** These islands are rich in wildlife and historic artifacts (page 79).

★ **Volcán Mombacho:** More than a gorgeous photo-op, Volcán Mombacho has a first-class set of hiking trails, an eco-lodge, and a canopy tour (page 80).

★ **El Mercado Viejo Craft Market:** Handmade pottery, leatherwork, and paintings are all handsomely displayed in a market designed to showcase Nicaragua's finest crafts (page 84).

★ **Volcán Masaya National Park:** Peer into the gates of hell, wherein dwell demon parakeets, then visit the museum of this popular national park (page 89).

★ **Laguna de Apoyo:** Get away from it all in what might be the coolest swimming hole in the country: an enticing volcanic crater lake ringed with forest (page 92).

★ **Catarina Mirador:** This crater lip's patio terrace, with one of the best panoramas in Nicaragua, often offers live marimba music to accompany your beverage (page 95).

★ **San Juan de Oriente:** Visit this town of potters' workshops where you can observe ceramics being made and browse pre-Colombian style ceramic pieces (page 96).

★ **Carazo Beaches:** Lounge in natural pools found in huge rocks that line these beaches (page 100).

A

ll within an hour of the capital, Granada, Masaya, and Carazo contain a taste of Nicaragua's must-sees. You'll find quaint colonial towns, smoking volcanoes, lagoons, traditional artistry, coffee farms, and the crashing tide of

the Pacific Ocean.

Granada's polished colonial architecture, horse-drawn carriages, and abundance of cafés, hotels, and spas—plus its strategic location—make it one of the country's most comfortable and popular spots for international visitors. Granada is a historical stronghold of conservatism. It is a striking juxtaposition of antique and modern, rich and poor, foreign and local. If you want to get a chocolate massage, eat a Middle Eastern dinner, and soak up some colonial charm, Granada is the place to go.

Just half an hour outside Managua, Masaya is a small town with a relaxed vibe. It's a city of artisans, metalworkers, leatherworkers, carpenters, painters, and musicians. In fact, no other region of Nicaragua is as blessed with a sense of artistry and creativity. Many of the handicrafts found in markets throughout the country are Masayan: hand-woven hammocks, terra-cotta pottery, musical instruments, and more. The charming Pueblos

Blancos, to the south and west of Masaya, are artisan villages. Make a day of pueblo hopping to visit workshops. In San Juan de Oriente you can watch a potter form a vase on a foot-spun wheel and buy pieces right out of the kiln for very reasonable prices. If you're eager to come home with something special, this is the place to find it.

Also outside Masaya are two must-see volcanic craters. Volcán Masaya is one of the world's most accessible volcanoes, one of only two on Earth where you can walk up to the crater lip and look inside. The region's most popular swimming hole, the Laguna de Apoyo, is a scenic 200-meter-deep crater lagoon. Lie on a floating dock, or kayak across it, surrounded by the sounds of birds and howler monkeys.

PLANNING YOUR TIME

There's a lot to see in this region. One day is enough time to see the major sites within the

---

Previous: Catarina Mirador; public art in Masaya. **Above:** Granada's cathedral as seen from the bell tower of Iglesia La Merced.

Granada and Masaya

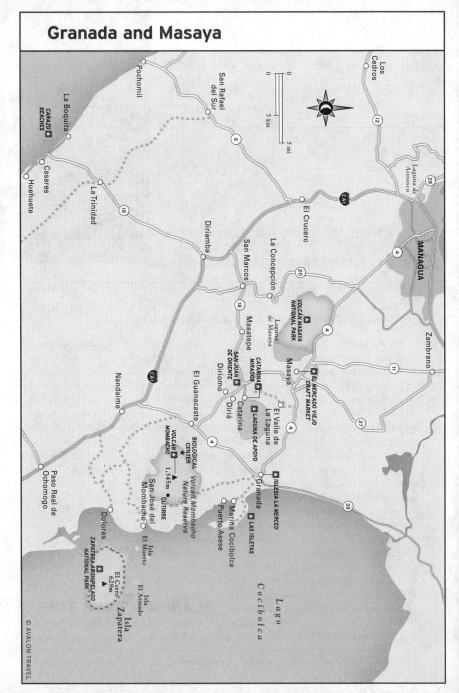

© AVALON TRAVEL

city of Granada. A lot of the city's charm lies in the interesting excursions reachable using Granada as a base camp. Leave half a day for a boat ride in Las Isletas, and another day for Volcán Mombacho. Naturalists can easily spend a long day on hiking trails, in the visitor's center, and on guided tours.

Most travelers devote a day or so to visiting the pueblos and markets in and around Masaya. It's possible to make Masaya your base for excursions, though many travelers opt to stay in Granada, which has a much wider selection of hotels and restaurants that cater to tourists. While you could conceivably day-trip to the Laguna de Apoyo, the hotel options make it a fun place to stay overnight. (When was the last time you woke up inside a volcano crater?) Just an hour to the west are the Carazo beaches. Spend the day soaking up the sun and surf in La Boquita, or stay a night and let the waves lull you to sleep.

Public transportation is frequent in this region, and it's easy enough to hop on a bus to get where you need to go. However, renting a car is a must if you're short on time.

Granada

Arguably Nicaragua's most picturesque town, Granada is an easy place to love. Much of its colonial architecture is remarkably intact and is being painstakingly restored. The colorful facades lining old narrow streets practically glow in the late afternoon sun. It's sultry and tropical here, and a fresh breeze blows off the waters of Lake Cocibolca. The views from along the lakeshore's broad, undeveloped shoreline—and the ever-looming silhouette of Volcán Mombacho—make for easy photos and good memories. At night the sky fills with stars and the neighbors come out to chitchat on their front stoops; inside even the most nondescript colonial facade is an open, private courtyard designed to capture the evening breeze.

See Granada from a horse-drawn carriage.

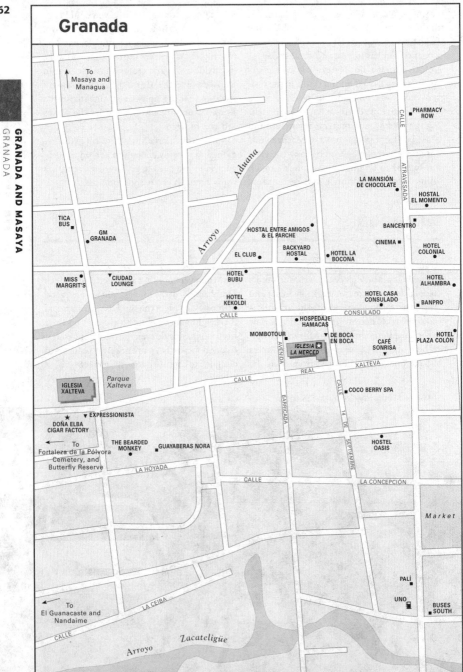

Granada

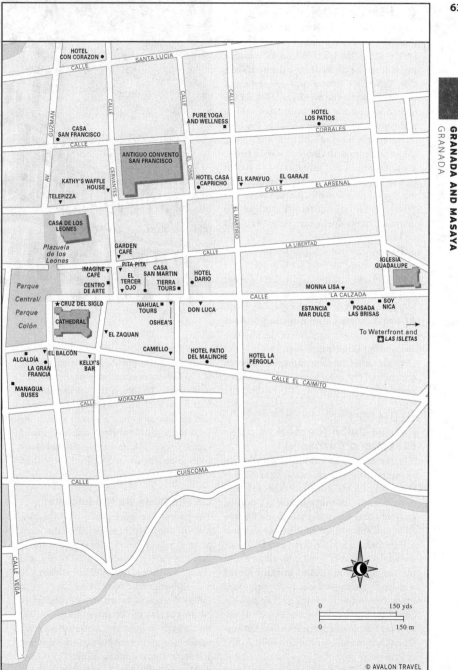

© AVALON TRAVEL

ORIENTATION

From Granada's central tree-lined plaza, a.k.a. the **Parque Central** and **Parque Colón,** look south to the giant Volcán Mombacho. Just behind the **cathedral** on the park's east side, **Calle La Calzada** runs due east about one kilometer to the municipal dock on the lake. A lot of the lodging and restaurants lie along this street or within a block or two of it.

At the lake, a paved road runs south along the water's edge to the *malecón* (waterfront), a tourist complex that's emptier than it should be due to its tendency to attract thieves (it's not a good idea to walk around a lot in this area). An easy taxi ride farther south are the marinas that provide boat access to Las Isletas and Zapatera.

West of the plaza is the **Xalteva** (pronounced, more or less, with a hard "h") neighborhood and eventually the cemetery and road to Nandaime. In this neighborhood, one block west of the Plaza, is **Calle Atravesada,** running north-south between the old 1886 train station and the bustling chaos of the municipal market. This is one of Granada's main thoroughfares and a modern commercial center for banks, movie theaters, and the like.

SIGHTS
Parque Colón (Central Plaza) and Cathedral

If Granada is the center of tourism in Nicaragua, then Granada's central plaza is the heart of it all. You'll pass through here dozens of times during your stay in Granada, and each time, sweat-drenched, you'll pause for something cold to drink. People-watchers will find it hard to leave, as the park is a steady stream of students gossiping, elderly men playing chess, and vendors hawking carved wooden toys, ceramics, jewelry, ice cream, and more. Order a glass of icy *fresco de cacao* at one of the corner kiosks, and enjoy the raucous bird-chatter in the treetops and the hustle and bustle of life in North America's first colonial city.

Cross the park to the magnificent

Granada's cathedral sits in the heart of the city.

cathedral on the plaza's east side. It's sometimes open to the public (even the bell towers). When the doors open for mass, it's worth a peek inside. The stone and wooden interior is dim and cool, and the bells echo overhead. Just outside the church's front step is the **Cruz del Siglo** (Century Cross), inaugurated January 1, 1900. Entombed in its cement are coins, pieces of art, and a gilded bottle from the 19th century.

La Plazuela de los Leones

The pedestrian space guarded by the cannon off the northeast corner of the main plaza is where Henry Morgan once set 18 cannons during his sacking of the city, and where, a century later, William Walker (the U.S. filibuster who once burned the city to the ground) was sworn in as President of Nicaragua. On the Plazuela's eastern side is the **Casa de los Leones,** a colonial-era home whose lush interior has been transformed into an international cultural center. Don Diego de Montiel, governor of Costa Rica, built the

Casa de los Leones in 1720. William Walker did not miss the opportunity to burn this place down, leaving nothing standing but the portal bearing the Montiel family crest (still visible). The unique, neoclassical colonnade facade was a product of the subsequent reconstruction. In 1987, the historical monument became the headquarters of the **Casa de los Tres Mundos Foundation** (tel. 505/2552-4176, www.c3mundos.org, daily 8am-6pm), bearing an art and music school, museum, historical archive, library, concert hall, literary café, bookstore, and exhibition space that hosts resident artists from around the world.

Antiguo Convento San Francisco

The **Antiguo Convento San Francisco** (1 block north and 2 east of the main cathedral, tel. 505/2552-5535, Mon.-Fri. 8am-5pm, Sat.-Sun. 9am-4pm, $2) and its trio of bells were once famously blue. Inside, set around open courtyards festooned with palm trees are centuries' worth of priceless artwork and 30 alter-ego statues collected a century ago from Zapatera Island. The carved basalt shows human forms with the heads of jaguars, birds, and crocodiles whose spirits were thought to flow through humans' souls—a rare look into the cosmology of Nicaragua's pre-Columbian peoples. There is also a large, to-scale replica of the city, and exhibits that represent the lifestyle of the Chorotega and Nahautl peoples. The convent was first built by Franciscan monks in 1529 and lasted 150 years before pirate Henry Morgan burned it to the ground. Since then it has housed William Walker's troops, U.S. Marines, a contingent of engineers surveying a possible canal route in the 1920s, and the National University.

Calle La Calzada

Walk east from Parque Colón toward the lake along Granada's hippest strip, recently reworked with a modern pedestrian-friendly design, but with an old feel featuring cobblestones, street lamps, and wide sidewalks. Halfway to the lake, stop at the 17th-century

Iglesia de Guadalupe, first built in 1626 and most recently refurbished in 1945. Continuing along the palm-lined boulevard, you'll reach the *muelle* and *malecón* (dock and waterfront) on the water's edge.

The Waterfront

At the lakeshore where the Calzada ends, stop and take in Granada's lacustrine panorama. Turn right and pass through "the rooks" (a pair of statues) to enter the **Centro Turístico,** a short row of restaurants and discos lining the lakeshore. This area has become attractive to robbers in the past few years and is often overrun with chayules (almost invisible biting water flies). Somehow this place fails to live up to its potential; it's not even good for swimming. From here, however, you can catch a cab south to where the boats depart for tours of the *isletas.*

★ Iglesia La Merced

Built in 1534, sacked and burned by Henry Morgan in 1670, then rebuilt, the church itself is pretty, located on the northeast corner of the intersection of the Calle Real and Avenida 14 de Septiembre. Ascend the tight spiral stairs of the **bell tower** (daily 10am-6pm, $1) for the single most spectacular view in the city. Look over an ocean of tiled roofs to the lake and *isletas,* with Volcán Mombacho over your shoulder. The scene changes over the course of the day; late afternoons are best when the shadows are long.

Fortaleza de la Pólvora and Cemetery

Built in 1748 to secure Granada's gunpowder supply from marauding pirates, **La Pólvora**'s (7 blocks west of La Merced, free) medieval architecture speaks of simplicity and strength: five squat towers and one heavily guarded gate with two oak doors. In the 20th century, both the city government and later Somoza's National Guard used the old fort and powder storage facility as a military garrison, and later a jail. These days it's a museum of arms or art whose exhibitions rotate regularly. Climb the towers for a breath of wind and a good perspective of the skyline, but watch your head and your step. Adjacent, the 10-meter-high arched stone walls known as **Los Muros de Xalteva** were erected by the Spaniards in the mid-1700s to separate Spanish settlements from those of the locals. There is a relaxing park across the street with interesting stone shapes.

Located at Granada's southwest corner, Granada's **cemetery** of enormous marble tombs—bigger than the homes of many Nicaraguans—shelters the bones of several centuries of elite from Granada's heyday, including a half-dozen presidents. Note the column-lined Capilla de Animas and the replica of the Magdalena de Paris, both built between 1876 and 1922.

Butterfly Reserve

At the **Nicaragua Butterfly Reserve** (2 kilometers down the dirt road to the right of the cemetery, tel. 505/8895-3012, nicaraguabutterflyreserve.wordpress.com, $5) tour the flight house filled with a magical array of butterfly species. You can also stroll around the grounds of this lush old fruit orchard. From the cemetery, it's 45 minutes on foot, or take a bicycle or pay $1 for a *moto* taxi.

RECREATION
Spas and Massage

The three blind masseuses at **Seeing Hands Massage** (Calle La Calzada in Hospital La Calzada and Calle 14 de Septiembre, across from Barba del Mono, tel. 505/8671-9770, massageseeinghands.blogspot.com, Mon.-Sat. 9am-5:30pm, 15-minute chair massage $5, 1-hour table massage $15) will give you a chair or full body massage. **Coco Berry Spa** (Calle 14 de Septiembre half a block south of the Iglesia La Merced, tel. 505/8466-6507, cocoberryspa.com, $30-40) is a full service spa that makes imaginative products using local products like cacao (don't miss the chocolate massage!) and volcanic clay. Their prices are extremely reasonable considering the quality of their products. **Pure Yoga and Wellness Retreats** (Calle Corrales, 1.5 blocks east of the Convento San Francisco, tel. 505/2552-2304, Purenica.com, daily) is a full service gym and yoga studio that has a variety of exercise and yoga classes as well as spa treatments. It's also home to a gigantic tortoise.

Boating and Swimming

Getting out on the water is the right way to enjoy this beautiful corner of Nicaragua.

Climb Iglesia la Merced's bell tower for the most spectacular view in the city.

Taking a boat trip through the *isletas* is the best way to do that.

Vladimir Torrez (at the end of the Centro Turístico Puerto Las Piedras Pintadas, tel. 505/8380-8196, tjorgevladimir@yahoo.com, $10/hour guided kayak tour, $20-40/hour boat tour, discounts for longer tours) is a recommended *lanchero* (boat operator), hired by many of the tour operators for his kayaks and motorboats. Vladimir and his team offer a variety of tour options. **Inuit Kayaks** (Centro Turístico, tel. 505/8691-0616, 2.5 hours minimum, $25/hour) rents kayaks.

The stand-up paddleboard trend has made it to Nicaragua and there are a few companies doing paddleboard tours of the *isletas*. **Livit Tours** (tel. 505/8085-7014, www.livit-water.com, $34-39, reservations must be made 24-hours ahead of time) is a company specializing in paddleboarding whose tours and paddleboard yoga classes leave from El Tercer Ojo restaurant twice a day.

To beat the heat, use the swimming pool at the **Mombacho Beach Club** (Calle Atravesada, across from Bancentro, tel. 505/2552-4678, daily 10am-6pm, $5), located inside Mansión de Chocolate. You can make spa and beauty appointments there as well, and these entitle you to use the pool. Swim laps, cool off, enjoy cocktails and light snacks, or check email in a chic atmosphere.

Bicycling

While biking around the city center can be complicated if you haven't oriented yourself first, there are plenty of other places to trek around town, including along the *malecón*. It's best to start early before the temperature rises. A bike ride down the Peninsula de Asese can be excellent, and the birdlife present there is astounding. In town, you can rent bikes at **Nahuatl Tours** (1 block down from the central square, tel. 505/8889-2461, nahualtours.com, $1/hr or $7/day) or, closer to the waterfront, **NicarAgua Dulce** (Marina Cocibolca, tel. 505/8802-0285, www.nicaraguadulce.com), where you can rent a beater bike. **De Tours** (Calle Corrales house #305,

northern side of the San Francisco Convent, tel. 505/2552-0155, www.detour-nicaragua.com), a tour operation committed to avoiding the use of fossil fuels, runs lots of bike trips to nearby sites and towns.

ENTERTAINMENT AND EVENTS
Bars and Clubs

There are three pub-style bars that are always full of traveler types on weekends. **Reilly's Irish Tavern** (Calle la Libetad, 1 block west of the Calzada, next to Imagine Café, tel. 505/7706-4157, daily from 9am) is probably the most popular bar among travelers. They have lots of themed nights and promotions as well as the best wings in town. **O'Sheas Irish Pub** (right on the Calzada, tel. 505/8454-1140 www.osheas-nicaragua.com, daily 8:30am-2am) is an Irish-owned pub that serves food and smoothies all day, and is a packed bar at night. Their specialty drink is the Jäger Thom (named after the owner), a dangerous combination of whisky, Jäger, and Redbull, served aflame. **Kelly's Bar** (Calle Caimito, 1 block east off of the Calzada, tel. 505/2552-2430, daily) is a sports bar turned club on the weekends. On Saturdays expect a $7-12 cover and an open bar.

A more romantic lounge scene can be found at **El Tercer Ojo** (Calle El Arsenal across from Convento San Francisco, tel. 505/2552-6451, Tues.-Sun. 11am-11pm). Try their swank tapas, wine, cocktails, and more. It's especially popular during happy hour (4pm-7pm). They are also now selling kombucha.

El Balcón (southeast corner of the central plaza, tel. 505/2552-6002, daily noon-10pm), on the second floor of the grand yellow-painted Gran Francia, offers the best aerial street-side balcony from which to watch the foot and horse traffic below as you sip your Centenario and enjoy the delicious bar menu.

Managua is better for dancing, but a tiny club scene exists in Granada. Casual and a little rowdy, **Inuit Bar** (inside the Centro Turístico, 505/8661-7655, Fri. and Sat. only)

Volunteering in Granada

If you can commit more than a couple of weeks and have decent Spanish, you can turn your vacation into something more than just travel by volunteering with one of several Granada-based organizations. Yes, you'll miss out on some hammock time, but look at what you'll gain:

Building New Hope (BNH) (U.S. tel. 412/421-1625, in Granada, call Donna Tabor at tel. 505/8852-0210, www.buildingnewhope.org), based in both Granada and Pittsburgh, Pennsylvania, is a nonprofit organization providing a number of ongoing programs with volunteer opportunities. BNH manages two neighborhood schools that welcome volunteer teachers' assistants. They assist the community library and reading-in-schools program (contact Carol Ann Rae). BNH is also on the lookout for music teachers for their **Rhythm in the Barrios** project (requires intermediate Spanish and one-month minimum commitment).

Empowerment International (519 Calle Libertad, tel. 505/2552-1653, U.S. tel. 303/823-6495, www.empowermentinternational.org) runs a community-based educational program for impoverished and at-risk youth. Direct work with the families and community is an integral part of their methodology, as are art and photography projects. They serve Villa Esperanza and Santa Ana de Malacos, two outlying communities of Granada. Intermediate Spanish is a must.

Hogar Madre Albertina (from Colegio Padre Misieri, 2 blocks north, hogardeninasmadrealbertina.com) is an underfunded home for girls where volunteers are sometimes welcome to read to or play games with the girls and help them with their homework. A one-month minimum stay and intermediate Spanish are required.

La Harmonía (Carraterra Masaya, 2 blocks west of La Colonia supermarket, eeap_aman@yahoo.com) is an organization for mentally and physically challenged children and young adults. They accept volunteers with basic Spanish who can teach handicrafts, weaving, haircutting, sign language, or have experience in special education.

La Esperanza Granada (Calle Libertad #307, tel. 505/8934-2273 or 8913-8946, www.la-esperanza-granada.org, info@la-esperanza-granada.org) focuses on education, especially with young children. Volunteers work in public schools on the outskirts of Granada; they tutor and teach arts and crafts, sports, English, and more. There is volunteer housing ($23/week) in the center of Granada; a one-month minimum stay and intermediate Spanish is preferred. They also have lots of experience with groups of international volunteers for short-term projects.

---

serves cold beer amidst reggaeton music. **WEEKEND** (in the Centro Turístico, tel. 505/8581-9549, Thurs.-Sun. $3-5 cover) is the trendiest club in town with live DJs and electronic music played at high volume. Make sure to take a taxi both ways and do not walk in this part of town at night.

Festivals and Events

A concerted effort to raise Granada's profile, the annual **Poetry Festival** (Feb.) is a knockout, drawing not only Nicaragua's most acclaimed literati and musicians (Gioconda Belli, Ernesto Cardenal, Norma Elena Gadea), but an astonishing array of poets and artists from around the world as well. The event capitalizes on the open spaces of several Granada landmarks, including cathedrals, the San

Francisco convent, and Granada's best plazas. If your trip coincides with this event, book your room early.

Berrinche Ambiental (Jan.) is another great festival that takes place in Granada. The programming focuses on youth and people who have "youthful spirits," using art, mime, and celebration to promote artistic expression and environmental consciousness. They offer lots of workshops and performances and always attract an international crowd.

Throughout the rest of the year, the **Casa de los Leones** (east side of Plazuela de los Leones, tel. 505/2552-4176) sponsors frequent events, including concerts by local musicians and visiting international artists. **Imagine Café** (tel. 505/2552-4672, imaginerestaurantandbar.com) is a restaurant in town that often has live music. Check their Facebook page (Imagine Restaurant and Bar) for upcoming events. Granada's humble movie theater, **El Teatro Karawala** (1 block west of the plaza), offers popular (often trashy) American movies.

SHOPPING

Though Masaya is the place most people look for artisan crafts, Granada offers a few unique shopping opportunities. There are several gift shops around the plaza, as well as frequent street vendors. The **municipal market** (1 block south of the plaza) spills up Calle Atravesada and is geared more for locals than tourists, but it is lots of fun to visit.

Cooperative El Parche Gift Shop (halfway down the block north of the Piedra Bocona, Calle 14 de Septiembre, tel. 505/8473-7700) is a cooperative store where local artisans display their products. While the products you find in many markets are often similar, this store has truly unique and creative items often made out of recycled products and local materials. A portion of their proceeds goes to doing workshops in rural communities on recyclable art and other techniques.

Soy Nica (Calle La Calzada in front of Carlos Bravo School, tel. 505/2552-0234, www.soynica.dk, Mon.-Thurs. 9am-6pm, Fri.-Sun. 9am-10pm) uses Nicaraguan leather to make stylish bags and other leather goods in a wide variety of colors. The workshop is right there in the store and you can stop in to see the process of working the leather.

Along the Calzada are a handful of boutiques selling clothes and accessories. **Centro de Arte** (Calle la Calzada, turn left 1 block from the Parque Colón, tel. 505/2552-6461, www.nicaragua-art.com, daily 6am-9pm) is an art gallery and store, which features pieces by local and international artists. You can also take art classes (from $6, come before 9am to sign up, children's classes on Sat.) and enjoy a coffee or sandwich at their Café de Arte.

Granada is *guayabera* country, and there are several places to buy these elegant Latin shirts. The best (and most expensive) shop is **Guayabera Nora** (east side of the Parque Central right around the corner from the Bearded Monkey, tel. 505/2552-4617). At **Sultan Cigars** (on Calle Vega across from the Plaza Central, tel. 505/8803-9569, eddyreyes78@yahoo.es, daily 8am-7pm), Eddy Reyes and family can make you a custom labeled case (your name on a cigar label) in a couple of hours; otherwise visit **Doña Elba Cigar Factory** (1 block west of Iglesia Xalteva, tel. 505/8860-6715, daily 7am-7pm). Antique lovers will adore **Casa de Antiguedades** (1 block north of Parque Colón on Calle Arsenal, tel. 505/8874-2034, haroldsandino@hotmail.com).

ACCOMMODATIONS

Granada lodging runs from youthful backpacker hostels to boutique-refurbished colonial homes. Much of the accommodations are located conveniently near Central Plaza. Interestingly, recent years have seen huge turnover in expat-owned places that appeared at the start of the real estate boom but then disappeared without a whisper. Locally owned places have mostly weathered the storm. Expect higher rates during the high season (Dec.-Apr.).

Under $25

★ **Hostel El Momento** (Calle el Aresenal 104, tel. 505/8457-6560, www.hotelgranadanicaragua.com, $8 dorm, $14-42 private) is the cleanest, most relaxed hostel around. They have new beds, trendy and comfortable common areas, a bar and restaurant, Wi-Fi, iPads available for use, laundry service, and they offer tours. The most hopping backpacker joint is a new place called **Backyard Hostal** (2 blocks west of Parque Colón on Calle Libertad, tel. 505/89842490, $7 dorm, $16-20 private). This place has a vibe of a backyard college party. They have a pool and a bar that are busy all day. They also have themed nights (movie nights, beer-pong tournaments) and offer tours. There is an open kitchen and a small food stand across the street where you can buy food to prepare.

Community Tourism near Granada

For those seeking a full-immersion cultural experience, the most obvious option is to sign up for a homestay with one of the many Spanish schools in Granada. This is a good option if you want to stay with a Nicaraguan family and still have access to Granada's many restaurants, Internet cafés, and other distractions. If you'd really like to get out there, consider arranging a few days (or weeks) with the **Unión de Cooperativas Agropecuarias Tierra y Agua,** also known as the **Earth and Water UCA** (Granada office: 75 yards west of the Shell Palmira, tel. 505/2552-0238, www.ucatierrayagua.org, turismo@ucatierrayagua.org, Mon.-Fri. 9am-4pm, $5/meal). The UCA is an association of rural farmers on the slopes of Volcán Mombacho and Isla de Zapatera National Park who will be glad to be your hosts. You'll stay in simple Nicaraguan lodging in La Granadilla or Zonzapote and eat typical food while getting to know a rural community. Local guides will take you horseback riding, hiking, fishing, and more. Cheap transport to and from Granada can be arranged. Income generated by your visit goes directly to a cooperative collective fund to pay for meals, guides, maintenance, etc., and to distribute to families involved. The UCA maintains a general fund for tourism, used for training and to make small loans for tourist-related projects.

GM Granada (in front of the Tica Bus station, tel. 505/2552-2910 or 8962-9954, gm-granada.com, GM@GMGranada.com, $11-30) is particularly popular for travelers coming up from Costa Rica on Tica Bus. This hostel is farther out of town than some of the other options (a 10-minute walk from the center), but this also gives it a calm vibe that some other hostels lack. Unlike some of its sloppy competitors, the pristine white walls and a clean blue pool give this place a sharp presentation.

Hospedaje Hamacas (Calle El Consulado, 250 meters west of Parque Colón, tel. 505/2552-0679, hostalhamacasgranada.com, $5 dorm, $8-15 private with a/c) is a locally owned basic hostel at a great price. They are owned together with Nahuatl Tours.

Hostal Entre Amigos (half block north of the Piedra Bocona on Calle 14 de Septiembre, tel. 505/8473-7700, hostalentreamigos.com, $5-25) is a small, laid-back hostel whose reception doubles as the **Cooperative El Parche Gift Shop.** They have special rates for people volunteering in Granada and also offer volunteer opportunities with their cooperative artisan shop. **Hostel Oasis** (1 block north, 1 block east of the local market, tel. 505/2552-8005, www.nicaraguahostel.com, $9 dorm, $20-45 private) is a laid-back place with a small swimming pool and a nice garden.

Past the restaurants of La Calzada are a handful of locally owned hostels whose locations can't be beat and are simple and economical. **Posada las Brisas** (Calle la Calzada, tel. 505/2552-3984 or 8885-3989, tcristac@hotmail.es, $12-20) is family-run, safe, and clean. Its features include wireless Internet, refrigerator, and kitchen access and fans, but no air-conditioning.

$25-50

Granada's midrange and upscale hotels offer remarkable value, each striving to offer an authentic but unique colonial experience with all the amenities. In this price range and above you can usually expect breakfast to be included as well as hot water, air-conditioning, private bathrooms, cable TV, artsy decor, and the ubiquitous open-air central patio with small swimming pool.

★ **Hotel Kekoldi** (3.5 blocks west of Parque Colón on Calle El Consulado, tel. 506/2252-4006, U.S. tel. 786/221-9011, www.kekoldi-nicaragua.com, Granada@kekoldi-nicaragua.com, $41-65) is spacious and colorful with well-planned architecture and plenty of open spaces. The pool is small, but the rooms are decorated with beautiful mosaics. Expect to find your towels folded into creative pieces of art.

Hotel La Pérgola (3 blocks east of Parque Colón on Calle El Caimito, tel. 505/2552-4221, www.lapergola.com.ni, info@lapergola.com.ni, $35-55) has 26 rooms with private baths and access to a gorgeous open balcony (for which the hotel is named), plus tour service and Wi-Fi.

Estancia Mar Dulce (Calle la Calzada, 3.5 blocks east of Parque Colón, tel. 505/2552-3732, www.hotelmardulcenicaragua.com, granadamardulce@hotmail.com, $30 without a/c, $40-55 private) is locally owned, clean, and professional. It has large, pleasant rooms and a spacious interior courtyard with a landscaped swimming pool.

El Club (3 blocks west of the northwest corner of Parque Colón, tel. 505/2552-4245, www.elclub-nicaragua.com, $30-90, includes continental breakfast) has a modern look with cozy, smaller rooms. They have a new whirlpool tub and there is a two-floor mezzanine room great for families. **Hotel Casa San Martín** (Calle La Calzada, 1 block east of the park, tel. 505/2552-6185, www.hcasasanmartin.com, reservaciones@hcasasanmartin.com, $41-66) has eight rooms, all with attractive hardwood floors.

For a nearby break 20 minutes north of the city, try **Hacienda los Malacos** (tel. 505/8485-3959, losmalacos.com, $35 pp dorm, $80 pp private room), a private nature reserve and eco-hotel, which offers all-inclusive hotel options and day trips. You can tour this farm/reforestation project on foot, on a bike, or on horseback and there is also great bird-watching and row boating on the properties.

$50-100

Run by a couple of dynamic and well-traveled ex-Peace Corps volunteer sisters, ★ **Casa San Francisco** (cattycorner to the Convento San Francisco, tel. 505/2552-8235, www.casasanfrancisco.com, csfgranada@yahoo.com, $55-95) is a charming colonial cluster of 19 decorated rooms. It features a small pool and is located in a quiet and central neighborhood. You'll also find a great on-site restaurant and bar called Bocadillos that specializes in tapas.

La Mansión de Chocolate (in front of Bancentro on Calle Atrevesada, tel. 505/25524678, mansiondechocolate.com, $80-200) is located inside Granada's largest intact colonial mansion (formerly known as Hotel Spa Granada). The beautiful house has been decorated using quirky architectural furniture, which creates an interesting juxtaposition. The pool is luxurious (watch out for the gang of ducks, they do not like to be touched). The hotel's spa, despite lack of trained masseuses, has interesting treatments, like the chocolate massage. The hotel also houses the Choco Café and Museum, which has an all-you-can-eat breakfast buffet and workshops on how cacao becomes chocolate.

With a feeling more like a private colonial mansion than a hotel, **Miss Margrit's** (2 blocks north of the Xalteva Park, look for a small sign, tel. 505/8983-1398, missmargrits.com, missmargrits@gmail.com, $70-90) is a beautifully restored home with seven rooms. It is located farther away from the center of town than other options, but comes highly recommended. Whether lounging by the pool, getting a massage, bathing in your jungle-like bathroom (some of the rooms have a garden inside), or playing billiards, you are guaranteed to feel pampered.

Hotel Patio del Malinche (Calle El Caimito, 2.5 blocks east of the central plaza, tel. 505/2552-2235, www.patiodelmalinche.com, $75-95) is a stunning restored home whose owners have taken a lot of care in collecting tasteful decorations and promoting local artisans. Sixteen rooms surround a huge patio, bar, and pool.

Hotel Casa Consulado (Calle el Consulado #105, 30 meters west of Banpro, tel. 505/2552-2709, U.S. 305/704-2078, info@hconsulado.com, $75-110) is a luxurious-feeling colonial building with bright colored walls and a pleasant pool and fountains. It has huge rooms with tile floors, some of which have lofts. This is a great space for families.

Hotel Casa Capricho (Calle El Arsenal, a block east of Convento San Francisco, tel. 505/2552-8422, www.hotecasacapricho.com,

$50-120), with nine rooms, an open kitchen, a dining room, and common areas is ideal for families. It's colorful and pleasant.

★ **Hotel con Corazón** (Calle Santa Lucia 141, tel. 505/2552-8852, www.hotelconcorazon.com, $60-100) has Scandinavian styling and works for a cause. In addition to the hotel, this is a foundation that invests heavily in the community, particularly in education. They have a charming little pool, 16 comfortable rooms, and a large swing. They also offer salsa classes.

Hotel Alhambra (northwest corner of the central plaza, tel. 505/2552-4486, www.hotelalhambragranda.com, $57-120) was Granada's first luxury hotel and has the best location in town, right on the park. Built around a pleasing landscaped patio, its 56 newly remodeled rooms (some with superb balcony views) have exposed wood beams and are tastefully decorated. The whole place has a classy, mahogany-enhanced ambience. ★ **Hotel Colonial** (20 meters west of the park's northwest corner, tel. 505/2552-7299, hotelcoloialgranada.com, $70-120) is newer, with 37 clean, well-appointed rooms (some including whirlpool tub) surrounding an outdoor patio, pool, and bar.

Staying at the ★ **Hotel La Bacona** (Calle La Libertad, 2 blocks west of the park, www.hotellabocona.com, hotelbocona@yahoo.com, tel. 505/2552-2888, $80-140) gives guests the feeling of living in colonial Granada. Each room has exquisite period furniture, cathedral ceilings, and ornate wooden doors, as well as four-poster king-size beds with luxurious draping. There are no TVs in the rooms and, in order to maintain the integrity of the building, the bathrooms are located outside of the rooms. The hotel also has modern amenities: a huge pool, Wi-Fi access, and an on-site spa. Half of La Bacona's profits are donated to a local NGO, La Carita Feliz, which has youth programming and serves free meals to thousands of local children.

Hotel Dario (3 blocks east of the central park, tel. 505/2552-3400, www.hoteldario.com, $90-104) has open walkways, gardens, and 22 rooms that make artful use of the available space. Request one of the rooms with small balconies facing Mombacho.

Over $100

A restored colonial mansion, the brand-new **Hotel Bubu** (Calle Libertad, from the BAC bank, 2.5 blocks west, tel. 505/2552-3432, hotelbubu.com, $140-160) has a modern design. Situated around a 13-meter lap pool, its five junior suites were built with every detail promoting airflow in order to avoid the need for air-conditioning. This hotel feels luxurious and exclusive; the second-floor terrace has a panoramic view of Granada where you can have a private breakfast or invite friends over for drinks. An intimate boutique hotel, **Hotel Los Patios** (Calle Corrales 525, tel. 505/25520641, lospatiosgranada.com, $90-175) features a range of indoor/outdoor spaces with a modern, minimalist Scandinavian design. Los Patios has five spacious rooms with beautiful tile floors. Its outdoor spaces feature a pool, green area, and giant chessboard. With a chic modern kitchen for guest use in the center, this hotel really feels like your own personal mansion.

One of Granada's first buildings (and one of a few that withstood the fire that consumed the rest of the city in the days of William Walker) has been painstakingly restored as ★ **La Gran Francia Hotel y Restaurante** (southeast corner of the park, tel. 505/2552-6000, www.lagranfrancia.com, $110-157). A careful blend of neoclassical and colonial elements in hardwoods, wrought iron, and porcelain characterize La Gran Francia's every detail, down to the hand-painted sinks.

Hotel Plaza Colón (on the west side of the park, tel. 505/2552-8489, www.hotelplazacolon.com, $109-234) has 26 large, elegant rooms with air-conditioning, hot water, cable TV, and ceiling fan; 6 rooms have vast wooden porches looking straight across the central plaza to the main cathedral, a beautiful (but sometimes noisy) vista. The other rooms face a quiet street or the sculpted inner courtyards and pool. A restaurant, bar, and wine cellar are on the premises, and parking is available.

FOOD

The Granada dining scene is in constant rotation, with old favorites disappearing, new contenders, and creative experimentation. Here are some favorite picks, but you won't go hungry if you simply stroll around.

The two major **supermarkets** are the **Palí** (on Calle Atravesada just south of the market) and **La Colonial** (from the Puma market, 1 block west) both open daily until 8pm or so. The local **market** (1 block south of the plaza) is a great place to buy fruits and veggies during the day. As many of the lower-priced *hospedajes* offer a kitchen and fridge, you can stretch your travel dollars immensely by using these markets.

Fritanga and Local Fare

Asados Don Chilo (in front of the cemetery, tel. 505/2553-4934, $5) is the best place in town for an authentic Nicaraguan meal. This buffet specializes in grilled meats served to you in a plantain leaf along with fried sweet or green plantains and cabbage salad.

Las Colinas Sur (from the Shell Palmira, 1 block south, 1 block towards the lake, tel. 505/2552-3492 or 505/8883-1522, $10-20) is a dirt floor rancho popular among locals for a nice meal with the family. They have all sorts

of Nicaraguan cuisine but their specialty is *guapote,* a fish caught in Lake Cocibolca. The restaurant is outside the center of town, so it might be best to take a cab.

In Granada, there are a handful of *fritangas*—roadside buffets that serve up fried Nicaraguan dishes at night. If you turn north four blocks down the Calzada and walk a block towards Calle La Libertad you will find a *fritanga* that serves its food in plantain leaves. Around the corner is another. There is also a popular one next to Ciudad Lounge. *Fritangas* are not recommended for the weak-stomached, but it is interesting to go and see the different options.

Cafés

Café Sonrisa (from the Iglesia La Merced, 50 meters towards the Parque Colón, tel. 505/8376-4881, Mon.-Sat. 7am-3:30pm, $1-9) is staffed completely by deaf Nicaraguan youth. This project was born not only to create employment for these youth, but also to give voice to a population that is so often ignored by hearing people. The menu is designed to help facilitate communication between waiters and customers. Many local venders and neighborhood folks have become regulars, picking up a great deal of the sign language

Sign language tips accompany the menu at Café Sonrisa.

posted all around. This is a great place to use Wi-Fi, lounge in the biggest hammock you have ever seen, or try your hand at hammock-making in the workshop next door, where at-risk youth weave hammocks for sale.

Espressionista (Calle Xalteva, across the street from the southern side of the Xalteva Church, tel. 505/2552-4325, Wed.-Sun. 11am-10pm) is a new trendy café that has put its efforts into demonstrating that Nicaragua produces high-quality products. You can enjoy top-notch Nicaraguan coffee along with one of their imaginative baked goods, like calala (passion fruit) cheesecake. They also serve artisanal beer made by a German who lives a few cities over, have a constantly rotating menu of food, and make their own ice cream. (Try the rose flavor that comes from Matagalpa roses!)

Garden Cafe (Calle la Libertad, 1 block east of Parque Colón, tel. 505/2552-8582, gardencafegranada.com, daily 7am-9pm, $2-12) is a wonderful respite from the heat, with a cool space to enjoy great breakfasts, gourmet sandwiches, salads, smoothies, and coffee drinks. The artsy patio is a great place to crank the Wi-Fi. **Kathy's Waffle House** (across from Convento San Francisco, daily 7am-2pm, $5-8) is the closest thing to a U.S.-style diner, minus its breezy outdoor patio, serving up delicious pancakes, biscuits and gravy, eggs and bacon, and omelets. The colorful space of **Café de los Sueños** (on La Calzada 3.5 blocks from the cathedral, tel. 505/8324-2913, $4-12) is a great place to get in Wi-Fi time while you enjoy tasty sandwiches and artwork that will make you smile.

Upscale and International

★ **El Tercer Ojo** (Calle El Arsenal across from Convento San Francisco, tel. 505/2552-6451, Tues.-Sun. 11am-11pm, $7-20) offers everything from Spanish tapas and sushi to Gorgonzola pasta, kebabs, and fine wine in a gauzy lounge of candles and soothing music.

For lip-smacking, upscale Nicaraguan dishes and steaks, don't miss ★ **El Zaquan**

(behind the cathedral, daily noon-11pm, $15-25). Your nose should lead you to the meat-draped open-flame grill and dishes like *churrasco jalapeño.*

Pita Pita (Calle Libertad, 1 block from the central plaza, tel. 505/5758-3870, www.depitapita.com, $4-10) is an authentic Middle Eastern restaurant that serves hummus with tahini imported from Lebanon, shawarma sandwiches, and other Mediterranean and Middle Eastern dishes. The food is very fresh—the owner has an organic farm where he grows the vegetables used in the restaurant.

For highly recommended vegetarian food try ★ **El Garaje** (512 Calle Corral, from Convento San Francisco 2.25 blocks towards the lake, tel. 505/8651-7412, Mon.-Fri. 11:30am-6:30pm, $3-10) or **El Kapayuo** (Calle El Martirio, 2 blocks north of the Eskimo on La Calzada, Tues.-Sun., $4-20). Both have slightly odd hours and might take a little asking around to find but are well worth it for their healthy vegetarian meals.

For fresh Middle Eastern food, **Camello** (Calle el Caimito, 2 blocks towards the lake from the central plaza, tel. 505/2557-7546, dinner daily, lunch only during high season, $5-10) serves falafel and shawarma as well as curry dishes and other international food.

Ciudad Lounge (Calle la Libertad, 5 blocks west of Parque Colón, tel. 505/2552-1543, Thurs.-Sun. 6pm-midnight, $10-35) is probably the swankiest place in town, with a quality wine list, martinis, cacao liquor, a daily changing menu of international foods, and cigars from Estelí.

Charly's Bar (from Petronic, 5 blocks west and 25 meters south, tel. 505/2552-2942, Wed.-Mon. 11am-11pm, $4-10) is an all-time schnitzel-flinging favorite on the western fringes of town, specializing in German cuisine, BBQ, and draft beer in a huge crystal cowboy boot. It's far from the center of town, but worth the taxi ride.

Locals and backpackers rave about the prices at **Telepizza** (Calle La Calzada, 2 blocks from the Parque Colón, tel. 505/2552-4219, daily 10am-10pm, large pies from $6, delivery available). The gigantic stuffed calzones may be one of the best deals in town. You'll find authentic pizza at **Monna Lisa** (Calle La Calzada, tel. 505/2552-8187, $5-12). Get real, thin-crust Italian pizza baked in a wood-fire oven at **Don Luca's** (Calle La Calzada, tel. 505/2552-7822, $6-12).

INFORMATION AND SERVICES
Banks
Banco de America Central (BAC) is on the southwest corner of the central plaza. **Banpro** and **Bancentro** are on Calle Atravesada, just a few blocks away. The sanctioned moneychangers are out in full force along this same section of Atravesada (they're on the street, waving wads of cash). You'll find **ATMs** in most banks and at the Esso gas station on the edge of town.

Emergency Services
The **police** presence is pretty serious in Granada. You'll note an officer stationed full-time in Parque Colón, and a lot of others patrolling to keep tourists safe. If you are a victim of crime, you can file a report by email (webdenunciagr@policia.gob.ni) or visit the **police station** (tel. 505/2552-4712) on the highway to Nandaime or the one 75 meters west of the cinema (tel. 505/2552-2977 or 505/2552-2929). The regional **Hospital Bernardino Díaz Ochoa** (on road to Managua), the biggest hospital in the area, is a few kilometers out of town. A private option closer to town is the **Hospital Privado Cocibolca** (on road to Managua, tel. 505/2552-2907 or 505/2552-4092). For minor treatments, the section of Calle Atravesada just south of the bridge is occupied by more than a dozen clinics, blood labs, and pharmacies.

Tour Operators
Most of the national tour operators listed in the *Essentials* chapter have offices in Granada

that provide local trips and transfers. In addition, here are a few Granada specialists:

Leo Tours (tel. 505/8842-7905, leotoursgranada@gmail.com, leonica1971@yahoo.com), run by Leopoldo Castillo, a Granada native, incorporates a community-minded spirit that will connect you to Nicaragua rather than just show you the sights. They can take you around Granada, Ometepe, Laguna de Apoyo, and Mombacho, or show by bike tour how the "rest" of Granada lives.

Café Las Flores-Mombotour (cafelasflores.com, from $30 pp) offers several different canopy tours, including their popular Tarzan Swing. They will pick you up, and you can be out the door of your hotel and on belay in 30 minutes. They offer a plethora of other tours including their specialty coffee tour.

Tierra Tours (Calle La Calzada, 2 blocks east of Parque Colón, tel. 505/8862-9580, www.tierratours.com, $55 pp for full-service camping trip) offers trips to Mombacho, Masaya, and through Las Isletas, where they can coordinate kayak tours as well. They are also gaining traction as the go-to place for travelers—usually Spanish language students—looking for long-term homestays. In addition to local tours of Granada, Masaya, and Catarina, Tierra offers night tours of Volcán Masaya and overnight cabins and tent platforms at a nearby Butterfly Reserve and coffee farm. Ask about shuttle service to other parts of Nicaragua, including León, where they have a sister office.

Amigo Tours (tel. 505/2552-4080, www.amigotours.net, bernal@amigotours.net), connected to the lobby of the Hotel Colonial, provides a higher-end option for tours, plus travel agency services like national airline bookings, car rentals, and transfers to and from Costa Rica.

GETTING THERE AND AWAY
In addition to the options that follow, most tour operators listed in this chapter offer

exclusive shuttles to and from San Juan del Sur, León, the dock for Ometepe, and the airport.

Bus
TO OTHER POINTS IN NICARAGUA

The easiest and most popular way to get here from Managua (or Masaya, which is on the way) is to grab a **COGRAN** *expreso* (1.5 blocks south of the central plaza's southwest corner, tel. 505/2552-2954). These medium-size express buses leave every 15-20 minutes daily 4:30am-7pm. (They stop service earlier on Sundays.) Another fleet of minivans *(micros)* leaves from Parque Sandino on the north side of Granada near the old railroad station, a few blocks from Parque Colón, with regular departures daily 5am-7:30pm. Both services leave from the UCA in Managua. From Granada, the same vehicles leave every 15 minutes daily 5:50am-8pm. If you don't mind not having a seat, you can catch either *micro* along Carretera Masaya. Note that the last bus of the day in either direction is usually the most packed.

Regular bus service from Rivas, Nandaime, and Jinotepe arrives to the **Shell Palmira,** on Granada's south side, just past the Palí supermarket. Buses to Rivas (1.5 hours) leave sporadically between 5:45am-3:10pm. Nandaime buses leave every 20 minutes. Jinotepe *expresos* take a mere 45 minutes compared to the nearly two-hour *ordinario* trip through the pueblos. Around the corner, behind the Palí, is the bus terminal with service to Masaya's city center (although any Managua-bound *expresos* will let you off along the highway through Masaya). Upon arrival at any of these locations, it's easiest to take a taxi to your hotel or Parque Colón; expect to pay about $1 per person.

TO COSTA RICA AND PANAMÁ

Avenida Arrellano, on the west end of Granada, is part of the San José and Panama City-bound routes for Central American bus lines. The two offices are located on the east side of the street. Reservations should be made at least two days in advance. For the **Tica Bus** terminal (half a block south of the Old Hospital, tel. 505/2552-4301), arrive at 6:15am for the 7am bus. **TransNica** (3 long blocks south of the Old Hospital, on the corner of Calle Xalteva, tel. 505/2552-6619) has three daily south-bounders, departing 6:30am, 8am, and 11am; be there a half-hour before departure. You should take a taxi ($0.50 pp) farther into town.

Boat
TO OMETEPE AND SAN CARLOS

Though the San Jorge ferry in Rivas is much more comfortable and direct way to get to Ometepe, it is possible to travel to Ometepe directly from Granada. Granada's crusty old ferry departs Granada's **municipal dock** (tel. 505/552-2966) Monday and Thursday at 2pm, arriving in San Carlos 6am. The price for a one-way passage between Granada and Ometepe is $10, but when lake is choppy, the ship will skip Ometepe altogether. The boat departs Granada on Mondays at 2pm (arriving in Altagracia, Ometepe around 6pm) and Thursdays at 3pm (arriving around 9pm). To get here from San Carlos, catch the ferry at 2pm, and from Ometepe, in Altagracia at midnight on Tuesdays and Fridays. It arrives at 4:30am on Wednesdays and Saturdays.

When weather permits, the boat stops at Altagracia before cutting across to the eastern lakeshore and port calls in Morrito and San Miguelito. The boat can get crowded and uncomfortable, especially around Semana Santa when the lake turns *bravo* (rough) and the weather is hot. Get to the port early and be aggressive to stake your territory.

A new option, the **Barco Turístico** ($20 first class, includes coffee and drink service; $13 economy), leaves Granada Fridays at 7pm, stopping only in Altagracia, then arriving in San Carlos the following morning at 6am. It departs San Carlos Sunday evening at 6pm. For more info, contact **La Empresa Portuaria** (tel. 505/2583-0256).

Near Granada

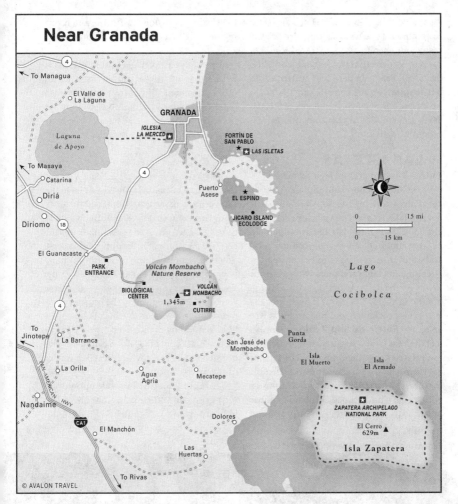

GETTING AROUND

Most of the top sights lie in the kilometer between the lake and the plaza, and they are all walkable. **Walking** is the best way to enjoy the city, and it's best to walk in the early morning when the temperature is still pleasant. You can also explore Granada's narrow streets via **horse and carriage** ($10-15/hour). Find the carriages along the western, shady side of the plaza. Please patronize only those drivers who seem to be taking good care of their animals. Though the situation is improving,

the occasional bag-o-bones with open saddle sores are still around. The pleasant tour will help orient you for the rest of your stay. **Taxis** are numerous and cheap (less than $1).

Car Rental

The **Budget** office (in the Shell Guapinol gas station on the road to Managua, tel. 505/2552-2323, reserve@budget.com.ni, daily 8am-6:30pm, car rental $30-110/day) rents cars and cell phones. There is huge demand for their 28-vehicle fleet, so reservations are necessary, especially in the high season. Hotels also often maintain a list of trusted cars and drivers, and many tour operators have extra vehicles. For car rentals, drivers, transfers, and four-wheel drive, call Peter van der Meijs at **Armadillo Nicaragua** (4 blocks north and 1.5 blocks west from the Shell Guapinol, tel. 505/8833-8663, armadillo-nicaragua.com, info@armadillo-nicaragua.com).

★ LAS ISLETAS

This 365-island archipelago formed when Volcán Mombacho erupted some 20,000 years ago, hurling its top half into the nearby lake in giant masses of rock, ash, and lava. Today, the islands are inhabited by a few hundred *campesinos* (country folk) and an ever-increasing number of wealthy Nicaraguans and foreigners who continue to buy up the *isletas* to build garish vacation homes on them. The natural beauty of the *isletas* is spectacular, and history buffs will enjoy the **Fortín de San Pablo,** a Spanish fort that was largely unsuccessful in preventing pirate attacks on Granada. The islanders themselves are interesting and friendly, maintaining a rural lifestyle unique in Nicaragua: Children paddle dugout canoes or rowboats to school from an early age, and

their parents get along by fishing and farming or by taking camera-toting tourists for a ride in their boats.

Almost every hotel and tour operator offers a trip to Las Isletas and may pair it with other excursions. There are a *lot* of options out there. For example, the Mombotour office in Granada offers an introductory three-hour kayak class ($34), which includes all equipment, sea kayaks, transportation, and a tour of the Fortín de San Pablo. For a more economical option, go right to the boat owners at the Marina Cocibolca. If you take a taxi to the southern end of the waterfront road there are many *lancheros* (boat drivers). Don't expect to haggle over prices, as gasoline is expensive (see for yourself at the dockside station). You'll pay about $10 per person for a half-hour tour, more for longer or farther trips. You can take a dip in the lake water or have your *lanchero* bring you to the cemetery, old fort, or **monkey island,** which is inhabited by a community of monkeys. If you want to eat lunch, ask your guide if you can stop at one of island restaurants or visit a local family who can serve you lunch.

There are a couple of upscale options for staying on one of the islands. The swankiest is **Jicaro Island Lodge** (tel. 505/2558-7702,

Rent a kayak to enjoy the natural beauty of Las Isletas.

Monkeys populate many of the *isletas*.

www.jicarolodge.com, $560 d, includes 3 meals a day), where you can watch the sun sink over the water from a beautiful two-story *casita* (cottage). A newer option with an up-close view of Mombacho is **El Espino** (tel. 505/7636-0060, www.isletaelespino.com, $120-195 d, includes transport and breakfast). The solar-powered lodge features a swimming pool, yoga platform, and massage facilities. They gladly accept day-trippers, call ahead for prices.

★ ZAPATERA ARCHIPELAGO NATIONAL PARK

About 34 kilometers south of Granada, Zapatera is an extinct volcano surrounded by Isla el Muerto and a dozen or so other islets, all of which comprise 45 square kilometers of land; the whole complex is home for some 500 residents. Zapatera is a natural wonder, rising 629 meters above sea level. Its virgin forest is rife with myriad wildlife such as parrots,

toucans, herons, and other waterfowl, plus white-tailed deer and an alleged population of jaguars no one ever seems to see.

These islands were enormously important to the Nahuatl, who used them primarily as a vast burial ground and sacrifice spot. The sites of **La Punta de las Figuras** and **Zonzapote** are particularly rich in artifacts and have a network of caves that have never been researched. Seek out the petroglyphs carved into the bedrock beaches of **Isla el Muerto.** An impressive selection of Zapatera's formidable stone idols is on display in the Convento San Francisco, but the islands' remaining archaeological treasures remain relatively unstudied and unprotected and (naturally) continue to disappear.

Officially declared a national park by the Sandinistas in 1983, the Zapatera Archipelago has never been adequately protected or funded. MARENA's thousand-page management plan document is just that—a document—while in reality, only one park ranger visits the islands a couple of times per month. It's no surprise then that inhabitants and visitors litter, loot the archaeological patrimony, hunt, and cut down trees for timber.

Visiting Zapatera

Access the islands from Granada's Puerto Asese, where you can strike a deal with returning Zapatera islanders or hire a tourist boat. The most reliable way is to arrange a trip with **Zapatera Tours** (tel. 505/8842-2587, www.zapateratours.com), a small company that specializes in creative lake tours, including overnight camping trips, fishing, and waterskiing. You can also inquire about Zapatera trips with any of the other Granada tour companies. With a fast, powerful motor, it's a 20-minute trip from Granada, partly over a stretch of open water that can get choppy.

There are a scattering of places to stay around the island, including a cheap dormitory and homestay options in Zonzapote. Or book a room at **Casa Hacienda Hotel Santa María** (tel. 505/8884-0606, santamariaislazapatera@gmail.com, $50 pp day use, $120 d, plus meals, transport, and fishing trips), where the Cordova family's 120-year-old tile-roofed ranch house has been outfitted with comfortably primitive double rooms with mosquito net, fan, and private bathrooms. The hotel is on a relaxing sandy beach, looking north toward Isla el Muerto and Mombacho.

★ VOLCÁN MOMBACHO

Mombacho is unavoidable. It towers over the southern horizon, lurks around every corner, creeps into your panoramic photos. In Granada, you are living in the shadow of a (fortunately gentle) giant. Every bit of cool, misty, cloud forest higher than 850 meters above sea level is officially protected as a **nature reserve** (tel. 505/2552-5858, entrance fee: $20 foreigners, $8 Nicas and residents, $10 students and children). This equals about 700 hectares of park, rising to a peak elevation of 1,345 meters, and comprising a rich, concentrated island of flora and fauna. Thanks to the Fundación Cocibolca, the reserve is accessible and makes available the best-designed and maintained hiking trails in the nation.

Overgrown with hundreds of orchid and bromeliad species, tree ferns, and old-growth cloud and dwarf forests, Mombacho also boasts three species of monkeys, 168 observed birds (49 of which are migratory), 30 species of reptiles, 60 mammals (including at least one very secretive big cat), and 10 amphibians. The flanks of the volcano, 21 percent of which remains forested, are composed of privately owned coffee plantations and cattle ranches. Maintaining the forest canopy is a crucial objective of Fundación Cocibolca, since this is where more than 90 percent of Mombacho's 1,000 howler monkeys reside (the monkeys travel in 100 different troops and venture into the actual reserve only to forage).

Although the majority of Mombacho's visitors arrive as part of a tour package, it is entirely possible to visit the reserve on your own, and it makes a perfect day trip from Managua, Granada, or Masaya. You'll start by taking a bus (or express minivan) headed for Nandaime or Rivas (or, from Granada, to Carazo as well); tell the driver to let you off at the Empalme el Guanacaste. This is a large intersection. The road up to the parking lot and official reserve entrance is located 1.5 kilometers toward the mountain—look for the signs. The walk to the parking lot is a solid half-hour trek, mostly uphill and in the sun. Water and snacks are available at the parking

the view from Volcán Mombacho

lot. Drink lots before and during this first leg of your journey. Once you arrive at the parking lot, you'll pay the entrance fee and then board one of the foundation's vehicles to make the half-hour, six-kilometer climb up to the Biological Station. The lumbering troop transports depart daily at 8:30am, 10am, and 1:30pm. The entrance fee includes admission to the reserve, transport to and from the top of the volcano, and insurance. If you've got the time, the shoes, and the strong legs, feel free to hike all the way up the steep road yourself. If you choose to walk, the cost reduces to $5 for foreign adults. Allow a couple of hours (and lots of water) to reach the top.

Trails

There is a short (half-hour) trail through the **Café Las Flores** coffee farm at the bottom of the volcano, where you wait for your ride up. Once on top, there are three trails to choose from: **Sendero el Cráter,** which encircles the forest-lined crater, and features a moss-lined tunnel, several lookouts, and a spur trail to the *fumaroles* (holes in the ground venting hot sulfurous air). The *fumaroles* area is an open, grassy part of the volcano with blazing wildflowers and an incredible view of Granada and the *isletas*. The whole loop, including

the spur, is 1.5 kilometers, with a few ups and downs, and takes 1.5 hours to walk. The **Sendero El Tigrillo** ($4) is a breathtaking 2.5-hour hike. The **Sendero la Puma** ($6) is considerably more challenging and requires that you go with a guide. This four-kilometer loop with several difficult climbs that lead to breathtaking viewpoints begins at a turnoff from the *fumaroles* trail; allow a minimum of three hours to complete it (bring lots of water). Well-trained, knowledgeable local guides (some with English) are available for the Sendero el Cráter ($7 per group, plus tip), Sendero el Tigrillo ($10), and are required for Sendero la Puma ($15). Note, because of the altitude and the clouds, the visibility from these trails may be much diminished on bad-weather days.

Volcán Mombacho Biological Center

Located at the base of one of Mombacho's 14 communications antennas, on a small plateau called Plan de las Flores at 1,150 meters, the research station is also an interpretive center, *hospedaje, cafetín,* ranger station, and conference center, technically completed in 2000 but still expanding. Find drinks and snacks here, including simple meals. Currently,

A truck will take you six kilometers up to the Biological Station on top of Mombacho.

the *albergue* (hostel; $50 pp, includes dinner and breakfast) has 10 dormitory beds in a loft above the interpretive center. You can also pitch a tent ($20) and buy meals on the side. To make a reservation, contact the **Biological Station** (tel. 505/2248-8234/35 or 505/2552-5858); or contact **Fundación Cocibolca** (tel. 505/2278-3224 or 505/2277-1681, www.mombacho.org) in Managua. Most tour companies will get you there; start with **Café Las Flores-Mombotour** (cafelasflores.com) or **Tierra Tours** (505/8862-9580, www.tierratours.com).

Canopy Tours

Put yourself on belay at the **Mombacho Canopy Tour** (tel. 505/8888-2566 or 505/8852-9483, gloriamaria@cablenet.com.ni, $40), located up the road from the parking lot, just before the road passes through the El Progreso coffee mill. Their 1,500-meter course involves 15 platforms and a 25-meter-long hanging bridge. Many tour operators offer a full-day Mombacho package that involves a visit to the reserve followed by a canopy tour on the way down, or you can arrange it yourself by calling Fundación Cocibolca.

Masaya

Masaya sprawls over a tropical plain nestled against the slopes of the volcano by the same name; at its western edge, paths carved by the Chorotega people trace the steep hillside down to the Laguna de Masaya. Twenty indigenous villages of Darianes used to cluster at the water's edge. Masaya was officially founded as a city in 1819 and has grown ever since. Several centuries of rebellion and uprising—first against the Spaniards in 1529 and later against William Walker's forces in 1856, the U.S. Marines in 1912, and a number of ferocious battles against the National Guard during the revolution—earned the Masayans a reputation as fierce fighters.

Travelers find Masaya less polished than Granada, and it's true that the streets and building facades in Masaya are less cared for. But Masayans are a creative people with many traditions found nowhere else in Nicaragua, such as their solemn, mysterious funeral processions. Your best introduction to these delights is Masaya's Mercado Viejo (Old Market), which is so pleasant and compelling that many visitors choose not to stray beyond its stately stone walls. But it's worth exploring further to people-watch in the central park and make your way over to the breezy *malecón* for the impressive views of the Laguna de Masaya 100 meters below.

ORIENTATION

Masaya sits due south of the Managua-Granada highway along the east side of the Laguna de Masaya. The street that runs north along the central plaza's east side is **Calle Central.** As you travel along it toward the highway, it becomes increasingly commercial. One block east of the southeast corner of the central plaza, you'll find the stone facade of the **Mercado Viejo** (Old Market). Six blocks west of the central plaza are the hammock factories, baseball stadium, and *malecón;* three blocks north are a handful of budget hostel options. Traveling due south leads to **Barrio Monimbó.** Going five blocks north puts you in the heart of the **Barrio San Jerónimo** around the church of the same name, situated at the famous *siete esquinas* (seven corners) intersection. The heart of Masaya is easily walkable, but one of the city's several hundred taxis (less than $1) or a public bus are recommended to get to the *malecón* or the highway.

SIGHTS

Masaya's central plaza is officially called **Parque 17 de Octubre,** named for a battle against Somoza's Guardia in 1977. Plenty of remaining bullet holes are testimony, plus two imposing command towers immediately to the west. It is a common meeting place for

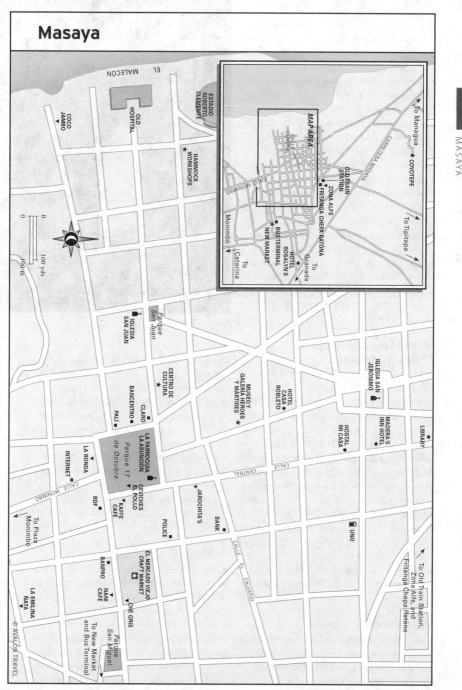

Masaya

© AVALON TRAVEL

Masayans of all walks of life, and is great for people-watching (it also has free Wi-Fi). The church in the northeast corner is La Parroquia La Asunción.

The triangular **Plaza de Monimbó** park on the southern side of Masaya comes to life every afternoon at 4pm as the throbbing social and commercial heart of the mostly indigenous Monimbó neighborhood. Climb the Iglesia San Jerónimo church four blocks north of the central plaza to get a great view of the city and its surroundings. Ask permission from one of the guards before heading up.

The **Museo y Galería Héroes y Mártires** (inside the Alcaldía, 1.5 blocks north of the central plaza, Mon.-Fri. 8am-5pm, donation requested) pays tribute to those Masayans who fought Somoza's National Guard during the revolution with a collection of guns and photos of the fallen. The highlight is the unexploded napalm bomb Somoza dropped on the city in 1977.

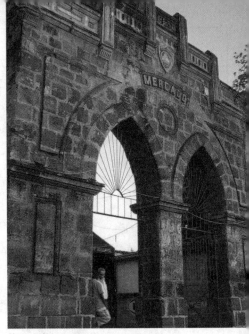
El Mercado Viejo

★ El Mercado Viejo Craft Market

All roads lead to **El Mercado Viejo,** built in 1891, destroyed by fires in 1966 and 1978, and refurbished in 1997 as a showcase for local handicrafts. Also known as El Mercado Nacional de Artesanías, or simply the "tourist market," El Mercado Viejo is safe, comfortable, and geared toward foreigners. You'll find all manner of delightful surprises: locally made leather shoes, brass, iron, carved wood, and textile handicrafts, plus paintings, clothing and hammocks. This is the best of what Nicaragua's talented craftspeople have to offer and it's the best reason to come to Masaya. Even if you don't buy anything, the market is an enjoyable and colorful experience. Of course, you pay for the convenience in slightly higher prices.

El Malecón

Cool off after an intense morning in the market on the windswept *malecón,* a beautiful cliffside promenade with long views over the Volcán Masaya crater lake to the north

and west. Set at the foot of the volcano, the Laguna de Masaya is 8.5 square kilometers and 73 meters deep in the center. It's also one of the country's most polluted lakes. While several trails, some of which were made by the Chorotegas themselves, lead the intrepid hiker down to the water's edge, this is no swimming hole. Dip your heels in nearby Laguna de Apoyo instead. The view is beautiful but the area is known for higher levels of common crime, so be extra vigilant with cameras and valuables. It's easily reached from the city center.

Artisan Workshops

Nicaragua's most treasured souvenirs, woven hammocks, are handmade by scores of Masaya families, taking 2-3 days each to make. The most obvious place to purchase one is in one of Masaya's public markets. More fun than simply buying a hammock, visit one of the many *fábricas de hamacas* (across from the old hospital on the road to the *malecón* and baseball stadium), most of which are in people's homes, clustered on the same block near the southwest edge of town. There you'll find at least a half-dozen family porch-front businesses; all of these craftspeople will gladly show you how hammocks are woven.

Sergio Zepeda is a third-generation luthier (maker of stringed instruments) at **Guitarras Zepeda** (200 meters west of the Unión Fenosa, tel. 505/8883-0060, guitarraszepeda@yahoo.com). His shop is only a block off Carretera Masaya, behind Hotel Rosalyn. Cheap children's and beater guitars start at $60; professional hardwood instruments with cocobolo rosewood back and sides, and imported red cedar, mahogany, or spruce tops can go for up to $800. Allow at least two weeks to order, or show up in his shop and see what's available.

ENTERTAINMENT AND EVENTS

Check out **Jueves de Verbena** (Mercado Viejo, Thurs. 5pm-11pm), which consists of dance, theater, art expos, music, and more, all presented in the Old Market on one of several stages. Rub elbows with the locals at the most popular local bar in town, **La Ronda** (south side of the central plaza), with beer, lots of space, and good appetizers. **Kaffé**

Café Bistro (western part of the central plaza, tel. 505/2522-2200) also often has live music on Saturday evenings; check their Facebook page for listings. **Zona Alf's** (behind the old train station, tel. 505/8981-5017) and **Coco Jambo** (by the *malecón*) are popular places to go dancing; take a taxi to the *malecón* at night instead of walking.

If you're here on a weekend during baseball season (Nov.-May), be sure to catch the local team, San Fernando, which plays in **Estadio Roberto Clemente** (on the malecón, from $0.50), named for the Puerto Rico-born Pittsburgh Pirate who died in a plane crash in 1973 delivering relief aid to Nicaraguan earthquake victims. The tailgating scene atop the *malecón* may be one of the most scenic in the world.

ACCOMMODATIONS

Along the highway and outside of town, Masaya's hotels tend to be pay-by-the-hour *auto-hotels*. These are mainly used for romantic escapades (nifty car park curtains hide license plates from spying eyes). In town, lodging is reasonable but not nearly as varied or polished as Granada.

Just a few blocks north of the central plaza there are a handful of small reasonably

Handwoven hammocks take 2-3 days each to make.

Masaya's Fiestas

Masayans celebrate all year long, observing various religious, historical, and indigenous rites with a wild collage of marimba music, traditional costume, poetry, painting, food, drink, and age-old customs. Costumes are a key element of the festivals and are often elaborate and gorgeous.

A few weeks before Easter, the celebration of **San Lázaro** features believers promenading with their ornately costumed dogs to thank their patron saint for keeping their household animals in good health.

In the **Festival of the Cross,** celebrated in May, in honor of La Señora de la Asunción, people exchange thousands of palm-thatch crosses to remember the miracle that occurred during the last eruption of Volcán Masaya's Santiago Crater, in which the virgin saved the city from hot ashes.

September through December are peak fiesta months in Masaya. Things get started with the official *fiestas patronales* (Sept. 20) in honor of Patron Saint Jerónimo. On the penultimate Friday of October, the **Fiesta de los Agüisotes** (Fiesta of Bad Omens) is a nod to Nicaragua's darker side: Folks dress up as scary figures from local legends, such as the *chancha bruja* (pig witch) and the *mocuana* (a woman who haunts La Mocuana Hill). This is a huge party night in the city and young people come from far and wide to dress up and go to the various parties around town, including a huge concert in the Old Market. The **Fiesta del Toro Venado,** on the last Sunday of October, is similar to Agüisotes, but it happens during the day. Masayans don disguises that poke fun at their favorite politicians, clergy, and other public figures.

Patron-saint celebrations end the first Sunday of December with the **Procesión de San Jerónimo.** This is perhaps the most stunning of Masaya's fiestas, as the statue of the city's patron saint is paraded through the streets amidst a sea of flowers. Every Sunday September–December features a folk dance of some sort, a competition between rival troops, or even dancers that go from house to house performing short dances to marimba music.

In mid-January, the **Festival of San Sebastian** explodes with life and energy in the indigenous Monimbó barrio. The celebration's highlight is the **Baile de Chinegro de Mozote y Verga,** in which participants engage in a mock battle, hitting each other with big sticks and finally coming together in a peace ritual.

Pieces and parcels of Masaya's festivals are found in the various *fiestas patronales* of the many surrounding pueblos, each of which present their own peculiar twist to the events. In mid-June, for example, San Juan de Oriente's party involves "warriors" dancing through the streets and whipping each other with stiffened bull penises.

priced hostels. ★ **Madera's Inn Hotel** (2 blocks south of the fire station, tel. 505/2522-5825, maderasinn.com, maderasinn@yahoo.com, $6 dorm, $15-45 private) is the nicest of the bunch; its 12 rooms occupy two floors set around a pleasant common room. You'll find friendly service, Internet access, parking, airport shuttle, tours, and laundry service. Some rooms have a fan and shared bath; more expensive rooms have private baths and air-conditioning.

One block towards the plaza there are four more budget hostels. **Hostal Mi Casa** (behind Fruti-Fruti smoothie bar and *cafetín*, tel. 505/2522-2500, $7-10 pp) has an open, colorful common space.

Found in an old colonial home near the church, ★ **Hotel Casa Robleto** (1.5 blocks south of Parque San Jerónimo, there is no sign so ask around, tel. 505/2522-2617, casarobleto@hotmail.com, $50 d, includes breakfast) is a well-run elegant bed-and-breakfast. The house is beautifully furnished with antique wooden furniture, like a locally made wooden chess set. The rooms have air-conditioning, Wi-Fi, and hot water.

FOOD
Fritanga and Local Fare

For authentic street food, visit Masaya's **Plaza de Monimbó** (across from the Don Bosco school, daily from 4pm). Vendors set up in the small triangular plaza. You'll find everything from standard finger-licking *fritanga* served on a banana leaf to hard-core snout-to-tail pig dishes and organ meat, such as that featured on the Travel Channel's *Bizarre Foods with Andrew Zimmern* "Nicaragua" episode.

Countless small *comedores* (cheap lunch counters) line both sides of the main street from the central plaza all the way up to the old train station. You'll find juicy, greasy, fried, and roasted treasures at one of several locally famous street grills: **Fritanga San Jerónimo** (a few blocks west of the church with the same name); **La Emilina Ñata en el Barrio Loco** (daily from 5pm), or Flat-nose Emilina's in the Crazy Neighborhood, open 'til its world-famous grilled beef runs out. After a late night party, **Fritanga La Chepa Ratona** (next to the old train station) is a popular option.

Cafés and Restaurants

Masaya has a burgeoning restaurant scene with a handful of new cafés and upscale restaurants. ★ **Kaffé Café** (across the street from the western edge of the central plaza, tel. 505/7725-2200, www.kaffecafebistro.com, $4-14) is a fine restaurant and café that serves elegant food, like delicious panini and toasted wraps. Vegetarians, don't miss the stuffed pepper with hummus. They also brew quality coffee, have a good selection of local and international beers, and often have live music on Saturday evenings. **Nani Café** (across the street from the south side of Mercado Viejo, tel. 505/2522-3909, lananicafe.com, $2-7) is a great place to cool off with air-conditioning and eat a quality Nicaraguan meal, or enjoy a pastry and cappuccino (complete with foam drawing). **Che Gris** (on east side of Mercado Viejo, tel. 505/2522-0394, www.restaurantechegris.com, $7-10) is an upscale bar and grill that offers traditional cooking in an air-conditioned setting. A lively, popular option is **Jarochita's** (north of the central plaza, tel. 505/2522-4831, daily 11am-10pm, $3-8), preparing Mexican cuisine with a Nicaraguan twist.

The iconic ★ **Ceviches el Pollo** (on western edge of the central plaza, tel. 505/8899-2776, www.cevicheselpollomasaya.com, $2-15) is known for its sky-high wooden tables and wide selection of fruit smoothies. Pick from 72 different smoothie combinations or order a fresh seafood ceviche. One of the waiters or, more likely the owner himself, will bring it up to easily 10 feet in the air.

Ceviches el Pollo

Fried Food Galore: Eating at *Fritangas*

fried foods typically found at the *fritanga*

For most Nicaraguans, the *fritanga* is a place in the neighborhood to buy prepared food for dinner. Nearly every neighborhood has at least one *fritanga*: a grill and maybe a few tables set up in front of someone's house where they sell food buffet-style and usually to-go. Most food at the *fritanga* is made just as it sounds: *frito* (fried). It's not recommended for the weak-stomached traveler, but it is worth taking a peek to get an idea of typical foods. The following terms will help you navigate:

carne asado: grilled beef
chancho (cerdo): grilled pork
enchiladas: Nicaraguan enchiladas are two tortillas filled with rice and shredded beef, folded in half, and deep-fried. Served with cabbage salad, ketchup, and crema (similar to mayonnaise).
gallo pinto: "Speckled Rooster" is rice and beans fried together with onion and sometimes green pepper or carrot.
maduro: fried ripe plantain, mashed and fried into a ball with a chunk of cheese in the middle
pollo asado: grilled chicken
repocheta: deep fried tortilla topped with refried beans, crumbled salty cheese, cabbage salad, and usually ketchup and crema
res: fried meat patty, basically a hamburger
tacos: Unlike Mexican tacos, Nicaraguan tacos are tortillas filled with shredded meat, rolled up, and deep-fried. Served as a side or with cabbage salad, ketchup, and crema (similar to mayonnaise). You can ask for them without condiments if you prefer.
tajadas: green plantain chips served as a side or with cabbage salad and a piece of fried cheese
torta de papa: mashed potatoes, with a chunk of cheese in the middle, fried into a ball

INFORMATION AND SERVICES

Hospital Hilario Sanchez Vásquez (on the highway toward Granada, tel. 505/2522-2778) is the biggest facility in town, though you are much better off driving to **Hospital Vivan Pellas** (on the highway before you reach Managua). The large, blue **police station** (half a block north of Mercado Viejo, tel. 505/2522-4222 or 505/2522-2521) is across from Norma's bakery. Besides the multiple **ATMs** within the Mercado Viejo, numerous banks are close by: **Bancentro** (on the west side of the central plaza) and a **BDF** (one block north of Mercado Viejo).

GETTING THERE AND AWAY

Nearly every southbound bus leaving Managua from Roberto Huembes passes Masaya, which is right on the highway, only 27 kilometers from Managua. Faster still are the Masaya- or Granada-bound *expresos* from the UCA leaving regularly 6am-7:30pm daily, arriving half a block north of Masaya's Parque San Miguel; from there, they depart for Managua 6am-8pm daily. The ride costs under $1. There is also *expreso* service between Masaya's Plaza de Monimbó and Mercado Oriental in Managua, 3am-7pm daily. Ordinary bus service leaves and arrives at the main terminal in the parking lot of the Mercado Nuevo. From any point of arrival, you can take a taxi to the center for less than $1.

Buses bound for Granada leave 6am-7pm daily from the UCA terminal in Managua, stopping along the highway in Masaya en route. You can catch one of these *micros* from the gas station on the highway in Masaya to get to Granada. To get here from Granada, hop any Managua-bound bus.

★ VOLCÁN MASAYA NATIONAL PARK

An extraordinary and easy day trip from Managua, Masaya, or Granada, **Volcán Masaya National Park** (tel. 505/2528-1444, daily 9am-4:45pm, $4) is Nicaragua's most impressive outdoor attraction and premier tourist site. There are very few volcanoes in the world where you can simply drive up to the crater edge and look into what the Spaniards declared to be the "mouth of hell." Masaya offers exactly this, and more. One of the most visibly active volcanoes in the country, Volcán Masaya emits a nearly constant plume of sulfurous gas, smoke, and sometimes ash, visible from as far away as the airport in Managua. From one of its craters, you can sometimes glimpse incandescent rock and magma. A visitor's center (where you'll be asked to park your car facing out "just in case") will help you interpret the geology and ecology of the site, as will the park's impressive nature museum. For the more actively inclined, hiking trails cover a portion of the volcano's slopes.

Volcán Masaya was called Popogatepe (mountain that burns) by the Chorotegas, who interpreted eruptions as displays of anger to be appeased with sacrifices, often human. In the early 1500s, Father Francisco Bobadilla

buses headed for Masaya

Near Masaya

placed a cross at the crater lip in order to exorcise the devil within and protect the villages below. Not long afterward, though, thinking the volcano might contain gold instead of the devil, both Friar Blas del Castillo and Gonzalo Fernandez de Oviedo lowered themselves into the crater on ropes. They found neither the devil nor gold and probably singed their eyebrows.

The park is composed of several geologically linked volcanic craters: **Volcán Nindirí,** which last erupted in 1670, and **Volcán Masaya,** which blew its top in 1772. The relatively new **Santiago Crater** was formed between the other two in 1852, and is inhabited by a remarkable species of parakeet that nests contentedly in the rocky side of the crater walls, oblivious to the toxic gases and the scientists who had thought such a sulphurous environment would be uninhabitable. You might see these *chocoyos del cráter* (crater parakeets) from the parking area along the crater's edge.

As for the sensation of "just in case," the danger is quite real. In April 2000, the Santiago crater burped up a single volcanic boulder that plummeted to earth, crushing an unfortunate Italian tourist's car in the parking lot. In April of 2012 the park closed temporarily due to the Santiago Crater's emission of incandescent material that caused a fire that spread across three acres.

Visiting Volcán Masaya

The exhibits at the Visitors Interpretation Center and museum include three-dimensional dioramas of Nicaragua and Central America, models of active volcanoes, and remnants of indigenous sacrifice urns and musical instruments found deep in the volcano's caves; there is also a display of old lithographs and paintings of the volcano as the Spaniards saw it. Consider one of several **guided tours** ($1-2 day tours, sign up at the visitors center), including an exciting night tour beginning at sunset ($10, call to reserve, minimum of 6 people). Of special interest is the walk to the Tzinancanostoc Bat Cave, a lava tube passageway melted out of solid rock.

Though most visitors only snap a few photos from the crater's edge before continuing on, the park contains several hiking trails through a veritable moonscape of lava formations and scrubby vegetation, making it easy to spend at least half a day here. Carry lots of water and sunscreen (there is little to

no shade). The worthwhile trails offer good opportunities to cross paths with some of the park's wildlife, including coyotes, deer, iguanas, and monkeys. The **Coyote Trail** will lead you east to the shore of the Laguna de Masaya.

Any Masaya- or Granada-bound bus from Managua (or Managua-bound bus from one of these cities) will drop you on the highway at the entrance to Volcán Masaya. If you have a car you can drive right up to the crater lip.

COYOTEPE

Just south of the volcano on a hill overlooking the highway, the battlements of fort **Coyotepe** (daily 8:30am-5pm, $2) overlook the city of Masaya. Take a cab or hike up the road. The view of Masaya, its lagoon, and the Masaya and Mombacho volcanoes, both great lakes, and the far-reaching surrounding countryside is worth it, and that's before you even descend into the dungeons. Built at the turn of the 20th century, this site witnessed a fierce battle between national troops and U.S. Marines in 1912. Somoza rehabilitated it as a particularly cruel prison. Today, Coyotepe is in the hands of the Nicaraguan Boy Scouts, who will accompany you through the pitch-black underground prison facilities in exchange for a small fee.

Volcán Masaya constantly emits sulfurous gas and ash.

NINDIRÍ

Just north of the highway between the entrance to the national park and the city of Masaya, Nindirí was the most important and densely populated of the indigenous settlements in the area up to 1,500 years before the arrival of the Spanish. Its name in Chorotega means Hill of the Small Pig, and its principal attraction is the 1,000-artifact collection in the **Museo Tenderí** (Mon-Fri. 8:30am-noon, tel. 505/8954-0570), named after a local cacique, which celebrates pre-Columbian culture. Ask around about the Cailagua site, with petroglyphs overlooking the Laguna de Masaya. Buses running between Managua, Masaya, and Granada will drop you off on the highway that runs along the edge of town. From there, you can take a taxi or walk a few blocks north to the center of town. Buses leaving from Masaya's Mercado Nuevo will take you direct into the city proper.

★ LAGUNA DE APOYO

Nicaragua's cleanest and most enticing swimming hole is the Laguna de Apoyo, just outside of Masaya. Actually a lagoon that formed in the drowned volcanic crater of the long extinct Volcán Apoyo, the lagoon floor reaches 200 meters in depth, the lowest point in all of Central America. Despite its continued seismicity—a minor earthquake in 2000 under the crater-rim town of Catarina caused Apoyo's water to slosh back and forth, wrecking a few homes—for the most part the volcano is considered dormant, and a thick green forest has grown up the slopes over the years. The valley of the lagoon is a national park and the slopes harbor a few hiking trails and are protected from further development by law. The crater hosts a few fish species found nowhere else on earth; scientists at the Proyecto Ecológico are studying them. If you hike through the forests, expect to observe species of toucan, hummingbirds, blue jays, howler and white-face monkeys (which are prone to fling their feces at you if you approach), and rare butterflies. There have been a few minor robberies over the years on the hiking paths, so carry as little of value as possible on a hike. There are few places on earth quite like this charming, isolated community.

Accommodations and Food

The number of places to eat or lodge along the western shore of the crater lake is continually improving, despite local grumbling about illegal development of the waterfront. At any establishment listed here, pay $5-10 to

The Laguna de Apoyo fills a long-extinct volcano.

stay for the day and enjoy the docks, kayaks, inner tubes, hammocks, and other facilities. The area has few stores or shops, and few services, so either pack your essentials before coming, or count on one of the local hotels or restaurants. Most hotels offer cheap shuttles from Granada, or you can hire a taxi or take a bus. All of the beachfront properties of the Laguna slope down towards the water and have lots of steps that require walking up and down to the waterfront.

★ **Hostel Paradiso** (300m north of the *triángulo,* tel. 505/2522-2878 or 8187-4542, hostelparadiso.com, paradisolaguna@hotmail.com, $10 dorm, $25-55 private, $7 for the day) is geared toward budget travelers, though you couldn't tell from looking at its beautifully landscaped property. Paradiso offers terraced patios, a floating dock, a delicious menu ($4-10), and the only bar open until 10pm in the area. Cheap transport from Granada is provided and leaves Hostel Oasis in Granada at 10am and 3pm, returning at 10:30am and 3:30pm. The dormitory has a fabulous sunrise view. This hostel organizes lots of activities during the week and offers Wi-Fi, free coffee, a volleyball court, petanque, Ping-Pong, yoga classes, windsurfing, and local crafts for sale. Ask about volunteer opportunities, or stay for a week and take Spanish classes.

The Monkey Hut (100m north of the *triángulo,* tel. 505/2220-3030, www.themonkeyhut.net, monkeyhulaguna@gmail.com, $14 dorm, $35-55 private room and cabaña, $6 for the day) and **Laguna Beach Club** (across from the *triángulo,* tel. 505/2520-2840, www.thelagunabeachclub.com, rememberlaguna@gmail.com, $12 dorm, $29-49 private room with fan, $6 for the day) are both found right at the entrance of the Laguna and are well-liked retreats with beautiful waterfront properties. Their recently renovated rooms provide a quiet, peaceful option for travelers. Both are popular spots for weekend day trips.

Proyecto Cocomango (500 meters north of the *triángulo,* tel. 550/7808-4384, proyectococomango.com, CocoMango.ni@gmail.com, $90/week) is a newly formed NGO working to promote educational and artistic opportunities as well as environmental protection for the Laguna de Apoyo and nearby communities. They are always happy to have volunteers stay at their volunteer house, where you can participate in a wide variety of small projects within the community. They work closely with Hostel Paradiso, so you can also volunteer while staying at Paradiso.

The ★ **Peace Project** (across from the public beach entrance, tel. 505/8266-8404, U.S. 301/880-7231, $8 dorm, $14-45 private room) is an NGO that has existed in various forms since the late 1980s and under its current leadership since 2011. The organization works in the local public schools teaching English classes, as well as hosting an after-school enrichment program, which focuses on computer skills, arts, and environmental stewardship. The Peace Project hostel is on the same property as the after-school program and the proceeds of the hostel and restaurant ($3-6) go towards supporting the project. Many visitors come to the Peace Project as volunteers and spend a minimum of three weeks at the hostel or living with families, while participating in the Peace Project's programming. Since many of the folks staying at the hostel are there long-term, staying at this hostel feels like hanging out on your friend's porch. Though its property isn't lakefront, there is quick and easy access to the public beach right across the street and they'll lug a kayak to the water for you. They offer scuba lessons and Spanish classes as well. To get here, follow the well-placed signs for "Proyecto de Paz" and turn right at the school (400 meters north of the *triángulo*). At the end of the road, turn left and go about 100 meters.

Casa Aromansse (1.5 kilometers north of the *triángulo,* tel. 505/2520-2837, casaromansse.com, sergecasaromansse@gmail.com, $50-65, includes breakfast), a new bed-and-breakfast located just a bit past the public beach, is a tranquil option for travelers interested in yoga and mindfulness. Casa Aromansse has six minimalist rooms and a French-Nicaraguan restaurant that focuses on vegetarian cuisine. The owner, Serge, is a yoga instructor and massage therapist offering Thai massage and yoga and meditation classes. He also does yoga teacher training courses and yoga retreats, which are advertised on their website. Casa Aromansse has a Spanish school for guests staying a minimum of one week.

Neither hostel nor hotel, **Guest House La Orquidea** (1.8 kilometers north of the *triángulo*, tel. 505/8872-1866, www.laorquideanicaragua.com, $120/night for 4 people, space for up to 6 people, $10 more pp, includes breakfast, separate room $70) is a stylish two-bedroom house, fully equipped for a relaxing stay. Features include a gorgeous balcony, boats, and water toys.

On the south end of the main road, **San Simian Eco-Resort** (3 kilometers south of the *triángulo*, tel. 505/8850-8108, www.sansimian.com, contact@sansimian.com, $47-60, includes breakfast) is a lovely waterside group of five private bungalows, each of which has a slightly different theme, built from natural materials like thatch and bamboo. The tasteful, rustic rooms have bamboo beds with comfy mattresses, mosquito nets, fans, and fun outdoor showers and gardens. Additional features include great on-site meals, a bar, and relaxing dock with water toys. Trailheads nearby lead uphill into the jungle and along the shore.

After several years of on-and-off neglect, a new management team has taken over **Apoyo Resort** (1 kilometer south of the *triángulo*, tel. 505/2220-2085, U.S. 562/631-7209, www.apoyoresort.com, $70-230, includes breakfast) and is bringing the property's 60 Caribbean-style villas back to their former glory. Apartments and suites (1-3 bedrooms) have hot water, bathtubs, air-conditioning, TV/DVD, and kitchenettes. An open-air shuttle will transport you from your cabaña to one of the three restaurants, two pools, or to the lakefront (meals $7-14, Wi-Fi available). Relax by the lakeshore and swimming pools, book a massage, or go boating, biking, and hiking.

Day-trippers are welcome with a $10 minimum purchase at the restaurant.

Getting There

The Laguna de Apoyo is a 20-minute ride from either Masaya or Granada, and an hour from the airport in Managua. There are two paved roads that go up and over the crater lip and down to the water's edge: one originates on Carretera Masaya, at a spot called *el puentecito* (the 37.5 Km mark on Carretera Masaya); the other branches off the Masaya-Catarina road. They join just before passing through the village of Valle de Laguna, where you'll turn right at the T, then make a quick left to begin your descent (pay $1 if driving, unless the guardhouse is empty). The road winds downward until it forks at a pulpería. This spot is known locally as *el triángulo* (the triangle). Turn left to go north, and right to go south.

A **shuttle** goes from the Oasis Hostel in Granada to Hostel Paradiso in the Laguna. It leaves Granada at 10am and 3pm and returns to Granada 40 minutes later ($3 each way). You can share a **taxi** from Granada or Masaya for about $15. Public **buses** headed for the Laguna cost under $1 and leave the main Masaya market terminal at 10:30am and 3:30pm; or you can hop one of the hourly buses for Valle de Laguna, then walk (30 minutes downhill), thumb a ride, or wait for a stray taxi. There is also a cooperative of taxis that leave from the Masaya market (once they fill up) and bring you to the top of the Valle for about $0.50. These taxis are tucked away in a hidden corner of the market. If you have enough Spanish to ask around and a little time to get lost, this is the cheapest option. If you are coming from Granada or Managua on a public bus, ask to be dropped at the entrance to the Laguna (the stop is called *el puentecito*), and then catch a taxi ($4 to the bottom) or hitch a ride. Three public buses can get you back up the hill, leaving at 6:30am, 11:30am, and 4:30pm (3pm on Sun. is the last bus).

The Pueblos Blancos and Carazo

Escaping the heat of Managua or Granada is as easy as a 40-minute bus ride to the Pueblos Blancos and Carazo, two regions that occupy a breezy 500-meter-high *meseta* (plateau) south of Managua and are thus far cooler and more relaxing. The Pueblos Blancos, or White Villages, are named for the pure color of their churches (some of which, naturally, are now other colors). They are separated to the north by the Sierras de Managua, to the east by the slopes of Volcán Masaya, to the south by the Laguna de Apoyo and Volcán Mombacho, and to the west by the dry decline toward the Pacific Ocean. Each town is well known for something particular—bamboo craftwork, wicker chairs, black magic, folk dances, Sandino's birthplace, crater lakes, beaches, or interesting festivals. Visiting the pueblos is an easy day trip best appreciated if you have a car, which permits you to tour furniture workshops, coffee plantations, and outdoor plant nurseries.

In nearby Carazo, the January celebration of San Sebastián is a dramatic and colorful festival not to be missed. Jinotepe and Diriamba are laid-back towns with refreshingly cool temperatures. Carazo is also the gateway to several Pacific beaches, which are quieter than their more developed neighbors and have beautiful natural pools.

ORIENTATION

Renting a car or taxi is the best way to visit the Pueblos, but you can get around almost as easily with the *expreso* microbus system. No more than 10 or 12 kilometers separate any two towns, all of which are easily accessible from Masaya, Granada, and Managua. Buses to Nandaime, Diriá, and Diromo leave from Huembes, continue south on the Carretera Masaya, and then turn west into the hills at various points, depending on the route. The Carazo buses—to Jinotepe and Diriamba—travel via Carretera Sur and leave from the

Mercado Israel Lewites and from the UCA terminal. Also leaving from the UCA are buses that go to Diriamba heading out Carretera Masaya and turning west before Masaya. In the market in Diriamba you can catch buses to the Carazo beaches.

★ CATARINA MIRADOR

This hillside pueblo clings to the verdant lip of the spectacular Laguna de Apoyo crater lake. Catarina Mirador is a blustery cliff-side walkway and restaurant complex at the edge of the crater with one of the best panoramic views in Nicaragua. Look for the distant red-tiled roofs and cathedral spires of Granada, broad Lake Cocibolca behind, and on a clear day, the twin volcanic peaks of Ometepe. Roaming marimba and guitar players will serenade you for a small fee (negotiate before they begin playing). Locals visit Catarina for its ornamental plant nurseries and the wares of local artisans and basket makers whose shops begin at roadside. Vehicles pay $1 each to enter the *mirador* (lookout point).

Plant lovers should make sure to check out **Ecovivero La Gallina** (close to the entrance to the town of Catarina, tel. 505/8872-7181, tours $5 pp), an 8 manzanas (around 13 acres) plant nursery. On the property of La Gallina grow a multitude of tropical plants including rare orchids and a one-of-a-kind pink cacao plant. A family of monkeys also visits the shady property almost daily. You can arrange a tour of the property and, if you call ahead, arrangements can be made for an English-speaking guide. Don't forget bug spray!

Hotel Casa Catarina (across from the central park, tel. 505/2558-0261 or 505/2558-0199, reservaciones@hotelcasacatarina. com, $45-90) is a three-star hotel with four floors and an on-site bar and restaurant. It has received mixed reviews from customers. ★ **Hotel Cabañas** (150m west of the Rotonda Catarina, tel. 505/2558-0484, $35) is outside of Catarina, along the highway. It has simple, charming cabañas and a swimming pool. The cabañas have air-conditioning, Wi-Fi, and cable TV; food is available if you request it in advance.

There are many restaurants within the grounds of the Catarina Mirador, which are all a little pricey and not very remarkable. Along the highway just before arriving in Catarina from Carretera Masaya is the famous restaurant **Mi Viejo Ranchito** (Km 39.5 Carretera Masaya-Catarina, tel. 505/2558-0473, miviejoranchito.com, $4-12), which has another location closer to Managua on Carretera Masaya itself. This restaurant serves high-quality traditional Nicaraguan food under a palm frond roof. It is known for its *quesillos,* a corn tortilla with fresh *quesillo* cheese (similar to string cheese), cream, and onions in vinegar on top. The Caballo Bayo sampler plate is a great way to try a variety of Nicaraguan specialties at once.

★ SAN JUAN DE ORIENTE

The community of San Juan de Oriente has been famous for its pottery for as long as anyone can remember. Nearby communities once poked fun at people from San Juan, calling them "comebarros" ("clay eaters") for their tendency to eat off of homemade clay plates. Recent generations of San Juan potters have expanded their craft and now make attractive ceramic vases, pots, plates, and more, in both a proud celebration of pre-Columbian styles and modern inspirations. Shop at one of the small cooperatives along the entrance to town, like **Quetzalcoatl Cooperative** (coopquetzalcoatl.jimdo.com), which also offers tours and lodging, or in the many tiny displays in people's homes as you walk through the narrow streets. Many artisans are glad to invite you back into their workshops for a tour where you watch them throw pots on a foot-spun pottery wheel. Most potters use artisanal tools made from household items like a shoe-heel or bike spoke. Their pottery is exquisite and in these shops they sell for extremely low prices.

DIRIÁ AND DIRIOMO

Named for the indigenous Dirian people and their leader, Diriangén (the famed rebel cacique and martyr whose spilled blood at the hands of the conquistadors is immortalized in Carlos Mejía Godoy's anthem, "Nicaragua, Nicaragüita"), **Diriá** and **Diriomo** face each other on both sides of the highway. Both towns are well loved for their unique celebrations

the view from Catarina Mirador

learning to make pottery in San Juan de Oriente

park has been restored as a library and museum. A 4,000-pound, solid bronze statue of the man, with the famous hat and bandolier of bullets around his waist, stands at attention at the east side of town. Niquinohomo's 320-year-old church is also worth a look.

MASATEPE

Masatepe (Nahuatl for "place of the deer") is a quiet pueblo of 12,000 that explodes in revelry the first Sunday in June during its famous **Hípica** (horse parade). Stick around after the festivities for a steaming bowl of Masatepe's culinary claim to fame: *sopa de mondongo* (cow tripe soup, washed with lime and cooked slowly in broth with vegetables), served hot in front of the town's gorgeous, architecturally unique church. Their *fiestas patronales* honor La Santísima Trinidad, the black Christ icon a Chorotegan found in the trunk of a tree during the years of the Spanish colony.

Outside of the city, both sides of the highway are lined with the workshops of the extraordinarily talented Masatepe carpenters, whose gorgeous handcrafted hardwood and rattan furniture is prized throughout the country. You'll wish you could fit more of it in your luggage (a set of chairs and a coffee table go for about $100), but console yourself instead with a comfortable, old-fashioned hardwood rocking chair. They'll disassemble and pack it down to airline-acceptable size for you for a small fee.

If driving to Masatepe from the south, save time for a meal at **Mi Teruño Masatepino** (on the east side of the road, just north of the turnoff for Pio XII and Nandasmo, tel. 505/8887-4949, $4-10), a delicious open-air restaurant featuring Nicaragua's traditional country cuisine.

MARIPOSA ECO-HOTEL AND SPANISH SCHOOL

Tucked into the forest off the road to the village of San Juan de la Concepción (a.k.a. La Concha, 12 kilometers west of Ticuantepe, under an hour from Managua), this unique hideaway has spurred a stream of rave

throughout the year, mixing elements of pre-Columbian, Catholic, and surprising regional traditions (like the "dicking" festival in which participants smack each other with dried-out bull penises, sometimes practiced in San Juan de Oriente as well). Diriá, on the east, has a *mirador* smaller and less frequented than the more famous one at Catarina, as well as additional trails down to the Laguna de Apoyo. Across the highway, Diriomo is renowned for its sorcery: The intrepid traveler looking for a love potion or revenge should seek out one of the pueblo's *brujos* (sorcerers) or at least read the book *Sofía de los Presagios*. Diriomo has a crater overlook of its own: **Diriomito Mirador,** which occasionally offers paragliding, or *parapente* (tel. 505/2522-2009).

NIQUINOHOMO

Niquinohomo, "the valley of the warriors" in Nahuatl, produced a famous warrior indeed: Augusto César Sandino, born there at the turn of the 20th century. Sandino's childhood home off the northwest corner of the reviews. **Mariposa Eco-Hotel and Spanish School** (tel. 505/8669-9455, www.mariposa-panishschool.com, average cost $350-400 pp per week all-inclusive) uses all of its revenue to fund a range of grassroots environmental and community projects. Guests are invited to help with the projects, from reforestation and chicken raising, to literacy, education, and animal rescue. The hotel and rooms, which use solar power, have excellent views of Volcán Masaya. There is an organic farm with coffee, bananas, free-range eggs, and lots of fruit. Meals are mostly vegetarian. Food that is not grown on their farm is bought as locally as possible. The rooms are decorated with local handicrafts, each with their own bathroom and fan. There is a fully stocked library, quality one-on-one Spanish school, and lots and lots of dogs. The school doubles as a dog shelter, so there is a constant stream of animals running around. There are volunteer and homestay opportunities as well. The all-inclusive Spanish school packages vary based on your interests.

CARAZO

Carazo is a group of small cities with refreshing cool temperatures that favor coffee production. The towns of Diriamba and Jinotepe make delightful lunch stopovers. From Diriamba you can reach the Carazo beaches, whose coastline is lined with huge rock formations and natural pools.

Jinotepe and Diriamba
DIRIAMBA

Diriamba's **Festival of San Sebastián** (third week of Jan.) is a religious, theatrical, folklore celebration uninterrupted since colonial days. Diriamba's celebration of the Holy Martyr San Sebastián stands above other pueblos' *fiestas patronales* as Nicaragua's most authentic connection to its indigenous roots. Featuring both pagan and Catholic elements, it is without rival in western Nicaragua, comparable perhaps only to Bluefield's Palo de Mayo. The festival's Dance of Toro Huaco is of indigenous ancestry and

features peacock feather hats and a multi-generational snake dance, with the youngest children bringing up the rear and an old man with a special tambourine and whistle up front. El Güegüense, also called the Macho Ratón, is recognizable for its masks and costumes depicting burdened-down donkeys and the faces of Spanish conquistadors. The Güegüense (from the old word güegüe, which means something like grumpy old man) is a hard-handed social satire with cleverly vulgar undertones that depicts the indigenous peoples' first impression of the Spanish—it has been called the oldest comedy act on the continent. UNESCO named the Güegüense dance a Masterpiece of the Oral and Intangible Heritage of Humanity. Be sure to try the official beverage of the festival: *chicha con genibre*, a ginger-tinted, slightly fermented cornmeal drink. Most of the masks and costumes in the productions are also for sale, as are homemade action figures depicting the various dance characters.

Visit the **Museo Ecológico de Trópico Seco** (in front of the police station, near the hospital, tel. 505/2534-2129, Mon.-Fri. 8am-noon and 2pm-4pm, $0.76 foreigners, $0.30 Nicas) for background on the region's unique dry tropical ecosystem. The MARENA office here ministers some of the local turtle-nesting refuges.

Hotel Mi Bohio (tel. 505/2534-4020, hotelmibohio.com, $35-70, includes breakfast) is a new hotel located in a colonial house near the museum with clean bright rooms, spa services, and one of the best restaurants in town on-site. **Restuarante Mi Bohio** (tel. 505/2534-2437, noon-9pm daily, $7-9) is a very typical Nicaraguan restaurant serving high-quality meat and seafood dishes.

Outside of town on the road to Managua, the ★ **Eco Lodge El Jardín Tortuga Verde** (tel. 505/2534-2948 or 505/8905-5313, www.ecolodgecarazo.com, rorappal@turbonett.com.ni, $25-45) is truly a pleasant and quirky guesthouse and plant nursery whose six clean, comfortable rooms are built around a beautiful jungle-like garden filled with statues. The

Nicaragua's First Microbrewery

Nicaragua's two basic beers, Victoria and Toña, dominate the beer industry. They are very light beers with only slightly different flavors that are refreshing served ice-cold, and well loved in Nicaragua. Inspired by the wide variety of microbrews he found in Seattle, a young Nicaraguan microbiologist started Cervecera Moropotente together with his brother-in-law in 2012. The brewery, "El Negrito," is located in Dolores, a small town near Jinotepe and Diriamba in Carazo. They have yet to set up tasting facilities on-site. At the time of publication, they were brewing a stout called "Lado Oscuro" (a creative combination of flavors including chocolate and coffee), a Blonde Ale called "19 Días," and a Pale Ale called "Citrus," in which they're experimenting with adding local fruits. And they've got a stockpile of recipes just waiting to be rotated into circulation.

Try the beer for yourself at one of two highly recommended restaurants near Jinotepe: **Makimaki** (from the University stoplight, 1 block east, 1 block south, half a block east), a reasonably priced sushi joint in Jinotepe; or **Casa del Campo** (Km 61 Carretera Nandaime), a classy restaurant that uses organic vegetables from its on-site organic garden.

You can find Moropetente's brews in Managua at **Layha Bistro** (in Altamira, from ProNicaragua, 1 block southeast), **Pia Bistro, Basil Bistro, Terraza Peruana,** and **Embassy Bar** (in Zona Hippos); in Granada at **Garden Café** and **Oshea's;** in San Juan del Sur at **La Carreta** (in front of Iguana); in León at **Yavoy** (50 meters west of Parque La Merced) and **Vía Vía;** and in Masaya at **Frankfurt.**

staff can show you around their converted coffee plantation, now rife with lush flowers and vegetation.

Go to the **Centro Comercial Gutierrez** (on the southeast corner of the San Sabastián Basilica) shopping center for a variety of food options, including La Nani Café, serving quality Nicaraguan dishes, panini, and waffles. Fratello's Italian restaurant is upstairs, as is Tsunami & Grill, which is popular on weekends.

JINOTEPE

Jinotepe (Xilotepetl, or "field of baby corn") is a sometimes-sleepy, sometimes-bustling villa of 27,000 set around **La Iglesia Parroquial de Santiago** (built in 1860) and a lively park shaded by the canopy of several immense hardwood trees. Thanks to a branch of UNAN, Jinotepe's student population keeps things youthful and lively, and its outdoor market is fun. Don't miss the beautiful two-block-long mural on the nursing school (3 blocks west of the park's northwest corner) and the towering statue of Pope John Paul II in front of the church. While you're there, enjoy an icy, chocolatey *cacao con leche* in the kiosk

under the shade trees of one of Nicaragua's shadiest parks.

The **Hotel Casa Mateo** (1 block north of the park and 2 west, tel. 505/2532-3284, U.S. tel. 410/878-2252, hotelcasamateo.com, $15 dorm, $40-65 private room, includes breakfast) has 40 rooms with TV, private bath, hot water, and fan. There's also laundry service, a guard for your car, a restaurant (called Jardín de los Olivos), conference room, and Wi-Fi. This is a nonprofit hotel run by Glenn and Lynne Schweitzer, pastors and missionaries from Maryland, to help fund Quinta Esperanza, a home for abused and orphaned children, preschool, and vocational center. They offer special group rates ($15-20 pp).

There are dozens of small, decent eateries. Managua expats actually drive here to enjoy ★ **Pizzería Coliseo** (1 block north of Bancentro, tel. 505/2532-2150 or 505/2532-2646, Tues.-Fri. noon-2:30pm and 6pm-10pm, from $6), a legitimate Italian restaurant run by Rome *originario* Fausto, who's been preparing delicious pizzas and pasta in Jinotepe for more than 20 years. ★ **Tian Lan Zu Shi** (1.5 blocks south of the UNAN turret, tel. 505/8739-2681, Mon.-Sat. 10am-4pm, $2-3) is a delicious and reasonably priced lunch buffet of creative vegetarian Chinese dishes, sometimes with a Nicaraguan touch. **Restaurante Hípico** is a cowboy-themed rancho found just outside of town, which serves authentic Nicaraguan specialties like *sopa de mondongo* (cow tripe soup) on Mondays and *sopa de albondigas* (chicken dumplings with corn meal) on Fridays.

GETTING THERE AND AWAY
Sleek *interlocal* microbuses leave for both Jinotepe and Carazo from the UCA in Managua until 9pm. Much slower *rutas* leave from Terminal Israel Lewites.

From Jinotepe, buses leave from the COOTRAUS terminal (along the Pan-American Highway directly north of the park) at all hours for Managua, Masaya, Nandaime, and Rivas. Microbuses ($1) to Managua leave from the unofficial Sapasmapa terminal on the south side of the Instituto Alejandro, 4:45am-7:30pm. The most comfortable choice is one of the *interlocales* to Diriamba and San Marcos queued up on the street 20 meters north of the Super Santiago. Only the front one will load passengers, departing when the van is full.

From Diriamba, a fleet of *interlocales* run to and from Jinotepe (about $0.25), daily 6am-9pm, from a spot right next to the clock tower. Walk east and take your first left to find *microbus expresos* ($1) to Managua's Mercado Israel Lewites and the UCA, 5am-8pm daily. A little farther east at the first *caseta* (booth) on the left, you can ask about all the buses that pass from Jinotepe (Managua: 4:30am-6pm daily; Masaya: 5am-6pm daily).

★ **Carazo Beaches**
La Boquita, Casares, and **Huehuete** are 35 kilometers due west of Diriamba. The road ends at the coast where you'll turn right to reach La Boquita tourist center (you'll pay a small fee to enter). A left at the coast takes you to Huehuete and Casares, which are both small fishing towns. These beaches attract mostly Nicaraguan families on picnics and outings and the odd foreigner in search of fresh fish dishes. On a big swell, the surf can be up at both places, and you'll likely be the only gringo in the lineup (rental boards are sometimes available). Just in front of MyrinaMar hotel and a very short walk south of the Boquita tourist center, the coast is lined with huge rocks that you can walk on when the tide is not at its highest. Pools form within these rocks like natural

the beach at La Boquita

whirlpool tubs with moss-carpeted flooring. Lounging in these pools is a great break from the tide and feels luxurious and peaceful. This area—particularly La Boquita—is best avoided during Semana Santa and New Year's Day when it is overrun by drunken mobs of vacationers.

When you walk into La Boquita there will be various ranchos (thatch-roofed restaurants) whose waiters will come over to try to pull you in. All of the restaurants are similar and serve good fish options. **Suleyka** (in the back left corner of the tourist center, $4-9) is the most relaxed of these and also has a decent hotel. **Suleyka Hotel** (tel. 505/8698-3355, swlagos@yahoo.com, $10-80) has simple rooms with air-conditioning and private bathrooms, and is right on the beach; the largest room can sleep 10 (in bunk beds). At La Boquita, there are a handful of interchangeable *hospedajes* with basic (occasionally filthy) rooms for under $15.

Just before La Boquita tourist center is an excellent B&B, **MyrinaMar** (del Empalme La Boquita/Casares, 1 kilometer towards la Boquita, tel. 505/8421-8306, myrinamar.com, $95-125 d). This pristine white house on the cliff in front of the beach has four beautifully designed rooms for 4-5 people. The upstairs suites have a second story loft and multitiered, stylish bathrooms, while the downstairs suite sleeps five in two rooms and has a fully stocked kitchen. The owners are two French doctors, one of whom is also a massage therapist who offers massage and acupuncture. They serve a superb multi-course breakfast using Nicaragua's tropical fruit varieties in creative ways.

Public transportation leaves from the main market on the highway east of the clock tower in Diriamba. Express microbuses leave every 20 minutes 6:20am-6pm daily for the ride to La Boquita (40 minutes, $0.75). Ordinario buses take 90 minutes and leave 6:40am-6:30pm daily. From the beach at La Boquita, buses depart 5am-6pm daily.

La Isla de Ometepe and San Juan del Sur

S outh of Managua, the land crumples into high cloudy ridges and the windblown peak of Las Nubes, and then falls off slowly until it spills into southwestern Nicaragua's plains. Here, Lake Cocibolca presses the land into a narrow belt

that barely separates the lake from the Pacific Ocean.

By the time the Spanish "discovered" this region, the Nicaraos (Uto-Aztecan people of southwestern Nicaragua) had been residents for at least seven generations. The modern day department of Rivas in southern Nicaragua is home to two of the major draws for tourists in the country—the alluring Isla de Ometepe and the beautiful Pacific coastal beaches.

These days, the town of Rivas is a transportation hub that draws less attention than the coastal communities of Tola and San Juan del Sur and La Isla de Ometepe, though it retains a colonial charm appreciated by many. But it's hard to compete with Ometepe for attention. The magnificent twin-peaked island rises like a crown from the center of Lake Cocibolca. An intensely volcanic island steeped in tradition and mystery, Ometepe was the ancestral home of the Nahuatl people and today is an alluring destination for

travelers, with its sandy beaches, swimming holes, hiking trails, and, of course, two breathtaking volcanoes: one hot, one cold (the former remains quite active).

Meanwhile on the coast, sunsets continue to paint the silhouettes of fishing vessels in crimson, and the mood in San Juan del Sur is low-key and fun. The noon sun is scorching, so life is languorous and measured, spent swinging in breezy hammocks, enjoying fresh fish and cold beer at seaside, or splashing about in the surf. While San Juan del Sur is the largest beach town, there is a host of less party-heavy alternatives up and down the coast.

PLANNING YOUR TIME

La Isla de Ometepe should not be missed on any but the shortest trips to Nicaragua. It offers in a nutshell a little of everything Nicaragua has to offer, from history to waterfalls and volcanic trekking to horseback

Previous: Buena Onda resort; riding a wave at Guasacate. **Above:** Reserva Charco Verde.

Look for ★ to find recommended sights, activities, dining, and lodging.

Highlights

© AVALON TRAVEL

★ **Charco Verde Reserve:** Verdant and cool, this gorgeous reserve is a lovely little eco-system with a sandy lakeshore beach in the shadows of tall trees (page 112).

★ **Río Istián:** Paddling a kayak through these still waters early in the morning or during sunset is a breathtaking experience (page 118).

★ **Volcán Maderas:** The lower slopes of this volcano are covered with petroglyphs dating from before Columbus (page 119).

★ **Cascada San Ramón:** The most popular attraction by far on Ometepe's south side is this stunning 180-meter waterfall (page 123).

★ **Surfing near San Juan del Sur:** This major surf center draws shredders and groms from all over. There are waves for all levels out here, and plenty of places that offer beginner lessons (page 138).

★ **La Flor Wildlife Refuge:** Even if you miss the spectacular nighttime turtle-nesting events, a simple walk along this protected beach and up the forested river is remarkable (page 149).

★ **Playa Marsella:** Gentle waves and a secluded beach make for all sorts of opportunities (page 151).

★ **Playa Gigante:** This magical little beach town, nestled in a beautiful, calm bay, is surrounded by some of the best beaches in the country (page 154).

La Isla de Ometepe and San Juan del Sur

riding, all in an environment travelers routinely rave about as relaxing and delightful. You could feasibly travel to and from the island in a single day, but such a short trip would be folly. Rather, allow at least two days and two nights (and an extra day and night if you'd like to hike a volcano, which is a full day activity in itself). Travel in this region requires careful coordination of transport, as you can easily lose up to a half day waiting for boats and buses. Traveling around Ometepe is never easy; local transport is slow and erratic (especially on Sundays) and

renting vehicles can be expensive. If you're visiting the island in February, when the annual Survival Run occurs, book rooms well in advance.

San Juan del Sur proper is a relatively small town; you could walk every street in a single morning. Most visitors spend at least two days and a night here. Beach lovers and surfers can stretch it into a full week using the town as a base to explore the surrounding beaches and coves. Buses, taxis, and shuttles in Rivas connect with most of the beach destinations to the north and south.

La Isla de Ometepe

The twin-peaked island of Ometepe (Nahuatl for "two hills") is remarkably insulated from the rest of the country by the choppy waters of Lake Cocibolca. Long before the Spanish arrived, the islanders considered Ometepe sacred ground, inhabited by gods of great power. Even today the island remains awash in myths and legends, some of which date back to the days of the Nahuatl. Today's islanders prefer their home to what they call "over there." In 1957, as Volcán Concepción rumbled and threatened to erupt, the government ordered the islanders to evacuate Ometepe; they flatly refused, preferring to die on their island than live anywhere else.

The slopes of the volcanoes echo with the deep roar of howler monkeys, and the air is filled with the sharp cry of thousands of birds. Ecologically, Ometepe has been called the edge of the tropics, as a dividing line between tropical and dry falls between the two volcanoes. Volcán Maderas is extinct. Its crater is filled with a shallow lagoon and its slopes are carpeted with more tropical and humid species, including actual cloud forest at the top. Concepción is an active volcano whose slopes are covered with tropical dry forest species. On December 8, 1880, Volcán Concepción erupted with such force that lava and smoke flowed out of the crater for nearly a year. The most recent mini-eruption was in 2011.

Ometepe's proud residents live a mostly agrarian lifestyle on the slopes of the twin Cenozoic volcanoes. The two principal towns, Moyogalpa and Altagracia, are formerly sleepy port towns and transportation hubs enjoying an upswing in tourism. Costs are lower here than on the neighboring Pacific coast. Many isolated areas on the island do not accept credit cards; take advantage of the ATMs available in town before heading out.

MOYOGALPA

Moyogalpa (Nahuatl for "place of the mosquitoes") is Ometepe's largest commercial center. In spite of its name, it's not that buggy, but rather a growing little town that's an easy place to base your trip, especially if you're planning to climb Concepción. The town sits at the western base of the volcano, making it a great place to watch the sunset beyond the lake. You'll find plenty of fine accommodations and food here, but I recommend basing yourself outside of the town to experience the more isolated sides of the island.

Sights

The best spot to watch the sunset is at the small lakeside **park** between the docks. At the top of the hill at the end of the main road, Moyogalpa's **Catholic church** is charming, with a bell tower just high enough over the tree line to afford you a decent view of the town, coastline, lake, and the statue of a boy urinating. **La Sala Arqueológica** (or El Museo, 9am-5pm, $1), located toward the top of the main street, has a small collection of pre-Columbian artifacts found on the island over the years. Owner and amateur historian Herman García and his wife Ligia are knowledgeable about island history and lore, and can point you to local artisan communities. The store in front of the museum sells contemporary works. Walk one kilometer along the lakeshore north of town to arrive at the wetlands and lagoon of **El Apante.** In the dry season, enjoy its rich birdlife while walking the nature trail around the lagoon.

Entertainment and Events

La Esquina Caliente (on the main street) is a popular place to drink and relax—good luck getting a table on game night. You'll find the weekend dancing crowd at **Disco Johnny Bar** (just north of the dock).

La Isla de Ometepe

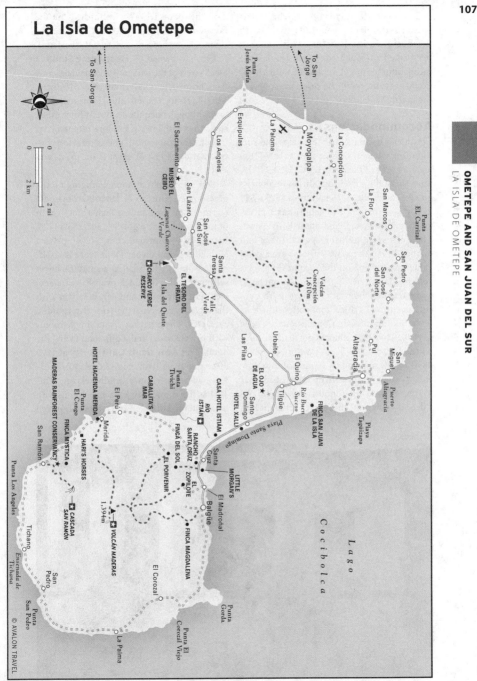

The town of Moyogalpa celebrates its patron saint, Santa Ana, June 23-26, with the **Baile de las Inditas.** This dance is performed in much the same way as the indigenous dance it replaced, with traditional costumes and the resonant sound of the marimba.

Accommodations

Consider a homestay in Moyogalpa and surrounding villages. **The Landing Hotel** (100 meters north of the dock, tel. 505/2569-4113, www.thelandinghotel.com, thelandinghotel@gmail.com, $7 dorm, $5 hammock, $15 s, $20 d, $30 apartments, $40 cabin) has a pleasant common space, and an attentive staff. The dorms are nothing special (dark and cramped), but the private rooms are a good value (ask for one on the second floor for a volcano view). There's garden space out back, a second floor hammock lounge with gym equipment, and a third floor patio with views of the lake and Volcán Concepción.

Hotelito Aly (1.5 blocks north of the dock on the left, tel. 505/2569-4196 or 505/8686-0830, www.hotelitoaly.com, hotelitoaly@yahoo.com, $7 dorm, $10 pp private bath) has 11 simple rooms set around a garden patio and a decent restaurant that serves three meals a day. The rooms feel a bit unfinished, but the family is friendly and helpful. The second floor balcony has a nice view of the volcano.

German-owned ★ **Hospedaje Soma** (3 blocks west of the park, www.hospedajesoma.com, hospedajesoma@gmail.com, $10 dorm, $20-40 private, $50-60 cabin) is the nicest option, although not quite central. Whitewashed structures with breezy, spacious rooms are set in lush landscaping. All guests receive a continental breakfast of eggs, fruit, toast, and coffee.

You'll feel right at home lounging on the breezy open patio at ★ **Hotel Ometepetl** (across from The Landing, half a block north of the dock on the right, tel. 505/2569-4276, ometepetlng@hotmail.com, $12-40 private bath, a/c). Local owner Doña Nora is a self-made woman who started a small business selling food by the dock over 40 years ago. Her staff is friendly and can help you with the logistics of preparing your trip (guides, cars, etc.). The hotel has clean, simple rooms with private baths and a gift shop facing the dock. The **American Café & Hotel** (100 meters up the hill on the right, tel. 505/8645-7193, www.americancafeandhotel.com, $20-40) has five spotless and spacious rooms with high ceilings, hot water, and reasonably priced

Hospedaje Soma

gringo-style breakfasts (café: daily 7am-4pm). **The Cornerhouse** (1 block north of the dock, www.thecornerhouseometepe.com, $25 s, $35 d) has a small sunny B&B above the café with cozy rooms.

Food

All the aforementioned accommodations serve food, including homemade Nica meals, the nicest of which is found at the restaurant at **Ometepetl** (across from The Landing, half a block north of the dock on the right, daily 7am-8pm, $2-5). **Los Ranchitos** (4 blocks up the hill from the dock, then half a block south, tel. 505/2569-4112, daily 7am-9:30pm, large pizza $6) is a favorite among locals and Peace Corps volunteers; its huge menu features surprisingly good pizza.

The trendy ★ **Cornerhouse** (1 block north of the dock, www.cornerhouseometepe. com, Mon-Sat. 7am-5pm, $3-6) has one of the best breakfast selections in town. Expect local coffee (from an espresso machine), fresh-baked bread, granola and jam made from scratch, and refreshing smoothies. They also sell *artesanía* (crafts) from local women's co-ops, who receive 100 percent of the sales.

Restaurante La Galería (2 blocks from the dock on the main road, daily 3:30pm-10pm, $4-10) serves delicious pasta dishes in a mellow atmosphere. Enjoy the art on the walls and smooth music while you wait on the sometimes-slow service. The bar/restaurant ★ **El Indio Viejo** (inside the Hospedaje Central, $3-7) offers smoothies, fish sandwiches, gringo burgers, burritos, and of course, *indio viejo* (a traditional corn-based stew). This is one of the only places I've found in the country where you can try a vegetarian version of the popular national dish. A good portion of their food is farm-to-table and organic, straight from their nearby *finca* (farm).

Information and Services

Get oriented at the Unión de Guías de Ometepe, or **UGO** (located to the left of the dock, tel. 505/8241-1794 or 505/8827-7714, daily 8am-5pm). This professional collective has enabled the local guides to share knowledge, formalize their training, and get sharp-looking uniforms to boot. Stop in and ask about bus schedules or places to stay. The offices for **Cacique Tours** (1 block up the hill, tel. 505/8417-8692) are equally knowledgeable and helpful. Both have INTUR-certified guides and can organize your volcano hike or island tour.

There are four **banks** in town, three of

Try vegetarian versions of popular national dishes at El Indio Viejo.

Alternative Tourism on Ometepe

There are numerous opportunities to support everyday Nicaraguans with your tourism dollars. From long-standing solidarity partnerships to sustainable agriculture work and research projects, Ometepe awaits those looking for something a little different.

HOMESTAYS AND COMMUNITY TOURISM

There are a handful of community-based tourism projects around the island. Experience authentic Nicaraguan living and invest in community tourism by spending a night with one of the families of **Puesta del Sol** (in the village of La Paloma, a few kilometers south of Moyogalpa, tel. 505/8619-0219 or 505/8695-7768, www.puestadelsol.org, $25/night). Accommodation rates include three home-cooked meals and filtered water. All bedrooms have a fan and access to toilets, but you'll share common spaces with dogs, chickens, and curious children. Rent a kayak or bike, and hang out in the small waterfront café. Learn to make *comida típica* in cooking classes ($10 pp), and try some of the locally made hibiscus wine. Basic Spanish will make your stay more enjoyable as the families involved don't speak much English. (Someone in the community does speak French, however.)

Pueblo Hotel Los Angeles (tel. 505/2569-4611 or 505/5720-1542, contact Carolina Flores Morales, pueblometepe1@gmail.com, $20/night pp) is a network of 15 women in the community of Los Angeles who host tourists in their homes. The cost of a stay includes three meals per day and a complete immersion experience. Aside from traditional tourism activities offered elsewhere on the island, the Pueblo Hotel members can arrange tours and a local youth organization rents bicycles.

At the foot of Volcán Maderas, **Mujeres de Balgüe** (tel. 505/8656-0857 or 505/8897-5035, trc. mujeresbalgue@yahoo.com, $8 pp) is a group of women who open their homes to guests. You'll get your own private room and you can arrange meals ($3 breakfast, $4 lunch, $4.50 dinner) with your family. It's best to arrange in advance, but once in Balgüe, you can check for availability at Comedor Isabel.

In Moyogalpa, **Escuela Hotel Teosintal** (2 blocks east of the dock, teosintalometepe09@ yahoo.es, $20 d) aims to provide an additional source of income for local producers and improve customer service and tourism services on the island. The theory is reinforced by the students' interaction with hotel guests. The hotel can arrange tours around the island or up to the volcanoes. The project, operating since 2005, can connect you with a network of agricultural cooperatives, many of which specialize in the production of sesame seeds for export.

which are located on the main strip (BAC, Banpro, and Bancentro). The **hospital** (3 blocks east of the park along the highway out of town, tel. 505/2569-4247) is more of a health center. For more serious ailments and injuries, go to the hospital in Rivas.

NEAR MOYOGALPA
La Concepción

More commonly referred to as "La Concha," this community three kilometers north of Moyogalpa is the start of one of the active volcano's more accessible trails. **Finca María Andrea** (tel. 505/8659-8964, $2 camping, plus

$5 to rent a tent) is a working family farm accustomed to serving breakfast to early morning hikers.

San Marcos

Just northeast of Moyogalpa along the "back way around the island" is the small community of San Marcos, home to a women's group that makes and sells ceramic pieces, including authentic replicas of pre-Columbian art. Ask around in town for the *taller de artesanía*.

Punta Jesús María

The long, sandy peninsula of Punta Jesús

VOLUNTEER OPPORTUNITIES

In the community of Santa Cruz, you'll find the **Fundación Entre Volcánes** (tel. 505/2569-4118, www.fundacionentrevolcanes.org, lorenaazteca41@yahoo.es), which runs projects all over Volcán Maderas focusing on environmental education, agriculture, and sustainable tourism. Opportunities range from assisting with school workshops to farm work and teaching composting techniques. You could also assist with community tourism trainings and marketing. Your Spanish should be at least conversational. Time commitments depend on the project.

In 2007, the folks at Hacienda Mérida founded the **Ometepe Bilingual School** (on the southwestern side of the island, tel. 505/8868-8973, contact Alvaro Molina, www.hmerida.com, alvaronica@gmail.com), a free afterschool English-language program for children in the rural community of Mérida. The school hosts international volunteers; student groups and individuals come from around the world. You can teach English to local elementary and high school students. There is a two-week minimum commitment, a $125 fee, and accommodations with a local family, or in the dormitories at Hacienda Mérida.

The **Maderas Rainforest Conservancy** (formerly the Ometepe Biological Field Station, Miami tel. 305/666-9932, www.maderasrfc.org, info@maderasrfc.org) is located near Merida, on the slopes of Volcán Maderas. They manage numerous forward-thinking conservation projects in surrounding communities, including a botanical garden on the lakeshore to serve as a refuge for endangered Blue Morpho butterflies. They also operate a field school for birding groups and research students. Tourists are welcome to sample the restaurant or stay at the station for a small fee.

AGRI-TOURISM

To learn about organic agriculture, permaculture, and horticulture, spend a couple of weeks at **Finca Bona Fide** (about 300 meters left of Finca Magdalena, tel. 505/8616-4566, www.projectbonafide.com, $20/night, less if you stay more than 1 week). Chris runs a beautiful farm, offers 18-day organic agriculture workshops (free for locals), has a nutritional kitchen in Balgüe, and offers farm work internships. Enjoy rustic lodging (a bunk bed or hammock on a raised platform) and three meals a day. Advance arrangements are preferred.

Similar agricultural work arrangements can be made at **La Finca Ecológica El Zopilote** (tel. 505/2560-1764, www.ometepezopilote.com). If you'll be sticking around more than a couple of weeks, ask about discounts. Finally, check out the **Fincas Verdes** network (www.fincasverdes.com) to get a lowdown on the various agricultural and conservation ventures being offered on the island.

María is lovely for swimming and relaxing in the dry season and submerges in the rainy season. The narrow kilometer-long sandbar is a good place to watch the sun set or enjoy a meal after a swim in the lake. The entrance is a long driveway just north of the town of Esquipulas that takes 15 minutes to walk. Take the bus and ask to get off at the picturesquely named **Punta de la Paloma** (Dove's Point). Don't leave bikes or valuables unattended here, as robberies aren't unheard of.

Stay nearby at ★ **Finca Samaria** (2 kilometers south of Punta la Paloma, tel. 505/8824-2210 or 505/8636-4886, $4 camp, $3 hammock, beachfront cabin $15, rooms $15-25) in Los Angeles. Rooms aren't fancy, but they're clean. Owners can organize fishing, horseback riding, and volcano tours. If you're just on a day trip, it's worth stopping for farm-to-table goodness at their restaurant **Playa Samaritano** (6am-9pm daily, $2-11), where you'll find homemade bread, paneer cheese and tofu, and delicious vegan options in addition to hamburgers and steak chimichurri.

Museo El Ceibo

Eight kilometers outside Moyogalpa in El Sacramento are the archaeological and currency museums at **Museo El Ceibo** (tel. 505/8874-8076, elceibomuseos.com, daily 8am-5pm, $5 each, $8 for both). The ranch was once a tobacco farm, and the archaeological museum is housed in the cellar formerly used for drying tobacco. The collection includes over 1,500 well-preserved pre-Columbian pieces from across the island, including unearthed funerary urns, jewelry, weapons, and tools of the Nahuatl dating back to AD 3000. The currency museum includes samples of Nicaraguan money dating all the way back to cacao—the only coin you can eat. Make a day of it: grab a bite at the **Bar La Herradura** (daily 7am-9pm, $3-8) followed by a languid dip in the lake. Or stay in one of the appealing new **cabins** ($68 d with a/c) and unwind in the large, well-maintained pool and enjoy free museum admission.

★ Charco Verde Reserve

Swim in the lake accompanied only by the call of the monkeys in the treetops and the whir of colorful birds. This is still a relatively wild area, with enough tall trees remaining to harbor some exciting wildlife. The entire area has been cordoned off to prevent development, leaving this cove an oasis of peace. Pay $2 to walk along one of three trails (totaling 4km) in the private nature reserve, one each for beginner, intermediate, and advanced experience levels. The easiest hike is flat and wheelchair accessible. You'll have amazing panoramic views of the island, and may see (or at least hear) howler monkeys, birds, and other wildlife. Bring bug spray. There is a lagoon in the reserve, but it's not recommended for swimming as it's full of algae.

According to legend, the enchanted city of Chico Largo lies beneath the lagoon. Some say that Chico Largo appears to people at night and offers to make a deal: wealth and prosperity during life, in exchange for their souls, which upon death, he converts into cattle. Many of the cows on the island, then, are the souls of Ometepe's previous generation, which opted for a life of decadence

pre-Columbian pieces at Museo El Ceibo

instead of hard work. In another version of the legend, the cacique Nicarao is buried with his solid gold throne along the edge of the Charco Verde. In this version, Chico Largo is a descendant of Nicarao and roams the area guarding and protecting Nicarao's tomb, as well as Ometepe's wildlife.

Some 50 meters from the reserve entrance is the **Paraíso de las Mariposas** (daily 7am-5pm, $5) butterfly reserve. Enjoy the beautifully landscaped garden before moving into the screened-in refuge, which houses 14 species of butterflies, including the endangered Blue Morpho. The entrance fee includes a peek at the on-site laboratory and an explanation of caterpillar transformation.

On Cerro Mogote, 100 meters down the road from the Charco Verde entrance, is **La Mirador del Diablo.** This hill is the highest point between the two volcanoes and provides excellent views. Hike up the short trail ($1 to access) to the lookout point, or do a **canopy tour** (tel. 505/8656-0522, daily 8:30am-4:30pm, $25 pp), which consists of 15 stations, a Tarzan swing, hanging bridge, and a 20-meter-high free fall or rappel.

ACCOMMODATIONS

The three nearest hotels are each owned by a different Riveras sibling. Each rents horses and offers boat and kayak trips along the shoreline, fishing trips, and horseback riding. **Hotel y Restaurante Charco Verde** (next to the reserve entrance, tel. 505/8887-9302 or 505/2560-1271, www.charcoverde.com.ni, charcoverde22@yahoo.es, $35-92) has easy trail access. Cute cabanas with tile floors, sunny windows, front porch, private bath, and air-conditioning can fit up to six people. The big lakefront restaurant has an air of luxury.

Up the beach is **Hotel Finca Venecia** (tel. 505/8887-0191 or 505/2560-1269, fincavenecia.com, hotelfincavenecia@yahoo.com, $25-50 cabin), a family-style guesthouse on a hundred-year-old farm on the beach. All rooms have hot water and air-conditioning. Ask for a lakefront cabin and watch the sunset from your private terrace. The restaurant serves well-prepared pasta, chicken, fish, and beef dishes. From here, it's an easy walk along the shore into the reserve of Charco Verde and to Playa Balcón. Right next door is **La Posada de Chico Largo** (tel. 505/8886-4069 or 505/8473-7210, chicolargo@yahoo.com, $10 dorm beds, $30 d), the most economic of the three. Despite their nickname, "Los Diablos" are accommodating hosts and their restaurant is good.

Valle Verde

The pirate's treasure is, in this case, an isolated retreat on a wide, black-sand beach rather off the beaten track. Reach the cove by getting off the bus at the entrance just beyond San José del Sur, then walking 15 minutes from the highway, following the signs. **El Tesoro del Pirata** (tel. 505/8927-2831 or 505/8566-8782, tesorodelpirata@gmail.com, $25 cabana, $5 pp camping) is located just far enough off the beaten track to encourage the local wildlife to whoop it up for you. Cabins are simple with private baths and can fit up

to four people. The owners recently added a small lakefront pool for guest use. The view is excellent, as is the swimming and boating, and they serve some of the best tasting fish on the island.

ALTAGRACIA

The second largest community on Ometepe and an important island port, Altagracia is more picturesque than Moyogalpa but plays second fiddle with regard to attractions and services. In 2000, National Geographic filmed a documentary about vampire bats here. While there are indeed many vampire bats, they are a threat only to the local chickens, which the bats suck dry by hanging from the chickens' nerveless feet.

Sights

El Museo Ometepe (next to the *alcaldía,* daily 9am-5pm, $1) has a few exhibits on the flora, fauna, and archaeology of Ometepe, including statues and ceramic pieces unearthed around the island. The **church courtyard** across from the park makes for a peaceful retreat with a few interesting pre-Columbian stone idols for added irony. You might get yelled at by a group of bright green parakeets that make their home in the roof of the dilapidated old church (right next to the new church). Across the street in the central park, you'll find the *artesanía cooperative* (daily 8am-4pm), comprised of local artisans who take turns working in the kiosk. Some of the pieces are original and exhibit the pride that the islanders have for their home.

From the park, walk east down a sandy road for 30 minutes, or bike, to the bay of **Playa Tagüizapa,** a fine sandy beach for swimming. You can pick up supplies in town for a picnic and make a lazy day of it. Located three kilometers north of the town of Altagracia, the port has boat service between Granada and San Carlos (Río San Juan). The road that leads to the port is shady and makes a nice, short walk—allow 45 minutes each way. On the way, you'll pass **Playa Paso**

Hiking Ometepe's Volcanoes

Ometepe's twin peaks are a siren's call for many intrepid backpackers, and hiking one or both is an intimate way to get to know the island. But do not underestimate the difficulty of the challenge before you: Both peaks are equally dangerous, for different reasons.

On either peak, a guide is *required,* and for good reason: The "trails" are unmarked, and branch dozens of times. On Maderas, an experienced hiker got lost in the crevices of the volcano's middle slopes and succumbed to dehydration and died. I recommend using a trained local guide from **UGO** (tel. 505/8827-7714, ugometepe@yahoo.com). You can hire a guide starting at $40 per group. **Cacique Tours** (tel. 505/8417-8692, office in Moyogalpa, informational kiosk in San Jorge port) is an excellent option, providing safe, experienced guides. **Berman Gómez** (tel. 505/8816-6971, ometepeisland@gmail.com) was the first bilingual guide on the island, and has since worked with BBC and *Survivor.* His prices remain reasonable, and his passion for wildlife makes his tours noteworthy.

VOLCÁN CONCEPCIÓN

Volcán Concepción (1,610 m.) is the **more arduous climb.** Large parts of the hike are treeless, rocky scrambles. Don't be surprised if the volcano is off-limits the day you arrive, as **Concepción is quite active,** and has spewn gas and ash on several occasions, including as recently as March 2010. The authorities prohibit climbs when the seismologists show conditions aren't safe. As you reach the volcanic cone, the wind that buffets you is cold until you reach the crater lip, where the volcano's hot, sulphurous gas pours forth (the clash of hot and cold air is responsible for the almost permanent cloud cover at the top of the volcano). On the off chance that the clouds thin, the view from the peak is unforgettable.

Allow a whole day for the full hike: five exhausting hours up and four knee-shattering hours down. Eat a hearty breakfast; take plenty of water, food, sun protection, and good shoes and socks to protect your feet.

Most travelers hike Concepción by way of the town **La Concha** (La Concepción). Following this trail until the forest ends is the most accessible hike, taking about five hours up and back. After that point, the trail continues steeply up, and is not recommended for inexperienced hikers. The trails that start at **La Flor** and **Moyogalpa** both meet up with La Concha's trail. There is an eastern approach from **Altagracia** that leads through an impressive amount of monkey-inhabited forest before hitting the exposed section. There are two southern trails in **San José del Sur** and **Los Ramos,** which are more difficult than the others due to their steep incline.

VOLCÁN MADERAS

Volcán Maderas (1,394 m.) is more accessible, and the volcano is **dormant,** if not extinct (in fact, there's a forested lake within the crater). It is thus **more frequently hiked,** but remains

Real, an out-of-the-way bathing beach you'll likely have all to yourself. If you're heading to the port to catch the boat to Granada or San Carlos, it's worthwhile to speak with the owner of Hotel Central. They offer pickup truck service to the port, so you don't have to carry your luggage that far. When the water is too rough, the boat may not show up at Altagracia at all, preferring to hug the eastern shore of the lake.

Entertainment and Events

Altagracia's *fiestas patronales,* in celebration of San Diego, are held November 12-18. In addition to the traditional festivities, the **Baile de las Ramas** (Dance of the Branches) is a major component of the celebration. The dancers tear off smaller branches of the guanacaste tree and hold them to their heads while dancing to imitate the worker *zompopo* (leaf-cutter) ants carrying leaves off to the anthills.

Volcán Concepción is still active.

equally dangerous and is responsible for at least two deaths since 2005. Maderas is a national park above 400 meters, and for good reason: It's really beautiful up there. You'll pass **petroglyphs** on your way up. When you reach the crater lip, the final descent to the mist-swept crater lake requires a rope and should not be attempted without proper safety equipment—make sure your guide packs rope.

The most commonly used trail to the top starts at **Finca Magdalena;** if you're not staying at the Finca Magdalena you must pay a trail fee to enter and pass through the coffee plantations. You'll pass a petroglyph or two on the way up. There are also nearby trails starting at **La Finca Ecológica El Zopilote** and **Albergue Ecológico El Porvenir.** Allow 4 hours to go up and 2-3 to come back down, and count on resting an hour at the crater lake (58 minutes of which you'll spend deciding whether or not to jump in the cold, mushy-bottom *laguna*). Some guides prefer hikers not swim here due to unseen submerged tree branches, which can cause injuries.

Another, more strenuous ascent leaves from **Mérida.** The first three hours include petroglyphs and a spectacular view from the *mirador* (lookout) but are an almost vertical ascent, leveling off into the upper reaches that one hiker calls "enchanted." All trails meet at the same spot before descending into the crater. For folks who aren't interested in the exhausting full trek, hike halfway up the Finca Magdalena trail to a coffee and rice-producing village, Las Cajillas. Nearby is a small waterfall, Cascada El Jerusalem—less impressive than San Ramón, but still worth the hike.

Accommodations and Food

Altagracia's accommodations are generally located within a few blocks of each other, so feel free to walk around and compare before settling in. One of the cheapest and friendliest choices is **Hospedaje Ortiz** (a block or so from the central park, $4-5 pp). **Hostal Edelma** (2 blocks north of the park, tel. 505/8417-8692, $8 pp) is a bit nicer. ★ **Hotel Central** (2 blocks south of the park,

tel. 505/2569-4420 or 505/8661-3858, doscarflores@yahoo.es, $6 pp shared bath, $10-12 pp private) is a traveler favorite, with a nicely furnished reading room, small garden, and helpful staff.

At **Hotel Castillo** (tel. 505/8856-8003 or 505/2569-4403, hotelcastillo@hotmail.com, $5 pp shared bath, $10-15 private bath), the upstairs dorm has a street-side balcony.

Information and Services

The small **Centro de Salud** (300 meters north of the park, tel. 505/2552-6089) can treat patients 24 hours a day, but for serious injuries have the owner of your hotel take you in a vehicle to the hospital in Moyogalpa, or head for the hospital in Rivas.

NEAR ALTAGRACIA
El Quino

Stay with a local family at **Hospedaje La Peñita** (tel. 505/8972-6299, famrampaiza@yahoo.es, $4 pp). The friendly owner has bikes to rent and will take you on a guided tour of the island. To get there, take the bus from Altagracia to El Quino (at the fork for the isthmus) and walk 300 meters north. This is about as close as you can stay to El Ojo de Agua.

Finca San Juan de la Isla

The beautiful and isolated ★ **Finca San Juan de la Isla** (tel. 505/8560-6977 or 505/8886-0734, www.sanjuandelaisla.com, $75-125) provides some of the nicest lakefront lodging on the island. Prices are higher than most other places on the island. Spend your time horseback riding on the beach, kayaking in the lake, or rent a bike or scooter to

visit the nearby El Ojo de Agua. A taxi from Moyogalpa runs about $20.

El Ojo de Agua

Located near the town of Tilgüe, on the northern part of the isthmus, **El Ojo de Agua** ($2) consists of crystal-clear, spring-fed waters captured in two natural, stone pools set in the middle of a gorgeous and colorful botanical garden. Swim in the revitalizing waters the way the Nahautls probably did, then climb out to drip-dry in the sun. It's the best swimming hole on the island other than the lake itself, and the water is the cleanest you'll find anywhere. Your entrance fee helps with maintenance, as does whatever you pay to take home some organic, herbal tea. Snacks (nothing fancy) are available at the little bar/shop (daily 7am-6pm). You can string up a hammock or set up a tent for the night ($3).

PLAYA SANTO DOMINGO

Playa Santo Domingo runs along the eastern side of the narrow wedge of land that connects the volcanoes of Concepción and Maderas, the product of rich volcanic soil that washed down from the slopes of both volcanoes over millennia, gradually

Playa Santo Domingo

connecting the two islands. The several-kilometer-long stretch of black sand on the northern part of the Istián Isthmus runs alongside the pueblos of Santo Domingo, San Fernando, and Santa Cruz. Its central location makes it the most convenient base for exploring the rest of the island. The swimming can be nice, but with the near-constant onshore breeze, the water is usually choppy and it can get very windy. If there are loads of *chayules* (gnats) when you visit, consider staying on another part of the island, away from the water, where these harmless but annoying little bugs are nearly nonexistent. Also note that in the rainy season water levels rise and the sandy beach all but disappears. Any time of year, expect great views of both volcanoes.

Athletes should check out the **Fuego y Agua** (fuegoyagua.org) race in February, which has been gaining a reputation as an exciting challenge among runners. There are four races: a 100K, 50K, 25K, and Survival Run ($75-225). The courses go along the lakefront and up and over both volcanoes. The Survival Run includes a variety of tasks, like harvesting plantains and building your own raft. If you're visiting the island in February, book a room well in advance.

Santo Domingo

The most services for tourists are along the part of the beach in the town of Santo Domingo where lodging and restaurants are clustered together along the main road. The charming stone cabins at ★ **Villa Paraíso** (tel. 505/2563-4675, www.hotelvillaparaiso.com.ni, $35 private room, $75-92 cabin) feature air-conditioning, fridges, satellite TVs, and hot water. The breezy waterfront restaurant is fabulous, or order food to the shaded beachside pool. Call early for reservations as the place fills up quickly, especially on weekends and holidays.

A budget-friendly option is the beachfront **Buena Vista** ($25 d), a pleasant, family-run place offering plain rooms with clean sheets and fans. Farther down the road is **Hospedaje El Bosque** (tel. 505/2569-4871, $8 dorm, $15 s, $25 d), located next to the family's *pulpería* (small grocery store). The beach is just across the street.

San Fernando

Just outside Santo Domingo in San Fernando is **Hotel Xalli** (tel. 505/2569-4876, www.ometepebeachhotel.com, $45-111) with seven luxurious rooms all with hot water, TV, ceiling fan, air-conditioning, room service, and

Villa Paraíso

Wi-Fi. Enjoy the breeze in a hammock under the trees on the lakefront property.

Two kilometers farther down the beach toward Maderas is Santa Cruz. The first place you'll come to is the **Sun Kite School** (tel. 505/8287-5023, www.kiteboardingnicaragua. com, info@sunkiteschoool.com), just across the street from the beach. The instructors are certified by the International Kiteboarding Organization and have 15 years of teaching experience. Kayaks ($12/hour) are available. The owners also rent a sunny little room ($15-30) next to the kitchen with two beds and private bath that can fit up to three people. At the small, open-air **Café de Paris** (daily Nov.-July 8am-5pm, $3-6) out front, you'll find yummy French dishes like crepes and quiche.

★ **Casa Hotel Istiám** (just outside San Fernando, before Santa Cruz, tel. 505/2569-4879 or 505/8844-2200, casaistiam@hotmail. com, $8 pp shared bath, $10 pp private bath, $35 d with a/c and private bath) provides enormous value, and its beach is clean and pleasant. The rooms are so-so but affordable, and the location is spectacular, with an impressive view of both volcanoes from the second-floor deck. The service is friendly and the restaurant good. Make reservations in Moyogalpa at **Hotel Ometepetl** (across

from The Landing, half a block north of the dock on the right, tel. 505/2569-4276, ometepetlng@hotmail.com), as they sometimes fill up. Camping is also possible.

★ RÍO ISTIÁN

The paddle trip in a kayak or canoe up the Río Istián is best early in the morning or during sunset but is worthwhile at any time. You slip into the still waters of a marshy isthmus deep with shadow from the tree canopy and raucous with the sounds of birds, all under the reflection of two volcanic peaks.

The best place to base your trip from is Mérida, which is just three kilometers away by kayak. Edgard Lacayo at **Aventuras en la Isla** (tel. 505/8356-5108 or 505/8557-6251, $15-25) runs kayaking and wildlife tours from nearby El Perú, just 20 minutes from the river mouth. **Caballito's Mar** (5 km from Santa Cruz, turn right at the signs and follow the dirt road to the lake, tel. 505/8451-2093, www.caballitosmar.com, fernando@caballitosmar.com) rents kayaks by the hour and offers a fun three-hour guided trip ($20-25) in which they'll point out the kingfishers, white herons, turtles, and caimans. You can easily stay in their basic dormitory ($5 pp) or just have a meal (traditional Nicaraguan

kayak tour of the Río Isitián

and lots of lake fish, $3). You can also rent kayaks at **Hacienda Mérida** (tel. 505/2560-0496 or 505/8894-2551, www.hmerida.com) or **Charco Verde** (tel. 505/8887-9302 or 505/2560-1271, www.charcoverde.com.ni, charcoverde22@yahoo.es). Allow half a day for the adventure, and bring sunscreen, snacks, and plenty of water. During the dry season (Feb.-Apr.), some parts of the river may be too shallow for kayaking. During heavy rains in October, wind may be too fierce to make the trip. There's a short trail that starts in Playa Santo Domingo (behind Casa Hotel Istiám) that will allow you to see part of the marsh. The shorter paddle to Isla el Congo, just offshore, is nice as well, but beware the monkeys!

★ VOLCÁN MADERAS

Maderas is officially a national park, which will hopefully encourage preservation of the thick forests. Maderas is a pleasant volcano to climb, since the hike is in the shade, and is less demanding than its truly active twin. A guide is now obligatory since a pair of hikers got lost and eventually perished on the mountain. Even if you're not a peak bagger, there's lots to do here, starting with a guided visit to the fields of old petroglyphs behind

Finca Magdalena and Albergue Ecológico El Porvenir, a relic of the island's Nahuatl past. There is mountain biking down the rutted roads to take a coffee tour, horseback ride, or kayak trip. In addition, a host of unique places to stay (many based on working farms, some using permaculture and principles of environmental sustainability) are fun and interesting.

Santa Cruz and El Madroñal

Hostal Espirales (tel. 505/8355-2531, $8 dorm, $14 d with shared bath, $18 d private bath) is a two-minute walk from beach access.

Let the lapping waves of Lake Cocibolca rock you to sleep at **Little Morgan's** (tel. 505/8717-6475, www.littlemorgans.com, $10 tree house dorm beds, $20-35 private cabana), named after the charismatic Irish owner's young son. Chill to the satellite tunes, play a game of pool, or hang out in the rancho's lookout point. You'll find it on the main road, on the edge of Santa Cruz heading towards Balgüe. There is a restaurant (daily 7am-8pm) and a bar that stays open late (if you're a light sleeper best ask for a bed closer to the water).

Its location at the intersection of two main roads makes **Rancho Santa Cruz** (tel. 505/8884-9894, www.santacruzometepe.com, santacruzometepe@gmail.com, $1 hammock,

Volcán Maderas

$2 camping, $6 dorm, $10-20 private) an excellent base from which to explore in either direction, as your chances of catching a bus or taxi double. The restaurant (breakfast $2, lunch and dinner $4-6) serves granola, yogurt, and pancake breakfasts and a selection of vegetarian options including pastas and curries for lunch and dinner. You can rent bikes ($5/day), and they can arrange horseback riding on request.

The cabanas at **Finca del Sol** (tel. 505/8364-6394, $37-47), directly across the road from Little Morgan's, are small and homey. The whole place is sun-powered and eco-friendly, including the composting toilets, and the Finca is less mainstream. Chat with welcoming hosts Cristiano and Sheri over a home-cooked meal.

A 15-minute walk up the trail from the main road in El Madroñal leads to **La Finca Ecológica El Zopilote** (tel. 505/8369-0644 or 8961-8742, www.ometepezopilote.com, $3 to set up your tent, $4 hammock dorm, $12-20 private cabin), a hillside cluster of thatch huts and platforms run by some peace-loving Italians and their pack of hound dogs. Follow the well-placed signs. Check out the organic products in the **gift shop** (daily 10am-6pm) in the old bus by the road. They offer free yoga classes for guests (visitors pay $3). Pizza nights (Tues., Thurs., and Sat.) are a hit with guests.

Across the road is a small café called **Jardín de Buhó** (on Finca El Delirio, Mon.-Sat. 8am-9pm), owned by well-known Nicaraguan artist Juan Rivas and his wife, Marta. They make a great stir-fry, but you'll also find *comida típica* (local food) and some Chinese dishes. On Wednesdays and Fridays they have free movie nights (6:30pm). Their small *hospedaje* (200 meters behind the restaurant, tel. 505/2560-1460, jardindelbuho@yahoo.com, $3 camping, $7 dorm, $15 private d with shared bath) is a short walk from a rocky lake beach. Marta is an anthropologist and offers archaeological tours ($5 each, minimum 5 people). The couple is interested in creating a shared artist space and is

the roadside gift shop at La Finca Ecológica El Zopilote

open to proposals from artists who want to share their skills with the surrounding local community.

Albergue Ecológico El Porvenir (tel. 505/2569-4420 or 505/2569-4426, doscarflores@yahoo.es, $10 pp private bath) is a peaceful hillside retreat with modern buildings, screened windows, volcano views, and lush tropical grounds. It's less ecological than it pretends, but you will nonetheless awaken to the sounds of the jungle. There is a one-hour trail to a lookout point with a great view of the isthmus and Concepción. If you're not a guest, you can visit for $1. It's a kilometer past Rancho Santa Cruz, and then 600 meters in from the sign on the road.

Balgüe

Balgüe is a convenient base for hiking Volcán Maderas. This *pueblito* has increasingly good lodging and food of its own. The stalwart of course is Finca Magdalena up on the skirts of the volcano itself, with petroglyphs and a compelling history, but various international

Finca Magdalena offers a great view of Volcán Concepción.

505/8811-3126 or 505/8216-9743, www.mitierraometepe.com, $6 pp, $25 private room) in the town of Balgüe proper is a family-run *hospedaje* with 10 clean rooms. Fernando and his family can rent you a mountain bike ($7/day), a *moto* ($25/day), or a horse ($7/hr), and can easily arrange a volcano hike or transportation to all the local hot spots in their minibus. Down the next dirt road, **The Lazy Crab** (from the Catholic Church, 100 meters east, 20 meters toward the lake, tel. 505/5718-2191 or 505/8281-5303, $3 hammock, $6 dorm, $14 private room) is a new option run by a young local who's trying to promote sustainable tourism options in the community. He's got four clean rooms with mosquito nets and shared bath as well as a private room with a private bath. He also can organize a volcano hike and a farm tour with local INTUR-certified guides. Ask about kayak, horse, bike, and *moto* rental.

★ **Finca Magdalena** (tel. 505/8418-5636 or 505/8584-9298, www.fincamagdalena.com, $4 to string up a hammock or camp on the porch, $4 dorm cot, $6-22 private room, $43 private cabin, and more expensive cottages) is a 26-family working coffee cooperative established in 1983. The 195-year-old wooden house, once home to a plantation owner, tends towards austere, but its bare rooms have a romantic air of nostalgia, and the staff is welcoming and sincere. Coffee tours (1.5 hrs, $8 pp), petroglyph tours (1 hr, $6 pp), and guided hikes up to the lagoon atop Volcán Maderas are available. To get to Finca Magdalena, take the bus to Balgüe (get off at El Bamboo) and follow the signs along the 20-minute walk up the road to the farm (arrive before dark).

★ **Casa del Bosque** (from bus stop at El Bamboo, 1.5 km uphill from Bonafide's sign, tel. 505/8585-8933, $35-45 d) is a beautiful, secluded, three-bedroom house with spacious high-ceilinged rooms located on the Café Campestre farm, just below Bonafide. It's solar-powered with composting toilets and cool spring water showers, and has ample hangout space, including a BBQ area, large couch, and a porch with rocking chairs. The paths through the surrounding farm make for nice

newcomers (and a couple of locals) now provide a much greater range of options.

Check out the local women's co-op **La Girasol** (75 meters up the hill from El Bamboo, tel. 505/8365-2288, ask for Claudia, Mon. and Wed. 2pm-5pm), which has created jobs and income for a group of women in the community. They craft lovely coin purses, e-reader and laptop bags, cosmetic bags, and purses. Pick out your own fabric if you like. You can also buy their products at The Cornerhouse in Moyogalpa, which gives the cooperative 100 percent of the sale.

The best maintained bikes in Balgüe are at Danilo Ortiz's place across from the soccer field. If you're having trouble finding him, he's more commonly known by his nickname, **Bro Chil** (tel. 505/8402-2525, Mon.-Sat. 8am-5pm, $6/day).

ACCOMMODATIONS

If you'd like to get to know a local family in Balgüe, try a homestay.

If you're on a budget, **Así Es Mi Tierra** (tel.

The Petroglyphs of Ometepe

In the days of the Nahuatls, Volcán Maderas was called Coatlán, "the place where the sun lives," and Concepción was known as Choncoteciguatepe, "the brother of the moon," or Mestliltepe, "the peak that menstruates." In the lush forests of the lower slopes of the two volcanoes, the Nahuatls performed complicated rituals in honor of many different gods: Catligüe, the goddess of fertility; Ecatl, the god of air; Migtanteot, the god of death; Tlaloc, the god of soil; and Xochipillo, the goddess of happiness. The Nahuatl gods were all-powerful and vindictive, and spent their days in the land where the sun rises doing what all-powerful gods do best—feeding on human blood.

The concept of a soul was an important part of the Nahuatl belief system, as were the concepts of an afterlife and some form of reincarnation. Their calendar consisted of 18 months of 20 days each, for a total of a 360-day calendar year. They believed in a cycle of catastrophic events that recurred every 52 years. According to that cycle, the Nahuatls stored grains and water in preparation for that year.

Scattered around the island of Ometepe, but principally on the **north and northeastern slopes of Volcán Maderas** (behind Finca Magdalena, Albergue Ecológico El Porvenir, and Finca Ecológica El Zopilote), are the statues and petroglyphs, carved around the year AD 300, that paid homage to the Nahuatl gods. **Spirals** are a consistent theme, representing perhaps calendars or the Nahuatl concept of time and space. It has been suggested that spirals may also represent the islands themselves, or that the twin-spiral shape of Ometepe gave the island even more significance to the islanders, as it fit in with their ideas about the cosmos. More mundane images can also be identified in the carved rocks: monkeys, humans hunting deer, and a couple in coitus, suggesting Nahuatl wishes for prosperity and fertility, or just a bit of monkey business.

walks during the day. The owner lives in a cabin on the property—far enough to be private, but close enough to find if needed. The town is not far and bikes are available for guest use. You can order food from Café Campestre if you don't feel like making the trek yourself. Breakfast is served B&B style on-site in the kitchen, which is otherwise open for guest use. Ask about renting out the whole house.

FOOD

Chepito's Comedor (across from Café Campestre, Mon.-Sat. 8am-8pm, $3-5) offers quality Nica dishes at a reasonable price. **Big Lake** (down the side road where Lazy Crab is located, turn left at the lake, daily 9am-9pm, $3-10) has the best location in town, right on the lake with a shaded outdoor eating area and small dock jutting into the lake for swimming. Their specialty is fish, but they serve a variety of meals to please meat lovers and vegetarians alike. This is a picturesque spot to unwind at the end of the afternoon.

★ **Café Campestre** (in front of the Pentecostal church, daily 9am-8:30pm, $3-6)

has some of the best organic, farm-to-table food in Nicaragua. The menu offers mostly international fare; highlights include handmade pasta, hummus, dahl, okra, lasagna, and beer batter crepes. Don't miss house-roast coffee that's grown in Cajillas on the side of Maderas. The moonshine on the menu will make my fellow Kentuckians feel right at home.

Nisyros (farther down the road, on the right past the bus stop, daily 8am-11pm, $2-7) is run by an Italian man and his son. They serve a changing menu of Mediterranean cuisine, but you can always count on pizza and free Wi-Fi. Keep walking and you'll see Argentinean-owned **El Bamboo** (at the turnoff for Finca Magdalena, Mon.-Sat. 11am-10pm, $3-12). Their menu boasts big sandwiches on homemade bread, homemade ravioli, tofu, and sauces, smoothies, and local, organic coffee.

Mérida

It's still difficult to get out here, but Mérida is steadily increasing services to tourists. A rigorous and none-too-obvious trail leads to Maderas's crater lagoon from Mérida; you can go down the way you came, or you can descend to the other side and emerge at Finca Magdalena or Finca Zopilote. But you absolutely must hire a guide, bring food and water, and get an early morning start: This is a serious hike for pros only.

Ride on horseback along the beach, through the forest, and beneath the full moon with **Hari's Horses** (300 meters east of El Pescadito, tel. 505/8383-8499, www.harishorses.com, harishorses@gmail.com, $10/hr), popular for his tours around the island on healthy, well-fed, trained animals.

ACCOMMODATIONS AND FOOD

Hari of Hari's Horses has bright, sunlit cabins at ★ **Finca Montaña Sagrada** ($45 d, includes yummy breakfast) with hot water and private decks complete with rocking chairs and amazing views.

★ **Hotel Hacienda Mérida** (tel. 505/2560-0496 or 505/8894-2551, www.hmerida.com, $5 camping, $8 dorm, $25-50 room with private bath, breakfast $5, dinner $7) is a friendly lakeside compound where second-floor balconies have views of the volcanoes and the lake. Take a swim from the private dock. They rent bikes and kayaks and can arrange hikes, fishing trips, tubing on the lake, and horseback riding ($5.50/hr); breakfast and dinner buffets are crafted with a nutrition focus from whole foods, many from the garden. Internet is available. The Nicaraguan owner, Alvaro Molina, speaks perfect English and is both a passionate advocate for and walking encyclopedia of Ometepe social causes. Ask about volunteer opportunities.

Farther down the road is ★ **Finca Mystica** (tel. 505/8751-9653 or 505/8119-1765, fincamystica.com, idigmud@gmail.com, $12 dorm, $35 private cabin), owned by a young U.S. family. Cabins are beautiful and made from organic materials. Their **Roots N Fruits Café** (daily 7:15am-8pm, $4-8) caters to all diets. Enjoy homemade raw chocolate, ginger beer, tasty baked goods, fresh bread and pizza from an earth oven, and locally grown house-roasted organic coffee.

Locally owned **Monkey's Island Hostel** (1 km south of Hacienda Mérida, tel. 505/8652-0971, $7 dorm, $12 shared bath, $20 private bath) has a friendly staff, boxy concrete rooms, and lousy feng shui. It's a short walk down some stairs to access the lake and sunset views.

San Ramón and Vicinity

Some 250 families fish and farm on Ometepe's least-visited shoreline, but it remains the "dark side of the moon": little visited but equally, if not more, compelling. Beyond San Ramón, the lonely east coast of Maderas is one of the most isolated spots in Nicaragua, connected tentatively by a poor excuse of a road with infrequent bus service. The locals are not used to receiving guests. It's potentially feasible to circumnavigate the entire volcano on foot or on a mountain bike (12 or 6 hours, respectively). The coast of Tichana hides lots of unexplored areas, including, reportedly, caves full of paintings as well as some petroglyphs near Corozal. There is one small *hospedaje* in San Ramón if you decide to stay the night. **Hospedaje La Cascada** (tel. 505/8573-3803 or 505/7847-6598, hospedajelacascadaometepe@gmail.com, $12 pp) is a five-room lakefront hostel with a small store and restaurant.

★ CASCADA SAN RAMÓN

It's a trek out to the isolated side of Maderas and then a two-hour hike uphill ($3 park entrance) to get to this waterfall, but it's well worth the effort. The signs say it is a three-kilometer trail, but it's likely more than that: allow three hours minimum, as a large portion of the trail is on an incline. Expect to get a little wet stomping through streams along the way. You can drive a four-wheel drive vehicle (or ride a horse) part way up to the water tank to skip past the exposed water pipes and head straight to the prettiest section of the hike. Otherwise, walk through avocado, mango, and lemon trees and up to a small parking area and hydroelectric plant. Once you enter the lush canyon, the humidity rises. You may have to scramble over some river rocks and at times the trail seems to disappear before it emerges a few meters ahead. At the waterfall you can bathe in an icy shallow pool and enjoy the view. You don't need a guide for this hike, but **Hari's Horses** (tel. 505/8383-8499, www.harishorses.com, harishorses@gmail.com) offers a popular horseback ride and guided hike to the waterfall ($40 pp) from Mérida. Having a local like **Berman Gómez** (tel. 505/8816-6971, ometepeisland@gmail.com) or one of the guides at **UGO** (tel. 505/8827-7714, ugometepe@yahoo.com) or **Cacique Tours** (tel. 505/8417-8692) to point out local wildlife along the way is invaluable.

MADERAS RAINFOREST CONSERVANCY

Four kilometers up the road from Merida, in the tiny village of San Ramón, the **Maderas Rainforest Conservancy** (formerly the Ometepe Biological Field Station, Miami tel. 305/666-9932, www.maderasrfc.org, info@maderasrfc.org) is a facility visited by student groups and researchers from all over the world. In addition to being active in numerous forward-thinking conservation projects in surrounding communities, MRC operates a field school on the volcano's slopes for undergraduate and graduate students in art and photography, primatology, ecology, bat ecology, botany, and other biological sciences. Tourists are welcome to sample the restaurant or stay at the station for a small fee.

GETTING THERE AND AWAY

Most visitors arrive by way of Rivas followed by a boat from San Jorge. Lake Cocibolca can get rough when the wind is high between November and February, at which times the larger boats are more comfortable. Avoid the roughest seas by traveling early morning and late evening, and sit near the center of the ferry where the rocking is slightest. The wind can sometimes contribute to ferries being cancelled altogether, so it's not a bad idea to plan a cushion of a day or two into your trip.

Cascada San Ramón

Boat from San Jorge

To access the dock, an employee of the municipal government will charge you $0.50. Boats from San Jorge on the mainland sail to Moyogalpa daily (1 hour). The trip offers great views of Omeptepe's towering volcanoes, and, barring rain, can be pleasant.

FERRY COMPANIES

The **Ferry Ometepe I and III** (tel. 505/8966-4978, $2.50) are big steel boats with radar and life jackets from whose roof you can travel in the fresh air. They depart San Jorge seven times daily 7:45am-5:45pm.

El Che Guevara (tel. 505/2563-0665 or 505/8694-1819, $2) runs from San Jorge to Moyogalpa at 7am and 4pm and departs Moyogalpa for San Jorge 11am and 5:30pm. A car and passenger ticket is $25, but make sure you reserve a spot in advance. Tickets can be purchased on board.

El Rey de Cocibolca (505/2552-8745, 505/8830-9995, 505/8691-3669 or 505/8833-4773, $2.50), a 1,300-passenger, four-story boat built in the Netherlands, plies the waters of Lake Nicaragua between San Jorge on the mainland and San José del Sur on Ometepe, a little town soon to become big thanks to the traffic. This boat departs from San José del Sur to the mainland at 7:30am and 3:20pm; from San Jorge to the island at 9:30am and 5pm. Bringing your vehicle costs less than $10 and the driver goes for free.

PRIVATE BOATS

The rest of the old San Jorge fleet provide a bumpier ride but are less expensive. These boats are independently owned and, unfortunately, rarely give honest information about the others; so if you're told, "The next boat doesn't leave for four hours," keep asking. Each company posts a sign with its own schedule; there is no main sign listing all the different times. UGO (office near the port in Moyogalpa, tel. 505/8827-7714) or Cacqiue Tours (kiosk in San Jorge port, tel. 505/8417-8692) will give you reliable information about the schedule.

From Moyogalpa to San Jorge, the *Karen María* leaves at 5:30am and 11:30am; the *Estrella del Sur* at 7am and 1pm; the *Santa Martha* at 6:30am and 3pm.

From San Jorge to Moyogalpa, the *Karen María* leaves at 9am and 1:30pm; the *Estrella del Sur* at 11am and 3:30pm; the *Santa Martha* at 12:30pm and 5pm.

From San José del Sur to San Jorge, the *Mozorola* leaves at 5:40am and returns from San Jorge at 2:30pm.

Boat from Granada and San Carlos

The Empresa Portuaria de Nicaragua (tel. 505/2552-2966 or 505/2552-4305) ferry leaves Granada on Mondays and Thursdays 2pm, arriving in Altagracia 6pm. The ship then continues onward to Morrito and San Miguelito on the southeastern lakeshore, arriving in San Carlos 5am.

On the return trip, the ferry leaves San Carlos on Tuesdays and Fridays 2pm, stops in Altagracia 11pm, and arrives in Granada at sunrise (4:30am). The price for a one-way passage between Granada and Ometepe is $9, but when seas are high, the ship will skip Ometepe altogether.

Air

Twice weekly flights land on the new landing strip several kilometers outside Moyogalpa on Thursdays and Sundays. Ometepe is part of the San Carlos-San Juan del Norte trip,

El Che Guevara ferry runs between San Jorge and Moyogalpa.

which means coming from Managua, the trip is short (20 min.), but the return is longer depending on where else passengers have booked flights. Book in advance with **La Costeña** (tel. 505/2298-5360, lacostena.online.com.ni). Flights depart Managua at noon and arrive at 3pm.

GETTING AROUND

Thanks to tourism, main roads have been paved and public transportation has improved on the island. You can take a slow public bus for under a buck, or you can catch a *colectivo* microbus. It's easiest to pay $20-35 for a taxi or private microbus to take you to the sites. If you're traveling with a cell phone and speak Spanish, it can be helpful to get your taxi driver's number so you can call later and make arrangements yourself.

You can also rent a motorcycle or scooter, or hitchhike. Once you've accommodated your stuff at your hotel, biking is an enjoyable, cheap, and relatively fast way to get around the island if you take it easy, drink plenty of water, and don't mind riding a clunker. Also try horseback riding, offered across the island, though there's no guarantee you'll get a well-trained, well-fed animal.

Bus

Buses are few and far between on Sundays, which remain a tough day to get around the island in anything but a rented vehicle, taxi, or by availing yourself of the services of your hotel.

In general, there's a bus in Moyogalpa to meet every boat. For the most up-to-date schedule, ask around the dock, or stop in the **UGO** office (north end of the port, tel. 505/8827-7714). A bus leaves for the town of Altagracia every hour 4:30am-7pm. Fully 90 percent of the buses leave the Moyogalpa dock, travel straight up the hill along the main street, stop at the park, then head east out of town on the road to Altagracia (passing through San José del Sur); the other 10 percent turn left, passing through La Flor and San Marcos on their way to Altagracia, which takes longer due to the rough road.

From Altagracia, buses depart for Playa Santo Domingo every hour on the hour. From Moyogalpa to Santo Domingo there are buses six times daily 8:20am-4:40pm. A bus passes through from Santo Domingo in the other direction 12 times daily 4:30am-5pm, but the schedule is sporadic.

Three daily buses depart for Balgüe from the dock in Moyogalpa, at 8:20am, 10:20am,

See Ometepe on horseback.

and 3:45pm, taking nearly two hours. Return buses leave for Moyogalpa at 5:30am and 1:30pm. Three daily buses leave Moyogalpa for Mérida at 8:30am, 2:40pm, and 4:30pm; from Altagracia buses depart at 7am, 10:30am, and 2pm (these buses continue to San Ramón, returning the following day starting at 5:30am). From Mérida to Moyogalpa, buses leave at 4am, 8:30am, and 3:30pm. If you board a bus in Moyogalpa that's heading to Maderas, remember you'll pass through Altagracia first. From Moyogalpa to Altagracia, it's approximately one hour, and from Altagracia to Balgüe it's about a half hour. The island is bigger than you think.

There is no direct public transportation between Balgüe and San Ramón, so you have to take a bus to *el cruce* at Santa Cruz and then catch a bus down the other road, depending on the direction you're going.

Car

Drivers should take care with the rocky and unfamiliar terrain. It's easy to damage your rental on Ometepe's back roads. There are no rental agencies on the island. Arrange a transfer with your hotel or a tour operator beforehand. Most hotels will gladly help to arrange tours as well, getting you up the volcanoes or on waterfall hikes, horseback rides, kayaking excursions, and other area attractions.

Rivas

Rivas is a languorous colonial town of traders and farmers. Hundreds of thousands of passengers traveling between New York and California passed through its streets in horse-drawn carts between San Jorge and San Juan del Sur; this was the only dry-land crossing of the entire gold rush journey. At about the same time, one of filibuster William Walker's first military defeats took place here. Nowadays Rivas is southern Nicaragua's most important city, a commercial center whose small population (under 50,000) helps it retain an old-world charm. Few travelers visit Rivas as a destination proper, but it remains an important companion town for San Juan del Sur and Ometepe, providing a better selection of medical, banking, and shopping services. Don't discount it as inconsequential: It's one of Nicaragua's more pleasant cities, charismatic and enjoyable in its own right, and has historical sites worth visiting.

Rivas is often hot because of its low altitude, but a cool lake breeze from Lake Cocibolca makes it bearable. Rivas is known as Ciudad de los Mangos due to the abundance of the trees in and around the city. swarms of chatty *chocoyos* (parakeets) feast on the fruit, their calls filling the skies around sunset.

SIGHTS

Rivas is the birthplace of several presidents of the republic, most recently, Violeta Barrios de Chamorro (Coalition, governed 1990-1997). **Chamorro's childhood home** is located across the street from the Iglesia Parroquial de San Pedro's south side. The modest **Emmanuel Mongalo y Rubio Monument** marks the final resting place of a local schoolteacher and hero who lived here in the mid-1800s. His actions during the Battle of Rivas resulted in the capture of William Walker.

Iglesia Parroquial de San Pedro

Rivas's obvious centerpiece is a well-loved historical monument repainted in 2007. Built in the 18th century, the **Iglesia Parroquial de San Pedro** (mass: Mon.-Fri. 7am and 5pm, Sat. 7am, Sun. 8:30am, 11:30am, and 5:30pm) has witnessed the California gold rush, William Walker, the Sandinista Revolution, and the 21st-century real estate boom. As you take in the details of the church's pleasing colonial design, remember that every single gold rush-bound passenger that traversed Nicaragua in the days of Cornelius

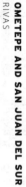

Rivas

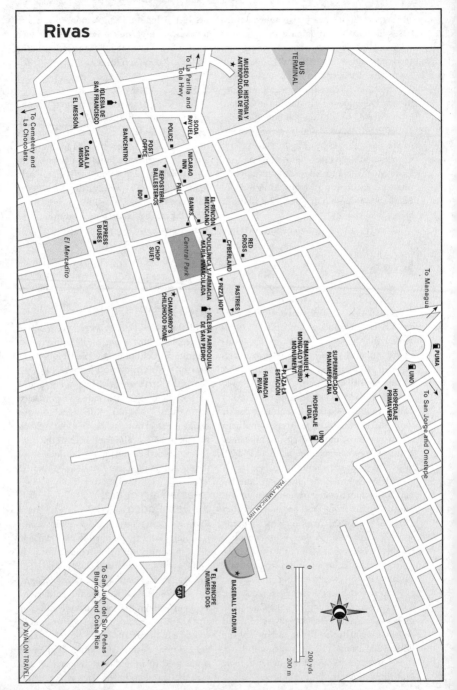

Vanderbilt's steamship line passed under its shadow. It is today, as always, a peaceful place to seek refuge. At the time of research the church's interior was being remodeled and only open for Sunday service. The rest of the week mass is held in the small chapel at the back of the church.

Iglesia de San Francisco

Four blocks west of the park at the town's center, the **Iglesia de San Francisco** was built in 1778 and was the first convent of the Franciscan friars. A beautiful statue commemorates the devotion of the friars to both God and their work. When construction of the nearby Bancentro began, an underground tunnel was discovered that linked the Iglesia de San Francisco with the plaza (the open area adjacent to the central park's north side); the tunnel passes beneath the old school (now a ruin one door east of Bancentro). Researchers speculate it was probably dug at the same time as the church, meaning it was in place and probably used during the Battle of Rivas, when the plaza was the site of a military barracks.

Museo de Historia y Antropología de Rivas

Rivas has its own history museum: the **Museo de Historia y Antropología de Rivas** (on the western side of town, tel. 505/2534-2129, Mon.-Fri. 8am-noon and 2pm-5pm, Sat. only in the morning, foreign travelers $2), in a 200-year-old house that was once part of a cacao and indigo plantation. Once known as the Casa Hacienda Santa Úrsula, on June 29, 1855, William Walker and his men were defeated here in a heroic battle that Nicaraguans are still proud of. The Battle of Rivas, as it became known, was one of the first manifestations of Nicaragua's growing sense of independence in the late 19th century. In fact, the people of Rivas claim "nationalism began in Rivas." The museum has a healthy collection of pre-Columbian pottery; domestic utensils from the 18th and 19th centuries including kerosene lamps, silverware, and hand tools; and several old maps of the region. The building itself evokes the lifestyle of the old farming community. The hours of operation are more of a suggestion than a rule, so stop by and try your luck.

ENTERTAINMENT AND EVENTS

El Principe Número Dos (next to the baseball stadium on the highway) is a popular bar, especially on Saturdays, and the restaurant is a

Iglesia Parroquial de San Pedro

staple among locals. **Chuperman** (new Plaza La Estación, 1.5 blocks west of the old Texaco, daily 3pm-midnight) and **El Nambaro** (new Plaza La Estación, 1.5 blocks west of the old Texaco, daily 2pm-midnight) are nearly identical smaller bars with shaded outdoor seating. A bit more interesting, though slightly seedy, is **El Rincón Mexicano** (1 block north of BanPro, daily 10am-10pm), which serves Nicaraguan versions of Mexican dishes, along with lots of beer. You're sure to be the only foreigner in the bar.

No one enjoys **baseball** as much as the people of Rivas. At last count, there were 138 officially registered baseball teams and more than 3,900 registered players in the municipality, with stadiums or makeshift diamonds in every village in the department! Attending a Sunday afternoon game ($1) in Rivas's main stadium on the highway is a great way to experience the city and the energy of its people. In lieu of chilidogs, there's plenty of *vigorón* (fried pork and yucca) and enchiladas in the grandstand.

ACCOMMODATIONS

Few travelers find a reason to spend the night in Rivas, and the Ometepe-bound tend to prefer the lakeside places in San Jorge. But if you're planning to catch an early bus on the highway, there's no reason not to spend the night. For budget travelers, ★ **Hospedaje Lidia** (half a block west of the old Texaco station, tel. 505/2563-3477, $10 pp shared bath, $12 private bath) is the most popular and has a dozen clean rooms situated around a pretty little garden, including large rooms for up to five people (groups ask about discounts). From here it's an easy walk to the highway to catch a bus north or south.

Hospedaje Hilmor (behind the Iglesia Parroquial de San Pedro, tel. 505/2830-8175, $6 s, $12 d with shared bath, $12 s, $18 d with private bath) is an option, though not quite as nice as Hospedaje Lidia. **Hospedaje Primavera** (next to the Shell station, $5 pp private bath) is a bare-bones lodge catering mostly to working Nicaraguan expats on their way to and from Costa Rica.

The **Nicarao Inn** (a block west of the park, tel. 505/2563-3234, www.hotelnicarao-inn.com.ni, $40 s, $50 d, includes breakfast) is efficient and modern with cable TV, air-conditioning, Wi-Fi, a guarded parking lot, pleasant lobby, and attentive staff. At the inn, you can arrange rides to San Juan del Sur and other parts. ★ **Casa La Misión** (southeastern corner of the Iglesia de San Francisco, tel. 505/2563-0384, $35-50) has character and large bathrooms, but no hot water. The highlight is the lovely, vine-covered, stonewall patio where you can enjoy your breakfast.

FOOD

Buy fresh pastries and juice at **Repostería Don Marcos** (a block east of the park), an easy breakfast en route between San Juan del Sur and the boat to Ometepe. If you've got some time, the outdoor seating at **Repostería Ballesteros** (across from the Nicarao Inn) lends itself to quality people-watching. Their pastries are a nationwide sensation.

Possibly the lowest-price lunch in town is **Soda Rayuela** (north side of the police station, daily 7am-8pm, $2-8), serving simple sandwiches, chicken, and burgers. Get your pizza fix at **Pizza Hot** (across the street from the Iglesia Parroquial de San Pedro, closed Mon.). Enjoy a slice at one of their outdoor tables. In the evening, street-side *fritangas* are plentiful. The dishes at **Chop Suey** (southwest corner of the park, daily 10am-9pm, $5-7 per plate), a Chinese place not far off the mark, have been subtly adapted to suit the Nicaraguan palate. **El Messón** (south side of Iglesia de San Francisco, tel. 505/2563-4535, daily 11am-2:30pm), serves a decent Nicaraguan buffet lunch as well as *caballo bayo*, a hearty stew.

★ **La Parilla** (1 block west of the historic museum, tel. 505/2563-1700, daily 11am-midnight, $5-10) is a nice option with outdoor seating preferred by locals for watching baseball games on TV. This is top-quality Nicaraguan food; you can't go wrong with anything off the grill. They serve the fanciest *tostones con queso* (fried plantains with cheese), with salad stuffed into cup-shaped fried plantains atop a thin layer of *frijoles molidos* (refried beans). **El Mariscazo** (800 meters south of the baseball stadium, tel. 505/2563-1077, daily 10am-9pm) is a popular seafood restaurant on the highway. Splurge on the grilled lobster.

INFORMATION AND SERVICES

Several well-stocked pharmacies in town make Rivas a good service stop for the San Juan del Sur beach crowd. **Policlínica y Farmacia María Inmaculada** (north side of the central park, tel. 505/2563-4935, Mon.- Sat. 7am-8pm, Sun. 8:30am-12:30pm and 4:30pm-7:30pm) is a pharmacy and private clinic providing doctors of various special- ties (consultation Mon.-Fri. 8am-5pm, Sat. 8am-noon). Another well-stocked pharmacy is the **Farmacia Rivas** (2.5 blocks east of the park at the intersection of the boulevard, tel. 505/2563-4292). For more serious issues, the **Hospital Gaspar García Laviana** (tel. 505/2563-3301) is located on the Tola highway.

There are several **banks** in town includ- ing BDF, Bancentro, Banpro, and BAC, all of which operate Monday-Friday 8:30am- 4:30pm, Saturday 8:30am-noon. Most are lo- cated on the main road near the central park. Internet cafés are easy to find around the city.

The **Costa Rican Consulate** in Rivas was temporarily closed at the time of research. The **police station** (tel. 505/2563-3732, rivas@ policia.gob.ni) is two blocks west of the cen- tral park.

GETTING THERE AND AWAY

Buses leave Managua's Roberto Huembes terminal for Rivas every 30 minutes. Several express buses depart before 8am. Express buses to San Juan del Sur and the border at Peñas Blancas will let you off on the highway at Rivas. They leave Huembes at 5am, 8am, 9:30am, and 3:30pm. While you can catch a bus easily on the highway, often these are standing room only. If you want a better

chance at getting a seat on an express bus to Managua, get a *triciclo* to El Mercadito.

A good way to reach Jinotepe, Masaya, Carazo, and the Pueblos Blancos is to take one of the express minibuses, which leave from El Mercadito on the south end of town about once every hour ($2.50). Regular buses leave from the market on the northwest side of Rivas: every hour for Jinotepe and Granada; every 25 minutes for Nandaime, Masaya, and Managua. The last bus for Managua leaves from the old Texaco station on the highway at 6pm. Four daily buses go to Belén and six to Las Salinas (9am-4:30pm).

To Costa Rica

Bus service to Peñas Blancas and the border (less than an hour, every 30-45 minutes, less than $1) runs 5am-5:30pm. You can also share a *colectivo*. On the highway there's a **Tica Bus** office (150 meters north of old Texaco station, tel. 505/8453-2228) in Pulpería la Diamante where you can buy tickets north or south. The bus passes by Rivas each morning bound for Costa Rica between 7am and 8am, and be- tween 3pm and 4pm every afternoon bound for Managua. Buy your tickets ($29 to San José, Costa Rica) the day before.

Taxi to San Jorge and San Juan del Sur

To San Jorge and the ferry to Ometepe, a taxi should cost you no more than $1 per person, whether you take it from the highway traffic circle or from Rivas proper. Ignore any taxi driver that tries to charge $2 or more, unless you're traveling after 10pm, when taxi prices go up. Taxis from Rivas to San Juan del Sur cost around $25, or $2 if it's a *colectivo,* which only run during daylight hours.

GETTING AROUND

A common landmark used in Rivas addresses is the old Texaco station *(la antigua Texaco),* which is now one of two Uno stations. Rivas is full of *triciclo* bike taxis eager for clients. These are known locally as ***pepanos*** after the first man in Rivas to ever use one (*"pepano"* was his nickname). You can catch a ride in one for about $0.60. Many taxi drivers prefer to work longer distances, as opposed to locally, but you can hail one to take you across town for under $1.

NANDAIME

Just south of where the highways from Granada and Carazo join to continue on to Rivas and the border, you'll pass by the mid-size city of Nandaime, located on the Pan-American Highway in the shadow of Volcán Mombacho. This is a humble, unassuming pueblo with the most basic of traveler's amenities, a small-town tranquility, and a passion for music. Nandaime's most famous son is Camilo Zapata, a key founder of the Nicaraguan folk style, who composed the song, "El Nandaimeño." Nandaime is also home to three *chichera* groups, ragtag bands composed of a bass drum, a snare, cymbals, a sousaphone, and loud, clashing brass. Known as "orchestras," they participate frequently in parades and bullrings, and their music is happy, loud, and scrappy.

On the southern side of the Mombacho volcano is a rural community tourism project, **Aguas Agrias** (tel. 505/2552-0238 or 505/8896-9361, turismo@ucatierrayagua.org), so-named for its lime-flavored waters. Local guides offer two-hour hikes ($3 pp) pointing out local wildlife, crops, and wonderful views of the volcano, ending at the Manares River for a swim in its natural clear waters sourced from beneath the volcano. Or, take a four-hour hike ($5 pp) to the hidden Laguna Verde, one of the lagoons of Mecatepe. Order a meal from the communal house before you leave, so it's ready on your return. Aguas Agrias lies 12 kilometers from the community of Monte Verde (located between Granada and Nandaime). If you're arriving via public transport, tell the *cobrador* to let you off at Monte Verde. From there you can take a moto-taxi ($4-5). You can also arrange private transport through UCA Tierra y Agua.

SAN JORGE

A traditional village with a strong Catholic spirit, San Jorge is primarily a port town and farming community that produces plantains. Nearby **Popoyuapa,** true to its Nahuatl-sounding name, cultivates cacao, the tree whose seed is used to produce cocoa and eventually chocolate, and which was once used by the Nicarao people as a form of currency.

The tiny lakeside port of San Jorge is your access point to La Isla de Ometepe and as such, most travelers breeze straight through it on the way to catch a boat. If you have an hour to kill before your ferry departs, there's no reason to spend it dockside sitting on your luggage. Some travelers find San Jorge a pleasant place to spend a night, and the locals are turning out increasingly acceptable hotel accommodations (mostly targeting the backpacker set). The port expansion was underway at the time of research, but it is expected to include a park and several kiosks, which will house tour operators and food vendors.

Be advised that at certain unpredictable times of the year, a southern wind brings plagues of *chayules,* small white gnats that swarm the lakeside in San Jorge and eastern shores of Ometepe. They neither bite nor sting but are relentless and always seem to wind up in your mouth.

Sights

Halfway down the long road to town, you'll pass under **La Cruz de España,** a graceful concrete arch that suspends a stone cross directly over San Jorge's main drag. This main street runs through town down to the water's edge and the docks. The monument commemorates—and is ostensibly built over the very place where—on October 12, 1523, Spanish conquistador Gil González Dávila and indigenous cacique Nicarao-Calli first met and exchanged words.

Across the street from the base of the arch is a **mural** commemorating the same event, with the words attributed to Nicarao: "The Spanish know about the flood, who moved the stars, the sun, and the moon. Where the soul was found. How Jesus, a man, is God and his virgin mother giving birth, and why so few men wanted so much gold." Many believe that the Spanish went on to refer to Nicaragua as The Land of Nicarao, which over time evolved into the modern word Nicaragua.

The squat **Iglesia de las Mercedes** is one of Central America's earliest churches. Built around the year 1575, it was renovated and re-painted a bright yellow in 2001. San Jorge's ki-lometer-long **beach** is hugely popular among Nicaraguans, who flock there during Semana Santa to enjoy the lake and the awesome view of twin-peaked Ometepe on the horizon.

Entertainment and Events

San Jorge celebrates its *fiestas patronales* annually April 19-23 (the date changes to ac-commodate Semana Santa when necessary), at which time you can expect the beach to be packed. San Jorge usually has a parade during the celebrations, and there are performances of traditional dances, including **Las Yeguitas** (The Dance of the Little Mares) and **Los Enmascarados** (The Dance of the Masked Ones). Neighbors in Rivas prefer this celebra-tion to their own patron saint celebrations.

Accommodations and Food

If you missed the last boat to La Isla and don't feel like backtracking to Rivas, book one of the rooms at **Hotel Hamacas** (less than 100 meters west of the dock tel. 505/2563-0048 or 505/8810-4144, hotelhamacas.com, $32 d with private bath and fan, $42 with a/c, includes breakfast).

You won't go hungry in San Jorge's nu-merous food-and-drink joints lining the beachfront, but neither will you be surprised by the menu: chicken, beef, fish, fries, burg-ers, and sandwiches. Near the dock entrance, expect to find higher prices aimed at tour-ists. Try the **mazorcas de cacao stand** (250 meters west of the dock, in front of the school), where you'll find a sweet of cacao mixed with sugar, cinnamon, pepper, and cloves unique to this region. Italian-owned **Bar y Restaurante El Navegante** (next to the dock, tel. 505/8601-1762, Wed.-Mon. 11am-8:30 pm, $4-10) is a decent place to wait for the ferry and enjoy the lakeside view. The menu has sandwiches, pastas, and a va-riety of delicious seafood options including salmon and snapper. **Sol y Arena** (north of the dock, $5-20) offers pizzas, pastas, and burgers.

Getting There

A taxi from Granada straight to the dock in San Jorge is about $30. From Managua, take any southbound bus from the Huembes bus terminal to Rivas and get off at the traffic circle on the highway. From the traffic circle in Rivas to the dock at San Jorge is four ki-lometers, accessible by Rivas buses once an hour ($0.25); they pass the traffic circle ap-proximately 20 minutes after the hour. If you don't happen to be there at that right moment, take a *colectivo* taxi to San Jorge ($1 pp; ignore anyone who tries charging more). (It may be easier to do this once you've left behind the crowd of taxi drivers who bombard passengers getting off the bus.) There is one Managua-San Jorge express, departing Huembes at 9am, arriving in San Jorge at 10:50am. The same bus departs San Jorge at 5pm, arriving in Managua at 6:50pm.

San Juan del Sur

This beach town has been changing and developing rapidly over the past few years and is really starting to give Granada a run for its money. With the construction of the town's new marina, locals expect cruise lines to bring herds of new visitors. Even so, when the waves die down and tourism slows, quite a few places close up shop (Sept.-Oct.).

The main show in town is the brightly colored day's end over the languid harbor waves. San Juan sunsets can go on for hours; make sure you're on the beach as the setting sun drapes the fishing boats in shadow and the rock face of El Indio dims behind the evening. San Juan del Sur's crescent-shaped beach washed with the gentle, warm waves of the protected harbor have been attracting travelers for a long time. In the 1850s, this quiet fishing village experienced its first brief boom as a transport hub for gold rush pioneers crossing the peninsula on Cornelius Vanderbilt's passenger route to California. This was also where many of William Walker's glory-seeking soldiers disembarked to join his ill-fated adventure. After the gold rush, the town sank into obscurity and tropical lethargy, where it remained for a century-and-a-half.

At the turn of the 21st century, San Juan del Sur again grew in international popularity to the steady drumbeat of high-profile international press coverage declaring the area a real estate hot spot. The area attracted a frenzy of property pimps, land sharks, and a flock of checkbook-toting prospectors scouring the coastline for a piece of the pie. The economic growth was not without scuffles, and there is still some tension, but some of the investment led to progress, new establishments, and healthy relationships between foreign investors determined to make money *and* a positive impact for their Nicaraguan colleagues.

SAFETY

San Juan del Sur is a nice town, but as tourists and foreigners increasingly populate it, thieves come out of the woodwork. Here are a couple of tips from the locals: avoid the beach after dark; keep your wits about you when walking around late at night. There's a

port in San Juan del Sur

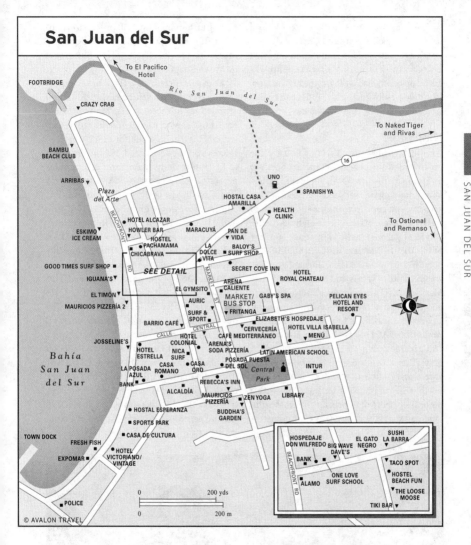

San Juan del Sur

© AVALON TRAVEL

nice quiet spot in the rocks on the north end of the beach for watching the sunset but it has a reputation for robberies. If your car is parked in town, be sure it's locked and valuables are stowed. Holdups sometimes occur on the roads to nearby beaches. A common tactic is to put some sort of obstacle across the road that the driver has to get out and move. There's no reason to stress about safety in San Juan del Sur, just be smart.

ENTERTAINMENT AND EVENTS

The community-run **Casa de Cultura** (on the main beach drag, tel. 505/8450-8990) offers classes to foreigners and locals. Most popular are dance lessons ($5 pp)—pick from salsa, merengue, *bachata*, or local *folklórico*. (Check out their *folklórico* presentation on Thursday evenings at El Timón.) They also offer free art classes for kids.

San Juan del Sur's mellow, year-round party scene picks up around Christmas, New Year's Eve, and Semana Santa when the town is flooded with visitors. Managuan club owners set up beach discos during the high season. Places come and go quickly, and it can be difficult to keep up with what's open.

Nightlife

An old favorite is the **Crazy Crab** (at the north end of the beach, 300 meters north of El Timón, daily 8am-5pm), popular for after-hours dancing on weekends. If you make it 'til 5am, you get a free *nacatamal*. Instead of walking, take a taxi home at night. Another San Juan del Sur classic is **Iguana's** (on the beach road, 50 meters west of the BAC, tel. 505/8635-5204, www.iguanabeachbar.com), which caters to locals and foreigners alike—Matthew McConaughey even showed up here once. The upper level deck heats up late night. **El Timón** (next door to Iguana's, 50 meters west of the BAC) offers a classier atmosphere and great happy hour prices (4pm-6pm). A bit farther down the strip is another enjoyable waterfront bar, **Arribas** (300 meters north of El Timón), an after-hours bar with a more chill vibe; things pick up after midnight. Open all day, **Big Wave Dave's** (25 meters

east of El Timón, daily 7:30am-10pm) is another fixture in San Juan's bar scene with a Margaritaville vibe. Check out live Blues night on Wednesdays.

As expats increasingly flock to this beach town, a plethora of exciting new options have cropped up in recent years. Many of these bars host theme nights like karaoke and trivia. **Howler Bar** (half a block north of Iguana's on the beach road, 100 meters north of El Timón, daily 10am-2am) is a popular new favorite. **San Juan del Sur Cervecería** (half a block east of the market, sjdsbrewers. com, sjdsbrewers@gmail.com, from 4pm daily) is one of the only places in the country where you can find a microbrew. Expect IPAs, wheat beers, and more creative options like Passion Fruit Ale. They give brewery tours (5:30pm, $15 pp). At Canadian-owned **The Loose Moose** (50 meters south of El Gato Negro, tel. 505/8255-6395) you can enjoy poutine and Caesars (a Canadian cocktail similar to a Bloody Mary) while watching a hockey game. It's a small place and fills up quickly. Farther down this road is **Tiki Bar** (from the market, 1 block west, half a block north, Mon.-Sat. 11am-11pm), where you can try a Tiki Bomb (coconut water and a shot of rum) served in the style of a Jaeger Bomb.

church in San Juan del Sur's central park

Belgian-owned **Rebublika** (one block west of the market, tel. 505/8282-7935, daily 8:30am-midnight) has a huge drink selection, BBQ, and trivia nights.

Festivals and Events

Sunday Funday (from 2:30pm, $30 pp) is one of the newer developments in the party scene and is popular among tourists but not among locals (for the debauchery that often ensues). It's a pool bar crawl starting at **Pelican Eyes** (on the hill above town, tel. 505/2563-7000, www.pelicaneyesresort.com), then moving to **Naked Tiger** (Km 138 on the highway outside of town, tel. 505/8621-4738, www.thenakedtigerhostel.com), and ending at **Hostel Pachamama** (from El Gato Negro, 2 blocks south, tel. 505/2568-2043, www.hostelpachamama.com, guests pay half price). Sign up at one of these three places the morning of. **Fight Night** (oxeventsfightnight. com, $11.50) runs four times throughout the year. Watch well-matched pros and amateurs, who train at the Gimnacio (a block east of the Catholic church), duke it out for local glory and bragging rights. Find the schedule on their website. Every March, expats organize the **Earthship Pitaya Festival** (earthship-pitayafestival.com), a weekend of parties, concerts, and a surf competition.

San Juan del Sur's *fiestas patronales* are June 16-24, with bull riding, pole climbing, greased pig catching, and Coca-Cola chugging contests, followed by **Procesión de la Virgen del Carmen** on July 17. Locals parade the icon, the Patron Saint of Fishermen, through town and to the docks where waiting boats take her (and as many locals as possible) for a lap around the bay. On **September 2** the town commemorates the tidal wave of 1992, a 62-foot monster that swept across Main Street, destroying many structures (and farther up the coast, entire villages, like El Tránsito).

San Juan del Sur has their own version of **Ahüizotes** (a copycat of the popular Masaya festival) on October 24 in which people dress as popular Nicaraguan myths and legends and parade through the streets at night. CANTUR organizes the **Aperatura del Verano** every weekend for four weeks leading up to Semana Santa. It includes concerts, *carnaval*-style parades, folkloric dance presentations, and a beach volleyball competition.

SHOPPING

During weekends, holidays, and cruise ship arrivals, street vendors from Masaya and as far as Guatemala and Argentina can be found in the **Plaza del Arte** (on the road in front of the beach). Most everyday items, including fresh vegetables and those dollar flip-flops you've been looking for, can be purchased in or around the **Municipal Market** (center of town, daily 7am-7pm). On Saturdays an **organic farmer's market** (7:30am-1pm) sets up in Big Wave Dave's.

There are some trendy surf shops popping up around town. **SanJuanSurf** (www.sanjuansurf.com) is a clothing line, sold at many local shops, run by Englishman Sean Dennis, who came eight years ago to surf, and never left. The clothing is handmade and designed in Nicaragua with profits donated to worthy causes. **ChicaBrava** (1.5 blocks north of El Timón, U.S. tel. 713/893-5261) stocks well-known clothing brands at their oceanfront store. **Auric** (from Barrio Café, 50 meters north, www.auricsurf.com, daily 9am-7pm, closes early on Sun.) sources their clothing from women-run Nicaraguan businesses, and the clothing is hand-finished locally. If you forgot your surf bikini, **Santosha Organic** (in front of Hotel Estrella, facing the beach, tel. 505/8458-1816, daily 10am-8pm) has got you covered. They also sell a variety of Nicaraguan-made artisan products, including chocolate, honey, coffee, and jam. They've started their own clothing line, Santosha Couture, and they sell Olibobolly dolls (olibobolly.com), which are locally made by Nicaraguan women. Your purchase pays for a second doll that is donated to a Nicaraguan child.

RECREATION

The **Sports Park** (next to the Casa de Cultura on the main beach drag) has **volleyball** and **soccer** facilities with league games on weeknights. During the rest of the day, the park is open for (often competitive) pickup games. Otherwise, expect soccer games to be played on the hard sand beach at low tide on either end of the bay.

★ Surfing

Most surfers make base camp in San Juan del Sur and then drive or boat out to the better breaks, though a lot of beaches are now also developing accommodations of their own. Many of the best breaks are only accessible by boat. There are plenty of hostels, tour operators, and surf shops that run daily shuttles to the nearest beaches: Maderas, Hermosa, Remanso, Yanqui, and Marsella.

An adequate selection of new and used surfboards is easy to find in San Juan. Local shredders Byron and Kervin López can be found in their shop, **Arena Caliente** (next to the market, tel. 505/8815-3247, www.arena-caliente.com). They'll rent you a board, drive you out to the beach, and teach you the basics for $32. **Baloy's Surf Shop** (a block east of El Gato Negro) is owned by another pair of Nicaraguan brothers who learned to surf on a secondhand board left behind by a tourist. They can arrange boards, gear, transportation, and lessons. Run by surfboard shaper Tom Eberly, **Nica Surf** (tel. 505/8934-3669, U.S. 760/473-9529, www.nicasurfinternational.com, info@nicasurfinternational.com) provides similar services and sells Eberly's namesake boards out of the local store.

Good Times Surf Shop (next to Iguana's, tel. 505/8675-1621, www.goodtimessurfshop.com, board rental $10/day) rents boards and sells new and used boards. They can help you arrange for ding repair, or head to **Mosco Repair** (outside Barrio Café), known for speed and quality. Good Times also offers trips to local surf breaks starting at $10 per person. **One Love Surf School** (next to Don Wildfredo's, tel. 505/8251-5525) offers two-hour classes for $30 daily. Beach shuttles are $5 and surf tours are $15.

ChicaBrava (tel. 505/8894-2842, www.chicabrava.com) is the first all-women's surf camp in Nicaragua, with high-end, all-inclusive packages that cover lodging, food, equipment, six days of instruction, and transportation. You can also stay at their flagship "cloud farm" nature retreat with many activities available, including a catamaran cruise.

surfing in San Juan del Sur

Sailing and Diving

The Pacific lacks the visibility of the Caribbean waters, but fish are plentiful and there's a sunken Russian shrimp boat offshore, so diving can be fun. The expert divers at San Juan's Nicaraguan-owned and -operated dive shop, **Neptune Watersports** (tel. 505/2568-2752 or 505/8903-1122, www.neptunenicadiving.com, $85 for two tanks, $350 for open-water certification), will rent you gear and take you underwater if you already have your license and are an experienced diver.

San Juan Surf & Sport (20 meters west of the market, tel. 505/8984-2464, sanjuandelsursurf.com, sanjuandelsurs_s@yahoo.com) offers tours and can take you fishing. Dario and his laid-back crew provide the equipment and will show you how to cast; you can keep any fish you catch. They have a new tour to the calm and remote Playa Blanca ($35 pp) that includes fishing, snorkeling, beer, and lunch.

SUNSET CRUISE

San Juan Surf & Sport (20 meters west of the market, tel. 505/8984-2464, sanjuandelsursurf.com, sanjuandelsurs_s@yahoo.com, $23 pp) offers a daily sunset cruise in a fancy *panga*. Expect great photo ops, a merry crowd, and an open bar. **Nica Sail n' Surf** (tel. 505/8980-1213, U.S. 281/960-7093, www.nicasailandsurf.com, nicasailandsurf@gmail.com, $75 pp) offers a popular afternoon sunset cruise with open bar and snorkeling to Playa Blanca and back on a catamaran. Check their website to join a trip or schedule your own. **Secret Cove Sailing Adventures** (secretcovesailingadventures.com, $50 pp), run by the inn of the same name, offer afternoon trips to the calm, remote Playa Blanca, which include lunch and snacks. You'll get back in time to watch the sun sink over the horizon from aboard the boat. You can also charter the *Pelican Eyes* yacht (tel. 505/2563-7000, $80 pp, $60 pp half-day) for an all-day jaunt, including lunch on a deserted beach and an open bar.

Canopy Tour

Da Flyin Frog (tel. 505/8611-6214, www.daflyingfrog.com, daflyingfrog@yahoo.com, Mon.-Sat. 8am-4pm, $30 pp) is a 17-platform, two-kilometer canopy tour through the trees with great views of the ocean. It's located just outside town on the Chocolata road; arrange free transportation directly from the company. The **Parque de Aventura Las Nubes** (tel. 505/5816-7205 or 505/5816-7297, Tues.-Sun. 8:30am-5:30pm), just three minutes from town, offers canopy tours, walking trails, rappelling, an iguanariam, and a playground for kids. You'll find some of the best views in the region of Ometepe Island and the coastal beaches, and may even see some monkeys. They'll shuttle you there from town for free.

Hiking

The statue of **Jesús de la Misericordia** (referred to locally as "el Cristo"), a 15-meter fiberglass thank-you note for the restored health of the gentleman who built Pacific Marlin (a neighborhood on the northern side of the city), is easily reached via the gated driveway past the Pacific Marlin neighborhood or the ladder that winds its way from about 500 meters around the rocks on the northern point of the bay. The steep walk takes about 30 minutes each way and leads to one of the best overlooks of the bay. You can walk 90 percent of the way for free; pay $1 to access the summit. For a panorama from the **antennas** that overlook the city, take a bus toward Rivas and ask the driver to let you off at Bocas de las Montañas. From there, head for an hour through the trees and pastures to the breezy and beautiful *mirador* (lookout).

Some 1,700-year-old **petroglyphs** are accessible via a 90-minute round-trip countryside walk beginning east of the Uno station. Consider asking for a local guide. Take a left (north), pass the school, and walk through a gate after about 500 meters; find the farmhouse and ask permission to cut through. Follow the water pipes and the river until you find the stone with the carvings. Continue upstream to the (rainy season only) waterfall.

Horseback Riding

Rancho Chilmate (tel. 505/8849-3470 or 505/8755-6475, www.ranchochilamate. com, $69 pp, $79 pp at sunset) offers popular outings on happy, healthy horses. Cowboy threads are available for all the photo ops you'll have during your trail ride through the forest and along the beach. Stay the night and enjoy a refreshing dip in the pool after your ride. Travelers rave about this place. You can also sign up for horseback riding along Playa Maderas and Playa Majagual at **Casa el Oro** (tel. 505/2568-2415, casaeloro.com, $30 pp). **Da Flyin' Frog Adventures** (tel. 505/8611-6214, www.daflyingfrog.com, daflyingfrog@ yahoo.com, $15 pp) offers horseback tours.

Skateboarding

Rancho Surf (tel. 505/8816-8748 or 505/8959-3820, www.surfranchnicaragua.com, free entrance, board rental $2/hour) has one of the only skate parks in the region, complete with flat bars, manual boxes, quarter pipes, and handrails, and with areas for all levels of experience. There's a skateboard shop on-site. Chill out in the pool with a beer when you're done. It's not in town, but you can catch a free shuttle here outside of Barrio Café five times daily 9:15am-9:15pm. Return shuttles make dropoffs five times daily 9am-9pm.

Spas and Yoga

There are free water aerobics (Tues. and Fri. 10am) at **Pelican Eyes** (on the hill above town, tel. 505/2563-7000, www.pelicaneyesresort.com). (It's worth going for the view alone.) **Zen Yoga** (southwest of the central park, tel. 2568-2008, www.zenyoganicaragua. com, $8 drop-in, packages start at $35 for 5 classes) offers daily classes in various styles including vinyasa and Yin yoga. They'll provide you with a mat for free. They also offer massages. **Nica Yoga** (just outside of town, tel. 505/8517-7573 or U.S. 805/426-5296, www.nicayoga.com, stay@nicayoga.com) offers daily yoga classes, individual guest accommodations, all-inclusive yoga retreats, and custom packages that include yoga and

surfing and more. Packages include fine food, San Juan's largest outdoor wooden yoga floor, and a saline lap pool open to guests.

Find shiatsu massage ($30/hr) or chiropractic work at **Elixir** (next to the Casa de Cultura, tel. 505/8971-9393, closed Sun.). **Gaby's Spa** (75 meters east of the market, tel. 505/2568-2654, massage $35/hour) offers shiatsu, Swedish, and deep tissue massages and reflexology in addition to standard manicures, pedicures, and facials. Both places are popular among locals.

The **Tranquila Spa** (at Pelican Eyes, tel. 505/2563-7000 x310, spa@pelicaneyesresort.com, massage $50/hour) offers massages, professional skin care, nail care, and salon services.

ACCOMMODATIONS

San Juan's lodging runs the gamut from grungy to luxe. The cheapest *hospedajes* are near the market, Nicaraguan owned, and usually extensions of someone's home. You may not encounter much of a "scene" at these places and a knock on the front door may be necessary if you return late at night. It is safe to assume that nicer hotels have backup generators and water tanks, but you should still ask unless you don't mind the occasional candlelit bucket bath. Note: prices listed here are high season prices (Christmas, New Year's, and Easter). During low season, you have more room to negotiate.

Under $25

There are still a few places around town where you can get a bed for under $10, but they are quickly disappearing. Surfers like to stay at centrally located **Hostel Beach Fun** (50 meters south of Barrio Café, tel. 505/2568-2441, $10 pp shared bath, $37 d with TV and fan, $10 more with a/c). The 16 rooms are small, but the owners are nice. You can rent an ATV (don't even think of driving it on the beach) or motorcycle for $20-30 per hour.

★ **Hospedaje Don Wilfredo's** (25 meters east of El Timón, tel. 505/2568-2128, www.hospedajedonwilfredo.com, $10 with

The Foreigner Effect

From about 2003-2008, San Juan del Sur saw an explosion in foreign investment, property development, and tourism expansion that had no precedent. Old properties were scooped up, hotels and vacation homes constructed, and restaurants opened. Throughout the southwest corner of the country, scrublands were turned into investment properties and gated retirement communities under the mantra of "Nicaragua is the next Costa Rica!"

Then it ended with a whimper. In 2009, amid a global recession and increasing uncertainty about Nicaragua's direction, the mood was sour and the verdict still out as to whether it was all worth it. The wave of investment was followed by foreclosures, half-built properties, and bitterness on both sides: Nicaraguans and foreigners.

On the Nicaraguan side are *campesinos* (country folk) who hastily sold their undeveloped land at rock bottom prices, then watched as their homesteads were turned into multimillion-dollar investment properties. Some Nicas now work as guards and maids at the new places. Others, though not all of them, have taken advantage of the short construction boom. Meanwhile, to encourage tourism, the mayor's office criminalized the raising of livestock and chickens within city limits, which hit a lot of San Juan del Sur's poor right in the belly.

On the North American side are the people who bought land during the frenzy but whose developments have not turned out as planned. In some cases, developers never connected water or power, nor built the roads they'd promised. Others blame the Nicaraguan government for suddenly enforcing forgotten taxes and the coastal law that prevents construction within 50 meters of the high-tide mark. Still others fell victim to contractors who ran off with prepayments and others whose workmanship was circumspect. Many investors have found that, far from being the next Costa Rica, Nicaragua was just too difficult to do business in, and they picked up and left.

The tension has boiled over in proxy battles, one of which was the case of Eric Volz, an American expat who was accused of killing his Nicaraguan ex-girlfriend, Doris Jimenez, in 2006. Evidence placing Volz in Managua at the time of the crime was rejected by the Sandinista judge in what observers called a "kangaroo court," while FSLN-organized mobs surrounded the courthouse bellowing for justice. Volz, who originally came to Nicaragua to edit a magazine called "El Puente" (as in "bridge" between Nica and gringo cultures) was declared guilty and sentenced to 30 years—the maximum—in prison. After 11 months in the horrific Tipitapa prison, he was released and fled the country (Eric Volz tells his story in *Gringo Nightmare,* St. Martin's Press, 2010).

For the moment, it seems both Nicaraguans and foreigners live in an uneasy detente, as some foreigners decide to pursue other interests and some have redoubled their efforts to be part of the local community. To the casual traveler, most of this will go unnoticed. But under the surface, the forces of globalization ensure that the battle between the haves and the have-nots will continue to be important.

Jean Walsh contributed to this story.

fan and private bath, $37 with a/c) is a terrific value. The hostel is centrally located just steps from the beach and has Wi-Fi and an open kitchen. The best way to make reservations is through their Facebook page. Ask for a room upstairs for good natural light and airflow.

On the other side of town, the relaxed **Hostel Esperanza** (half a block south of BDF Bank, tel. 505/8754-6816 or 505/8471-9568, www.hostelesperanza.com, hostelesperanzasjs@gmail.com, $10 dorm, $25 private

with shared bath, $30 private) includes breakfast, coffee, and oceanfront views. **Casa Oro** (tel. 505/2568-2415, www.casaeloro.com, $11 dorm, $32 private) is a popular dorm-style youth hostel just west of the central park. They run three convenient beach shuttles daily, undercutting the competition Wal-Mart-style, to the chagrin of the smaller tour operators and taxi drivers. Guests love the daily surf report and travel info, lockers, TV lounge, and free make-your-own pancakes on the weekends.

★ **Hostel Pachamama** (2 blocks north of El Gato Negro, tel. 505/2568-2043, www.hostelpachamama.com, dorm $10, private room $25-35) is a laidback spot with two locations half a block apart. The larger location has a popular bar and is generally rowdier; both have small pools and similar accommodations. Most nights they have activities including beer pong and themed parties with contests (winners receive free passes to Sunday Funday).

At the entrance to town, **Hostel Casa Amarilla** (25 meters west of the gas station, tel. 505/8568-9174 or 505/8882-7174, info@bonvoyagenicaragua.com, $10 dorm, $25 private) has complimentary coffee and free bicycle use for guests. They'll let you hang your hammock for $5. If you don't need sleep, **Naked Tiger** (Km 138 on the highway outside of town, tel. 505/8621-4738, www.thenakedtigerhostel.com, $12) has the party scene for you. They have a beautiful infinity pool with some of the best sunset views in the area. They're a bit outside of town, but they offer free shuttle service from Barrio Café every two hours 8:10am-2am.

Casa Romano (half a block east of the BDF bank, tel. 505/2568-2200 or 505/8788-5920, $20 d) is a pleasant family-run spot with

great natural light and airflow. It's in the quieter south end of town.

Find a warm welcome, kitchen, and parking at **Rebecca's Inn** (25 meters west of the park, tel. 505/8675-1048, martha_urcuyo@yahoo.es, $16-20, all with private bath), run by Martha, who grew up in this house and can tell you about the local lore in English. **Posada Puesta del Sol** (across the street from Rebecca's Inn, tel. 505/2568-2532, lalacard98@yahoo.com, $10 shared bathroom, $15-20 d) has five simple rooms and gives deals to students studying Spanish in town.

$25-50

★ **Maracuyá** (from El Gato Negro, 1 block north, 1 block east, on the hill, tel. 505/2568-2002, www.maracuyahotels.com, $11 dorm, $35 d, $60 studio) has the best view in this price range from the highest point in the middle of town. The dorm price is quite a steal for the quality and location. Price includes a pancake and fruit breakfast on a breezy rooftop terrace. They also offer yoga classes ($10).

A few doors down, **Secret Cove Inn** (tel. 505/8672-3013, www.secretcoveinn.com, rjesq@aol.com, $28 d, $33 with a/c) is a little U.S.-owned bed-and-breakfast with Wi-Fi, free calls to the U.S., and bicycles; they also

the smaller of Hostel Pachamama's two locations

Cruise Ships: *Los Cruceros* Cometh

In 1998, the Holland America Line added San Juan del Sur as a port of call on several of their cruises. The announcement sparked hope in the people of San Juan del Sur, who began preparing their sleepy town to receive the thousands of cruise ship passengers scheduled to disembark.

After years of regular biweekly stops, whether or not *los cruceros* have benefited San Juan del Sur depends entirely on whom you ask. The Careli Tours company, which enjoys a monopoly on the buses and guides who whisk passengers straight from the dock in San Juan to day trips in Granada or Masaya, isn't complaining. These passengers never set foot in San Juan proper, and the few hundred who decide to remain in town do not spend much money in restaurants or hotels. A few bars have made a good business catering to thirsty crewmembers, but passengers themselves don't do much onshore imbibing or eating. The *ciclo* taxis and their drivers that cart passengers to and from the dock are imported from Rivas and few of the crafts vendors that display along the tree-lined beachfront strip are Nicaraguan. In fact, the majority of San Juaneños have not gained a dime from the arrival of the cruise ships and would only notice their absence by the lack of tinted-window bus convoys rumbling past their doors every two weeks.

A new $2.5 million tourism project (underway at the time of research) will allow large ships to more easily dock in the bay, and hopefully will help to convince cruise ship companies of San Juan del Sur's appeal. Concerned cruise passengers should attempt to leave some dollars behind for someone other than their ship-sponsored tour operators, whether in San Juan del Sur or in other Nicaraguan cities they visit. And if you like what you see, come back and spend a night or two.

offer sailboat tours and weekly rates. **Barrio Café Hotel** (1 block west of the market, tel. 505/2568-2294, barriocafesanjuan.com, $39-59), located above the café of the same name, has eight pretty and clean rooms. The second floor rooms have the better view. First floor rooms are separated from the café only by shrubbery.

$50-100
★ **Hotel Villa Isabella** (across from the northeast corner of the cathedral, tel. 505/2568-2568, villaisabellasjds.com, $85 d) has rooms with private bath, air-conditioning, TV, heated pool, and family-friendly condos ($175, 6 people). This pristine, 13-room bed-and-breakfast is two minutes from the beach and offers business services, full wheelchair accessibility, and free calls to the United States and Europe. Their breakfast is no meager continental affair: homemade waffles, cinnamon rolls, banana pancakes, breakfast burritos, fresh fruit, and great coffee.

Royal Chateau Hotel (1 block east of the market, tel. 505/2568-2551, www.hotelroyalchateau.com, $50-98) is Nica-owned, and

their friendliness, the security of the compound, private parking, a big wooden porch with traditional adobe-tiled roof, and a filling breakfast make the Royal Chateau an easy pick. **Hotel Colonial** (half a block from the park, tel. 505/2568-2539, www.hotel-nicaragua.com, $48 s, $54 d, includes breakfast) has 12 rooms and decent parking. The lush interior garden is a lovely place to relax.

★ **La Posada Azul** (half a block east of BDF bank, tel. 505/2568-2524, www.laposadaazul.com, $46-64 d) has lovely rooms and a small pool. Tasteful decor, lazily spinning wicker ceiling fans, and classy wood-grained ambience echo the remodeled building's 100-year history. **La Dolce Vita** (1 block west of Uno, tel. 505/2568-2649, ladoclevita.sjs@gmail.com, $45-100, includes breakfast) is located near the entrance to town and has private rooms with air-conditioning and TV set around a pleasant open-air patio. Ask about free movie nights on the rooftop terrace.

Over $100
Pelican Eyes Hotel and Resort (on the hill

above town, tel. 505/2563-7000, www.pelican-eyesresort.com, $130-500) was one the first high-end resorts of its kind in Nicaragua, offering fully equipped homes with kitchenettes and outdoor decks. Despite ongoing property disputes and management changes, the place trucks on. There are two bars, a world-class restaurant, and three infinity pools overlooking the ocean. Their **Bistro La Canoa** is one of the best places in town to enjoy a sunset. Go for happy hour, otherwise a margarita can set you back $7. There's also an on-site spa and sailboat to charter.

The oceanfront boutique **Hotel Alcazar** (150 meters north of El Timón, tel. 505/2568-2075, hotelalcazarnicaragua.com, $90-149) is aesthetically pleasing in every sense. Each room has unique decor. Services include in-room spa treatments, tour organization, laundry services, and free coffee and tea. Expect luxurious wooden lounge chairs and a front-row seat to San Juan's stellar sunset.

Built in 1902, the ★ **Hotel Victoriano** (on the waterfront, tel. 505/2568-2005 or 505/2568-2091, www.hotelvictoriano.com.ni, reservaciones@hotelvictoriano.com.ni, $105-194) has retained the classic feel of that time. It has 21 rooms, giant four-poster beds, and all the amenities: little shampoo bottles, bathrobes, beautiful lobby, pool, air-conditioning, TV, hot water, private parking, and Wi-Fi. The hotel is located at the quieter south end of town.

Long-Term Accommodations

Weekly or monthly rentals are easy to arrange, both in San Juan proper and in the hills surrounding the city. Most Spanish schools in town have packages combining lessons and a homestay, which can be arranged (whether or not you are attending class) for around $100-250 per week including three meals a day. Most places will cut you a deal if you stay more than a few nights. **Secret Cove Inn** ($200/month) rents a small room with private bath. **Hospedaje Don Wilfredo's** (25 meters east of El Timón, $350/month) rents rooms with private bath

the pool at oceanfront boutique Hotel Alcazar

and air-conditioning. They're always full, so reserve in advance.

For something fancier, see **Vacation Rentals Nicaragua** (www.vacationrentalsnicaragua.com), **Vacation Rentals by Owner** (www.vrbo.com), or **Home Away** (www.homeaway.com), or stop by **Aurora Beachfront Realty** (tel. 505/2568-2498, U.S. tel. 323/908-6730, www.aurorabeachfront.com). A fully furnished two-bedroom place goes for $950-1,700 per week and a big house is double that. Nearly all homes come with swimming pools and sweeping ocean views.

FOOD

Fear not the municipal market: you can eat three tasty and filling *corriente* (standard) meals a day at one of the four counters inside for under $3. Evenings, try Juanita's *fritanga* (on the street where the buses leave). Nearly every *hospedaje*, hotel, and beach restaurant makes a variety of breakfasts, usually for $2-3. Locally owned *sodas* (cafés) offer Nicaraguan standards for $3-4. Nowadays you can find any kind of food here, from sushi and crepes to Indian food and Mexican tacos.

Cafés

Expat-owned ★ **El Gato Negro** (50 meters east of the BAC, daily 7am-3pm, $3-8) serves freshly roasted coffee and good breakfasts, including bagels and cream cheese, in a bookstore setting and focuses on environmental and social responsibility. They are emphatically not an Internet café, but they'll let you use their Wi-Fi. Expect to pay an extra dollar for charging your device. **Barrio Café** (1 block west of the market, daily 6:30am-10pm, $4-10) makes first-rate espresso drinks and serves breakfasts with coffee and mimosas. They have some interesting cocktails, including a chia and flaxseed martini.

A mellow bar with eclectic music, darts, and a great menu, including a monster Philly cheesesteak, **Big Wave Dave's** (25 meters east of El Timón, $4-7) is open early for breakfast, then serves bar food and drinks all day long. The ample horseshoe bar is a good place to hang out and chat with your compatriots.

★ **Buddha's Garden** (with Zen Yoga, southwest of the central park, tel. 505/8321-1114, www.buddhasgarden.net, Tues.-Sun. 9am-8pm, $5-8) serves raw vegan "ice cream," smoothies, salads, and creative meals in a mellow ambiance.

Seafood

A row of virtually identical thatched-roof *rancho* restaurants (daily until 10pm, $5-14) runs along the central part of the beach, serving fresh fish and shrimp and lobster dishes. **Josseline's** (at the southern end) offers delicious fish dishes, a notable vegetarian soup, and a pleasant atmosphere. **El Timón** is a longtime favorite of Nicaraguans and tourists alike. Some say it has the best service of all the *ranchos*. It's also one of the most expensive.

★ **Bambu Beach Club** (from the pedestrian bridge, 75 meters south, tel. 505/2568-2101, Wed.-Mon. from 11am, $7-12) is a Mediterranean-influenced restaurant with stylish decor and cool bathrooms. Serving seafood, sandwiches, and entrées, it has a full bar, relaxed beach hangout with a pool, seaside cinema, and acoustic concert space.

Upscale and International

Vintage (in Hotel Victoriano, on the waterfront, tel. 505/2568-2005 or 505/2568-2091, $8-22) is a classy beachfront restaurant popular for its lobster dishes. **Menú** (20 meters east of the central park, tel. 505/2568-2063, Wed.-Mon. 11:30am-10pm, $5-12) serves big plates of *comida típica* (typical Nica food) on sleek wooden tables. This is the best place in town to try Nicaraguan classics like *indio viejo* (corn-based stew) and beef stew.

Bar y Restaurante La Cascada (in Pelican Eyes, on the hill above town, tel. 505/2563-7000, breakfast and lunch from $7, dinner $11-20) offers tables set above the village with a prime view of the ocean and sunset. The chef is world class, serving delights such as parmesan-crusted baked mahi over herb spaetzle. Sample from the exotic tropical drink menu.

★ **Mauricio's Pizzería** (just west of the playground at the municipal park, tel. 505/2568-2295 for delivery, daily from 5pm, from $5 pizza pie) is easily one of the most popular restaurants in town, with great pasta and real Italian pizza by the slice. Ask Mauricio for a shot of his homemade *limoncello* after your meal. **Arena's Soda Pizzería** (tel. 505/8816-3302, Tues.-Sun. noon-10pm, $4-10) is a small locally owned place with a full menu of pizzas and pastas.

Nicaraguan-owned **Sushi la Barra** (25 meters east of El Gato Negro, $4-7 per roll) is identifiable by its bright red paint and white "sushi" letters on the entrance. Don't be scared of the hole-in-the-wall appearance, the chef has been well trained, and serves up a delicious sushi roll with thoughtful presentation. **Taco Spot** (across the street from Sushi la Barra, daily 11am-4am, $1-4) is popular among the late-night crowd and those missing spicy food. (*Picante* does not appeal to the Central American palate.) This is the closest

I've gotten to an authentic street taco south of Mexico—beware the red sauce.

INFORMATION AND SERVICES

From home, check out sanjuandelsur.org or www.sanjuansurf.com, where many businesses post their updated rates. **INTUR** (northwest corner of the park, Mon.-Fri. 8am-5pm) can provide helpful information on local guides and activities, and free maps and flyers—if you can catch them in the office. Pick up a free copy of *Del Sur News,* a weekly bulletin of community news and events in English and Spanish, at many places around town.

Banks

Nearly all of the nicer hotels (and some restaurants) accept major credit cards. The three banks in town all have **ATMs. BDF** (half a block from the Casa de Cultura), **BAC** (in front of Alamo), and **Bancentro** (next to Big Wave Dave's) all offer similar services, but none will cash travelers checks. **Banco ProCredit** has an ATM 1.5 blocks west of the market.

Emergency Services

For basic medical needs, the **Centro de Salud** (at town entrance, tel. 505/2568-2320, Mon.-Sat. 8am-7pm, Sun. 8am-noon) provides free consultations. For any serious medical concerns, plan a trip to Rivas, as the Centro is typically understaffed and crowded. The **police station** (75 meters north of the port, tel. 505/2568-2382) is on the main beach road.

Laundry

Most of the nicer hotels provide laundry service, as will the inexpensive hotels if you strike a deal. If you'd rather go to an independent *lavandería* (laundromat) with modern machines, **Gaby's** (uphill from the market, tel. 505/8837-7493) charges $5 per load (wash, dry, fold). There are plenty of other folks with "Laundry" signs posted around town as well.

Spanish Schools

What better place to learn Spanish than at the beach? There are several options in this category. For a full week of one-on-one classes and homestay with meals expect to pay around $250; hourly rates hover around $8. Or, create a custom study plan for yourself that works with your schedule. The **Latin American School** (north side of the central park, tel. 505/2568-2158, www.nicaspanish. org) is a nonprofit co-op of local teachers who aim to impart social, political, and cultural awareness along with the Spanish language. **Veronica's Spanish School** (near the Palí, tel. 505/8888-6567, www.sjdsspanish.com) and **Spanish Ya** (from the UNO station 100 meters north, 505/2568-3010 or 505/8898-5036, www.spanishya.com, info@learnspanishya.com) are both popular options. The **Casa de Cultura** (tel. 505/8450-8990) offers Spanish classes ($8/hour).

GETTING THERE AND AWAY
To Rivas, Managua, and Granada

The trip from Managua is about 2.5 hours in your own vehicle or express bus but 4 hours in an *ordinario*. From Managua, the absolute fastest option is by express shuttles that leave from the airport. **Adelante Express** (tel. 505/8850-6070, www.adelanteexpress.com) charges $45-60 one-way, depending on the time of day. Traveling with others will cost you less. For guaranteed service, make your reservation at least 24 hours in advance. **Nica Adventures** (tel. 505/2552-8461, www.nica-adventures.com, info@nica-adventures.com) also has comfortable shuttles from San Juan to other cities. A private shuttle from Managua through most San Juan del Sur companies or hostels will cost about $80.

Regular express buses make the trip to Rivas (2 hours, $3 pp) leaving from Huembes market about every hour 10am-4pm (the last bus is the best). Slow, crowded *ordinario* service (4 hours, $2.50) is direct to San Juan del Sur from Huembes market. It operates

Volunteering in San Juan del Sur

If you'd like to spend some time working with the community, the environment, or the children of San Juan del Sur, there are a couple of options.

The **San Juan del Sur Biblioteca Móvil** (www.sjdsbiblioteca.com), located across the street from the park, is the first lending library in Nicaragua, a country largely devoid of libraries that loan out books. They serve as the town library and also bring books to 31 outlying communities. Besides helping monetarily, voluntourists can teach English, organize books, read to youngsters, or join staff on a visit to a rural school. A formal volunteer program for librarians, library school students, and others is held twice a year. Book donations are always welcome.

Comunidad Connect (tel. 505/ 2568-2731, www.comunidadconnect.org, info@comunidadconnect.org) is a local nonprofit with a bilingual, multicultural staff, dedicated to supporting sustainable economic and community development. They run the Sports Park by the beach, helped start a municipal recycling program, work with real estate agencies and developers to facilitate private sector donations to community projects, run a small business development initiative, and invite voluntourists like yourself to help with their projects. CC can arrange an all-inclusive homestay with a local family, volunteer projects, Spanish lessons, and excursions to their organic coffee farm.

Nonprofit **Escuela Adelante** (www.escuelaadelantenicaragua.org, escuelaadelante@outlook.com) is a new English school that will prepare school-age kids for bilingual high schools. They'll also provide adult English classes to employees in local businesses. They welcome native English speakers who are willing to help with conversation practice, fundraising, and translating written materials.

10am-4pm. The handlers at the Huembes bus terminal can get aggressive. They will grab your bags out of the taxi, push you onto a slow Rivas bus, claim it's an express, and then demand a tip. Read the windshield of the bus and ask the other passengers to verify.

Once in Rivas, you can take an *ordinario* from the market, a *colectivo* ($2 pp), or taxi from the highway bus stop ($20-25) the rest of the way to San Juan del Sur. After dark, *colectivos* don't run and taxi prices double.

From Granada there are several shuttle services worth taking, all of which cost more than the bus but more than compensate in saved time and frustration.

Express buses leave San Juan del Sur from the corner in front of the market at 5am (this is the nicer *lujo* (luxury) bus), 5:55am, and 7am. Four buses stop in Rivas on their way to Managua, leaving at 5am, 5:40am, 7am, and 3:30pm. *Ordinarios* to Rivas (1 hour) leave every hour 6:30am-5:30pm. You can also catch a *colectivo* taxi to Rivas ($2 pp), which leaves when it's full, 4am to 3pm or 4pm near

the market. Tell the driver you're going to Managua and they'll leave you at the bus stop in front of the gas station, and then catch any northbound bus toward Managua (look for *expreso* on the window for a faster ride). The trip to and from Rivas takes 30 minutes by car and 45-60 minutes by bus.

To Costa Rica

To the border at Peñas Blancas, get a ride to La Vírgen in a bus or taxi, and then catch a lift south; the first Rivas-Peñas Blancas bus passes at 7:30am. Or book a ticket with **Tica Bus** (near the market, tel. 505/2568-2427) or **TransNica** (transnica.com) at their San Juan del Sur offices. Also check with the shuttle services.

From the Costa Rican border at Peñas Blancas, buses for Rivas leave every half hour. Get off at **Empalme la Vírgen** and flag a bus, taxi, or ride going between Rivas and San Juan del Sur. The beach is 18 kilometers due west of La Vírgen; taxis from the border to San Juan charge $25-35.

GETTING AROUND

You won't need a taxi to get around town (you'll only see them trolling for passengers to Rivas and the beaches). From one end of town to the other it's a 15-minute stroll. **Elizabeth's Hospedaje** (near the bus stop) rents bikes.

To travel up and down the coast, you'll need a sturdy and preferably four-wheel drive car or a decent mountain bike and some stamina. Taxi drivers hang around the main road and can take you up and down the coast, but if you are going surfing for the day, you're better off catching a ride with one of the surf shops, or with the "gringo shuttles" from Casa Oro or other hostels. Water taxis operate from in front of Hotel Estrella.

Alamo (tel. 505/2568-2746, alamonicaragua.com), in front of El Timón, rents cars from their lot, including a selection of 4x4 trucks. **Budget** (on the waterfront, tel. 505/2568-2005 or 505/2568-2091) has a desk in the Hotel Victoriano. Arrange a car and driver in advance by contacting **Ricardo Morales** (2.5 blocks south of Hotel Villa Isabella, tel. 505/8882-8368, richardsjds@hotmail.com), a San Juan native with a few four-wheel drive vehicles and a great deal of local contacts and knowledge. He'll pick you up at the airport or in Granada.

BEACHES SOUTH OF SAN JUAN DEL SUR

Between San Juan del Sur and Ostional on the Costa Rican border are a number of excellent beaches. The Ostional bus will take you there, if you can afford to wait; otherwise, do like everyone else and bum a ride with someone with a vehicle, including the several shuttle options leaving from San Juan del Sur's center. You'll first pass through Barrio Las Delicias, which includes San Juan del Sur's stadium and cemetery, followed by a fork in the road known as El Container. Turn right here to get to **Playa Remanso,** about a kilometer down a path infamous for robberies: Don't go alone. It'll take 25 minutes to get there on rough dirt roads. This slow surf break is great for beginners, so

expect to share it with all the new friends you met over beers last night. There's a shady outdoor bar right on the sand where you can purchase snacks and drinks at inflated prices. At low tide, look for bat caves, tide pools, blowholes, and various wildlife. (Don't hang out too long after dark. It gets dodgy.)

Walking 30 minutes south around the rocks brings you to **Playa Tamarindo,** followed by **Playa Hermosa** just under an hour later (it's a 20-minute walk from the bus stop at El Carizal, farther down the road toward Ostional). The $3 fee to access Hermosa helps maintain the beach and the bathroom facilities. Ask in the surf shops in town about safety precautions and public access to these beaches. A night at **Playa Hermosa Beach Hotel** (tel. 505/8671-3327,

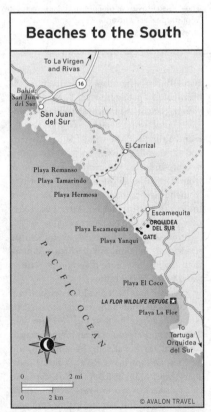
Beaches to the South

info@playahermosabeachhotel.com, $18-55) includes free breakfast and Wi-Fi, and they'll shuttle you out for free if you stay more than one night. They offer surf lessons (2 hours, $23) and board rental ($10/day).

A 30-minute drive south of town is **Playa Yanqui**. This powerful and fast wave that rolls into a giant beach was almost destroyed by one of the new developments when the owner decided to build a "viewpoint" going out into the sea. An effort by local surfers and activists prevented the construction and, for now, this break remains one of the best in the area. Look for a sign at a fork on the main road before you get to the Yankee Beach development; go right and then left at another sign, then over a hill for a photo-worthy view of what awaits. Park ($3) at the small house on a hill at the south end of the beach to prevent theft, or at low tide you can park right on the beach.

Places to stay in this area are limited. Stay in a rustic cabin at **Lomas del Bosque** (a few kilometers down the road to La Parcela, tel. 505/5840-0022, www.hostellomasdelbosque.com, $3 hammock, $10 pp dorm, $30 d) and wake up to the roosters while assuring your tourist dollars support the local community. Go horseback riding, butterfly watching, and let your host, Don Miguel, point out the various tropical plants and crops.

★ **Orquidea del Sur** (tel. 505/8984-2150, www.orquideadelsur.com, $175-200 d) is a high-end retreat with a luxurious pool perched atop the hills. Book in advance.

Playa El Coco

Eighteen kilometers south of San Juan, this jewel of a beach is great for swimming, fishing, and access to the turtles at La Flor. This is where you'll find **Parque Marítimo El Coco** (tel. 505/8999-8069, www.playaelcoco.com.ni, lodging from $185), an extensive compound on a wide beach with a popular restaurant called **Puesta del Sol** (daily 8am-8pm, from $7). Accommodations range from furnished apartments to fully equipped bungalows and houses. Weekend packages are reasonable for

groups. Houses ($240-280) have air-conditioning, satellite TV, hot water, and kitchen, and sleep up to eight people. Come prepared with supplies. There is an on-site minimarket, plus bike rental, Internet, and a new conference facility. Buses leaving from San Juan del Sur's market for Ostional (7am, 11am, 1pm, and 5pm) will drop you off on the road to El Coco.

★ La Flor Wildlife Refuge

One of the two Pacific turtle nesting beaches in Nicaragua, the park at **La Flor** (foreigners $8 pp entrance, $18 per tent for camping) is managed by the governmental environment agency MARENA. The park participates in turtle conservation, and will let guests help release baby sea turtles back into the ocean, which is possibly the most adorable thing you'll ever see. Make sure you catch one of the nighttime *arribadas* (mass nesting events) that occur during the crescent moon July-February. For camping here, bring your own gear. Guards offer 1.5-hour hikes ($10 per group) around the reserve, pointing out coastal wildlife and plants. Casa Oro in San Juan del Sur runs shuttles during the season. Public buses to Ostional pass by the reserve entrance.

Ostional

This picturesque bay and community at the extreme southwestern tip of Nicaragua is still more of a fishing town than a tourist destination, but curious visitors can seek out the rural tourism cooperative, **COOPETUR** (tel. 505/8913-3975 or 505/8498-6650, communitytours@yahoo.es), for tours of the area and nearby bays, snorkeling, horseback riding, hiking, and fishing, along with simple accommodations. All trips are about four hours and have a local guide, whether by boat or horseback. A portion of the profits goes toward 30 university scholarships for promising youths of the community. Buses from Rivas to Ostional pass through the San Juan del Sur market at 7am, 11am 1pm, and 5pm (2 hours to Ostional). They depart from the center of Ostional at 5am, 7:30am, and 4pm,

Turtle-Viewing Etiquette

The Olive Ridley (or Paslama) sea turtle *(Lepidochelys olivacea)* is an endangered species well known for its massive synchronous nesting emergences. These seasonal occurrences, called *arribadas,* take place several times during each lunar cycle in the July-February nesting season and, at their peak (Aug.-Oct.), result in as many as 20,000 females nesting and laying eggs on a single beach.

In Nicaragua, the two beaches that receive the most turtles are **Playa Chacocente** and **Playa La Flor,** both on the southwestern Pacific coast. Playa La Flor, located about 15 kilometers north of the Costa Rican border and 18 kilometers southeast of San Juan del Sur, is a 1.6-kilometer-long beach that has been protected as part of a wildlife preserve. Hatchings have been less successful every year. Fly larvae, beetles, coyotes, opossums, raccoons, skunks, coatimundi, feral dogs, pigs, and humans all prey on Olive Ridley sea turtles in one form or another. High tides and beach erosion sweep away other eggs, and once they emerge from their shells, they are pounced on by crabs, frigate birds, caracara, vultures, and coyotes before they can reach the sea. Once in the water, they must still battle a host of predatory fish.

In general, females lay two clutches of eggs per season and remain near shore for approximately one month. The mean clutch size of the females differs from beach to beach but averages 100 eggs; incubation takes 45-55 days, depending on the temperature, humidity, and organic content of the sand.

The *arribadas* and hatching events both occur during the night. Witnessing these phenomena is an unforgettable experience. Tourism can protect the turtles, as it provides an incentive to continue protection efforts, but it can just as easily be disastrous (since the first edition of this book was published, the rangers have been permitting people to "swim with the turtles," an injurious practice). It is too easy to harass, injure, or frighten the turtles if you're not careful. Don't count on park rangers to tell you what's acceptable. Please pay close attention to the following rules during your expedition:

- Always **maintain a distance** of at least three meters, and never get in front of the turtle. Always watch the turtle from behind. Do not form a circle around the turtle; this can be very stressful for it.

- Do not use your **camera's flash** when taking pictures of turtles coming out of the sea, digging a nest, or going back to the ocean. The light can scare them back into the ocean without laying their eggs. The only time that you can take a picture of them is when they are laying eggs. The flash will not disturb them as much, as they enter a semi-trance state.

- Keep your **flashlight** use to a minimum; use a red filter over the lens or color it with a temporary red marker. If the moon is out, use its light instead.

- If **camping,** place your tents beyond the vegetation line so as not to disturb the nesting turtles.

- Do not dig out any **nests** that are being laid or are hatching.

- Do not eat **sea turtle eggs,** whether on the beach or in a restaurant. Despite their undeserved reputation as an aphrodisiac, the raw eggs may carry harmful organisms and their consumption supports a black market that incentivizes poaching.

- **Do not touch,** attempt to lift, turn, or ride turtles.

- Do not interfere with any **research** being performed on the beach (i.e., freeing hatchlings from nest boxes).

- Do not throw **garbage** on the beach.

Shaya Honarvar, PhD, Department of Bioscience & Biotechnology, Drexel University, contributed to this piece.

but confirm with the driver and anyone else you can find waiting around.

BEACHES NORTH OF SAN JUAN DEL SUR

To get to **Maderas** or **Marsella,** stop by any of the surf shops in San Juan. Rides cost $10 round-trip. If you're driving, access these beaches via the road to Chocolata, just east of the Uno station. Much of this road served as the old railroad grade for a railroad never built. After seven kilometers, turn left at Chocolata to a fork in the road: left goes to Marsella and Maderas, right to **Majagual.** The drive out, on a newly paved road through the ex-mayor's cattle ranch, is simply beautiful. It takes about 20 minutes to reach either beach.

Playa Nacascolo

This small cove just north of San Juan del Sur is an hour's walk from town. (A taxi will charge about $10 each way.) There are some beautiful vacation home rentals in this bay. In the hills above the beach is **El Jardín** (tel. 505/8659-1795 or 505/8880-2604, www.eljardinhotel.com, info@eljardinhotel.com, $65-120 d), a beautiful boutique-style hotel with impressive views of the area. Its isolated location makes it a great place to unwind (and to enjoy French cuisine from the terrace). To get your money's worth, ask for a room with a view.

★ Playa Marsella

This pleasant, breezy beach is one of the closest to San Juan del Sur. You can drive right up to the sand, making it a popular day trip for Frisbee throwers and sunset watchers. On the weekends, a small restaurant on the beach serves ceviche, fried fish, and cold beer. Just can't tear yourself away? Stay five minutes away at ★ **Empalme a las Playas** (located at the fork in the road between Maderas and Marsella, tel. 505/8803-7280, www.empalmealasplayas.com, $50-85 with breakfast), a small private resort. Monkeys lull you to sleep and birdcalls are your morning

Beaches to the North

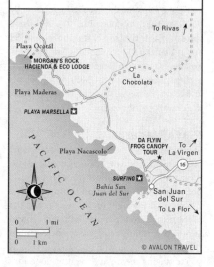

© AVALON TRAVEL

alarm in these four bamboo cabins surrounded by trees.

Marsella BeachFront Hotel's (tel. 505/8194-4666, marsellabeachfronthotel.online.com.ni, $49-250) rooms are farther removed from the restaurant and pool areas and enjoy an excellent sunset view, but you can see just as well from the infinity pool. Bed-and-breakfast **Casa Pelón** (tel. 505/8387-1241, www.casapelon.com, $25 shared bath, $35 private) offers stand-up paddleboarding lessons, surf lessons and rentals, kayaking, yoga classes, horseback riding, sport fishing, and participates in local turtle conservation efforts. To get here, follow the road to Marsella straight to the beach. Casa Pelón's entrance is the last driveway on the right before Concha's Restaurant. Look for the sign. Next door, the **Lil' Aussie Hut** (tel. 505/8385-6644, www.aussiehut.com, aussiehut@gmail.com, $6 day pass, $10 camping with your own tent, $40 d) is an open-air thatch roof structure with king-size beds that attracts more of a party crowd.

To get here from San Juan Del Sur take Chocolata Road (near the Palí) headed north. After four or five kilometers you'll see the turn off to Playa Marsella and Playa Maderas on your left. Keep left at the first fork in the road. You will come to a second fork, where you'll see signs for the beach. To get here by bus, take the "Chocolata Bus" ($0.76) which leaves opposite the Irish House in San Juan del Sur at 10am and 12:30pm daily. The bus travels along Chocolata Road, and will drop you at the intersection of Playa Majagual, Maderas and Playa Marsella. Then it's about a 2-kilometer walk to the beach.

Playa Maderas

One of the most consistent, easy-to-access surf breaks from San Juan, Maderas is enjoyed for its medium-speed hollow wave that breaks both right and left, best on incoming tides. There's parking right on the beach, and the place turns into a popular hangout around sunset. Surf shops bring groups here several times a day, so you won't be surfing solo. If you're staying the night here, it's a good idea to bring some supplies with you, as there's no store nearby. There's no public transport, but you can catch a ride from Casa de Oro or one of the surf shops in town.

Hostal los Tres Hermanos (tel. 505/8460-7464, manuelantoniocascante@hotmail.com, $10 pp dorm, $20 s, $30 d), a simple wooden bunkhouse with a kitchen, offers lodging right on the beach, cheap meals ($2 breakfast, $5 lunch), and rents boards by the hour.

Matilda's (a short walk north along the beach, tel. 505/2456-3461 or 505/8818-3374, $4 camping, $8 pp dorm, $5 *casita,* $25 private) has tiny private *casitas* for sleeping that look like oversize doghouses. The location is perfect for swimming and you're welcome to use the communal kitchen. **Buena Vista Surf Club** (tel. 505/8863-4180 or 505/8863-3312, www.buenavistasurfclub.com, info@ buenavistasurfclub.com, $130 d, includes breakfast and dinner, minimum stay 2 nights) leans towards luxury and is located in the hills above Maderas, from where you can watch the waves while doing yoga on an incredible wooden deck. **Mango Rosa** (1.5 km from the beach, tel. 505/8403-5326, www.mangorosanicaragua.com, $139 d) has a friendly staff, pool,

volleyball court, hammocks, restaurant, and bar under a shady *rancho.* They've built an environmentally friendly sewer system and are careful about energy use—you'll get a bill separate from your room costs.

Surf instructors Liz and Scott at ★ **Rancho Cecilia** (tel. 505/8489-9452, www.ranchocecilianicaragua.com, info@ ranchocecilianicaragua.com, $65-85 d, minimum stay 2 nights) will make you feel right at home in their jungle paradise. The building has big porches for lounging, and operates on solar energy.

Morgan's Rock Hacienda & Eco Lodge

Playa Ocotál is the home of a much-hyped eco-lodge at the vanguard of Nicaragua's up-scale tourism market. ★ **Morgan's Rock Hacienda & Eco Lodge** (tel. 505/8670-7676, www.morgansrock.com, $268 d cabin) is an exclusive resort surrounded by a 1,000-hect-are reforestation project and an 800-hectare private nature reserve. Its 15 elegant, hard-wood cabins are built into a bluff above the crashing surf on the beach below. As few trees as possible were felled during construction, so you'll have to walk a 110-meter-long sus-pension bridge through a lush canopy to reach your cabin, which is the most luxurious and beautiful tree house your childhood fantasies ever dreamed up. The structures, as well as the main lodge, which features a gorgeous infin-ity pool, were designed with all local materials and feature ingenious architecture and atten-tion to detail.

You're on vacation here, so no phones or Internet, but there's plenty to do: sun-rise kayak tours of the estuary, tree-plant-ing excursions, and tours of their shrimp farm and sugar mill, where they brew their own Morgan's Rum. More than 70 workers are employed to grow and produce much of the restaurant's vegetables, dairy products, herbs, and other needs. Cabin rates include three meals (lunch and dinner are both three courses), a couple of beers, all you can drink of local, nonalcoholic beverages, and one tour a day. Prices vary by season, so call or email to reserve your room. The facilities and services are for guests only, so sorry, no day-trippers. The resort can organize ground transportation for you. If you have your own vehicle, make a right just before entering the town of San Juan del Sur, at the sign that says "Morgan's Rock 8km," then follow the signs and rocks with yellow "MR" painted on them for about half an hour.

Tola and Popoyo

Ten kilometers west of Rivas is the agricultural community of Tola, gateway to the steadily improving shore road and a string of lonely, beautiful beaches that make up 30 kilometers of Pacific shoreline. The word is out and land prices are rising, but the beaches west of Tola are still far less developed than San Juan del Sur and retain some of their fishing village character. Tola is famous in Nicaragua as the subject of a common expression: *Te dejó esperando como la novia de Tola* ("He left you waiting like the bride of Tola"), which recalls the real-life soap opera of a young woman named Hillary, who, on the day of her wedding, was left at the altar at Belén while the groom, Salvador Cruz, married his former lover, Juanita.

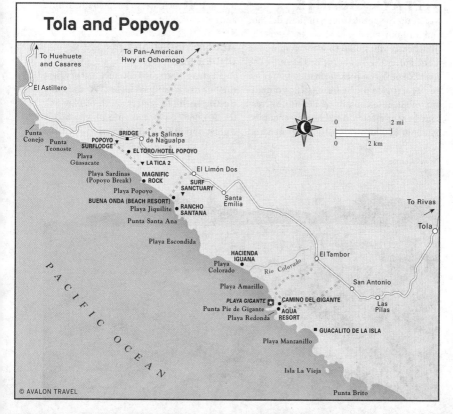

Tola and Popoyo

© AVALON TRAVEL

TOLA

In Tola proper, many travelers have stayed and worked with Doña Loida (an influential Sandinista leader, elected mayor in 2004) of **Asociación Esperanza del Futuro** (on the road that leads from the park to the baseball field/basketball court, about 100 meters past the baseball field, tel. 505/2563-0482, www. para-nicaragua.de/AEF/INDEX.htm, loid-anet@hotmail.com), who can help arrange cheap room and board from a week to six months. Her foundation provides educational workshops to local *campesinos* (country folk) as well as a library, sewing co-op, and gardens; classes in guitar, agriculture, herbal medicine, and computers are offered. There are a few decent eateries in Tola, the most popular of which is **Lumby's.**

★ PLAYA GIGANTE

North up the coast from San Juan del Sur, and an hour outside Rivas, Gigante is the first beach you come to after Tola and is named after the Punta Pie de Gigante (The Giant's Foot), the rock formation you'll see on the left side of the beach. The community of Gigante consists of a beautiful crescent beach; a few dozen homes occupied by about 800 locals, mostly fishermen and people working in the nearby resorts; several restaurants and hotels; and a few surf camps. Surfing has had a big impact on the community's economic situation, and it's continuing to grow. Get here before it's so developed that it's unrecognizable.

If you want to spend a week or more learning Spanish on the beach, this is a great place to do it. The beachside **Pie de Gigante Spanish School** (tel. 505/2560-1450 or 505/8652-7502, www.nicaraguaspanishlessons.com, spanishgigante@gmail.com) provides one-on-one lessons with teachers who have 10+ years of experience. They can organize a homestay immersion with a local family ($100 pp, minimum 1-week stay, includes private room and three meals a day).

Avoid this beach during Semana Santa, when it gets crowded with locals who camp out on the beach, get phenomenally drunk, and run cockfights.

Accommodations
UNDER $50
Right at the beach road entrance, left of where the bus drops off passengers, ★ **Cabinas de Gigante** (25 meters south of Blue Sol, tel. 505/8667-5498, $10 pp, $40 with a/c) is a great option for budget travelers. This is a

Playa Gigante

quiet, family-run place that offers basic private rooms with comfy double beds and the option for air-conditioning. The family's restaurant is just across the sandy dirt road.

If you're looking for a scene, **Camino del Gigante** (tel. 505/8743-5699, www.gigante-bay.com, gigantebay@gmail.com, $5 to camp on the beach, $10 dorm) is the place to be. The dorms sleep dozens of people and are located behind the bar. They also own a cabin, which has private rooms and a smaller dorm, and a B&B with private rooms with air-conditioning. The latter two share a nice pool. To get there, walk down the road towards the left end of the bay and pass the park, then follow the signs. The bar is somewhat pricey, but is a popular hangout spot. They run tours and rent gear as well.

★ **Monkey House** (tel. 505/8255-7547, $10 dorm, $25 d with shared bath) has the best view in town at the top of the rock formation on the right end of the bay. It's the perfect spot to lounge in a hammock and watch the sunset. The accommodations themselves are sparse, but all beds have mosquito nets and all rooms have a fan. The owner rents surfboards and paddleboards and gives lessons ($40 for 2 hours). To get there, follow the uphill road that starts at the right end of the beach, and take the first left. There's no obvious sign, just walk around the back of the house.

Hotel Brio (tel. 505/8833-3300 or 505/5749-8756, www.hotelbrio.com, $26-65 with fan and private bath) sits atop a hill 300 meters back from the beach, with ocean views and Wi-Fi. They also have two 25-foot *pangas* for surfing and fishing tours. **Dale Dagger's Cool Places to Stay** (daledagger@gmail.com, $18-45) is where you'll find the man himself. Dagger was the first foreign surfer to come to Nicaragua and scout the waves (he shipwrecked here in 1993 and never left), and his knowledge of the coastline is unparalleled. He's got six different lodging options, including a dorm as well as luxury options.

OVER $100

These are resorts on private property farther removed from the community. **Giant's Foot Surf Lodge** (tel. 505/8449-5949, U.S. 562/888-1518, www.giantsfoot.com, from $900/week) rents out two adjacent beachfront lodges with air-conditioning, fan, and private bathroom. Amenities include table tennis, a fire pit, hammocks, DVDs, books, and board games. Weeklong packages include everything except your airfare; discounts are available in the off-season.

Monkey House, Playa Gigante

At **Dale Dagger's Surf Lodge** (www. nicasurf.com, speak@nicasurf.com, $2,095/ week), you get cushy digs, a ride from the airport, all meals, and unlimited trips to some of the best and least-known breaks in Nicaragua, returning to the luxury of air-conditioning, wireless Internet, and running hot water.

★ **Aqua Wellness Resort** (tel., U.S. 917/338-2116, 505/8739-2426, 505/8849/6235, aquanicaragua.com, contact@aquanicaragua. com) is situated in a natural lush tropical forest setting within a private beach cove. This resort, secluded and peaceful, is ideal for a relaxing beach holiday. They also offer holistic yoga, meditation, and spa treatments that nourish the soul.

Food

Some big, airy *ranchos* (thatch-roofed restaurants) sit right on the beach: **Miramar** (next to the Spanish school, $4-7) is one of the better choices. **Buena Vista** (up the road at the top of the hill, daily 8am-10pm, $4-7) has similar fare and is a great lookout point. **La Gaviota** (50 meters from Blue Sol, on the beach, $4-11) is famous for its *plato típico de Gigante* featuring seasonal seafood. **Blue Sol** (at the main entrance to the beach road, daily 8am-10pm, $4-12) is popular for its huge fish tacos.

Buy your own fresh seafood in the mornings from three local *acopios* (storage houses) and buy everything else from **Pulpería Mena** (50 meters south of Blue Sol, daily until 8pm).

★ **Party Wave** (50 meters south of the *pulpería,* Mon.-Fri. 7am-4pm, Sat. 8am-4pm, Sun. 8am-2pm, $3-5) offers delicious sandwiches, smoothies, and even Vietnamese coffee. They also run the only cyber café in town and rent paddleboards ($5/hour) and snorkel equipment ($3/day). Stop by the **farmer's market** (in front of Blue Sol, Sat. 9am-1pm).

Getting There and Away

It's easier than ever to get to this beach town, but it's still a trek. Take the Las Pilas bus from Rivas at 2pm daily (except Sun.). It returns at 7:30am and 3pm. Otherwise, take the Las Salinas bus from Tola or Rivas ($1.50) and get off at the first entrance to Gigante (30-40 minutes). You'll have to walk a sweaty 40 minutes, or hitch about six kilometers to reach the beach. Taxis on this road are few and far between, but anyone driving a pickup will probably let you hop in back. You could also contract a taxi from Rivas for $25, not bad if you can fill the cab.

PLAYA COLORADO

This beach is widely recognized as having two of the most consistent and best breaks in the area: **Colorado** and **Panga Drops.** The land behind this beach is privately owned, and the best way to get here is to take a shuttle from San Juan del Sur or rent a 4x4. To rent a vacation home from the gated community on this beach, contact Iguana Surf Rentals, who run **Hacienda Iguana** (tel. 505/8736-0656, iguanasurfrentals.com, $375-700). Their fully furnished homes have pools and air-conditioning. They also offer beachfront condo rental ($150-300). You'll have access to the community pool and golf course.

PLAYA SANTANA AND JIQUILITE

Just south of Popoyo, this beach is west of a small community called Limón with just a few places to stay, many of which are closed in October, when the waves just aren't worth it. Take the bus in Rivas that leaves for Las Salinas or El Astillero. Get off in Limón #2. From there it is about a half-hour walk to the beach, or you can hop in a moto-taxi ($4). A taxi from Rivas costs about $25. The 2700-acre resort at **Rancho Santana** (tel. 505/8882-2885 or U.S. 310/929-5221, reservations@ranchosantana.com, $300 d) encompasses five beaches offering surfing, fishing, snorkeling, and horseback riding. Relax by the clubhouse pool, do some yoga, or get a massage. The on-site car rental agency makes it easy to get around.

Villa Jiquilite (north of Playa Santana, tel. 505/8883-8678 or 505/8884-1467, ww.villajiquelite.com, villajiquelite@gmail. com, $15 dorm, $25 d with a/c) has basic clean rooms with shared bath and a small pool shaded by a large almond tree. They serve food from the beachside restaurant.

★ **Buena Onda** (a few minutes walk north of Villa Jiquilite, tel. 505/8809-0794, www.buenaondaresort.com, $15 pp dorm, $35 shared bath, $45-55 private) is just south of Playa Sardinas, where you'll find the Popoyo surf break. The resort is a two-minute walk from the beach, has a beautiful large pool, a mini-halfpipe (boards available), and many other activities like snorkeling and horseback riding. Rates double during the holidays.

The Surf Sanctuary (tel. 505/8894-6260, $60/day house, $1,250/week pp all-inclusive) is a surf camp with restaurant, bar, TV, Internet, movies, and the works. Guests enjoy a private house with four beds, bath, hot water, air-conditioning, private porches, and pool.

LAS SALINAS DE NAGUALAPA

Las Salinas is a humble fishing community. In town, **La Tica** (tel. 505/7855-4030, $10 pp) is a popular restaurant and *hospedaje*. Nearby **hot springs** are worth exploring if you get sick of the beach (ask at La Tica for directions). The springs are also used by local families to wash clothing, so they're not exactly pristine.

Buses to Las Salinas leave from Tola and Rivas throughout the day ($1.50), passing the entrance to Playa Gigante along the way.

GUASACATE AND POPOYO

A few kilometers west of Las Salinas, **Guasacate** is a huge stretch of gorgeous and mostly remote shoreline—beautiful by any standard. The community of **Popoyo** was wiped out by a tsunami decades ago and is technically located south of Playa Sardinas. This whole area is commonly referred to as Popoyo nowadays. Staying at Playa Guasacate puts you near the Popoyo and Outer Reef breaks. The walk from Guasacate to Santana is a good long haul in the hot sun.

Many of the restaurants and hotels in this area are European-owned, unlike mostly gringo San Juan del Sur, and there's a range of accommodations from weekly surf camps to midrange hotels to cheap crashpad *hospedajes*. The entrance to Guasacate is three kilometers down the first left-hand road after crossing a bridge in Las Salinas. The road runs two kilometers more along the ocean until it dead-ends at Playa Guasacate (just 5 minutes from Playa Sardinas and the Popoyo surf break), with a handful of hotels

mini-halfpipe at Buena Onda resort

and restaurants sprinkled along the two-kilometer stretch. If you're here, you're probably here to surf; in case of disaster, take your board to **Popoyo Ding Repair/La Tiendita** (200 meters before the road dead ends, tel. 505/8464-9563, www.popoyodingrepair.com, board rental $10/day), a small shop that repairs, rents, and sells boards and other handmade surf accessories. Stock up on necessities at **La Tica 2** (end of the road across from La Bocana del Surf, tel. 505/8873-0521), a hostel and general store catering to most of the beachfront community.

Accommodations
UNDER $25
★ **Hotel La Bocana del Surf** (end of the road on the west side, tel. 505/8599-0847 or 505/8391-9118, gerardomena@yahoo.com, $8 pp) is the best value in town. Rooms are dark and lodging is spartan, but the views from the porch are spectacular. They have Wi-Fi and a restaurant on the first floor.

Italian-owned ★ **Wild Waves Guesthouse** (across from Popoyo Ding Repair, tel. 505/8578-6102, www.wildwavesnicaragua.com, wildwavesnicaragua@gmail.com, $10-14 dorm, $25 s, $30 d, $40 with a/c) has pleasant, well-kept rooms and a roadside

hammock patio. The open kitchen is clean and has complimentary coffee throughout the day.

Popoyo Beach Hostel (tel. 505/8722-2999 or 505/8953-2814, $10 dorm, $20-30, $40 with a/c) has three dorms and a private upstairs room with a balcony. They've got Wi-Fi, an open outdoor patio with a bar, and a kitchen for guest use. They rent boards ($10/day) and offer surf lessons ($30 for 2 hours).

$25-50
El Club del Surf (600 meters from the end of the road, tel. 505/8456-6068, www.clubdelsurf.com, $40 d) has Wi-Fi and six charming doubles with cable TV, air-conditioning, and private bath. Be sure to get a room facing the ocean.

La Vaca Loca B&B (500 meters from the end of the road, tel. 505/8584-9110, www.lavacalocaguasacate.com, lavacalocaguasacate@gmail.com) is a thatch-roof bed-and-breakfast above a coffee shop. Their two rooms have a shared bath and large four-poster beds with private balconies. There's ample lounge space facing the ocean, plus a third-story loft with a lone hammock.

★ **Vibra Guesthouse**'s (next to Wild Waves, across from Popoyo Ding Repair, tel. 505/8322-9065, vibraguesthouse@gmail.com,

Guasacate is a huge stretch of gorgeous and mostly remote shoreline.

Magnific Rock

$30 s, up to 5 people $70) two pretty rooms are simple, but you'll appreciate the attention to detail. Each has a private bath and can house up to five people. Guests are welcome to use the shared kitchen.

$50-100

Hotel Popoyo (left side of the road at the end of a short driveway, behind El Toro, tel. 505/8885-3334, www.hotelpopoyo.com, closed Oct., $50-80 d, includes breakfast, $100 apartment) has a spacious room with a king-size canopy bed, plenty of windows, bamboo roof, air-conditioning, and cable TV. There's a pool out back and a few hammocks slung under the *rancho*.

Magnific Rock (end of Playa Sardinas, tel. 505/8916-6916 or 505/8237-7417, www. magnificrockpopoyo.com, $70-100 d, from $1,295/week all-inclusive) sits high on a rock directly between the Guasacate and Santana beaches, providing a spectacular 280° view. It's popular among local surfers for its parties and live music.

OVER $100

Popoyo Surf Lodge (U.S. tel. 321/735-0322, www.surfnicaragua.com) pioneered the local surf scene in the 1990s. The owner, JJ, is a ripping, born-again surfer who also preaches at the local church. Reservations and packages are available online. Drop-ins (no surf pun intended) are accepted in the off-season.

Food and Nightlife

★ **La Vaca Loca** (500 meters from the end of the road, Wed.-Sun. 8am-1:30pm, $3-7) and **Dutch's Deli** (50 meters from the end of the road, Mon.-Sat. 6am-4pm, $3-7) are the only veritable coffee shops in this area. Their food is all made fresh from scratch. **El Club del Surf** (600 meters from the end of the road, tel. 505/8456-6068, $5-11) features affordable Italian specialties and a variety of fresh salads (tuna, chicken, Caprese) and, of course, wine. For great Italian pizza and calzones, go to **Viento Este** (600 meters from the end of the road, Mon.-Sat. 6pm-10pm, $5-10), which regularly hosts live music and surf movie nights.

The most popular eatery in Guasacate is **El Toro** (behind Hotel Popoyo, east side of the road, tel. 505/8885-3334, $5-10), with an airy dining area and a great selection of meatless treats such as gazpacho, hummus, pasta, and veggie burritos. Rum and cokes are $1 during happy hour (4pm-6pm). **Los Amores del Sol** (next to La Bocana, daily 8am-8pm, $3-12) is a well-liked beachfront restaurant and full bar where you can watch the waves roll in or just enjoy the meticulously landscaped grounds.

Getting There and Away

At least one bus a day leaves Roberto Huembes market in Managua bound for El Astillero via Ochomogo (not Tola) at 2:30pm and arrives at the entrance to Popoyo 6pm ($3). From San Juan del Sur or Costa Rica, you'll drive through Rivas and Tola, following the signs to Rancho Santana, then continue past this development's gates until you reach Las Salinas. Buses depart Rivas about every hour. A taxi to Guasacate from El Astillero costs $7, from Rivas $30. The road to the beach leads past several austere salt flats, from which the nearby town of Las Salinas gets its name. Ignore the signs pointing to Popoyo, which lead to the former town farther from the break.

EL ASTILLERO AND BEACHES TO THE NORTH

Most of the little deserted beaches in the 10-kilometer strip between Las Salinas and El Astillero don't even have names. **El Astillero** itself is a fishing village full of small boats and is, in fact, the first safe boat anchorage north of Gigante. North of El Astillero, the road turns inland away from the coast. Accessing the beach anywhere along this area requires a boat and a lot of dedication. Ask around in El Astillero. There are plenty of underemployed sailors and fisherfolk that would be glad to strike a deal with you if you're interested in exploring the coastline. Buses take three hours departing Rivas at 5am or Nandaime's market at 9am and 2pm. They return to Rivas at 7am and 10am and to Nandaime at 6am and 1pm.

Just south of the town of El Astillero, ★ **Las Plumerias** (tel. 505/8979-7782, or 505/8969-1809, www.lasplumerias.com, $60-75 d) offers comfy bungalows on well-manicured grounds and an infinity pool. Price includes three meals and unlimited soft drinks and beers. French owners Emeline and Etienne are both trained surf instructors and offer surfboard rental, guides, and lessons. Another option is the beachside **Hostal Hamacas** (50 meters north of the school, tel. 505/8810-4144, www.hostalhamacas.com, $30 d, $45 with a/c). They have a nice pool, but no Wi-Fi.

Beachfront resort lodging can be found just outside of town at **Punta Teonoste** (www.puntateonoste.com, $164-328 d) in one of 16 freestanding villas. The design strikes a balance between luxury and rustic (guests enjoy the open-air showers). There's also an on-site spa and free horseback riding and surfboards available to guests.

RÍO ESCALANTE-CHACOCENTE WILDLIFE REFUGE

One of the only Nicaraguan Pacific beaches where the Paslama turtle (Lepidochelys oliveacea) lays its eggs, and the Tora Turtle (Dermochelys coriacea), the Torita Turtle (Chelonia mydas), and the Carey Turtle (Eretmochelys imbricata) also lay eggs, is at **Refugio de Vida Silvestre Río Escalante-Chacocente** (www.chacocentenicaragua.com, $5), a protected wildlife area whose beach provides habitat for numerous other species as well, including white-tailed deer, reptiles, and many interesting types of flora. There's lots to do, including guided wildlife tours to three different lookout points, hot springs and a waterfall, turtle observation ($7.50-10 pp), and visiting local bee keepers ($17.50-20 pp). Organize activities through **COSETUCHACO** (tel. 505/8603-3742 or 505/8481-1202). Campers can bring their own tent or stay in the research center's wooden bungalows. There's no running water here and solar electricity lasts for about four hours every night. Food from the restaurant should be ordered at least three days in advance. There is also a local group of women who collect plastic bag trash from the beach and weave it into bags that are sold in Managua and online. The project, Tejiendo por la Naturaleza, clears the beach for the turtles and creates income for local women.

Getting to Chacocente isn't easy, which, for the sake of the turtles, is just as well. Take a bus to El Astillero, where you'll find the reserve's tourist center. To get there, the turnoff from the Pan-American Highway is just south of the Río Ochomogo bridge, or take a taxi from Rivas (90 minutes, about $40). Coming from the north, during the dry season you can take the unpaved road from Santa Teresa.

Peñas Blancas and the Costa Rica Border

Peñas Blancas is the official border crossing into Costa Rica. A major effort continues, with financing from the United States, to make this border crossing a bottleneck and entrapment point for drug traffickers headed north. Many of the buildings you see in the compound are inspection points for the hundreds of tractor-trailers that cross the border daily. Needless to say, this is one place you don't want to be caught smuggling furs. Sniffing dogs are common.

Border hassles can last 1-7 hours. The wait is longest a week before and after Christmas, Easter, and during any Nicaraguan election, when the hundreds of thousands of Nicaraguans living across the border are traveling to and from their country. Afternoon is the best time of day to cross. Usually you can squeeze through in an hour.

CROSSING THE BORDER

The border is open Monday-Saturday 6am-10pm and Sunday 6am-8pm. There is a fee for exiting ($2-5) and entering ($10-13) Nicaragua. Inside the customs and immigration building, find a branch of Bancentro, which can help you change money. Its schedule is generally tied to that of the border post itself. If you change with a *coyote*, be sure you know the exchange rate and do your math ahead of time so as not to lose too much money.

A **passport** and some **cash** is all that's required of North American and European travelers, but don't forget to get stamped on both sides of the border to avoid subsequent headaches! To enter Costa Rica, Nicaraguan citizens must have a Costa Rican visa from the consulate in Managua. Upon entering Nicaragua, most North American and European travelers are granted a 90-day visa.

By law, folks entering Costa Rica must have a ticket to leave the country. They usually don't check, as long as you're dressed like you have money. If they do, you lose your place in line and go to the table outside, where Transport Dendu will sell you an open-ended ticket from San José to Managua.

Entering Nicaragua with Your Vehicle

Rental vehicles cannot cross the border. If you are driving your own vehicle, the process to enter Nicaragua from Costa Rica is lengthy but usually not too difficult. You'll present your title *(Título de la Propiedad)*, as well as your driver's license and passport. Get proper stamps from Hacienda (Timbres de Hacienda), and a property certificate from Hacienda. Also make sure you have a current tag and *Tico* insurance; all of this can be taken care of in the town of Liberia, just to the south. You will be given a 30-day permit ($10) to drive in Nicaragua. Should you lose the permit, you will be fined $100. Travelers driving their own vehicles north from the border will be forced to pass through a dubious "sterilization process" on the Nica side, in which the exterior of the vehicle is sprayed with a mystery liquid to kill porcine and bovine diseases. This costs $1 and takes five minutes unless the line is long. Roll up the windows and remove exposed food from the car. You can now rent a car with **Budget** (505/8645-4050) at the border. The office is located in the Duty Free Tienda.

CONTINUING INTO COSTA RICA

International bus services like Tica Bus, TransNica, NicaBus, and King Quality are popular ways to get across the border easily and comfortably. In many cases, the bus has a helper who collects your passports and money and waits in line for you. The disadvantage is that the bus won't pull away from the border post until every single traveler has had their papers processed, which can be time-consuming (waits up to 4 hours are not unheard of). More confident travelers like to take a Nicaraguan bus to the border, walk across to Costa Rica, and take a Costa Rican bus to San José, which is often faster. Express buses from Managua to Peñas Blancas depart Mercado Huembes at 5am, 8am, 9:30am, and 3:30pm. Buses and microbuses leave the market in Rivas every 30-45 minutes.

After crossing the border, you've got two choices: Buy a ticket to San José from the TransNica booth across from customs (6-8 hours, $10 pp), with eight departures daily at 5:15am-6pm. Or, get a Liberia-Pulmitan bus to Liberia (2 hours, last bus 5:30pm, $3 pp). From Liberia, 14 daily buses go to San José (3-5 hours); buses leave every 20 minutes to the Nicoya Peninsula and its beaches. You can overnight in **Hotel Liberia** (tel. 506/2666-0161, www.hotelliberiacr.com, $13 pp dorm, $35-40 d), which is safe, pretty, and clean.

León and the Volcanic Cordillera

Look for ★ to find recommended
sights, activities, dining, and lodging.

Highlights

© AVALON TRAVEL

★ **León's Museums:** Begin your art immersion at La Casa de Cultura and then continue around the corner to the fabulous Centro de Arte Fundación Ortiz-Gurdián (page 170).

★ **Volcano Boarding on Cerro Negro:** Whether you go on a toboggan or a modified snowboard, hurling yourself down a steep pitch of tiny black pebbles on an active volcano is a scream (page 174).

★ **Las Ruinas de León Viejo:** As old as Nicaragua's colonial history, this legitimate archaeological dig exposes the bones of Spain's earliest settlement (page 181).

★ **Las Peñitas Beach:** Popular with beginning surfers, Las Peñitas has relaxing and peaceful accommodations at the ocean's edge that offer easy access to the impressive Isla Juan Venado (page 183).

★ **Isla Juan Venado Wildlife Reserve:** Visit the sea turtle reserve August-December and you may be able to witness these impressive creatures return to shore to lay their eggs (page 184).

★ **Telica-Rota Protected Area:** Peer into the crater of an active volcano and, if you're lucky, see lava glowing below (page 185).

★ **Padre Ramos Wetlands Reserve:** If you're into isolated beaches and protected bird-filled estuaries, the bouncy trip north is worth it (page 195).

★ **Volcán Cosigüina Natural Reserve:** Visit hot springs and check out the spectacular views of El Salvador and Honduras across the Gulf of Fonseca (page 196).

I n León and Chinandega, you can delve into the volcanic half of "the land of lakes and volcanoes." Explore the Ring of Fire by peering into a crater lake at the top of Cosigüina, catching a glimpse of lava at night from Telica, or sliding down

Cerro Negro at high speeds. The high temperatures may make you feel like you're actually *inside* a volcano, but to beat the heat, just head to the coast, where you'll find beaches that are quickly becoming surfer favorites. You will find long stretches of sand, black from volcanic rocks, which are less crowded than those farther south in San Juan del Sur.

At different points in history León has been the capital of Nicaragua, as well as a breeding ground for poetry and revolution. Nicaragua's literary legend, Rubén Darío, spent much of his childhood, and, later, the end of his life, in this colonial city. It was also here that the young poet Rigoberto López Perez, disguised as a waiter, assassinated the first of the Somoza dictators. Today, León is a university town filled with cathedrals and cafés that still plays an important cultural role and boasts a lively nightlife.

Chinandega has historically been the agricultural center and home of the country's main port. You will find much of the country's sugar and rum production in Chichigalpa, with San Cristobal, Nicaragua's tallest active volcano, looming in the distance. Today, blossoming eco-tourism projects that benefit local communities allow you to kayak through mangroves and estuaries and visit sea turtle reserves in northern Chinandega.

PLANNING YOUR TIME

León has a wide range of activities, so plan on at least one day to visit the museums and cathedrals of the city, another if you plan to hike a volcano, and another if you head to the shore. Las Peñitas, Isla Juan Venado, Padre Ramos, and other points outside León require more effort to reach but are excellent destinations for those traveling on a slightly slower schedule. It's worth slowing down in fact, so you can paddle through the estuaries and observe the wildlife (like nesting turtles on Juan Venado). It is also one of the places

Previous: looking out over a crater lake from Cosigüina; La Iglesia El Calvario in Chinandega. **Above:** La Catedral de León.

León and the Volcanic Cordillera

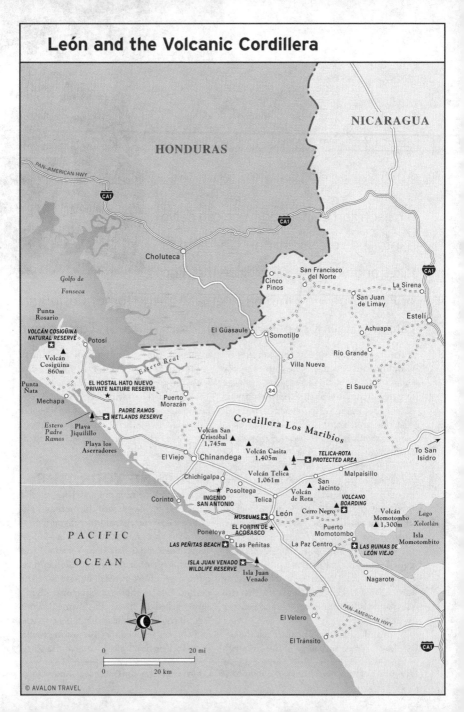

© AVALON TRAVEL

where visitors stay to study Spanish both in and around the city. There is plenty to do, whether you come for two days or two weeks. In general, getting around on public transportation is easy in this region. Buses and *interlocales* run regularly and are inexpensive. To reach some of the volcanoes, secluded beaches, or nature reserves, drivers will need four-wheel drive vehicles or transport through a tour operator.

León

The principal metropolis of the low-lying Nicaraguan northwest, León has had several incarnations over the centuries. The Spaniards first built the city along the shores of Lake Xolotlán, but they picked up and moved when Volcán Momotombo shook the ground beneath their feet. Modern León is at once a dusty provincial capital and an architectural delight. Traditionally designed colonial homes, churches, universities, and immense cathedrals stand shoulder to shoulder in a tropical torpor that keeps city life to a low but exciting hum. León is an easily walkable city, with a plethora of interesting cafés and restaurants, Latin America's largest cathedral, and an ambience quite unlike anywhere else in Nicaragua. Its longtime political rival, Granada, may have more fresh paint and international adoration, but León remains an irreverent, unique city where tourism is an afterthought, not a necessity.

ORIENTATION

León is laid out in the traditional colonial grid system with the central park and cathedral at the center. It sprawls impressively in all directions. The main bus terminal and market are nearly a kilometer northeast of the main plaza, and Barrio Sutiaba is 12 blocks due west. A *zona rosa* of sorts is developing along 1 Calle SO as it extends westward from the southwest corner of the plaza. Most of the town's nightlife is condensed here. University campuses are primarily just north of the plaza.

SIGHTS

The shady and pleasant **Parque Rubén Darío** (a.k.a. **Parque de los Poetas,** a block

LEÓN
LEÓN

La Catedral de León

León

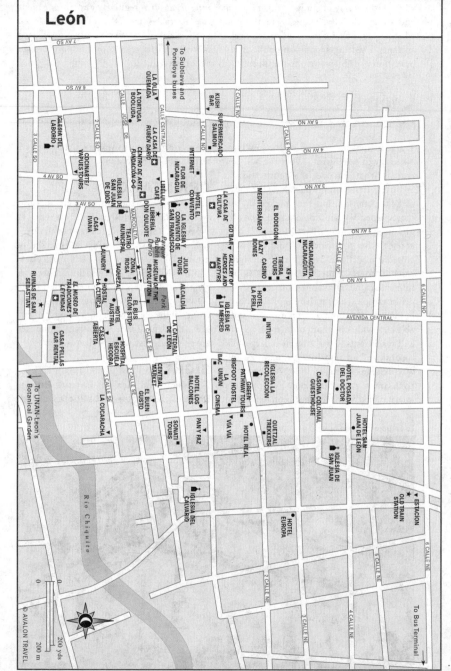

west of the central park) pays tribute to four famous Nicaraguan writers, all sons of León: Azarías H. Pallais (1884-1954), Salomon de la Selva (1893-1959), Alfonso Cortés (1893-1969), and the beloved Rubén Darío (1867-1916).

León's **Old Train Station** (2 blocks north of the Iglesia de San Juan), built in 1884, was Nicaragua's first and most majestic. The creepy, yet captivating **El Fortín de Acosasco** sits on a grassy hill just south of the city, providing phenomenal views of the entire Maribio volcano chain. Conservative President Sacasa built it in 1889 to keep an eye on the Liberals that would overthrow him four years later. Abandoned until Anastasio Somoza took interest and rehabilitated it, El Fortín has since served as both a military base and jail. It is presently abandoned once again, though the city has invested a small amount to seal off the dangerous dungeons and to slap on some fresh paint. At the time of research it was under construction. From the Sutiaba church, it's an easy 45-minute walk (don't go it alone), or $6 by taxi: Go one block east and head due south up the hill along the shady dirt road.

A short ride outside the center of the city you'll find an oasis in **UNAN-León's Botanical Gardens** (tel. 505/2311-4012, jardinbotanicoambiental@ct.unanLeón.edu.ni, daily 8am-4pm, foreigners $4). Because of the trees and the microclimates in the gardens, the air is much cooler than other parts of the city. You'll find flora from all parts of Nicaragua, including faraway places like Bosawás and Corn Island. There are picnic tables where you can enjoy a peaceful lunch. Check out the butterfly gardens as well. Catch a taxi or a *camioneta* from the central park that stops at the Politécnico La Salle in Sutiaba, then walk about 800 meters to the gardens (there will be signs pointing you along the way). You can reserve guided tours for groups and stay the night (cabin $20, bring your own tent $8).

La Catedral de León

La Catedral de León (near the central park, $3) is the largest cathedral in Central America and the modern city's focal point. In 2011 it was declared a UNESCO World Heritage site and has been undergoing repairs and getting a fresh coat of brilliantly white paint. One (probably apocryphal) story claims that the architect accidentally switched two sets of plans while on the ship from Spain, and the larger of the two cathedrals, originally intended for Lima, Peru, was built in Nicaragua.

a native plant at UNAN-León's Botanical Gardens

A Walking Tour of Churches and Ruins

Begin your walking tour at La Catedral de León, near the central park, then head either northeast or southwest to view the following churches and ruins.

NORTH AND EAST FROM THE CENTRAL PARK

Iglesia de la Merced, 1.5 blocks north of the main cathedral, is the church considered most representative of León in the 1700s. It was originally built in 1762 by the Mercedarian monks, the first order of monks to arrive in Nicaragua during the years of the conquest. It is essentially baroque in style but has neoclassical elements in the front and colonial on the south side. It faces a small but lovely park popular amongst León's skateboarders. Particularly attractive is the church's side bell tower.

Passing the Iglesia de la Merced and walking two blocks east along 2 Calle NE, you'll find the yellow **Iglesia de la Recolección** on the north side. This church has the most perfect baroque style of the León churches and a massive, functional bell tower. It was built in 1786 by Bishop Juan Félix de Villegas and is the only church in León constructed using carved stone.

From the Iglesia de la Recolección, continue one more block and turn north. Walk two blocks until you reach the picturesque **Iglesia de San Juan.** The old train station is a block farther north from the east side of the church. Built 1625-1650 and rebuilt in the 1700s, the Iglesia de San Juan's architecture is a modern interpretation of neoclassicism. This neighborhood of León will give you a good feel for what León was like in the 1700s: church, park, small houses of adobe using traditional *taquezal* construction techniques, and the nearby market.

Walking four blocks south down the same road, you'll find the **Iglesia del Calvario** on your left side. It is set at the top of broad steps on a small hill overlooking one of León's narrow streets. Renovated in the late 1990s, Calvario was built 200 years before in a generally baroque style, but with neoclassical ornamentation in the front that reflects the increasing French influence in Spain in the 18th century. Inside are two famous statues known as *El Buen y el Mal Ladrón* (The Good and the Bad Thief).

The cathedral was constructed in 1747 at the request of Archbishop Isidoro Bullón y Figueroa and inaugurated in 1860 as a basilica by Pope Pius XI. It's an imposing and majestic baroque structure whose grandeur is magnified by the open space of the park in front of it. The **Tomb of Rubén Darío** is a notable element of the cathedral—look for the golden statue of a lion. The cathedral holds the mortal remains of the musician José de la Cruz Mena and several religious figures. Look for the famous *Cristo de Pedrarias*, a painting that once hung in the cathedral of León Viejo. The particularly beautiful **Patio de los Príncipes** is a small courtyard of Andalusian design, with a fountain in the center and colorful beds of flowers. Rooftop tours are highly recommended. The entrance fee is worth it to stand among the white towers and domes that

form the roof of the Catedral de León and for the unsurpassed view of the city and nearby volcanoes.

★ Museums

León's museums are exceedingly eclectic, covering the political, natural, and all things cultural. Start at **La Casa de Cultura** (from Iglesia y Convento de San Francisco, 1 block north, 20 meters east, tel. 505/2311-2116, Mon.- Sat. 8am-noon and 2pm-7:30pm, free), housed in an old colonial home. The collection of artwork includes a disparaging painting of Ronald Reagan and Henry Kissinger. This is a good place to find out about all kinds of cultural classes and activities.

La Casa de Rubén Darío (from Parque Ruben Darío, 2 blocks west, tel. 505/2311-2388 or 505/2311-6509, Tues.-Sat. 8am-noon and

SOUTH AND WEST FROM THE CENTRAL PARK

La Iglesia y Convento de San Francisco, three blocks west of the park on the north side, and across the street from the Casa Museo Rubén Darío, contains two of the most beautiful altars of colonial Nicaragua. The church was built in 1639 by Fray Pedro de Zuñiga and rebuilt and modified several times afterwards, notably in the mid-1980s to restore the damage done to it during the Revolution. Its small, tree-lined courtyard is a pleasant place to escape from the hot sun and relax.

Turning and walking a block south, you come to the unassuming Iglesia de San Juan de Dios, built in 1620 as a chapel for León's first hospital (now gone). Its simplicity and colonial style reflect the wishes of Felipe II when he designed it in 1573.

Two blocks farther south and one short block to the west is the Iglesia del Laborío, a graceful, rural-feeling church in the old mixed neighborhood of El Laborío.

on the roof of La Catedral de León

This church, one of León's earliest, formed the nucleus of the working-class neighborhood that provided labor to León's wealthy class in the 17th century. The street from Laborío east to the Ruinas de la Ermita de San Sebastián is known as Calle la Españolita and was one of the first streets built in León.

The Ruinas de la Ermita de San Sebastián consist of the shattered remnants of the outer walls, and inexplicably, the intact bell tower. The Ermita was built in 1742 on a site long used by the indigenous people for worship of their own gods. It suffered major damage in 1979 during Somoza's bombardment of León. El Museo de Tradiciones y Leyendas is across the street.

2pm-5pm, Sun. 8am-noon, $1-2 donations accepted) is a glimpse into 19th-century León. Nicaragua's favorite son lived here with his aunt and uncle until the age of 14. Fellow poet Alfonso Cortés later inhabited the same house as he battled insanity (his room still has the iron bars he bent during one attempted escape). Darío's bed and the rest of the furnishings of the museum are typical of middle-class León in the late 19th century, as is the building itself, built from adobe with a clay-tile and cane roof. On display are original copies of his most famous works translated into several languages and copies of a magazine he published in Paris. The silver crucifix given to him by Mexican poet Amado Nervos, correspondence from when Darío was the consul to Argentina and ambassador to Spain, and period coins and currency are also displayed.

Occupying two facing buildings, the Centro de Arte Fundación Ortiz-Gurdián (1 block west of Parque Rubén Darío, tel. 505/2311-2716, www.fundacionortizgurdian. org, Mon.-Fri. 9am-5pm, Sat. 9:30am-5pm, Sun. 9am-4pm, $1, free Sun.) has reputedly the best collection of Latin American artwork in Nicaragua, with an emphasis on colonial America.

El Museo de Tradiciones y Leyendas (Barrio Laborío, tel. 505/2315-4678, Mon.-Sat. 8am-noon and 2pm-5pm, Sun. 8am-noon, $1) celebrates Nicaragua's favorite folktales: the golden crab, La Carreta Nagua, the pig-witch, and La Mocuana. The building itself is the former XXI jail and base of the 12th Company of Somoza's National Guard. Built in 1921, XXI meted out 60 years of brutal torture. The mango tree that now shades this museum was planted by a prisoner and watered from the same well that was used for electric shock and water-boarding sessions.

To learn about Nicaragua's revolutionary history, take a tour with a veteran as your guide at the **Museum of the Revolution** (across the western side of the central park, daily 8am-5pm, $2). The somewhat sparse relics in the museum are not the real draw, rather the opportunity to talk to the ex-combatants who lived the experiences first-hand. You can also make a quick stop at the **Gallery of Heroes and Martyrs** (half a block west of Iglesia de la Merced, daily 9:30am-5pm, $1 contribution), maintained by a group of mothers who lost their children during the war.

Murals

Although many murals from the revolutionary period were painted over after the Sandinistas lost the elections in 1990, around the city you can still find murals telling Nicaragua's history, in addition to new street art popping up. Perhaps the most famous is located across from the north side of the main cathedral: a long, horizontal piece telling the history of a proud and turbulent nation. Starting on the left with the arrival of the Nahuatl, the mural traces the planned inter-oceanic canal, the exploits of William Walker, Sandino's battle with U.S. Marines, the revolution of 1979, and a utopian ending image of a fertile, peaceful Nicaragua. Flanking a doorway across the street, a colorful Sandino steps on Uncle Sam's and Somoza's heads. One block to the west, the CIA, in the form of a thick serpent, coils through the Sandinistas' agrarian reform, literacy campaign, and construction efforts, to strike at a Nicaraguan hand at the ballot box. Near the UNAN you will find a mural representing students who struggled to keep 6 percent of the budget for education designated in the Constitution. Newer murals can be found around the 23 de Julio basketball court near Iglesia de la Merced.

"Sandino lives" mural in León

Barrio Sutiaba

The indigenous neighborhood of Sutiaba (Maribio for "land of the big men") retains a trace of both its cultural identity and political autonomy. Besides the thrill of walking the streets of a village predating Columbus, note several interesting ruins here. Just about any of the microbuses that circulate through León will take you to Sutiaba if you're not up for the 12-block walk.

La Catedral de Sutiaba, beautiful in its aged simplicity, is second only to the Catedral de León in size and is the keystone of the community. Construction began in 1698 and finished 12 years later, but the indigenous inhabitants of Sutiaba kept worshiping their own gods despite Spanish proselytism. In an effort to get the locals into the church, the Spanish mounted a carved wooden image of the sun representing the local god on the church ceiling, a compromise that left everyone satisfied, even if, during a church service the Spanish and locals were simultaneously worshiping different gods. The beautifully crafted sun remains, as do the immense wooden columns that evoke the kind of forest that surrounded León 300 years ago. Next to the cathedral is the Casa Cural, which predates the cathedral of Sutiaba by 160 years but was rebuilt in 1743.

Museo Adiact (across the street from La Catedral de Sutiaba on the north side, Mon.-Fri. 8am-noon and 2pm-5pm, Sat. 8am-noon, $1-2 donation) is a run-down but captivating museum that houses many of the area's archaeological treasures. Sadly, some of the better idols and statues were stolen in the late 1980s and sold to foreign museums.

A small **park** (5 blocks east of La Catedral de Sutiaba's southern side) is dedicated to the last cacique of Sutiaba, Adiact, and his daughter, Xochilt Acalt. **El Tamarindón** (from La Catedral de Sutiaba, 3 blocks south and 2 blocks west) is an enormous, gnarled tamarind tree from whose branches the Spanish hung the last cacique. To modern Sutiabans, the tree still represents the rebelliousness of the indigenous people and is a source of much community pride.

There are two sets of ruins in Sutiaba, **Las Ruinas de Veracruz** (1 block west of La Catedral de Sutiaba, set in high weeds) and **Las Ruinas de Santiago** (1 block north of the cathedral on the other side of Calle Central, look for a small sign). The church at Veracruz was Sutiaba's first, built sometime around 1560 and abandoned in the late 1700s due to its small size. The eruption of Volcán Cosigüina in 1835 caused its subsequent collapse. The church at Santiago, constructed in the early 1600s, is significant because its small square bell tower remains intact.

ENTERTAINMENT AND EVENTS
Nightlife
BARS AND DISCOS
It's no surprise that a university town like León has a thriving nightlife. For student-centered beer gardens, roam the university area in the two blocks north of the main plaza. The nicest *discotecas* and bars are clustered on a

single block called the *zona rosa* (on Calle 1 SO between Avenida 1 and Avenida 2), a tongue-in-cheek swipe at Managua's more impressive and similarly-named hot spot. Walk west from the southwest corner of the main plaza.

For dancing, the best disco with the most varied music selection is **Oxígeno** (zona rosa, the sign says O2, Wed.-Sat. from 8pm), where things start picking up around 11pm. There are several other popular options on the same block, including **Zona Illiom** (zona rosa, tel. 505/ 2315-2842). **Bohemios** (80 meters west of the antiguo Teatro Municipal, tel. 505/8810-2039) is a club with a lively dance floor and a VIP section if you're feeling like going out in style. If you're ready to stay out until dawn, head to **K9** (15 meters north of Casino La Perla), one of León's only after-party spots.

At **Taquezal** (half a block west of the central park's southern end), depending on the night, you can try out your bachata or salsa moves, sing your heart out at karaoke, or dance to throwbacks on 1980s night. They also serve a varied menu ($5-9). Try the Nicaccino, cappuccino with a shot of Nicaraguan rum, or ask for a new Nicaraguan microbrew. Across from Parque La Merced, the **Don Señor** complex—disco (Tues.-Sat. from 8:30pm, $2 cover), restaurant, downstairs dive, and upstairs patio lounge with a view of the nightlife—attracts the college crowd and foreigners. The restaurant and the bars are open for lunch and dinner, and close late on Saturdays.

Go Bar (2 blocks north, 25 meters east of Parque de los Poetas, tel. 505/2311-1400, Sun.-Thurs. 6pm-midnight, Fri.-Sat. until 2am) is an LGBTQ-friendly bar and dance club. They host regular parties and events like karaoke nights. Not into the typical club scene? **Kush Bar** (1 block west of the Salman) offers an alternative environment with live music including punk rock and reggae shows.

LIVE MUSIC
Several bars and cafés host a weekly live music night. Friday nights at **Vía Vía** (75 meters south of the Servicio Agrícola Gurdián,

tel. 505/2311-6142, www.viaviacafe.com) are a must; for current listings, ask the folks at **CocinArte** (across from the north side of La Iglesia el Laborío). On Wednesdays, go to **La Olla Quemada** (1 block west of La Casa de Rubén Darío) with a nice atmosphere and variety of performing artists; Thursdays are salsa night, where you may find León's salsa aficionados dancing *casino* or *rueda* salsa. **Tequetzal** (half a block west of the central park) regularly hosts live music.

Theater

El Teatro Municipal José de la Cruz Mena (1 block south of the southwest corner of the central park, tel. 505/2311-1788) is the cultural heart of the city, open to the public for half-hour theater tours during the day with all kinds of events at night. Some big-name performers prefer León over Managua.

Festivals and Events

June 1 is the celebration of Somoza's defeat in León. August 14 is **La Gritería Chiquita,** when devout Catholics celebrate being spared from Cerro Negro's frequent eruptions. The first week of December is huge, with loud, firework-festooned celebrations of the Immaculate Conception. León celebrates its *fiestas patronales* on September 24 and the weeks surrounding it. León's **Semana Santa** celebrations are acclaimed throughout Nicaragua as the nation's most lively. In addition to tons of food and drink, local artisans craft religious scenes in beds of colored sawdust worked painstakingly by hand.

SHOPPING

León is a dream for thrift store lovers. Find plenty of used clothes in the various *pacas* (named for the enormous packs of used clothing that arrive from the U.S.) lining the streets. Check out **Flor de Nicaragua** (75 meters west of the San Francisco Church, in front of Libélula café, tel. 505/2311-7313) for Nicaraguan crafts and art such as ceramics and handmade bags. **Kaman** (just off the southwest corner of the plaza, Mon.-Sat.

9am-6pm with a break for lunch) has crafts and clothes from around Latin America, artsy postcards, and some Nicaraguan children's books. For beautiful handmade weavings made by a family co-op in León, visit the home/studio **Textiles La Fé** (6.5 blocks north of the Recollection Church, tel. 505/8867-0074, textillafe@gmail.com).

For books (and old Sandinista money), look for the sidewalk vendors near the plaza. The best shop is **Librería Don Quijote** (2 blocks west of the park, Mon.-Sat. 8am-7pm), an interesting new and used bookshop that sells many old Sandinista titles. There's a sprawling market near the bus terminal and a smaller one immediately behind the cathedral with a selection for local shoppers, but not many crafts.

RECREATION
Baseball

León has won more baseball championships than any other city in Nicaragua. Catch a game during the season (Jan.-May). Ask any taxi driver when the next game is and if they'll take you to the stadium on the edge of town.

★ Volcano Boarding

Careening down the black sands of Cerro Negro on a modified snowboard is León's most exciting outdoor adrenaline rush. The slope is a full 40° in places and the ride is fast and hot. Stand-up boards get bogged down, but sitting down, you can build up some serious speed (Bigfoot has clocked clients at over 59 mph). Wear sturdy shoes, long pants, and long sleeves. Plan on a 60-minute climb and a 45-second descent in a hot, rugged landscape. Half-day trips run about $29 per person. The **Bigfoot Hostel** (tel. 505/2315-3863, www. bigfootnicaragua.com) runs daily trips, which include an orange jumpsuit, goggles, gloves, and pads. **Vapues Tours** (tel. 505/2270-1936) and **Tierra Tours** (tel. 505/2311-0599, tierratour.com, tierratour@gmail.com) also make daily trips to Cerro Negro with experienced guides, and can pick you up and drop you off at your hotel. This adventure has its risks:

volcano boarders climbing up Cerro Negro

less meet-other-travelers vibe, check out ★ **Casona Colonial Guesthouse** (half a block west of Parque San Juan, tel. 505/2311-3178, $17-45). Its eight rooms, each with queen bed, private bath, hot water, and a fan, represent one of the best bargains in León, complete with high ceilings, flower-filled courtyard, and beautiful wooden furniture.

The city's many international-oriented hostels each cater to a slightly different style. **La Tortuga Booluda** (1.5 blocks west from the San Juan de Dios church, tel. 505/2311-4653, www.tortugaBooluda.com, $5 dorm, private room $10-30) offers a breezy courtyard and has common hangout areas and a communal kitchen excellent for meeting other travelers. La Tortuga feels homey and features a nice book exchange, billiards, coffee, and Wi-Fi. The only meal served is free pancake breakfasts for guests, a fun morning ritual.

Enter ★ **Vía Vía** (75 meters south of the Servicio Agrícola Gurdián, tel. 505/2311-6142, www.viaviacafe.com, $5 dorm, $15-25 private) through its popular multicultural café and information area, then continue walking into a quiet, colonial-style patio where a small selection of dorms and private rooms surround a gorgeous garden. There are two six-bed dorms, and four rooms with private baths, high ceilings, and fans. The building was reportedly built by an Italian in 1760 for his Nicaraguan mistress and her servants. Ask about Spanish classes and salsa dance lessons.

Bigfoot Hostel (from Banco Procredit, half a block south, tel. 505/2315-3863, www.bigfootnicaragua.com, $7 dorm, $21 d) caters to backpackers, surfers, and anyone else who enjoys sipping a delicious mojito while seated in a small, footprint-shaped swimming pool. This is the biggest hostel in León, so expect a lively party scene. **Lazy Bones** (2.5 blocks north of Parque de los Poetas, tel. 505/2311-3472, www.lazybonesLeón.com, $8 dorm, $20-30 private) is centrally located. The kicker here is the pool, still a rarity in León hotels. Lazy Bones seems to be a quieter option in this price range, offering free lockers, billiards, computers, and lounge space.

Many who try it walk away unscathed and with an intense adrenaline rush, while others leave with broken bones or serious scrapes if they take a tumble.

ACCOMMODATIONS

Dozens of hotels range from backpacker hostels to midrange and luxury hotels, and increased experience with foreign tourists is bringing the quality and the service up. You will sleep well here.

Under $25

Casa Ivana (across from the Teatro Municipal's south side, tel. 505/2311-4423, $6 dorm, $17 s, $19 d) is the best Nicaraguan-owned option, with seven clean, quiet, safe rooms with private baths along a long garden in a family house. **Hostal La Clinica** (around the corner from Casa Ivana, tel. 505/2311-2031, $5 dorm with fan, up to $25 with a/c) is a low-key, friendly, Nicaraguan-owned *hotelito* with a veritable jungle growing in the central patio. For a Nicaraguan family-oriented,

$25-50

Hotel San Juan de León (on the north side of the Plaza Iglesia de San Juan, tel. 505/2311-0547, www.hsanjuandeLeón.com, from $35, includes breakfast) has 20 smallish rooms with fan and private bath (option for a/c) on two floors surrounding a tasteful courtyard and kitchen for guests' use. **Hotel Real** (from the Iglesia Recollección, 1.5 blocks east, tel. 505/2311-2606, hotelreal.León@gmail.com, $40 s, $50 d, includes breakfast) is an excellent, friendly, family option with 14 well-equipped rooms in a nicely furnished, comfortable home with Wi-Fi. Compare several rooms to see what you prefer. Don't miss the lookout point upstairs.

The imposing 30-room compound of **Hotel Europa** (from Iglesia de San Juan, 1 block south and 1 east, tel. 505/2311-6040, heuropaLeón@hotmail.com, $25-35) has been around since the 1960s, when it catered to the train passenger crowd. Recently remodeled and kept clean, it offers a restaurant, lounge areas, Wi-Fi, guarded parking, and its own water and electricity supply.

$50-100

★ **Hotel Posada del Doctor** (1 block west of Parque San Juan, tel. 505/2311-4343, www.laposadadeldoctor.com, $45-60) offers 11 lovely, fully equipped rooms around a bright and pleasant garden.

Expect old colonial stateliness in the 20 wood-adorned rooms at ★ **Hotel Los Balcones** (3 blocks east of the cathedral, tel. 505/2311-0250, www.hotelbalcones.com, balcones@turbonett.com.ni, $47 s, $64 d, includes breakfast). Upstairs rooms have small balconies overlooking the street, plus standard amenities: TV, air-conditioning (discount if you don't use it), hot water, and Wi-Fi. In the center of León, **Hotel Austria** (from the cathedral, 1 block south and half a block west, tel. 505/2311-1206 or 505/2311-7178, www.hotelaustria.com.ni, from $50) is a practical hotel with 35 spotless, modern, air-conditioned rooms with TV, phones, and hot water (heated by solar panels). There is

a continental breakfast and guarded parking for your vehicle. There is an on-site restaurant and comfortable space for relaxing or meetings.

Over $100

Hotel El Convento (next door to the San Francisco Church, tel. 505/2311-7053, www.elconventonicaragua.com, from $92) offers bathtub-equipped rooms with lots of space and history. Parts of the hotel were built with stones used in the convent's original 1639 construction. From the beautiful centerpiece garden and fountain to the long, cool corridors adorned with art and antiques, El Convento impresses. In addition, the hotel offers business and conference services, a ballroom, a restaurant, and local tours for guests.

The rooms at ★ **Hotel La Perla** (1.5 blocks north of Iglesia de la Merced, tel. 505/2311-3125, www.laperlaLeón.com, from $94) are among the classiest anywhere in Nicaragua, combining old-style elegance and antiques with modern comforts like plasma screen TVs and Wi-Fi. This 150-year-old home was lovingly restored by owners with a passion for architecture and history. The two presidential suites sport mirrored dressers, king beds, and mini-bars, both on the second-story balcony with superb views of León's tiled roofs and churches. Hotel La Perla is also a veritable museum of fine art. The hotel offers an excellent breakfast and small pool for guests, plus a white-cloth restaurant with hearty fajita and pasta dishes.

Long-Term Accommodations

A college town, León caters easily to those looking to stay on longer. "Room for Rent" posters are found around the universities and on bulletin boards of the main hostels. In general, expect to pay $150-200 a month for a room with shared kitchen and up to $400 a month for furnished apartments. Check with **Jordan Clark** (1 block and 20 meters north of Parque de los Poetas, tel. 505/2311-0957, 8840-2476, www.nicaraguarealestateLeón.com) or **Green Pathways** (www.greenpathways.

Local Guides and Community Tourism

Who better to show you around León than someone who grew up here? Some of these community tourism projects are made up of people living at the base of the active volcanoes where acid rain and ash often damage crops. Eco-tourism injects much-needed income into the area.

Padre Ramos Tours (tel. 505/8469-9453 or 505/8454-5351, padreramostours@yahoo.com) is a cooperative of guides who can take you to climb the volcanoes San Cristobal and Cosigüina, as well as give tours of the Gulf of Fonseca and the Padre Ramos wetlands. They're one of the few tour groups that have equipment to take you into the crater lake of Cosigüina for a swim.

At the entrance to Cerro Negro you will find a small information center, a *ranchón,* some bathrooms, and a friendly and informative local tourism cooperative called **Las Pilas-El Hoyo** (tel. 505/8495-5672 or 505/8640-7837, www.laspilaselhoyo.com, laspilaselhoyoLeón@yahoo.com, $5). The entrance fee supports conservation efforts and pays a portion of the members' salaries. Cooperative guides can take you on hikes in the area, including the two taller volcanoes, El Hoyo and El Pilas; a nearby swimming hole; and a large reservoir with some of the best views in the country. Sleep nearby at **Eco Albergue El Pilar** (7km from Cerro Negro, 505/8495 5672 or 8744-8124, $15 dorm, $25 private, laspilaselhoyoleon@yahoo.com) run by the cooperative Las Pilas-El Hoyo.

A new cooperative of local guides from the Cosigüina peninsula can take you on hikes of the volcano and through the Estero Real. Contact the coordinator **Don Inés Aquino** (tel. 505/8777-7519) for more information. Among the guides are incredibly knowledgeable locals working on conservation projects on the reserve. They recently tracked down two lost European tourists who had ventured out without a guide by having them describe what types of trees were around!

Telica-Rota Tourism Cooperative (COTUR) (www.TelicaVolcano.com) offers tours either by foot or on horseback to the impressive crater of Volcán Telica, where you can sometimes catch a glimpse of lava. They offer hikes of the surrounding nature reserve including a tour of a bat cave. A new cabin and eco-friendly restaurant are in the works.

The **San Cristobal Tourism Project** (tel. 505/2341-0901, mazzanticlau@gmail.com) can provide local guides to take you up the largest active volcano in Nicaragua or to explore the coffee plantations and forests around the base. They offer options to stay in newly renovated eco-lodges.

In the city of León, explore Sutiaba with **RAISUT R.L.** (tel. 505/8941-3449, omarelim@gmail.com). This cooperative of women are León's "food sherpas," offering a gastronomic tour perfect for foodies. The name of the group translates to "Roots of Sutiaba." They will meet you at your hotel and take you to the market to pick up ingredients for your choice of a traditional Nicaraguan dish, such as *nacatamales* or *indio viejo,* and then teach you how to make it. They offer additional cultural experiences such as learning traditional Nicaraguan dances and visiting a local farm.

com); both keep lists of long-term rentals in León and shared houses on the beach.

FOOD

Of the several huge supermarkets, the most centrally located are **La Unión** (1 block east of the cathedral, Mon.-Sat. 7:30am-8pm, Sun. 8am-6pm) and the new **La Colonia** (in Barrio Zaragoza).

Fritanga and Local Fare

The best finger-lickin' *fritanga* (street-side barbecue and fry-fest) in town is **El Buen**

Gusto (a couple blocks east of the cathedral's south side, Mon.-Sat. 10am-10pm, less than $4). Mix and match from their sidewalk smorgasbord and hubcap grill. The carne asada at the **Estación** (near the old train station, $2-5) offers strong competition for León's best *fritanga* crown; there you'll find several large grills serving mountains of *gallo pinto,* plantains, and fried cheese to an appreciative crowd. When in doubt, or on a Sunday evening when everything else is closed, head to the food grills behind the main cathedral.

Don't be discouraged by this restaurant's

popular name: ★ **La Cucaracha** (3.5 blocks east from the Hospital Heodra, tel. 505/2311-4474, $2-5) is one of León's oldest and most frequented local spots. The nondescript exterior leads to a pleasant back patio that is always crowded. Their specialty is bean soup *(sopa de frijoles)*. (Even when it's boiling outside, Nicaraguans enjoy a good soup to help them sweat and cool off, often accompanied by some rum or beer.) I love the white beans *(frijoles blancos)* served with caramelized onions, cheese, and a hot tortilla.

El Lobito (4 blocks south and a half block east from the Texaco in Sutiaba, tel. 505/ 2311-4146, $2-5) is another León classic. You may be serenaded by mariachis while you enjoy typical Nicaraguan dishes and cold beers. **Pescaditos** (1 block south, 1.5 blocks east from the Sutiaba Church, tel. 505/2311-2684, $3-6) serves tasty fresh seafood and large portions. You can pick out the fish you want before they grill or fry it up.

Cafés

Libélula's (around the corner from La Casa de Rubén Darío, tel. 505/8493-4505, Mon.-Sat. 7:30am-9:30pm, Sun. 8:30am-8pm, $2-8) name comes from a poem by the beloved writer Rubén Darío. It's a popular, centrally located café where you can enjoy smoothies and coffee drinks, including some with liquor (if you need that extra kick). They also serve breakfast, crepes, sandwiches, and main courses.

Take some time out of the heat for a drink or dessert at **Café Rayuela** (1 block north of Iglesia y Convento San Francisco, half a block west, tel. 505/8753-3555), a cute new café run by two young women from León and Chinandega who met at the university. This café serves local products such as organic coffee from a women's cooperative in Somoto and locally made jams and *rosquillas*. The café also hosts cultural events and literacy programs for youth.

Run by a friendly Nicaraguan/Italian couple, **Nicaragüita, Nicaragüita** (2 blocks north of Iglesia de la Merced and 90 meters west, tel. 505/8377-7222, daily 8am-9:30pm, closed Wed.) describes itself as a café/restaurant with Nicaraguan culture and Italian style. They offer lots of vegetarian options and a menu that represents both countries' cuisines. In the evening, the café transforms into a candlelit haven to relax before going out while you sip coffee or a $2 glass of wine. Check out their book exchange in the back.

The French bakery/café **Pan y Paz** (1.5 blocks east of the corner of the banks, tel. 505/8956-5070, Mon.-Sat. 7am-7pm) lives up to its name with tasty baked goods and a peaceful interior courtyard where you can enjoy your treats.

Upscale and International

The restaurant and coffee shop at **CocinArte** (across from the north side of La Iglesia el Laborío, tel. 505/8854-6928, daily 11am-10pm, $6-8) has an incredibly varied and creative menu, including Indian and Middle Eastern dishes found nowhere else in Nicaragua, plus a small selection of chicken and traditional dishes. The reading and lounging space boasts chessboards and tasteful art.

The ★ **Mediterráneo** (2.5 blocks north of Parque de los Poetas, tel. 505/2311-0756, daily 7am-midnight, $6-10) is one of the best options for Italian dishes and pizza. At night on the back patio you can eat under the stars peeking through the leaves of the avocado trees.

Stop in for some tasty Cuban food at **Campestre La Habana** (on the road towards Poneloya, tel. 505/8329-6261, $5-12, pay $2 for pool access) that you can wash down with mojitos or daiquiris. The gregarious Cuban owner is also experimenting with a location in the center of León called **El Bodegón**. Some dishes are traditional Cuban fare like *lechón* (grilled park) and *yucca con* mojo (yucca with garlic sauce), while others display a fusion of Cuban, European, and other Latin American cuisines.

Casa Abierta (2 blocks south and half a block east from the cathedral, on the southern side of Hospital Heodra, tel. 505/2311-0313,

$7-15) is unassuming from the outside. Tucked inside you'll find a restaurant with a beautiful pool and patio, as well as a yoga studio. The name references a song by the Nicaraguan band, Duo Guardabarranco. Both vegetarians and meat-eaters will be happy with the varied menu.

INFORMATION AND SERVICES

Bancentro is one block north of the cathedral. Most of the other banks in the city are clustered in the same area. **ATMs** are located one block east of the cathedral in the **BAC** (open 24 hours with guard, *córdobas* or dollars), at La Unión Supermarket, at gas stations, and in Plaza Siglo Nuevo shopping center.

The **hospital** (1 block south of the cathedral) is in the center of León, though you're probably better off in one of the two private clinics with emergency rooms. **Policlínica la Fraternidad** (in the San Felipe neighborhood, 1 block north and 25 meters east of the San Jose Church, tel. 505/2311-6838) and **Policlínica Occidental** (tel. 505/2311-2722) face each other from opposite sides of the street. Even there, on weekends and after normal business hours, they may not have a doctor on-site.

Tourism Information and Tour Operators

The government **INTUR** office (2.5 blocks north of the cathedral, tel. 505/2311-3682) has brochures, postcards, and updated bus schedules. They are also a good resource to connect you to upcoming community tourism projects and guides. Also visit the student-run **Information Office** (near the northeast corner of the plaza on the side of the new *alcaldía*'s (mayoral) office), which also offers mounds of brochures, plus a gang of eager UNAN co-eds waiting to help you with local information and maps, and to practice their English. Both offices operate Monday-Saturday during normal business hours, including a two-hour lunch break. Also check in the **Casa de Cultura** for local tour services

and classes, and nearly all the youth hostels maintain up-to-date bulletin boards.

León has a number of tour operators that can organize local adventures or trips to other parts of the country, such as **Green Pathways Tours** (tel. 505/2315-0964 or 505/8917-8832, www.greenpathways.com, greenpathways@gmail.com), **Sonati Tours** (tel. 505/8591-9601, www.sonati.org, tours@sonati.org), and **Tierra Tours** (tel. 505/2311-0599, tierratour.com, tierratour@gmail.com). However, with a little extra effort (and usually less money), you can reach local guides and community-run tourism projects blossoming throughout the León/Chinandega region.

For city tours and day trips to nearby sites like León Viejo, San Jacinto Hot Springs, Isla Juan Venado, and others, you can start with **Julio Tours Nicaragua** (Calle Rubén Darío, 1 block east of Iglesia y Convento San Francisco, tel. 505/8625-4467, www.juliotoursnicaragua.com.ni, info@juliotoursnicaragua.com.ni). Julio is popular for his relaxed, homespun services and comes highly recommended.

GETTING THERE AND AWAY

From Managua, take an express *interlocal* from the UCA (best for Masaya and Granada connections) or Mercado Israel Lewites (less than 2 hours, $2). They depart as soon as the microbus fills up 5am-7:30pm. In León, they'll let you off at the main bus station (La Terminal) in the northeast corner of the city grid. If you'd rather not deal with public transportation, ask tour providers and hostels in town about shuttle transport between Granada, San Juan del Sur, and other destinations.

In León, you'll find transportation to most points at La Terminal (except Poneloya and Las Peñitas; buses to these beaches depart from their own terminal in Mercadito Sutiaba). Big yellow buses and small white *interlocales* depart 4am-7pm for both Managua and Chinandega. There are also a few daily expresses to Estelí 4am-3:10pm

LEÓN

Hiking the Maribio Volcanoes

Each volcano along this chain is unique and offers a different sort of adventure. Start early and bring a minimum of three liters of water per person. None of these hikes should be attempted without a guide because unaccompanied tourists have gotten lost and injured. Luckily you won't have any trouble finding a local guide since community tourism projects are growing at the base of many of these volcanoes.

MOMOTOMBO

1,300 meters, 8 hours round-trip

The quintessential cone-shaped volcano, Momotombo rises up from the shores of Lago Xolotlán in a particularly menacing posture, and history has proven that the menace is real. Momotombo is climbable, but it's not easy, especially when you hit the loose volcanic gravel that comprises the upper half of the cone. Your triumphant reward will be one of the best views possible of Lago Xolotlán without use of an airplane. From the Ruinas de León Viejo, head out of town to the main highway and turn right (north) along the highway. Follow that to the geothermal plant, where you'll have to convince the guard to let you through to hike. They're sensitive about people traipsing across their installation, so honor whatever promises you make.

TELICA

1,061 meters, 5-7 hours round-trip

Despite its tendency to spew ash over its namesake town, Volcán Telica makes for a good climb. Take a bus from León to Telica, then follow the road to the community of La Quimera and keep going until the road disappears beneath your feet and becomes the volcano. Alternatively, access the volcano from Santa Clara, the town adjacent to the Hervideros de San Jacinto.

CERRO NEGRO

675 meters, 2 hours round-trip

This is the most frequently active volcano in the chain (its last eruption was August 1999). The lowest and youngest of the Maribios, Cerro Negro rises like a black-sand pimple from the land-

(departure depends on when they fill up) and to Matagalpa 4:20am-2:45pm.

International Transport

Most Central American bus routes include a stop in León. **Tica Bus** (2 blocks north of the San Juan church in Viajes Cumbia traveling agency, tel. 505/2311-6153, www.ticabus.com) offers buses to most Central American capitals and Mexico. Two blocks west of the San Juan church is an authorized **TransNica** agency (tel. 505/2311-5219) with bus service to Costa Rica, Honduras, and El Salvador.

Viajes Mundiales (from the cathedral, 3 blocks north, half a block east, tel. 505/2311-6263 or 505/2311-5920, viajesmu@ibw.com.ni, Mon.-Fri. 8am-noon and 2pm-6pm, Sat. until

1pm) is a full international agency and official representative of major airlines.

GETTING AROUND

To get anywhere within the city, **taxis** charge $0.75 during the day and $1.25 at night per person. Small city buses and converted pickup trucks also crisscross León and charge about $0.25; ask about your destination before getting on.

Don't miss León's answer to London's double-decker bus tours: **El Bus Pelón** (The Bald Bus, Sat.-Sun. 5pm-10pm, free) runs 30-minute rides around the city, sometimes featuring live *chichero* music. Line up at the southwest corner of the central park. The locals love it!

The only official car rental agency in León

scape, completely free of vegetation and scorching hot when there is no cloud cover. A road leads from León to the base; from there, follow the makeshift "trail," part of which will have you scrambling over awkward rocks and fighting surprisingly strong wind. The trail loops around the steaming crater, which the brave may enter at their own risk. If the gaseous wind blows across your path, move fast to get out of it. You can also descend into the second crater accessible from the summit, again at your own risk. Getting out of this one is much harder and much hotter, so make sure you are in good shape. Going down is easy: run, skip, and hop down the backside or zoom down on a board. There are a number of approaches; the most common heads due east from León, near the town of Lechecuago. Leave early in the morning to beat the heat and avoid the afternoon thunderstorms. The metals in Cerro Negro attract lightning better than the taller volcanoes nearby, so don't test it.

SAN CRISTÓBAL

1,745 meters, 8 hours round-trip
This is the granddaddy of volcano hikes in the Pacific region. It's long but the grade is moderate and even easy compared to some of the other volcano hikes. You'll need a guide to help you wend your way through the myriad fields, farms, and fences that obstruct the path upward (and which change every planting season).

COSIGÜINA

860 meters, 6 hours round-trip to edge of crater, 11 hours round-trip to crater lake
Literally, it's a walk in the woods and then you're at the vegetation-carpeted crater lip with crazy views. Start walking from Potosí, or rent horses. Head back along the road toward the community of La Chacara, where the slope of Cosigüina is most amenable for climbing. From the edge of the crater, you can see across the Gulf of Fonseca into El Salvador. For those up to the extra challenge, there are some tours that can take you down into the crater lake, such as Padre Ramos Tours. To do so you will need to use ropes. Since the hike is longer, it can be broken into a two-day camping trip. Be careful: Hikers have died on this volcano.

is **Dollar,** run out of the Casa Pellas dealership (tel. 505/2311-3371) in the southern part of town. You'll need a four-wheel drive if you're driving up to Cosigüina or on surf safari to coastal roads. They can order up special cars (roughly $100/day) from Managua or Chinandega if you give them time. You can also find individual cars and drivers for rent by inquiring through the main tour operators and your hotel.

SOUTH OF LEÓN
★ Las Ruinas de León Viejo

The sleepy ruins of Spain's first settlement in Nicaragua, **Las Ruinas de León Viejo** (Mon.-Sat. 8am-5pm, Sun. 8am-4pm, hours strictly observed by bribe-resistant guards,

$3 plus a small fee to take photographs or video) make for an easy day trip from León. Francisco Hernández de Córdoba founded the first León in 1524. Pedrarias Dávila governed it. After two years, for reasons unknown, Dávila had Hernández de Córdoba decapitated in the town square. In 1610, Volcán Momotombo erupted, burying the site under ash. But León may have already been abandoned following a series of premonitory earthquakes that convinced the settlers to look elsewhere for a place to call home. (Momotombo has erupted several times since then, most recently in 1905.)

Dr. Carlos Tünnerman and a team from the National University (UNAN) first uncovered the ruins of old León in 1966. In

2000, archaeologists found the remains of both Córdoba and Dávila and placed them in an on-site mausoleum. León Viejo is now a UNESCO World Heritage Site. The Nicaraguan Culture Institution has completed fascinating excavations and has trained many local guides, most of whom are friendly and speak passable English.

The ruins are located just adjacent to Puerto Momotombo. Turn off the highway at La Paz Centro (at the statue of an indigenous warrior). Most travelers go on tours organized by their hotel or a tour company in León, but you can do it by yourself as well. Catch a bus from León to La Paz Centro, then take either an 8am or 11am bus to the ruins. The last return bus from the ruins departs at 3pm. For more info, call the **Palacio Nacional de la Cultura in Managua** (tel. 505/2222-2905, ext. 112).

Volcán Momotombo and Momotombito Island

Volcán Momotombo is the most challenging Pacific volcano to climb, and it is one of Nicaragua's more active volcanic peaks. While the small town of El Cardón, on the other side of Volcán Momotombo is closer, the town itself is difficult to get to from the highway.

Momotombo's little sibling, **Momotombito Island,** was once a pre-Columbian religious sanctuary, when the islet was called Cocobolo. Today, it is an uninhabited natural reserve of tropical dry forest. First, head to the town of Puerto Momotombo, where for the right price, many fishermen will be eager to transport you the 25 kilometers along the north shore of Lake Managua to the island. Bring water and supplies to last two days in order to camp on the island, and don't pay your boatman until he returns to take you off the island. The island reportedly contains petroglyphs and the faintest remnants of the previous civilization who would be horrified to see what has become of their precious lake.

Nagarote

About halfway between Managua and León,

Quesillos

Quesillos, a snack of mozzarella-like cheese, sour cream, and vinegar-soaked onions wrapped in a hot tortilla, is a classic Nicaraguan street food. Nagarote and La Paz Centro are the most sought out places for this creamy, salty goodness in León. The towns' rivalry over the best *quesillo* extends to who holds the record for the world's largest *quesillo.* Although they have some competition to the southeast as Chontales recently made a 1,233-foot-long *quesillo,* breaking the last record (and feeding 4,000 people!). You'll find roadside restaurants that cater to León-Managua travelers, many of whom plan their trips around a stop in Nagarote or La Paz Centro just to grab a bite. One favorite is **Quesillos Güiligüiste** (off from the main road in La Paz Centro).

the historic village of Nagarote's claim to fame is an enormous, old *genícero* **tree** (2 blocks north and 1 block west from the central park) dating to the time of Columbus, whose broad branches shade the small market. The tree is next to a **statue of Diriangén.** Nagarote has a **Casa de Cultura** (1 block south of the tree).

WEST OF LEÓN

Exactly halfway to the coast from León, look for the turnoff to **Rancho Los Alpes** (Km 100.5, León-Poneloya road, tel. 505/8803-7085, rancholosalpes@gmail.com), an old-style ranch house with nice rooms filled with handmade furniture and interesting antiques. This is an excellent spot for groups, with service and tour opportunities, excellent food and barbecues, as well as horseback riding and other day trips to beaches and volcanoes.

Poneloya and Las Peñitas Beaches

Only a 20-minute drive toward the coast from León (on a road completed in 2009), Poneloya has been a playground of the Leónese elite for generations. Nearby Las Peñitas is better developed for foreign travelers who come looking for beginner surfing waves and nature excursions into the Isla Juan Venado Wildlife Reserve. During Semana Santa, hotels at both beaches swell to capacity and double their rates.

PONELOYA

The road from León splits when it reaches the coast. The right fork leads to Poneloya. Poneloya has a vicious undertow that makes it dangerous for casual swimmers; bathers die every year. The *estero* (estuary) is safer than the ocean, a fact not overlooked by lots of children who come to splash around.

Marítimos (150 meters west of the entrance on right-hand side, tel. 505/2317-0378, $30 d) is the only hotel in town, remodeled in 2010 and now offering 15 rooms with private bath, fan, and air-conditioning. It's simple and not quite on the beach, but essentially clean. A better option is a five-minute boat ride away, on Isla Los Brasiles. There, the **Surfing Turtle Lodge** (tel. 505/8640-0644, www.surfingturtlelodge.com, $12 dorm, $35 d) has one dormitory and several rooms or the option to pitch a tent, plus surfing lessons and rentals, horseback riding, biking, yoga, massages, fishing, and turtle-watching.

For food, **El Pariente Salinas** is the only restaurant in the middle of Poneloya. A better option is to walk north up the beach to La Bocana, where you will find a group of restaurants, all of which let you choose a fish to be fried whole. The last one, **El Chepe** (La Bocana, $4-10), is the best, and the only establishment in the area that accepts credit cards.

★ LAS PEÑITAS BEACH

Las Peñitas is more popular than Poneloya among beginner surfers, since the waves are mellower and there are many boards for rent. It's a rare exception along this stretch of Nicaragua's Pacific shoreline, where the waves are less forgiving than the beaches around San Juan del Sur; they break faster and with more force, and the currents are stronger.

Traveling several kilometers south along the coast will bring you to a series of accommodations that make up Las Peñitas, presented here in order from north to south. **Playa Roca** (3 miles south of Poneloya, tel. 505/2317-0224, www.playaroca.com, $7 dorm, $25-45) has two dormitories, eight cozy rooms, and a popular bar-restaurant (Sun.-Thurs. until midnight, Fri.-Sat. until 2am). The view of the rocks and the waves is one of the best on the beach and the large *pasillo* (patio) is ideal for reading, playing pool, and watching the sunset.

Hotel Suyapa Beach (tel. 505/2317-0217 or 505/8885-8345, www.suyapabeach.com, info@suyapabeach.com, $35-90) is a modern, well-kept hotel and restaurant with 22 rooms around a small pool. The food and service here is reportedly the best on the beach.

French-owned **Hotelito El Oasis** (tel. 505/8839-5344, www.oasislaspenitas.com, aixpat426@hotmail.com, $7 dorm, $20 d) has reasonable rates, spacious rooms, and slow service. But what's the rush? Rooms have fans and private baths. Enjoy the small *rancho* and hammock area with a great second-story view of the beach. Like most other places on the beach, they rent surfboards and can arrange tours of Isla Juan Venado or Spanish lessons ($4/hour). Around the corner and past the local bars of Los Cocos and El Calamar, you'll find the **Lazy Turtle** (tel. 505/8546-7403, thelazyturtlehotel@gmail.com, $30, includes breakfast), run by a Canadian couple who got tired of the cold. They serve tasty Mexican food and burgers, including a noteworthy veggie burger. **Restaurante y Cyber Manojito** (tel. 505/8789-2804, reynercalderon@yahoo.es) offers seafood, cocktails, surf lessons, and local tours.

At the end of the road, ★ **Hotel de la Playa Barca de Oro** (tel. 505/2317-0275, www.barcadeoro.com, info@barcadeoro.com, $7 dorm, $32 cabana) remains the clear favorite among travelers, with its range of accommodations from dorms to cabanas (includes fan, mosquito net, and private bath) that sleep up to four. The food here is fantastic. La Barca looks directly out to the northern tip of Isla Juan Venado, only 100 meters away across a protected lagoon. They can help you arrange all kinds of local (and inland) excursions. You can also rent kayaks and horses and hire sportfishing guides and locals for massages and pedicures.

GETTING THERE
Buses for Poneloya leave every 45 minutes from the Sutiaba Mercadito, from early in the morning until 6pm. They stop first in Poneloya, idling for 10 minutes, then continue to Las Peñitas; the trip to the end of the road at Barca de Oro takes about 30 minutes with the new road. You'll save time if you take a taxi from León ($8-10, not bad if you have three or four people to split the cost). The last bus back to León leaves Barca de Oro at 6:30pm, so you can easily do a day trip and end up back in your colonial room in León for dinner.

★ Isla Juan Venado Wildlife Reserve

The 21-kilometer strip of tropical dry forest, mangroves, and inland estuary south of Las Peñitas provides habitat for hundreds of species of migratory birds, as well as crocodiles and other wetland creatures, and is also an important nesting beach for sea turtles.

Many León-based tour operators run trips to Isla Juan Venado, but you can just as easily go to the **visitor's center** (down the beach from the Barca de Oro, tel. 505/8330-5947 or 505/8629-3823, odgqnic@gmail.com) to arrange a tour with the community's cooperative. Or better yet, arrange your trip at least one day in advance, especially if you plan on a sunrise excursion, when you'll see the most wildlife (late afternoons are good, too). Take sun protection and lots of water. They offer different boat tours ($40-100 depending on your destination). Also available are nighttime turtle-viewing trips (seasonal, Aug.-Dec., $10) with necessary guided camping ($10). The cooperative recently opened a rustic cabin if you would like to spend the night

on the island, which is when you will see the most turtles laying eggs or recently hatched turtles braving their way to the ocean. Some of the hazards in the reserve include caimans, bees, snakes, and crab and turtle egg hunters frustrated by poverty, so bringing a local guide is a really good idea.

The community helps with reforestation of the mangrove forests, turtle monitoring, and other types of ecological research in cooperation with the organization FUNDAR. Like many protected areas in Nicaragua, Isla Juan Venado is co-managed by the local community and an NGO, in this case LIDER. This is one of the most successful examples of the COMAP (co-management) program in Nicaragua, and the ranger station can be a good source of information on this topic, as well as other issues concerning the flora and fauna of the reserve.

You can also access the reserve from the rustic community of Salinas Grandes on the south side of the island, where you can rent kayaks and stay in beachfront *ranchos* at **Rigo's Guest House** (tel. 505/2311-3306 or 505/8868-1569, rigosampson@gmail.com). Make arrangements at least one week in advance to make sure that Rigo is ready.

El Velero and El Tránsito Beaches

Local surf information (there are several world-class waves in the region) is fiercely guarded by those in the know. These beaches have enormous potential for tourism, and a few surf tour providers operate out of nice homes along the coast. One of those is **Surf Tours Nicaragua** (tel. 505/8438-4522, U.S. tel. 619/946-3434, www.surftoursnicaragua. com, surftoursnica@gmail.com), offering all kinds of activity-based, all-inclusive packages. If they have space, they may accept you for nightly rates.

South from León, the gorgeous two-kilometer stretch of white-sand beach known as **El Velero** (The Sailboat) has tremendous tourist potential but is occupied by summer homes for wealthy Leóneses. Buses for Puerto Sandino and El Velero leave from the station at León. The limited options for travelers are not cheap and have fallen into total disrepair. It's better to visit for the day.

A quiet fishing community 60 kilometers from Managua along the old highway to León, **El Tránsito** was devastated by the tidal wave of December 1992. The Spanish helped them recover and built what is now the new town on the hills above the old one, which was at the shoreline. The swimming here can be tricky, as there's a strong undertow that will pull you north along the cove. Walk south along the shoreline to see the rock formations and popular swimming holes behind them. These rocks run parallel to the shoreline and buttress the full blow of waves. Splash around in one of them at high tide, when the waves strike the rocks and rush up and over in an exhilarating saltwater shower. Ten minutes' walk north along the shoreline takes you to the wreckage of **El Balneario,** an old abandoned vacation spot. Enjoy cheap, cold beer and fresh fish on the south end of the village. Buses leave Managua from Mercado Israel Lewites daily 11:15am, 12:40pm, and 2pm. Buses leave El Tránsito daily 5am, 6am, and 7am.

The active Volcán Telica has a tendency to spew ash.

NORTH OF LEÓN
★ Telica-Rota Protected Area

At the Telica-Rota reserve you can have the thrilling and breathtaking experience of standing at the edge of an active volcano. You can also enjoy hikes with stunning views of the rest of the Maribios volcanic chain. If you choose to hike up from San Jacinto, where you can enjoy bubbling muddy hot springs, take a bus to any town off the Telica/San Isidrio highway, such as Malpaisillo and El Sauce, and ask to be dropped in San Jacinto. You can also arrange a tour with Telica's tourist cooperative. Take a bus from León towards Chinandega and ask to be dropped off at the entrance of Telica, where a new visitor's center is in the works, and you can arrange to meet up with a guide. At the moment you either need to hike from the entrance or have a vehicle with 4WD to get closer to the crater.

Los Hervideros de San Jacinto

On the southeast flank of 1,061-meter Volcán Telica, **Los Hervideros de San Jacinto** (daily 7am-5pm, $1) are a warren of boiling mud pits and thermal vents, which have formed a veritable martian landscape not far from León. The vents testify to the region's geothermal electric potential, an opportunity that has not gone unnoticed by potential foreign investors that continue to explore the idea of producing energy from the vast reserves that are forming the vents. To get there, take a bus from León bound for Estelí, San Isidro, or Malpaisillo and get off at the town of San Jacinto (approximately 25 kilometers from León). The entrance is marked by an enormous arch and a posse of women and children selling "artifacts" from the hot springs. The boys will offer to guide you around for $1 or less, which is worth it, considering the danger of falling into a scalding mud bath. Community-based tourism projects and trail improvements are in the works, as is a new hotel.

El Sauce

In the foothills of the Segovia Mountains, a 90-minute drive northeast of León, the village of **El Sauce** (rhymes with WOW-seh) was once the eastern terminus of the railroad that received inland-grown Nicaraguan coffee bound for the port at Corinto. In the 1800s, caravans of mules lumbered into town laden with thousands of pounds of coffee beans. El Sauce has since faded into a sleepy cowboy village whose pride and joy is a breathtaking **colonial church** built in 1750 in tribute to the patron saint, Nuestro Señor de Esquípulas (also known as El Cristo Negro, or the Black Christ). El Sauce celebrates its *fiestas patronales* during the third and fourth weeks of January and attracts a massive pilgrimage (as many as 25,000 people!) from all over Nicaragua to view the Black Christ icon.

El Sauce makes a fine first stop on pueblo-hopping routes toward Achuapa, San Juan de Limay, and Estelí. Buses run daily from Managua and León.

ACCOMMODATIONS AND FOOD

There are a couple of places to eat in town, and several simple *hospedajes* for lodging: try **Hotel Blanco** (from the *Alcaldía*, 1 block south, 1 block west, tel. 505/2319-2403, $8 s, $12 d with fan, $16 s, $20 d with a/c) or **Hotel El Viajero** (from Casa Cural 50 meters east, tel. 505/2319-2325, $3 shared bath, $5 private bath and TV). If you're going to stay here though, a better option is to sample El Sauce's unique community-based tourism project, **Sauce Aventuras** (1 block west of the bus station, tel. 505/2319-2239 or 505/8691-8939, sauceaventuras@gmail.com). They rent bicycles ($5/day, $2/two hours) and provide local history tours. Ask to see the church, the railroad line (with great views), swimming holes in the river, farm tours, and more. They also manage the **Casa Huéspedes** guesthouse program ($16/night with 3 meals, $11/night with breakfast only), where you can stay in a local home.

Their most spectacular offering is an overnight excursion to **Los Altos de Ocotal.** The Ocotal mountain peak is one of the most spectacular views in Nicaragua. Stay with a host family ($8, includes breakfast) or in a cabin ($5-8). There are hiking trails, horseback riding, and various tours all in gorgeous pine forest (tours $3.50-4 pp). Pick up organic coffee and export-quality pine needle baskets. You can reach the cooperative in a *ruta* (small truck, $1 pp) that leaves the bus station daily 2pm and comes back to El Sauce 7am.

Chinandega

The provincial capital of Chinandega is the last major town before the Güasaule border with Honduras, and also the gateway to Nicaragua's distant corner of the Gulf of Fonseca. It's a town you'll get to know well if you are stocking up for a visit to the desolate coastline or the unvisited crater wall of Volcán Cosigüina. It's also undisputedly the hottest corner of the nation.

The same threatening volcanoes that loom over the city of Chinandega and its surrounding plains are also responsible for the high fertility of the soil. Chinandega suffers the same poverty as the rest of the nation, but also boasts a prosperous community of old and new money, based primarily in sugar, bananas, peanuts, sesame, soy, and shrimp. The agricultural activity of the region and proximity to the northern borders and Port of Corinto make Chinandega Nicaragua's most important agribusiness center. The U.S. marines occupied Corinto in the late 19th century. Later, the United States illegally mined the harbor during the Contra war. Cotton was the number-one cash crop in the 1960s, but the deforestation and agro-chemicals essential to its production caused monumental environmental damage that affects life to this day. In recent years, Nicaragua has started exploring organic cotton production.

More Nicaraguans migrate from Chinandega than from anywhere else in the country except Managua. Many head north to America, unlike in other parts of the country, where people mainly migrate south to Costa Rica. So you may find Chinandeganos who speak English or know your neighborhood.

ORIENTATION

You can easily see Chinandega's colonial churches and central market in a couple of hours before stopping to catch your breath. Chinandega's two hubs of activity are the area surrounding the *Mercado Bisne* (from the English word business) and the town center, or simply, *el centro*. The Mercadito is located two blocks north of the central park, and the Central Market a few blocks east of the park, along the Calle Central. La Rotonda los Encuentros and the Texaco StarMart are both important reference points you'll pass on your way into town. Everything is walkable, but drink lots of water. Taxis are plentiful and cost $0.40 within city limits; *ruta* buses in town are $0.10.

SIGHTS

Chinandega's picturesque churches are worth a look. Check out **La Iglesia El Calvario's** (in Barrio El Calvario) white- and blue-tiled ceiling, the colonial **Our Lady Santa Ana Parish** (in the central park), the sky-blue facade of the **Sanctuary of Our Lady of Guadalupe** (from the Uno, 50 meters north), and the austere exterior of **Saint Anthony Church** (2 blocks south of the central park), historically frequented by the city's moneyed crowd.

ENTERTAINMENT AND EVENTS

For dancing, especially on Saturdays, the **Dilectus Disco** (east of town on the road to León) is popular with well-off locals, but overpriced and ridiculously loud. If you prefer a looser, younger crowd and still want air-conditioning, try **Montserat** (on the highway to Güasaule, Wed. is mariachi night), or better still, **La Terraza** (on the road to El Corinto), which has an open-air *rancho* (thatch-roofed restaurant). It's pleasant, with dancing on the weekend, decent food, and a clean swimming pool!

ACCOMMODATIONS

Backpacker hostels with dormitories haven't made a splash in Chinandega yet like they

Chinandega

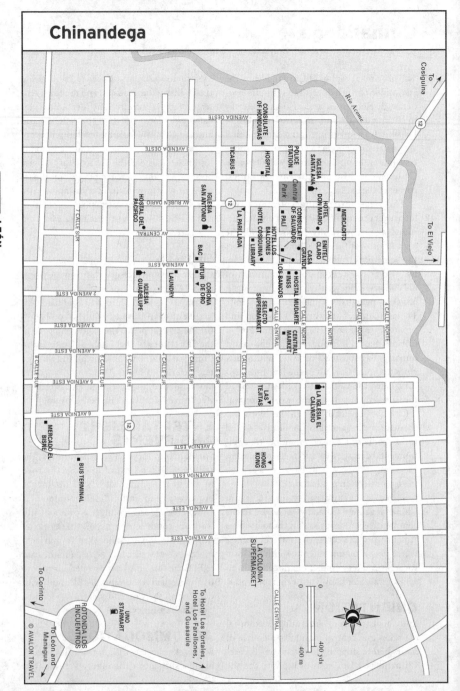

© AVALON TRAVEL

have in León, but you will find many cozy hotels as well as more upscale options that are still reasonably priced for their level of luxury.

Under $25

The centrally located **Hostal Mudarte** (next to the INSS, tel. 505/2341-2820 or 505/7741-6241, hostalmudarte@gmail.com, $12 single w/fan, $25 single with a/c) is affordable, with friendly hosts and simple but pleasant rooms named after different attractions in Chinandega. The owners also have a neighboring smoothie shop.

Hotel Don Mario (170 meters north of Enitel, tel. 505/2341-4054, hoteldonmario@hotmail.com, from $20 d) offers a peaceful space decorated by the owner's own artwork and filled with plants and flowers hanging from the interior courtyard. Rooms include cable, Wi-Fi, private bathrooms, and some have air-conditioning.

$25-50

Centrally located **Hotel Los Balcones** (75 meters north of the corner of the banks, tel. 505/2341-8994, www.hotelbalcones.com, Chinandega@hotelbalcones.com, $40-75, includes breakfast) is an excellent option offering free Wi-Fi, hot water, cable TV, and laundry services. If it is booked, they can send you to their nearby sister hotels: **Hotel Cosigüina** and **Hostal del Pacífico.**

Hotel San José (2.5 blocks north of the corner of the banks, tel. 505/2341-2723 or 505/8474-6845, hotel_sanjose@hotmail.com, includes breakfast and coffee, $30 s, $40 d) is a cozy family-run hotel with a back terrace, hot water, air-conditioning, cable, and Wi-Fi.

Casa Grande (tel. 505/2341-4446, www.hotelcasagrandenicaragua.com), one of Chinandega's longest standing hotels, was going through renovations at the time of research, so check their website for updates. The friendly owner, Don Álvaro, helps organize volcano expeditions to San Cristobal with newly trained local guides as part of a community tourism project or arrange lodging at the foot of Nicaragua's tallest active volcano at their cabin, **La Hacienda Las Rojas,** where they also produce coffee.

Over $50

Hotel Los Portales (500 meters north of the Rotonda Los Encuentros, tel. 505/2342-9190, www.hotelosportales.com, reservaciones@hotelosportales.com, $75-200) is an elegant, luxurious option conveniently located off the Pan-American Highway. Choose from one of the plush rooms or suites and then lounge by the pool or soak in the views of the San Cristobal volcano from the terrace.

Hotel Farallones (300 meters north of Hotel Los Portales, tel. 505/2342-9160, www.faralloneshotel.com, info@faralloneshotel.com, $70 s, $90-100 d) offers upscale accommodations and includes its own pool, club, bar, and karaoke.

FOOD

There are two fully stocked supermarkets here: **El Palí** (in front of the park) and **El Selecto** (3.5 blocks east of the park). Food choices range from every type of street food imaginable in thousands of coolers, stands, and baskets all over town, to the *comida corriente* (meals less than $2) in any of the markets, to a host of expensive restaurants. Good Salvadoran *pupusas* are found in the central park. Or head to Calle Central to **Las Tejitas** (7 blocks east of the park, open evenings, under $3). This may be the best *fritanga* in Nicaragua, a bold statement indeed, but so say the stream of regular clients. Sit outside on the sidewalk and enjoy a heaping plate of juicy roasted chicken, *gallo pinto, tajadas* (fried plantain chips), and any number of deep-fried delicacies. Another good *fritanga* is **La Parrillada** (about 100 meters south of Palí, tel. 505/2341-3745, open all day, $4-8) with free delivery and buffet, grill, fry, and rotisserie options.

The best Chinese food, and in an air-conditioned setting, is **Hong Kong** (2.5 blocks east of the Esso station, $4-8). Nicaraguanized Chinese food is at **Corona de Oro** (1.5 blocks east of Iglesia San Antonio, $5), with large portions and good service.

Many fancy restaurants abound along the highways in and out of town, including **Restaurante Los Vitrales** (Hotel Los Volcanes, Km 129.5, Carretera a Chinandega, tel. 505/2341-1000, Sun.-Thurs. 6am-11pm, Fri.-Sat. untill midnight, $8-11). Options include juicy, bacon-wrapped filet mignon.

INFORMATION AND SERVICES

INTUR (1.5 blocks south of Selecto, tel. 505/2341-1935, chinandega@intur.gob.ni) maintains an office full of brochures and has a staff who are surprisingly helpful as long as you sign in. Find lots of useful info about lodging, restaurants, tours, and sites at visitchinandega.com.

In town, you'll find the **police** (the entire block along the west side of the central park) and the **hospital** (across the street to the south of the police). Moneychangers work the streets near the central market. Most of Chinandega's **banks** are clustered on *la esquina de los bancos* (corner of banks), two blocks east of the park. Find **ATMs** at **Banco America Central** (BAC), **StarMart,** and **On the Run.**

For laundry, head to **Lavamatic Express** (north of Iglesia Guadelupe, tel. 505/2341-3319, Mon.-Sat. 7am-9pm, Sun. 8am-5pm).

International Consulates

Local consulates include **Consulate of El Salvador** (eastern side of the corner of the banks, tel. 505/2341-2049, Mon.-Fri. 8am-2pm), **Honduran Consulate** (across from Claro, tel. 505/2341-0949, Mon.-Fri. 8:30am-4:30pm), and **Costa Rican Consulate** (half a block north from Banpro, tel. 505/2341-1584, Mon.-Fri. 8:30am-5pm, Sat. until noon). When applying for an El Salvador visa, leave your passport before 11am.

GETTING THERE AND AWAY

The main bus station is at **Mercado Bisne** (past Rotonda los Encuentros). From La Rotonda, highways run north to Somotillo and the border with Honduras at Güasaule, southeast to León and Managua, south to Corinto, and three daily buses to Matagalpa. Service to Managua, León, and the border runs daily 4am-7pm. A second bus station located at **El Mercadito** (north of the central park) provides service to all points north: El Viejo, Jiquilillo, Potosí, Cosigüina, and Puerto Morazán.

Even though there is a **Tica Bus** agency in town, those traveling north into Honduras or El Salvador will have to go to Managua to catch the bus, which no longer stops in Chinandega. Any foreigner entering El Salvador must have a visa. Get yours at the Salvadoran Consulate. Contact tour companies in León for the latest.

Car rentals starting at $35 a day are available at the **Avis** (in Hotel Cosigüina) and **Budget** (in Hostal Las Mañanitas). There is also a **Dollar** office (Casa Pellas).

EL VIEJO

A few kilometers west of Chinandega, El Viejo is a cheerful town of some 50,000 Viejanos. Less service-oriented than its big neighbor, El Viejo can still launch you on your next adventure. El Viejo is much older than Chinandega. Originally an indigenous community called Tezoatega, for the fierce cacique who once ruled it, the town was renamed for the old Spaniard who arrived in 1562 carrying a sacred image of the Virgin Mary. According to legend, when the Spaniard tried to sail back to Spain, the Virgin created a hurricane so that she would be returned to her new home in Nicaragua. The old man complied, and the image soon became the most important Virgin Mary in the country. Her fame has lasted through the centuries, and in 1996 the Pope himself recognized her when he came to declare El Viejo's church a *Basilica Minor*.

Buses arrive half a block north of the basilica, across the street from the market where you'll find the cheapest eats. Buses called *interlocales* back to Chinandega leave from the basilica, one block west of the park, and run until about 11pm.

Sights

The **Basilica of the Immaculate Conception of Mary** in the center of town is impressive. Its famed statue of Mary is still located here, and the baptismal font dates back to 1560.

Entertainment and Events

Nightlife in El Viejo is exciting for a small city. The clean and well-liked **Lety's Bar** (north of the basilica), formerly Tezoatega (well known even in León), has good food and service, lots of music, and karaoke on Thursdays and Fridays. **La Piscina** (2 blocks north of the basilica and half a block east) is almost as good, with dancing Thursday-Saturday. Their swimming pool costs $0.75 to use on Sundays.

El Viejo's *fiestas patronales* are the week of December 6, with firework-spitting bulls every night, culminating in the **Lavada de la Plata** (at the basilica), when even the

president and national ballet show up to help wash the church silver.

Accommodations

There are few good accommodation options, so you may opt to stay in Chinandega or León. An option in town is **Charly's Hotel and Restaurant** (20 meters north of the Petronic gas station, tel. 505/2344-0287, hotelrestaurantecharlys@hotmail.com, $20-30) with several simple rooms with air-conditioning, cable TV, and Wi-Fi. The adjacent restaurant/bar has karaoke and music some evenings. The owners strive to create an inclusive environment free of discrimination based on sexual orientation or gender.

CHICHIGALPA

Set in the middle of hundreds of square kilometers of sugarcane are Chichigalpa's **Ingenio San Antonio,** Nicaragua's largest and most powerful sugar refinery, and the **Compañía Licorera,** Nicaragua's alcohol monopoly and source of all the Toña, Victoria, Flor de Caña, and Ron Plata you've been drinking. The two companies belong to the wealthy Pellas family, who founded the sugar refinery in 1890 and have produced

El Viejo's Basilica of the Immaculate Conception of Mary

Sugar Cane's Unsavory Side

Researchers are looking into a mysterious epidemic of kidney disease of unknown origin among Nicaraguan agricultural workers, particularly amongst sugar cane workers in León and Chinandega. This disease is killing thousands of people throughout Central America or leaving them too sick to work. Different theories about the cause of this disease include chronic dehydration from years of working in the overbearing sun, a rare virus, and exposure to chemicals used on sugar plantations. Although no solid link has been made yet between herbicides and the epidemic, sugar cane workers have protested sugar companies in Managua and Chichigalpa.

This is reminiscent of a scourge of health problems banana workers in the region experienced, allegedly from a chemical that some U.S. companies continued using abroad for years even after it was banned in the United States. To this day some U.S. fruit companies are embroiled in disputes about the effects of these agro-chemicals on banana workers' health. Several years ago the Nicaraguan government gave banana workers, mainly from Chinandega and León, homes to replace their camp of makeshift tents of black tarps and banners in front of the National Assembly in Managua where they had been protesting off and on for years. Today they are brightly painted homes of all colors of the rainbow, but you may still see camps of protesting sugar cane workers.

sugar and liquor ever since (except 1988-1992 when the Sandinista government briefly expropriated it).

It's worth the quick bus ride from León or Chinandega into the small town of Chichigalapa for a tour of the **Flor de Caña museum** (tel. 505/2342-9150 ext. 3868 or 505/8588-3039, tours $20 foreigners, $7 nationals). Many hostels can help arrange a tour or call the plant directly in advance to make a reservation. Tours run at 9am, 11am, 2pm, and 4pm. Learn from the friendly, knowledgeable guides how rum is produced from sugar cane to the bottle. Along the way you can taste free samples of delicious aged rum that is arguably among the best in the world.

CORINTO

Nicaragua's primary port complex is the reason for Corinto's existence, linking Nicaragua with the shipping lines of the Pacific. Corinto is 20 kilometers southwest of Chinandega with a couple of halfway decent beaches and a small range of simple hotels and seaside restaurants. Corinto's 20,000 inhabitants live on 49 square kilometers of what is actually a barrier island, connected to the rest of Nicaragua by two small bridges.

Sights and Entertainment

Playa Paso Caballo is located on the northern tip of the island. All buses from Chinandega pass by here before continuing to the center of town. Be careful, as the rip currents are notoriously strong, and keep a close eye on your possessions on these beaches. Several *ranchos* on the beach provide shade, food, and alcohol, but a growing number have succumbed to the beach erosion that began when a spooky, wrecked tanker that had been there for years was finally scrapped. In town, what was once the **Old Railroad Terminal and Customs House** (next to the old railroad station, tel. 505/2342-2383) is now a museum in tribute to the old train. It's well worth a visit.

Accommodations and Food

The family-run **Hospedaje Vargas** (about a block west of the Uno station where buses arrive, tel. 505/2340-5814, $6/s shared bath, $8/s private bath) is simple and has fans in all 10 of its rooms. **Hospedaje Luvy** (1.5 blocks north of the central park, tel. 505/2342-2637, $12 d with fan, shared bath) is similar. All 10 rooms in the **Hotel Central** (across from the port, tel. 505/2342-2380, $40 with a/c, private bath, cable TV) enjoy a view of Corinto's dock operations.

As always, your best bargain is the *comida corriente* in the town market. Otherwise, numerous *cafetíns* dot the town and a row of restaurants flank the town beach. **Restaurante Costa Azul** (1 block south of the *alcaldía*, from $5) and **El Peruano** (1 block south of the *alcaldía*, from $5) have typical meat and seafood dishes. They are pleasant, breezy, open-air *ranchos* with views of the harbor and

islands; hours are casual and all are easy to find, just head downtown and ask. Also consider **New Orleans** (1 block east of the mini-supermarket, $4-10), run by a returned Nica who spent ages in New Orleans, Louisiana's French Quarter.

The best restaurant in town is **El Español** (on the main road to Chinandega, near the bridge from which you can jump into the water, tel. 505/8887-7740, daily 11am-8:30pm, $4-10). The owner makes a mean sangria.

Northwest Coast and Cosigüina Peninsula

Although a trip to the scenic crater that makes up the highest point of Reserva Natural Volcán Cosigüina is the center point of a trip to this area, you can also take a horseback ride, explore, fish, or lounge on the beach.

Access to this northern region is from the Nic-12 highway, most of which was paved with financial support from the U.S. government in 2009. There's no real coastal road to area beaches, only side spurs from Nic-12. Some of the side roads are in better condition than others. Four-wheel drive is still necessary to explore this area. Buses to Cosigüina's scattered northern villages and beaches leave from Chinandega's Mercadito and make stops in El Viejo before continuing northwest. Many of these destinations only have bus service once a day, which means you'll be making an overnight trip if you don't have your own wheels. Most visitors rent a vehicle or arrange a transfer with their hotel.

PLAYA LOS ASERRADORES

Playa Los Aserradores is quiet and desolate, with impressive surf good only for experienced wave-shredders. Beginning surfers will have better luck at nearby Aposentillo and Bahía Santa María.

As you come off the highway before

reaching the coast, look for signs for the turnoff to ★ **Al Cielo Restaurant and Cabañas** (tel. 505/8993-4840, www.alcielonicaragua.com, cabin $20-60, meals $8-13). This gem sits on top of a hill with lovely views of the surrounding mountains and the ocean in the distance. Two friendly French expats, who seriously know their food, prepare delicious Mediterranean meals that are sought out by Nicaraguans from around León and Chinandega. Don't miss their creative rum infusions such as chile with honey and pineapple with vanilla. Spend the night in one of their six cabins, each equipped with its own porch and hammock to enjoy the view, or relax in the pool. Your hosts can help you set up surfing, horseback riding, or kayaking trips and also teach you the French game *petanque*.

Hotel Chancletas (tel. 505/8868-5036, www.hotelchancletas.com, contact@hotelchancletas.com, $10 pp dorm, $35-85) is perched on a grassy rise. Activities include surfing, kayaking, deep-sea fishing, stand-up paddle, volcano tours, horseback riding, and whale-watching (Dec.-Mar.). If all of that makes you exhausted, relax in a hammock or enjoy the full bar and restaurant. Miami native and owner Shay O'Brien is a great source of information and can point the way to nearby breaks. Reservations are a must. Chancletas can also be booked for private retreats.

Joe's Place (near the José de la Cruz Mena school, tel. 505/8804-5646, www.nicaragua-surfhotel.com, portunica@gmail.com, $7 pp) is an affordable, small, family-run hotel. They offer four rooms/dorms that sleep 2-8 people. It's a 20-minute walk to the beach or you can arrange a boat to take you from the nearby estuary to reach a good surfing spot. (They also offer trips to a secret spot.) If you'd like to try your hand at fishing, Joe, an avid sailor and fisher, can take you out on his boat. Doña Aleyda serves fresh seafood and fruit smoothies.

There are also a handful of surf resorts that only offer all-inclusive surf and yoga retreats, such as **El Coco Loco** (www.cocolocoresort.com), home to pro-surfer Holly Beck's all-women surf and yoga retreats, **Surf With Amigas,** and **Rise Up Surf** (www.riseup-surf.com), founded by the former owner of the popular Bigfoot Hostel in León.

This area is also home to Nicaragua's only luxury yacht-docking option, **Marina Puesta del Sol Resort** (www.marinapuest-adelsol.com, from $185), an incongruous mul-timillion-dollar, 600-acre development with gorgeous suites and a dockside restaurant (sandwiches $6-9, seafood entrées $12-23), all with stunning views over the estuary to the San Cristóbal volcano. They have a beach area and pool for events. The rooms are well equipped and nicely laid out. The restaurant offers a huge menu. The Marina hosts the Flor de Caña International Fishing Tournament during the first weekend of December.

There are two daily Los Aserradores buses, leaving from the Mercadito in Chinandega. Buses leave Chinandega around 12:30pm for these areas and return the next day at 5am.

JIQUILILLO AND PADRE RAMOS

Less than a one-hour bus ride from El Viejo, **Playa Jiquilillo** is on a northwest-pointing peninsula of beaches that make this area either a beautiful day trip or an extended, lazy stay of paddling through the wetlands and lazing on the beach. Avoid it during Semana

Santa, when it's overrun. The area remains deserted and undeveloped. Buses make the round-trip from Chinandega to Jiquilillo five times daily 7am-4:30pm. The bus to Jiquilillo continues up the coast, through the Los Zorros barrio, and arrives at the end of the road in the community of Padre Ramos.

A simple fishing village of some 150 dispersed families, **Padre Ramos** is the gateway to the neighboring protected wetlands, and consequently the site of several grassroots tourism projects. You can get a quick boat ride to the community of Venecia across the estuary, where you'll find long stretches of utterly deserted beach. The entire area is a breeding ground for sea turtles, the eggs of which are laid and hatch November-January.

Accommodations and Food

The first lodging you'll reach is owned by a local family: **Vista del Pacífico** (tel. 505/8872-0436, $10-15 with shared bath) has simple, second-story rooms. Enjoy the breeze and view from the hammock on the balcony. Below is a restaurant ($5-10) serving seafood and Italian pizza. To get here, look for a big yellow sign just past the elementary school. Next door you'll find **Don Wilson** (tel. 505/8647-1615), originally from Puerto Cabezas on the Atlantic Coast of Nicaragua. He's famous in town for his delicious coconut and banana breads that he bakes from his home and walks around selling fresh from the oven. If you call in advance he can prepare Caribbean dishes that are hard to find on the Pacific side such as *rondón*, a coconut based soup with fresh seafood.

★ **Rancho Esperanza** (on the main road after Vista del Pacífico, tel. 505/8680-0270 or 505/8879-1795, www.rancho-esperanza.com, rancho.esperanza@yahoo.com, $8 dorm, cabin from $20) is a unique, community-centric operation offering a cluster of bamboo huts and dormitories. You can also pitch a tent or hammock ($5). There is electricity and fans, ecological toilets, lockboxes, books, surfboards, a community garden, and games. Experience low-impact natural living with projects like a kids' club and community center that actively benefit the village. Ask about special rates for volunteers (3-week minimum, some Spanish required). The hostel offers great local food ($2-5 per meal) and will organize excursions to nearby Padre Ramos estuary and Volcán Cosigüina.

Monty's Beach Lodge (just past Rancho Esperanza on the left, tel. 505/8473-3255, www.montysbeachlodge.com, $20 dorm, $35-65 private room, includes breakfast, meals $7-12) offers all inclusive weekly packages or daily rates. You can surf the waves as well as the net with Wi-Fi. They have surf and boogie boards for rent. In addition to the beach, you can lounge by the pool, play volleyball, rent a kayak, or enjoy yoga. Ask about setting up fishing tours, volcano boarding in Cerro Negro, hiking volcano Cosigüina, or kayaking through the mangroves.

Rancho Tranquilo (farther up the beach, tel. 505/8814-2245 or 505/8968-2290, $7 dorm, $20-28 private hut) has beachside bamboo-thatch huts with cement floors, mosquito nets, and shared toilets and showers. Features include a good learning beach for surfing and an open *rancho* right at the waterline. Ask about English-teaching and Spanish-learning opportunities. Rancho Tranquilo collaborates with the neighboring turtle rescue project and sometimes you might find a small turtle nursery on-site.

Ecolodge La Trinchera (near the Padre Ramos estuary, tel. 505/8758-5214 or 505/8382-8560, info@fincatrinchera.com, $12 pp in private room with shared bath) is a quaint cabin. If you're on a tight budget, or just love the great outdoors, you can rent a hammock for the night ($4). Run by a family from El Viejo, the lodge helps arrange tours to kayak through the nearby mangroves or hike through the surrounding tropical dry forest. Seafood lovers can tour the family's shrimp farm and then taste a fresh shrimp cocktail at the end.

In Padre Ramos, dine at **Bar Zulema** ($5-10) or **Don Roque**'s traditional *ranchos* ($5-10) on the water's edge.

★ PADRE RAMOS WETLANDS RESERVE

Relax in the gentle waters of this protected estuary, laze in a hammock under the shade of a nearby *palapa,* or be lulled to sleep on a deserted starlit beach. **Padre Ramos Wetlands Reserve** is a little-visited part of Nicaragua that will reward you with an expanse of serene coastline and an overflowing supply of hospitality, wilderness, community, and culture.

The estuary is a decidedly mellower place to swim than the ocean and is home to all the wildlife (especially birds) you could hope to see. Check out the visitor's center when you arrive to ask about fishing and boat trips into the wetlands.

One of the best ways to explore Estero Padre Ramos is by sea kayak, paddling amongst the birds, sea turtles, and mangroves that inhabit this rich environment. **Ibis Exchange** (tel. 505/8961-8548, U.S. tel. 415/663-8192, www.ibiskayaking.com, $35-120 pp) has new, safe boats, professional guides, unique expeditions, plus delicious meals, kayak gear, and camping equipment for day tours and overnight adventures. All ages and skill levels are welcome. Ibis Exchange offers eight-day package tours that include León, Estero Padre Ramos, and Juan Venado Nature Reserve. Contact Ibis's local contact (tel. 505/8460-4854).

PUERTO MORAZÁN AND ESTERO REAL

Here's a chance to forge a trail on your own: The decrepit inland port town of **Puerto Morazán** is the gateway to the magnificent and sinuous **Estero Real Wetlands Reserve,** whose mangrove-filled estuary provides habitat for countless marine species and birds. The estuary is gorgeous, even if its "protected" status has been largely ignored by government officials and the shrimp industry over the years. Take a bus from El Viejo and ask around for a local guide or boat driver. The mayor's office may help guide you in the right direction. You won't be disappointed by the extraordinary variety of wildlife, nor by the amazing view of Volcán Cosigüina.

EL HOSTAL HATO NUEVO PRIVATE NATURE RESERVE

North of El Viejo, just past the community of El Congo, but before you reach the volcano, is **El Hostal Hato Nuevo** (tel. 505/2341-4245 or 505/8865-9683, www.hatonuevo.com, from $40); look for a steep driveway on the right. This unique, elegant stone home in the middle of the forest has seven comfy rooms and an old-ranch feel with plenty of shade and hammocks. The owner, Mareano, is a native of Chinandega who has studied art in London and Mexico City and whose custom-crafted paintings and furniture fill the place. He's a wonderful cook too, so even if you're not spending the night, try calling ahead for a relaxing meal. Located on a 600-plus-acre natural reserve, there are nature trails, horse-back riding, and wetlands, beach, and volcano expeditions available.

MECHAPA VILLAGE AND REDWOOD BEACH

This tiny fishing village on the Pacific coast of Volcán Cosigüina fronts a long, gorgeous, nearly-empty beach that stretches northwest to the cliffs at Punta Ñata (travel to the cliffs by horseback or car at low tide only). Ask for Captain Odel Yoel Gaitán, an experienced sailor who'd be happy to take you fishing or surfing in his *panga.*

There are few services in the area and only one place to stay: **Redwood Beach Resort** (tel. 505/8996-0328, U.S. tel. 800/583-4289, www.redwoodbeachresort.com, info@rbr-mechapa.com, $129-229), an isolated, North American-owned beach retreat especially popular with foreign diplomats and well-off Nicaraguans. Some packages include meals, most of which are fresh from the sea. Cheaper rates with fewer meals or during low season are available. The eight wooden cabanas are elevated one-room structures with fan, op-tional air-conditioning, private bathroom, and comfortable porches only meters from the pounding surf. You can laze around the beach, hunt *moro* crabs, and much more.

One bus a day leaves Chinandega at 1:30pm for Mechapa (3 hours); it departs the village the following morning at 4am. A more pleas-ant option is to travel by vehicle to Jiquilillo then arrange with the Redwood folks to be picked up by boat.

★ VOLCÁN COSIGÜINA NATURAL RESERVE

From the volcano's rim you have amazing views of the crater lake below and a panorama of the Gulf of Fonseca and Padre Ramos es-tuary. Much of this hike is shaded by forests on the reserve and along the way you may catch a glimpse of local fauna and hear the call of endangered birds that conservationists are working to protect. The trail from Potosí takes three hours uphill and two more hours downhill. You can also take boat tours into the Gulf of Fonseca to see the *islotes,* which are stunning rock formations created from a volcanic eruption. If you want to soak your muscles after your climb, take a dip in the hot springs. To get here, take a bus to Potosí from Chinandega ($2).

POTOSÍ

Potosí, a small fishing village on the east coast of the peninsula at the base of Cosigüina, was a trading port with El Salvador until the Contras blew it up in the 1980s. In re-cent years boats have begun transporting people between El Salvador and Nicaragua again, meaning you can skip the lengthy bus ride by land if you're planning on heading to some of El Salvador's beaches. Many hotels in Jiquilillo, Playa Aserradores, and Potosí can help you arrange transport or you can contact **Tierra Tours** (www.tierratours.com). You'll need to stop by the lonely immigration office at the end of a dirt path to get your passport stamped and pay the exit fee.

On the road toward Potosí, at the tiny vil-lage of La Piscina, is an interesting commu-nity-based tourism effort called **Ramsar Lodge** (tel. 505/8963-2719, www.ecodetur. com, cosiguinatour@gmail.com), located near cemented-in hot springs and providing rustic wood-and-thatch huts with communal hangout area equipped with a *rockola* (jukebox). Ramsar is run by a cooperative that supports conservation projects in the area and offers tours of the volcano, wetlands, and *islotes*.

A few more kilometers up the road, as you enter Potosí, look on your right for the locally owned **Hotel Brisas del Golfo** (tel. 505/2231-2238, $15) with five clean, private rooms with fan at a very reasonable price. Don Rafael Castro and his wife can prepare you three meals a day and help organize your volcano expedition.

If you're on the peninsula in May, ask about the three-day festival on Meanguera, an El Salvadoran island.

You can reach Potosí at the end of a three-hour bus ride from Chinandega; about six buses leave daily (less than $2 each way).

HONDURAN BORDER AT EL GÜASAULE

Located 1.5 hours north of Chinandega, **El Güasaule** (migration office tel. 505/2346-2208) is the principal Pacific-side border crossing with Honduras. It is six kilometers beyond the town of Somotillo, where you'll find a large number of trucker and traveler services. At the actual border, there is a Bancentro branch and basic food services.

El Güasaule is open 24 hours, and there is always heavy truck traffic and road repair problems on the Nicaraguan side. It costs $2 to leave Nicaragua and $7 to enter the country. A passport and some cash are all that's required of North American and European travelers.

If you are driving your own vehicle, the process to enter Nicaragua is lengthy but usually not difficult. You must present the vehicle's title, as well as your own driver's license and passport. You will be given a temporary 30-day permit ($10) to drive in Nicaragua. Should you lose the permit, you will be fined $100.

There are numerous and regular buses traveling between the Bisne Terminal in Chinandega and El Güasaule, and the main international bus lines (Tica Bus, etc.) heading to Honduras and El Salvador pass through León on their way to the border.

Though Nicaragua and Honduras are neighbors, the contexts and crime rates are very different. Make sure to research your destination in Honduras and take extra precautions when traveling, such as taking trusted taxis and avoiding traveling after dark.

The dormant Volcán Cosigüina is now filled with water.

Estelí and the Segovias

As you travel north and up out of the sultry Pacific lowlands, your introduction to Nicaragua's hilly interior begins with the Sébaco Valley, green with rice, carrot, and onion fields. Steaming hot sweet corn products will be abundant from here on out. The Pan-American Highway struggles upward to the pleasant city of Estelí, the "Diamond of the Segovias," then continues through mountains and valleys dotted with rural villages whose inhabitants are proud to call themselves *norteños*. Most folks here get along by subsistence farming and ranching, while cash crops like tobacco and coffee reign. A few communities boast talented artisans in pottery, leather, and stone. Underneath the north's gentle exterior of pine trees and tended fields are minor ruins of ancient cities, deep pools and cascades, and rugged communities of farmers and cowboys.

The north of Nicaragua is poorer than the rest, and suffers acutely from drought, poor soils, and deforestation: Nowhere else is the six-month dry season so intense. The challenging living conditions however make for a hardy and hardworking people, quick with a smile or a story. The curious and unrushed traveler will not regret breaking away from the highway and going deep into this northern countryside.

PLANNING YOUR TIME

It takes 5-7 days to hit the highlights of this area. Spend a day at the gem of this region—the Somoto Canyon—then catch the last bus back to Estelí, Nicaragua's capital of tobacco. With a second day, focus on nearby attractions like those at El Tisey and Miraflor reserves (the latter of which is worth a second day), or check out the highland border town of Ocotal and its surrounding *pueblos* (small villages). If you're really curious, travel the long loops eastward toward Jalapa, and you'll be rewarded with excellent camping opportunities, mysterious hot springs, and a glimpse into the region's rich indigenous roots. This region is well connected by buses.

Previous: soapstone *gordita* on the road to San Juan de Limay; rustic Miraflor. **Above:** hand-rolling cigars in a factory in Esteli.

Look for ★ to find recommended sights, activities, dining, and lodging.

Highlights

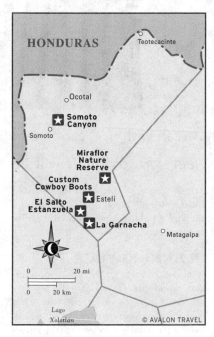

★ **Custom Cowboy Boots:** Don't leave Estelí without a pair of custom-made leather boots for long rides into the wild—or just dancing, northern-style (page 206).

★ **El Salto Estanzuela:** Estelí's premier swimming hole is at the base of a 15-meter waterfall. Hike, ride horses, or take a swim (page 210).

★ **La Garnacha:** Take in stunning vistas and the scent of pine trees while learning about this small community's diverse industries, including cheese making, organic coffee, artesanía, and vermicomposting (page 212).

★ **Miraflor Nature Reserve:** This is the best place in Nicaragua to get back to nature—and spot exotic wildlife like the elusive quetzal (page 213).

★ **Somoto Canyon:** The nicest swimming hole north of Estelí is a great example of responsible community-run tourism (page 220).

Estelí and the Segovias

© AVALON TRAVEL

Estelí

Spread across a flat valley 800 meters above sea level, Estelí is an unassuming city whose 110,000 merchants, ranchers, artists, and cigar rollers are prouder than most. In Nahuatl, Estelí means something like "river of blood," an apt moniker for an area so saturated with Sandinista rebels in the days that led up to the 1979 revolution that Somoza carpet-bombed the city (ask locals where to find *la bomba,* a relic from the air strikes). But these days, most Estelíanos live a bucolic life of farming and commerce. People are attracted to Estelí for two main reasons: to learn about the city's revolutionary legacy and to visit the nature reserves that surround it.

ORIENTATION

Buses to Estelí will deposit you in one of the two bus terminals (COTRAN Sur and COTRAN Norte) on the east side of the highway. Express buses bound farther north for Ocotal and Somoto will drop you off at the nearby Shell Esquipulas. In either case, take a cab to the central park ($0.50) to start your exploration. Estelí is quite possibly the only city in the country to name avenues (north-south) and streets (east-west), a system ignored in lieu of the tradition of counting blocks from known landmarks.

The two avenues that border the park, and one additional avenue on either side, make up the bulk of the commercial district. Avenida Central, on the west side of the park, hosts the greatest number of businesses and restaurants.

You're essentially safe in Estelí, but in the barrios east of the highway and west of the river, be especially cautious.

SIGHTS
El Parque Central

Estelí's newly renovated **central park** is a hub of mellow activity and a magnet for local characters. Buy an ice cream cone, kick back on a bench, and watch it all swirl by. The **Iglesia de San Francisco** was built in layers starting in 1823. Today it is a modern building, with stately columns, a neoclassic facade, and twin bell towers topped with crosses.

La Galería de Héroes y Mártires

La Galería (half a block south of the cathedral, tel. 505/8419-3519 or 505/2713-7763, Mon.-Fri. 8am-5pm, donations accepted) is one of the only surviving projects of the Association of Mothers of Heroes and Martyrs of Estelí, a support group of 300 women who lost children during the battle against Somoza's National Guard. The gallery itself is a single room in what was once one of Somoza's jails, filled with memorabilia from the days of the Revolution—photos of Estelí as an urban battleground, quotes from Sandino and Che Guevara, weaponry and shell casings, and portraits of young men and women killed in action, sometimes accompanied by uniforms and other personal effects. If you have solid Spanish, listening to the stories of the parents of lost soldiers who will show you around the museum is a powerful and recommended experience for understanding Nicaragua's history. Call Guellermina "Mina" Meza ahead if you are interested in visiting over the weekend and to confirm someone will be there to receive you during the week.

Connected to the Galería is the less powerful but still interesting **Museo de Historia y Arqueología** (Mon.-Fri., closed Wed. 9am-noon), with a small display of petroglyphs, artifacts, and revolutionary photos.

The **Casa de Cultura** (in the same building as the Galería, on the south side) offers a series of music, art, and dance classes to the public. It often has a display of local artists in its spacious lobby. The Casa regularly hosts cultural events, especially around the national

Estelí's Murals

One way to understand a little about the history, culture, natural diversity, and social issues of the "Diamond of the Segovias" is to view its murals, most of which were painted by children and young muralists and are distributed throughout the city. Murals began to pop up in Estelí in the late 1980s during a transitional stage of the country's history when the civil war was ending and presidential elections were being held. The idea was to empower the people while reclaiming Nicaraguan culture and promoting children's participation in society. The creation of the murals was invariably tied to further community activities and social work.

After two years of covering the walls of the Batahola Cultural Center in Managua with murals created by students and community members, the founders of what would come to be known as the **Fundación de Apoyo al Arte Creador Infantíl** (FUNARTE, tel. 505/2713-6100, www.funarte.org.ni) began doing mural workshops in Estelí. Today FUNARTE is run by some of the early participants and boasts a full schedule of art classes throughout the year, including classes for children with different abilities and teenagers who are in prison. Their students have contributed to well over 100 murals in Estelí, and often demonstrate a process in which they reflect upon social issues affecting their communities. Volunteer with FUNARTE to learn more about the great cultural work they do.

holidays. Go by the office to ask about events during your visit.

Cigar Factories

In Estelí there are about 10 serious cigar producers, few of which offer individual tours. Most businesses are *zonas francas* (free-trade zone factories), which prohibits them from selling their product within Nicaragua.

To visit the factories it is best to contact **Puro Norte Tours** (tel. 505/8415-2428 or 505/8551-5137, puronortetours@gmail.com or infopuronortetours@gmail.com, $40 for a group of 3, $10 each additional person) or **Tree Huggers Tours** (1 block east and 1 block north of the cathedral, tel. 505/8496-7449 or 505/8405-8919, $5 pp) to arrange a tour. **Tabacalero Santiago,** the factory visited by the Tree Huggers tour, has cigars for sale as part of the tour. Otherwise, there are local cigars for sale in most of the hotels and hostels around town.

Local Craft Lessons

There are a few different options for trying your hand at local crafts. In the **Casa de Cultura** (in the same building as the Galería, on the south side), sign up for a workshop on how to make cards out of recycled materials

(ask for Juan Carlos). Cándida at **Tarjetas Ambietales** (half a block east of the southern side of the Cine Nancy, tel. 505/2714-2237, www.environcards.org) creates a variety of crafts out of recycled paper. She'll be glad to teach you her trade.

ENTERTAINMENT AND EVENTS

Estelí's festival season is clearly December, when there is some sort of activity practically the whole month, including the famous *Hípica* (horse parade) and *Purisima,* celebrating the Virgin Mary with free take-aways at every house.

Nightlife

Considering it is far from any beaches or larger cities, Estelí has quite an eclectic nightlife, offering dive bars, mixed local and foreign crowd scenes, salsa, and live music. The nightlife scene in Estelí is mostly overrun with pricey bars where young Estelíanos come dressed to the nines. Be warned: a foreigner in flip-flops will stand out like a sore thumb.

Café Luz (from Hotel Mesón 1 block east, tel. 505/8441-8466, www.cafeluzyluna.com) is one of the only places that'll take you if you didn't bring your club clothes. Here you will

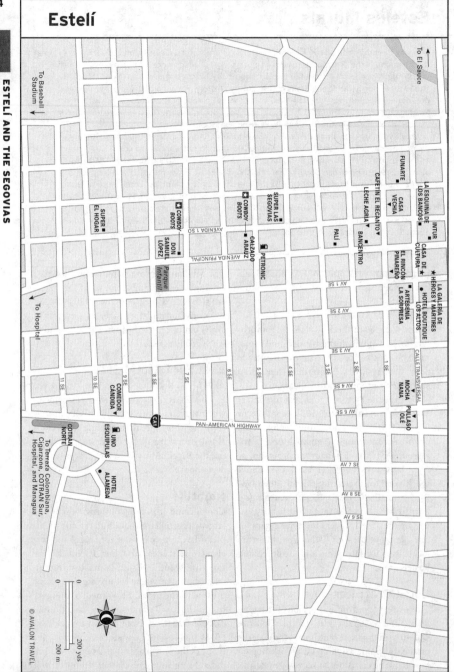

Estelí

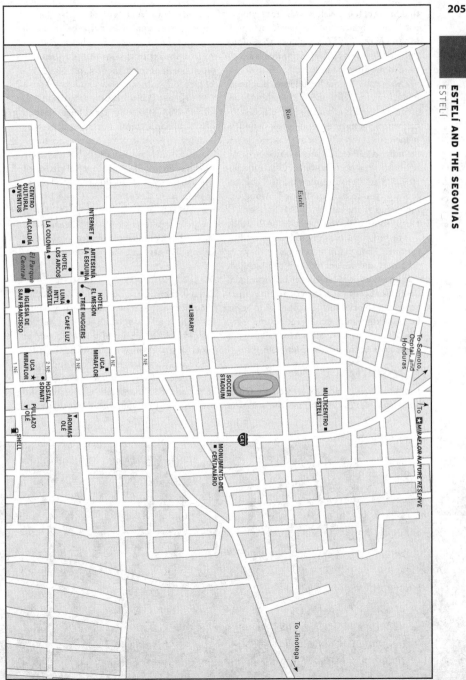

CENTRO CULTURAL JUVENTIUS
ALCALDÍA
LA COLONIA
INTERNET
EL Parque Central
HOTEL LOS ARCOS
ARTESENIA LA ESQUINA
LUNA INT'L HOSTEL
IGLESIA DE SAN FRANCISCO
HOTEL EL MESON
TREE HUGGERS
CAFÉ LUZ
LIBRARY
1 NE
UCA MIRAFLOR
2 NE
3 NE
4 NE
5 NE
UCA MIRAFLOR
HOSTAL SONATI
PULLAZO OLÉ
AROMAS OLÉ
SHELL
SOCCER STADIUM
MULTICENTRO ESTELÍ
Río Estelí
To Somoto, Ocotal, and Honduras
To ★ MIRAFLOR NATURE RESERVE
CAT
MONUMENTO DEL CENTANARIO
To Jinotega

find many of the travelers who are staying in Estelí and a bohemian, low-key local crowd. **Mocha Nana Café** (half a block west of the Pullaso Olé) often has live music that is advertised in the different hostels.

Cigarzone (in the Justo Flores neighborhood, from the Petronic Sur 75 feet south, tel. 505/2713-7595) is considered the classiest locale where young professionals rub shoulders in their finest threads. The bar has two floors, including a VIP section and a variety of drink options. **Paparazzi** (in front of Cigarzone, tel. 505/2713-6410) has a sports bar feel but still requires you to be well dressed. Along the same lines on the same strip is **Puro Ron** (75 meters south of Petronic, tel. 505/8425-9401).

The rest of the bars in Estelí are more like cantinas. Though full of local flavor, they can get rowdy and are not highly recommended. Karaoke is as popular as ever in Nicaragua, and Estelí keeps pace. **La Confianza** (from Payless, 1.5 blocks north) is the place to be for beers, talking, and catching interesting regulars. The atmosphere allows for talking but also boasts lots of space and karaoke.

SHOPPING

Provided you're not interested in fruits and vegetables (in which case you want the *mercado* on the south end of Estelí), the entire length of **Avenida Principal** is lined with boutiques and a variety of clothes stores.

Two shops, **Artesanía La Esquina** (1 block north of the cathedral, tel. 505/2713-2229, Mon.-Sat. 8am-6pm) and **Artesanía La Sorpresa** (1 block south of the cathedral, tel. 505/2713-4456), each have a huge selection of Nicaraguan arts and crafts from all over the country. In general, prices are cheaper in the Managua and Masaya markets, but for locally produced items, like soapstone carvings and Ducualí pottery ($3-10), these are good places to shop. **Café Luz** (1 block east and 1 block north of the cathedral, tel. 505/8441-8466), the sister restaurant to Luna International Hostel, has a number of talented local artists selling their arts and crafts products.

★ Custom Cowboy Boots

Estelí is the place to buy handmade leather goods like belts, saddles, and cowboy boots: Find them all along the southern half of Avenida 1 SO. A pair of quality cowhide boots (or snakeskin, or iguana skin, the latter of which is an endangered species and might get confiscated at your home customs office) go for about $100 and take a week to make when custom fit to your foot. **Calzado Arauz**

cigars fresh from a rolling factory

Smokin' Nicaragua

Estelí's most industrious crop is tobacco for the production of cigars. After being harvested from fields across the region, it's sent to factories in urban areas where it's then rolled and exported. It all began with the 1959 Cuban revolution, when capitalist Cuban cigar lords found their businesses liquidated into the new socialism. These artisans of the finest cigars in the world quickly gathered illicit caches of the precious tobacco seeds their families had been cultivating for centuries and fled to Miami. From there, it was only a couple of years before they discovered Nicaragua.

The core of the old Cuban cigar aristocracy moved to Estelí and, with their precious seeds from the homeland, began turning out world-renowned cigars once again. They endured another popular revolution in 1979, the ensuing civil war and land redistribution, and then survived the cigar boom and bust of the 1990s, followed by the waters of Hurricane Mitch that tore through fields in 1998. But the business is sunk deep into the rich soil, and the handful of familial cigar dynasties that first came to Nicaragua 30 years ago are still rolling world-class cigars.

Cigar making is a proud family tradition here, and there's no denying the craftsmanship of a fine cigar, but consider the other side of the coin. Organic tobacco is grown in Nicaragua, but barely. Most production employs massive quantities of chemicals, which invariably find their way into the earth and water as well as workers' lungs, hands, and feet. Tobacco handlers often absorb the toxic elements of the leaf, and although at least several of Estelí's factories have impressive, airy environments for their workers, conditions for the rollers are often no better than the worst sweatshops. Additionally, many *campesinos* (country folk), in an effort to make ends meet, grow this cash crop on their land for these companies, leaving little to no room for their own food production, and quickly diminishing the quality of the soil for future production. And the history burns on. Almost all of the cigars are consumed in the United States.

(2 blocks south of supermarket Las Segovias, calzadoarauz@yahoo.es) is the first in a line of options and is recommended for high quality handmade leather goods along with **Don Samuel Lopez** (4 blocks south of supermarket Las Segovias, Mon.-Sat.).

ACCOMMODATIONS

Estelí's climate is such that air-conditioning is often unnecessary and many of the hotels only have fans. Also, because of the cool weather, the majority of the hotels have hot water in the showers. The hot water comes out of an electric showerhead that typically has three options: a full circle (hot water), a half-filled circle (lukewarm water), and an open circle (cold water).

Under $25

★ **Luna International Hostel** (1 block east and 1 block north of the cathedral, tel. 505/8441-8466, www.cafeluzyluna.org, $9 dorm, $25 private) is one of the most popular places in town for travelers. The hostel, along

with their cattycorner sister businesses Café Luz and Tree Hugger Tours, are run as a nonprofit social enterprise, which uses 100 percent of their profits to support a wide variety of projects in the area, providing financing and micro-loans to community tourism ventures, the arts, nutrition, and housing projects. They also run workshops along with a Library Bus that travels to rural areas providing access to books. Ask about volunteering.

★ **Hostal Sonati** (3 blocks east of the northern edge of the cathedral, tel. 505/2713-6043, www.sonata.org, $10 dorm) is a new option in town whose profits are completely directed toward environmental education. They offer a variety of workshops to youth, including creating various mosaics using recycled products that you're sure to see around town. They have a communal kitchen, cozy spaces for chilling, and a variety of tours.

The eight rooms at **Hotel El Mesón** (1 block north of the cathedral, tel. 505/2713-2655, $23-27) have private bath and fan (a few with a/c). This place is quiet and clean, and the hot water makes January mornings a lot more bearable. They have parking, a bar and restaurant, a garden, a travel agency, car rental, and will change traveler's checks. **Centro Cultural Juventus** (tel. 505/8923-6283, $7 dorm, $20-25 apartment) is a quirky little hotel and Spanish school (Spanish classes $6/hour) decorated with bamboo and natural materials. They also have a "waterfall bathtub," where you can relax while 1.5 gallons of water pound your back per second.

$25-50

If you're more interested in a relaxing evening than a night in town, ★ **Hotel Cualitlán** (from COTRAN Sur, 2 blocks south, 4 east, and 1 north, tel. 505/2713-2446, $35-40) is a walled-in guesthouse compound unlike any other in Estelí. It has a verdant sitting area with a tree-canopy roof, soothing music, and a creative menu geared to the international traveler. Choose one of several delightfully appointed cabanas—something like Swiss chalets—set around the lush tropical courtyard, all with hot water and cable TV.

Over $50

The pleasant **Hotel Los Arcos** (1 block north of the cathedral, tel. 505/2712-6720, www.hotelosarcosesteli.com, info@hotelosarcosesteli.com, $50-95, includes breakfast) is run by a Spanish development organization in a charming colonial edifice. All profits go toward development activities like their schools, continuing education programs, and street children.

FOOD
Cafés and *Comedores*

★ **Mocha Nana** (half a block from Parque Infantíl on Avenida Central, tel. 505/2713-3164, Mon.-Sat. 9am-7pm) is a perfect respite from the afternoon sun. In addition to fine cappuccinos, mochas, coffee, and espresso, they have bagels, waffles, and a small English language bookstore and trade library. **Café Don Luis** (25 meters north of Bancentro, tel. 505/2713-0178, Mon.-Sat.

7am-10pm, Sun. 1pm-9:30pm) is known for its coffee, breakfast food, crepes, and salads. Among locals, it is one of the most popular cafés in Estelí.

★ **Café Luz** (1 block east and 1 block north of the cathedral, tel. 505/8441-8466, daily 7am-10pm) serves a variety of international fare and *comida típica* that is particularly appealing to the *gallo pinto*-weary traveler. Café Luz is a great place to spend a few hours on the Internet or socializing with fellow travelers while sipping coffee or eating veggie burgers or vegetarian *nacatamal* (a rare find). The café is one-third of a nonprofit-social enterprise with all proceeds supporting community-driven projects in the department.

The menu is simple, healthy, and home-grown at ★ **La Casita** (across from La Barranca, south entrance, tel. 505/2713-4917, Mon. 1pm-7pm, Tues.-Sat. 7am-7pm, Sun. 9am-7pm, closed first Mon. of every month). Yogurt, home-baked breads, fresh cheeses, vegetables, granola, juices, and coffee drinks are all served in a pleasant garden atmosphere along the shore of a babbling brook. It's on the Pan-American Highway a few kilometers south of the city. Take an *urbano* bus to the hospital, then walk south around the bend in the road; or hail a taxi for about $1.50—it's well worth the trip. In addition to featuring wonderful food and mellow music, La Casita sells local crafts and plants, including herbs, ornamentals, and much more.

Leche Agria (2.5 blocks south of the corner of the banks, daily 8am-7:30pm) serves excellent *quesillos* (cheese and tortilla snack), cheeses, and lunch plates. **Cafetin El Recanto** (2 blocks south of the park, Mon.-Sat. 7am-5pm) has an extensive collection of quality *rosquillas* (a traditional Nicaraguan cookie made from corn and cheese) and lunches at a good price. A good place for groups or travelers passing through along the Pan-American Highway, **Comedor Cándida** (in front of the UNO Esquipulas gas station, tel. 505/2713-7630) serves traditional Nicaraguan food buffet style.

and continue downward. You ve reached Don Alberto's when gn welcoming you to the *Galería Piedras* (rock sculpture gallery). *nas!*" until the dogs hear you and you to come on in. Usually, Don he back, so follow the path past into the woods where you will carvings and benches. Call out erto comes to find you. It can at the top of the mountain, so to bring a sweater.

nacha

l community of **La Garnacha** agua's greatest success stories tourism and cooperative de- vas founded as an agricultural the 1980s when families dis- var moved here to farm com- the transition to a different lel in the 1990s, each family p of their land, but various together to form an associa- y runs most of the town's eco- ts.

tion produces Swiss cheese; fertilizer, and vegetables; and ts. Local artisans sell their

Garnacha's *mirador*

goods in the shop. Profits go to their nonprofit association and, despite the fact that some areas make much higher profits than others, the people who work in the various areas all make the same salary.

In the soapstone carvings shop, observe the young men carving wood and soapstone mined within the community. Be sure to visit the natural medicine pharmacy for a consulta- tion ($2, free with a tour). To figure out which herbs you need, the pharmacist will pass you different bags of plants and, as you push your finger and thumb together, will see how easily she can pry your fingers apart.

The association runs a tourism project and has a variety of wooden cabins ($20-35), an area with private rooms, and a restaurant, which serves their vegetables and handmade cheese ($3-5). It gets cool at night so bring a sweater and socks! Call **Pablo** (tel. 505/8658- 1054) to make reservations. **Hospedaje Familiar El Carrizo** (tel. 505/8524-4764, $15/ day, includes meals, plus a tour of their or- ganic garden) is a lodging option. They have a tree-house room. They can also help set up homestays.

To get to La Garnacha, take a bus leav- ing Estelí (daily except Wed.) at 6:30am or 1:30pm. In a car (or as a more adventurous

International

★ **El Rincón Pinareño** (3 blocks south of the cathedral, tel. 505/2713-4309, daily 11am-10pm, $4), a two-floor family-run es- tablishment in a pleasant environment, serves excellent authentic Cuban cuisine. It's worth waiting on the slow service for a plate of food large enough to satisfy any appetite.

For Italian, head straight for **Casa Vechia** (1 block south then 1 block west of the corner of the banks, tel. 505/2713-2569, Mon.-Sat. 11am-9pm, $10). You can't go wrong with the *fettuccine frutti di mare.* **Dough Pizza** (half a block west of supermarket Las Segovias, tel. 505/2713-7777, $5-13, $2/slice) serves some of the best Nicaraguan-style pizza in town. Located off the Pan-American Highway, **La Terraza Colombiana** (2 blocks south of the Maxi Palí, tel. 505/2713-7509, $10-20) has great views of the surrounding mountain range and an elegant menu of Colombian favorites.

For a splurge, try ★ **Pullazo Olé** (from the UNO station, 1 block west, tel. 505/2513- 2569, www.pullazoole.com, daily 11am- 10pm, $8-20) and join the fierce Nicaraguan debate over the best beef in the nation. They also serve fantastic sausages and desserts. They have recently opened an upscale café: **Aromas Olé** (3 blocks east of Hotel Mesón, tel. 505/2713-5239, $10-15) has a full menu of fusion style food including coffees, cocktails, crepes, sandwiches, and entrées.

INFORMATION AND SERVICES

There are three respectable banks at *la esquina de los bancos* (the corner of banks, 1 block west and 1 south of the park); one block south is **BAC,** the only bank that changes dollars. All have **ATMs,** as does the Texaco station on the northern border of the city. The street *coyotes* (moneychangers) are safe and often give a bet- ter exchange rate than the banks. You'll usu- ally find bunches of *coyotes* at various corners of Estelí, including one block east of the cor- ner of the banks. These will be the gentlemen sitting on the corner holding or shaking loads

of money in mysterious dark sunglasses. Don't let their appearance sway you. They have cer- tification (often worn on a lanyard) to show they are legit.

El Hospital Regional de Estelí (tel. 505/2713-6305) is located just south of the city, but for minor cuts and bruises, Avenida Principal's many private clinics are a better option. The **police station** (tel. 505/2713- 8159 or 505/2713-2615, esteli@policia.gob.ni) is located on the main highway, toward the northern exit.

Tourism Information and Tour Operators

INTUR (half a block west of the cathedral, 2nd Fl. of Plaza Plator, tel. 505/2713-4432, Mon.- Fri. 8am-5pm) has helpful staff that can point you in the direction of the department's many attractions and valuable guides.

Socially responsible eco-tourists will want to head for **Tree Huggers Tours** (1 block east and 1 block north of the cathedral, tel. 505/8496-7449 or 505/8405-8919, daily 8am- 8pm), an incredible resource for planning trips in the region. Staff can provide you with basic information about bus schedules and lodging options. They also offer fairly priced tours to destinations around Estelí. Tree Huggers is part of the nonprofit social enter- prise that works together with the hostel and café across the street. All of their profits go to investing in community-led projects.

One of those projects supports the rural community tourism cooperative in the Miraflor reserve. They'll set you up with a guide to visit Miraflor ($15/group) and con- nect you with a homestay ($24 pp, meals in- cluded). They offer city tours, cigar tours, tours to the Tisey nature reserve ($15 with guide on public transport, $50 private trans- port, homestay available), and day trips to Somoto Canyon ($30 with local guide).

GETTING THERE AND AWAY

Find the bus schedules posted in English on the wall of Tree Huggers Tours office (1 block east and 1 block north of the cathedral, tel. 505/8496-7449 or 505/8405-8919, daily 8am-8pm). Express and ordinary buses for Estelí leave from Managua's Mayoreo terminal. Seven *expresos* per day bound for Managua pass Estelí (2.5 hours, $3). If you're arriving from Honduras, buses depart frequently every day from Somoto and Ocotal, the last one leaves 5pm.

From Estelí, *ordinario* buses leave the **COTRAN Norte** (tel. 505/2713-2529) at regular intervals for Ocotal, Somoto, and points north 4am-5pm. Buses leave **COTRAN Sur** (tel. 505/2713-6162) for Managua, Matagalpa, León, Tisey, and La Garnacha. From COTRAN Sur there are dozens of daily buses to both Managua and Matagalpa, leaving from the wee hours until 6pm; three express buses to León depart 5:45am and 6:45am from COTRAN Sur and 3:10pm from COTRAN Norte. A few microbuses leave for León daily: 8:30am, 9:30am, noon, and 2pm (they leave when they fill up, and competition is fierce).

GETTING AROUND

Estelí is a long city. You can cut short the walking by hopping a cab for the fixed price of $0.50 anywhere in the city (except La Casita restaurant on the south side of town). *Urbano* buses ($0.25) are safe to ride and run a big loop around the city, including up and down the main avenues and nearby barrios.

Agencia de Viajes Tisey (in Hotel El Mesón, tel. 505/2713-3099, fax 505/2713-4029, barlan@ibw.com.ni) is a modern and professional agency that deals with airlines, international reservations, and Budget rental cars. **Casa Estelí** (on the Pan-American Highway, 20 meters south of the monumento centenario) has a **Budget** rental car office with four-wheel drive trucks (about $60/day). The **Dollar** car rental agency (with the Toyota dealer on the highway) has economy sedans ($35/day) and pickup trucks ($60/day).

wildlife in El Tisey Nature Reserve

EL TISEY NATURE RESERVE

Ascending into the Tisey Nature Reserve, you will notice a change in landscape as the cool air fills your lungs and the aroma of pine reaches your nostrils. This is the southernmost point in the Western Hemisphere where you'll find pine forest, and the huge moss-covered trees are lined with hundreds of species of orchids. This area is also home to some inspiring communities and cultural sites. There's more to see than you'll likely have time for, so plan a few days at least.

★ El Salto Estanzuela

El Salto de Estanzuela (outside the city on the way to the Tisey Nature Reserve) is a gorgeous 15-meter cascade. Plunging into a cold, shady pool, beneath the waterfall, you can actually swim past the falls and perch on the rocks behind them. Unfortunately, this site can only be visited during the rainy season (Sept.-Jan.). The road to Estanzuela

El Salto Estanzuela

branches off the Pan-American just south of the new hospital and is sandwiched between two *pulperías* where you can stock up for the journey. You can hike to the waterfall from the highway or rent a bike and leave it with the caretakers at the entrance. The five-kilometer walk should take 60-90 minutes each way. It's an easy hike but has lots of ups-and-downs. Otherwise, hop a bus for the 20-minute ride (buses leave COTRAN Sur at 6:30am and 1:30pm). When you arrive you will see an *arteseanía* shop on the left and gated field to the right. Enter through the gate where the family who lives at the entrance will charge you $1.50 to hike down to the falls. There have been a few instances of robbery along here, so be alert. To be extra careful, go with a guide from one of the hostels. Head downward for 10 minutes until the track veers to the left. Follow the path down and you will see a set of stairs. You should now be able to hear the falls.

A bumpy 1.5 hours down the road from Estanzuela is **Eco-Posada Tisey** (tel.

505/2
$10 d
They
show
mos
veg
met
view

Do
Es
Vi
m
ca
D
ar
hi
ca
a
P
t
v
t
j
l

a green gate
know you ha
you see the si
Escultura en
Call out *"Bue*
someone tells
Alberto is in
the house and
see rocks with
until Don Al
get windy up
you may want

★ La Gar
The small rur
is one of Nica
of community
velopment. It
cooperative in
placed by the
munally. With
economic mo
took ownersh
families came
tion, which tod
tourism projec

The associa
organic coffee,
medicinal pla

the view from La

traveler), you can also go to the town of San Nicolás (along the Pan-American just south of Estelí, take any bus going south) and follow the road towards San Nicolás for nine kilometers until you see a sign for "Rancho Don Luis" towards community La Tejera. Turn right and, after following the road for 3.5 kilometers, turn left at the road junction to La Garnacha. After 1.5 kilometers, you will reach the community La Garnacha. This walk can be done in a few hours on foot or by looking for rides along the way.

★ MIRAFLOR NATURE RESERVE

More than a trip into Estelí's misty mountains, a visit to Miraflor is a trip backward in time. Miraflor is unabashedly rustic, natural, and unpretentious. Declared a protected natural reserve in 1990, this rudimentary tourist infrastructure was developed by locals, with their own sweat and labor and in the absence of any external help.

Miraflor as an entity is a little vague. There's no town, per se, or even a real center. Rather, 5,000 Mirafloreños live dispersed throughout the 206 square kilometers of the reserve in nine geographically dispersed but socially united communities. The protected area of Miraflor is privately owned, cooperatively managed in many parts, and almost entirely self-funded by associations of small-scale producers. Most notable among these is the **UCA Miraflor** (Unión de Cooperativas Agropecuarias Héroes y Mártires de Miraflor)—not to be confused with the University of Central America—an association of 14 small farmer cooperatives and 120 families living within the protected area. UCA Miraflor is primarily an agricultural credit and loan institution, but it has also tackled issues such as community health and education, organic agriculture and diversification of crops, cooperative coffee production, gender and youth groups, and conflict resolution. Tourism, Miraflor's greatest potential, was just an afterthought.

Lodging and recreation are divided into three unique levels: the **lower, medium,** and **high zones.** Some visitors spread their time out over 3-4 days to properly visit each part. The lower zone is dry forest, while the highest zone at 1,400 meters above sea level, is a jungle with cloud forest, impressive waterfalls, and a better chance to see monkeys.

Visiting Miraflor

You can certainly visit parts of Miraflor in a day trip from Estelí, but consider experiencing the unique and friendly lodging options. Trained local guides ($15-30 per tour) point out local wildlife, flora, and fauna and help you make the most of your trip around the reserve.

Start with a call or visit to the tourism office of **UCA Miraflor** (from the north side of the cathedral, 2 blocks north, 2 blocks east, tel. 505/8661-0434 or 505/2713-2971, www.ucamiraflor.com, miraflorcommunitytour@yahoo.com, Mon.-Fri. 8am-noon and 1pm-5:30pm, Sat. 8am-noon and 1pm-3pm) in Estelí. The nonprofit tourism office **Tree Huggers Tours** (across from Luna International Hostel, tel. 505/8496-7449 or 505/8405-8919, www.treehuggers.cafeluzyluna.org, info@cafeluzyluna.com, daily 8am-8pm) works closely with the community and provides the same thoughtful service. Folks at either place will present your options and help arrange lodging, tour guides, and horse rental, taking care to distribute guests fairly among the various families who have agreed to host guests.

Miraflor is remote, cloud-covered, and sometimes downright chilly. Be prepared for inclement weather (buy a sweatshirt at one of Estelí's used-clothing stores) and bring your own bottled water. A flashlight or candles will be helpful on that midnight walk to the latrine.

Every attraction in Miraflor is privately owned, often by local *campesinos*. Your financial support leads to the continued preservation of these magnificent forests, because, "hey, this would be a great place to chop down the trees and plant some beans."

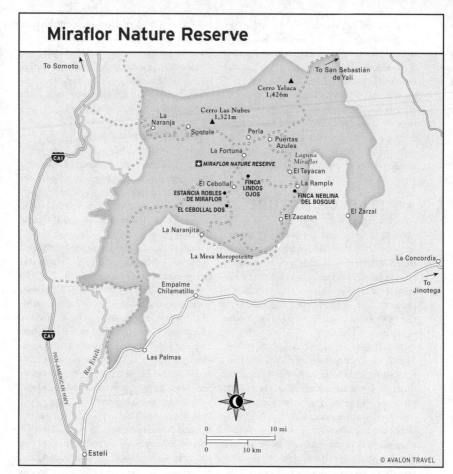

Miraflor Nature Reserve

Recreation

The most impressive thing about Miraflor is its remarkable biodiversity. The distinct bird species number 236. That's nearly 40 percent of all bird species in the country, including four species of the elusive quetzal (*Pharomachrus mocinno*); toucans; the *ranchero* (*Procnias tricaruntulata*), with its three dangling chins; and the Nicaraguan national bird, the *guardabarranco*. **Bird-watching hikes** are $30 per person.

Miraflor is one of the richest and most unexplored **orchid-viewing** regions anywhere. Among the more than 300 identified species is

an enormous colony of *Cattleya skinniri* (the national flower of Costa Rica), not to mention scads of bromeliads and a museum of other orchids from throughout the reserve. Orchid lovers should base themselves in the medium zone.

The *campesinos* at Miraflor will gladly show you their cutting-edge lifestyle, including organic compost, natural pest management, watershed protection, live fences, crop diversification, soil management, reforestation, worm farming, and environmental education. In addition, Miraflor's small-scale, fair trade, organic coffee cooperatives and

bus to Miraflor

Jinotega. It's so remote you have to go on **horseback** ($33, $9 each additional rider) to get there and back in the same day. The forests are replete with mysteries, such as the *casa antigua,* a 1,200-year-old foundation in the Tayacán area, surrounded by dozens of other unearthed *montículos* (mounds). Archaeologists haven't even begun to investigate the rest of them.

Accommodations and Food

Start with a call or visit to the UCA Miraflor office or Tree Huggers Tours in Estelí. They will help arrange ★ **homestay lodging** ($20/night pp, includes all meals), taking care to distribute guests among the various *campesino* families who have agreed to host guests. Campers can pitch a tent ($5 pp). Lodging is distributed between four main communities, and they'll ask you to pick a zone: either the cloud forest with the community of La Rampa; the middle zone (best for birders as it has more species diversity) with the communities of Sontule and El Cebollál; or the low, dry zone with the communities of Coyolito and La Pita. Ask about package trips that include meals, guided hikes, and organic agriculture demonstrations. Wherever you stay, you'll be off grid and disconnected.

There are several other options throughout Miraflor for those who need their privacy. Wind down after dark around a cozy bonfire at **Finca Nebilna del Bosque** (tel. 505/8701-1460 or 505/8666-5245, www.neblinadel-bosque.com, $27 pp, includes meals). Their comfy bamboo cabins fit up to four people. To get there, walk 300 meters from the bus stop at La Rampla.

In the community of El Cebollál, German-owned **Finca Lindos Ojos** (from La Rampla 2 kilometers west, 50 meters north, tel. 505/2713-4041, $28 pp) offers clean, comfortable rooms on a beautiful property. The largest accommodation in Miraflor is **Estancia Robles de Miraflor** (tel. 505/2713-9451, www.estanciaroblesdemiraflor.com). They

cupping lab (in Cebollál) are among the nation's finest. **Coffee tours** are $70 for a group of seven.

Short **hikes** (from $15 pp) are possible through any of the hundreds of pockets of forest, but ask your guide to take you on one of the more adventurous trips. Although difficult to access, the 60-meter waterfall at **Salto de la Chorrera** is one of the wildest spots in the lower zone of the reserve. In the same zone are the **Caves of Apaguis,** dug in pre-Columbian times by gem seekers, and which have been occupied ever since by *duendes* (dwarves), as any local will inform you. The mature cloud forest of **Los Volcancitos** is Miraflor's highest point at 1,484 meters and is a known habitat for howler monkeys and quetzals. If the monkeys don't snatch away your binoculars, expect fantastic views from El Tayacán, Cerro Yeluca, Cerro El Aguila, La Coyotera, and Ocote Calzado. **Barranco Blanco** is a 50-meter-high waterfall on the edge of the reserve bordering offer freestanding cabins on a working farm with restaurant and pool.

Getting There and Away

Until the road from Estelí is paved, expect bumps, dust, and mud on the slow ride into the hills. You should make arrangements in Estelí beforehand, rather than just showing up in Miraflor. There are five buses a day from Estelí that follow three different routes. To get to the **highest zone,** catch a two-hour bus 6am, noon, or 4pm from COTRAN Norte to Yalí, Miraflor. Get off at La Rampla or Puertas Azules, depending on where you're staying. To get to the **medium zone** in El Cebollal, buses leave from COTRAN Norte 6am and 1pm, take two hours, and pass through Sontule and La Perla along the way. One Cebollal-bound bus leaves from the Texaco Star Mart 6am and 2:15pm passing through El Coyolito and La Pita (it doesn't run on Sun.). Fare is less than $1.

Returning to Estelí, buses take a little longer than two hours. They depart El Cebollal 8am and 3pm, passing through La Pita 8:15am and 3:15pm. Another bus (the one that doesn't run on Sun.) leaves El Cebollal for Estelí 6:30am, going through Sontule 7:15am, and La Perla 7:50am. The bus from Yalí passes by Puertas Azules 6:45am, 11:15am, and 3:45pm, followed by La Rampla 7am, 11:30am, and 4pm. Hitching in this remote area of the Estelí countryside is difficult, as there are not many rides.

CONDEGA

The 9,000 inhabitants of the Tierra de los Alfareros (Land of the Potters) eke out a living raising cattle, corn, and beans, as did the Nahuatl centuries before. Truckloads of pre-Columbian pottery have been dug out of area cornfields, and the tradition lives on today with a women's pottery cooperative in Ducualí Grande. Before the revolution, only three *terratenientes* (landowners) owned all the land from Condega to Yalí. Condegans proudly supported the Sandinistas, which led to lots of harassment from Somoza's National

Guard (Commandante Omar Cabezas once hid out for months with his troops in the mountains outside Condega, reportedly in a cave near El Naranjo). In 1979, the Sandinista government confiscated those properties and redistributed them to the locals.

Contra soldiers found easy pickings in the unprotected farms of the Canta Gallo Mountains east of Condega, where several major skirmishes took place during the 1980s. Most locals remember the horror stories. In 1998, Hurricane Mitch destroyed more than 200 homes and two of the three local industries (a cigar box factory and a tannery).

Sights

Toward the end of his grip on power, Somoza took to strafing the northern regions with his air force. When, on April 7, 1979, the Sandinistas downed one of his planes, it was considered a major victory and huge morale booster. Follow the dirt road behind the cemetery, then 100 meters to the top of the hill to the downed airplane in **Parque Mirador El Avión**—now a monument—complete with a simulated airport control tower viewing platform. The original blue and red dot symbol of the Somoza Air Force has been replaced by the stars and bars of the U.S. Air Force. Ignorance or revisionist history? You make the call.

The **Casa Cultural Conthecatl** is a former command post of the National Guard. In its musical instrument workshop you can order a custom-made guitar, *guitarrón,* or violin.

The **Julio Cesár Salgado museum** (central park, tel. 505/2715-2330, Mon.-Fri. 9am-5pm, Sat. 8am-noon, reading room Mon.-Fri. 1pm-5pm, $0.50), named after the town's first archaeologist, has a collection of pre-Columbian ceramic work that local farmers have unearthed. Take in some baseball weekends at the **ball field** (north of town), or catch the *fiestas patronales* on May 15, traditionally the first day of the rainy season—a double cause to celebrate in this rain-starved region.

Just outside of town is the **Taller de Cerámica Ducualí Grande** (pottery $1-7), an artisan's workshop founded in the 1980s. The 13 workers continue to create charming ceramics using simple wheels and firing the pieces in a woodstove. To get there, take a bus north about two kilometers and get off where a large concrete sign points west to the workshop. Follow that road one kilometer across the bridge and through the community of Ducualí Grande. Turn left when you see the small church, and look for the white sign on the right side.

Accommodations and Food

Pensión Baldovinos (south side of the park, tel. 505/2715-2222, $8 pp) has been a town landmark for decades. It has five simple double or triple rooms with private bath and decent meals. **Hospedaje Framar** (next door to Pensión Baldovinos, tel. 505/8353-4647, $5) is clean, offering seven dark rooms with shared bath; doors close at 10pm.

★ **Hostal and Mirador La Granja** (half a block east of the park by the Catholic church, tel. 505/2715-2357, $15 s, $20 d) has simple, bright, and airy rooms with private bathrooms. Their balcony offers a splendid view of the surrounding mountains. **Campestre La Granja Hospedaje** (from Instituto Marista, 1 kilometer east, tel. 505/2715-2521, $10 pp) is in a beautiful location with lots of greenery and a pool.

Stop in for an ice-cold *cacao* drink or fresh *quesillo* at ★ **Lacteos La Gualca** (on the Pan-American Highway, tel. 505/2715-2128, daily 6am-9pm), which sells locally produced cheese, yogurt, wine, honey, and coffee.

Getting There and Away

Any bus that travels between Ocotal, Somoto, or Jalapa and Managua or Estelí can drop you off on the highway in front of Condega, a two-block walk from the center of town. Buses leave Managua every hour 5am-5pm. Or take the Yalí-La Rica buses from Estelí (5am-4:10pm). Make sure to ask if the bus goes through Condega, as there are two routes to Yalí. Express buses will let you off on the highway by the cemetery; *ordinarios* will let

you off in front of the park. From Condega, walk out to the Instituto on the highway to try to catch north- or south-bound *expresos,* or wait for slow buses at the park.

PALACAGÜINA

The town of Palacagüina is best known as the pastoral setting for Carlos Mejía Godoy's revolutionary religious anthem, *"Cristo de Palacagüina."* In the song, the Christ child's *campesino* parents, José and María, are dismayed when, instead of becoming a carpenter like his father, he wants to be a guerrilla fighter.

Most *ordinario* buses (not *expresos*) traveling between Estelí and Somoto or Ocotal pass through Palacagüina. If you take an *expreso,* the walk from the highway into town will be long and dusty, but there are usually taxis waiting for just a few *córdobas.*

Coffee Cooperative

One of Nicaragua's largest fair trade coffee cooperatives, **PRODECOOP** is comprised of 38 smaller co-ops with 2,300 coffee-growing families. They export as many as 30,000 *quintales* (100-pound bags) a year. This is a great place to learn about coffee production and the meaning behind that ambiguous buzzword "fair trade." The cooperative's **Hotel Palacagüina** (for reservations: Estelí office, 75 meters west of the corner of the banks, tel. 505/2713-3268 or 505/2713-3236, www.prodecoop.com, $10-25) houses and feeds guests in accommodations atop the cupping lab overlooking the drying beds, which bustle with activity during the harvest. There is also a swimming pool and an awesome 360-degree view of the surrounding hills. They even have Wi-Fi. There are no English-speaking guides, so it's best if you come armed with some basic Spanish. The coffee compound is between Palacagüina and the northern exit to the highway.

SAN JUAN DE LIMAY

Since 1972, Limay's claim to fame has been its *marmolina* (soapstone) sculptors, trained by a priest named Eduardo Mejía so that they could improve their living conditions, develop their talent, and market their beautifully polished long-necked birds, kissing swans, iguanas, and Rubenesque women. A core of local carvers still lives and works in Limay, and you can watch them work and purchase some pieces with little effort. In town, ask around for the *artesanos de piedra*. **Taller Casco** (from the *Colegio Felicita Ponce*, 1.5 blocks east, tel. 505/2719-5228, ocascodavila@yahoo.es) has a large collection of pieces starting at $4.

Nearby, **Río Los Quesos** meanders outside the city limit. Ask a local to show you the **Poza La Bruja** swimming hole, ringed with pre-Columbian petroglyphs. Find an adequate place to bed down for the night at **Hostal Las Gordas** (a yellow corner building located half a block north and 1 block east of the police station, tel. 505/8444-0976, $4 pp).

The hour-long trip out here is worth it for the amazing views reaching past the volcanoes in León to the Gulf of Fonseca.

Along the road from Estelí to Limay is the **Corredor de las Gordas,** part of INTUR's investment in its Ruta de Café project. Eleven *gorditas* (statues of chubby women) are scattered along the highway, and nine more in Limay itself. Each sculpture took about a month to create, weighs 2 tons, and cost upwards of $2,000. They hold different objects representing distinct communities in the area. The largest—*la Gorda de la Sirena*—welcomes you at the turnoff from the Pan-American Highway. Half an hour outside Limay, at the *Gorda del Café,* do like the locals and stop for a bite at **Comedor Chilito** ($1), where a local woman serves homegrown coffee roasted on the *comal* (griddle) alongside delicious *güirilla* (a corn and cheese dish), *cosas de orno* (corn-based baked goods), and home-cooked meals.

San Juan de Limay is a 44-kilometer bus ride from Estelí that traverses a 1,000-meter mountain pass through coffee fields. Buses follow two routes to Limay (via La Shell and via El Pino) and leave Estelí's COTRAN Norte at 8:45am, 9:15am, 12:15pm, and 2pm.

artisan at Taller Casco carving a two-ton *gordita*

Somoto

Located on the south side of the Pan-American Highway as it veers westward toward the Honduran border at El Espino, Somoto is an average-size city of 15,000 and capital of the department of Madriz. Tucked into the Cordillera de Somoto at 700 meters above sea level (the highest point of this range is Cerro Tépec-Xomotl at 1,730 meters), Somoto enjoys a fresh climate most of the year. Somoto is known for its donkeys, *rosquillas* (baked corn cookies), and blowout carnival each November. A tributary of the Río Coco traverses the city.

U.S. Marines built an airstrip here, three blocks south of the park (now lost forever under a modern development), to try out a military technique they'd just invented: the air strike. They used the base in Somoto to bomb Ocotal in the 1930s in a failed attempt to root out General Sandino. These days, the *Ciudad de Burros* (City of Donkeys) has not much more to offer than a quiet evening in its quaint and friendly park and a pleasant, village ambience.

SIGHTS

La Parroquia Santiago de Somoto is one of Nicaragua's oldest churches. Construction began in 1661, 86 years before León's great cathedral. If you're around Somoto on the eighth of any month, consider joining the religious masses on their pilgrimage to the tiny community of **Cacaulí,** all hoping for a glimpse of the Virgin Mary. Ever since she appeared to a young farmer named Francisco in the late 1980s, thousands of people have arrived to try to repeat the miracle. They each carry a clear bottle of holy water, which they hold up to the sun at exactly 4pm. The Virgin—not parasites—should appear in the water. Whenever the eighth falls on a Sunday, the believers turn out in larger numbers.

Pass through the **Mercado Municipal 19 de Julio** to rub shoulders with the locals,

mostly farmers. Or check out the two scenic view overlooks: The first is west of the city and offers a quick, easy walk and a rewarding view. The second, **Mirador de Canopy Castillo** ($1), has a small café and a four-cable canopy tour that looks steeper than it should be: Be cautious.

ENTERTAINMENT AND EVENTS

Somoto's *fiestas patronales* fall on July 15-25, but the town is more famous for the **carnival of November 11** (or the second Saturday of the month), when it celebrates the creation of the department of Madriz in 1936. All of Nicaragua's best party bands make the trip north, each setting up on one of seven stages, plus mariachis, dance parties, and the standard bull and cockfighting.

ACCOMMODATIONS AND FOOD

Hotel Rosario (on the north side of the park, tel. 505/2722-2083, www.hotelelrosario.wordpress.com, $12 s, $18 d, meals $3) has simple, clean rooms with private bathrooms, and serves home-cooked meals. Ask for an airy second-floor room for easier access to the balcony and less noise.

The **Hotel Colonial** (half a block south of the church, tel. 505/2722-2040, $20 s, $30 d, includes breakfast) has a new restaurant and large patio, rooms with private bath, cable TV, and parking. **Hotel El Portal del Angel** (1 block west, 1 south of the police station, tel. 505/2722-0244, portalhotel@yahoo.com, $35 s, $55 d) was constructed in 2008 and has tidy rooms, a restaurant, and an upstairs bar with a nice view of the mountains.

For a real country experience set up lodging with the family at ★ **Finca Mejía** (tel. 505/8616-3729 or 505/8414-9731, finca_mejia@yahoo.com, $6 pp, $2 meals). Rooms are adequate, and you'll be glad to find a toilet instead of a latrine. Learn to make tortillas and milk cows in the morning, and enjoy the star-speckled sky by night. The farm is perched on the edge of the canyon, and boasts a couple of fantastic lookout points. It's a perfect spot for camping ($1).

Comedor Soya (in front of the park) serves soy with a smile. All kinds of surprising and cheap meals are available. The market is full of other delicious treats, all of them fried. For excellent smoothies, cakes, and locally grown coffee, check out **Aroma's Café** (1.5 blocks east of Farmacia del Pueblo, tel. 505/8532-6816).

Comedor Bamby (2.5 blocks west from the Enitel office, Mon.-Sat. 8am-8pm) is a great place for lunch on just a few dollars. A lunch buffet is served 11am-2pm, or until they run out of food. Many working people in Somoto frequent the spot, so it pays to get there early.

★ **The Almendro** (across from the Colonial, daily 10am-9pm, from $5) was mentioned in a Mejía Godoy song *("el almendro de donde la Tere")*. Try the house specialty, *curbina al ajillo* (fish in garlic sauce). **Akasos** (from ENITEL, 1 block south, 50 meters west, tel. 505/2722-0120, $8) serves quality beef, fish, and fresh veggies in a tasteful environment.

INFORMATION AND SERVICES

There is a **bank** across the street from the *alcaldía* (mayoralty). **Profamilia** (1 block north of the police station, tel. 505/2722-2753, www.profamilia.org.ni, Mon.-Fri. 8am-5pm, Sat. 8am-noon) is a modern health clinic. The **Hospital César Augusto Salinas Pinell** (next to the Red Cross, tel. 505/2722-2037) is the local public option. The **police station** (tel. 505/2722-2311, madriz@policia.gob.ni) is a couple of blocks south of the COTRAN terminal.

GETTING THERE

Buses to Somoto from Estelí (1 hour, $1.50) run every hour 5:30am-5:20pm. There are also regular express buses from Mayoreo in Managua (3 hours, $4).

★ SOMOTO CANYON

Dramatic cliffs cast shadows over Somoto's best swimming hole. Float through limpid, cool pools penned between the lush vegetation of the 100-meter high canyon walls, home to cliff bats and rare birds. The deep pools are separated by shallow sections that preclude boating. Rather, spend all day splashing from pool to pool. Bring water

Somoto Canyon

Somoto's Tasty Treat

Although *rosquillas* (crunchy rings of salted corn-dough baked with cheese) are baked in adobe wood-burning ovens all over Nicaragua, Somoto is particularly renowned throughout the country for the quality of this baked treat. When they're not baked the traditional way, you'll find them as flat, molasses-topped *ojaldras* or thick nugget-pockets called *pupusas*. Serve them up with a cup of steaming hot, black coffee, still fragrant with smoke from the wood fire, and enjoy: The two tastes naturally complement each other. The two main producers in town are **La Rosquilla Somoteña Betty Espinoza** and **Rosquilla Garcia,** both two blocks west of the COTRAN on either side of the street. *Somoteñas* are the most famous regional variety of *rosquillas*. If you're traveling anywhere else in the country, they make a cheap, simple gift, greatly appreciated by any Nicaraguan.

shoes for the canyon tour, as sharp rocks can tear up bare soles. You'll likely be there all day, so a picnic lunch is a good idea. And, most important, bring plastic bags to keep things dry. During the height of the rainy season (Sept.-Oct.), the current may be too strong for swimming. During these months it's safest to take a guide.

This trip is easiest and most rewarding with a guide who knows the canyon. You can organize a tour at the main entrance at the bottom of the canyon, or arrange in advance. The local guide coordinator is **Henry Soriano** (tel. 505/8610-7642), who can be found at the entrance to the canyon. Private operator **Namancambre Tours** (tel. 505/2722-0826 or 505/8821-8931, www.namancambretours. com, $40 pp) has routed a climb up one of the cliff walls, and will take you there and provide climbing equipment, plus a local guide for a canyon tour. Guides will bring a waterproof bag for keeping things dry along with lifejackets, and can show you the safest spots to jump off the rocks into the water.

To make your own way, follow the road past the entrance at the gate for 15 minutes or so until you reach a river. Follow it upstream to a spot where boats are parked. Pay for a ride, and the driver will take you as far into the canyon as a boat can go. You'll arrive at a point where there are inner tubes available to rent. From there you can swim into the canyon and walk along the shallow parts. The canyon is very deep for long stretches, and there are no places to walk alongside the river once in the canyon, so swimming is necessary (a life jacket is highly recommended). When you're done, turn around and make your way out the way you came in.

This is possible as a day trip from Estelí, though it's nearly three hours each way, and the last express bus back to Estelí leaves at 3:30pm. Catch a bus to Somoto, then another to El Espino (every 45 minutes or so), getting off at the entrance (25 minutes from Somoto) at the bottom of the canyon. About 200 meters down the path is a gate and cabin, with guides available. Pay the entrance fee, and organize a tour with a local guide.

EL ESPINO BORDER CROSSING

The least used border crossing in Nicaragua, El Espino is open 24 hours. To get there from Somoto, take one of the regular buses ($0.50) that head toward El Espino, or chip in for a cab (about $5). It's a 20-minute ride from Somoto. At the crossing, you first receive and fill out an immigration form at the booth next to the steel railroad crossing-style gate, then proceed 100 meters up to the little building on the right where you'll pay $3 to exit or $12 to enter. You should not need another visa for Honduras.

Continuing bus service into Honduras is just over the hill and runs until 4:30pm. Get there early to avoid traveling in the area after dark. Even though these countries are neighbors, their contexts and crime rates are very different. Do your research about where you are going in Honduras and take extra precautions when traveling.

Ocotal

Built on a thick bed of red sand and surrounded on all sides by mountains draped with green Ocote pines, Ocotal is the last major settlement before the Honduran border at Las Manos and the unbroken wilderness that stretches eastward to the Caribbean. In the early 1930s, General Sandino and his men were firmly entrenched in the mountains north of Ocotal, and the U.S. government, intent on capturing him, sent in the Marines. Based in Ocotal, they scoured the countryside around Cerro Guambuco and built the country's first airstrip in Somoto, from which they launched strikes on the city of Ocotal, the first city in the history of the world to experience an air raid.

Since 2000, the city has seen a lot of development and the feeling of Ocotal is one of progress. For most travelers, Ocotal may be nothing more than a place to sleep before hitting the border, but for many coffee growers and subsistence farmers, it's still "the big city" for supplies and business. Here you are indeed getting close to the frontier, however, and you only have to head a mile out of town in any direction before you are back to the rutted dirt roads, soporific cow towns, and sweeping valleys that make Nicaragua at once so charming and so challenging.

ORIENTATION

Buses will deposit you at the Shell station (referred to as "la chel") located towards the north of the city right across from Hotel Frontera. Two main *entradas* (entrances) to the city, one from the south, and another from the highway to the west, meet at the northwestern edge of the town center. If you enter from the west, pause at the top of the monument to San Francisco to appreciate the layout of the city before continuing into town. Most of the commercial activity occurs between the park, the market, and around the Shell station on the highway. Ocotal is walkable but

has numerous taxis anyway. Expect to pay about $0.50 during the day and $1 after 10pm for taxis.

SIGHTS
Centro Histórico

Start with the three-naved **Iglesia de Nuestra Señora de la Asunción** in the center of town. Construction began in 1804, and the northern bell tower (the left one) wasn't completed until the 21st century! Two centuries of inhabitants have taken the liberty of scratching their names into its soft adobe walls, including U.S. Marines in the 1930s. The church looks out over Ocotal's **central park,** one of Nicaragua's most gorgeous. Shady and green, it fills up in the evenings with sparrows and gossiping *campesinos*. As the sun goes down, the church is set aglow, making for a lovely scene.

Half a block west of the park's southwest corner, the **Casa de Cultura** (across the street from restaurant Llamarada del Bosque) boasts an impressive collection of photos of gringo military defeat and General Sandino's resistance. Yes, "boast" is the right word there. Ironically, the Marines lodged their troops in the Casa de Cultura as well as most buildings surrounding the park during their stay in Ocotal.

Mirador la Fortaleza

South of town and across the river is the museum built to commemorate the battles of Sandino and his army against the "Yanquis." Completed in 2009, it is less inspiring than the view of Ocotal it commands, as it is perched on the top of a hill.

ENTERTAINMENT AND EVENTS

Disco Sky Dancing (3 blocks south and 1 block west of the central park) attracts young clientele. **La Quinta del Moncho** (on the

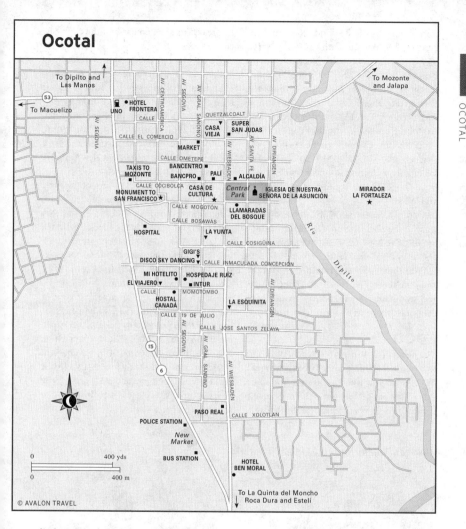

Ocotal

© AVALON TRAVEL

highway south of the city) is popular among the young after-work crowd. Ocotal celebrates its *fiestas patronales* August 14-15, when you can expect to find *Ocotaleños* blowing their hard-earned cash on horse shows, live music, gaming tables, and the like.

ACCOMMODATIONS

Ocotal has nearly a dozen cheap and spartan *hospedajes*. Backpackers will do fine in secluded **El Viajero** (7 blocks north and 1 block east from the bus station, tel. 505/2732-2954,

$10-20), offering TV, private bath, and Internet. A remodeling, including an addition of 10 rooms, provides rooms with higher amenities. It's quiet and clean, and the service is exceptionally friendly in an area not really accustomed to tourists. If you're on a budget, better go with **Hospedaje Ruíz** (across from Mi Hotelito, $5 pp). Rooms are dark and share a bathroom, but the place is clean.

Mi Hotelito (del Instituto Nacional, 2 blocks west, half a block north, tel. 505/2732-3071, $7-20) is a clean, no-frills option with rooms varying in size and shape and including TV, private bath, and hot water. ★ **Hostal Canadá** (half a block south of Mi Hotelito, tel. 505/2732-0309, $8 pp) is named for the family's second country of residence. It's a great value: clean, homey, and simple with private baths, TV, and attentive staff.

Hotel Ben Moral (about 1 kilometer from the police station on the first entrance to the city, tel. 505/2732-2824, $15-35) is a favorite for quality and price. Rooms include private bath, phone, TV, air-conditioning, hot water, and Wi-Fi.

Ocotal's finest is ★ **Hotel Frontera** (east of the Shell station, tel. 505/2732-2668 or 505/2732-2669, $23-73), with private bath, phone, and TV, plus a slick poolside bar, conference room, parking, Internet, restaurant, and pleasant airy porches overlooking the city and mountains. More expensive rooms are by the pool; cheaper rooms are in the back.

FOOD

The menu in these parts is chicken, steak, and fish (most of the fish comes from Managua). ★ **Llamarada del Bosque** (on the south side of the park, Mon.-Sat. 6:30am-8pm, $2) is a favorite, serving three meals buffet-style.

Its breakfasts are renowned for the city's best coffee.

La Yunta (1 block east and 1 south of *hospedaje* El Viajero, closed Mon., $4-8) is high quality and pricey, with live music many Thursdays and karaoke on the weekends. **Gigis** (a block south of La Yunta, tel. 505/2732-2967, Thurs.-Tues. 11am-10pm, $5-10) has burgers and pasta served by a Nicaraguan who spent years in New York. He makes a mean steak sandwich.

La Esquinita (5 blocks south of the park, daily 7:30am-3pm, $5) is immaculately clean, with generous portions. ★ **Casa Vieja** (from the Super San Judas, half a block north, tel. 505/2732-2559, Tues.-Sun. 5pm-11pm, $3-6), in a charming 100-year-old home with exposed earth walls, is a local favorite for its elegance, quality, and economy.

For great food and an amazing view of Ocotal, head out of town a few kilometers toward Estelí to **Roca Dura** (tel. 505/8853-7696 or 505/8834-6949, Mon.-Thurs. 10am-11pm, Fri.-Sun. 10am-12:30am, $4-9) for chicken, steak, burgers, and a truly impressive view. A taxi there will run you about $1, or $0.25 by bus, daytime. This place is rapidly becoming the weekend party spot.

Iglesia de Nuestra Señora de la Asunción

Ocotal's San Francisco monument

INFORMATION AND SERVICES

The Ocotal **INTUR** office (from the central park, 3 blocks south, 1 block west, 1 block south, tel. 505/2732-3429, Mon.-Fri. 8am-5pm, Sat. 8:30am-noon) is better than most regional branches. They train waiters and hoteliers, and organize cultural exchanges with other parts of Nicaragua. **Banks** are easy to find around the park. The **police station** is on the highway near the southern entrance to the city. For health-related needs you'll find the **Hospital Modesto Agurcia Moncada** (from Banic, 3 blocks west, tel. 505/2732-2491) and the **Centro de Salud** (5 blocks south of Telcor, tel. 505/2732-2430).

GETTING THERE AND AWAY

At least 11 express buses leave Managua's Mayoreo terminal for Ocotal (3.5 hours, $4), stopping along the highway in Estelí to pick up additional passengers. Most of these are Jalapa-bound and will drop you along the way.

Sixteen buses ply the route between Somoto and Ocotal daily 5:45am-6:30pm. If you miss the *expreso* buses, there are countless additional, painfully slow ordinary buses from Mayoreo.

The last Managua-bound *expreso* bus from Jalapa leaves Ocotal at 3:30pm and saves you around an hour to get to Estelí or Managua. The last *ordinario* heads south for the capital at 5:30pm.

OCOTAL TO LAS MANOS
Dipilto

Continue north past Ocotal on the highway, and you'll come to the small town of Dipilto, about a half hour from the border at Las Manos. Originally founded in response to gold mining in the area, Dipilto is now home to internationally renowned coffee production. Visit cooperative UCAFE's **Centro de Catación de Café** in town to learn how coffee beans are evaluated. Tour the historic mines on **Cerro La Coquimba,** and appreciate the mount's panoramic views along the way. Locals worship the miraculous image of *la Virgen de la Piedra* found on a rock on the banks of the Río Dipilto. The image was brought here in 1947 and has been credited with many blessings and miracles since. Grab a bite in town at **Pinal del Río** (100 meters west of the police station, $3-5). Buses leave frequently from Ocotal's terminal (30-minute ride).

Crossing the Border at Las Manos

The Honduran border is 24 kilometers north of Ocotal, and open 24 hours. You will be charged $2 to leave Nicaragua and $7 to enter (or $4 exit, $9 entry after normal business hours or on weekends). There are several small eating booths, a coffee shop, two places to change money, and not much else. Fill out the immigration form at the little gray building and walk 100 meters farther down the road to the immigration building to pay and get your exit stamp. Honduran buses to Danlí stop running after 4:30pm. To get to the border from Ocotal, take a bus (5am-4pm, $1) or a cab (around $10-20, depending on how hard you bargain). You should not need another visa for Honduras.

OCOTAL TO JALAPA
Mozonte

An easy day trip from Ocotal, Mozonte, of largely indigenous descent, is notable for its workshops of potters who produce ceramics from a particularly fine clay. You'll come across a variety of ceramic pieces for sale along the highway. As in other parts of the north, pine crafts (in the form of earrings, baskets, pot holders) are common here. The folks at the **Casa de la Comunidad Indígena** (tel. 505/8228-2766 or 505/8353-8451, Mon.-Fri. 8am-noon and 2pm-5pm) can point you to the workshops of local artisans, and also can set up workshops ($4 pp) to teach you their craft.

The **Mirador Loma Santa** is an impressive lookout point atop a hill a couple of blocks from the town center, immediately obvious upon arriving in Mozonte. At the end of a long and steep stairway you'll come to a ruin of an old chapel next to an image of *la Virgen de Guadalupe*. Every December 12 the stairs are lined with people making offerings to the Virgin. **Templo Parroquial San Pedro y San Pablo** (in the central plaza) holds the remains of Monseñor Nicolás Antonio Madrigal y Garcia, who is in the process of canonization by the Vatican. The church dates back to the 18th century and holds sacred relics from the colonial era.

You can spend the better part of a morning (start the hour-long walk from Ocotal early to avoid the heat) in Mozonte admiring the craftsmanship of the potters and the town's local charm. For a quicker trip, hop on an *interlocal* (15 minutes, less than $1). They park near the highway and leave as soon as they're full. The trip ends in the town center.

San Fernando and Cerro Mogotón

San Fernando is a picturesque village of thick adobe-walled homes set around the town park and **Templo Parroquial.** Its 7,000 inhabitants live on more than 200 individual coffee farms and produce an estimated 25,000 *quintales* (100-pound bags) of coffee annually. More famous than its coffee, however, are its inhabitants, who since the colonial days have been lighter-skinned and more Spanish-looking. Many have blue or light brown eyes. How do they do it? Just don't ask about those last name combinations: Herrera-Herrera,

chapel ruin at Mirador Loma Santa in Mozonte

Urbina-Urbina, and Ortez-Ortez, though many attribute the blue eyes to the town's occupation by the U.S. Marines 1927-1931. Life revolves around coffee in San Fernando, and many homes double as coffee-processing mills *(beneficios)*.

A nearby hike is to the **Salto San José,** where water rushing off the Dipilto mountain range cascades into a small pool. Take a bus to the community of Santa Clara and get off across from the ball field, turn left (north), and walk 6-8 kilometers to the river. To be sure of the trail, hire a local kid to take you.

You can stage a hike to **Cerro Mogotón,** Nicaragua's highest point (2,106 meters) from San Fernando, 20 kilometers away. The trail follows the Achuapa River about an hour before making a steep climb into the cloud forest. At its peak, you'll reach a small plaque marking the northern border with Honduras. The hike can take as long as eight hours up and back. A guide is essential, as the trail isn't well maintained and there still may be active mines on the mountain. **Roberto Castellano and Bayardo Jimenez** (tel. 505/2732-2267 or 505/8827-0595, www.cerro-mogotonnicaragua.dorosevich.com, $60 pp) in Ocotal will take you there. Look for a new tourism project promoted by INTUR, which will include rustic lodging and horseback riding on Cerro Mogotón.

Buses leave frequently from the terminal in Ocotal (30 minutes, $1).

Ciudad Antigua

Ciudad Antigua was the second Spanish attempt to settle Nueva Segovia. (The remnants of the first settlement, built in 1543 at the bequest of then-governor Rodrigo de Contreras, are called Ciudad Vieja, and can still be seen at the junction of the Jícaro and Coco Rivers.) The wooden doors of the **Iglesia Señor de los Milagros** still bear the scorch marks of one attempted sacking of the city by pirates. You can pore over some well-loved religious pieces and a few historic documents and other colonial structures that survived the onslaughts of the 19th century at the **Museo Religioso de Ciudad Antigua** (next to Iglesia Señor de los Milagros, Mon.-Fri. 8am-4pm). Stay in town at the humble **Hospedaje La Esperanza** (from backside of the church, 2 blocks south, tel. 505/8353-1457, $5). Buses depart from Ocotal daily 5am, 9am, and noon.

San Nicolás Tree Farm

The farm at **Finca Forestal San Nicolás** (Pan-American Hwy. between Ocotal and Jalapa, tel. 505/8856-5105 or 505/8858-2205, $3.50 pp, $8 pp cabin, $5 pp dorm, $4 pp camping, $3-4 meals) aims to prove that farmers can produce crops without destroying the surrounding forest. There are two hiking trails on the property, one of which leads to a lovely *mirador.* They offer private cabins, a dorm, camping, and meals for visitors with advance notice. Any Jalapa-bound bus will drop you at the entrance road.

Don Alfonso's Hot Springs

Just four kilometers from the San Nicolás farm in Aranjuez are **Don Alfonso's *aguas termales*** ($1). Little waterfalls pour into the spring as hot mist rises around bathers. The cooperative COODETUR (tel. 505/2737-2031) has constructed five places where you can relax in the natural sauna. You can even have yourself a hydrotherapeutic mud bath.

There's a sign on the Ocotal-Jalapa highway at a farm belonging to Doña Domingo. A Jalapa- or Ocotal-bound bus will let you off there. She'll sell you a ticket, which you then present to the guard who lives in a house on the property. The entrance is about two kilometers past her farm. The property is about 30 kilometers from Jalapa.

Jalapa

Tucked back in one of Nicaragua's farthest populated corners, Jalapa enjoys a cool, moist microclimate suitable for the production of tobacco and vegetables that its drought-stricken neighbors could only hope for. Only four kilometers from the border, it is surrounded on three sides by Honduras and only surpassed in its remoteness by nearby border outpost

Teotecacinte. That isolation made Jalapa prime stalking ground for Contra incursions from three nearby bases in Honduran territory: Pino-I, Ariel, and Yamales. The city of Jalapa was flooded with refugees from farming communities farther afield in response to Contra attacks like that of November 16, 1982, when a Contra unit kidnapped 60 *campesinos* at Río Arriba. Muddy and isolated, Jalapa is a peaceful and laid-back place these days, most concerned with good tobacco and coffee harvests. The whole town comes to life every year at the end of September for the **Festival de Maíz** (Corn Festival).

Look for local *artesanía* of baskets made of coiled and lashed pine needles: beautiful baskets, potholders, earrings, and other items. Visit artisan **Doña Gloria** at her farm (10 kilometers outside of Jalapa) for a demonstration of her craft and she'll let you try your hand at it ($7.50 pp). If you'd like to stay for lunch ($4 a plate), she'll prepare you something. To get here take a taxi from Jalapa (be sure you agree on a pickup time).

As founding members of local tourism co-op COODETUR Las Segovias, **Hotel Campestre El Pantano** (8 blocks west of Procredit Bank, tel. 505/2737-2031, www.hotelelpantano.com, $4 camping, $10 pp dorm, $25 d) can help you find plenty of ways to spend time in the surrounding countryside. They offer clean lodging with Wi-Fi, hot showers, and an attentive staff. Start your day in their restaurant with a delicious breakfast and cappuccino. Campers can rent tents ($3) and get a hot shower ($3).

Five express buses leave for Managua 4am-1:45pm. Expect to pay $2 to be dropped in Ocotal, $4 to Estelí, and $5 for the whole six hours.

The Matagalpa and Jinotega Highlands

Look for ★ to find recommended
sights, activities, dining, and lodging.

Highlights

★ **La Catedral de San Pedro de Matagalpa:** One of the north's finest structures, this gorgeous cathedral can be spotted from anywhere in town (page 238).

★ **Centro Cultural Guanuca:** Rub shoulders with Matagalpa's enlightened citizens and visitors while you enjoy stimulating theater and great music (page 239).

★ **White Water Rafting on the Tuma River:** Get an adrenaline rush while you crash over the rapids on the Río Tuma (page 251).

★ **El Macizo de Peñas Blancas:** Hike through an enchanting jungle with a great rock massif looming over head (page 252).

★ **Hotel de Montaña Selva Negra:** A hotel quite unlike any other, Selva Negra has enough farm tours, mountain hikes, good food, and quiet, peaceful relaxation to rest any weary soul (page 253).

★ **La Fundadora:** One of the country's best options for community tourism, La Fundadora's Eco Albergue is a great spot to relax with some hot coffee, then explore the Datanlí el Diablo nature reserve (page 255).

East of the Pan-American Highway is a rugged region of blue-green hillsides, thickly forested mountains, and small, farming villages of adobe homes and clay-tile roofs. It is unlike anywhere else in the country.

As highlands go, Nicaragua's center is not that high—barely 2,000 meters above sea level. But, coming from the torrid plains around Granada and Managua, the cool pine-scented air is a welcome surprise. Coffee's preference for shade has encouraged the preservation of much of this region's forests, and mornings resonate with birdcalls and the bellowing of howler monkeys.

Draped over the curves of rolling hills, Matagalpa is the more elegant of the region's two big cities, with a gargantuan cathedral and several big, shady parks. Jinotega is smaller and snugly nestled among the northern mountains at a higher altitude. Emphasizing its sense of isolation are the green walls of the valley that cradles it; even the cathedral in the town's center is dwarfed by the immensity of nature in its lush plaza. Jinotega remains a cowboy town and feels like the end of the road—the gateway to the thousands of remote kilometers that separate the Atlantic coast from the rest of Nicaragua.

Periods of tremendous violence and warfare have racked the mountainous north for over a century. In the early 1930s, Augusto César Sandino fought U.S. Marines here; 40 years later came the revolution. Far more devastating than either of those conflicts, however, was the Contra War, when travelers along the region's few roads were frequently ambushed and soldiers raided villages as a matter of course. In the 1980s, farmers learned to tend their crops with rifles slung over their shoulders. The past decade of peace has transformed Matagalpa and Jinotega into an agricultural powerhouse. Gone are the thousands of cold, wet, and hungry guerrilla soldiers that muddily marched through these hills. Today's *norteños* instead struggle against rural poverty, drought, and the whims of the world coffee market.

Previous: city of Matagalpa; man-made lake at Hotel de Montaña Selva Negra. **Above:** La Catedral de San Pedro de Matagalpa.

The Matagalpa and Jinotega Highlands

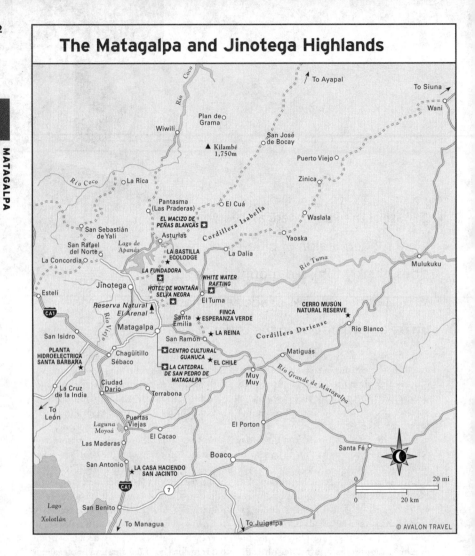

© AVALON TRAVEL

PLANNING YOUR TIME

Two or three nights is sufficient for seeing Matagalpa and Jinotega, but allow an extra day or two if you plan to explore any of the surrounding countryside. Those looking for a peaceful mountain retreat often spend 2-3 nights at either Hotel de Montaña Selva Negra, La Fundadora, or with a homestay program run by a coffee cooperative. Combining such a trip with a night or two in the city can easily consume five or six days—more if you visit the more remote communities. Buses are easy to use in this region, though having your own vehicle is useful if you're short on time. East of Matagalpa, 4WD is useful, and necessary in the rainy season.

The Road to Matagalpa

The highway from Managua climbs from the verdant plains of sugarcane and rice up through a series of plateaus with long horizons and broad panoramas before reaching the long mountain valleys that characterize the north. Most travelers take an express bus straight through this landscape and beeline for the mountains, but Matagalpa's dry lowlands hide a few interesting places if you have your own vehicle, or some extra time.

LA CASA-HACIENDA SAN JACINTO

A must-see on the high school curriculum of all Nicaraguan history students, the **Casa-Hacienda San Jacinto** (Carretera Norte, Km. 39.5, tel. 505/8761-6852), north of Managua, merits its own roadside statue. The monument guards the turnoff to the battlefield of San Jacinto and depicts a defiant Andrés Castro standing atop a pile of rocks. This is the site where, in 1856, the Liberals—supported by William Walker and his band of filibusters—and Conservatives battled fiercely. Conservative Andrés Castro, out of ammunition, picked up a rock and hurled it at the enemy, killing a Yankee with a blow to the head and becoming a symbol of the Nicaraguan fighting spirit that refuses to bow to foreign authorities.

Three kilometers east of the highway (a flat, 20-minute walk), the **museum** (Tues.-Fri. 8:30am-4pm, Sat.-Sun. 9am-4pm, $4) at the restored San Jacinto ranch house is run-down and little visited except by occasional hordes of high school students. You can explore the period relics and admire the displays. If no one is working the ticket window, shout until the caretaker rides her bike down from the main building. Bring water: There are no facilities at the site itself, though you can find something to eat in nearby San Benito.

LA LAGUNA DE MOYOÁ AND LAS PLAYITAS

After conquering the first big ascent on the highway from Managua (known as Cuesta del Coyól), you'll be greeted by the Laguna Moyoá on the west side of the highway and the swampy Laguna Tecomapa to the east (unless it is a dry year, when both disappear). Geologists believe they are the remnants of the ancient Lake of Sébaco, a giant reservoir that formed the heavy clay soils of today's Sébaco Valley. A tectonic shift ages ago sent the Río Grande de Matagalpa flowing eastward toward the Atlantic instead of into Lake Xolotlán through Moyoá, and the lake gradually disappeared.

The locals do a good business catching fish out of Moyoá, mostly *mojarra* and *guapote,* both good for eating and both of which you'll see held up on strings along the side of the road. Visit the lagoon through a new tourism project run by the **Asociación Pobladores de Moyoá** (tel. 505/8976-5557 Tomás Moreno). Spend the day here swimming, fishing, and relaxing, or rent a horse or *lancha* (boat) and tour the area. Birds you might see at Moyoá include *playeritos, piches, zambullidores,* and several types of heron.

The ***hospedaje*** ($6 pp) is inexpensive and rustic (expect latrines, instead of commodes). The association can also set you up in a **homestay** ($6 pp, plus $2 meals). Whether you go for the day, or stay the night, be sure to call ahead to ensure that there will be a boat waiting for you. To get there, take any bus headed to or from Managua, and tell the *ayudante* to let you off at Pesca Frito (Km 69 on the Pan-American Hwy.). From there one of the *lancheros* will take you across the lake ($2).

SÉBACO

No matter where you travel in the north of Nicaragua, at some point you'll pass through

Sébaco. Located right where the highway splits to take travelers to Estelí and the Segovias (fork left) or Matagalpa, Jinotega, and the northeast (fork right), Sébaco, a.k.a. the "City of Onions," is known throughout the region for its lively roadside commerce. If you're traveling at night, Sébaco is a sudden blast of streetlights, traffic, and bustle after two hours of darkness since Managua. While travelers are more typically interested in the Uno station's restrooms, most Nicas pick up fresh produce like carrots, beets, and of course onions, at one of the many identical stands on the true roadside market. Sébaco's aggressive road vendors will scale the side of your bus and display their goods through your window. If you have a long bus ride ahead of you, this is a good place to pick up bags of fruit juice, snacks, or veggies, which make good gifts for your Nicaraguan hosts.

In 1527, the Spanish founded the city of Sébaco on the banks of the Río Viejo alongside the indigenous settlement of Cihuacoatl, capital of the Chontales people. After a major flood put the town under water in 1833, Sébaco was moved to the hill east of town, where the remnants of Sébaco Viejo can still be found: The **Templo Viejo** houses a simple collection of archaeological artifacts, including pieces of pottery and ceramics, some small statues, and a wooden carving of the deity Cihuacoatl. When they moved, the residents of Sébaco packed up their buildings piece by piece and transported the materials to the new location, where they reconstructed the buildings to approximately their original form. Since then, the houses slowly crept down the hill and back to the water's edge, waiting for history to repeat itself. And that's exactly what happened. In 1998, Sébaco was

hit so hard by Hurricane Mitch it became one of the primary obstacles separating Managua from the north.

Although there are a few cheap places to crash in town, you'd be much wiser to continue to Matagalpa or Estelí, both a 45-minute drive away. The dozens of decent roadside restaurants offer similar menus of chicken, tacos, beef, and sandwiches. Sébaco has several banks, a telephone office, and a private health clinic.

CHAGÜITILLO

About four kilometers north of Sébaco along the highway to Matagalpa, Chagüitillo is a small community with access to several dozen pre-Columbian petroglyphs scratched into the stone walls of a canyon outside the village. The sites are known locally as **Santuario Salto el Mico** (once a sanctuary where the still-visible lunar calendar was observed) and **Santuario los Venados.** Relics depicting monkeys, shamans carrying human heads, and hunting scenes line the banks of the Aranca Burba stream. Local guides can easily help you find the two streambeds and show you the petroglyphs. Both sites are an easy walk from the center of town.

Chagüitillo is the source of a water project for the city of Matagalpa, and engineers digging the trenches for the pipelines have unearthed many additional artifacts. Some are scattered amongst the many houses of the community, but you can find most of them at the **Museo Precolombino** (300 meters north, 100 meters west, 50 meters south from the bridge at Km 107 on the highway to Matagalpa, tel. 505/8837-7535 or 505/7623-0414, Mon.-Fri. 8am-5pm, Sat. 8am-noon, $2). Tours of the museum are around $5.

Matagalpa

The department of Matagalpa is the most mountainous in Nicaragua, and its capital city remains true to form. Matagalpa lies blanketed over the rolling valley floor beneath it, creating steep climbs for pedestrians (and impressive views). Nicknamed "The Pearl of the North," Matagalpa's true precious stone is a ripe, red coffee bean, the production and harvest of which is essential to the regional and national economy. Matagalpa enjoys clean, mountain air, but clean water is in dreadfully short supply due to deforestation and human contamination. The surrounding mountains have been mostly scraped clean of trees, but during the wet season, they turn emerald green and remain so throughout December, when the coffee harvest turns the city into a lively center of coffee pickers, prospectors, packers, and processors.

Nahuatl influence is prominent in Matagalpa, particularly in regional vocabulary, which retains much pre-Columbian vocabulary. In the second half of the 19th century Matagalpa saw a flow of German immigrants who arrived in Nicaragua to develop gold mines in the east. Once they realized how perfect the climate was for the cultivation of coffee, their interest switched to the crop that would define Nicaragua's economy for the next 150 years.

Tourists will prize Matagalpa as a welcome respite from the heat of the lowlands, plus a chance to sip the best coffee in the world while plotting forays deep into the mountains. Ignore the inflated population sign as you enter the valley. The latest figures put Matagalpa's urban population at just over 100,000.

SIGHTS
Parque Darío
Grab a bench in the revamped Parque Darío (in front of El Templo de San José de Laborío)

and buy a crushed ice *raspado* (shaved ice) to enjoy while people-watching. There are lots of trees jammed into the park's tiny confines, and come sunset the branches fill with thousands of birds. A permanent fixture in the park is a vendor with rows and rows of handmade ceramic piggy banks for sale, none of which costs more than $3.

El Templo de San José de Laborío
El Templo de San José de Laborío sits at the edge of the Parque Darío at the south end of town. It's probably as old as the colonial presence in Matagalpa, but no one is quite sure exactly when it was built. It was rebuilt in 1917 on top of its old foundation, but underneath that foundation are the ruins of another that date to at least 1751, and possibly a bit earlier. In 1881, an indigenous uprising used the church as its garrison.

La Casa Cuna Carlos Fonseca
Matagalpa was the birthplace of the founder of the FSLN (Sandinista National Liberation Front), Carlos Fonseca. The house he was born in has been converted into a museum. Known as **La Casa Cuna Carlos Fonseca** (1 block east of Parque Darío's south side, tel. 505/2772-3665, Mon.-Fri. 8am-noon and 2pm-5pm, small donation), the tiny corner building has the original brick floors, mud walls, and tile roof, as well as an interesting assortment of documents, photos, and memorabilia, including Carlos's typewriter and his gear from military training in Korea.

La Iglesia de Molagüina
The history of **La Iglesia de Molagüina** (in the center of the city) has been forgotten. It was probably constructed between 1751 and 1873, though those dates have been questioned by historians. Simple and monastic, it is a

Matagalpa

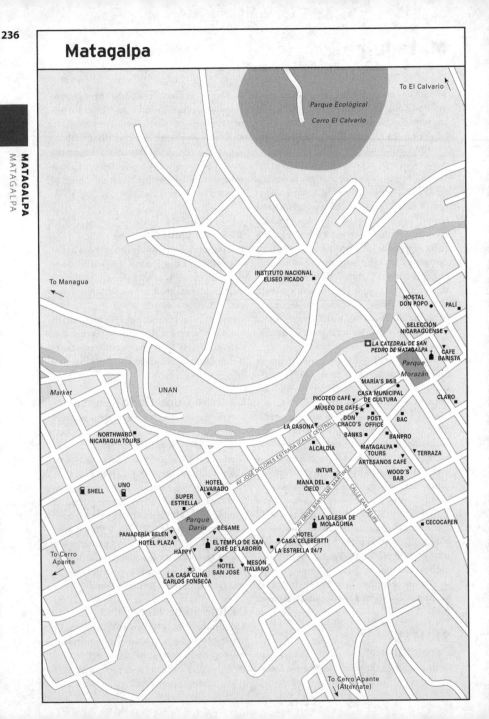

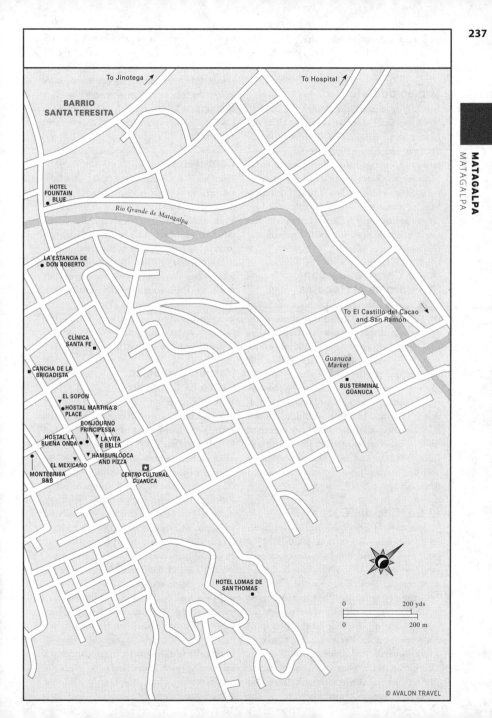

To Jinotega

To Hospital

BARRIO SANTA TERESITA

HOTEL FOUNTAIN BLUE

Río Grande de Matagalpa

LA ESTANCIA DE DON ROBERTO

To El Castillo del Cacao and San Ramón

CLÍNICA SANTA FE

Guanuca Market

CANCHA DE LA BRIGADISTA

BUS TERMINAL GÜANUCA

EL SOPÓN

HOSTAL MARTINA'S PLACE

BONJOURNO PRINCIPESSA

HOSTAL LA BUENA ONDA

LA VITA E BELLA

HAMBURLOOCA AND PIZZA

EL MEXICANO

MONTEBRISA B&B

CENTRO CULTURAL GUANUCA

HOTEL LOMAS DE SAN THOMAS

0   200 yds
0   200 m

© AVALON TRAVEL

well-used and well-loved church: Molagüina is home to a Catholic order of nuns and the College of San José.

Museo de Café

Recently revamped, the **Museo de Café** (1 block south of Parque Morazán, on Calle del Comercio, tel. 505/2772-0587, Mon.-Fri. 8am-12:30pm and 2pm-5:30pm, free) displays interesting murals and photographs from Matagalpa's history, plus a small collection of indigenous artifacts. You'll find interesting info (in Spanish and English) about the history of coffee in the region, starting with the German immigrants who started growing the first plants here.

★ La Catedral de San Pedro de Matagalpa

At the northeastern end of town, **La Catedral de San Pedro de Matagalpa** (mass daily 6pm) was a disproportionately large cathedral—the third largest in the nation—when it was built in 1874, reflecting the opulence of Matagalpa at the time. The cathedral is built in the baroque style, with heavy bell towers set at both sides and an airy, spacious interior. It's the most prominent building in town and is easily visible from the hillsides north of town on the road to Jinotega. The cathedral's interior is crisp and cool, tastefully adorned with bas- and medium-relief sculpture, carved wood, and paintings.

El Castillo del Cacao

The **Castle of Chocolate** (200 meters north of Las Marías Esso station, tel. 505/2772-2002, www.elcastillodelcacao.com, Mon.-Sat., tours $6 pp) is the Willie Wonka factory of Nicaragua, located a five-minute cab ride from the city center. You can tour the factory, visit a chocolate museum, and learn about the production of organic chocolate in Nicaragua. Nicaraguan cacao is known as a *landrace,* or a traditional variety almost identical to pre-Columbian cacao. It has a rich, complex, nuttier flavor than the heavily cultivated and hybridized strains grown elsewhere in the

world. The best time to go is when the factory is in full swing (Tues.-Sat. 9am-2pm). Call ahead to make sure someone will be available to give tours. To get the most thorough tour of the factory and an interpreter, contact **Matagalpa Tours** (tel. 505/2772-0108, $15-22). Price includes transport, entrance fee, and a snack.

Cemeteries

There are two adjacent cemeteries on the hillside east of the city, a 30-minute walk from town. One is for locals and one for foreigners, a rare arrangement in Nicaragua. Both contain headstones hand carved from dark rock, something seen only in Matagalpa. Buried in the cemetery higher up on the hill in the local section is one of the most famous casualties of the 1980s war: **Benjamin Linder.** An American, Linder was an avid juggler and unicyclist, and his headstone reflects those passions, along with some doves, the symbol of the peace he never lived to see.

Parque Ecológico Cerro El Calvario

This lookout point high above Matagalpa provides visitors with a breezy view of the entire city. The **Parque Ecológico Cerro El Calvario** (tel. 505/2772-0162 or 505/8528-8136, daily 8am-noon and 2pm-5pm, $0.20) offers the cheapest canopy tour in Nicaragua ($2). That may be because it's the shortest, at 300 meters in length and consisting of just two stations. There's also a children's playground and a two-story observation deck. To get here, take a 15-minute taxi ride ($4) from the city center. Vehicles use the main road up the hill, which passes through Santa Teresita, not the safest neighborhood in town. If you want to walk, you can trudge up the mountain from the other side—20 steady minutes up a steep incline. Start at the Instituto Nacional Eliseo Picado (INEP) and walk seven blocks west. Eventually you'll come to an iron and brick gate, which is the road to the park. With 300 meters more climbing sharply up, you'll arrive at the entrance.

ENTERTAINMENT AND EVENTS

Matagalpans celebrate their *fiestas patronales* on September 24, and the anniversary of their becoming a city on February 14. Every September there is a rowdy country fair that brings in crowds from the north and east, and cattle traders from all over the country. This is the best time of year to catch Matagalpa's traditional music of polkas, mazurkas, and *jamaquelos,* performed by the roving street bands that play at restaurants. The fourth weekend in August you can enjoy all the delicious corn products Nicaragua has to offer at the **Feria Nacional del Maíz.** A similar fair celebrates coffee in December.

The **Arabesco Academía de la Danza de Matagalpa** (25 meters west of the Iglesia Bautista) puts on dance presentations several times a year. If there's going to be a show, they advertise it at the **Casa Municipal de Cultura** (next to the fire station, tel. 505/2772-4608). Both places offer dance classes from Zumba to salsa and merengue. Classes are free at the Casa Municipal.

★ Centro Cultural Guanuca

The **Centro Cultural Guanuca** (1.5 blocks south of La Ermita de Guadalupe, tel. 505/2772-3562, www.grupovenancia.org, Thurs.-Sat.) has a convivial open-air bar surrounding a stage and sometimes dance floor. They host music, dance, theater, artsy international films, and both local and global activism. The place is renowned for its free shows every Saturday night. Grupo Venancia is a nonprofit women's group that runs the center and can probably be called ground zero of Nicaragua's feminist movement. It was founded in 1990 and in addition to the gathering space, runs urban and rural workshops on women's rights and domestic violence. Ask about their published materials, ways to volunteer, and try to catch their Saturday morning radio show, "*La Hora Lila,*" on Radio Yes (FM 90.1) at 8:30am.

Nightlife

There's no doubt that Matagalpinos like to shake their boots. Matagalpa's various *discotecas* are generally open Thursday-Sunday nights, but the only consistently happening night—with guaranteed crowds and electric dance floors—is Saturday.

The bohemian hang of choice is **Artesanos Café Bar** (half a block up from Banpro next to Matagalpa Tours, tel. 505/2772-2444, Tues.-Thurs. 4:30pm-midnight, Fri.-Sun. 4:30pm-2am), sometimes with live music from around the country. Try out your salsa skills on Friday nights, when that's all they play. **Wood's Bar** (next door to Artesanos Café Bar, tel. 505/2772-5199, Mon. 4pm-1am, Tues.-Thurs. noon-2am, Fri.-Sun. midnight-3pm) is a lively drinking spot among younger folks, especially on karaoke nights (Wed. and Fri.). Completing the local nightlife trifecta, **Terraza** (across the street) is always hoppin' on weekends.

Open all week for mediocre lunch and dinner, **La Casona** (from the Alcaldía, 2 blocks east, 15 meters north, tel. 505/2772-3901) comes alive as Matagalpa's premier Friday night fiesta, with live music in a crowded, open-air back patio. More mature revelers and couples enjoy the hassle-free dance floor at **Rincón Paraíso** (Km 125 on the Managua-Matagalpa Hwy., tel. 505/2775-4451).

SHOPPING

The north's famous black pottery—darkened by a particular firing technique—is unique in Nicaragua, where pottery is typically a natural reddish-orange color. Multiple shops bearing the name **Cerámica Negra** are spread throughout the city, offering similar selections, but if you are looking for a specific location, a kiosk is located in Parque Darío. Even La Vita e Bella restaurant offers an excellent variety of ceramics and jewelry.

Telares Indígenas de Nicaragua (in the front of the building shared with Matagalpa Tours, Mon.-Sat. 8am-6pm) offers a great selection of local crafts. The store has the widest selection of sturdy hand-woven bags from the nearby community El Chile. **Centro Girasol** (a bright yellow corner building right across the first bridge as you enter Matagalpa from Managua, tel. 505/2772-6030) has local crafts, jams, honey, coffee, and yogurt.

RECREATION
Hiking

Immediately recognizable by the giant cross on its peak, **Cerro Apante** (1,442 meters) towers above Matagalpa. Officially, it is a nature reserve (entrance fee 30 *córdobas*, or $1.50), though most of its steep flanks are privately owned, covered by thick vegetation and a handful of small farms. Apante is a well-preserved piece of tropical humid forest that contains decent stands of oak and pine, as well as several hundred types of wildflowers. It protects an important source of water for the city (*apante* is Nahuatl for "water") and is crisscrossed with many small trails that lead to its streams and lagoons, all of which are easily accessed by foot from the city.

The two routes to the top both begin by standing at the northwest corner of Parque Darío (in front of Hotel Alvarado). Walking south on the *calle principal* will take you up to the Apante neighborhood on the edge of town (also serviced by the Chispa-Apante *rapibuses*). Continue up the road, keeping the summit to your left and continually asking if you're on the right track to *el cerro*. From the same corner in town, travel due east up a road that climbs steeply, eventually deteriorating into a rutted road. The road switches back a few times, ending at a hacienda atop a saddle in the Apante ridgeline. From there, find a footpath to the top. The actual summit is off limits, and is guarded by a caretaker and his dog, but the nearby ridge offers a breathtaking view. You can link the two hikes into a three-hour loop; bring lots of water. Consider a night tour with a local guide.

Tours

Start by picking up a map at the **Centro Girasol** (a bright yellow corner building right across the first bridge as you enter Matagalpa

from Managua or 2 blocks south and 1 west from the COTRAN Sur, tel. 505/2772-6030). The *Treasures of Matagalpa* map (less than $2) benefits local children with disabilities, and outlines a number of walks, but be warned—although it still serves for some trails, it hasn't been updated in years.

Matagalpa Tours (half a block east of Banpro, tel. 505/2772-0108 or 505/2647-4680, www.matagalpatours.com) is a guide service, travel agent, and backcountry outfitter, run by a Dutch expat named Arjen. Let them arrange a variety of packages including kayaking and rafting expeditions, Bosawás camping treks, coffee plantation tours, and community tourism. Arjen has explored, hiked, and camped throughout the Nicaraguan countryside and has even drawn a number of trail maps. The Bosawás tours are major wilderness excursions that need to be arranged long in advance. Their newest tour is an eight-hour white-water rafting trip on the Río Tuma ($130 pp, less with large groups). They share space with Colibrí Spanish School, run by his partner Noelia, and the artisan store Telares Indígenas de Nicaragua.

Run by English-speaking local Guillermo Gonzalez (a.k.a. Memo), **Nativos Tours** (tel. 505/2772-7281 or 505/8493-0932, nativotour@hotmail.com) is a great choice for your expedition. This nature-lover offers what you'd expect—coffee tours, Apante and Arenal hikes—but he'll also take you running in the city (6 km, $10 pp), on Cerro Apante (12 km, $25 pp), or to La Poza del Corazón (6 km, $15 pp). Individual prices decrease with larger groups. If you're looking to *bacanalear* (party), Memo will take you out for a night on the town, showing you Matagalpa's best nightlife based on your interests (from $20 pp, drinks not included).

Northward Nicaragua Tours (tel. 505/2772 0605, www.adventure-nicaragua. com) creates customized adventure and sport trips based on your interests. Their experienced, English-speaking tour leaders embody an extensive knowledge of Nicaragua and an earnest desire to share its beauty. They work with local guides and promote environmental conservation. Ask about mountain biking trips and bouldering and rappelling opportunities in the area.

ACCOMMODATIONS
Under $25

Hotel Alvarado (across from Parque Darío's northwest corner, tel. 505/2772-2830 or 505/2772-2252, $12 s, 15 d) is run by a friendly Christian doctor couple who also run a pharmacy downstairs. Ask for one of the top-floor rooms, which boast private bathrooms, a breeze, and views of the city and mountains from the small balconies. If their eight rooms are full, ask about their other location across town.

Owned by the same Italian-Nica couple that owns the restaurant across the cobblestone alley, ★ **Bonjourno Principessa** (across from La Vita e Bella, tel. 505/2772-2721, $12 pp dorm double with shared bath, $30 d with private bath, includes delicious breakfast) is a slice of tranquility in the midst of the bustle of the city. Rooms are clean and comfy with hot water and Internet. The rooftop terrace is a great spot to laze in a hammock and enjoy the view.

A peaceful respite in the heart of Matagalpa, ★ **Hostal La Buena Onda** (3.5 blocks east of the Cancha de la Brigadista, tel. 505/2772-2135, www.labuenaonda.com.ni, $8 pp dorm, $30 d) has become a backpacker staple. Its name roughly means "good vibes." The hostel occupies a large, two-story house where travelers can lounge in the garden patio hammocks. There are five communal rooms, each with bathroom, hot shower, and handcrafted wooden bunk beds. You have free coffee and tea available all day. *Buena onda,* indeed.

Hostal Martina's Place (from the Cancha de la Brigadista, 1.5 blocks east, tel. 505/2772-3918, www.martinasplace-hostal.com, $9 pp dorm, $28 d) has a backpacker vibe with a familial spin—it's run by a Spanish family out of their home. (Martina is the name of their daughter.) Rooms are clean and the well-kept garden patio is breezy. A kitchen space is available for guest use, although breakfast is included in private room prices.

If you're looking for an affordable escape from the city, try the clean rooms and pleasant garden at **Hostal Ulap Yasica** (Km 133 on the highway to La Dalia, tel. 505/2772-6443, U.S. tel. 512/487-6850, www.hostalulapyasica.com, $10 dorm, $25 s, $30 d) on the outskirts of town. A six-hour hiking trail begins 200 meters from the hostel's front door, and you're 10 minutes closer to Selva Negra from here. You'll pay double the taxi fare, but it'll still cost under a dollar to get out here (tell the driver you're going to Parador Yasica).

$25-50

Hotel Lomas de San Thomas (350 meters east of Escuela Guanuca, tel. 505/2772-4189, $35 s, $45 d) lords over the city, a mustard-colored, three-story establishment on a breezy hill just east of town. The 25 rooms have private bath, hot water, TV, and telephone, many with an excellent balcony. It gears itself for business conventions and the NGO crew, offering conference rooms, fax, Internet, and a tennis court. To get there, leave the highway at the third entrance to Matagalpa and pass straight through town following the signs. At the eastern edge of Matagalpa, turn left and climb the hill on a cobblestone road to the hotel.

The restaurant at **Las Praderas** (from Shell La Virgen, 200 meters north, tel. 505/2772-4708, $43-51 d) serves an appetizing steak. And hey, the hotel is nice, too. Its spacious, spotless rooms feel more private than others in this price range, and all have air-conditioning, Internet, and hot water. Out front is a guarded parking lot.

$50-100

María's B&B (on Calle 30 de Marzo, from BANPRO, 1 block east, 20 meters north, tel. 505/2772-3097, www.mariasbnb.com, $46-66) is comfy, cozy, and centrally located. Rooms are elegant and simple, but you'll most appreciate the homey feel and plush sofas in the sunlit common areas. The B&B has private

Cool Beans: What Makes Gourmet Coffee

As much as 80 percent of Nicaraguan cooperative-produced coffee can be considered "quality coffee" because it fills the following internationally recognized requirements:

- Arabica beans (not robusta), grown at an altitude of 900 meters or higher, are used.

- Beans are large, and the lots are aromatic, well sorted, and free from broken or burned beans and small stones.

- Beans are given one month to sit during processing and are not de-hulled until just before shipping.

- Beans are transported in sealed containers and are adequately stored by the purchaser.

- Upon roasting, the beans are sealed immediately in special one-pound vacuum-packed bags that prevent the introduction of light, air, and moisture, but permit carbon dioxide to escape.

- The consumer can buy the coffee in whole-bean form, not ground.

parking. ★ **Hotel San José** (behind the San José Church, tel. 505/2772-2544, $50 d, $60 with a/c) offers simple, tidy rooms with hot water, ceiling fans, Wi-Fi, TV, and air-conditioning. Staff are friendly and helpful.

Over $100

Splurge at urban oasis ★ **Montebrisa Boutique B&B** (3 blocks east of Parque Morazán, tel. 505/2772-4292, www.monte-brisa.com, $105-117 d), where you'll find modern amenities in a stylish art deco ambience. The remodel of the family's 1950s home (surrounded by a lovely garden, and an enormous cement wall) highlights all its original architectural details. There's nothing quite like it in the region.

FOOD

The locally owned **Super Estrella** (tel. 505/2772-5404, daily 7am-9pm) is the first **grocery store** open and the last one to close. The smaller **La Estrella 24/7** (from Hotel Bermudez, 1 block north, tel. 505/2772-0257) is the best (and only) option for late nights and early mornings.

Coffee Shops and Cafés

There is no shortage of joe up here where it's produced, and there are plenty of coffee shops

competing for your *córdobas*. ★ **Selección Nicaragüense** (half a block south of the cathedral, daily 8am-10pm) never fails to impress, with chocolate, smoothies, and cakes. **Café Barista** (north side of the cathedral, tel. 505/2772-3183, daily 7:30am-10pm) offers the full barista experience plus crepes, panini, smoothies, and sweets. Both cafés have a second location near Parque Darío. **Barista Coffee of Heaven** (from Citibank, 1.5 blocks south, tel. 505/2772-3646, Mon.-Fri. 10am-9pm, Sat. 9am-9pm, Sun. 7am-9pm) offers crepes, salads, breakfast, and fancy coffee drinks with a celestial theme.

Sniff around east of Bancentro and you will surely catch a whiff of warm, fresh breads and pastries wafting out from **Panadería Belén** (tel. 505/2772-4158, Mon.-Sat. 7:30am-6pm). Make sure you stop in for a *nacatamal* if you're here on the weekend. They have a second location on the south side of Parque Darío.

★ **Bésame** (northeast corner of Parque Darío, Sun.-Thurs. 11am-9pm, Fri.-Sat. until 10pm) is a small café that has everything to please a sweet tooth. Best of all? Homemade sorbet-style ice cream in all sorts of inventive flavors. Try as many as you like for less than $1 each in tiny scoops called *besitos* ("little kisses"). I recommend Amigos con Derechos ("friends with benefits"), a delightful combination of lavender and blueberry.

Artesanos Café Bar (half a block east of Banpro, next to Matagalpa Tours, tel. 505/2772-2444, daily 7am-3pm) is one *norteño*'s cathedral to coffee. Proprietor Noel Montoya offers a close look and taste of Nica beans at their best, and is happy to introduce you to the art of roasting and brewing. Mix the black liquor with Flor de Caña. Open for breakfast and dinner, Artesanos is one of the most relaxing hangouts in the city, especially in the morning. Local artists' paintings and murals decorate the walls of this old colonial building, and an enormous old tree grows out of the back patio.

Comida Típica

Local snacks and simple dishes are Matagalpa's specialty. There's tasty street food in both parks. As always, it's *vigorón* or *chancho con yucca* (both include pork and yucca served on banana leaves). During the lunch hour, several *fritangas* at Parque Morazán serve a more robust menu.

One of the friendliest and most famous *comedores* (cheap lunch counters) is ★ **Don Chaco's** (1.5 blocks east of the Alcaldía, tel. 505/2772-2982, Sun.-Fri. 7:30am-6pm, $2-5), where in addition to heaping plates of *comida típica* (with great veggie options), you'll find a delicious *batido* (smoothie) menu of fruits, vegetables, and even soymilk. If you prefer buffet, lunch-line style, with a smorgasbord of Nica food lined up in front of you, the ragingly popular **Maná del Cielo** (1.5 blocks south of Banco Uno, Mon.-Sat. 7am-8pm, Sun. menu only 7am-10pm, $3-5) will satisfy. It's owned by a retired baseball player who played in Nica's pro leagues for a number of years. Good luck getting a table at lunchtime.

To taste the sweet goodness of Matagalpa's best *güirila* (a sweet-corn pancake wrapped around a hunk of salty *cuajada* cheese, $0.60), you'll have to brave the chaos of the crowds that cluster around the smoky stands across the street from Palí. For a hearty bowl of soup head to **El Sopón** (1.5 blocks east of the Cancha de la Brigadista, tel. 505/2772-5159, Fri.-Wed. 9am-9pm, $4-5).

Everybody loves Don Tano's **Picoteo Café** (1 block south of Teatro Perla, tel. 505/2772-6000, daily 11am-10pm, $2), serving chicken, burgers, pizza, and lots of beer. The walls are covered with platitudes painted on wooden plaques.

La Casona (on the main drag, across from the mayor's office, daily 9am-11pm, $3-4)

MATAGALPA
MATAGALPA

Satisfy your sweet tooth at Bésame.

offers a lunch buffet and a variety of bar-type foods. It's open later on weekends when it turns into a popular bar. Look for the big 7-Up sign outside.

Upscale and International

One of the cornerstones of Matagalpa's dining scene, ★ **La Vita e Bella** (tucked into an alley in the Colonia Lainez, exactly behind Buena Onda, tel. 505/2772-5476, Tues.-Sun. 12:30pm-10:30pm, entrées under $4, large pizza $6) serves Italian and vegetarian dishes, and desserts that will make you glad you found the place. This is possibly the best restaurant in the city for non-chicken and non-beef dishes. There's an excellent wine selection. A new, similar option is **Mesón Italiano** (half a block west of Hotel Bermudez, tel. 505/2772-2369, daily noon-9:30pm, $6-15).

The mellow ambience at **El Mexicano** (from la Doctora Rizo 75 meters east, tel. 505/2772-3732, Mon.-Sat. 11am-9pm, $4-6) sometimes includes live music. From quesadillas to *chalupas* to *chilaquiles*, plates are authentically Mexican—a rare find in Nicaragua.

The best steak in town is at **Toro Bravo** (from the UNAM, 2 blocks north, tel. 505/2772-3240, www.restaurantetorobravo. com, daily 11am-11pm, $5-7), located in a handsome adobe building that offers elegant outdoor seating. For a California burger, ★ **Happy** (southeast corner of Parque Darío, tel. 505/2772-2958, www.happy-matagalpa.com, Tues.-Sat. 11:30am-2:30pm and 5:30pm-9:30pm, Sun. 11:30pm-2pm, $3-7) is where you want to be. U.S.-Nica co-owners bring high-quality culinary skills and hospitality service straight from California to Matagalpa, offering a variety of dishes to please any palate.

INFORMATION AND SERVICES

The friendly **INTUR** (from Citibank, 1.5 blocks south, tel. 505/2772-7060, intur-matagalpa@gmail.com) staff can point you

Volunteering in Matagalpa

Various Matagalpan organizations accept volunteer help from time to time if you'd like to make this your home for a few months or more. The **Movimiento Comunal** (tel. 505/2772-3200, marcxilo@yahoo.com) deals with indigenous rights issues and fights against water privatization. Contact them to discuss volunteer opportunities that fit with your schedule and abilities. **Escuela Especial La Amistad** (from the *antiguo* Royal Bar, 1 block north) works with kids and young adults who have special needs. Stop by and ask how you can help out. The women's sewing group **Telares Indígenas Nicaragua** can use help with a variety of communications and promotions tasks, from taking photos to website design, and much more. Stop by the store in front of the Matagalpa Tours office. An initiative of Matagalpa Tours, **Proyecto de Educación Ambiental Aguali** (www.aguali.net) promotes local environmental education through puppet shows and workshops. Ask about helping out in the Matagalpa Tours office. For more volunteer opportunities, contact **La Escuela de Español Colibrí** or **Centro Girasol.**

in the right direction during your stay in Matagalpa.

Banks

There are a half-dozen banks in Matagalpa—**BAC, Banpro, Citibank, Bancentro,** and **Banco Mercantíl**—and a fistful of money changers that hang out around the southeast corner of Parque Morazán. The banks are mostly clustered in a three-block strip, starting at the southeast corner of Parque Morazán. Nearly all have **ATMs.**

Emergency Services

While there is **Hospital Cesar Amador Molina** (north end of town on the highway to San Ramón, tel. 505/2772-2115), you'll get better medical treatment at the **Clínica Mil**

Flores (from the Banco Mercantíl, 1 block east, half a block north, tel. 505/2772-2944) or **Clínica Santa Fe** (from Semáforos de Salomón López, 2.5 blocks east, tel. 505/2772-5121, www.clinicasantafe.net), which operate 24 hours a day. Local **police** (tel. 505/2772-3511) can be found half a block south of Parque Morazán.

Laundry

Most hostels and hotels can organize a load of laundry for you. Washing your clothes at **Lavandería Cuenta Conmigo** (from Ixchen, 3.5 blocks south, tel. 505/2772-6713, www.lavanderia.cuentaconmigo.info, $3-5 per load) helps out Cuenta Conmigo, an organization that works to strengthen the marginal aid to people with psychosis in Matagalpa. Cost includes one ironed item per load.

Spanish Schools

For 10 years now the **Escuela de Español Colibrí** (half a block east of Banpro, tel. 505/2772-0108, www.colibrispanishschool.com) has been providing excellent one-on-one tutoring and instruction to foreigners looking to learn not just the Spanish language, but also about Nicaraguan history and culture.

They offer flexible schedules as well as local homestay options and apartment rentals. The school is run by a local Nicaraguan woman whose partner runs Matagalpa Tours out of the same space, although the businesses remain separate entities. A package of 20 hours of classes plus a homestay costs $318. Hourly prices are $9-10.

GETTING THERE AND AWAY

Express buses from Managua leave the Mayoreo bus terminal every hour 5:30am-5:30pm bound for Matagalpa or Jinotega (2 hours, about $3). If heading north from Granada or Masaya, you can bypass Managua by grabbing one of two direct buses (less than 3 hours) from the Masaya bus terminal, leaving at 5am and 6am. From León, there are two daily expresses, leaving at 4:30am and 2:45pm (3 hours, $2.50). Matagalpa-bound buses leave every half hour, starting about 5am from Estelí (last bus leaves at 5:45pm) and Jinotega (last bus leaves at 7pm). There is one direct bus from Chinandega to Matagalpa, leaving at 5am.

Matagalpa has two bus terminals. Which one you head to depends on your destination. At the south end of town, **COTRAN**

COTRAN Sur bus terminal in Matagalpa

Sur (tel. 505/2772-4659 or 505/2603-0909) services Managua, Estelí, León, Masaya, and Jinotega. There's a public bathroom ($0.18) and several small *pulperías*. At the ticket window you can buy a seat on the express buses to Managua, which depart every hour 5:15am-5:15pm. No other bus tickets are sold here; pay on the bus. Non-express Managua-bound buses, known as *ruteados,* leave every half hour 3:30am-6pm. Direct buses to Masaya leave daily at 2pm. There's a second bus at 3:30pm, which doesn't leave on Thursday and Sunday. To León via San Isidro and Telica, there are two daily expresses, leaving at 6am, 3pm, and 4pm. There are also *interlocales* minivans that leave whenever they fill up; or take any bus bound for Estelí, get off at the Empalme León, and catch a bus to León (departing every 20-30 minutes). There is a constant flow of buses to Estelí and Jinotega, leaving every half hour 5am-5:40pm (Estelí) and until 6pm (Jinotega). One direct bus to Chinandega leaves Matagalpa at 2pm daily.

At the north end of town, the **COTRAN de Guanuca** services the interior of Matagalpa, including El Tuma-La Dália, San Ramón, Río Blanco, Muy Muy, and Bocana de Paíwas. The ride to San Ramón (45 minutes) costs $0.30. Buses to points east depart every 15-60 minutes until around 4:30pm.

GETTING AROUND

Matagalpa is a good city for walking, except for all those hills. The taxi fare within town is fixed at $0.35, unless you're going far, in which case you'll pay double. Expect the driver to pick up other passengers along the way. City buses ply three different routes back and forth across town, and cost about $0.10. Particularly useful is the bus route called El Chispa.

For car rental, **Budget** (Km 130, tel. 505/2772-3041 or 505/2266-6226, reserve@ budget.com.ni, from $35/day) has a small lot at the La Virgen Shell Station, just as you enter town from the south. **Dollar** (from Claro, 1 block south, tel. 505/2772-4100, www.dollar. com.ni, $40/day) has an office in Casa Pellas.

EAST OF MATAGALPA

Heading into the geographic heart of the nation, travelers encounter broad hillsides of shiny coffee bushes beneath shady canopies, plots of corn and beans, and small communities of tile-roofed adobe houses sitting among the rugged mountains that are the eastern reaches of the Cordillera Dariense. The lands east of Matagalpa made good training grounds for the guerrillas that followed Fonseca into battle against Somoza's troops in the 1970s. Today, the *campesinos* in the folds of these mountains live much the way they have for centuries, even as governments, revolutions, and natural disasters have swirled violently around them.

The major communities and commercial and transportation centers of the east, Río Blanco, Matiguás, and Muy Muy, offer rudimentary accommodations. Don't expect any luxury rides here: The roads east of Matagalpa are some of the most neglected in the country, notably the stretch between Siuna and Mulukuku, which is practically impassable during the wettest months of the year. That said, you will be traveling through some of the most beautiful and least visited parts of Nicaragua.

San Ramón and Vicinity

Only 12 kilometers from Matagalpa, the village of San Ramón is nestled in a lovely valley at the base of several steep hills. This peaceful, friendly hamlet is about 10 square blocks and surrounded on all sides by green farms and forests penetrated by a number of roads and trails. San Ramón has two parks, a health clinic, a gas station, and a number of nonprofit and coffee-related administrative offices. Because of sister-city relationships with Catalan (Spain), Henniker (New Hampshire), and Durham (North Carolina), small groups of wandering foreigners are not uncommon. San Ramón adeptly hosts both foreign groups and individuals in one of several guesthouse and homestay programs.

Use San Ramón as a rural alternative to Matagalpa (travel to and from the city is a

La Ruta de Café

Both international coffee merchants and *café-turistas* can travel a circuit of coffee cooperatives scattered through the mountains of Jinotega, Matagalpa, and the Segovias. As a participant in this Ruta de Café you can sample coffee in special cupping labs and visit coffee-growing families and their farms, which are often enchanting cloud forests shrouded in cool mists. Stay for a couple of hours or a couple of days, living and eating meals with the families, picking coffee, and learning about all stages of the process. You'll even learn what organic, bird-friendly, and fair trade-certified coffees are (visit www.fairtradeusa.org and www.globalexchange.org for details).

To experience the most activity, arrange your visit during the peak of the harvest, usually mid-December-February, when you'll see rows and rows of freshly harvested coffee drying in the sun along the highway to Matagalpa. Make your arrangements in advance with the ecotourism project of the **UCA-San Ramón** (in front of the central park in San Ramón, tel. 505/2772-4478, www.tourism.ucasanramon.com, turismo@ucasanramon.com). They can arrange anything from an afternoon coffee cupping at CECOCAFEN's Sol Café *beneficio* (coffee-processing mill; $7 pp) to a day trip, visiting some of their farmers, to a multi-night excursion, staying in *campesino* homes and touring farms (or even putting some work in during the harvest). Trips include transportation and food, and hikes (with pick-ups) can be arranged between towns. Prices fully depend on the trip. Or consider a stay at **Finca Esperanza Verde** (outside San Ramón, www.fincaesperanzaverde.org), an acclaimed accommodation and working organic coffee farm.

In Jinotega, **SOPPEXCA** (Society of Small Coffee Producers, Exporters, and Buyers, 1 block west of the Ferretería Blandón, tel. 505/2782-2617, www.soppexcca.org, soppexcc@tmx.com.ni) is eager to serve as your tour guide of the region, arranging any number of hikes, trips, and homestays among its growers in the surrounding hills. Their office and cupping lab is located in Jinotega. (This co-op of 15 families sells to brands Peet's Coffee and Sustainable Harvest in the United States.)

There are several welcoming coffee cooperatives in the hills north of Estelí with similar tours available.

cinch), or sample one of the short local excursions, such as the walk to La Pita coffee cooperative. On the way, you'll pass the 100-year-old ruins of the Leonesa mine, overtaken by moss, ferns, and giant ceiba trees. Local tourism association **ADETURS** (next to la Casa del Niño, tel. 505/8652-0426 or 505/8907-6748, turismoensanramon@gmail.com) can hook you up with a local guide. They also set up homestays ($22 pp) in town. Guests get private rooms, and sometimes even a private bathroom, with three meals.

The **UCA-San Rámon** (southside of the central park, tel. 505/2772-5247, 505/8927-9067, or 505/8927-9066, turismo@ucasanramon.com) is an association of fair trade coffee cooperatives. Their main office in town can connect you with a few nearby communities that have developed coffee-related tourism initiatives. La Pita is the only one of these that has an English-speaking guide.

Overlooking the town of San Ramón is **El Sueño de la Campana** (tel. 505/2772-9729, www.fundacionlacampana.es, $12 pp dorm, $30 d), located just down from the gas station, across the creek at the bridge and on the left. This is not only a hostel, but a Spanish NGO that works to create sustainable job opportunities for women and young people. The hostel has 11 rooms from dormitory accommodations to private cabins. There is a restaurant with excellent *comida típica*, laundry service, library, Internet, 24-hour reception, and trails on the property. Stay as a guest or get involved in some of the projects.

One of the only true restaurants in San Ramón is **Las Orquideas** (southside of the central park, tel. 505/2772-5279, $4-8), serving typical fare in a classy dining room with billowing curtains at every window. The hotel ($12 pp dorm, $40 d with a/c and hot water) offers dorm beds and spacious upstairs rooms. There are plenty of more casual eateries, including tasty *comedores* along the sidewalk across the highway from the Shell station. **Doña Nelys Arauz** (under $2) serves heaping plates of originally styled Nica food. **Doña Aracely** (half a block east of the Alcaldía, tel. 505/8961-5903) opens her *fritanga* for dinner.

Buses to and from San Ramón are frequent, leaving the Guanuca terminal every hour or so 6am-7pm, in addition to the many other eastbound buses that pass through San Ramón on their way elsewhere. There's also a *colectivo* taxi service ($0.76), which leaves as soon as the vehicle is full. A direct cab from Matagalpa costs about $5.

LA REINA

Three kilometers east of town is the coffee-growing community of La Reina (also referred to as Monte Grande) where local tourism **Cooperative Danilo González** will be happy to host you and teach you about the harvesting process of the coffee bean. Green Mountain Coffee in the United States buys shade-grown coffee directly from the co-op. Spend a day learning about the co-op and the production process behind your morning coffee. Get there early so you'll have time to scale the steep hillside (about 45 minutes) and enjoy a spectacular view from the top. With an extra half-day you can visit the old gold mine on a two-hour historical tour, part of which involves wading through a cave in knee-deep water. Organize a homestay ($20 pp) with a local family. You'll get your own private room, and eat meals with the family. To visit La Reina, contact the **UCA-San Rámon** (tel. 505/2772-5247, 505/8927-9067 or 505/8927-9066, turismo@ucasanramon.com). To get there on public transport, catch a bus (departing hourly from 5am) in Matagalpa at COTRAN Guanuca heading to Cerro Colorado, El Coroso, La Mula, or Matiguás and tell the *ayudante* to let you off at La

river in San Ramón

Reina. Then plan on a short hike up the road to the community.

LA PITA

Also outside of San Ramón is the community of La Pita, originally founded by miners searching for gold in the area. Nowadays, folks here harvest coffee, corn, and beans. There's also a women's *artesenía* cooperative that creates beautiful stationery and other products from handmade paper, decorated with flower petals. Cooperative Denis Gutierrez can provide you a guide to take you to the four old gold mines on the mountain, one of which is a 46-meter-deep chimney mine. They also offer coffee tours and a hike to a nearby waterfall. Find *hospedaje* at their small **Eco Albergue** ($20 with three meals). The four double rooms each have private bathrooms and impressive views. The lodge was built by a French organization to make it easier for tourists to visit the community. There's no public transportation here. You could walk from town in 40 minutes, or take a cab ($4). To visit La Pita contact the **UCA-San Rámon** (tel. 505/2772-5247, 505/8927-9067 or 505/8927-9066, turismo@ucasanramon.com).

FINCA ESPERANZA VERDE

Finca Esperanza Verde (FEV, tel. 505/8775-5338, 505/2772-3586 or 505/8775-5341, www.fincaesperanzaverde.org, $24-46 pp bunks depending on group size, $95 cabin, $10-12 meals) is a cool, green getaway 18 kilometers outside of San Ramón and 1,180 meters above sea level. Travelers will find a range of peaceful accommodations, as well as beautiful sunsets, delicious food, and a menu of educational and recreational activities. FEV was founded in association with the Durham, North Carolina-San Ramón Sister City Project, but is now privately owned.

The property features several waterfalls, a butterfly house and breeding project (tours $8 pp), and a spring-fed, potable water supply. In November-February, pick, process, and sort the coffee beans, then follow the coffee to Matagalpa where it is sun-dried, sorted, graded, cupped, and exported. Or just relax on the hammock terrace watching the jungle and the sunset.

The lodge and cabins, built of handmade brick and other local materials, can accommodate up to 26 people and are equipped with solar electricity, flush toilets, sinks, and warm sun showers. The bunks and private cabin for two with a view come with private toilets. Meals include fresh juices, fruits, vegetables, and eggs from neighboring farms, and of course, homegrown organic coffee.

If you have a vehicle with moderate clearance (and four-wheel drive for the rainy season), FEV is a 40-minute drive from San Ramón. Follow the road to Yucúl, then turn left and follow the signs to the *finca*. By bus, take the Pancasan-El Jobo bus from the COTRAN Guanuca terminal in Matagalpa, and get off in Yucúl past San Ramón; then follow the signs to FEV, a beautiful 3.5-kilometer uphill walk that should take under an hour. Don't forget to bring a long-sleeve shirt and a rain jacket.

EL CHILE

El Chile has been famous for its weavers for centuries. This was one of the last communities to stop wearing homespun fabrics after the influx of pre-manufactured garments in the early 20th century. The women of El Chile continued weaving until 1942, when the Somoza regime banned the cultivation, spinning, and weaving of cotton and other fabrics. The reason for this prohibition is unknown, though some theorize that it was to free up labor for the fields of nearby landowners, or to weaken the culture and demoralize the people (or both). Whatever the reason, the effect was a total cessation of the craft for more than three decades. After the revolution, the Sandinistas made a point of reviving the lost indigenous weaving techniques, and in 1984, 80 women were trained, some of whom formed three weaving groups in El Chile that still exist today: **Telares Indígenas Nicaragua, Tejidos Indígenas de El Chile,** and **Grupo La Malinche en Sonzapote.** Weaving began as a cultural revival and today has become a productive and self-sustaining business.

You won't find any hotels or restaurants here. If you contact them in advance, **Telares Indígenas Nicaragua** (telaresnicaragua@matagalpa.info) can set you up with food and a homestay. You can visit the weavers on your own, but they aren't accustomed to receiving curious tourists. You'll get more information out of a guide from Matagalpa Tours, whose 5-6 hour tour includes interpreting, transport, a meal, and a hike up Cerro El Chile ($45 for two people, less with larger groups).

To get there on your own, take a bus from Matagalpa's COTRAN Norte (Guanuca) headed to San Dionisio or Esquipulas, departing 8am, 9am and 10:30am. Get off at the junction to El Chile and walk 30 minutes to the weavers' house. The short hike boasts beautiful mountain views. To get back, return to the highway and take a bus to Matagalpa, which pass by at 12:30pm, 2pm, 3pm, and 4:30pm.

Muy Muy

There's not a whole lot of town here, but you're out here for the nature anyway. The town's Nahuatl name refers to otters, which were once plentiful in the surrounding rivers. Grab a bite at **Coffee Angels** (the old Estación Roma, tel. 505/2777-2227, daily 9am-10pm, $3-5) or the **Oasis** restaurant (in the center of town, tel. 505/2777-2066, daily 8am-10pm, $3-6). Nature lovers will be happy at the 170-acre **Ecological Farm El Escondido** (tel. 505/8661-9439 or 505/8821-2423, www.el-escondido.com, $30 cabin, $2-4 meals), which is mostly covered with thick tropical forest. There are a couple of quiet cabins on the property. You can learn about the coffee harvest, go horseback riding, or swim in the Río Escondido. There are four hiking trails to explore: La Poza Azúl, El Salto, El Martiñeno, and La Cascajera. Keep an eye out for sloths, howler monkeys, orioles, and toucans. Make your own pizza in the outdoor wood-burning oven, or ask your hosts to take the grill to the river for a BBQ. In Muy Muy, you can find a taxi to El Escondido for $5. The entrance is four kilometers along the Santa Fe road.

From Managua take a bus headed to Río Blanco from El Mayoreo ($3.75), or from the Guanuca terminal in Matagalpa.

Río Blanco and Cerro Musún Nature Reserve

Cerro Musún encompasses the 1,460-meter peak of the same name and is still the haunt of some of Central America's more elusive mammals, like the puma. (You may catch sight of one on a night tour.) There are three different trails. The shortest is **La Golondrina** (7 km), starting in Río Blanco. Along the way you'll see waterfalls over 50 meters high, and an appreciable amount of wildlife: birds, reptiles, and amphibians, along with an ample variety of orchids, bromeliads, and tree species. The longest hike, **El Mojón** (12 km), takes you all the way to the top in 5-6 hours (up and back). At the top of the massif, you'll be shrouded in cloud forest. The **Bilampi** hike leads to an 80-meter waterfall where a small hydroelectric plant generates electricity for nearby communities. Hire a volunteer park ranger to lead you through the reserve ($8 for up to 8 people, plus $4 entrance fee). Contact **Fadir Rojas** (tel. 505/8403-3885, fadirrojas@gmail.com).

The town of Río Blanco is your jumping-off point for hikes in this tremendous reserve area. Rest and fuel up at **Hotel y Restaurante Bosawás** (at the exit to Matiguás, tel. 505/2778-0160 or 505/8697-9042, $10-12 with fan, $20 with a/c) or **Hotel Nicarao** (across from Findesa, $10 pp). While you're in town, check out the statues in the Catholic church, artifacts from the pre-Columbian civilizations that occupied these lands. They left behind some petroglyphs at the river's edge (visible only during the dry season). Start searching near the red hanging bridge on the exit to Barrio Martin Centeno.

Two express buses (4.5 hours) leave for Río Blanco from Managua's Mayoreo terminal five times daily 4am-2:30pm. Additional service (3.5 hours) is available from the COTRAN Guanuca in Matagalpa every 1.5 hours. You can also get a bus here from Boaco (3 hours), which leaves every hour.

NORTH OF MATAGALPA
Santa Emilia and El Cebollál Waterfall

It's an easy day trip to the farming community of **Santa Emilia** (marked by a left turn at about Km 145). A bit farther, you'll find a 15-meter waterfall spilling impressively into a wide hole flanked by thick vegetation and a dark, alluring rock overhang. The falls are known alternately as Salto de Santa Emilia and Salto el Cebollál. With the new establishment **Ecolodge Cascada Blanca** (tel. 505/2772-3728 or 505/8966-2070, $30-50 d), it's increasingly being referred to as La Cascada Blanca. During the dry season, white water gushes into the river below, creating a pleasant swimming hole. After heavy rains, however, water blasts wildly over the rocks, splashing visitors watching from the metal hanging bridge. Follow the trail into the caves behind the waterfall for a more intimate experience of its natural beauty. Entrance for day-trippers is $2.

The ecolodge has a **restaurant** (daily 9am-5pm, $3-6) serving local fare and vegetarian options. They also offer lodging options, including camping in the aforementioned caves ($4, bring your own tent). Access is just beyond the Puente Yasica, a bridge at about Km 149; look for a small house and parking area on the right, where a soft-drink sign reads Balneario El Salto de Santa Emilia. You'll be asked to pay a $1 parking fee unless you're just jumping off the Tuma-La Dalia bus.

El Tuma and La Dalia

Intimately connected to the Contra War of years past, El Tuma and La Dalia are local commercial centers serving the local farming region. Both host resettlement camps where Contras gave up their weapons in exchange for a piece of land to farm. ★ **La Sombra Eco-Lodge** (tel. 505/8455-3732 or 505/8468-6281, www.lasombraecolodge.com, sombra_ecolodge@yahoo.es, $45-55 pp, or $15 for the day) is an ecotourist facility set in a private forest reserve on about 200 hectares of shade-grown coffee and hardwoods. Stay in their enormous, wooden lodge house, with spacious balconies overlooking the greenery, where the

price includes three meals and coffee, tours of the butterfly and frog farms, hiking, and swimming in Cascada El Eden. They also lead guided trips on horseback.

About 10 kilometers (15 minutes) southwest of La Dalia in the Río Tuma, **Piedra Luna** is a rainy season-only swimming hole formed by the waters of the Río Tuma swirling around a several-ton rock sitting midstream. The swimming hole is easily seven meters deep, and local kids come from all over to dive off the rock into the pool. How did the rock get there? Ask the locals, who will relate the fantastic legend of the spirits that carried it there from someplace far away.

Find buses to Tuma-La Dalia at the Guanuca terminal in Matagalpa ($2). You can take a taxi from town to La Sombra ($5). From Managua, take a bus from El Mayoreo bound for Wasala, which passes by these towns.

★ WHITE-WATER RAFTING

The Río Tuma starts at the Apanás Lake outside of Jinotega and turns into the Río Grande before emptying into the Caribbean Sea. Along this waterway are class 3 rapids (sometimes 4) and miles of untouched forest. **Matagalpa Tours** (tel. 505/2772-0108 or 505/2647-4680, www.matagalpatours.

white-water rafting on the Río Tuma

com, $130 or less depending on group size) is the only tour operator that offers white-water rafting in the country. They offer a five-hour paddle starting at El Tuma-La Dalia for up to 10 people. Cost includes transport from Matagalpa, lunch, and all necessary equipment.

★ El Macizo de Peñas Blancas

Located in the department of Jinotega on the road that leads between El Tuma-La Dalia and El Cuá, the cliffs of Peñas Blancas (1,445 meters) are several hundred meters high and carved out of the top of a massive hillside. This is unquestionably one of the most stunning natural sights in northern Nicaragua and the widely respected Gateway to Bosawás. At the top of the cliff is the **Arcoiris** ("rainbow") waterfall, gorgeous and little known. The cliffs and waterfall are easily visible from the highway.

The hike is much easier in the dry season. You'll pass through a series of humid forest ecosystems of orchids and mossy trees. Near the falls, the wind is full of spray. The hike up and down can be done in two hours but expect to get extremely muddy and wet during the rainy season. Guides (about $5) leave regularly with groups from the Centro de Entendimiento con la Naturaleza (CEN). There's a longer hike (4 hours) that leads to the top of the *macizo* (massif), where the waterfall splashes over the cliffs for some unforgettable views.

There are a few options for hikers that want to stay the night. **GARBO-Cooperativa Guardianes del Bosque** (tel. 505/8641-3638 or 505/7711-0623) is a cooperative of local coffee farmers who will be glad to give you a tour of their farms ($8-10). The co-op has a humble *hospedaje* (400 meters from Empalme la Manzana, $6 dorm, $12 private cabin, $3-4 meals). One member of the co-op, **Don Chico** (tel. 505/2770-1359) has basic rooms available in his home for similar prices. The family restaurant out front is a great spot for a home-cooked breakfast. The **CEN** (tel. 505/8852-6213, www.cenaturaleza.

the Arcoiris waterfall at Peñas Blancas

org, cenbosawas@gmail.com, $100 d cabin, $70 d private room, $27 dorm) is an NGO and research center that works to preserve the surrounding nature. They have creatively-built cabins, as well as rooms and dorms, available for tourists with community dinners open to all ($4-7). Prices include meals and hikes.

Take the El Cuá-Bocay bus from Matagalpa (leaves Guanuca station five times daily 6am-1:30pm). Get off at Empalme La Manzana (about 14 kilometers before El Cuá) in the community of Peñas Blancas. Walk 500 meters along the road and you'll come to a series of lodging options. A Matagalpa-bound bus passes the entrance to the reserve at 2pm.

THE MATAGALPA-JINOTEGA HIGHWAY

The sinuous mountain road between Matagalpa and Jinotega is considered one of the most scenic roads in all of Nicaragua. You'll pass neatly arranged coffee plantations shaded by rows of cedar and pine, banana trees, and canopies of precious hardwoods.

There is also an endless succession of vegetable and flower fields, and roadside stands that sell farm-fresh goods. A set of small farm stands along the road are evidence of the rich harvests of this area. Whether you want to eat them or just photograph them, the stacks of fresh cabbage, carrots, and greens are a culinary feast for the eyes. The stands are typically run by the family's older children, who might sweet-talk you into making a purchase.

The Matagalpa-Jinotega Highway was first opened around 1920 by the English immigrant and coffee farmer Charles Potter for use by mules and wagons taking coffee from his farm to Matagalpa. No small feat of engineering, the road had to negotiate over 100 curves, the worst of which was the Disparate de Potter (still legendary). A stubborn old man, Potter built his road in spite of the naysayers, and it's said he used the road to carry a piano—strung atop two mules—all the way to his farm. At Km 143, there's now a restaurant bearing the name **El Disparate de Potter** (tel. 505/2772-2553 or 505/8621-3420, daily 9am-8pm, $5-8) that caters to tourists who want to take in the long valley panoramas, which are often breathtaking: Momotombo and the Maribio volcanoes are visible when the sky is clear.

★ Hotel de Montaña Selva Negra

Twenty minutes north of Matagalpa, **Hotel de Montaña Selva Negra** (tel. 505/2772-3883 or 505/2772-5713, www.selvanegra.com, reservaciones@selvanegra.com, from $15 hostel, $30 d, $95 private bungalow) has been an anchor in Nicaragua's tourism scene since well before there ever *was* a tourism scene. With a name meaning Black Forest, it remains popular for people looking to hike, dine, and monkey-watch, though San Ramón and La Sombra now provide healthy competition.

The resort is, at its heart, a coffee farm by the name of La Hammonia, owned and run by Eddy Kühl and Mausi Hayn, third- and fourth-generation German immigrants and members of the founding families of the country's coffee industry. The farm—considered one of the most diversified in Central America, and winner of the 2007 Sustainability Award from the Specialty Coffee Association of America—is based on the German tradition of chalets set around a peaceful pond with access to short hiking trails up the adjoining 120-hectare hillside and along its ridge. Rooms range from a spot in the youth hostel to a double overlooking the lake to a private bungalow. There are larger

MATAGALPA
MATAGALPA

cozy cabin at Hotel de Montaña Selva Negra

bungalows for groups and families. The restaurant serves hearty, home-cooked meals using organic ingredients produced entirely on the farm. You'll dine on a gorgeous outdoor patio overlooking the water. Needless to say, the coffee is superb and fresh (and sold at Whole Foods Market in the United States).

Selva Negra is a birder's paradise with 300 species of birds. Try to spot them with one of the professionally trained bird guides. Tours ($15-20 pp) of the coffee farm, flower plantations, the cattle, and livestock start at 7:30am, 9:30am, and 2:30pm—in Spanish, English, and German when Mausi is available. Almost everything on the farm is recycled, even the plastic bottles, which are used as pest control. The half-hour tour ($5 pp) is an amazing education in permaculture and innovative organic methods. Or you can easily rent a horse for the day and ride the many roads that crisscross the plantation on your own. In 2000, the Kühls built a gorgeous, orchid-adorned stone chapel for the wedding of their daughter, and they now rent out the facilities—chapel, horse-drawn carriage, and fresh-cut flowers—for guests who come to get hitched.

Expect to have a chat with the owners while you're there. Eddy is a wealth of knowledge, a prolific writer, and a well-loved amateur anthropologist. Many of the family's ideas have come from the suggestions and talents of the guests who visit them.

An old military tank on the side of the road 15 minutes' drive north of Matagalpa, a relic from the revolution, marks the entrance to Selva Negra. Jinotega-bound buses from Matagalpa will drop off here (tell the driver you want to get off at Selva Negra, or Km 140). Then walk a mile down a shady gravel road to the entrance gate.

El Arenal Reserve

True to form in this wet northern region, **Reserva Natural El Arenal** (look for the sign at Km 142.5 on the Matagalpa-Jinotega Hwy.) is covered in giant old oaks often obscured by a misty cloud forest. Reportedly, the oldest tree in the country can be found on this hill. At 40 meters high and 2.5 meters in diameter, it's estimated to be around 500 years old. On these slopes the Jiguina River is born, which contributes to the city of Matagalpa's potable water and 35 percent of its electricity. The reserve covers an area of over 14 square kilometers and its highest peak is over 1,500 meters above sea level. The existing hiking trails vary in difficulty and length, providing accessible conditions for any visitor.

The Eco Albergue in La Fundadora is a peaceful mountain retreat.

You'll come across monkeys, armadillos, and a variety of birds, including the sacred quetzal. In the various farms you'll find coffee, vegetables, basic grains, and many varieties of orchids. Tour operators in Matagalpa offer a variety of trips to El Arenal.

On the northern side of Cerro Arenal is the **Hotel de Montaña Aguas del Arenal** (tel. 505/8886-3234, aguasdelarenal@gmail.com, $30 d, $50 cabin), with clean, pleasant rooms and cabins. Everything about this place invites you to enjoy the calm serene vibe, from the striking natural beauty to the friendliness of your hosts. Accommodations have private baths and hot-water showers. Vegetarians will be satisfied with their options for meals. Guests receive a free farm tour in Spanish, English, German, or Italian. The hotel is 2.8 kilometers from the Matagalpa-Jinotega Highway (the same turn off for the reserve) outside Aranajuez. From the Empalme El Porvenir, it's 50 meters south, 10 meters uphill, 50 meters south. Pick up service is available from Matagalpa.

The **Colectivo de Mujeres de Aranjuez** in the town of Arenal is a women's group who studies and shares natural medicine techniques. The initiative was created to contribute to the holistic health of local families and has also created alternative income for participants. They sell herbs and homemade marmalade.

★ La Fundadora

At the foot of Datanlí el Diablo is the coffee-growing community of La Fundadora. Tucked away in the mountains some three kilometers from the highway, it was once home to the hacienda of the Englishman Charles Potter. Founded in 2001, La Reforma cooperative in the community of La Fundadora is younger than most in Nicaragua. A few years ago in an effort to diversify its income and create sustainable development, they constructed the **Eco Albergue** (tel. 505/8855-2573 or 505/8929-7439, www.fundadora. org, info@fundadora.org, $15 s, $20 d, $6 dorm, $4 camping or $1 with your own tent) with the help of local NGO Culculmeca. It has quickly gained a reputation as one of the country's gems of community tourism. Five private cabins are scattered over a hilly property around a garden and main building where food is served and the kitchen is available for guest use. (There are a couple of eateries in town, five minutes away.) The fantastic views of mountains stretching out on all sides lend a feeling of serenity. Hang around on the porch of your cozy cabin (with hot-water shower) and snuggle around a roaring bonfire at night.

From here there's a nice hike into the Datanlí el Diablo reserve that leads you to La Bujona waterfall. If it's not too cold, jump in for a swim. (You have to walk through fenced-in private property to access the waterfall, but the folks at the Eco Albergue have a key.) Or go on horseback ($25).

There are two buses that will drop you at La Fundadora, leaving Matagalpa's Guanuca terminal at 1pm and 2pm ($1). Any other time of day, you can catch a bus between Jinotega and Matagalpa (less than $1) and get off at the Empalme Las Latas and walk three kilometers over rolling hills lush with trees and coffee plants to the Eco Albergue.

Jinotega

Walking the cobbled streets of Jinotega, you can't help but feel you're at the edge of the world, with hundreds of kilometers of wild, lush mountain country beckoning to the east, where the pavement stops, the roads turn rutted and bumpy, and accommodations dwindle, at least the kind where they fold the edge of the toilet paper into a little triangle. Jinotega is replete with fragrant valleys of orange groves, white corn, plantains, sweet vegetables, and a whole lot of cattle. In between the farms, Jinotega is open space—virgin forest, small freshwater lagoons, stately mountain ranges, and the mighty Río Coco (which forms the northern border of the Jinotega department) and the Río Bocay.

The name Jinotega is said to come from the Nahuatl name Xilotl-Tecatl ("place of the jiñocuabo trees"; also translated as "the place of the eternal men and women"). Indeed, the natives who lived in this peaceful valley enjoyed healthy and prosperous existences and were known to live to more than 100 years of age. Jinotega was possibly the worst affected department in Nicaragua during the 1980s, when Contras and Sandinistas fought each other on the mountain roads and deep valleys. Since then, Jinotega has voted steadfastly against the Sandinistas, who they claim are responsible for 10 years of devastation.

Nowadays, "The City of Mists" is the watering hole and commercial center for the department. Farmers from the north and east inevitably find their way here to do their business; to serve them, Jinotega City has developed into a clean, prosperous community. Gateway to the wide-open expanses of the east, Jinotega is at once charming and thrilling. Travelers enjoy it because the high elevation gives it a pleasant climate. (Don't forget your sweater!)

ORIENTATION

Jinotega occupies the bottom of the steep-walled bowl formed by the mountains that surround it on all sides. The highway passes along its east side, and the cemetery is at the western edge.

SIGHTS

There are few traditional tourist sights in Jinotega, but lots to see and do. Jinotega was the scene of a few ferocious battles during the revolution years, and it was down by the riverside in Jinotega where much-loved Sandinista commander German Pomares (a.k.a. El Danto), who had been instrumental in the operation that led to political prisoner Daniel Ortega's release from jail, was killed in battle. A carefully maintained red-and-black **memorial** marks the spot where he was killed.

In front of the **Catedral San Juan Bautista,** the **central park** is a gathering place for families, and folks looking for a Wi-Fi signal (free signal in the park). At one time, it was common to find wild monkeys in the old-growth park canopy of *lechito* trees. Nowadays a family of sloths has made their home in it.

Don Pilo is a second-generation medicine man who lives in an unknown location in the mountains west of Jinotega city. On Tuesdays and Fridays, he climbs down out of the mountains with bags of herbs and potions and sets up camp at the cemetery to sell them. He's a well-loved town character who some put off as a charlatan and others consider a true magician and physician. Regardless, both rich and poor wait for him to see if he can cure their ills, from intestinal parasites to bad marriages and spurned lovers. The cures are all natural and brewed out of the strong medicinal plants of the region.

The town **cemetery** is an interesting place

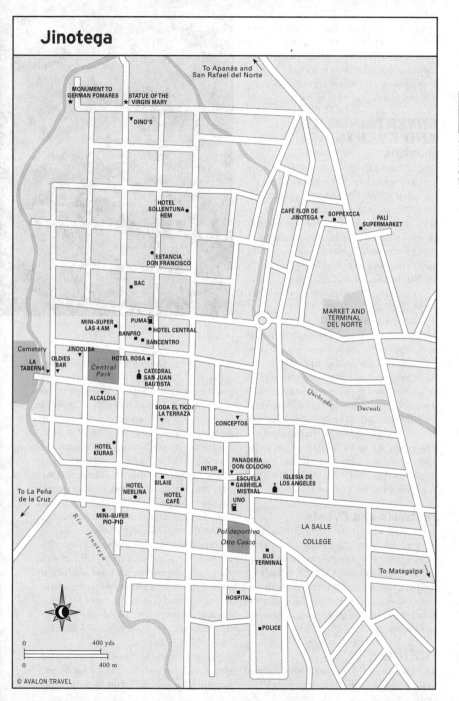

Jinotega

To Apanás and
San Rafael del Norte

MONUMENT TO
GERMAN POMARES

STATUE OF THE
VIRGIN MARY

DINO'S

HOTEL
SOLLENTUNA
HEM

CAFÉ FLOR DE
JINOTEGA

SOPPEXCCA

PALÍ
SUPERMARKET

ESTANCIA
DON FRANCISCO

BAC

MINI-SUPER
LAS 4 AM

PUMA

HOTEL CENTRAL

BANPRO

BANCENTRO

MARKET AND
TERMINAL
DEL NORTE

Cemetery

JINOCUBA

OLDIES
BAR

HOTEL ROSA

Central
Park

CATEDRAL
SAN JUAN
BAUTISTA

LA
TABERNA

Quebrada

Ducuali

ALCALDIA

SODA EL TICO/
LA TERRAZA

CONCEPTOS

HOTEL
KIURAS

PANADERÍA
DON COLOCHO

INTUR

ESCUELA
GABRIELA
MISTRAL

IGLESIA DE
LOS ANGELES

HOTEL
NEBLINA

SILAIS

HOTEL
CAFÉ

UNO

To La Peña
de la Cruz

Río Jinotega

MINI-SUPER
PIO-PIO

Polideportivo
Otto Casco

LA SALLE

COLLEGE

BUS
TERMINAL

To Matagalpa

HOSPITAL

POLICE

0   400 yds

0   400 m

© AVALON TRAVEL

to wander. The graves started at the entrance to the cemetery and have worked their way south over time. The victims of the war in the 1980s are located at the south end of the plot. Some of the older gravestones are particularly ornate and well crafted in stone.

ENTERTAINMENT AND EVENTS
Nightlife

One of the better bars in town, and a common expat hangout, is **La Taberna** (on the right just before the cemetery gate, closed Mon.) serving food, booze, and unique cocktails. This place takes the cowboy motif to an extreme with a woven bamboo roof and barstools with saddles. However, the carefully partitioned and cozy feel lends a romantic air. **Bull's Bar** (from Silais, 2 blocks north, 2 blocks east) is a popular alternative in the chill bar scene.

There are two small discos in town. Start with the tried-and-true **Conceptos** (not far from the center of town), formerly a house but was converted into a dance hall with a house-party feel. The newer **Insomnia** (Barrio Llano de la Cruz, from the *monumento de la cruz*—the cross monument—100 meters northeast, tel. 505/8651-3781, $1 cover) is insanely popular with young folks. In the words of one Jinotegano, it's up to "Managua standards." There's generally karaoke until 1am. It's outside of town, so you'll need to spring for a taxi to get there and back (about $5).

Festivals and Events

Folks from all over the north of Nicaragua show up for Jinotega's *fiestas patronales* (May 1-May 15). The *fiestas patronales* of San Juan de Jinotega are June 24. In addition (perhaps just to round out the year with parties), the *Aniversario de la Creación del Departamento de Jinotega* is celebrated on October 15.

HIKING

La Peña de la Cruz atop the western wall of the Jinotega valley makes a popular climb

Misty mountains surround Jinotega.

for a Saturday morning up to where the cross is planted. The hike is 60-90 minutes, and you'll be rewarded with an impressive view of the city and the verdant valley of Jinotega. If visibility is good, you can see all the way to Apanás Lake. The cross isn't the original. Locals say its predecessor was bigger and "better"; it was said to have stopped an avalanche from crashing down and covering the city. But, the modern cross is illuminated, thanks to an electric cable that climbs the steep hillside. Look for the shining beacon of Christianity at night from the city. Start at the cemetery and follow the paved road on the left from the gate. You'll see a graffitied sign identifying the start of the hike, after which you'll pass through a fence and start upwards on the dirt road. You'll soon come to the beginning of a stairway that winds all the way up the mountain. (I lost count, but it's something like 1,000 stairs in total.)

The eastern wall of the valley is steeper and longer, and there are no trails. That doesn't stop many locals from making their way to the top for a look around. Plan on two hours for this one. The easiest way to do it is the steep, windy dirt road that climbs abruptly out of the city and snakes its way to the top of the ridge. By road, it's around an hour on foot, but it's still not an easy walk, as the road is exceptionally steep. Watch your step on the loose gravel.

ACCOMMODATIONS

Until recently, Jinotega's chief clientele were the small-scale farmers of the east who come to see a dentist, sell some corn, and have their boots fixed, as evidenced by all the under-$4 *hospedajes* that spot the neighborhood around the market. The following are some more "upscale" options. As you choose your lodging, remember to ask about hot water: This is about the only area in Nicaragua where you'll want it.

Under $25

Hotel Rosa (behind the cathedral, $4-5 pp) is the oldest gig in town, and 100 years ago, when it first opened its doors, it was the only gig in town. Its 19th-century feel remains in massive wooden beams, simple rustic rooms, and a laid-back atmosphere. The 30 rooms are somewhat dark and dingy.

★ **Hotel Neblina** (from the Polideportivo Otto Casco, 2.5 blocks west, tel. 505/2782-2899 or 505/8153-4069, hotelneblinajinotega@gmail.com, $15 s, $20 d, includes breakfast, $5 more with a/c) has simple, pretty, and clean rooms with hot water and TV. For a great view, ask for a second-floor room facing the western mountains. **Hotel Central** (1 block from the park, tel. 505/2782-2063, $20 d) is indeed central and features a massive lobby leading back to 23 well-lit rooms not much larger than their beds. There are nice rooms upstairs with cable TV, private bath, and hot water.

Hotel Sollentuna Hem (3 blocks north, 2 blocks east of the central park, tel. 505/2782-2334, hotelsollentuna@gmail.com, $20 d, breakfast $2, lunch and dinner $3) is owned by a Swedish-Nica woman. The hotel's name is Swedish for "home of the green valley." In

business since 1988, the hotel has 17 different rooms (Scandinavian clean, with a unique, mismatched style) with private baths and hot water. Meals are available, and she can accommodate vegetarians. Complete laundry service is offered, as are tours of her farm on the outskirts of town.

$25-50

★ **Estancia Don Francisco** (from the main Puma station, 250 meters north, tel. 505/2782-2309 or 505/8465-7861, www.estanciadedon-francisco.com, estanciadonfrancisco@gmail.com, $40-50 d, includes breakfast) welcomes you with its plush sofas in a sunlit sitting room. Rooms are varied (one has a balcony) and include WiFi, TV, and private bathroom with hot water. There is a verdant garden in the courtyard, bar, and parking. Rooms at **Hotel Kiuras** (from the cathedral, 1.5 blocks south, tel. 505/2782-3938, $20 d) have private baths, TV, and Wi-Fi. There's also a delicious café out front.

Over $50

Jinotega's classiest accommodation, the ★ **Hotel Café** (1 block west, half a block north of the Uno station, tel. 505/2782-2710, www.cafehoteljinotega.com, $63-67 d, includes breakfast) stands head and shoulders above the rest with its 16 tidy, comfortable, and tastefully decorated rooms, taking up two stories and surrounding a lush garden and spiral staircase. The rooms feature private baths, hot water, cable TV, telephones, desks, and air-conditioning. There are mini-suites for a few bucks more. You'll find valet parking and laundry service. Hotel Café accommodates groups and has a conference room, business center, and great views of the surrounding city and countryside, as well as Jinotega's nicest restaurant and bar. Hotel staff can assist in planning your visit and tours of the area.

FOOD

Meals are simple but hearty in this neck of the woods. There are no real fine dining options (except in the Hotel Café). After dark, the streets fill with *fritangas* (street-side barbecues and fry-fest), and families open their front doors to create cheap eateries in their living rooms and front parlors. You can eat your way to greasy happiness for under $2 with no effort at all. Start at the southeast corner of the park and stroll the two main streets through a sea of enchiladas, *papas rellenas* (stuffed and fried potatoes), and *gallo pinto* (the national dish of rice and beans).

★ **Soda El Tico** (in front of Colegio La Salle, tel. 505/2782-4530, daily 8am-5pm, $3-6), a local lunch favorite, is just east of the park and has a clean and inexpensive lunch buffet and simple menu. **La Terraza** (upstairs from Soda El Tico, daily 10am-10pm) is a tranquil spot to sip some coffee and enjoy a dessert. **Dino's** (from the Virgin Mary statue, 1 block south, tel. 505/2782-2137, daily 8am-10pm, $7-10) is a popular option for pizza, and it turns into a hangout after dinnertime.

If you need a break from Nica food, **Jinocuba** (from the Alcaldía, 5 blocks north, tel. 505/2782-2963, Wed.-Mon. open from noon) serves up delicious Cuban cuisine like *lechón* (grilled pork), and of course, mojitos. The **Restaurante Borbón** (at the Hotel Café, tel. 505/2782-2710, $6-15) is the most upscale option. They feature a full wine and foreign drink list at the bar, and the chicken cordon bleu is spectacular.

For baked goods hit **Panadería Don Colocho** (northside of the Escuela Gabriela Mistral, tel. 505/2782-2584, Mon.-Sat. 8am-6pm), which has earned a reputation among locals for its great bread and cakes. Be sure not to miss ★ **Café Flor de Jinotega** (tel. 505/2782-2617), located next to the Soppexcca coffee exchange, a small-scale coffee producers' cooperative (it's more commonly referred to as Soppexcca). Here you can have a cappuccino as good as any in Nicaragua, check out educational displays on coffee and coffee economics, and check out packages as they're sold in the United States (by brands like Peet's and Thanksgiving). Hit it before or after you get on the bus for the hinterlands at COTRAN Norte.

INFORMATION AND SERVICES

The local **INTUR** office (from Polideportivo Otto Casco, 1 block north, tel. 505/2782-4552) can give you a lot of useful information about the area. *Promotor* Martín is passionate about his work, and will make you love Jinotega as much as he does.

There's a bank on practically every corner in Jinotega. All the major players, including **Banpro, Bancentro,** and **BAC,** are present. Bank hours are standard; check your firearm at the door, please. The most reliable **ATM** is found at BAC (1.5 blocks north of the central park).

Centro de Salud Guillermo Matute (next to Barrio German Pomares, tel. 505/2782-3807) is the local health center, adequate for your most basic ailments. More immediate issues can be taken care of at the **Hospital Victoria Motta** (in Barrio 20 de Mayo, tel. 505/2782-4206), though if you have the means, it's best to go to Managua. If you're staying at Kiuras, you're in luck—the owner is a doctor.

GETTING THERE AND AWAY

Buses leave every half hour from COTRAN Sur in Matagalpa 5am-6pm. Find an updated schedule on the board above where the bus parks.

The southern bus terminal (under construction at the time of writing) is located across from La Salle (a Catholic high school). Several eateries line the road behind the station, where you can relax and wait for the bus to leave, as the terminal doesn't have any facilities for passengers.

Buses to Matagalpa (1 hour) leave every half hour 5am-6pm. Buses head south to Matagalpa and Managua, including several express buses that make one stop along the highway at Matagalpa without entering the city itself, then continuing straight on to Managua. Express buses to Managua (3 hours, $4) leave every hour. Ask ahead to find out what your options are. The last one leaves at 4pm, but you can also catch a bus to Matagalpa and continue south from there.

Buses leave for Estelí from the COTRAN terminal on a long, roundabout overland route that may require making a connection in La Concordia or San Rafael del Norte. The northern terminal also has regular bus service to San Sebastián de Yalí and La Rica, via San Rafael del Norte and La Concordia, from where you can get back-road bus service to Estelí—a fun way to make a loop through some really beautiful country. It is much easier to get to Estelí by simply taking any Managua bus to Sébaco, and transferring to a northbound bus heading to Estelí, Ocotal, Somoto, or Jalapa.

Buses leave for points inland in Jinotega and beyond, including El Cuá, San José de Bocay, San Rafael del Norte, and Wiwilí. There are five express buses for Estelí, 5:15am-3:30pm. There are 10 regular buses for San Rafael del Norte, departing 6am-6pm. Regular buses for Wiwilí (7 hours) depart 4am-1:15pm. Regular service to El Cuá-Bocay (4 hours) begins daily at 4am. There is regular service to Pantasma (2 hours) about once per hour until 4:40pm. Pantasma buses go past Asturias and the dam at Lago de Apanás.

GETTING AROUND

With a cool climate and not too much traffic, Jinotega is pleasant for walking. There are no city buses, nor is there need for them. Several taxi cooperatives circulate the city streets and will take you across town for $0.35.

EL VALLE DE TOMATOYA

Located just north of the city of Jinotega on the road to San Rafael del Norte, this is the home of a women's cooperative that produces the region's famous black pottery. The production of black pottery is a little more intricate than other types of ceramic arts, and in fact there are only two other countries where it's produced: Mexico and Chile. These women have produced beautiful pieces of art, including faithful replicas of pre-Columbian designs, as well as many utilitarian pieces.

Grupo de Mujeres de Las Cureñas has some fine pieces for sale. Buses from Jinotega heading to San Rafael can let you off along the way.

LA BASTILLA ECOLODGE

La Bastilla (tel. 505/2782-4335 or 505/8654-6235, www.bastillaecolodge.com, $15 camping, $20 dorm, $45 s, $70 d, includes breakfast) is not only an eco-lodge, but also a rural entrepreneurship school. The profits generated by the hotel are reinvested back into the school. Rustic, cozy cabins fit up to four people. All come with their own balcony and solar-heated showers in private en-suite bathrooms. There are dorms for those on a budget, and luxury camping platforms, which include large tents and private bathrooms. There is complimentary coffee all day. Food (lunch and dinner $5-10) is prepared with fresh ingredients from the school's farm. There's plenty to do here: coffee tours, bird-watching, and hiking. The location has the added benefit of being close to Apanás Lake, which provides the option for kayaking.

La Bastilla is about 20 kilometers from Jinotega city in the Datanlí el Diablo Nature Reserve. From Jinotega travel by bus from the COTRAN Norte bound for Pantasma, or rent a 4WD vehicle in Matagalpa for the bumpy, country road. Following the road towards Pantasma, you will pass El Puente de Jigüina. After the bridge take the second entrance on the right. La Bastilla Ecolodge is approximately 5 kilometers from the entrance. If arriving by bus, the lodge can pick you up from the Technical Centre ($2 pp). They can also set up private transportation from Jinotega ($35).

LAGO DE APANÁS

Apanás Lake is the largest artificially constructed body of water in Nicaragua. Luís Somoza Debayle's administration created it in 1964 by damming the Río El Tuma, flooding the broad valley just north of Jinotega, which contained pasture, small farms, and an airstrip. Today, Apanás Lake is a long, irregularly shaped lake. It feeds the twin turbines at the Planta Hidroeléctrica Centroamérica, which produces 35 percent of the nation's hydropower. Hurricane Mitch nearly sent the whole works downstream in 1998, and the government has been negotiating since 1999 to find a way to repair the damaged spillway and return the dam's safety structures to normal, while the IMF and World Bank have been trying to privatize the whole system. The lake itself is picturesque, but equally impressive are the remains of the damaged spillway. On the lake side of the road are the remains of a military base built in the 1980s to prevent Contra troops from destroying the dam.

A stretch of waterfront has been developed to make the lake more accessible to tourists in the town of Sisle. Here you'll find **Mirador y Comedor Norita** (tel. 505/8651-2336 or 505/8367-8443), which offers a lovely lookout point from which to enjoy your lunch. You can fish for giant tilapia and *guapote*, or take a dip. The **Cooperativa de pescadores "El Conejo"** (Javier Altamirano tel. 505/8367-8443) rents boats and kayaks. Or inquire at the restaurant **El Chilamate** (tel. 505/8625-5306 or 505/8787-7658) about rentals. There are several grassy areas at the lake's edge where you can jump in the surprisingly cold water of Apanás. From the dam, walk along the highway in either direction and choose your place. The lake is safe. There are no underwater structures or water intakes to fear, and the water is deep and refreshing. Obviously, stay away from the spillover drain.

To get to the dam, take any bus headed toward Pantasma and get off at Asturias (60-90 minutes from Jinotega). The highway crosses the dam, so you'll know when you've arrived.

SAN RAFAEL DEL NORTE

This remote, cloud-shrouded town has a cool climate and is surrounded by green hills year-round. San Rafael served as the proving grounds for the general's legendary battles with the U.S. Marines in the 1930s. Sandino's wife was a San Rafaelina, and Nicaraguan folk musician Carlos Mejía Godoy wrote moving lyrics about love and war in Sandino's hills there.

Sights

Some call **La Iglesia de San Rafael del Norte** (on the north side of the central park) the most beautiful church in all of Nicaragua. Pastel-colored windows admit a calming light in which to view the many bright murals, reliefs, and shrines. Many Nicaraguans distinguish between Sandino the man and Sandinismo as practiced by Daniel Ortega. Look closely at the inside left wall of the church, where a painting of the devil implies that Daniel has betrayed the ideals of Sandino.

The church was a project of Italian priest Odorico d'Andrea, who gave much more than that to this town, including a health clinic, library, and several neighborhoods for the poor. From his arrival in 1953 to his death in 1996, Father Odorico achieved virtual sainthood among the people of San Rafael and surrounding communities. His image, a smiling man in plain brown robes, can be seen all over town. Many believe he performed miracles and that his body has not decomposed. You can check for yourself at its resting place, called the **Tepeyac Retreat Center** (5 blocks north of the central park) on the Cerro de Tierra Colorada, the hill overlooking the town. Ascending the stairs, you'll pass the 12 stations of the cross until you reach the shrine on top where the tomb lies, as well as gorgeous views. An impressive stand of old trees shades the hilltop. Virgin pine forests carpet the countryside.

Recreation

There are some precious **swimming holes** around San Rafael, the easiest of which to access are in the two creeks that meet at Los Encuentros restaurant, a 10-minute walk on the road to Yalí. You can also **hike** into the gorge that runs on the north edge of town; descend from the Hospedaje Rolinmar, and then start upstream to where cold water rushes out of a narrow canyon.

Zip-line over the Nicaraguan countryside five minutes north of San Rafael del Norte with **Canopy La Brellera** (tel. 505/2784-2356 or 505/8976-6360, daily 8am-4:30pm, $15 pp).

The 12 platforms and short return walk take about an hour.

Accommodations and Food

There are great eats at **Doña Chepita's** ($2-4), and there are two places to stay. ★ **Hotel Casita San Payo** (2.5 blocks north of the park, tel. 505/2784-2327, www.hotelcasitasanpayo.com, $13 s, $17 d) is a cute family-run place that doubles as a local watering hole. **Comedor y Hospedaje Aura** (on the main street east of church) is a typical Nicaraguan *hospedaje* catering more to the traveling *campesino* than foreign traveler.

Near San Rafael del Norte is the private nature reserve ★ **Finca el Jaguar** (tel. 505/2279-9219, www.jaguarreserve.org, $70 pp private cabin, $35 pp dorm), a 105-hectare stretch of land, of which 60 percent is cloud forest. The coffee *finca* (estate) was established to monitor over-wintering survival of migratory birds, and now offers a variety of lodging options and a unique way to get under the forest canopy. Cabins have private baths and terraces. There's solar-powered hot water in the showers. Prices include three meals and a guided tour. They require reservations in advance. From COTRAN Norte in Jinotega, catch a bus to Santa Fe-La Reforma and La Providencia (1pm, 2pm, and 3pm). The drive by bus to El Jaguar takes 1.5 hours. Get off at the Empalme del Carril and walk 2 kilometers to El Jaguar. They can set up private transportation for guests as well.

Getting There

Buses pass through San Rafael del Norte regularly on the route between Jinotega and San Sebastián de Yalí/La Rica. There is also one express bus to Managua that leaves at 4am, passes through Jinotega at 5am, and continues south through Matagalpa to Managua. The same bus leaves Managua's Mayoreo at 3pm and retraces the route to San Rafael del Norte, arriving after 7pm. *Expresos* leave Jinotega for San Rafael five times daily 8am-5:30pm. They depart for Jinotega five times daily 6:15am-3:45 pm.

EL CUÁ, SAN JOSÉ DE BOCAY, AND AYAPAL

El Cuá (2.5 hours outside of Matagalpa) is best known for Benjamin Linder, the only known American casualty of the Contra War. El Cuá and **San José de Bocay** are illuminated by mini-hydroelectric power plants he helped design and implement. Both towns were completely enveloped in conflict during the 1980s, overrun first by Contras and then by the FSLN. Today it's a logical place from which to visit Peñas Blancas.

Of El Cuá's three *hospedajes* (and various *pensiones*) travelers prefer **Hotel Chepita** (on the main street, toward La Pavona exit, tel. 505/2784-5158 or 505/8437-1531, www.hotelchepita.com, reservaciones@hotelchepita.com, $10 s, $20 d), run by an affable Anglophone Nicaraguan woman by the name of Josefa. She has 16 rooms with fan, TV, and Internet access. There are plenty of eateries around town, with little variance between them, but you might try **Típicos Mi Tierra** (from the Empalme La Chata, 800 meters towards Bocay, tel. 505/8299-1606, $3-5). There's not much nightlife here, but **Roka Club** (off the highway north of the center) is a large and popular bar with a pool.

There are a few *hospedajes* in Bocay, the nicest of which is the simple hotel **Five Star** (from Petronic, half a block south, tel. 505/8919-3860, $3-5), which incidentally earned an INTUR rating of one star. You'll find a few small eateries and a gas station.

Ayapal is a small community on the banks of the Río Bocay. From here, you can hire boats to take you downstream to several Miskito communities (not cheap), or visit the surprisingly expansive **Cuevas de Tunowalam,** a sandstone cave structure north of San José de Bocay. Guides are available through Hotel Chepita in El Cuá.

WIWILÍ

The upstream capital of the Río Coco region lies snug near the Honduran border and a long, bumpy, five-hour slog north of Jinotega. Wiwilí is a mestizo town, meaning it's of Spanish, not indigenous, origin. The

The Assassination of Ben Linder

As the only reported incident in which a United States citizen was killed by Contra soldiers, Benjamin Linder's death had enormous repercussions, stemming primarily from the fact that he was shot with weaponry purchased by his own government, and by soldiers carrying out a hotly contested policy of violence supported by the same government. Linder's death was elevated to the status of martyrdom by those that shared his values.

Oregon native Ben Linder graduated from the University of Washington in 1983 with a degree in mechanical engineering. After graduation, he came to Nicaragua like thousands of other *internacionalistas* to help the revolution reach the poor. In mid-1985, Linder moved to Jinotega to help install a mini-hydroelectric plant in the town of El Cuá. This was an area overrun with raiding Contras, and the danger in the region was real. But his engineer's passion for solving problems led him farther into the bush, to San José de Bocay, to repeat the success he'd had at El Cuá. In Bocay, the Contra were everywhere. On April 28, 1987, Linder and a crew of Nicaraguans crossed paths with a squadron of Contra that had been stalking Sandinista supporters. He, and several others with him, were assassinated at point blank range by a bullet to the temple.

The political repercussions were enormous. The Sandinistas, the Contras, and the U.S. government all angrily accused each other. Though the Contras claimed that Linder had been dressed in combat uniform, was carrying a weapon, and that Linder's team had fired the first shots, the evidence did not support it. That an American had been killed in Nicaragua, with a bullet also paid for by the American people, resonated deeply.

Linder was buried in a small, neat grave in the Matagalpa cemetery. His legend and inspiration live on. The peaceful community of San José de Bocay has been electrified, courtesy of the Benjamin Linder Mini-Hydroelectric Power Plant, constructed after his death. The Benjamin Linder School is down the road, and one of Bocay's more newly settled neighborhoods was christened Barrio Benjamin Linder.

In the early 1990s, when the Sandinistas handed power over to Doña Violeta's administration and it became obvious the great socialist revolution of the 1980s was not to be, most of the international crowd packed up and returned home. What Ben Linder set out to do—bring progress and hope to the people whose lives are the most difficult—is an ideal that did not die with the Revolution. The **Asociación de Trabajadores de Desarrollo Rural Benjamin Linder** (The Benjamin Linder Association of Development Workers, 25 meters south of the Hotel Bermúdez in Matagalpa, tel. 505/2612-2030, www.atder-bl.org) continues to do what Linder was doing the day he was killed: build small-scale hydroelectric plants to promote rural development. The association is managed by Linder's coworker Rebecca Leaf. To learn more about Ben, visit the Quaker House in Managua, the Ben Linder Café in León, or read the book *The Death of Ben Linder: The Story of a North American in Sandinista Nicaragua* by Joan Kruckewitt (Seven Stories Press, 2001).

strikingly beautiful town of Waspám, 550 kilometers downstream, is the other anchor at river's end, and is mostly indigenous.

Wiwilí is split by the Río Coco, which runs through the middle of town. Several hundred inhabitants of Wiwilí lost their lives to the river during Hurricane Mitch, and political fallout outlasted the storm. Post-Mitch, the two sides of the community went their own separate ways to find international aid, and subsequently decided to become independent. While they retained the same name,

Wiwilí on the north side of the river is now part of the department of Madriz, while Wiwilí on the south bank remains part of Jinotega. Both are important port towns with access to the deep waters of the Río Coco.

Local coffee cooperative members of **ASDECK** (tel. 505/8410-9068 or 505/8410-9064, guided hikes $20 for the day) can lead individuals or groups on community-led tours to nearby **Kilambé National Park** and other surrounding treasures. In the park you'll find a series of waterfalls: Cascada Caballo

Blanco, Cascada Borbollones del Diamante, and Cascada Quebraditas Yacalguas. **Hostal las Orquídeas** (tel. 505/8410-9068, diamanteki@yahoo.es, $5 dorm, $15 d, $3-4 meals) is a good base for hiking the reserve, but can only fit seven people.

There are a few decent *comedores* and accommodations in Wiwilí: **Hotel Central** (from the Red Cross, 75 meters south, tel. 505/8548-8436, $6 pp with shared bath, $20 d with private bath) and **El Hotelito** (from the central park, 1 block northwest, half a block southwest, $7 s with shared bath).

To get here, take the road to Santa María de Pantasma, which begins 10 kilometers north of Jinotega on the Jinotega-San Rafael del Norte Highway. Buses leave daily from Jinotega.

Chontales and Cattle Country

East of Lake Cocibolca lie hundreds of thousands of hectares of rolling hillside in a broad ecological transition zone where undulated, scrubby pastureland gradually unfolds into the pine savannas and wetlands of the Caribbean coast.

It's less populated than the Pacific region— Chontales and Boaco residents are easily outnumbered by their cattle. It's the cattle that make this area famous. Chontales ranches produce more than 60 percent of Nicaragua's dairy products, including dozens of varieties of cheese and millions of gallons of milk.

The flavor of Chontales and Boaco play no small part in the flavor of Nicaragua as a whole, from the cowboys, to the wide open sky, to the pre-Columbian relics and the small-town lifestyle. This entire region is firmly off the beaten path, so expect to be the only tourist for miles in most of the towns and sights. Boaco is known for its exceptional dairy products and makes a reasonable base for treks or drives into the hills between Boaco and Matagalpa Departments. Juigalpa is a much bigger and more economically active urban center that remains an overgrown cowboy town. Here you'll rub shoulders with cowboys and *campesinos* (country folk) sporting

their cleanest boots on their twice-a-month trip to the city to pick up supplies, strike a few deals, and do their errands.

Juigalpa's patron saint celebrations in mid-August are among the best in Nicaragua and draw a crowd from as far away as Managua to enjoy the elaborate bull-riding competitions, horsemanship contests, and traditional dances, all under the magnificent backdrop of the Amerrisque mountain range. Originally settled by the Chontal people, these mountains remain little explored, and the continual discovery of ancient statues and sculpture imply the grandeur of the mysteries this area still retains.

PLANNING YOUR TIME

Many travelers treat this region as an uninteresting and unavoidable expanse to be traveled through as quickly as possible en route to Nicaragua's Río San Juan or the Atlantic coast. But travelers who tire of the Granada

Previous: cattle grazing in Boaco; rodeo in Juigalpa. **Above:** *El Bailante* statue in Boaco.

Look for ★ to find recommended
sights, activities, dining, and lodging.

Highlights

★ **Santa Lucía:** The most charming and picturesque of Boaco's mountain villages, Santa Lucía is rich with gorgeous mountains, river valleys, and hiking trails (page 275).

★ **San José de los Remates and Esquipulas:** These cowboy towns offer great opportunities to hike, ride horses, see petroglyphs, and cool your heels in a waterfall (page 275).

★ **Camoapa:** Visit this small town to shop for intricate straw craftwork, including beautiful hats, boxes, and fans (page 277).

★ **Museo Arqueológico Gregorio Aguilar Barea:** This warehouse of statuary is filled with treasures the Chontales carved long before Columbus (page 279).

★ **Punta Mayales Nature Reserve:** Generally open February-May, this reserve on Lake Cocibolca is a beautiful escape and a fine example of rural tourism (page 283).

Chontales and Cattle Country

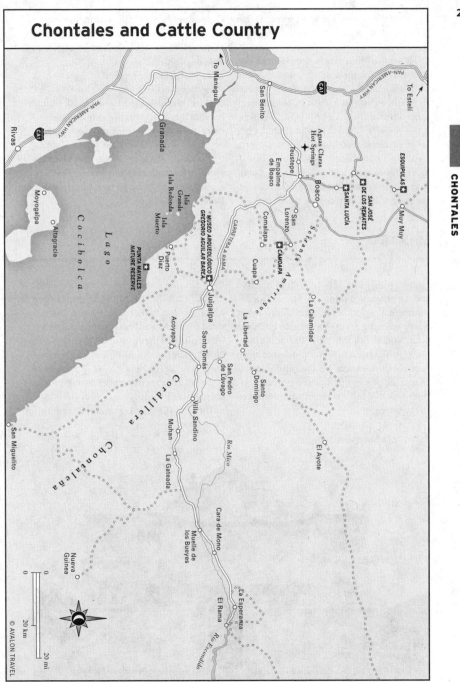

© AVALON TRAVEL

hype and the overwhelming presence of other foreigners will be amply rewarded with a trip to Chontales.

How much time you'll need depends on your inclination for adventure and ability to forgo some creature comforts. You could easily spend a day and a night in one of many quiet agrarian towns like Boaco, Camoapa, and Cuapa. The attraction is simply a bucolic, rural lifestyle. Most towns in the area have some basic accommodation and small local sites of historical, cultural, or geologic interest. Add an additional day if the bouldering and hiking opportunities in Cuisaltepe or Cuapa whet your appetite, and another day on horseback in San José de los Remates (you can even continue on the little-traveled high road to Matagalpa).

Public buses connect most of the region. In some of the smaller towns there are only a few buses that run daily, and it's best to ask around because they don't always run on schedule. If there isn't a bus at the time you want, you can get a ride or take a taxi out to the highway (*empalme de Boaco* for Boaco, *empalme San Fransico* for Camoapa), where buses pass constantly between San Carlos, Rama, Juigalpa, Boaco, and Managua.

Boaco

Nestled snugly in a 379-meter-high notch in the Amerrisque mountains, Boaco is a departmental capital and an agriculture center whose soil struggles to support both cattle and corn. Modern Boaco (the city's name is a combination of Aztec and Sumu words that mean "land of the sorcerers") is the third incarnation of the city. In the 18th and 19th century, two previous Boacos were built and destroyed in the same place.

The modern city of Boaco began on a hilltop and crept down the hillside into a valley. It literally has two different levels, the elevated city center and lower commercial sector, which earned it the nickname The City of Two Floors. (The fact that, compared to the rest of Nicaragua, Boaco has an unusual number of houses that have two or more floors reinforces the moniker.)

During the Contra War, Boaco was

Parroquia de Santiago Apóstol

Boaco

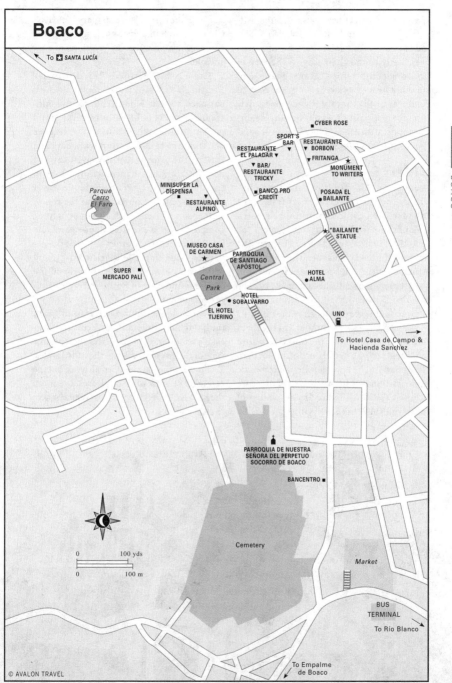

To ✚ SANTA LUCÍA

CYBER ROSE

SPORT'S BAR
RESTAURANTE BORBON
RESTAURANTE EL PALADAR
FRITANGA
BAR/ RESTAURANTE TRICKY
MONUMENT TO WRITERS

MINISUPER LA DISPENSA
BANCO PRO CREDIT
POSADA EL BAILANTE

Parque Cerro El Faro
RESTAURANTE ALPINO

"BAILANTE" STATUE

MUSEO CASA DE CARMEN
PARROQUIA DE SANTIAGO APÓSTOL

SUPER MERCADO PALÍ
Central Park
HOTEL ALMA

HOTEL SOBALVARRO
EL HOTEL TIJERINO

UNO

To Hotel Casa de Campo & Hacienda Sanchez

PARROQUIA DE NUESTRA SEÑORA DEL PERPETUO SOCORRO DE BOACO

BANCENTRO

0   100 yds
0   100 m

Cemetery

Market

BUS TERMINAL
To Rio Blanco

To Empalme de Boaco

© AVALON TRAVEL

spared from direct battles. But in the hillsides that surround, the city violence dislodged countless *campesinos,* all of whom eventually found their way to the city of Boaco seeking refuge. Many decided to stay, and Boaco has swelled over the past 20 years, faster than it can provide for its new inhabitants, most of whom occupy neighborhoods of small concrete homes around the outskirts of the city.

SIGHTS

Learn about Boaco's history and see an impressive private collection of artifacts at the **Museo Casa de Carmen** (on the north side of the park behind Café Carmen, tel. 505/2242-1053, free). The museum is the hobby of the town's doctor and former mayor, Armando Incer. It is best to visit Dr. Incer in the afternoons or call ahead to make sure he is not with patients.

Boaco's churches neatly serve the residents of the city's two levels without forcing them to traipse up and down the hill. **Parroquia de Nuestra Señora del Perpetuo Socorro de Boaco** (in the lower level) is an elaborate nontraditional church whose architecture is nearly Greek orthodox. Inside, statues of Jesus and the Virgin Mary line up side by

side with the carved stone statuary of Boaco's Chontal and Sumu ancestors, an intriguing compromise between the religions of new and old.

The freshly painted **Parroquia de Santiago Apóstol** (at the top of the hill) has been a Boaco landmark since the mid-1800s. Mass is held daily (several times daily on the weekends), when the ringing of the church bells fills the town square and scatters the pigeons. On any given day you may find folkloric dance presentations in front of the church. *El Bailante* **statue** (1 block east of the church and at the top of a steep set of steps with the same name), complete with snake stick in one hand and brass knuckles in the other, depicts a dancer participating in the folkloric reenactment of a battle between the Christians and the Moors found only in Boaco during its *fiestas patronales.*

Boaco's highest point is **Cerro El Faro,** the lighthouse without a sea. A concrete pedestal and tower, the Faro offers a panoramic view of the city and valley of the Río Mayales. Technically, the tower is open all week, but the caretaker closes it when he pleases. Evenings, the Faro is one of Boaco's more popular places to steal a few kisses.

Parroquia de Nuestra Señora del Perpetuo Socorro de Boaco

ENTERTAINMENT AND EVENTS
Nightlife

Boaco's sole disco is **Mango's Ranch** (a kilometer or two out of town along the highway to Muy Muy). Its relaxing atmosphere is perfect for a drink and some traditional Latin music: salsa, *cumbia,* and merengue are popular, along with the occasional Mexican *ranchera* cowboy song. By 10pm, the dance floor is packed, especially when there's live music. Take a taxi for $1. There are many bars in town offering cheap beer and a relaxed atmosphere until about 11pm. In the center of town, **Sports Bar** (in front of Borbon restaurant, daily) is a popular cantina that serves reasonably priced bar food.

Festivals and Events

Boaco's patron saint is Santiago Apóstol, and the **fiestas patronales** in his honor are particularly interesting and historic. The festival lasts the entire month of July, during which time the saint's statue is paraded daily from one neighborhood to the next. The crux of the ceremony is July 23-25, when the procession is accompanied by dancers whose performance tells an elaborate tale of the expulsion of the Moors from Spain.

ACCOMMODATIONS

Many of the hotels and *pensiones* near the bus terminal and along the main road of Boaco's lower level do a brisk trade in prostitution and romantic getaways for young couples and are best avoided. Boaco has constant problems with water, so be prepared to grin and bear it with a bucket shower if need be. A brand new hotel, **El Hotel Tijerino** (on the south edge of the park, tel. 505/2542-2798, $20-35, hot water, a/c, $35 includes breakfast) is the most upscale lodging in town. Rooms are modern and the ones in the back have great views. The hotel has a restaurant and bar.

★ **Hotel Sobalvarro** (next to El Tijerino, tel. 505/2542-2515, $15-30, $30 includes breakfast) has been lodging travelers and passers-through since before the Revolution and still retains the faded charm of yesteryear. It has a few rooms with air-conditioning in a once grandiose building of wooden rooms set around a courtyard with a balcony overlooking the lower half of town. **Hotel Alma** (from the east side of the Iglesia Santiago, half a block south, tel. 505/2542-2620, $8-15) has basic rooms with either private or shared bathroom, plus a nice view of the city.

Posada El Bailante (down the block from the dancer's statue, tel. 505/2542-2380,

CHONTALES
BOACO

Boaco is known as the "City of Two Floors."

www.posadaelbailante.com, info@posadael-bailante.com, $20-25) is easy to recommend. It offers cable TV, Wi-Fi, and air-conditioning in all 22 rooms.

Hotel Casa de Campo (Km 98 on the highway between Boaco and Río Blanco, tel. 505/5767-6422, hotelcasadecampo@yahoo.es, $15-30) is a classy new hotel located just outside of town. This quaint country home is a relaxing place to take a dip in the pool. They also have a popular restaurant and event venue. Check their Facebook page for concert listings.

FOOD

Several restaurants on the top "floor" of Boaco serve traditional Nicaraguan dishes, burgers, and sandwiches. Pastries and snacks are for sale in the park. They go well with a shake from **Hotel Sobalvarro** (on the south edge of the park, tel. 505/2542-2515), where you can also grab a sandwich or burger, all served on the best front porch in the city.

A little pricier than the others, ★ **Restaurante Alpino** (from La Kodak half a block north, $2-12) is the most highly recommended restaurant in town. Try their beef *churrasco* (grilled steak) and seafood. Locals and foreign NGO workers like **Restaurante Borbon** (Barrio Olama, from the Banco ProCredit, one block east, half a block north, $4-7), which is known for its *pollo al vino* (chicken cooked in wine) and pork chops, among other classics, plus huge glasses of *fresco* (fresh juice).

For a classic Nicaraguan meal, visit the unnamed ★ *fritanga* (half a block south of Borbon, $2) for dinner. Enjoy their finger-licking good grilled meats atop a mound of *verde* (plantain chips) or *maduro* (sweet fried plantain) and with plantain leaf plate.

Hotel Casa de Campo (Km 98 on the highway between Boaco and Río Blanco, $5-12) and **Hacienda Sanchez** (from the Instituto Nacional de Boaco, 100 meters west, 200 meters north, $5-12) both have pleasant restaurants that are popular with families on the weekend.

INFORMATION AND SERVICES

There are two banks in Boaco: in the lower part, **Banpro** (on the main street); in the upper part, **ProCredit** (1 block north of the backside of the church). There is a **Western Union** (near the market, Mon.-Sat. 8am-4:30pm), a **post office** (1.5 blocks north of the church on the left side), and a **pay phone** (out front of the post office, Mon.-Fri. 8am-5pm, Sat. until noon). One of the better Internet joints is **Cyber Rose** (near the writer's monument), which has six computers and a nice smoke-break balcony.

GETTING THERE AND AWAY

Buses to Boaco leave every 30 minutes or so from the Mayoreo terminal in Managua (2 hours, $1.50). Two microbuses leave from the terminal in Boaco (2 hours, $1.50) daily 6:30am and 12:30pm. Regular buses leave every 30 minutes for Managua until 5:40pm.

Five buses leave for Santa Lucía (45 minutes, under $1) daily 10:30am-5pm. Buses bound for Río Blanco (3 hours, $2) and Muy Muy leave 5:50am-5pm. For traveler masochists, the 12-hour Boaco-Siuna kidney-bruiser goes over some of the worst dirt roads in the nation.

AGUAS CLARAS HOT SPRINGS

Locals say the *aguas termales* at Aguas Claras are heated by an underground volcano. That's probably not too far from the truth given Nicaragua's seismicity. In 2000, an entrepreneur channeled the geothermal-heated waters into pipes and a series of concrete pools protected by palm-thatch roofs. The resulting **Aguas Claras Hot Springs and Hotel** (7 km west of Empalme de Boaco, tel. 505/8856-7306, $35 d with a/c, $2 day use) and resort complex has six pools available to the public and another two reserved for hotel guests. The complex is far from fancy, but the pools are clean and professionally maintained. The water is extraordinarily warm, and is therefore most enjoyable at night. While you lounge in the pool, you can order from an extensive menu of traditional Nicaraguan food and drink. The hotel features 17 private rooms. Credit cards are accepted for hotel and restaurant expenses, but not for the entrance fee.

During Semana Santa and weekends in the dry season, the hotel can fill quickly, so make reservations. The *aguas termales* are tough to reach by public transportation.

★ SANTA LUCÍA

The town of Santa Lucía was created in 1904 by decree of President José Santos Zelaya in an effort to concentrate the dispersed and poorly administered farming communities of the hillsides north of Boaco. More than a century later, Santa Lucía remains a picturesque and enchanting village in a valley ringed by green mountains.

Santa Lucía itself doesn't have hotel rooms or fancy restaurants but travelers sometimes come for the scenery around Cerro Santo Domingo, the long rocky precipice of Peña La Brada, and **Las Máscaras petroglyphs** in the valley of the Río Fonseca. For hikes in the Santa Lucía area, **Don Osmin** (505/8943-7343) and his *compañeros* from the Paradiso Verde nature club are the right people to accompany you. He is a fun tour guide and can be found in the Claro office, where he works.

Salto de los Américas is a seven-meter waterfall with a deep pool, located a short walk up the river off the road to Boaco (2 km before arriving in Santa Lucía). Several families of monkeys live in the area. **Peña La Brada** is a cliff edge outside town, with an amazing panoramic view of Boaco and beyond. There are several natural destinations nearby including a group of caves that Don Osmin can accompany you to if you call in advance.

There are no official accommodations in Santa Lucía. **Comidería El Cipres** (in the park, tel. 505/254-91005 or 505/8943-7343, ask for Doña Lucinda) specializes in grilled

meat and can make rooms available if given prior notice.

A direct bus leaves from Managua for Santa Lucía at 10:30am (3 hours, $1.50), bypassing Boaco entirely. The same bus leaves Santa Lucía for Managua early in the morning. Two different roads can bring you to Santa Lucía from Boaco. The faster route leaves Boaco at 10am and returns at noon. The trip takes 30-45 minutes. The second route takes over an hour and leaves from Boaco at noon, returning around 3pm (it passes the Empalme de Boaco on the way back if you want to leave town). The buses sometimes leave early, so get there ahead of time.

★ SAN JOSÉ DE LOS REMATES AND ESQUIPULAS

These picturesque cowboy towns can be the backdrop to your guided horse tours and hikes to local waterfalls. Catch a ride to **Cerro Cumaica-Cerro Alegre Natural Reserve,** which lies between the two towns and is accessible from either one. The weather here is usually a perfect 20°C (70°F) with a slight breeze almost year-round. Consider visiting both of these towns on the back road to Matagalpa. The bus trip is bumpy, but the views are grand. One of the main attractions is the "original black Jesus." In fact, thousands of national and international pilgrims descend each year on Esquipulas during the *fiestas patronales* (January 14-15) to catch a glimpse of their saint icon, **El Señor de Esquipulas,** housed in one of the best-kept churches in Nicaragua. Locals believe that only due to the power of their patron saint was the town spared from all the wars that over the centuries engulfed the surrounding hills.

In San José de los Remates, **Jorge Isaac** (tel. 505/2542-2359) will help you find accommodations in the 10-room town hostel (hot water) or with a local family. Also look for **Doña Rosinda** (from Claro, half a block east), who is involved in the San José tourism committee and can help you get horses, guides, or maps. The view from **Cruz del**

Hikes in the Boaco Area

LA CEBADILLA

Around the turn of the 20th century, a farmer from the mountain town of Cebadilla was surprised to see the Virgin Mary appear before him amongst the rocks where he was tending his cattle. The site has been treasured by locals ever since. La Cebadilla is no easier to get to than it ever was. This is an out-of-the-way corner of the region. At one time a small chapel was erected in honor of the Virgin, and there was a small well where it was said the water was blessed. Today, the chapel has mostly fallen to bits.

The day hike starts 1.6 kilometers east of Empalme de Boaco, where on the south side of the highway there's a dirt road leading south to the community of Asedades and a steel sign with a picture of the Virgin Mary and the words La Cebadilla. The road leads south one kilometer to Asedades, a community of adobe houses, flower gardens, and rocky fields. It's imperative that you find a guide in Asedades to take you up the mountain to La Cebadilla. There are many small footpaths that lead up the hill, but they intertwine and none is more obvious than the others. The walk up the hill takes 3-4 hours. Take water and food (and make sure you have something to share with your guide). The walk back to Asedades can take 2-3 hours. Your guide will recommend that you stay at the top of the hill through midday and do your walking in the cool of the afternoon.

At La Cebadilla, you may or may not have visions of the Virgin Mary, but you will certainly have a fantastic view of the valley below and the hills of Boaco to the east, sometimes all the way to Lake Nicaragua.

CAMOAPA'S MOMBACHO

In the early 1900s, Nicaraguans from Granada transferred their homes and possessions to Camoapa to try growing coffee on the area's hillsides. They chose the slopes of one mountain in particular because of its rich soils and named the peak Mombacho, in memory of their Granada homeland. Camoapa's Mombacho is a forested mountain with a rocky protuberance jutting out of the top. It is lined with several coffee plantations and a handful of radio towers and makes a pleasant day hike from Camoapa. Long ago, Mombacho was the site of a moonshine distillery, the products of which were sold under the name Mombachito.

Hiking the hill is significantly easier than hiking Cuisaltepe and offers a beautiful view of Camoapa's open ranges. From Camoapa, the road to Mombacho can be accessed by the Salida de Sangre de Cristo (*Sangre de Cristo* is the name of a church found along the first part of that road). From Claro in the center of Camoapa, walk six blocks west, crossing over a small bridge and arriving at the public school. Turn right at the school and head north until you see the Iglesia de Sangre de Cristo. Continue on that road until you reach Mombacho. The hike from town takes 3-4

Milenio is worth the walk: On a clear evening, you can see the lights of Granada and Cerro Negro in León.

Esquipulas, in the department of Matagalpa, is similar, but has its own charm, waterfall, and friendly tourism committee representative: **Doña Berena** (tel. 505/8426-8238 or 505/2772-9262, berenatellez@gmail.com). She can arrange visits to Salto de Limón in the nearby Cumaica Nature Reserve, petroglyph walks, and all-inclusive tourism packages with rural, cultural, and historic elements in and near Esquipulas. Ask about **Cerro El**

Padre (a giant granite rock on top of a large hill) and the *miradores* (lookout points) that some of the locals are putting up in their backyards. Don't ask about the *cususa*, corn mash moonshine as clear as water and as strong as gasoline. The area is famous for it.

For food, try **El Quelite** or **El Campero,** both on the main street. **El Hotelito** (near the park, tel. 505/2772-9132, $11) has seven cozy rooms.

Four buses leave Teustepe daily. A direct bus from Managua's Mayoreo terminal leaves daily at 12:30pm (2 hours, $2).

hours. There's a dirt road that leads up Mombacho from Camoapa to the radio towers. In Nahuatl, *mombacho* means "steep," so be prepared.

PEÑA LA JARQUÍNA

At the entrance to Camoapa on the southeast side of the highway (to your right as you head toward Camoapa) is a broad, rocky cliff face at whose base is a hardwood forest. This is Peña la Jarquína, named after a prominent local family. It's an easy 90-minute hike from the entrance to Camoapa, around the backside of the hill to the top. Skilled climbers might find it makes a suitable technical ascent. The rock is solid and has plenty of cracks, and is almost assuredly unclimbed.

CUISALTEPE

Unless you breezed by it on the midnight bus to El Rama, Cuisaltepe inevitably caught your eye: a massive, rocky promontory that juts out of the hillside between San Lorenzo and the entrance to Camoapa. Approaching it from the west, its silhouette resembles the tip of an upturned thumb, pointing in the direction of the highway. In Nahuatl, Cuisaltepe means "place of the grinding stone"; it was a good source of the volcanic rock the indigenous peoples used for making long, round stone implements with which to grind corn into dough. Cuisaltepe was the home of the last cacique of the region, Taisigüe.

Hiking Cuisaltepe is no casual endeavor. More than 300 meters high, much of the south side of the rock is a series of vertical crevasses and overhangs and much of the rest of it is prohibitively steep. However, there is one summit approach—from the north side of the rock—that you can reach from Camoapa. Hike with caution. The climb takes six hours round-trip, but adjust that estimate according to your own hiking ability. Wear good shoes, as much of the route is loose, slippery gravel.

Your point of entrance is the road to Camoapa. Any bus traveling between Managua or Boaco and the east will take you there, leaving you at Empalme de Camoapa (also called San Francisco) along the highway. A better option is to take a direct bus to Camoapa: 10 leave daily from Managua (5 on Sun.). From the highway, the road that leads to Camoapa climbs 25 kilometers. Get off the bus before you reach Camoapa at Km 99, where a small turnoff to the west leads to the community of Barrio Cebollín with a little red bus stop at the entrance. Access to the summit is neither obvious nor easy, and involves climbing partway up, crossing the small forest in a notch in the hillside, and then climbing the ridge to the summit. You can find guides in Barrio Cebollín in the first house on the left after you pass the school (the house nearest to the utility pole). Euclídes and brothers know the mountain well and climb it periodically.

★ CAMOAPA

A cow town of 13,000 set in the mountains east of Boaco, Camoapa got its name from a Nahuatl phrase that can be translated either as "place of the parrots, place of the dark rocks," or "place of the yams." (How's that for precision?) Once an indigenous community ruled by the cacique Taisiwa, it was later absorbed by the Spanish settlers and incorporated under the name San Francisco de Camoapán. Camoapans boast that they have the toughest bulls and best horses around.

Today, besides its renowned dairy production, Camoapa is best known to Nicaraguans for its production of woven straw hats and other products. In the 1960s, a school for promoting the art of weaving was formed, and the art passed through several generations. There are still several hundred weavers in Camoapa. Walk west of the park to find a few different homes with display cases filled with beautiful hats, boxes, and fans. The pieces are made from intricately and tightly woven strips of fibrous white *pita*, a kind of processed straw.

★ **Hotel Las Estrellas** (7 blocks east of the church's north side, tel. 505/849-8549, $10-20, hot water), a former auto-hotel turned honest, offers the best value rooms in its price range. Small but close to town, **Hotel Taisiwa** (along the main road, $5 with private bath) has 11 rooms. In addition to **Atenas** (next to Radio Camoapa, tel. 505/2549-2300, $3-5), solid meals are found at **Camfel** (1 block west of the church's north side, $3-6), a clean place run by seven women; and **Bosquecito** (just down the road that leads to Comalapa, $3-5), a restaurant filled with potted plants and flowers.

Buses from Managua to Camoapa depart Mayoreo Monday-Saturday 4:30am-4:10pm (2.5 hours, $2). The Sunday schedule provides fewer buses. Buses to Managua depart from the shady side of the church (whichever side that is as the day progresses), Monday-Saturday 6:25am-5pm. A minibus shuttles between the Empalme del Camoapa (San Francisco) and Camoapa, but it's irregular. Your best bet is to catch a ride.

COMALAPA

In 1752, Friar Morel de Santa Cruz visited Comalapa and said, "This is a town of Indians located in a land that's stony, mountainous, and fenced in by hills. Its church is of straw, reduced and indecent, lacking a vestry, but possessing an altar...100 families and 484 persons both Indian and Ladino." Comalapa is largely the same 250 years later, though the church is now a quaint stone structure. Access to Comalapa is through Camoapa, 20 kilometers down the road. There is one bus per day, leaving Camoapa at 6:30am. The same bus leaves Comalapa at 4pm. At other times of the day, hitch a ride with pickups traveling between the communities, or try hiking a piece of the road.

Camoapa's straw crafts are admired across the country.

Juigalpa

The last big settlement on the road southeast to El Rama (or south to San Carlos and the Río San Juan), Juigalpa is a prosperous city of 70,000 cattle ranchers and farmers. Juigalpa bears the traces of its indigenous roots in elaborate statuary and other archaeological pieces still being discovered in the mountains east of town. Juigalpa in Aztec means "great city" or "spawning grounds of the black snails." Its first inhabitants were likely the Chontal, displaced from the Rivas area by the stronger Nicaraos. They resisted the Spanish occupation fiercely in the 16th century, rising up no fewer than 14 times to attack the installations of the colonial government.

Upon Nicaragua's independence, the land that comprised Chontales and Boaco was controlled by Granada. In 1858, the Department of Chontales was formed. In the 18th and 19th centuries, travelers bound for the gold mines of Santo Domingo and La Libertad crossed Lake Cocibolca, landed in Puerto Díaz, and spent a night in Juigalpa before proceeding.

SIGHTS
★ Museo Arqueológico Gregorio Aguilar Barea

Juigalpa's most interesting attraction is the **Museo Arqueológico Gregorio Aguilar Barea** (from the central park, 2.5 blocks east, tel. 505/2512-0784, Mon.-Fri. 8am-noon and 2pm-4pm, Sat. 8am-noon, less than $1), an airplane-hangar-like building housing a collection of more than a hundred examples of pre-Columbian statuary uncovered in the folds of the Amerrisque mountain range. Ranging 1-7 meters tall, the pieces are reminiscent of totem poles, elaborately carved in high- and low-relief, with representations of zoomorphic figures and humans (the latter often clutching knives or axes in their hands, or presenting their arms folded across their chests). The statues, thought to be 1,000 years old, were the work of the Chontal people, driven to the east side of Lake Cocibolca by the more powerful Nicaraos some 1,500 years ago.

Unlike the Nahuatl and Nicarao, relatively little is known about the Chontal

CHONTALES
JUIGALPA

pre-Columbian statuary in the Museo Arqueológico Gregorio Aguilar Barea

Juigalpa

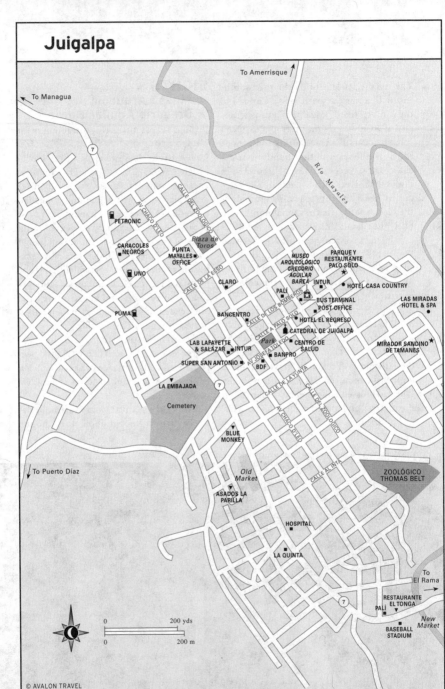

To Amerrisque

To Managua

To Puerto Díaz

Río Mayales

PETRONIC

CARACOLES NEGROS

PUNTA MAYALES OFFICE

UNO

PUMA

AV CHICO DIEO

CALLE DEL ZOOLÓGICO

Plaza de Toros

CALLE DE LA ESSO

CLARO

PALÍ

MUSEO ARQUEOLÓGICO GREGORIO AGUILAR BAREA

PARQUE Y RESTAURANTE PALO SOLO

INTUR

HOTEL CASA COUNTRY

BUS TERMINAL
POST OFFICE

LAS MIRADAS HOTEL & SPA

BANCENTRO

CALLE DE LOS BOMBEROS

CALLE A PALO SOLO

HOTEL EL REGRESO

CATEDRAL DE JUIGALPA

LAB LAFAYETTE & SALAZAR

INTUR

CALLE JOSEFA TOLEDO

Park

CENTRO DE SALUD

MIRADOR SANDINO DE TAMANES

SÚPER SAN ANTONIO

AV JOSEFA TOLEDO

BANPRO

BDF

LA EMBAJADA

CALLE DE LA VUNTA

CALLE DEL ZOOLÓGICO

AV CHICO DIEO

Cemetery

BLUE MONKEY

Old Market

CALLE AL INTA

ZOOLÓGICO THOMAS BELT

ASADOS LA PARILLA

HOSPITAL

LA QUINTA

To El Rama

PALÍ

RESTAURANTE EL TONGA

New Market

BASEBALL STADIUM

0   200 yds
0   200 m

culture and its statues, more of which are continually being discovered in the Amerrisque range. The museum was built in 1952 by the well-loved former mayor of Juigalpa, Gregorio Aguilar Barea. It also exhibits Nicaraguan coins from across two centuries, gold figurines, original paintings by the museum's namesake, and several historical paintings and photographs. The building has an open front, so even if the gate to the museum is locked, all the statues can be seen from the street.

Parks

The view from **Parque Palo Solo** (at the north end of town) is elevated above the surrounding streets, giving the impression of looking over the bulwark of a fortress. The fortress feeling isn't entirely accidental: Juigalpa was built at the top of the hill to offer it some means of defense from the Miskito and Zambo peoples who once raided it from those same mountains 200 years ago. The park was built by Mayor Aguilar Barea in the 1960s and named after the one tall tree that dominated its center. The tree has since been replaced by a fountain adorned with images of the mainstays of the Chontales economy: corn and cattle. A restaurant at the edge of the park serves fancy lunches and dinners.

Juigalpa's **parque central** (in the center of town) is a green, orderly, and clean place, whose statue of a boy shining shoes was made by a former mayor who spent his early years earning money as a shoe-shine boy. The statue bears the inscription: "Hard work dignifies a man." The walls around the base of the park are covered in lovely mosaics. In front of the park sits the town's simple **Catedral de Juigalpa,** constructed in 1648. Stop in for a look at its pretty stained-glass windows.

For the best view in town, visit the **Mirador Sandino de Tamanes,** a newer park located on the edge of town. To the east, there are breathtaking views of nearby mountain ranges. To the west, a huge silhouette of Sandino frames a birds-eye view of the city. This is a nice place to sit on a bench and have

a quiet moment along with the whispering couples with whom you will most likely share the space.

Zoológico Thomas Bell

Zoológico Thomas Bell (tel. 505/2512-0861, Tues.-Sun. 9am-noon and 1pm-5pm, $1) is a popular attraction for local tourists, especially during Juigalpa's *fiestas patronales*. Here you will find an impressive collection of native animals as well as animals from around the world. With a focus on conservation and saving local endangered species, the zoo is home to 58 local species, including different species of macaws, parrots, and toucans. You can also see jaguars, the peccary (a pig-like mammal), and wild cats. It is difficult for the zoo to maintain the budget it needs to properly maintain the animals, so keep in mind that you won't find the standards you are used to in North America zoos. Due to lack of resources, the animals are sometimes underfed, and access to specialized veterinary attention can be difficult.

ENTERTAINMENT AND EVENTS
Nightlife

The best disco in town is **La Quinta** (out on the highway, Sat. night only). Second best is **Caracoles Negras** (half a block south of the Petronic station along the highway, formerly Hotters), which picks up the slack on Sunday night and appeals to the cowboy crowd more than La Quinta. **The Blue Monkey** (from the stoplight at the cemetery 1 block south, 25 meters west) is a new bar that's popular with young people in town and has a hopping dance floor on weekend nights.

Festivals and Events

Juigalpa's *fiestas patronales* (Aug. 11-18) attract visitors from the entire nation and even Honduras and Costa Rica. Much of the festivities take place on the north side of town in the Plaza de Toros, but you'll find parties, bull riding, rodeos, and horseback games all over the place at all times. In one of these, called the *carrera de cinta*, mounted riders gallop underneath a wire from which a small ring is suspended. If a rider successfully puts a pencil through the ring at full gallop, he can present it—and a kiss—to the woman of his choice among the contestants vying to be queen of the festival. The woman who receives the most rings is crowned the queen.

ACCOMMODATIONS

Many of Juigalpa's cheapest *hospedajes* are intended to be occupied one hour at a time; travelers should avoid these.

Hotel El Regreso (east—rear—side of the church, tel. 505/8735-5040, $8-18) is the most economical option with three floors and a friendly owner. At the time of research, they were planning construction on the front of the building, including putting in a restaurant. A more polished option in town, **Hotel Los Arcángeles** (behind the church, tel. 505/2512-0847, $50 with a/c and hot water) has 13 rooms with king-size beds and an extensive collection of religious statues and figurines in the front room. ★ **Hotel Casa Country** (Parque Palo Solo at the north end of town, tel. 505/2512-2546, $25-30) has nice rooms in an old home, all with private bath, air-conditioning, and TV.

Posada la Casona (300 meters south of the Asunción Hospital, tel. 505/2512-4759 or 2512-4759, hotelposadalacasona.com, $15-35) is found on the highway leaving town to Rama and is popular with national business people. It has 14 basic rooms, air-conditioning, hot water, and the option to purchase breakfast.

The fanciest place in town is ★ **Las Miradas Hotel & Spa** (next to 7/24 restaurant, tel. 505/2512-4525, hotellasmiradas@ hotmail.com, $50, includes breakfast). You'll find the most stunning view in the city and the surrounding mountains with luxury accommodations (hot water, a/c, Wi-Fi). Plans for a pool and other amenities are in the works. Make reservations in advance.

FOOD

Juigalpa has a variety of food, often at reasonable prices, and naturally, with massive quantities of beef and dairy on the menu. Case in point: ★ **La Embajada** (difficult to find, but everyone knows it, just ask around, $10/ pound). The only thing on the menu is beef ribs, ordered by the pound, which comes with a huge hunk of *cuajada* cheese and a tortilla bigger than your head. This family has been serving meat by the pound from the back patio of their house for three generations

Check out a rodeo during Juigalpa's *fiestas patronales*.

and is famous for Tía Mercha's secret marinade. Native Chontaleño Daniel Ortega has made appearances here, and the bigwigs of Chontales also frequent it.

Restaurante Palo Salo (along the far side of the Palo Salo Park, $7-11) can't be beat for its beautiful views of the city and the nearby mountain ranges.

A great place to try local meats for a good price, **Asados la Parilla** (from the Chele Varga Hospital, 1 block south, tel. 505/8212-5117, $3-6) is not in the center of town, but definitely worth the taxi ride. For more upscale dining along the highway to El Rama, try **Restaurante La Tonga** ($4-6), or the newer **Restaurante y Hotel La Hacienda** ($8-15), which is also a conference center.

The old movie theater is now a **Palí** grocery store; **Supermercado San Antonio** has a better selection and is locally owned.

INFORMATION AND SERVICES

For Internet, check behind the Texaco station, or just walk around town. There is an **ATM** located off of the central park outside the Banpro. The **INTUR** tourist office (1 block east of the museum) can provide you with brochures and recommendations on where to stay and what to do.

One of the better pharmacies in town is **Farmacia La Salud** (at the northwest corner of the park, tel. 505/2512-0932). **Hospital La Asunción** (on the southeast side of town along the highway) doesn't have very good facilities. A better option for travelers is the **Lab Lafayette & Salazar** (2 blocks west of the park, tel. 505/2512-2292), a private clinic and doctor's office. There is a **Centro de Salud** (Mon.-Fri. 8am-9pm, Sat.-Sun. 8am-1pm) across the street from the church.

GETTING THERE AND AWAY

Microbuses to Managua (2.5 hours, $3) depart from the north or east side of the church at 6am and 1:40pm. The larger buses depart Juigalpa from the cramped bus terminal in the market. Ask around to be sure from where your bus departs. Buses leave hourly for El Rama 4:30am-1:30pm and every half hour to Managua 4am-5pm. You'll also find daily service to Boaco and other local destinations.

PUERTO DÍAZ

It's a short ride from Juigalpa down to the village of Puerto Díaz, a sleepy lakeside town of fishing families that pretty much live on what they catch. Puerto Díaz doesn't have any facilities for travelers but is worth a day trip on a lazy Saturday to see how the "far" side of the lake (the world across the lake from Granada) lives. There are various restaurants along the water where many families come to eat and enjoy the view. Buses leave from Juigalpa at 5am, 2pm, and 5pm. From the bus terminal, they cross the highway at the Esso station before working their way slowly down to the shoreline.

★ PUNTA MAYALES NATURE RESERVE

Located an hour from Juigalpa, **Punta Mayales** ($1) is home to 250 species of birds including owls and hawks; mammals like porcupines, anteaters, sloths, and monkeys; and an incredible assortment of flora with a backdrop of Lake Cocibolca and the Isla de Ometepe and Zapatera volcanoes. There are three cabins of various sizes, plus five trails, ranging 1-3 kilometers, and each offering a unique view of the peninsula.

Stop in the **Juigalpa office** (in the Ameri-cable office, from the Esso gas station 30 km southeast, tel. 505/2512-2322 or 505/8830-2770, arbagar@yahoo.com) to arrange a day trip or an overnight stay. You can camp here or stay in one of their cabañas ($12-15). Ask about all-inclusive packages and having food prepared. A land tour is $6 with the option to take horses. The river tour is $5. Caiman-watching trips are easily arranged. The reserve is closed during the rainy season. It's generally open February through May, but it depends on the yearly rainfall so call ahead.

Hikes Near Juigalpa

EL MONOLITO DE CUAPA

The Cuapa Monolith is a 75-meter-high chunk of granite that projects like a giant needle out of a field, as though it dropped from the sky and pierced the ground. It's first visible on the bus ride to Cuapa.

Climbing El Monolito isn't easy, but it isn't impossible either. It's a hike, not a technical rock climb. The locals in Cuapa know all the trails that lead there, and any young *campesino* will be glad to show you the way to the top to see the cross. From the town of Cuapa, it's a 2.5-hour hike to the top, including several extremely steep sections. Hike with good shoes. Locals recommend not climbing it on particularly windy days. Ask around for Nicolás, an English-speaking resident of Cuapa (originally from Bluefields), who can be a guide. He runs a tire repair shop next to Parque Zapera.

SERRANÍA AMERRISQUE

A powerful backdrop to Juigalpa, the Amerrisque mountain range forms a rocky backbone to the history of the city. Most of the archaeological pieces in the Juigalpa museum were unearthed in the Amerrisques, and countless other sites have yet to be explored. Although the area is undeveloped for tourists, the rocky peaks make a tempting hike and the locals claim the east side of the range contains several caves.

Your starting point is the road called the Camino de la Vaticana, built by Rome and Holland in the late 1990s. It will lead you nine kilometers east toward the range and the tiny farming community of Piedra Grande. From there, you can strike into the hills to explore. You can try hitching a ride out there to trim down the flat, boring part of the hike, but it won't be easy, as traffic along the road is sparse at best. There are few communities along its length. Consider hiring a pickup truck in town. A group of five travelers offering $15-20 might be able to convince someone to drive them out there. Try to swing a deal for the ride back while you're at it.

Daniel Molina (tel. 505/2512-2940) can serve as a guide. He speaks English and can arrange a trip out to the mountains, where he'll help you find a local guide to show you the trails.

CUAPA

Tiny, isolated Cuapa was once an anonymous farming town in the foothills of the Amerrisque mountain range. In 1985, Contras attacked and took control of the town, capturing Sandinista mayor Hollman Martínez. They later released him when the townspeople pleaded for his life, but 12 other Sandinista activists were marched out of town and executed at the roadside. When the Sandinista military got wind of the Contra occupation, they dispatched a truckload of 40 soldiers to defend the town. Contras ambushed the vehicle, killing nearly all of them. A small roadside **monument** bearing the Sandinista flag commemorates both the civil servants and the soldiers killed during the war.

Cuapa is famous among devout Catholics.

In the early 1980s, the Virgin Mary appeared to local farmer Bernardo Martínez, relaying the following message: "Don't preach the kingdom of God unless you are building it on earth. The world is threatened by great danger." Devout Catholics were overjoyed at the appearance, but the moment was rapidly politicized. Some claimed the Virgin's message was a coded recrimination of the Sandinista government. The Sandinistas responded by clamping down on all press coverage of miracles not previously accepted by the Vatican. An elaborate and well-maintained statue and sign greet you at the entrance to Cuapa with *"Bienvenido a la Tierra de María"* ("Welcome to Mary's Land"). Believers from all over eastern Nicaragua flock to Cuapa on May 8, the anniversary of the day the Virgin first appeared. Silvio Sirias's novel, *Bernardo and the Virgin,* is a fascinating fictionalized account of the events surrounding the apparition.

Whether you've come to see the shrine or to climb the impressive, needlelike **monolith** outside of town, Cuapa isn't a bad place to spend the night. One option for the climb is to arrive in the evening, spend the night in Cuapa, and set off to climb the monolith the following morning. Find accommodations and meals at **Restaurante Hospedaje La Maravilla** ($3-4 rooms). The hotel fills up June 19-27, when Cuapa celebrates its patron saint, San José.

Six buses leave Juigalpa for Cuapa daily 6am-6pm. Buses from Cuapa to Juigalpa leave from the town center daily 6am-4:30pm.

Solentiname and the Río San Juan

The Río San Juan carries the waters of Lake Cocibolca to the Caribbean through a lush landscape of extensive nature reserves and broad cattle ranches. The biggest town in the area, San Carlos, has transformed from edgy port town to

quaint destination. You'll inevitably pass through it on the way to various adventures. Offshore, the Solentiname Archipelago is a quiet group of islets of striking natural beauty, as pertinent to the revolution years as to Nicaragua's prehistoric past, and the source of some of the country's best-known paintings.

Take a boat down the river towards the Atlantic, a windy, sun-baked ride back through time. El Castillo, one of Spain's most permanent colonial legacies, remains little changed from the 17th century and the days of marauding pirates. From there, downstream fishing village follows pasture follows rapids, until you reach San Juan de Nicaragua, remote and untamed.

Parallel to the Costa Rican border, the river has been contested by politicians between the two countries for centuries. In spite of relentless "El Río San Juan is ours!" chest thumping in Managua, as in most border zones, the communities along the river live symbiotically

with their neighbors. Families in this zone are a mesh of *Nicas* and *Ticos*; many give birth in Costa Rica to provide their babies with dual citizenship (and better work opportunities). Many towns use the Costa Rican *colón* instead of, or in addition to, the *córdoba*.

This region isn't part of the casual traveler's itinerary, but if you can invest a little more time than usual, the dramatic landscapes and remoteness will impress you. The tourism potential here is enormous.

PLANNING YOUR TIME

Allow at least a full week for exploration of this region. Make your plane reservation from Managua to San Carlos early; seats fill up fast. Outside of San Carlos, expect about 25 percent higher costs for most goods in this isolated region (35 percent more on Solentiname). Use your time in San Carlos to find updated boat schedules, make contact with downstream river lodges, and stock up

Previous: sunset in Solentiname; Rio San Juan near El Castillo. **Above:** pet macaw at Albergue Celentiname, San Fernando.

Look for ★ to find recommended sights, activities, dining, and lodging.

Highlights

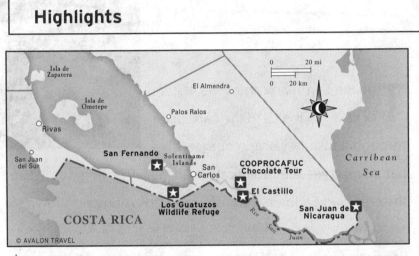

★ **Los Guatuzos Wildlife Refuge:** This is one of the best places in the south to get down and dirty with nature. Start by identifying a few of the 411 species of tropical birds (page 296).

★ **San Fernando:** One of the Solentiname archipelago's jewels, this island features a museum, a hiking trail, spectacular sunsets, and a wonderful community of farmers, fishers, and artists (page 301).

★ **COOPROCAFUC Chocolate Tour:** Learn to make your own chocolate at a cacao

farmer's cooperative outside of Boca de Sábalos (page 303).

★ **El Castillo:** In this town, the mighty embattlements of a historic mud-river fortress have watched over the river since the days when pirates prowled the coastline (page 305).

★ **San Juan de Nicaragua:** Remote and thick with history, San Juan de Nicaragua is an adventure in itself. Spot manatees in a nearby lagoon or trek through a nature reserve to visit the indigenous community at Canto Gallo (page 308).

Solentiname and the Río San Jaun

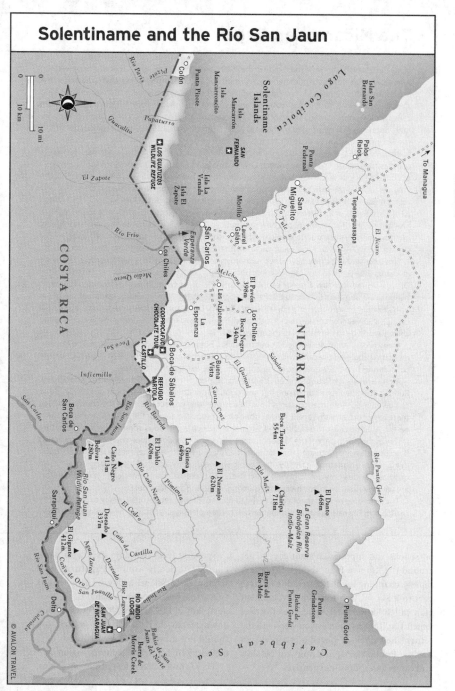

© AVALON TRAVEL

The Nicaraguan Canal

Since the Spanish colonized the region in the 1500s, the prospect of a canal that could connect the Atlantic and Pacific oceans glimmered as a distant hope for colonizers, imperialists, and politicians across the world. When U.S. tycoon Cornelius Vanderbilt began his steamship business during the California Gold Rush in the 1850s, Nicaragua convinced the world it was the best place for a canal, and Vanderbilt made some of the first moves towards realizing it. There's a one-kilometer long waterway still referred to by locals as *el canal*, along with a 150-year-old sunken dredge, in the Río Indio near San Juan de Nicaragua.

But while the U.S. was discussing plans in Nicaragua, France's canal project in Panama was in disarray. Desperate French landowners in Panama paid a lobbyist to convince U.S. lawmakers of concerns about volcanic activity surrounding the proposed Nicaragua route, and in 1902 the Panama Canal deal was signed. Nicaragua continued negotiations with Japan, inciting U.S. Secretary of State Philander Knox to support a 1909 revolt to oust dictator José Santos Zelaya. When two U.S. citizens who'd been fighting with the rebels were executed, Knox sent in the Marines and supported the placement of a new president. In 1914 the Bryan Chamorro treaty was signed, guaranteeing that Nicaragua would not build a competing canal—unless it was backed by the United States. (Another Nicaraguan dictator, Anatasio Somoza, abolished the treaty in 1970.)

Since those days, there have been numerous conversations with governments and private investors interested in Nicaragua's canal potential. In 2014, to the surprise of his citizens, Daniel Ortega signed into law a major canal investment project with Chinese telecommunications billionaire Wang Jing. Similar to the Panama Canal deal, the Nicaraguan government has given Jing's investment group, Hong Kong Nicaragua Canal Development Investment Company (HKND Group), a 50-year concession over the canal with a chance to renew for another 50 years. Meaning it likely won't be in the control of the state until 2114.

Many Nicaraguans are excited about the canal, but just as many are concerned. The government has predicted the canal will lift 400,000 Nicaraguans out of poverty by 2018—a big number considering that three quarters of the population lives on less than $2 a day.

Many are worried about the environmental impact the canal will have on Lake Cocibolca. Rumors and allegations are flying left and right, but neither the government nor HKND group has given much information about how they expect this project to impact the country. In fact, there have not been any recent studies done of the proposed area for the canal (from Punta Gorda on the Atlantic coast to San Juan del Sur in the Pacific). Indigenous communities in the nature reserves that form part of the Mesoamerican Biological Corridor (which connects forests across five countries) are protesting their imminent displacement. Researchers at the Humboldt Center in Managua estimate at least 109,000 people will be directly affected by the mega-project. No one has any idea how dredging will affect the largest lake in Central America. Five urban centers are wholly reliant on its freshwater for drinking, including San Juan del Sur.

Though some remain skeptical as to the fulfillment of the megaproject, many expect it will be carried out. The real question Nicaraguans are contemplating is, is it a step forward, or a step back?

on snacks and supplies. It's not easy to get around the Río San Juan, though things are rapidly changing for the better, due in large part to a $14 million tourism development plan called La Ruta del Agua, the effects of which you'll see as soon as you step onto the refurbished dock or paved airstrip at San Carlos. Public transportation can be slow and capricious, but is inexpensive.

Spend at least two days in Solentiname. Plan strategically around Papaturro boat schedules to spend a day or two in Los Guatuzos. Spend a day in Sábalos, an hour upstream of El Castillo. Don't head farther downstream than El Castillo (which you should not miss) with fewer than four days including flights to and from the region.

There's little cell service outside San Carlos.

Several businesses listed here have Costa Rican numbers (beginning with 506). If you have a local cell phone, Claro seems to reach further than Movistar in this region.

San Carlos

Surrounded on three sides by a watery horizon, San Carlos's sky is frequently pierced by bright rainbows sparked by afternoon showers. A sleepy river town of about 10,000 people, it has served as a raucous and spirited way station for many travelers over the centuries. Founded in 1527, San Carlos is one of the oldest colonial towns on the continent. San Carleños are a lively bunch. Many were born elsewhere in the country and ended up here on their way to somewhere else—field hands on their way to Costa Rican harvests, border soldiers on leave from remote posts, and lake and river merchants trading with Chontales cattlemen.

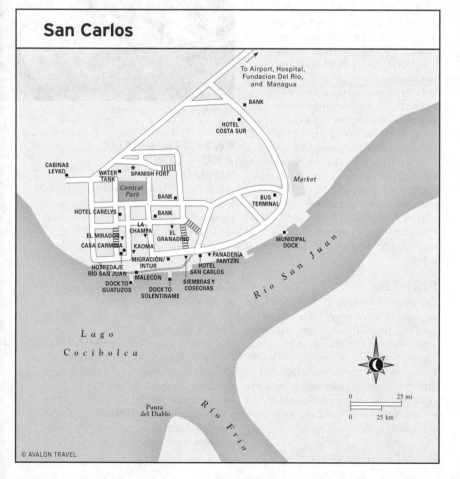

San Carlos

All foreign travelers in the Río San Juan region are obliged to pass through San Carlos, the departmental, economic, and transport hub of the region. The city has cleaned up its act and greatly improved in the last few years, with an increasing number of services (the region's first ATM was installed in 2009). There are garbage cans on every corner, street sweepers, and newly painted homes, adding appeal to San Carlos and its scenic views of Lake Cocibolca.

ORIENTATION

The main center of San Carlos is only about a dozen city blocks, all south of the central park on the flank of a hill looking south over the water. The waterfront can be a little confusing if you find yourself in one of the narrow market aisles, but, all in all, there's not much actual "town" in which to get lost. Main Street runs along the waterfront, from which the city sprawls northward along the highway to the hospital and airport. If you are landing at the airstrip, grab a taxi to take you the couple of kilometers into San Carlos (5 minutes, less than $1). The bus station is slightly north of the town center, across from the gas station and docks. Arriving by boat dumps you right in the middle of the *malecón* (waterfront). Taxis charge a fixed rate of $0.50 per passenger. No taxi should charge you more than $1 to get anywhere in town.

SIGHTS

The old **Spanish fort,** as the highest lookout point in town, enjoys a nice view of the town and lake. Its cultural center and library were founded with Cuban support—to wit, countless volumes of communist propaganda—and has since been supported by the Netherlands. At the *mirador* (lookout), you'll find old cannons, a romantic sunset setting, and one of the nicer restaurants in town.

live music at the Carnaval Aquático

ENTERTAINMENT AND EVENTS
Nightlife

Locals make their way to **La Champa** (half a block north of the waterfront park), a bar so popular, its name has become a verb among locals (as in, "Let's go *champear!*"). Bars line most streets throughout town, with the rowdiest ones down by the waterfront; try the **Granadino** (20 meters east of Lafisse) or the **Kaoma** (in front of the waterfront park) for a mellower vibe.

Festivals and Events

The annual **sportfishing competition** (Sept.) is a big deal for Nicaraguan anglers and attracts crowds from across the world for prizes like outboard motors and more. Enjoy the *fiestas patronales* on November 4. San Carlos's **Carnaval Aquático** (Nov.) is a cultural display of dancing, food, live music, and decorated riverboat floats. Its exact date fluctuates, but it attracts thousands of regional (and some international) tourists, so make hotel reservations early.

ACCOMMODATIONS

San Carlos's shabbier *hospedajes* on the main drag charge as little as $4 per person, but you get what you pay for. If you're short on cash, try **Hospedaje Río San Juan** (on the *malecón*, tel. 505/2585-0451, $4-5 pp), a cheap but relatively secure family-run joint with a tidy little *comedor* (eatery) overlooking the waterfront.

Casa Carmina (in front of Kaoma, tel. 505/2583-0289, $12 s, $20 d) is a nice, small hostel with five rooms and charming decor. All rooms have the option for air-conditioning, at a higher cost. **Hotel Costa Sur** (200 meters north of the bus station, in front of Banpro, tel. 505/2583-0224 or 505/8853-6728, hotel.costasur@hotmail.com, $10-30 with fan or a/c) has clean rooms and Wi-Fi, but it can be noisy from street traffic.

★ **Hotel Carelys** (half a block south of the park, tel. 505/2583-0389, $15), also known as Aquiles or Doña Coco, is a family-run hostel consisting of 16 rooms, the cleanest and most pleasant rooms in the city. Each includes private bath, fan, TV, and complimentary

drinking water. **Cabinas Leyko** (2 blocks west of the church, tel. 505/2583-0354, leykou7@yahoo.com.es, $20-47) is a popular choice. Its 22 somewhat damp and dark rooms start with a simple double with fan, but they have some nice higher-end alternatives with air-conditioning and cable TV as well—have a look at the room first. They also rent kayaks and can arrange tours in the area.

FOOD

The row of *comedores* (lunch counters, daily 6am-10pm, $3 for a big plate) alongside the bus station offers the best cheap meals in town. ★ **El Granadino** (across from the court, tel. 505/2583-0142, daily 10:30am-10pm, $8-9) serves the best food in town with a great view of the lake. Popular **Kaoma** (on the *malecón*, tel. 505/2583-0293, daily 9am-11pm, $4-12) has a similar menu and is open late on weekends. **El Mirador** (on the *mirador*, tel. 505/2583-0377, Mon.-Sat. 7am-10pm, $4-8), aptly named for the landmark on which it sits, has good food and pleasant lake views from the outside seating area. Try the fish fillet while you enjoy the sunset.

Next to the migration building, take a break from the sun and stop in Siembras y Cosechas (open daily) for a fresh fruit smoothie. On the

A parade of floats are judged at the annual Carnaval Aquático.

same street, ★ **Panadería Pantzín** (next to the Hotel San Carlos) is one of the only places in town you'll find anything stronger than instant coffee. The bakery serves delicious pastries and breads, with proceeds going to an NGO that works with local women who've experienced domestic abuse.

INFORMATION AND SERVICES

There's access to free (but slow) public Wi-Fi in and around the central park. **INTUR** (in the migration building, tel. 505/2583-0301, riosanjuan@intur.gob.ni) can provide a brochure or two about the region as well as an updated list of boat and bus schedules. On the street directly in front of the dock for Papaturro is the office for **CANTUR** (tel. 505/2583-0266, Mon.-Fri. 8am-5pm), which provides contacts for private transport services and a list of tours and local tour operators who offer trips throughout the region.

Banks

You need lots of cash down here. Small bills are best. Some of the main area lodges take credit cards, but always confirm. **LaFisse** (1 block east of the park, tel. 505/2255-8888x1, Mon.-Fri. 8:30am-4pm, Sat. until noon) has a 24-hour **ATM.** They will exchange dollars and Euros, but will not deal with traveler's checks. There are plenty of *coyotes* (moneychangers) down by the migration office, trading *córdobas,* dollars, and *colónes.* Otherwise, head for the **Western Union** (southwest of the church).

Emergency Services

There is a **police station** (3 km from the center of San Carlos on the road to Managua, tel. 505/2583-0350) and a **fire station** (tel. 505/2583-2149). **Hospital Luis Felipe Moncada** (tel. 505/2583-0244) is north of town on the highway; or try the **Centro de Salud** (half a block west of the *Escuela Autónoma*, tel. 505/2583-0361), located behind the hospital. San Carlos's medical services may be okay for minor problems, but for

any real emergencies, you're better off chartering a boat south to the hospital in Los Chiles, Costa Rica (1 hour or less by boat) or trying to get a flight to Managua.

Tourist Operators

Most lodges and hotels can arrange daily trips and activities, or hire a local guide in San Carlos. Ronny Zambrana of **Ryo Big Tours** (tel. 505/8828-8558, 505/8380-5395, or 505/8829-3944, ryobigtours@hotmail.com) is part of a growing group of professionally trained young Nicaraguan guides. They specialize in 6-8 day tours of the main sights along the river (from $400). They are part of a local tour guide effort and can recommend unique tours throughout the area.

Many national tour operators based in Granada and Managua offer package trips to the Río San Juan region. To paddle the Río San Juan and camp along its banks, contact **Green Pathways** (in Managua, tel. 505/8917-8832, www.greenpathways.com) and ask about their 12-day Río San Juan kayak expedition (3 people minimum, 2 weeks advance notice).

GETTING THERE AND AWAY
Air

There are two weekly 50-minute flights from Managua (Thurs. and Sun. noon, $110 one-way, $165 round-trip). The view as you arc over the lake and volcanoes is stunning. The plane continues on to San Juan de Nicaragua before returning. It departs San Carlos for Managua at 2:15pm, immediately after landing and unloading. For tickets, contact **La Costeña in Managua** (tel. 505/2263-2142, lacostena.online.com.ni). In San Carlos, the La Costeña office is run by **Jorge López** (tel. 505/2583-0048), but it's best to reserve your seat online. If you buy a ticket at the terminal, you'll need to pay in cash. Reserve your spot as far in advance as you can. Flights fill up fast. Getting on the waiting list and trying to go stand-by works more often than you would think for a 12-person plane.

Freshwater Sharks

After thousands of years of hunting in the brackish outflow of the Río San Juan, Nicaragua's freshwater sharks made their way up the river and formed a healthy population in Lake Nicaragua. The *Carcharhinus leucas* became the only shark in the world able to pass between saltwater and freshwater. Humans later became both victims and hunters of the shark (for more info see Edward Marriott's book, *Savage Shore*). Indigenous tribes on Ometepe worshipped the shark, sometimes feeding their dead to it. This fear and reverence only faded when the Asian market for shark-fin soup helped to create an industry around harvesting the famous fish, culminating in the late 1960s, when Somoza's processing plant in Granada butchered up to 20,000 sharks a year. Today, the only freshwater shark in the world is seldom seen, although it is still inadvisable to swim in the waters near San Juan del Norte.

Bus or Car

From Managua it's six hours (300 kilometers) to San Carlos by bus ($6) or car. Buses leave Managua's Mayoreo market seven times daily 5am-6pm. Buses leave for Managua six times daily 2am-8pm. In San Carlos, buses for all destinations leave from the terminal near the municipal dock.

Boat
TO GRANADA AND OMETEPE

Two weekly boats run between Granada's municipal dock and San Carlos. The ferry leaves Granada Monday 2pm and Thursday 5pm, making stops at Altagracia in Ometepe 3-4 hours later, followed by Morrito and San Miguelito, before arriving in San Carlos 14 hours later. Foreigners pay $10 for padded first-class seats with air-conditioning. There is also a VIP suite for $110. The same boat departs San Carlos bound for Granada on Tuesdays and Fridays at 2pm. Be there at least an hour in advance to get your ticket.

This boat passes Ometepe around 1am, where you can get off at Altagracia. The boat gets crowded at times, especially around Semana Santa, when the hot easterly winds chop the lake into steep swells, and the voyage degenerates into a 16-hour puke-fest. At other times of the year, the long ride is generally pleasant. Sailing west is always easier than sailing east. Buy your ticket from San Carlos at the Empresario Portuario (at the end of Calle Calzada, hours vary to match boat schedules) on the main drag (la Calle Comercio).

DOWN THE RÍO SAN JUAN

All boat tickets are sold at the Empresario Portuario (by the gas station). Inside you'll find up-to-date schedules and advance ticket sales for its fleet of *lanchas*. All boats for El Castillo also stop in Boca de Sábalos. The fast boats leave at 10:30am and 4:30pm to El Castillo ($5) and Sábalos ($4). The first slow boat to El Castillo (2-3 hours) leaves San Carlos daily 8am.

Slower colectivo boats to San Juan de Nicaragua (a.k.a. San Juan del Norte) leave on Tuesdays, Thursdays, and Fridays at 6am and return on Thursdays, Saturdays, and Sundays at 5am (11-12 hours, $13). The fast boat leaves San Carlos Tuesdays and Fridays 6am, returning from San Juan del Norte Thursdays and Sundays 5am (6 hours, $25).

Arrange private boat trips at CANTUR, or directly with a *panguero* (private boat owner). Armando Ortiz's **Viajes Turísticos** (1 block from the Western Union, tel. 505/8839-2878 or 505/8828-8550, viajesturisticosortiz@hotmail.es) specializes in private tours and transfers. Rising gas prices make chartered trips cost hundreds of dollars. As the demand for transportation continues to grow and shift, so do boat schedules. Check departure times well in advance, and be sure to get a second (and third) opinion.

RÍO FRÍO BORDER CROSSING

Boating south into Costa Rica begins with a visit to the *migración* office (on the *malecón*, tel. 505/2583-0361, daily 7am-6pm). There are usually three boats to Los Chiles, Costa Rica (1 hour, $9), at 10:30am, 1:30pm, and 4pm. The 1:30pm boat will only leave once its full, or not at all. Sundays there are boats at 11am and 1:30pm. To leave Nicaragua, it costs $2, and to enter it costs $12.

Once in Los Chiles, Costa Rica Migración is located 200 meters up the road from the dock, where you *must* get stamped. Daily direct buses depart for San José (5 hours, $5) at 5:30am and 3:30pm.

Boats leave Los Chiles to San Carlos daily noon and 4pm ($9). A second town by the name of Los Chiles is about two hours northeast of San Carlos, in Nicaragua. Be sure to distinguish between the two when asking for directions.

★ LOS GUATUZOS WILDLIFE REFUGE

The 438-square-kilometer strip between Nicaragua's southern border and Lake Cocibolca is a protected wetlands and wildlife reserve replete with myriad species of animals and inhabited by some 1,700 fishermen and subsistence farmers in 11 small communities. The locals are descendants of the Zapote and Guatuzo (or Maleku) peoples as well as the mestizos who arrived in the late 19th century to cultivate rubber. These same *huleros* reverted to the slave trade when the world rubber market crashed, selling Guatuzos for 50 pesos a head to the gold mines of Chontales. Today, only a handful of full-blooded Maleku exist, mostly over the border in Costa Rica.

In the 1930s, settlers introduced cacao to the region, which, because of the crop's need for shade, preserved much of the area's original forest canopy. When plummeting cacao prices and a deadly fungus wiped out the industry in the 1970s, hardwood logging ensued. Only military conflict in the 1980s stopped the logging, but it also drove nearly the entire population of Los Guatuzos into Costa Rica. When families returned in the early 1990s, the area's ecosystem was still largely intact, and the new government quickly acted to protect it from destruction.

Caimans are plentiful along the river.

Today, residents count on the richness of their natural surroundings to attract visitors and scientists. No fewer than 411 species of birds have been observed here. Between February and April, flocks of migratory species fly through in spectacular concentrations. Los Guatuzos contains dense populations of crocodiles; caimans; feral pigs; jaguars; and howler, white-faced, and spider monkeys. This is also home to a rare, ancient species of fish called the gaspar *(Actractoseus tropicus),* a living, armored relic of the Jurassic age that uses its snout and fangs to eat other fish, crabs, and even small turtles.

The narrow river's fauna-rich jungle gradually swallows you as you approach the community of Papaturro, located 40 kilometers from San Carlos, up the Río Papaturro, which drains the slopes of Costa Rica's northern volcanoes. Arrange birding safaris, fishing trips, kayak excursions, nighttime wildlife safaris, boat trips in the wetlands and lake, and tours of local villages (tours $30-40 pp). In Papaturro, a multiplatform suspension canopy bridge behind the Centro Ecológico research station allows for incredible bird and wildlife viewing in the upper reaches of the rainforest. Ask your host for tours, or at one of the *comedores*. Bring quick-drying clothes and adequate protection from the sun, rain, and especially bugs.

Accommodations and Food

Howler monkeys and birdcalls will wake you bright and early in Los Guatuzos. In the river community of Papaturro, ★ **Cabañas y Comedor Caiman** (immediately west of the main dock, tel. 506/8676-2958, www.cabañas-caimanlosguatuzos.com, armandogcarballo@hotmail.com or aillenm@hotmail.com, $12 pp, $18 with breakfast) has a cozy two-room cabin right on the river. It's solar-powered and nearly mosquito proof, quite a feat in the middle of the jungle. Owners Aillen and Armando will make you feel right at home, and can lend boots for trekking through the muddy paths around the community. Armando offers an incredible wealth of knowledge and passion for nature from over 20 years of working in the jungle.

Arrange your meals in the surrounding community. Locals ask that you divide your business as best you can between the three

comedores ($8 a plate). It's a little pricey for your standard Nica fare, but you get quantity and quality for your money.

Another option is only a five-minute boat ride from San Carlos. **Hotel La Esquina del Lago** (tel. 505/8849-0600, www.riosanjuan.info, travelangler@gmail.com, $30 s, $40 d, with breakfast) grew from a French expat's world-class sportfishing trips and area nature tours. Despite cold water and some broken fixtures, the rooms are homey and charming. Accessible only by boat, the jungle lodge feels incredibly remote, with views of surrounding volcanoes and all kinds of tours and water activities. They offer all transfer services, boats for your use, 24-hour electricity, Internet, and package deals with meals and tours included.

Getting There

From the west dock near the CANTUR office in San Carlos, *colectivos* leave for Papaturro Monday-Wednesday and Friday 9am (4 hours, $4 pp); the trip stops at the small island of Chichicaste, where fried fish and soup are available ($2). The boat returns to San Carlos Monday, Tuesday, Thursday, and Sunday, leaving Papaturro at 8am. The fast boat ($6) takes half the time. It leaves Tuesdays and Saturdays 10am from San Carlos, returning

SOLENTINAME SAN CARLOS

Los Guatuzos Wildlife Refuge

Monday and Friday 9am. Or you can rent a private *panga* ($120), which can take up to 10 people to Los Guatuzos in only 1.5 hours.

ESPERANZA VERDE

Part of the Guatuzos Reserve, this 5,000-hectare protected area is part of an effort to reforest and protect the overgrazed watershed of the Río Frío and the Río San Juan. From the dock of Esperanza Verde and the military post, walk 500 meters downstream to the **Centro de Interpretación Ambiental Konrad Lorenz,** and a row of six guest rooms with 20 beds ($45 pp with transportation and food); inquire about

special rates for NGOs, students, and Nicas. One-day tours from San Carlos can be arranged. The barren area immediately surrounding the guest facilities is uninteresting, but a 40-minute walk up the road brings you straight into the heart of the rainforest—monkeys, 200 species of birds, giant spiders, and potentially even pumas. There are a total of three trails and numerous aquatic trips. Contact Leonel Ubau with **FUNDEVERDE** (in Hotel Cabinas Leyko in San Carlos, tel. 505/2583-0354, fundeverde@yahoo.es). Located 15 minutes from San Carlos, take any *colectivo* heading up the Río Frío toward Los Chiles.

The Solentiname Islands

The 36 volcanic islands in southern Lake Cocibolca have a long history of habitation. Signs of its original residents are abundant in the form of petroglyphs, cave paintings, and artifacts. Somoza's logging companies deforested most of the archipelago, and Boaco cattlemen cut the rest to make pasture. But much of the forest has been allowed to regenerate, and the rebirth has attracted artists and biologists from all over the world. Fishing, of course, remains a mainstay of the islanders' diet. Today, 129 families (about 750 people) share the archipelago with an amazing diversity of vegetation, birds, and other wildlife.

Solentiname's best-known attraction is the creativity of its inhabitants, a talent Padre Ernesto Cardenal discovered in 1966 when he gave brushes and paint to local *jícaro* carvers. Cardenal, recently returned from a Trappist monastery in Kentucky, formed a Christian community in Solentiname and stayed on Isla Mancarrón to work and write for the next 10 years (he is locally referred to as "El Poeta"). Under his guidance, the simple church at Solentiname became the heart of Nicaragua's liberation theology movement, which represents Christ as the revolutionary savior of the poor. Cardenal's book, *The*

Gospels of Solentiname, is a written record of the phenomenon.

Cardenal later became the Sandinista Minister of Culture and formed the Asociación Para el Desarollo de Solentiname (Solentiname Development Association, or APDS). Under APDS, the arts continued to flourish and receive much attention from the rest of the world. Today, no fewer than 50 families continue to produce balsa-wood carvings and bright "primitivist" paintings of the landscape and community.

ORIENTATION

Essentially, only the four largest of the nearly three dozen islands are inhabited: Isla Mancarrón, Isla San Fernando (a.k.a. Isla Elvis Chavarría), Isla la Venada (a.k.a. Isla Donald Guevara), and Isla Mancarroncito. Only the first two have services for tourists. Staying on the island requires you to plan your meals ahead, as there aren't many restaurants in Mancarrón or San Fernando. Ask your host about including food in your room rate.

The best **tour guides** are folks from the area. Ask your host at your hotel or hostel for a tour of the area. It is possible to get a fully guided, four-day exploration of the entire

The Solentiname Islands

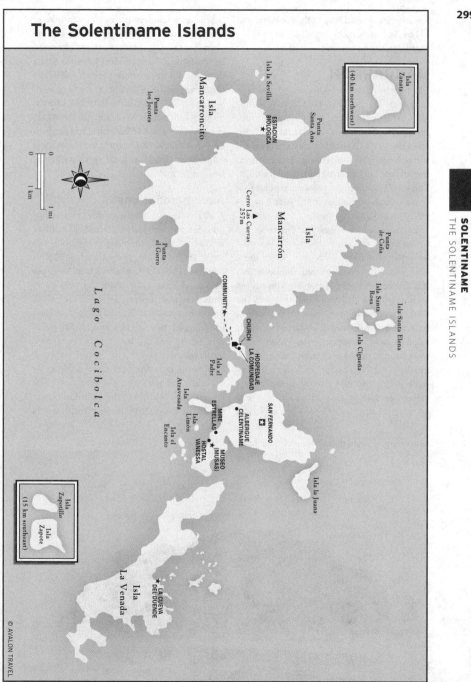

© AVALON TRAVEL

Solentiname archipelago and the Río Papaturro in Los Guatuzos, including all its natural, archaeological, and cultural attractions.

MANCARRÓN

The biggest (20 square kilometers) and tallest (at 257-meter Cerro las Cuevas) island, Mancarrón is populated by 34 families, about 200 people. The "town" of Mancarrón, built up in the 1980s, is simply a cluster of houses, a health center, school, church, and *pulpería*, five minutes up the paved path from the dock. The whole community is based around this center. Much of the rest of the island is privately owned and off-limits.

Ernesto Cardenal's project began in the 1960s in the church **Nuestra Señora de Solentiname** (daily 6am-6pm, $1 for tourists), which he reconstructed and designed. It is unlike any house of worship you've ever seen, featuring children's paintings on the whitewashed adobe walls, a unique crucifix sculpted by Cardenal, and an altar decorated in pre-Columbian style. To get there, walk straight up the path from the dock. The nearby APDS compound includes a library (with Internet access), a museum ($1), an art gallery, a display of indigenous artifacts, and an eclectic collection of books in a variety of

languages, including the complete works of Ernesto Cardenal. There are other works on liberation theology, plus the original primitivism painting by local resident Eduardo Arana that helped start the whole project. Ask if they can show you the 1970s BBC video documentary about the Solentiname Islands. Cardenal no longer maintains a residence in the APDS compound but visits frequently. You can visit the priest's former home (next to Hospedaje la Comunidad, free). The front porch is a breezy lookout point.

Accommodations

A local collective of families offer various options for accommodations. **Hostal Familiar El Buen Amigo** (turn left at the dock and walk 5 minutes along the path, tel. 505/8869-6619, hostalbuenamigo@gmail.com, $8-12 pp, $4-5 meals) has small cabins surrounded by fruit trees and flowers. Three of the rooms have a private bath. They offer tours of surrounding islands and also run a small pulpería, where you can buy a soda, Toña, or a bottle of rum.

Turning right from the dock, a two-minute walk will take you to a group of white houses, which is where the community was originally located. Walking right, towards

one of the many islets that make up the Solentiname archipelago

the water, you'll come to ★ **Hospedaje La Comunidad** (tel. 505/2277-3495, solpita@hotmail.com, $30 pp small cabin, $40 pp big lakefront cabin, rates include meals), which offers some of the prettiest rooms in Solentiname. The pricier rooms have big wooden porches complete with hammocks and rocking chairs, as well as bathrooms with bidet and a naturally lit shower. **Catalanica** (next to Hospedaje La Comunidad, tel. 505/8793-9320, reservas@catalanica.com, $18 pp) has a similar set up with fans and mosquito net, but meals are extra. There are a few other hostels scattered around the community.

★ SAN FERNANDO

In the 1980s, San Fernando was dubbed Isla Elvis Chavarría ("La Elvis") for a young martyr who participated in the 1977 raid on San Carlos and was subsequently captured and killed by the National Guard. Folks in the area never did stop calling it by its former name. The island has a health center, a school (Escuela Mateo Wooten, named after the Peace Corps volunteer who led its construction in the mid-1990s), a museum, a library, small shop, hiking trails, and a *mirador* with pre-Columbian petroglyphs. This is the best sunset view in the archipelago. For maximum enjoyment, I recommend grabbing a Toña and taking a dip in the lake at dusk.

El Museo Archipiélago de Solentiname (at the top of the steep path out of town, Mon.-Sat. 7am-noon and 2pm-5pm, $1) was built in September 2000 to preserve and display the natural and cultural heritage of the Solentiname Islands and its people. The flowers along the path on your way up were planted to attract butterflies and hummingbirds. Inside, local artists have painted scenes of the islands' early history. Also find interesting maps of the area, archaeological information, and a display of traditional fishing techniques and the balsawood carving process. Behind the museum there's a model organic avocado and balsawood plantation and a weather station. If you find it closed during its hours of operation,

ask around for Yelma, the local curator, caretaker, and key master.

Accommodations

Doña María Guevara has been running the ★ **Albergue Celentiname** (tel. 506/8503-5388 or 506/8500-2119, celentiname7@yahoo.es, $35 d, includes 3 meals) since 1984 on a beautiful point at the western edge of the island. All of the electricity in the hotel is solar generated. The eight cabanas all have private bath. Sit on your private porch and watch the hummingbirds flitting through the bushes while the water laps against the shore below. The picturesque main porch has priceless flower-framed views. Kayaks and fishing gear are available for rent. Make reservations in advance if possible (email is best).

Several hundred meters east, with his own dock on the southern shore of the island, **Don Julio** rents three rooms in his rustic and comfortable, lakefront homestead called Mire Estrellas ($8-10 each). Don Julio runs trips to other islands, and his brother, Chepe, runs transport to and from San Carlos and can arrange custom trips around the islands as well. Chepe's family runs a small hostel called **Hostal Vanessa** (tel. 505/8680-8423 or 505/8740-8409, jose.sequierapineda@gmail.com, $10-15 dorm, $25 private).

LA VENADA

Also referred to as "La Donald," for its official name, Isla Donald Guevara's namesake was martyred alongside his *compañero* Elvis Chavarría. La Venada is home to Rudolfo Arellano, one of the original artists from the islands. His family has a total of seven artists now who exhibit their work at the family house on the south side of the island. Paintings start around $25.

On the other side of the island is **La Cueva del Duende,** an important archaeological site that the islands' past inhabitants believed to be the entrance to the underworld. They painted faces to represent their ancestors, thought to reside there, and left other markings including a female fertility figure. The small nearby island **El Plato** has a petroglyph of an adult and child figure. For both of these, visibility is best at the peak of the dry season (Mar.-Apr.), but if the rainy season is light, you still have a good chance of seeing them. These will be most interesting for history buffs, but there's plenty of wildlife to see on the way. You can arrange the tour with your host or through CANTUR.

MANCARRONCITO

Mancarroncito is the best-preserved, wildest, and least inhabited of the main islands. Its steep, thickly vegetated hills rise to a 100-meter peak. In a cave on the island is the **Pared de las Ánimas,** filled with ancient drawings of the islands' former inhabitants. It's only accessible during the dry season (Mar.-May). The **Estación Biológica** on the island is run by local organization **Fundación del Río** (tel. 505/2583-0035, fdrio@turbonett. com.ni, $11 pp lodging, $5 meals). It offers lodging for up to 10, meals, and guide services around the reserve. Make reservations in advance by contacting Fundación del Río. Their main office is in San Carlos.

OTHER ISLANDS

Zapote and Zapotillo are the two closest islands to the mainland and are both owned by APDS, which has essentially decided to leave them alone. **Zapote** is a key nesting area for a variety of birds and turns into a whitewashed, foul-smelling squawk-fest November-April, when some 10,000 breeding pairs representing around 30 different species build nests there. The rest of the year you can still observe the 15 species that reside there permanently. Watch the reproductive mayhem from your boat only, as landing there disturbs the birds. Locals do go to the island periodically

to collect the rich compost created by all the bird dung. Smaller **Zapotillo** has less bird activity and a more sordid history, involving a fruit farm, an orphanage for boys, and a pedophile Evangelist priest who was eventually chased into Costa Rica, barely escaping with his life.

Located just off the western tip of La Elvis, **El Padre** became a howler monkey sanctuary when a single breeding pair introduced in the 1980s subsequently reproduced into a family of some 50 members. **Isla la Atravesada,** just off La Elvis and to the east of Isla el Padre, is privately owned by a Nicaraguan. Its northern shore is a nesting area for crocodiles March-June, and so is best avoided around that time.

GETTING THERE AND AWAY

From San Carlos, slow *colectivo* boats depart Tuesday and Friday 1pm for the archipelago (2 hours, $4 pp). The return trip leaves Solentiname Tuesday and Friday 4:30am, arriving in San Carlos in time to catch a bus to Managua at 8am. **TranSol** now runs a faster one-hour trip leaving daily from San Carlos at 3pm and returning at 9am ($10 pp). Should you want to leave the islands at any other time, private boats start at $180. CANTUR can arrange transportation to Los Guatuzos or San Carlos.

GETTING AROUND

If you are on a budget, getting around the islands will be your biggest challenge. You can either catch a free or discounted ride in someone's *panga,* or you can rent a kayak or canoe and do some paddling. Almost anyone with a boat will rent you their guide services, and there's room for negotiating. The more people per trip, the cheaper for each individual.

Down the Río San Juan

The 190-odd-kilometer journey to the sea takes you down the broad, lethargic Río San Juan through forests and isolated cattle farms. You'll have the opportunity to stop in several villages, isolated clusters of stilted homes, or in one of several river resorts and research stations. There are a few minor *raudales* (rapids) where the channel suddenly narrows, including the infamous *Raudal el Diablo* in front of El Castillo. Enormous silver *sábalos reales* (tarpon) are often seen rising just upstream from these fast waters. Downstream of El Castillo, things become decidedly wilder, especially on the Nicaraguan side, where the enormous Gran Reserva Río Indio-Maíz spills over the left bank. Finally, you'll reach San Juan del Norte, with all its ghosts, and a long sandbar, beyond which lies the Caribbean.

BOCA DE SÁBALOS AND VICINITY

A two-hour *lancha* ride from San Carlos brings you to this town, six kilometers upstream of El Castillo. Boca de Sábalos is a working town of about 1,200 souls, located at the mouth of one of Río San Juan's nearly 1,000 tributaries. It's actually the de facto seat of the El Castillo municipality (it was transferred here from El Castillo temporarily during the war, and then never moved back).

Sights

El Quebracho Wildlife Reserve, located in the part of the biosphere reserve allocated for ecotourism development, has two trails (one of which is self-guided) through a wildlife-rich setting. The reserve can accommodate up to 25 people ($20 pp, includes three meals) and guides can be hired ($10/day, discounts for groups larger than 10). Count on spending the night, as its isolation makes day trips challenging. Make arrangements at the office of **Fundación del Río** (a block south of the Alcaldía in Sábalos, tel. 505/2583-0035),

which owns and operates the reserve, or the main office near the hospital in San Carlos.

You can also hike down the Río San Juan to the 100-year-old, half-buried hulk of the **steamship wreck.** However, without a guide (or *very* good directions), it's easy to get lost. To go tarpon fishing, get a permit from the town MARENA office (hook only, no spears), and then hire a guide and boat to take you to just above the Toro Rapids, less than five minutes down the Río San Juan.

★ COOPROCAFUC CHOCOLATE TOUR

COOPROCAFUC (tel. 505/8390-5978 or 505/8441-5958, COOPROCAFUC@yahoo.es, $30 pp tour) is a cooperative of cacao farmers in the community of Buena Vista. They offer "chocolate tours" of the entire process of chocolate making, from planting to harvest to creating delicious chocolate products. During the tour you'll zip-line across a river and learn to make your own chocolate. The tour includes land transport to and from Boca de Sábalos (30 minutes). Don't forget to buy some chocolate to take home.

The co-op will gladly set you up with *hospedaje* in one of the family's homes ($4), or if you'd rather, rent a room at **Hostal Ricgema** ($10 pp). You can take a collective taxi ($2 each) from Sábalos to the Quebracha reserve, then walk 3.5 kilometers to the community. A private taxi will charge you $20. You can also get a hold of COOPROCAFUC through Jacamar (tel. 505/8441-5958 or 8910-0001, asociacionguiasjacamar@yahoo.com).

Accommodations
IN BOCA DE SÁBALOS

Walking straight up the road from the dock, you'll come to the beautiful hardwood ★ **Hospedaje Kateana** (tel. 505/2583-3838 or 505/8744-9278, $10) on your right, offering a variety of 14 clean rooms, some with private bath, all in a nice homey setting. Inquire in the *puplería* below for a room.

★ **Hotel Sábalos** (across the river from the main dock at the confluence of the Río Sábalos and the Río San Juan, tel. 505/8659-0252 or 505/2271-7424, www.hotelsabalos.com.ni, hotelsabalos@yahoo.com, $15-27 pp, includes breakfast) was built on a big deck over the water. The view from the porch might be the best in the entire Río San Juan area. Enjoy hot water, private bathrooms, classy accommodations, a restaurant ($4-7 meals), and a *panga* that can take you on tours around the area. They'll gladly shuttle guests back and forth across the river as needed.

NEAR BOCA DE SÁBALOS

Contemplate the night sky from a hammock at the **Grand River Lodge** (outside the community of La Esperanza, tel. 505/8936-3919 or 505/7892-8374, www.hotelgrandriverlodge.com, grandriverlodgehotel@gmail.com, $7 dorm, $15 s, 20 d private cabin with bathroom, $3 to camp with your own tent or hammock). They offer a variety of tours and recreation, including horseback riding, chocolate tours, sportfishing, hiking, kayaking, and canoeing. By boat, ask the *lanchero* to leave you at their dock. Or, take a bus from San Carlos. Tell the *busero* to leave you at the Grand River Lodge. Then walk 300 meters from the sign on the road.

★ **Sábalos Lodge** (tel. 505/8823-5514 or 505/2278-1405, www.sabaloslodge.com, sales@sabaloslodge.com, $35-75, includes breakfast) has 10 riverside bamboo and wood cabins with thatched roofs, hammock lounge, and a dining area. For true nature lovers, "adventure" cabins are open-air structures with private baths. Meals ($5 breakfast, $8-12 lunch and dinner, huge portions) and the service are excellent. Hiking trails and inner tube floats are available, plus free pickups from the Sábalos dock and tours to nearby cacao farms, nighttime caiman watching, and the Indio-Maíz biological reserve. The lodge is a 5-minute boat trip (or 15-minute walk) downstream from Boca de Sábalos.

open-air cabin at Sábalos Lodge

Located downstream from Boca de Sábalos on "river right" (assuming you're traveling downstream) before reaching El Castillo, **Montecristo River Lodge** (tel. 505/8649-9012, www.montecristoriverlodge.com, montecristoriver@yahoo.com, $75 all-inclusive) is a calm, riverside resort offering sportfishing, birding, hiking trails, horseback riding, and tours of local cacao farms and reforestation projects. They have a variety of rooms on a neatly kept compound and private nature reserve of 120 acres. They can transport you to area reserves and Solentiname. Your all-inclusive package includes three meals, three walking tours, trail hiking, and horseback riding; ask about discounts. You can also go kayaking or horseback riding ($25 pp).

Tour Operators

The best way to see what this area has to offer is to take one of the many tours offered by local guides. **Jacamar** (tel. 505/8441-5958 or 505/8910-0001, asociacionguiasjacamar@yahoo.com) is a local association of tour guides. They have a kiosk right in front of the dock where you can inquire about tours, rent a kayak ($12), or just ask for directions. The fudge they sell to promote their cacao farm tours is some of the best chocolate you're likely to find in Nicaragua.

Shane Tours (tel. 505/8431-2390, juliomurillo50@gmail.com) is part of the association and run by Don Julio Murillo, who speaks English. He organizes a variety of tours on and around Río Sábalos, and rents canoes and kayaks with or without a guide. He can also arrange a 6 to 8-day all-inclusive adventure trip to San Juan del Norte ($300 pp) that includes kayaking and diving around historic sunken steamships. Inquire at the kiosk to contact him.

Just outside of town, **Cooperativa de Servicios Múltiples** (tel. 505/8624-7666 or 505/8495-5446, cosemucrim_organico@yahoo.es) offers a "chocolate tour" of a cacao farm and the chocolate-making process.

Getting There and Away

The boats (slow boat $3, fast boat $4.50) that make the trip to El Castillo from San Carlos and back every day stop at Boca de Sábalos and the lodges upon request. Buses leave daily from the terminal in San Carlos to Boca de

Sábalos (1 hour) every hour on the hour 7am-11am and at 1pm, 2pm, 4:30pm, and 7pm, with reduced service on Sundays.

★ EL CASTILLO

The town of El Castillo (pop. 1,500) has neither roads nor cars—reason enough to visit. The town's not accessible by land, so most folks can't drive a car, but nearly all of them can drive a *panga*. Residents make their living principally in the tourist industry, in addition to working on cacao farms in the surrounding hills, fishing the river, commuting to the sawmill in Sábalos, the palm oil factory up the Río San Juan, or one of the resorts along the river. El Castillo celebrates its *fiestas patronales* on March 19.

Sights

Built in 1675, *la fortaleza,* the fortress of El Castillo de la Pura Inmaculada Concepción de María, was strategically placed with a long view downriver, right in front of the torrent Raudal el Diablo (still a navigational hazard). At the time, it was the largest fortress in Central America with 32 cannons and 11,000 weapons. Now dark, moss-covered ruins, *la fortaleza* is one place you should not miss.

Celebrating 500 years in the Americas, the

The fortress of El Castillo sits high above the Río San Juan.

government of Spain restored the fortress at great cost, building an historical museum and lending library, plus the nearby school and Hotel Albergue. The **museum** (Mon.-Fri. 8am-noon and 1pm-5pm, Sat.-Sun. 8am-noon and 1pm-4pm, $3) is small, but interesting, showing the history of the fortress and a collection of arms and other items dating as far back as the 1500s, including a pile of cannon balls and early rum bottles. Most signs are translated into English. A nearby butterfly farm, **Mariposario El Castillo** (tel. 505/8924-5590, $3 foreigners, $2 Nicas, $1.50 students), was also built by the Spanish, although much more recently.

Recreation and Tours

Run by municipal tourism cabinet, **La Caseta de Información Turística** (in front of the main dock, Mon.-Sat. 8am-12:30pm and 3pm-6pm) is the first stop for most tourists. The attendant can help with directions, lodging options, renting kayaks, and organizing tours of the surrounding area with local guides who are part of the cabinet. Prices keep rising as El Castillo becomes more popular. The most popular tours promoted at La Caseta are jungle hikes or chocolate making at a nearby cacao cooperative ($75-85, up to 5 people). Unfortunately smaller groups pay the same minimum price. They offer a variety of other options including horseback tours and nocturnal caiman watching. Charter a fishing boat ($140/day). Rent a kayak for three hours ($15 pp). If you plan to hike in the nearby reserve at Bartloa, buy your pass here first ($3).

There are plenty of other guides who advertise along the main road offering similar tours. Your host can certainly help arrange tours. It's best to shop around a little to compare tours and prices. **Juan Ardilla** (tel. 505/8938-8552) offers a five-day camping tour from San Juan de Nicaragua to El Castillo. Alfonso at **Agencia Tropical** (in front of El Chinandegano, tel. 505/8431-2389), a member of the local cacao co-op COODEPROSA, offers chocolate tours of his land parcel ($15 pp, minimum of 2 people).

Nena Lodge & Tours (1 kilometer west of the dock, tel. 505/2583-3010 or 505/8821-2135) offers tours of the Indio Maíz Reserve ($70-80 for 2 people, $80-90 for 4 people) as well as night tours on the river ($45 for up to 4 people). Check out their sister's handmade *artesenía* store a couple houses down, **Artesanía y Manualidades Yorleni** (daily 8am-7pm). It's a little space with a lot of variety of artisanal crafts, most made by Yorleni herself.

Accommodations

Hospedajes are popping up all over town as word spreads about this tourist destination. Most are downstream from the dock. The ones closest cost $5 a night but don't offer much.

Farther along the path, **Nena Lodge & Tours** (tel. 505/2583-3010 or 505/8821-2135, www.nenalodge.com, nenalodgeandtours@yahoo.es, $10 s, $25 d with private bath) is on your right above the family home. It has clean sheets and a streetside balcony. A little ways down on your left **Casa de Huespedes y Restaurante El Chinandegano** (tel. 505/2583-3011, $8 pp shared bath, $12 private bath, includes breakfast) offers simple, homey rooms right on the river.

The two-story, wooden **Hotel Albergue El Castillo** (follow the stairs next to La Caseta, tel. 505/8360-2163 or 505/8939-3119, PEACRISTINA19@yahoo.es, $15 s, $25 d with private bath, includes breakfast) was built in 1992 with the help of the Spanish government. Its comfortable double balcony overlooks the town, the river, and rapids beyond. It sleeps up to 35 people, with shared bath.

For those with more flexible budgets, there are a couple of nice options. **Hotel Victoria** (very end of the road leading downstream from the dock, tel. 505/2583-0188, $35 s, $60 d, includes breakfast) is new, and has hot water and air-conditioning. There is a second floor balcony with hammocks and a river view. The elegant restaurant on the first floor sells artisanal chocolate from the nearby cacao farm. They offer chocolate tours directly to guests.

comfy upscale lodging at Hotel Luna del Río

★ **Hotel Luna del Río** (90 meters east of the main dock, tel. 505/8624-6263, riosanjuannicaragua@yahoo.es, $45 s, $60 d, includes breakfast) is a cozy little eco-lodge just upstream of the Ruedal del Diablo. Watch the tarpon jumping from the porch while enjoying your complimentary hot chocolate. They serve real coffee and the attentive staff offers tours. They use LED electricity, a solar-powered water heater, organic detergent, and high efficiency air-conditioning units. Five percent of their income goes towards buying supplies for the local school.

Upstream of the dock is one of the newer additions to the area, **Hotel Lara's Planet** (tel. 505/8637-1440, www.hotellarasplanet. com, $40-75 s, $80-90 d), with a huge deck jutting into the river that offers a panoramic view of the river and fort. All rooms include balcony, fan, drinking water, mini-fridge, TV, and lock box. The more expensive rooms are the biggest you'll find anywhere along the river.

Food

When they're in season, find delicious and frighteningly large river shrimp at **El Cofalito** (just west of the dock, daily 7am-8pm, $5-13) served on an airy, open second-story deck. ★ **El Chinandegano** (1 kilometer west of the dock, daily 7am-9pm, $2-3 breakfast, $5-6 lunch and dinner) is the best value for local fare. **La Orquidea** (next to the Nazareno church, $3-10) serves meals along with smoothies and fresh juice.

If you need a break from *gallo pinto* and instant coffee, ★ **Border's Coffee** (daily 8am-10pm, $3-4 breakfast, $7-8 lunch and dinner) specializes in pastas and curry dishes. They have an espresso machine, fresh juices, and milkshakes, all in a great ambience. To get there, turn right down the path just past the bridge next to Hotel Victoria. ★ **Lara's Planet** (upstream of the dock, daily 6am-9pm, $5-11) serves homemade yogurt using milk from the dairy farm across the river. They cook with vegetables fresh from their garden and even make their own delicious coconut cream.

Getting There and Away

Lanchas colectivas to El Castillo (fast boat $5, 3 hours; or slow boat $3.50, 5 hours) depart San Carlos seven times daily 8am-4:30pm. It's best to be at the dock at least a half hour before the boat is scheduled to leave. The last fast boat makes part of the journey after dark, which is more dangerous. Returning boats leave for San Carlos every hour 5am-7am and at 2pm (Sun. only at 5am and 2pm), with two fast boats at 5:30am and 9:30am.

To go downstream, ask around the dock or at La Caseta. Boats for San Juan del Norte pass through on Tuesday and Friday 9am. They head upstream on Thursday, Saturday, and Sunday, passing El Castillo in the early afternoon. It costs $13 to get to San Juan del Norte from El Castillo and $23 on the fast boat, which is more than worth it for the four hours it saves you.

RÍO SAN JUAN WILDLIFE REFUGE

This two-kilometer-wide belt that follows the north side of the river is part of the **Río Indio-Maíz Biosphere Reserve,** a 3,618-square-kilometer virgin rainforest. The first access point to the Refugio is six kilometers downstream of El Castillo (or about 3 hours by boat from San Carlos). The western border of the reserve is the Río Bartola at its confluence with the Río San Juan. Arrange a hike through La Caseta in El Castillo, or stay in the community of Bartola, 1.5 hours outside the town.

The eco-lodge and research station, **Refugio Bartola** (tel. 505/8446-3657 or 505/8772-5868, www.refugiobartola.com, $44 d, $7-13 meals, $30-80 tours, no more than 5 people per tour) has 11 rooms on the corner of the protected area with wonderful views of the river. The compound is surrounded by rainforest and fueled by solar energy but is remote and difficult to contact; email is your best bet. You may need to wait until you're in El Castillo where they can be contacted through La Caseta.

★ **Basecamp Bartola** (tel. 505/8913-8215, indio.maiz@gmail.com) is a community initiative run by Cooperativa de Turismo Sostenible Bartola Sol y Luna that offers hiking trails, wildlife tours in traditional wooden boats in Río Bartola, and, as they're also associates of COODEPROSA, chocolate tours. They invite visitors to camp in tents set on raised wooden platforms. They offer a variety of tour and lodging packages ranging from $179 for one night and two days, to $215 for two nights and three days for 2 people. Reserve ahead for transport from El Castillo.

★ SAN JUAN DE NICARAGUA

Still commonly referred to by its previous names, San Juan del Norte or Greytown, this settlement near the mouth of the river is located 100 winding kilometers beyond El Castillo. This hot, historic village in Nicaragua's extreme southeast corner is home to about 2,000 residents representing Creole, indigenous Rama, and mestizo roots. The village is not accessible by land, so most locals can't drive a car, but they all know how to use a *lancha*.

This area has played an important role in Nicaragua's history. Sir Charles Grey, governor of Jamaica, first seized the land for the English in 1848 and built the rowdy port of Greytown, which lasted about 150 years. When the British pulled out, it melted into

San Juan de Nicaragua

a forgotten backwater, and these days nothing but a historic cemetery of segregated plots with both British and American headstones remains.

Present-day San Juan lies hidden in the brackish swamps at the confluence of Río Indio with the Río San Juan. San Juan del Norte suffered during the Contra War in the 1980s, during which time Hurricane Joan also flattened it. By the 1990s, the town consisted of just three buildings, but has since grown to accommodate interested tourists and the September fishing tournament. Plans for a new marina in the town are included in the country's most recent canal scheme.

Services are limited, and so is the water and power supply. (Much of the community uses solar power.) There is public Internet access in the library and mayor's office (la alcaldía). There are no ATMs or banks in town, so bring plenty of cash.

Sights

There's not a lot to do in the town proper, and leaving requires a boat, so expect to pay for at least one tour while you're here. Or, rent a kayak and paddle around yourself. The most popular attraction in the immediate area, for its historical appeal, is the **colonial cemetery,** located in Greytown's former location along the airstrip, a short boat ride away across the mouth of the river. Just beyond is the Caribbean. Though often rough and not suitable for swimming, there are some bays where you can swim. To get there you'll need to negotiate a price with a *panguero* (*panga* driver) who knows the coast. There are a couple of hiking trails behind the community. They're not well marked, so locals highly recommend taking a guide.

Tours

One of the more popular tours is to Rama indigenous community **Canto Gallo** in the Indio Maíz Reserve, where you can still see the stone remnants of former generations. It's a few hours north from San Juan, so you'll need to stay the night. A 45-minute boat ride to nearby lagoons **San Juanillo, La Barca, Silico and Plaüellas** (all connected by small rivers) for a day of swimming and hiking will run 3 people about $50 each. Other popular tours include a visit to the **Laguna Manatí,** where you're likely to see manatees. The **Laguna Macquengue** is a great spot for bird-watching.

Don Enrique and his four INTUR-certified sons at Hotelito Evo (tel. 505/2583-9019 or 505/8624-6401) offer several tours including a coastal excursion, a visit to the **Cangrejera** (the largest coconut farm in Central America), night tours, sportfishing, and visits to the Rama indigenous community. They offer a half-day trip to historic Greytown that includes hiking ($50 for 2 people), and a two-day trip, including hiking, camping in hammocks, food, transportation, and a visit to Canto Gallo ($400 for 4 people).

Cabinas Jardín de los Ramas owner **Porfirio Duarte** (505/8841-8130 or 505/8504-2908) specializes in sportfishing tours ($250/day) and also offers Canto Gallo tours ($400). **Augencio Salmón** (tel. 505/8832-9003) is INTUR-certified, speaks English, and comes highly recommended.

Coulson Tours (tel. 505/8909-7635 or 505/8414-9761, coulson.tours@gmail.com), in addition to abovementioned tours, works with the Wildlife Conservation Society and runs a marine turtle tour (Mar.-Aug., $50 pp). Guides Edgar (of Cabinas Escondite) and Adonis speak English.

Accommodations and Food

The town is small, and everything is in walking distance. **Hotelito Evo** (from the Enitel antenna, 3 blocks southwest, tel. 505/2583-9019 or 505/8624-6401, www.hostalevo.com, evohotel@yahoo.es, $15 s, $20 d) has seven clean rooms, all with fans and mosquito nets, five with private bath. Ask about adding breakfast to the price.

For a rustic feel, try the thatched-roof cabins in **Cabinas Escondite** (tel.

505/8414-9761, $15 pp with private bath and mosquito net) owned by Nicaraguan Rastafarian Edgar (more commonly referred to as Rasta). Reserve ahead so he can set up a room for you. He's also a chef who serves one of the best meals in town. Just give him a heads up and let him know you're coming. To find Rasta's *cabinas* ask around near the military post at the north end of town (where the third walkway ends). Turn left there and walk behind the second house on your right.

The nicest option in town is the family-run ★ **Cabinas Jardín de los Ramas** (from the dock walk 700 meters east, tel. 505/8841-8130 or 505/8504-2908, $25-50, includes breakfast). Cabins are scattered under the trees and have pretty wooden private baths, mosquito netting, and fans. The restaurant (Mon.-Fri. 10am-midnight, Sat.-Sun. noon-midnight) is right on the water.

For dancing at the go-to weekend spot, head to **Bar y Discoteca Sabor Tropical** (3 blocks east of the dock, Fri.-Sat. 7pm-midnight). The restaurant (Tues.-Sun. 10am-1pm and 4pm-midnight) is on the second floor. **El Tucán** (50 meters east from the courthouse, tel. 505/8419-5356, daily 7am-9pm, $5-12) has a *hospedaje*, which floods in the rainy season. The owner's son Alfredo gives tours and rents kayaks. Both venues offer typical local fare like fish and rice and beans.

★ **Restaurante y Hospedaje Familiar** (on the waterfront, $12-20 with private bath and fans) has two bright, airy rooms with a shared porch offering the best view in town. The restaurant (daily 6:30am-9pm) makes *nacatamales* on weekends.

Getting There and Away

The easiest way to get to San Juan del Norte is by plane from San Carlos. **La Costeña** (tel. 505/2263-2142, www.lacostena.com.ni) runs flights to and from on Thursdays and Sundays (30 minutes, $55, $102 round-trip). A flight all the way back to Managua stops in San Carlos along the way (1.5 hours, $110 one-way).

Reserve early; the 12-passenger plane fills up fast. For a cheaper option, a couple of *pangas* now make the trip three days a week, stopping in El Castillo. The slow boat ($13 each way) takes at least 11 hours. The fast boat ($25) takes half the time. For the fast boat, you pay the same price from El Castillo. Buy your downstream ticket at the San Carlos municipal dock or at La Caseta in El Castillo the day before your trip.

There is a scheduled weekly *colectivo* service between San Juan del Norte and Bluefields on Wednesdays 8am. The *colectivo* ride along the coast is run by a man called **Chacalín** (tel. 505/8355-8745, 4-5 hours, $35 pp). He makes the return trip on Fridays at 9am. He's also available for private trips.

Although the Tortuguero Park is just across the border in Costa Rica, there is no immigration post this far east. The closest place to cross is Los Chiles, leaving from San Carlos.

THE RÍO INDIO LODGE

Fall asleep to the sounds of the jungle in the multimillion-dollar, five-star **Río Indio Lodge** (tel. 505/2580-0813, 506/8382-3860, U.S. tel. 866/593-3168, www.therioindiolodge. com, reservations@bluwing.com, $150 pp), a self-described ecotourism and sportfishing resort geared to the luxury adventure traveler. It's located in the forest in front of a 150-year-old dredge at the mouth of what was to have once been the Nicaraguan canal. Costa Rican owned and operated, the Río Indio has a lakefront swimming pool filled with treated rainwater as well as a refuge space used by MARENA for healing animals.

Accommodations are outdated, and I ran across a few broken fixtures, but your money is well spent with the lodge's friendly expert guides who run tours and fancy sportfishing trips on the Río San Juan. Price includes your choice of a tour of historic Greytown cemeteries or a two-hour wilderness hike, and a night tour for alligator spotting, as well as Wi-Fi, laundry service, three meals, and all the rum you can drink. They'll add another tour for every day you stay. Other activities include guided fishing trips, bird-watching, kayaking, hiking, and visits to nearby lagoons.

Sign up for the weeklong Bushmaster Survival School ($1,950), a wilderness training which will teach you basic survival skills in the Nicaraguan jungle. The course includes three straight days of sleeping in waterproof camping hammocks, fishing, finding edible plants, and learning to find drinking water.

Reserve in advance for airport or dock pickup, 10 minutes away in a *panga*.

Bluefields and the Corn Islands

The Atlantic coast of Nicaragua is a land unto itself. Nicaragua's vast semi-autonomous Caribbean regions are influenced more by the English than the Spanish, and more by indigenous and African ancestry than by mestizos.

(Though the "Spanish," as western Nicaraguans are known, are quickly moving in and catching up.) The vast majority of Nicaragua's 450 kilometers of Atlantic coastline are unexplored, undeveloped, and unapproachable, and the culture on the sunrise side of Nicaragua is distinctly Caribbean. The sentiment is so strong, the name Autonomous Region of the South Atlantic (RAAS) was recently changed to Autonomous Region of the South Caribbean Coast (RACCS), and the north is now officially the RACCN. However, you'll still hear "RAAS" used in everyday conversation.

The Atlantic coast is languid and lazy, but it's got an edge, too, in the form of bitter poverty and a history of drug-related danger. It also has sultry mangrove estuaries, white, sandy beaches, and a relaxed lifestyle. The warm, humid breezes smelling of coconut palms and vegetation are a nice break from the dry, dusty highlands. Bluefields is a quintessential Caribbean port town, with enough

fresh seafood to wear you out, an oppressive afternoon sun, and a no-hurry attitude. Corn Island and Little Corn Island are another scene altogether with soft sand beaches and rustling palm fronds, plus an isolated feeling that's hard to find elsewhere.

PLANNING YOUR TIME

Big Corn Island is worth a night or two unless you really crave remoteness, in which case you should beeline to Little Corn, the more rustic of the pair, where 2-4 days will provide ample opportunity to dive and explore the reefs. With 2-3 more days, head back to Bluefields (plan on a whole day of travel if you go by boat), and catch a boat to Pearl Lagoon the next morning. Book a trip to the Pearl Cays for the next day, and then spend the afternoon checking out Awas, or poking around town. If you have a couple more days, relocate to Orinoco or Wawachang.

If you're traveling overland from Managua,

Previous: bikers on Big Corn Island; Long Beach, Big Corn Island. **Above:** the main dock at Big Corn Island.

Look for ★ to find recommended
sights, activities, dining, and lodging.

Highlights

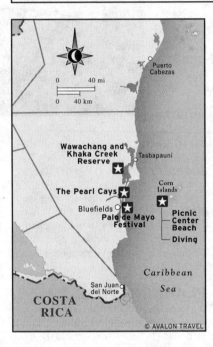

★ **Palo de Mayo Festival:** Sensual and rhythmic, Bluefield's joyous May Day celebration is one of the flashiest shows in the country (page 319).

★ **The Pearl Cays:** These 18 tiny islands rest in calm, clear waters chock full of marine life. Spend a day swimming, snorkeling, and relaxing on the beach (page 328).

★ **Wawachang and Khaka Creek Reserve:** Venture up the Wawachang River to this guesthouse and beautiful forest reserve, one of Nicaragua's best community-based ecotourism ventures (page 329).

★ **Picnic Center Beach:** This Corn Island classic is an uninterrupted crescent of white-sand hedonism (page 334).

★ **Diving near the Corn Islands:** Snorkel, swim, or scuba to experience the reefs and marine life just offshore of either Corn Island (pages 335 and 341).

Bluefields and the Corn Islands

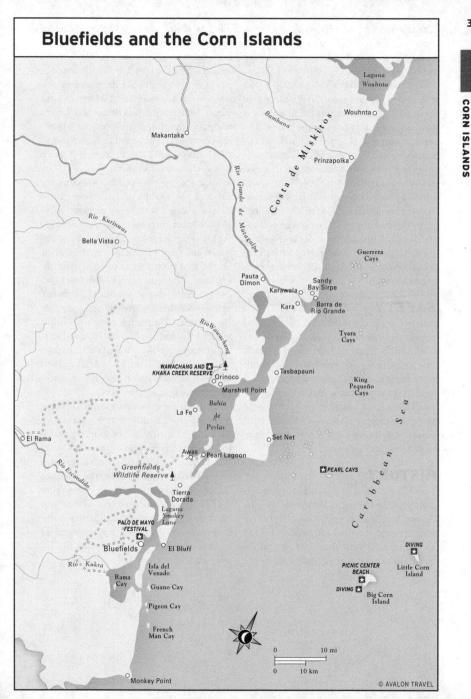

© AVALON TRAVEL

schedule one day for the trip and another to recover in Bluefields. If you have a day to kill waiting for a ride to the islands, spend the day swimming in El Bluff.

The Atlantic coast receives 3,000-6,000 millimeters of rain annually (with the higher levels falling in southern RACCS), making it among the wettest places on the planet. The rainy season is punctuated by hurricanes in September and October and can extend well into December, sometimes longer. The end of December is marked by cool, "Christmas" winds. Most visitors come during the period between late January and April when it's generally dry and sunny. The biggest crowds arrive for Christmas, Semana Santa (the Holy Week before Easter), and during various regional fiestas, when making reservations is a good idea.

SAFETY

International drug trafficking continues to impact the Atlantic coast of Nicaragua, including Bluefields and the Corn Islands, which have in the past seen incidents of both petty crime and more serious assault against tourists. In recent years, Bluefields has seen a decline in drug-related crime, due in large part to the capture of some well-known local *narcos*. Still, it's not a bad idea to stick to the beaten path in these parts.

HISTORY

The Atlantic coast of Nicaragua was originally populated by native Miskito, Mayangna (Sumu), and Rama people, who settled along the rivers and coastline and lived on fishing and small-scale agriculture. Its general inhospitality kept it free of foreign influence

until the 1700s, when the English organized the Atlantic coast into a British protectorate, establishing "Miskito Kings" whom the British educated, armed, and maintained in power. In 1860, the British departure was followed by the advent of North American businesses, which established timber and banana company camps. Bluefields became a thriving commercial center with regular steamship connections to New Orleans, Baltimore, Philadelphia, and New York.

Such was the state of Bluefields and the Atlantic coast when dictator José Santos Zelaya ordered a military occupation in 1894. General Rigoberto Cabezas deposed the Miskito government, and officially united Nicaragua from the Atlantic to the Pacific for the first time. Once united to Spanish-speaking Nicaragua, Managua felt free to tax and ignore the Atlantic coast, and Zelaya and successors roundly abused indigenous rights for centuries. The foreign companies began to withdraw, and Sandino and his anti-imperialist troops brutally attacked those tempted to linger. In the aftermath, the Atlantic coast has decayed into a state of corruption, financial mismanagement, and poverty.

Costeños were decidedly apathetic about their supposed Sandinista "liberation" in 1979 and many were hostile to it after major FSLN errors in the region. Since the Contra War ended, Spanish-speaking Nicaraguans have arrived en masse, putting the black and indigenous populations in the minority for the first time ever. Tensions rise as these new "Spaniards" (as Costeños have always referred to mestizos) seek housing and employment and attempt to import their culture to their new home.

Bluefields

Bluefields is a rich waterfront melting pot of nearly 50,000 souls representing six different ethnic groups, many of whom make a living in the fishing and timber industries, or working on cruise ships, where their bilingual skills are prized. The city has never been connected to western Nicaragua's highway system and can be reached only by water or air. Bluefields Bay remains an important Atlantic port, and the city itself is the capital of the RACCS and home to two universities. Despite all the activity, unemployment is acute and this town is no stranger to petty crime. There's not whole lot to do in town, but it makes a great base for trips to nearby sights. Do not miss the Palo de Mayo celebrations, an exuberant and erotic calypso-inspired dance and music event, unique to the city and celebrated fervently throughout the month of May.

ORIENTATION

Bluefields streets run parallel to the coast between the airport, several-kilometers south of town, and Lomas Frescas, its northernmost neighborhood. Several small barrios lie between these points, none of them more than a few blocks large. Barrio Central is the most traversed part of town, spreading west from the municipal wharf downtown. Parque Reyes is located three blocks west of the waterfront road. Avoid neighborhoods Beholden and Cotton Tree after dark. Always take a cab after midnight.

SIGHTS

Bluefields does not offer much in the way of sightseeing, but if you're up for a stroll, there are a few places to visit. Start near the wharf at the red-roofed **Moravian church,** originally built in 1848 with English, French, and Caribbean influence, the first of its kind on the Central American coast. Hurricane Joan destroyed it in 1988, so the actual structure is just a few decades old. About two blocks

west, the whitewashed wood and stained-glass Catholic **cathedral** is captivating, airy, and modern.

An affiliate of the BICU university, the **Historical Museum** (on 2nd Fl. of the CIDCA building, Barrio Punta Fría, tel. 505/2572-2735, 8am-noon and 2pm-5pm Mon.-Fri., $2) is worth a visit to learn about the region's past. They have a collection of historical objects and fascinating photos of Bluefields before Hurricane Joan and the last Mosquito King, as well as various early indigenous artifacts from all over the region.

TOUR OPERATORS

Travel the RACCS with an experienced local guide from **Atlantic Tour** (north side of the Alcaldía, tel. 505/2572-2259 or 505/8813-8329, www.rightsideguide.com/atlantic-tour, altlantictour@hotmail.com, Mon.-Fri. 9am-5pm). The company offers day trips to Rama Cay, El Bluff, and tours of both urban and rural Bluefields. You can book an overnight trip to the Pearl Cays, which includes a tour of Pearl Lagoon and its surrounding villages.

Maintained by a Texan who moved to Nicaragua in 2008, **Right Side Guide** (www.rightsideguide.com) has lots of useful info about the region, including up-to-date transportation schedules.

ENTERTAINMENT AND EVENTS
Nightlife

You'll hear the reggae bumping wherever you go, from dance hall, roots, *soca, punta,* and Palo de Mayo to reggae *romántica,* and of course long sets of Bob Marley. Interestingly, the Atlantic coast's second favorite is U.S. country music, which locals proudly call their "coastal music."

For dancing, **4 Brothers** (Barrio Punta Fría, 6 blocks south of the park, Thurs.-Sun. 9pm-3am) has been the heart of the Creole

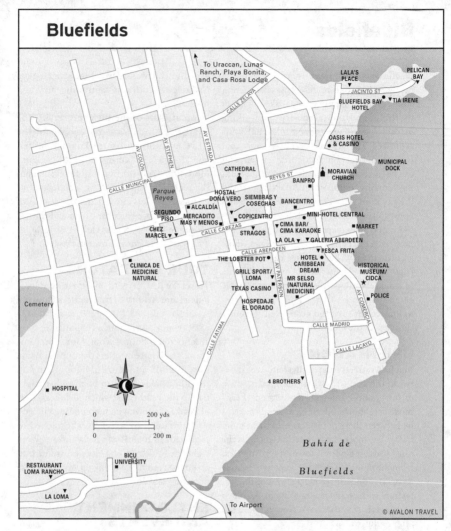

Bluefields

© AVALON TRAVEL

social scene since the 1990s. Expect a small, cramped juke joint with a wooden-plank dance floor and ice-cold beer. You'll need that beer to help you master the sensual Caribbean "hug-up" grind.

Cima Bar (Barrio Central, half a block from Bancentro on the left, 2nd Fl., tel. 505/2572-2782, daily 5pm-3am) draws a lively Creole crowd with its intimate dance floor. **Cima Karaoke** (above Cima Bar, Thurs.-Sat. 8pm-3am) offers louder music, a spacious

dance floor, a longer bar, and a more diverse crowd, but there's rarely karaoke. Chill out on the second-floor balcony at **Stragos** (Barrio Central, next to Cima, daily 3pm-midnight), the local sports bar.

Pelican Bay (Point In, daily 11am-11pm) is best in the afternoon when you can look out over the water, but you'll enjoy the ocean breeze at any time of day. This is a calmer environment in which to enjoy your nightcap. Half a block down the road, the lively

A Few Creole Expressions

Put your Spanish dictionary away in Bluefields—you're in Creole country! Creole is a complete language system that's in the process of being documented, and books are being written to teach Creole students to read and write in their first language. The campaign slogan is: *Kriol iz wi langwij, mek wi rait it!* (Creole is our language, let's write it). At times, the rhythms of the Costeño tongue are difficult to understand, but not so tough to speak. And, of course, coastal communication slides easily in and out of English and Spanish. For instance, *"Dem aprovecharing beca dem mama no de"* means "That person is taking advantage of the fact that his mother is not home." Listen for the following expressions and try them out if you're feeling up to it.

"She done reach Raitipura." She arrived at Raitipura.
"How you mean?" Explain that please.
"No feel, no way." Don't worry, it's okay.
"I no vex." I'm not angry.
"Dat nasty." That's awesome!
"That ain't nothing." Thank you.
"Check you then." Goodbye.
"Make I get tree o dem." Give me three of those.
"She feel fa eat some." She's in the mood to eat.
"He own" His.
"It molest we." It bothers us.
"Nice." "It's all good," or goodbye.
"Uno jus keep walking." You all just keep walking.
Wabool Cassava pounder, or penis
Coco Coconut, or vagina

Thanks to "Dr. G.," a.k.a. Georgie Cayasso, Bluefields native and distinguished Creole linguist.

Lala's Place (Point In, tel. 505/8840-7531, daily 11am-3am) offers dancing at night and delicious *rondón* (seafood stew) at meal times. **Lady D's** (Barrio Pantasan, in front of Distribuidora Marin) is a *rancho* (thatch-roofed restaurant), popular as both a bar on weekends and a restaurant all week long.

Festivals and Events

The **Crab Soup Festival** (Aug. 27-28) is a commemoration of the islanders' emancipation from British slavery in 1841. The governor of this then-British protectorate, sitting miles away in Kingston, Jamaica, was authorized to pay slave owners compensation for the loss of their "assets," while the newly freed slaves scrambled to put together a meal out of what was most handy—crabs. Be sure to catch the crowning of Miss Corn Island, Miss Coconut, and Miss Photogenic.

The city's birthday is October 11. Celebrations last throughout the month of **October.** October 28 is the anniversary of the 1987 passage of the Autonomy Law; its commemoration features cuisine competitions between all the ethnic groups. This is a great time of year to sample the foods of the coast, learn about the autonomy process (and its history), and meet community leaders and politicians. Although the **November 9-11** celebration of Garífuna culture is best in Orinoco, Garífunas make merry throughout the region with live music and plenty of food.

★ PALO DE MAYO FESTIVAL

Also known as the *¡Mayo Ya!* festival, Bluefields's **May Day** celebration is unique in Central America. In Bluefields, May falls on the cusp of the rainy season, and the entire month is a bright burst of colors, parades, costumes, feasting, and most importantly, dancing around the maypole. Every night is a party, and the festival comes to a rip-roaring peak at the end of the month with the celebration of the *tululu* dance, starting in Old Bank and parading through Beholden, Point In, Central, and Cotton Tree neighborhoods.

In Bluefields, the Palo de Mayo refers to the month-long celebration in Bluefields, Pearl Lagoon, and the Corn Islands, and also to the name of a dance and style of music. The dance has gotten progressively more sensual in recent decades, sometimes appearing as simulated sex on the dance floor (conservative Costeños have started a movement to return the dance to its more respectable origins).

SHOPPING

Visiting the town market on the municipal dock is a dark, damp experience, with cramped stalls in an ugly metal building, but it's interesting nevertheless, especially if you need to stock up on homemade cheese and buns. **Joyería y Artesanía Gutierrez** (Barrio Central in front of the SOS Farmacia) sells Caribbean-inspired woodcarvings, which you'll also find at some hotel shops. **Julio Lopez** (Barrio 19 de Julio), a Garífuna originally from Orinoco, and **Leo Bolanos Padilla** (Barrio 19 de Julio, tel. 505/2572-0070) are renowned local artisans. Find Julio Lopez in front of where INAFOR used to be; find Leo Bolanos Padilla *contiguo donde fue la cocotera* ("next to where the coconut trees used to be"). **Mr. Rene Hodgson** (tel. 505/2572-1658) is a talented, self-taught Creole painter and local Adventist pastor whose work is frequently displayed at the Bluefields Bay Hotel (Point In, tel. 505/2572-2143).

ACCOMMODATIONS

This is one place where "roughing it" in the cheapest flophouses (there are a few obvious ones near the dock and market) is asking for trouble. If you do decide to go for one of the budget hotels, assess both its security measures and the kind of people hanging around. Insist on a window with screens or a mosquito net. Avoid the Pension López, famous for drunk men and hourly room rentals.

Under $25

Hospedaje El Dorado (Barrio Punta Fría, across from the Cruz Lorena, tel. 505/2572-1435, $8 with private bath, $5 shared bath) is one of the best options if you are determined to stick to a strict budget. The hotel offers relatively clean, well-maintained rooms with private bath and cable TV. **Lobster Pot** (on the main drag in Barrio Central, tel. 505/8731-5961, $5 s, $6-10 d, $12 with private bath) is owned by a Creole-speaking Cayman Islander who runs a large establishment that rents many of its rooms to permanent guests. The clean rooms with a shared bath have Wi-Fi and are better than some other rundown places. Ask for a cooler second floor room. Family-run **Guest House Campbell** (Barrio Fátima, tel. 505/8827-2221, $11-12) offers adequate private rooms with fan, TV, and bathrooms.

★ **Hotel Doña Vero** (half a block west and half a block south of the cathedral, tel. 505/2572-2166, $12-17) is by far the best budget option: clean, airy, and centrally located. They have a new pool out back that gets lots of sun in the morning. **Mini-Hotel Central** (Barrio Central, across from Bancentro, tel. 505/2572-2362, $16 with fan, $30 with a/c) has been a mainstay of Bluefields since 1983 and its 10 rooms are nearly always booked. It has a popular restaurant and outside veranda, and clean, well-maintained rooms with private bath and cable TV.

$25-50

★ **Hotel Jackani** (Barrio Punta Fría, 20 meters south of police station, tel. 505/2572-0440 or 505/8850-8754, hoteljackani@gmail.com, $27 s, $37-47 d plus taxes) is a new hotel run by a mother and daughter duo. Rooms have private baths, hot water, TV, and are spotlessly clean. Enjoy the ocean breeze from a rocking chair on the second-floor terrace. Nearby **Hotel Caribbean Dream** (Barrio Punta Fría, 30 meters south of the main

Giant shrimp are abundant on the Caribbean coast.

market, tel. 505/2572-0107, $22-32 d) offers spacious, well-appointed rooms with private bathroom, closets, cable TV, air-conditioning units, hot water, Wi-Fi, a stuffy on-site restaurant, a bright atmosphere, and an upstairs veranda.

Bluefields Bay Hotel (Point In, tel. 505/2572-2143, $20-25 with fan, $28-37 with a/c) is near the dock, away from the hustle and bustle of the *centro,* yet still within walking distance. It's a uniquely Costeño establishment that operates as a hotel school. It has clean, if slightly shabby, rooms, hot water, and air-conditioning. It's located right in front of the Tía Irene Restaurant, which is also staffed by students.

Over $50
★ **Oasis Hotel** (on the corner near the municipal wharf, tel. 505/2572-0665, reservacioneshoteloasis@yahoo.es, $55-70 plus tax, includes breakfast) was opened in 2005 by a North American businessman who also owns the two casinos in town (one of which

is on-site). This is the classiest hotel in town, with both carpeted and hardwood floors, Wi-Fi, and decent views. The handful of spacious rooms each have a lovely large bathroom, minibar, safe, TV, and air-conditioning. There are a few larger suites, and the top floor is a ridiculously huge two-bedroom presidential apartment ($160/night) with a whirlpool tub overlooking the bay; it used to belong to a foreign playboy.

FOOD
Street Food and *Fritanga*
In Bluefields, Creole *fritanga* (street-side barbecue and fry-fest, usually $1) features stewed chicken with a savory brown and salty sauce, served in a small, plastic bag with *tajadas* and Creole cabbage salad. The mestizo version of *frito* consists of fried or slow-roasted chicken plus all your favorites from Spanish-speaking Nicaragua. Try **Berjas Blancas** (Barrio Central, across the street from Movistar) or **Comedor Plata** (Barrio Central, next to Movistar, tel. 505/2572-1694) specializing in chicken and beef *frito*. You'll also find local fare like *rondón* and almond *posol* (a sweet corn drink).

Cafés
It can be hard to find a breakfast spot as most places open around 11am. Hotels that serve breakfast are your best bet. Pancakes, sausage, and eggs are scarce in Bluefields. Eat like a local at **Cafetín Dominguez** (Barrio Central, on the same corner as Radio Zelaya, $3), where you can get a hearty plate of *gallo pinto* and eggs. Find fruit salads and smoothies at **Siembras y Cosechas** (Barrio Central, tel. 505/8912-6453, Mon.-Sat. 8am-9pm, Sun. 11am-9pm) next door to Hotel Doña Vero. ★ **Galeria Aberdeen** (Calle Aberdeen, tel. 505/2572-2605, Mon.-Sat. 7am-9pm, Sun. 7am-2pm, $1) is the only coffee shop in these parts. They serve fresh-ground, export-quality Nicaraguan coffee in an airy, high-ceilinged establishment with great ambience. They've got a selection of German beers and a respectable wine list. Galeria Aberdeen is

Sea to Soup: Atlantic Coast Cookin'

Atlantic coast cuisine is marked by its simplicity and freshness. That lobster on your plate was probably picked off the ocean floor this morning; the fish were swimming hours ago. The only way you'll get fresher fish is by cooking it on the ship or eating it raw: **ceviche** with limejuice, tomato, and onion. Seafood on the Nicaraguan Atlantic is cheap by international standards, delicious by anyone's standards, and well worth the wait (most Bluefields restaurants are slow, even by Nicaraguan standards). If your travel complaints don't evaporate in the garlicky steam of lobster under your nose, then you obviously are going to need to spend another couple of days.

Start off with **yellowfin, snapper,** or **sea bass,** grilled or fried. **Conch,** when tenderized correctly, is soft and delicate, less briny than other seafood but with a soft texture. Or enjoy a **lobster** *al vapor,* bulging with delicate white meat you can pull from the shell with your fingers, and drenched in butter and lime.

Mixed soup is served in a helmet-sized bowl choked with crab, lobster, conch, and fish marinating in coconut milk. Not hearty enough? Then reach for *rondón,* or rundown, a thick stew of fish (or endangered turtle), vegetables, and coconut milk thickened with starchy tubers and plantains. In August, don't miss the Corn Island **Crab Soup Festival,** when Costeños cook tons of soft crabmeat into a festival you won't forget. Atlantic coast crabmeat is particularly soft, with a delicate flavor unique to the tropics.

You don't have to stick to seafood to eat well on the Atlantic coast. Even the *gallo pinto* tastes better here: That's because it's cooked in sweet coconut oil. Between meals, fill up with **coco bread,** football-sized loaves of soft, rich wheat flour cooked up with coconut and served hot out of the oven. Another treat is kind of like cinnamon rolls but without the cinnamon: **hot coconut bun** is sweet and sticky.

located *donde fue Los Pipitos* ("where Los Pipitos used to be").

Mission House (in front of the central park) is a great spot for coconut bread. Try the moist Coco Cake for a true coast snack: grated taro with coconut milk, cinnamon, nutmeg, and sugar.

Nica and International

Mini-Hotel Central Café (Barrio Central, across from Bancentro, tel. 505/2572-2362, $4-12) offers a wide range of well-prepared Nicaraguan and Costeño dishes at reasonable prices. **Iris Foods & Honey Sweets** (Barrio Central, 1 block south of Movistar, tel. 505/8929-4382, daily 10am-10pm, $8) offers a classic Creole kitchen featuring stew beans and dumplings, *rondón,* and coconut rice and beans.

La Ola (1.5 blocks east of Pesco Frita, daily 9am-10pm, $4-8) has all the typical local dishes, plus a few with Chinese influence. Enjoy your meal from the second-floor patio

overlooking the street. **Segundo Piso** (next to Parque Reyes, tel. 505/2572-0109, $5-7) makes local pizza that comes pretty close to the real thing.

Upscale

Grill Sport (Barrio Central, next to Texas Casino) is a hip restaurant in town, specializing in seafood, vegetarian, and salads. After 4pm, the bar and dance floor upstairs are popular with the moneyed Creole crowd. **Loma** (Calle Colón, near BICU) is another semi-elegant option with a view from your table, a long menu, and steep prices. Feel free to drink the ice (they have a water purification system for ice and fresh drinks) in a delicious piña colada or a fresh fruit punch.

★ **Tía Irene Bar and Restaurant** (behind Bluefields Bay Hotel, daily 11am-9pm, $4-9) is located over the water. Its one-of-a-kind view of the bay and reliable quality have kept this restaurant a local favorite from the time it was known as Manglares. You can't go wrong with seafood at ★ **Pelican Bay** (Point In, tel. 505/2572-2089, daily 11am-11pm, $7-15).

Luna's Ranch (Barrio Loma Fresca, almost across from URACCAN, daily 10am-10pm, $8) is a well-known restaurant in the newer part of town. Decorated with the traditional thatched-roof design, the restaurant offers great food, midrange prices, and a professional staff. **Chez Marcel** (Barrio Teodoro Martínez, near Pizza Martinuzzi, tel. 505/2572-2347, $7-15) is another longtime standby, especially if you're craving a steak.

INFORMATION AND SERVICES

For the best chance of securing a decent computer without a long wait, check out the original Bluefields cybercafe, **Copicentro** (Barrio Central, tel. 505/2572-2232, Mon.-Sat. 8am-5:30pm), offering Internet access ($0.75/hour) and international phone calls to the United States ($0.10/minute).

The **INTUR** office (across from the police station in Cotton Tree, tel. 505/2572-1111, inturbluefields@hotmail.com, Mon.-Fri. 8am-noon and 1pm-5pm) can't hold a candle to CIDCA, the **Research and Documentation Center for the Atlantic Coast** (50 meters north of the police station, Mon.-Fri. 8am-5:30pm with a break for lunch). CIDCA makes available to the public a wide selection of materials about Caribbean cultures and languages, including several Miskito-only publications in the first-floor library.

Banks

There are two banks on the Atlantic coast: **Banpro** (in front of the Moravian church, Mon.-Fri. 8am-4:30pm, Sat. 8am-noon) and **Bancentro** (around the corner from Banpro, on Calle Cabezas, Mon.-Fri. 8am-4:30pm, Sat. 8am-noon). Both banks feature 24-hour **ATM** service, though the one at Banpro dispenses the money in much more reasonable denominations (100 *córdoba* vs. 500 *córdoba* bills, which can be hard to change in Bluefields).

Moneychangers are on the corner between the two banks and are both safe and useful. **Doña Vero** (half a block west and half a block south of the cathedral) will change money at the store next to her hotel. The town hall (or Palacio) has a 24-hour ATM booth (east of the park, across the street).

Emergency Services

Emergency services include a **fire department** (north of the Moravian church, tel. 505/2572-2298), **police** (on the same side of the street, 3 blocks south, tel. 505/2572-2448), the **Red Cross** (Barrio Fátima, tel. 505/2572-2582), and **Hospital Ernesto Sequeira** (5 long blocks south and west of the park, tel. 505/2572-2391 main switchboard, 505/2822-2621 emergency). The best local private clinic is **Clínica y Farmacia Bacon** (next to Bancentro).

GETTING THERE
Air

La Costeña (Bluefields office tel. 505/2572-2750, www.lacostena.com.ni) offers regular daily flights between Bluefields, Managua, and Big Corn Island. Three daily flights leave Managua for Bluefields (1 hour, $82 one-way, $126 round-trip, plus $18 if you buy online). The flight between Corn Island and Bluefields costs $64 ($99 round-trip). From the Bluefields airport take a taxi for the several-kilometer approach to town (fixed price $0.60 pp, expect to pay the same amount every time you get in a taxi here).

Boat

There are no roads connecting Bluefields directly to the Pacific coast. The closest you can get is Rama. Then you'll hop in a boat for the last leg of the journey. This route is cheaper than flying. It isn't difficult, though it is long (8-12 hours total).

All boat transportation to Bluefields is found at the Rama municipal wharf, near the last bus stop. *Pangas* cast off from the dock as they fill up, 5:30am-3:30pm

(1.5-hour trip to Bluefields, $9 pp), but won't leave at all if they're short on passengers. They arrive at the municipal wharf downtown. There are larger ships that carry freight and passengers between El Rama, Bluefields ($4 pp), and Corn Island ($16 pp), but they are slow. The **Captain D** freighter (tel. 505/8850-2767, transportemaritimo-normand@gmail.com) leaves El Rama every Monday 8pm. It's best to arrange transport with them in advance.

GETTING AWAY
Boat

Heading back to Managua, buy a ticket for both a *panga* to Rama and your bus fare to Managua in advance at the municipal dock ($16 pp). *Pangas* leave for El Rama 5:30am-noon and 1pm-3:30pm as they fill up ($10 pp).

Passenger-boat traffic to El Rama, Pearl Lagoon, Orinoco, and Pueblo Nuevo (up the Wawachang River) originates from the main municipal dock. Pay the $0.20 entrance fee at the dock entrance (second door on the right after the gate). They leave when they're full; get your name on a list upon arrival, and don't go anywhere. Trips to El Bluff ($2 each way) originate at a much smaller MINSA dock

next to the municipal market (inquire at the market).

There's one small weekly boat to Big Corn Island run by the **Empresa Portuaria Nacional** on Wednesdays 9am, and returning the next day (6 hours, $10 pp). Get in line at the municipal dock before 8am on Wednesday to ensure you get a ticket. If you choose this route instead of flying, take lots of water, sun protection, a barf bag, and a sense of humor. Ask the crew to stow anything you want to keep dry below deck.

Captain D (office in Bluefields across from Oasis Casino, tel. 505/8850-2767) makes weekly runs to Bilwi ($33) departing Bluefields on Wednesday 11am, overnighting on Big Corn ($10 pp), and leaving Thursday 8pm for the RAAN. This trip only happens if they have enough freight, so call ahead. They occasionally make runs to San Andres Island, which is technically part of Colombia.

Rumors about scheduled weekly boat service between Bluefields and San Juan del Norte to the south appear to finally be true. The choppy ride along the coast (4-5 hours, $35 pp) is run by a man called **Chacalín** (tel. 505/8355-8745) from San Juan del Norte. He leaves from San Juan on Wednesdays 8am, departing on Fridays 9am.

boat traffic outside Bluefields

Spiritual Practices of the Atlantic Coast

A distant cousin to the voudoun ("voodoo") of Haiti and Benin, Obeah refers to sorcery, folk magic, and other religious practices brought by Central and West African slaves to the Americas. Using herbal teas and baths, charms, amulets, and prayer, Obeah is best described as a method of communication with the supernatural world, and a means of calling on metaphysical powers through shamanistic rituals.

On the Atlantic coast, Obeah is a large part of the culture, and every Costeño believes, just a little, in its power. Contrary to popular belief, Obeah is not always used for negative purposes. Often times Costeños pay a practitioner to influence events in a person's favor; to achieve success in a particular endeavor; or to find out the answer to an important question (such as who is my husband sleeping with, or who stole my cows). However, amongst the Miskito and Afro-Caribbean peoples, negative Obeah is not unheard of: Locals will even resort to Obeah revenge rather than the police department.

There is no need to fear Obeah (unless you take away another's lover). Moreover, the way that most Costeños approach Obeah is indicative of their overall spiritual perspective on life. For example, in Creole culture, there is a strong nine-day ritual that follows a person's death. As soon as the person is pronounced dead, word begins to spread amongst the Creole community. The family's closest friends and family quickly arrive at the house to clean, cook, and receive the multitudes that will soon come to accompany the family during their grief. This set-up appears to be like a party without the music—crowds of people eating, drinking rum, and talking. On the ninth night, the night before the person is finally buried, the same friends and family of the deceased remove all bed linens, tablecloths, and curtains from the home. At midnight, all present sing to the spirit of the deceased to signal that it is now time to ascend to heaven. It is widely believed that failure to perform this ritual will cause the spirit of the dead person to wander the earth as a miserable ghost, causing harm to the living.

In Bluefields, Mr. Selso (tel. 505/8845-4137 or 505/2572-2176) is a traditional and fascinating Miskito **"Bush Docta"** and Obeah practitioner who is highly sought after for spiritual, emotional, and medical issues that doctors trained in Western medicine have been unable to resolve. The small **Clinica de Medicina Natural en Terapias Alternative** (Barrio Teodoro Martinez, Avenida Cabeza, in front of Escondite bar, daily 5:30pm-8pm) is a natural medicine clinic offering beach flower therapy, healing massage, and medicinal plants. For more information on Obeah, check out the novels and memoirs of Jamaica Kincaid, or *Vampire The Masquerade*, *Unburnable*, and *Brown Girl in the Ring* by Nalo Hopkinson.

Contributed by Phoebe Haupt-Cayasso, trip leader and experiential learning consultant with experience working with students in Bluefields and Atlantic coast communities.

GETTING AROUND

Bluefields is small enough that you should need a taxi only to go to the extremes of town (the URACCAN campus at the north and the airport at the south), or when you feel unsafe. Two nearly identical bus routes run 6am-7:30pm. Get on and off where you like for $0.25.

EL BLUFF

Once connected to the mainland before 1988 when Hurricane Joan breached the bar, El Bluff is an industrial platform and important port that happens to be adjacent to a gorgeous little Caribbean white sand beach. Reconnected in 2006 by a pedestrian walkway, El Bluff makes an exotic day trip for *blufileños* tired of the "big city." But it only attracts the most adventurous foreigners. Spend a lazy day walking up to the small lighthouse for a 360° view before jumping into the water to cool off.

Take a Bluefields *panga* (from the MINSA dock next to the municipal market in Bluefields) to get to El Bluff (30 minutes,

$1.50). *Pangas* embark as soon as they fill up with 12 passengers. The last boat returns to Bluefields around 4pm. From the park, walk until you see a paved path on your left and follow it through a residential area until it ends (10-15 minutes). Keep going straight for about 200 meters at which point you will be able to see the beach. (The mounds of stone scattered along it were intended for a pedestrian bridge.)

RAMA CAY

Fifteen kilometers south of Bluefields is Rama Cay, ancestral home of the Rama people. About 800 souls live on this small island. According to historians, the Rama people are originally descended from the Chibchas and Aruac Rama from the Amazon basin; several oral histories explain how the Rama came to occupy this isolated island at the end of the 17th century. Rama culture is now disappearing. Only a small handful of elders still speak the language.

There is a community tourism initiative on the island that offers homestays and tours. Ask around for a tour of the island ($4, or $7 with lunch). Or, take a trip to the nearby El Padre Island for an afternoon of swimming and hiking ($8). Getting to Rama Cay is an easy *panga* ride (1 hour, $6) from Bluefields. You can also book a trip with **Atlantic Tour** (tel. 505/2572-2259) from Bluefields.

GREENFIELDS WILDLIFE RESERVE

On the outskirts of Kukra Hill, **Reserva Silvestre Greenfields** (tel. 505/2278-0589 or 505/8428-8403, www.greenfields.com.ni, info@greenfields.com.ni, $30 s, $50-100 d) is a protected reserve, characterized by its scenic beauty, silence, and proximity to nature. Privately managed as an ecotourism business, you can hike more than 25 kilometers of trails, canoe through jungle watercourses, or rest and enjoy the silence surrounded by lush vegetation. Price includes lodging, meals, and guided tours. You can make this a day trip ($30 for 1-2 people or $50 per group, up to 6 people, no lodging, no meals) and enjoy excursions with guides by foot or canoe, the botanical park, the bathing pier, and more. All trips must be previously arranged and reservations need to be received at least four days in advance. Camping in the reserve is an option.

PEARL LAGOON

Tucked away one lagoon north of Bluefields, Pearl Lagoon (Laguna de Perlas) is a small community whose natural splendor is a welcome respite from Bluefields. Its sandy streets are easily explored on foot. This little village gives access to local Miskito communities and the enchanting Pearl Cays. The locals earn their living from the water. You'll see boats of the five companies that deal in fishing and fish processing tied up along the docks or moored in the lagoon. Denmark and Norway have been active in the economic development of the region, constructing municipal piers in Pearl Lagoon, Haulover, Tasbapauni, Kakabila, Brown Bank, and Marshall Point to assist local fisherfolk in getting their catch to market.

Sights

Don't miss the **"the great gun,"** as the locals lovingly call the iron cannon mounted in front of the municipal dock and surrounded by a small garden. Embossed with the seal of the British Empire and the year 1803, it dates back to the protectorate. The clean architectural style of the most eye-catching building in town, the whitewashed **Moravian church,** was typical of the period. Attending an evening service there is memorable (dress appropriately).

Entertainment

Don't miss a night of reggae at one of Pearl Lagoon's several small *ranchos,* or clubs, the most popular of which is **Bar Relax** (one block north of the Moravian church, Mon.-Thurs. 3pm-midnight, Fri.-Sat. 3pm-2am, Sun. 4pm-1am).

Pearl Lagooners love **baseball** and compete on teams with names like the Buffalos,

Pearl Lagoon's whitewashed Moravian church

Mariners, Young Stars, Hurricanes, Sweet Pearly, First Stop, Young Braves, and the Haulover Tigers. Watch them battle it out at the stadium (Sat. and Sun. Sept.-Feb.).

Accommodations

The best of the family-run guesthouses is ★ **Green Lodge Guesthouse** (half a block south of the dock, tel. 505/2572-0507, www. pearllagoonhotel.com, $8 s or $9 d shared bath, $16 private), a pleasant place on the main drag. The entrance is charmingly obscured by overgrown flower bushes and trees. Also known as Hotel Estrella, for the Spanish translation of its Miskito name, **Hospedaje Slilma** (half a block east of the Claro tower, tel. 505/2572-0523, slilma_gh1@yahoo.com, $7-20) has several clean rooms in a two-story structure near the lagoon. Upstairs rooms are cooler and have private baths.

Casa Blanca Hotelito y Restaurante (tel. 505/2572-0508, $10-30 private bath and a/c) is clean and well liked with airy rooms. It's run by a Danish-Creole couple intent on

making your trip pleasurable. To get there, walk west straight down the road with the Claro tower. You'll see it a couple of blocks after the baseball stadium.

Two rustic cabins jut out from behind the restaurant ★ **Queen Lobster** (200 meters north of the dock, tel. 505/2572-5028 or 8662-3393, www.queenlobster.com, $35 d), each with its own private balcony, creating the most romantic getaway in Pearl Lagoon. The clean and friendly **Hotel Casa Ulrich** (400 meters north of the dock, tel. 505/8907-1483, www. casaulrich.com, $8 pp dorm, $10 s or $12 d with shared bath, $35 d private) is a popular spot for groups.

Food

Miss Betty's ★ **Coconut Delight** (across from the wharf, look for the wooden "bakery" sign above the door, daily 8am-8pm) bakery is the place to go for pastries, smoothies, sweets, and real coffee. Be sure to try the traditional ginger cake known as *toto*. **Comedor Eva** (in the side street across from Claro, $4) offers good home cookin'. There's no menu, just stop in and ask what she's got. ★ **Casa Ulrich** (400 meters north of the dock, tel. 505/8907-1483, daily 6am-10pm, $6-9) is the best meal in town, and possibly in the region, prepared for you by a multilingual Swiss- and French-trained chef. The shrimp omelet with fresh-cracked peppercorn is outrageously popular.

Queen Lobster Restaurant (100 meters north of the municipal dock, daily noon-11pm, $6-12) has a tranquil setting on the lagoon and serves mostly seafood and mixed dishes. Eat local fare in the yard under the stars at **Warner's Place** (from the Moravian church, 1 block west, half a block south, tel. 505/8426-7565, $3-5).

The **Casa Blanca Hotelito y Restaurante** (a couple of blocks after the baseball stadium, daily 7am-8pm, shrimp from $7, lobster from $12) has the most varied menu in town, served in a pleasant ambience.

Information and Services

You won't find a bank here, so be sure to hit

the ATM before leaving Bluefields. The store with the Western Union sign out front will change your dollars. You can withdraw money with a card at the store with the green Banpro sign (half a block west of the evangelical church in front of the wharf), but they'll take a cut for the service.

The **health clinic** is a few blocks south, to the right of the Moravian church. Four **pharmacies** can take care of basic medical needs. For more serious medical emergencies, you will be strapped into a *panga* and rocketed off to Bluefields. With that in mind, stay safe. The **police** are located next to the red and white Claro tower.

The **INTUR** office (1st Fl. of the wharf building, tel. 505/8920-9863, svelasquez@ intur.gob.ni) is new and still getting on its feet. You'll be better off talking to the folks at **Kabu Tours** (from wharf, 1 block south, known as the turtle house, tel. 505/8714-5196, www.kabutours.com, info@kabutours. com), an association of local tour guides who joined together with the help of the Wildlife Conservation Society as part of an effort to protect endangered sea turtles—a popular ingredient in local cuisine. A trip to the Pearl Cays around nesting time (June-Nov.) is guaranteed to be unforgettable. They offer an overnight camping tour ($229 pp or less) and a couple of other packages to the Cays, as well as community tours of the surrounding villages.

Getting There

The *panga* trip from Bluefields up the Río Escondido and then north through a complex network of waterways to Pearl Lagoon is a beautiful ride (1 hour, $7). On the way, you'll pass several shipwrecks, and the active dock at Kukra Hill, named after a long-assimilated cannibalistic tribe. There's usually a quick stop for passengers in Haulover, minutes south of Pearl Lagoon. Go to the municipal dock in Bluefields to sign up for the Pearl Lagoon *panga* at least an hour before you want to leave (the first boat leaves around 9am). Get your name on the list, and then stick around: Boats leave as soon as they

have 20 passengers, all day until 3pm. The last *panga* back from Pearl Lagoon leaves between 1pm and 3pm but won't leave if it isn't full. Stop in the first story of the wharf building for daily schedules.

To skip Bluefields entirely, you can take a bus from El Rama (4 hours, $5) north over a rough and unpaved road. It will drop you off at the basketball court (1 block west of the main drag).

★ THE PEARL CAYS

Most of the 18 specks of land that make up the Pearl Cays archipelago remain untouched and relatively accessible, though a few cays were at one point being built up by wealthy foreigners, and controversy over their ownership resulted in the declaration of the Pearl Cays as a wildlife refuge. The cays (pronounced "keys") spread east starting at three kilometers from a small Miskito coastal village called Set Net. Hire a boat from Pearl Lagoon and enjoy the ride through the harbor, into the open Caribbean, then up the empty coastline to the cays. Spend the day swimming and snorkeling in pristine clear blue water.

The Wildlife Conservation Society has made efforts to protect the marine environment of these cays, which provides a crucial breeding, developmental, and migratory habitat for species like the endangered green and loggerhead sea turtles, and especially for the critically endangered hawksbill turtle. Turtle nesting season is June-November.

So far, the Pearl Cays have zero tourist facilities (though one resort has come and gone, and more may follow). Bring water and your Gilligan's Island survival kit to be safe. (Most guides include lunch in the package price.) Arrange a trip through Kabu Tours, La Casa Blanca, or Queen Lobster in Pearl Lagoon. A round-trip *panga* ride to the Pearl Cays costs $150-300, so the more people chipping in, the cheaper it'll be. If you find yourself sharing one of the islets with local fishermen cutting down coconuts and telling fishing stories over a fire on the beach, feel free to strike up a deal for some fresh seafood for the grill.

VILLAGES NEAR PEARL LAGOON

Awas

The town of Pearl Lagoon sits on the southeast side of a small prominence jutting out into the bay. West of the town is the broad, shallow lagoon-beach community of Awas. This half-hour walk down a flat, paved road will cross a saltwater estuary and a small footbridge. When you get to the Miskito community of Raitipura (Miskito for "on top of the cemetery"), turn left and follow the road to Awas. A *caponera* (motorbike taxi) will bring you out here from Pearl Lagoon for less than $1. Walking alone is not recommended. Take advantage of the **Bar and Restaurant Tropical View** (tel. 505/8765-8500 or 505/8844-8084, Fri.-Sun. 10am-6pm), built out over the water. Go for a swim and watch the sunset from the dock. Local guide Orlando lives in a small wooden house (100 meters from the restaurant) and will be happy to spend a couple of hours taking you on a canoe ride and sampling local cuisine in his home.

Tasbapauni

Farther up the coast, on the Caribbean side of the land, is the community of Tasbapauni (2 hours from Pearl Lagoon), set on a thin strip

of land right between the Caribbean and the lagoon, close to the Man of War Cays. Both the town and the cays contain incredibly natural beauty. There is one place to stay: **Mini Hotel, Bar & Restaurant Yadosh** ($10) with seven rooms with private bathrooms; the restaurant offers a wide variety of seafood. Beware of the sand flies when the breeze is not blowing (same with visiting Set Net). From Bluefields, you can go directly here via *panga* ($13 each way).

★ Wawachang and Khaka Creek Reserve

Located about a kilometer up the river from Wawachang, Khaka Creek Reserve is the epitome of the local, grass-roots ecotourism movement that provides alternate means of subsistence in a delicate ecosystem. Run by the Foundation for the Autonomy and Development of the Atlantic Coast of Nicaragua (FADCANIC), modern tourist facilities include hiking trails to cabins and trained guides knowledgeable in local flora and fauna.

Founded by a small group of passionate Creole leaders in the early 1990s, FADCANIC manages a number of successful development programs. The **Wawachang Center**

Awas is a great place to watch the sun set.

(tel. 505/8930-0248, geovasandoval@yahoo. com, $5/night, $4/meal, $10 for trail guide) is FADCANIC's largest microcredit program. Stop by it to visit the Agro-Forestry high school and walk the fields, seedling nursery, and model farm. The Wawachang Center is ideal for ecological research and is equipped with solar energy, Internet access, screened windows, and purified water. The guesthouse offers seven rooms that can accommodate 25 people, one with a double bed and private bath. There's another *albergue* (hostel) in the **Khaka Creek Reserve** (opposite side of the river and a kilometer north, tel. 505/2570-0962), which offers similar services.

To arrange your trip from Bluefields, stop by the **FADCANIC** office (in Barrio Punta Fría, tel. 505/2572-2386, www.fadcanic.org. ni) and speak with any of the Agro-Forestry or Wawachang staff. To get here, catch the Pueblo Nuevo *panga*, departing Bluefields on Sundays and Wednesdays ($12 pp each way), and returning on Mondays and Thursdays. It passes Wawachang and the Khaka Creek Reserve on the way to Pueblo Nuevo. Either way, reserve your return seat in the boat on your way upstream.

ORINOCO

Orinoco is the southernmost home of the Garífuna people, a distinct ethnic group with strong West African roots unique to Central America. In 2001, UNESCO proclaimed the Garífuna language, music, and dance a "Masterpiece of the Oral and Intangible Heritage of Humanity." Their dancing, drumming, and singing manifests strong African roots. Don't miss the Garífuna Arrival Day in Nicaragua and National Day for the Garífuna People on November 19, featuring talented Garífuna singers, drummers, and dancers from the coast, as well as from Belize, Honduras, and Guatemala.

Nearby **Marshall Point** is a typical, small Creole community. You can reach Marshall Point by going to Orinoco and then walking (20 minutes) or hiring a *panga* to take you around the corner. Do not walk alone. And here's a tip: Grease the edge of your shoes with a thick line of Vaseline as you arrive in Orinoco and Marshall Point, as grass lice can be abundant.

Invite community leaders Frank Lopez, Ramon Martinez, and Fermin Gonzalez to lunch to hear about the history and culture of the Garífuna and Orinoco. You may witness a *walagallo* or *dugu* (ceremony), a healing ritual that has been known to bring people back from the brink of death. The spirit of an ancestor appears to someone in a dream, giving the specific recipe for that particular *walagallo*. Dancing, singing, and sacrificing of chickens continues until the dying person gets up from the sickbed to start dancing, signifying to the crowd that he or she has been cured.

Accommodations and Food
The most popular lodging option in Orinoco is the **Hostal Garifuna** (tel. 505/8927-0123 or 505/8648-4985, $13-20, meals $4-7), a nice guesthouse with seven large rooms and a pleasant area for relaxing. Arrange to eat your meals at the hostel to experience authentic Garífuna cooking. The owners can help direct all your activities and transport in the area. Local guide and music teacher Kevin Sambola is one of several guides who offer community tours, highlighting traditional medicine techniques and cuisine ($10 pp).

In the community of Marshall Point, **HQ Bed & Breakfast** ($10) is a great value with large hammock-laden porches and spacious rooms with TV and fan. Although breakfast is not included in the price, you can request it the night before. Owners offer horseback tours and boat rides.

Try to sample some *fufu,* a cassava dish common throughout West Africa, or the Garífuna *ereba* or *bami,* flat bread also made from cassava.

Getting There and Away
From the municipal dock in Bluefields, take a *panga* into the Laguna de Perlas (the water body, not the town) to Orinoco

The Road to El Rama

If you've got a few extra days to spare, consider the overland route to Bluefields from Managua, which leads through some out-of-the-way corners of the country. The road is in better condition than ever, though this land route requires stamina and patience. Most people leave Managua for El Rama at night, then board a predawn *panga* and soak up two hours of fresh air during a sunrise trip down the Río Escondido to Bluefields (bring a sweater for both parts of the trip). This route offers you a true appreciation for Nicaragua's sheer girth, and the Atlantic coast's geographical isolation. If you're interested in breaking up the long trip, plan on making a couple of stops along the way.

Heading east out of Managua, the route leads through southern **Boaco,** continuing south into the charming city of **Juigalpa,** where you can check out a museum and admire the views. Farther east in **Chontales,** between Villa Sandino and La Campana, are hundreds of pre-Columbian petroglyphs in situ, around which the **Parque Arqueológico Piedras Pintadas** (tel. 505/8850-2121, $2) was developed in 2008 with help from Finland. From Villa Sandino, it's 20 minutes by bus, but you can easily walk it. Stay in Villa Sandino at **Hotel Santa Clara** (tel. 505/2516-0055, maisalar@hotmail.com, $25 with a/c and hot water, $20 with fan) or at the more economical **Hospedaje Chavarria** (across from the Medical Center). El Rama is 1.5 hours east of Villa Sandino.

and Marshall Point. The famous "hardway *panga*" ($11 one-way) leaves Bluefields on Mondays, Thursdays, and Saturdays, and returns to Bluefields on Mondays, Tuesdays, Thursdays, and Fridays. You can sometimes catch this boat from Pearl Lagoon, depending on whether or not they filled up with passengers in Bluefields (check in the wharf office). You can also occasionally catch the Pueblo Nuevo boat.

EL RAMA

At the eastern terminus of the highway from Managua, El Rama straddles the frontier between Atlantic and Pacific more perceptibly than any other Nicaraguan town. A longtime riverine port and trader town, El Rama is a melting pot of 50,000 people, where mestizo cattle traders meet Caribbean steamer captains, and dark-skinned Creoles mix with "Spaniards" from the Pacific. The name Rama is a tribute to the Rama people who once inhabited the shores of the Siquia, Rama, Escondido, and Mico Rivers.

The typical traveler spends no more than 15 minutes in El Rama between getting off the bus and onto a boat to Bluefields. The folks at El Rama are interested in developing

a tourism infrastructure; they just haven't figured it out yet (the first step should be to pick up all the garbage). Any adventuring you do in the region will require ingenuity and patience. Divided by rivers and swamps, the lands around El Rama are teeming with places to explore and look for wildlife.

Accommodations and Food

Lodging here is generally affordable and unvaried. Clean and quiet **Hotel García** (from the bus stop where the monument used to be, half a block towards the river, tel. 505/2517-0318, $5 s, $6-10 d) is the best budget option. The second floor rooms are slightly fancier with air-conditioning and a view of the river. Or try **Hospedaje Solidaridad Tres Rios** (a few hundred meters up from the dock, on the left along the main drag, tel. 505/2517-0152, $3-5), with very basic rooms, run by a nice family.

Casa Huesped Río Escondido (next to Restaurante El Expreso, tel. 505/2517-0287, $12-15) has tidy rooms with private baths. **Nuevo Oasis del Caribe** (1 block south of the bus station, tel. 505/2517-0264, $12 s $16-24 d) is similar, though not quite as nice. Rooms have private bath, fan, and TV.

★ **Eco Hotel El Vivero** (Km 293 on the highway from Managua, tel. 505/2517-0281 or 505/8351-8523, www.ecohotelvivero.com, ecohotelvivero@outlook.com, $10-16) is a quiet, peaceful place within a private reserve, located two short kilometers from the city of El Rama. Flowers and trees surround the wooden cabins, and the restaurant serves decent meals.

Restaurante El Expreso (1 block east of Claro, tel. 505/2517-0043, $8) is slow anyway, but serves good seafood, soups, chicken, and steak. The **Eskimo** sells sandwiches in addition to ice cream. A good *fritanga* sets up shop evenings near the market.

Getting There and Away

Buses to El Rama leave from Managua's Mayoreo terminal ($5) daily 3am-9pm. Two express busses leave the Ivan Montenegro Terminal at 6am and 9pm (4 hours, $5). Express buses don't linger in Juigalpa or stop along the road, shaving two hours off the trip. All boat transportation to Bluefields is found at the municipal wharf: *pangas* cast off from the dock as they fill up, 5:30am-3:30pm (1.5-hour trip to Bluefields, $10 pp). **Captain D** (tel. 505/8850-2767) makes weekly runs Tuesday 8pm from El Rama to Bluefields ($4), continuing Wednesday 11am to Corn Island ($16), before continuing (about once a month) to Bilwi on Thursday.

Big Corn Island

Eighty-three kilometers due east of Bluefields Bay's brackish brown water, the Corn Islands are a pair of Tertiary-period volcanic basalt bumps in the Caribbean. Formerly home base for lobster fishermen and their families, the islanders are increasingly turning to tourism for their future. How well the fragile island ecosystem will support it will determine the fate of the islands.

Big Corn Island is 10 square kilometers of forested hills, mangrove swamps, and stretches of white coral beaches. The mangrove swamps and estuaries that line several stretches of coastline are crucial to the island's water supply, and the islanders have fiercely resisted attempts by foreign investors to drain or fill them. Of the six sea turtle species swimming off Nicaragua's shores, four live in Caribbean waters. On land, Corn Island boasts three endemic species of reptiles and amphibians, all threatened by the continued swamp draining. The highest points are Quinn Hill, Little Hill (55 and 57 meters above sea level, respectively), and Mount Pleasant (97 meters).

HISTORY

Pirates on their way to maraud the coast of Central America and Nicaragua's Río San Juan first visited here in the 16th century, sometimes by accident after the reefs tore the bottom of their ships open. But Corn Island was inhabited long before that by the Kukras, a subtribe of the Mayangnas whose penchant for consuming the bodies of their enemies inspired the first English visitors to call them the Skeleton Islands. The Kukra were eventually assimilated into the Miskitos. Nowadays, the native Creole population shares the island with an increasing number of menial laborers from the mainland, who have overtaken the Creoles in number and have increased the island's total population to nearly 12,000. Native islanders are direct descendants of several infamous European pirates, as well as English royalty and plantation owners. Don't be surprised if you meet people with names like Kennington, Quinn, Dixon, or Downs.

ORIENTATION

From most places a walk to Brig Bay, which is the "downtown" area, is around 2.5 kilometers

Big Corn Island

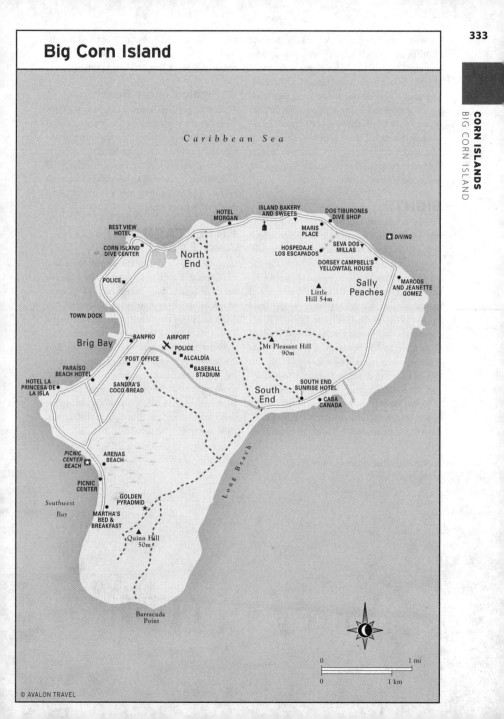

Caribbean Sea

HOTEL MORGAN

ISLAND BAKERY AND SWEETS

DOS TIBURONES DIVE SHOP

BEST VIEW HOTEL

MARIS PLACE

DIVING

CORN ISLAND DIVE CENTER

HOSPEDAJE LOS ESCAPADOS

SEVA DOS MILLAS

North End

DORSEY CAMPBELL'S YELLOWTAIL HOUSE

POLICE

Sally Peaches

MARCOS AND JEANETTE GOMEZ

Little Hill 54m

TOWN DOCK

BANPRO

AIRPORT

Mt Pleasant Hill 90m

Brig Bay

POLICE

POST OFFICE

ALCALDÍA

PARAÍSO BEACH HOTEL

BASEBALL STADIUM

HOTEL LA PRINCESA DE LA ISLA

SANDRA'S COCO BREAD

South End

SOUTH END SUNRISE HOTEL

CASA CANADA

PICNIC CENTER BEACH

ARENAS BEACH

Long Beach

PICNIC CENTER

Southwest Bay

GOLDEN PYRADMID

MARTHA'S BED & BREAKFAST

Quinn Hill 50m

Barracuda Point

0   1 mi
0   1 km

© AVALON TRAVEL

(20 minutes). You can walk the length of the island in under an hour. A paved road circumnavigates the island and bicycles can be hired at some hotels and Corn Island Car Rentals. The municipal docks are in Brig Bay with *panga* service to Little Corn, and the airport is nearby. El Bluff, the southern tip of the island, at the end of Long Beach on the eastern side, and Southwest Bay on the other side, is the most remote part of the island. It's best not to wander around alone.

SIGHTS

The incongruous **Golden Pyramid** on the top of Quinn Hill was built in 2006 by the Soul of the World society, a group whose members believe Quinn Hill is one of eight spots in the world where the vertices of a cube—with a diameter the same as the earth itself, and placed inside the Earth's orb—intercepts the land surface of the globe. Got that? The other vertices are found in the Cocos Islands (Indian Ocean), Hawaii, Santiago de Compostela (Spain), South Island (New Zealand), Buryat (Siberia), Tierra del Fuego (Argentina/Chile), and the Kalahari desert (Namibia).

Long Beach, or Long Bay, is the largest beach on the island, running the length of its southeastern side. It's a bit windier than Picnic Center Beach, but isolated and beautiful. There are just a couple of hotels and one restaurant providing services to tourists.

★ Picnic Center Beach

The most popular swimming beach, South West Bay is a long, golden crescent of soft sand and turquoise water, with a smattering of restaurants and not-so-cheap hotels. Popularly known as Picnic Center Beach for the hotel and restaurant located there, this beach is not private and you can throw a towel or chair down where you please.

ENTERTAINMENT AND EVENTS

On weekends, the locals dance to island rhythms at **Bambulay** or at **Nico's** on the beach in South End. Take a taxi, as it's hard to get out here on your own. In "town," bar **Sky** (2nd Fl. of the building next to the bank, Thurs.-Sun. 8pm-1am) is the go-to spot.

Corn Islanders are serious about their **baseball:** A league of eight teams (including two from the Little Island) play in the stadium east of the airport. On **August 27,** Corn Islanders celebrate their ancestors' emancipation from slavery. On that date, crab soup can be found in abundance.

dock at the end of the Southwest Bay beach, Big Corn Island

RECREATION

There's not much hiking here, but for a short **walking** adventure, tackle the shore between the Gomez's hotel in Sally Peachy and the South End Cemetery, or break a sweat on the 20-minute hike up Mount Pleasant where the view from the top is well worth the effort. A path leads up to Mount Pleasant opposite the Casa Canada. When you reach the local school, take the path that winds up behind the school to the left. Or, go with local guide **Vilma Gomez** (tel. 505/2575-0144 or 505/8848-8136, vilgomezz@ hotmail.com) to learn about the history of the island along the way.

There are plenty of reefs along the beach in Sally Peachy and North End for **snorkeling,** and most hotels can rent you snorkel gear ($5). Both dive shops offer two-hour snorkeling trips ($25), as well as longer trips to Blowing Rock.

Colorado native Joey Saputo of **Stand Up Paddle** (tel. 505/8735-8516, joeysaputo@hotmail.com) offers a two-hour paddleboard and snorkeling tour ($25). See the whole island from the ocean, circling it on a paddleboard. Rent one of his boards at Picnic Center or Dos Tiburones ($12/hour).

★ Diving

Three distinct layers of reef, composed of more than 40 species of coral, protect the north side of the island. The diving and snorkeling are impressive, and divers regularly see nurse sharks, eagle rays, and lots of colorful fish. Unfortunately, the reefs closest to shore have deteriorated over the past decades, victims of overfishing, predatory algae (which grow as a result of increased nutrient levels in the water from sewage runoff), sedimentation, storm damage, and global warming. **Blowing Rock** is a rock formation with lots of color and dozens of varieties of tropical fish. Any of the island's dive shops will take you there. A few sandy stretches of beach along the north shore allow you to get into the water. One good one is in front of Dorsey Campbell's Yellowtail House.

A mother and son from the U.S. co-own a full-service, modern dive shop in North End. **Dos Tiburones Dive Shop** (tel. 505/2575-5167, www.divecornisland.com) offers scuba gear and the services of PADI- and SSI-affiliated dive-masters. They offer an introductory course ($335), a two-tank dive ($65), and a dive at Blowing Rock ($95). The shop's Dive Café offers fresh-ground coffee and smoothies you can sip from a lawn chair on the beach out back. **Corn Island Dive Center** (across from Best View Hotel in North End,

beach on Big Corn Island

tel. 505/8851-5704 or 505/8735-0667, www. cornislanddivecenter.com) is PADI-affiliated and offers similar services: a dive at Blowing Rock ($85), two tanks ($65), and snorkeling ($25). Not sure if you want to get certified? Or, need to brush up on rusty skills? Try it out or do a review ($65) at either shop.

ACCOMMODATIONS
Under $25

Stay with the family of ★ **Marcos and Jeanette Gomez** (from the Km 4 marker, walk towards the beach until you see a bright yellow house, tel. 505/2575-5187 or 505/8548-3360, $10) who rent three clean, safe rooms in their home and a three-bedroom cabin ($12/room) with patio facing the beach. It's a great spot to watch the sun come up. **Dorsey Campbell's Yellowtail House** (near Marcos and Jeanette Gomez, tel. 505/8909-8050, $25) offers two self-catering private cabins and accompanied snorkel trips from the shore out to the reefs ($20 for 2 hours). Dorsey knows the reefs better than anybody. Neither place offers meals, but Seva's Dos Millas is conveniently around the corner.

Ms. Danette offers three comfy rooms in her home, known as **Maris Place** (near Dos Tiburones, tel. 505/2575-5235 or 505/8650-6811, $25). Expect a clean room with private bath and two mouthwatering meals a day.

Hotel Morgan (North End, near the cervecería, tel. 505/2575-5052 or 505/8835-5890, kerrygean.morgan@gmail.com, $15-25) has six cabins with simple rooms with air-conditioning, fridge, TV, and private bath.

$25-50

Locally owned, wonderfully clean **South End Sunrise Hotel** (3 minutes from the airport, tel. 505/8828-7835, www.southendsunrise.com, $50-60 d) has 15 spacious double rooms with air-conditioning, TV, and hot shower. Access to Long Beach is five minutes down the road.

The ★ **Picnic Center Hotel & Restaurant** (Southwest Bay, tel. 505/8437-6501, $41-53) enjoys the best uninterrupted

cloudy skies over Big Corn Island

crescent of white sand on the island. Rooms are a little overpriced for the quality of the services, though they are well equipped with air-conditioning, TV, queen-size beds, and private baths and superb hot showers. The restaurant is an enormous, palm-thatched open-air patio.

$50-100

★ **Paraíso Beach Hotel** (tel. 505/2575-5111, www.paraisoclub.com, info@paraiso-club.com, $45-70), tucked away on its own grounds in Barrio Brig Bay, has 14 brightly painted cabana-style rooms with private baths, fan or air-conditioning, laundry service, plus food and drink service to guests on the nearby beach. They also have a honeymoon suite. Snorkeling trips are available, as are Swedish massages (from $20). Under Dutch management since 2005, the hotel offers excellent service.

La Princesa de La Isla (Walua Point, tel. 505/8854-2403, www.laprincesadelaisla.com, info@laprincesadelaisla.com, $55-70, reservation only) is a secluded beachfront hotel, run by an amiable Italian family, who offer excellent cuisine and cappuccinos. It is at the south end of Brig Bay and accessed by a beach road that passes by the shrimp processing plant.

The secluded **Martha's Bed & Breakfast** (next to Capitanía, tel. 505/8835-5930 or 505/2575-5260, marthasbb@aol.com, $50-60 d) feels more like a hotel, but it's run out of Ms. Martha's home at the quiet end of Southwest Bay. Rooms are spotless, and price includes Wi-Fi, air-conditioning, TV, hot water, private bath, and a hearty breakfast at her beachside eatery. This end of the beach is so seldom frequented that it feels private.

On the north side of the island try out "glamping" (camping in luxury accommodations) on Little Hill at ★ **Hospedaje Los Escapados** (the Australian next to the dentist in Sally Peachy, hospedaje_los_escapados@y7mail.com, $50-65). The Australian owner has three large "tents" set up like cabins on wooden decks. One has a large attached bath and porch with an ocean view. The others have detached baths, but all have convertible beds, mini-fridge, and Wi-Fi. A homemade breakfast of crepes, oatmeal, or fruit is included in the price.

Over $100

★ **Casa Canada** (tel. 505/8644-0925, Canada and U.S. tel. 306/861-9224, www.casa-canada.com, casacanadaresort@gmail.com, $90-115 d) has a superb location at South End overlooking a turquoise bay and reef. The resort is classy and luxurious, from sumptuous towels and hot showers to the minibar, cable TV, air-conditioning, fridge, and coffee machine. Each cabin features king-size beds and overstuffed sofa and chairs. Dip in the infinity pool, or explore the beach and rocks. The restaurant serves excellent seafood and strong coffee with Canadian breakfasts.

Arenas Beach (South West Bay, tel. 505/2575-5223, www.arenasbeachhotel.com, info@arenasbeachhotel.com, $98-127) has 26 rooms and large, clean, and well-equipped bungalows with deck verandas, all finished in tropical timber. It has a boat bar (daily 10am-6pm) and lounge chairs on the beach, and next door you can rent golf carts to tour the island.

FOOD

The restaurant industry is growing on Big Corn. A standby is **Seva's Dos Millas** (north side of the island, daily 8am-9pm, $7-12), which has seen better times, but still serves reliably tasty seafood and ice-cold beer. At

Rent a simple beachfront cabin from Marcos and Jeanette Gomez.

★ **Maris Place** (near Dos Tiburones, Wed.-Mon. 8am-9pm, $5-12), Ms. Danette sells some of the best food on the island. Her front porch and living room fill up around dinnertime with folks who come for her excellent cooking. There's no menu, but she's always got burgers, lobster, fish, and shrimp (and if you're lucky, breadfruit). Ask her about cooking classes.

Paraíso's restaurant **The Buccaneer** (Barrio Brig Bay, daily 6am-10pm, $5-8) has one of the better menus on the island. **La Princesa de la Isla** (Walua Point, tel. 505/8854-2403, $15-22) is the only Italian restaurant on Big Corn, specializing in homemade pastas and ravioli. It's worth coming out here just for the strong espresso. Reservations are required for lunch and dinner.

Check Ms. Adele's **Cool Spot** (shorefront in Sally Peachy right around the corner from Jeanette and Marcos Gomez) for her delicious coconut bread and some fresh coconut water. Fill up on coconut bread, which usually comes out around midday. **Island Bakery and Sweets** (at Km 2.5, tel. 505/2575-5015, Wed.-Mon. 8am-9pm) has a diverse and delicious choice of pastries and cakes to choose from.

INFORMATION AND SERVICES

Cell phone services are available from the two main local carriers, Movistar and Claro, or roaming from your own phone. Internet is available at most hotels on the island and **Comisariato** (close to the gas station). **Banpro** is the only bank on the island, occupying a new building in Brig Bay, at the corner where the road turns parallel to the airport runway; they have the only **ATM** on the island. Dive shops and larger hotels take credit cards, but some only take Visa; check before you go. There is a small and improving **hospital** with limited ability and a **police** station (next to the new gym, near the Alcaldía).

GETTING THERE
Air
La Costeña (Corn Island tel. 505/2575-5131, www.lacostena.com.ni) offers three daily flights to Corn Island from Managua with a stop in Bluefields ($107 one-way, $165 roundtrip). Buying your ticket at the airport will save you the extra fees you incur with an online reservation. Reserve in advance; these flights fill up fast.

Boat
The quickest ride is the Río Escondido boat, run by the Empresa Portuaria Nacional, which leaves the municipal dock in Bluefields to Corn Island on Wednesdays and returns on Thursdays from Corn Island's municipal dock to Bluefields, ($10 one-way). It leaves Bluefields at 9am, but the line starts when tickets go on sale at 7am in the ticket office next to the dock entrance. The six-hour trip on this little boat is not for the weak-stomached traveler. Plan on four hours on the open sea surrounded by vomiting passengers. **Captain D** (office in Bluefields across from Oasis Casino, tel. 505/8850-2767) makes weekly runs to Bilwi ($33) departing Bluefields on Wednesdays 11am, overnighting on Big Corn ($10 pp), and leaving Thursday 8pm for the RAAN, returning to Big Corn on Saturday before heading back to Bluefields. The last leg only happens if they have enough freight, so they may head straight back to Bluefields on Friday night. Call ahead to check.

GETTING AROUND
From the airport building, it's a five-minute taxi ride ($0.70 day, $1.50 night) to almost anywhere on the island, though buses circulate about twice per hour ($0.35). It's easy to get most places on foot, and worth the walk to properly take in the scenery. Taxis pass consistently along the paved roads, and are easy to flag down. Avoid walking around Bluff at the southern tip of the island without a guide, as this area is isolated and not accustomed to wandering tourists.

Corn Island Car Rentals (next to Arenas Hotel, tel. 505/8643-9881 or 505/2575-5222, nestort0110@hotmail.com) offers golf carts (from $25 for 2 hours), scooters, and motorcycles (don't forget your driver's license), and boat rides. They also have diving and fishing gear.

Little Corn Island

A humble, wilder version of Big Corn, "La Islita" is a mere three square kilometers of sand and trees, laced with footpaths and encircled by nine kilometers of coral reef. Little Corn is a delicate destination, visited by an increasing number of travelers each year. There are clever accommodations for several budgets to meet the demand, but rough boat transport from Big Corn—an experience one traveler likened to pursuing a *narco-panga* across 15 kilometers of open swell—will help hold the masses at bay. Bring a flashlight, your snorkel gear, and a good book.

Little Corn Island is irregularly policed by volunteers and has experienced a handful of violent attacks on tourists in recent years. The security situation is sometimes better, sometimes worse. Ask at your hotel for the latest news and advice on staying safe. Above all, don't walk alone on the beaches, or at night. For medical needs, you can find a meager health clinic just south of the Hotel Los Delfines. Anything complicated requires a *panga* ride back to the big island, or even Bluefields.

ORIENTATION

Unless you make special arrangements with your *panga* driver to take you elsewhere, you will be let off at the southwestern-facing beach, where you'll find a cement sidewalk that runs the length of the village. This is called the "front side" by islanders and is the center of most social activity. Walk north along that sidewalk, turning right at the school and you'll come to the baseball field. Just past the school on the left, walk up to the lighthouse for a great view, or follow the dirt track onward through forests and fields to the north beach and Yemaya Hideaway (the island's only resort) and Derek's Place. Just south of the dive shop is another track that leads across to the "breezy side" of the island and the Casa Iguana. You can walk from one end to the other in about 45 minutes.

ENTERTAINMENT AND EVENTS

The best place on the island to sip a drink and enjoy the gorgeous waterfront view of the big island on the horizon is **Habana Libre** (50 meters north of the dock), owned by Ronaldo, a Cuban transplant to the island. They offer the best mojito on the Atlantic coast, with mint fresh from the garden. The bar is home base for the Island Braves baseball team. The **Happy Hut** (behind Café Tranquilo), a Rasta-colored building on the front side, is a grinding good time on weekends. They often have live music but don't seem to have any regular hours. **Café Tranquilo** (200 meters south of the dock, between the two dive shops) is a popular hangout day or night. Stop in for happy hour (daily 5pm-7pm).

RECREATION

Beach hikes, snorkel excursions, and lots of time reading and swinging in your hammock will fill your day. **Casa Iguana** offers fishing, snorkeling, and picnic trips, and most of the beachfront hotels have snorkel gear for rent. For a rewarding hike, walk to the school, turn right, and follow the sidewalk to its end; then follow the footpath up and to the left to reach the **lighthouse** (about 20 minutes from the waterfront), perched on Little Corn's highest

Little Corn Island

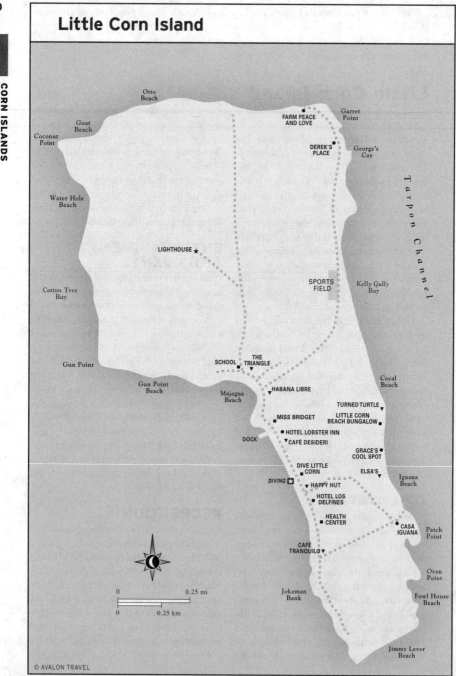

© AVALON TRAVEL

Rent a *panga* and driver for fishing and diving expeditions.

peak. You can climb up to get a view of the entire island.

Walking all the way to **Yemaya Hideaway** on the north end of the island is well worth it to enjoy the sparkling blue water and well-kept beach complete with lawn chairs. Expect to pay resort prices at the beachside bar and the hotel restaurant.

★ Diving

Little Corn's delicate reef system is unique for its abundance of wildlife and coral formations, including overhangs, swim-throughs, and the infamous shark cave. Most dives around the island are shallow (less than 60 feet), but a few deeper dives exist as well. The island's bigger scuba shop, **Dive Little Corn** (south of the new pier on Pelican Beach, tel. 505/8856-5888, www.divelittlecorn.net), operates out of a wooden building. They offer morning and afternoon dives for novice through advanced divers, night dives by appointment, hourly and all-day snorkel trips, PADI certification, and kayak rentals. Hotel

Los Delfines has **Dolphin Dive** (tel. 505/8917-9717, www.dolphindivelittlecorn.com, info@ Dolphindivelittlecorn.com), which offers PADI certification.

Fishing

Within a couple kilometers of shore, you'll find schools of kingfish, dolphin, amberjack, red snapper, and barracuda. Fly fishers can catch tarpon and bonefish right from the beach, or **Casa Iguana** (www.littlecornfishing.com, info@littlecornfishing.com, $50 pp) will take you out. Boat trips can be arranged with a number of locals, or at Hotel Los Delfines. Ask around on the front side for a good deal. Spearfishing is illegal on the island due to its severe impact on local reef ecosystems.

ACCOMMODATIONS

A variety of accommodations are available on Little Corn, from palm-thatch huts to cabins to conventional hotel rooms with color TVs to resorts. ★ **Grace's Cool Spot** (tel. 505/8617-0239, $15 pp), a locally run establishment and backpacker favorite with bright beachside cabins and hammocks slung from the coconut trees, is just meters from the shoreline.

Get back to nature (that's why you came to Little Corn, after all) at **Derek's Place** (on the beach south of Yemaya, www.dereksplacelittlecorn.com, dereksplace@gmail.com, $70-100 d). Derek has been here for years. Shack up in raised cabins with electricity and breezy porches looking over the reef. Delicious international meals are available in their communal dining room, as are snorkel trips and transfers.

Hotel Los Delfines (100 meters south of the wharf, tel. 505/8411-3572, www.losdelfineslittlecorn.com, hotellosdelfines@hotmail.com, $50-80) has 18 air-conditioned concrete and glass bungalows on the water. They'll be glad to arrange trips for you and private boat transport from Big Corn.

Located on the cliffs of the southeast, breezy side of the island, **Casa Iguana** (www.

casaiguana.net, casaiguana@mindspring.com, $35-75) consists of raised, wooden cabins clustered around a communal, hilltop lodge where guests gather to eat, drink, and listen to the waves. The 15 cabins are a clever compromise between rustic simplicity and comfort, and include soft mattresses, outdoor showers, private, breezy porches with hammocks, and shelves full of books. Join the other guests each morning for breakfast, lunch, and each evening for happy hour and family-style dinner, frequently the day's catch. Casa Iguana provides snorkel gear rental, fishing trips ($59 pp), and satellite email. Casa Iguana is 100 percent off the grid, operating purely on solar energy. They compost and use biodegradable products.

★ Little Corn Beach & Bungalows (southwest side of the island, tel. 505/8333-0956 or 505/8662-7033, www.littlecornbb.com, info@littlecornbb.com, $79-209) is impressive: Their eight bungalows have private bathroom and small kitchen, just steps from the water. Co-owner/architect, Scot Smyth (winner of an Innovative Builder of the Year Award from the Northern Colorado homebuilders association) has ensured his eco-friendly design includes shower water from rooftop rain barrels, and coming soon, wind and solar power. The owners have sponsored several veterinary clinics on the island, resulting in the spaying and neutering of hundreds of pets; ask how you can help. They've constructed a yoga and massage studio on the property called **Firefly.** Ask about health and wellness packages.

Hard to find but worth the effort, **Farm Peace Love** (www.farmpeacelove.com, paola@farmpeacelove.com, $75 suite, $90 cottage, minimum 3-night stay) offers rich, fresh Italian and Caribbean dinners from local ingredients ($18 prix-fixe) and a classy guest suite including breakfast. They have a fully-equipped cottage with bedroom, living room with futon, and full kitchen. They'll pick you up in a boat at the wharf to avoid the 45-minute overland trek. Ask about weekly and monthly rates, or low-season (May-Oct.)

discounts. Reservations are required. Snorkeling and horseback riding are available.

FOOD
Nearly every accommodation offers meals. **Elsa's Great Food and Drinks** (east side of the island, closed Sun., $6-9) offers just that, but slowly, in a beachside barbecue setting. **The Triangle** (next to the school, $6-9) is a great spot to find coconut and home-cooked meals. Owner Alfonso also offers snorkeling and fishing trips. **Hotel Lobster Inn** ($6-10) is more formal and offers chicken and steak. Knock on the door at the blue house past the school to inquire about **coconut bread.**

Located halfway on the trail that divides the island, **Rosa's Restaurant** (Mon.-Sat., breakfast $4, lunch and dinner $6) serves tasty made-to-order meals all day. There are good menu options for vegetarians and vegans, including delicious curry.

The immensely popular ★ **Café Tranquilo** (on the front side between the dive shops, tel. 505/8336-3068 www.tranquilo-cafe.com, daily 10am until the bar closes, $3-12) offers a widely varied menu featuring freshly brewed coffee, salads, fish tacos, and authentic smoked BBQ. There's free Wi-Fi, a book exchange, and gift shop. Italian-run **Café Desideri** (next to Café Tranquilo, tel. 505/8412-6341, Tues.-Sun. 9am-10pm, $6-12) is a popular spot serving delicious seafood dishes. Breakfast includes French press coffee and homemade granola and yogurt. Don't miss the dessert menu!

The ★ **Turned Turtle** (at Little Corn Beach & Bungalows, daily 7:30am-10am, noon-3pm, and 5:30pm-8:30pm, breakfast $4-6, lunch $4-8, dinner $9-15) is the most upscale option on Little Corn, serving four-course meals in the evening. They have an impressive breakfast menu of coconut French toast, mini-waffles, and vegan burritos.

GETTING THERE AND AWAY
Three scheduled *pangas* ply the route between Corn Island and Little Corn Island ($7 each

way) and are coordinated with the departure and arrival of the two rounds of daily flights. Fast boats depart from Big Corn Island (30 minutes) around 9am and 4pm; departing Little Corn Island 7am and 2pm (pay a $0.20 harbor tax). A slower red boat (1 hour) leaves at noon.

The trip to Little Corn is often choppy and rough. During the windiest time of year (Dec.-Apr.), the port authority can stop shuttle service until conditions are safer. Expect to get wet regardless of the weather. Seats in the front afford a more violent bashing; seats in the back are prone to more frequent splashes of spray. The *pulperías* across from the dock on Big Corn sell heavy, blue plastic bags that fit over a backpack for less than $1, an essential investment for keeping your gear dry. A number of larger fishing boats travel between the islands, and these may agree to take on a paying passenger. See Miss Bridgett for the day's schedule.

Puerto Cabezas and the Río Coco

Isolated from the rest of Nicaragua by vast tracts of inaccessible forest and coastline, the municipality of Puerto Cabezas, its capital Bilwi, and the Río Coco watershed are remote and wild.

Spanish-speaking Nicaragua has always felt nationalistic about its right to alternately claim and ignore this far-off corner of the country. Managua has incited neighboring Honduras over the subtleties of the border, yet the only road to Puerto Cabezas degenerated into bumpy oblivion decades ago, making Bilwi somewhat of an island in itself. Tourism is undeveloped throughout this region, which for some travelers makes it all the more enticing.

This is far and away the most indigenous region of Nicaragua, where Miskito is heard more than Spanish. At first glance, Puerto Cabezas and the Río Coco might have the air of a drowsy backwater unchanged through the centuries. But to the contrary, the area is affected by many modern issues, including drug trafficking, global lobster prices, and international development projects.

The Río Coco is Central America's longest river and the cultural and spiritual heart of the Miskito people, who live a traditional lifestyle on both banks of the waterway. The whole region burned white-hot during the revolution years, and the scars run deep. These days the rhythm of the days revolves around fishing and farming, as it has for centuries.

Inland, the "mining triangle" is composed of the three pueblos of Siuna, Bonanza, and La Rosita. The area no longer produces the quantity of gold or guerilla warriors it once did, but there is yet a pioneering feel to the area, which is still host to a Canadian gold mining company and a few casinos in the town of Bonanza. This area is one jumping-off point for the country's most rugged adventure, an expedition into the sprawling and untamed Bosawás Reserve.

PLANNING YOUR TIME

This region doesn't figure prominently into many travel itineraries. Though it's easy enough to hop a puddle jumper in Managua

Previous: Miskito hut; Bilwi's main dock. **Above:** The Creole Moravian church, Bilwi.

Look for ★ to find recommended sights, activities, dining, and lodging.

Highlights

★ **Moravian Churches:** The Moravian religion took root early on Nicaragua's Atlantic coast and remains an important influence. Join a Sunday church service given in the Miskito language (page 349).

★ **Tours to the Miskito Communities:** AMICA, an association of indigenous women, will take you to Nicaragua's indigenous fishing communities, which are practically a country unto themselves (page 355).

★ **Waspám:** The spiritual home of the Miskito people is also the gateway to Central America's longest river, the Río Coco. It's about as rough and remote as you can get in Central America (page 355).

★ **Bosawás Biosphere Reserve:** No corner of Central America is wilder or less explored than this unbroken stretch of cloud forest (page 359).

Puerto Cabezas and the Río Coco

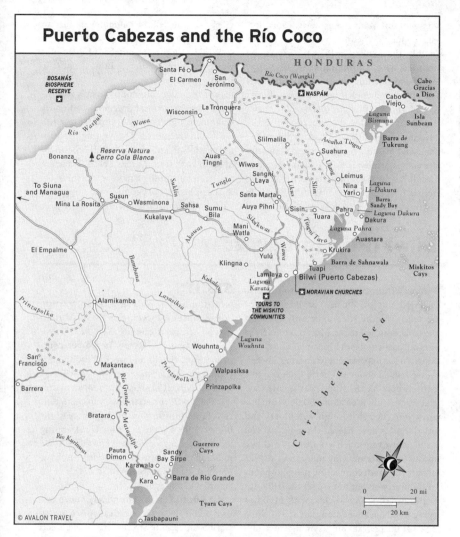

for an hour-long flight to Bilwi, Waspám, or the mining triangle, always plan more time than you think you'll need when traveling in these areas. Once on land, moving between towns requires ample patience and flexibility. Plan a day or two in Bilwi and a few days to head up the coast or to nearby villages.

HISTORY

Renamed "Puerto Cabezas" in the 1900s after President Zelaya took control of the coast to unify the nation, the city of Bilwi has seen more glorious days. Testimony to the wealth of Puerto Cabezas during the lumber boom of the 20th century is the enormous wooden dock that juts into the Atlantic, built in the mid-1940s. (It was destroyed during Hurricane Felix in 2007, but its ruins are still visible.)

Somoza was well liked in the northeast. He largely left the Atlantic coast to its own devices and Costeños generally viewed the goings-on in Managua as news from a foreign country. When the Sandinistas arrived to unite the country in 1979, the Revolution collided with a growing sense of Native American autonomy worldwide. Indigenous leaders soon disputed Sandinista authority to rule the Atlantic coast. The Sandinistas retaliated by forcing the relocation of entire Miskito communities and razing villages. Ten thousand Miskito villagers resettled in refugee camps, while another 40,000 escaped to Honduras. In 1985, Minister of the Interior Tomás Borge conciliated, and the Río Coco communities have slowly rebuilt original villages in the delicate autonomy granted to the two departments of the Atlantic coast.

While a significant number of Puerteños work in government jobs—Bilwi is not only the departmental capital, but also the center of the indigenous community's government—several thousand were laid off under Chamorro's government, and the city has never quite recovered. The Nicaraguan military patrols the northern Atlantic coast and Miskito Cays from its naval base. There are scattered jobs in the timber and fishing industries, and many people are looking for a legitimate way to earn a living.

Bilwi (Puerto Cabezas)

Far away from everything, Puerto Cabezas (referred to as just "Puerto" or "Port") is connected to Pacific Nicaragua only by semipassable, seasonal roads. Most travelers fly to this outpost city from Managua. The city of Bilwi, in the department of Puerto Cabezas, is itself also known as Puerto Cabezas. It is entirely possible that you'll be the only traveler in this town of about 50,000 inhabitants, but enough foreign volunteers and missionaries have passed through that you won't draw too much attention. In Bilwi, most streets are nothing more than streaks of bare red earth connecting neighborhoods of humble wooden homes set on stilts. It's a glimpse of many worlds, with Miskitos tying wooden canoes alongside steel fishing boats at the pier. It's an easy walk from anywhere in town to the water's edge. Fledgling recreational beaches aren't quite ready for tourists, and the water between them is shallow and rocky. The Mayangna inhabitants named it Bilwi because the leaves *(wi)* were full of snakes *(Bil)*. These days you should worry less about serpents than the increasing drug traffic slowly impacting the social norms of the region: You are closer to trouble here than elsewhere because of that same remoteness.

SIGHTS

Near the center of town is an interesting house/museum/hotel, the **Casa Museo** (Barrio Aeropuerto, tel. 505/2792-2225, Tues.-Sat. 9am-4pm, Sun. 10am-2pm, free), commemorating the life and work of Judith Kain Cunningham, a local painter who passed away in 2001. A prolific artist, her subject matter was the Río Coco and the Miskito communities of the Waspám. Also on display are works of macramé, sculpture, artifacts celebrating local indigenous movements, and more. A free museum guide is available Monday-Saturday. Free art classes are offered to children on Saturdays 2pm-4pm.

La Bocana (at the north end of town just past Kabu Payaska restaurant) is a sandy Caribbean coast beach that has a reputation for being a bit dangerous (enjoy its tranquil beauty from afar). The tourism association in barrio El Cocal has recently created a community police force to increase security, and it seems to be making a difference. If you do wander down here, don't bring valuables, and go with a group. A small beach dubbed **La Bocanita** (at the opposite end of the town's shoreline) offers a couple of restaurants to attract pleasure seekers.

The **CIDCA** library (across from the

The Struggle for Indigenous Self-Determination

When the FSLN (Sandinista National Liberation Front) came to power, the Sandinistas attempted to incorporate the developing Miskito indigenous movement into their own organizational structure. Uninterested in being part of any group led from Managua, the indigenous people of the Atlantic coast instead organized themselves into the political group MISURASATA. Its leaders hoped to convert the entire region into an autonomous, self-governing indigenous reserve.

The Sandinistas met resistance with violence and repression, forcefully relocating Miskito villages to refugee camps and burning the old villages to prevent roving bands of Contras from making use of them. This cemented the Miskito's mistrust into hatred.

Then, in 1987, the government signed an autonomy statute and guaranteed self-rule and first-class citizenship for all minority groups, permitting them to use their own languages, common land, and have a say in the use of their natural resources. Two coastal governments were formed, responsible for governing trade, and administering health and education.

The Miskitos who found their way into the ranks of the Contras in the 1980s organized themselves into a group called **Yatama** (Yapti Tasba Masraka Nanih Aslatakanka, or Sons of the Mother Earth). At the war's end, the Yatama Contras disbanded, exchanging weapons for land and converting to a political party. During the departmental elections of 2000, violence erupted when Yatama was excluded from the ballot. Yatama vowed that unless they were permitted to participate, there would be no elections. The military engaged in armed confrontations with protesters; several were killed. Yatama accused President Alemán of trying to politically eradicate the indigenous community.

Yatama leaders were wooed into an alliance with the Sandinistas for the 2006 elections. Sandinistas on the Atlantic coast now complain that Yatama has effectively displaced them. How long it will be before the FSLN feels it has to retake control remains to be seen; the FSLN has never been comfortable with independent-minded allies.

PUERTO CABEZAS
BILWI (PUERTO CABEZAS)

stadium) has a wealth of up-to-date information about the area. Wander through the aisles of the **Miskito market** (2.5 blocks north of the central park, daily 7am-3pm), full of produce from the surrounding communities, seafood, meats, natural medicines, and more. It's the biggest market on the Caribbean coast. Stop by Mr. Gaston's butcher stand around 11am for fresh fried pork rinds and a good story.

★ Moravian Churches

Bilwi is more Moravian than Catholic, and its quaint churches betray the region's separate history. Nearly every neighborhood has a Moravian church. This is the only place on earth you can hear a service given in Miskito; try the **Central Miskito Church** (in the center of town). On a street lined with old Creole houses is the **Creole Moravian Church** (behind the Central Miskito Church), where you can hear a service given in English. The barrel-shaped **Catholic church** (in the center of town near the water) is replete with stained glass. The remnants of the former Catholic church stand behind it.

ENTERTAINMENT AND EVENTS

Karaoke Payito (Barrio 19 de Julio, half a block west of Radio Caribe, tel. 505/8834-6665, Mon.-Fri. noon-midnight, Sat. noon-2am) is a small, low-key bar with a proclivity for 1980s and '90s music and cold beer without the booming sound systems that prevail in most of Bilwi's discos and bars. Find cheap beer and no drama at **Barcito Doña Ruth** (3 blocks south of the stadium), Bilwi's resident dive bar, which has a mellow, welcoming vibe.

For dancing, **Zenith** (Barrio Thelma Morales, 100 meters south of la Ochoa, tel. 505/8413-9262, open 24 hours) is Bilwi's

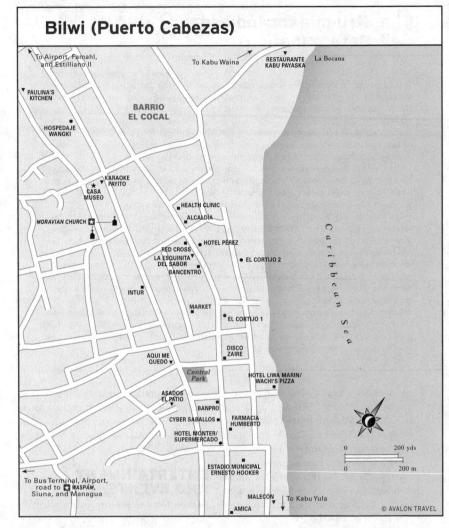

Bilwi (Puerto Cabezas)

overall most happening nightlife venue. **Malecón** (at the end of the road behind the stadium, tel. 505/8826-1177, daily 11am-2am) has inside and outside tables overlooking the beach and two dance floors that start throbbing on the weekends. *Soca* and salsa beats throb at **Disco Zaire,** and a group of other discos that surround the park.

El Bohemio (on the road to Lamlaya, tel. 505/2792-1087, daily 11am-2am), just outside the city, offers a mellow ambience in a thatch-roofed *rancho*. Go for the live music on Sundays.

Semana Santa in Puerto Cabezas is an unforgettable event during which many overseas Puerteños return home. The town sets up dozens of thatch *ranchos* at La Bocana beach, and the 24/7 party lasts at least a week: food, drink, music, and nonstop Caribbean grinding.

Relax in Casa Museo's shady garden.

SHOPPING

You'll see plenty of *artesanía* made from Tunu tree bark. The bark is soaked for a few days and pounded repeatedly until the artisan is left with a soft fiber. It's then dyed and used for constructing sturdy bags, hats, wallets, and purses. Nuri at **Artesanías Gill** (Barrio Pedro Joaquín Chamorro, Casa E 15, tel. 505/8747-3903) makes particularly nice things out of Tunu, which she sells at her workshop next to the Radio Impacto de Dios, uphill from Cable Vision.

Winger Wilson is a fantastic woodcarver who lives in Barrio Filimon Riviera, down the alley that parallels the river on the road that connects the police and the Moravian Creole church. **Jimmy Webster** (home is behind Colegio Jac) is an 85-year-old furniture maker who speaks English and knows a lifetime of good stories.

Dario Salgado (in Barrio Filimon Riviera) makes the nicest jewelry in town out of a variety of shells and seeds. (Abstain from buying the turtle shell products.) He only

sells it out of his house. Past the police station heading towards San Luis, take the second left after the speed bump, and then look for the sign on right.

ACCOMMODATIONS
Under $25

Family-run **Hospedaje Wangki** (3 blocks south of the airport, tel. 505/2792-1545, $8 shared bath, $12-17 private bath) has 15 decent rooms with your choice of shared or private bath, with or without air-conditioning. Breakfast is available.

★ **Casa Museo** (near the center of town, tel. 505/2792-2225, casamuseojudithkain@hotmail.com, $13-28) was built in and around the museum, and has as much character as you'd expect to find in an artist's home. A handful of accommodations on wooden stilts with bright, well-appointed rooms surround a central garden with sprawling comfy sofas, tables, benches, and other sitting areas. The on-site café serves breakfast and lunch as well as coffee and sodas throughout the day. The family also owns shore-side **Hotel Liwa Mairin** (Barrio Libertad, from the Banco del la Producción, 1.5 blocks east, tel. 505/2792-2315, $13 s, $17 d with fan). Rooms are spacious with Wi-Fi, fan, TV, and screened windows; some have air-conditioning. You can catch a glimpse of the ocean through the trees from the second story balcony. The downstairs café serves breakfast, salads, and coffee during the day, and by night becomes **Wachi's Pizza** (daily 3pm-10pm).

Hotel Pérez (on the main drag, tel. 505/2792-2362, $20-25) has eight rooms with good natural light set in an old wooden house. Some rooms have air-conditioning and mini-fridge, but all come with private bath and use of the kitchen. There's a small pool out back. Ask about discounts if you plan to stay a few nights.

★ **El Cortijo 1** (1 block south of the mayor's office, tel. 505/2792-2340, $17-29, breakfast $5) is on the main drag in a charming old wooden house with a large back porch overlooking a pleasant garden. Ask for an upstairs room with high ceilings, air-conditioning, private bath, and cable TV. There's also a small, sunny back room with a single bed ($14). **El Cortijo 2** (2 blocks east of El Cortijo 1, tel. 505/2792-2340, $17-29, breakfast $5) is more elegant and sits atop a bluff over breaking surf. Guests enjoy stained hardwood interiors, a wonderful ocean-facing deck, and a semi-private beach at the bottom of the stairs. Ask for a room with a private balcony.

$25-50

★ **Hotel Monter** (across from the baseball stadium, tel. 505/2792-2669, www.hotelmonternicaragua.blogspot.com, hotelmonter@gmail.com, $35-58, includes breakfast and Internet) is a class act, with a large, breezy, open-air patio centrally located above the Supermercado Monter. Rooms with balconies are the nicest (and the only ones with sunshine). All rooms have private bath, air-conditioning, and fans. Airport transfer is included in the price.

FOOD

Bilwi has a good selection of simple *comedors* (cheap lunch counters), typically offering barbecue beef and chicken. ★ **Asados El Patio** (Barrio Libertad, half a block west of Indio,

tel. 505/2792-2221, Wed.-Sun. noon-midnight, $2-5) is a popular spot for coconut-flavored *gallo pinto* and other typical fare. There is always a line in front of the grill at **Aquí Me Quedo** (kitty-corner from the central park, $3-4). You can order tacos and a milkshake at **La Esquinita del Sabor** (across from the Alcaldía, $1 tacos), a favorite *comedor* serving three square meals a day.

At the **Sport Cafetín Membreño** (Barrio 19 de Julio, tel. 505/2792-1730, Mon.-Sat. 10am-9pm, Sun. 1:30pm-9pm, $4-5), grab a stool at the counter or on the patio for Mexican fare or a cheeseburger and fruit drink. The owner, a nice guy with impeccable English, retired in 2009 from working cruise ships out of the southern United States. For traditional local food, **Paulina's Kitchen** (near the cemetery, in front of Bodega PMA, daily 11am-2pm, $3-5) has *gallo pinto* with coconut, *rondón*, and other regional meals. Get there early before the food runs out.

There are a handful of nice restaurants throughout town, all offering essentially the same menu of shellfish, fresh fish, soups, beef, and chicken. At the north end of town, the best meal in the city is at ★ **Restaurante Kabu Payaska** (Barrio Cocal, tel. 505/2792-1620, daily noon-midnight, $7-10), serving

fritanga at Aquí Me Quedo

seafood on a beautiful grassy lawn overlooking the ocean.

There are two good restaurants near the airport: ★ **Famahi** (next to the airport, tel. 505/2792-1614, daily 10am-midnight, $6-10) is open for three hearty meals a day. Their breakfast and house *mondongo* (tripe soup) are their specialties. Famahi also serves Chinese-inspired dishes. **El Esteliano II** (near the airport, $6-10) is a local favorite, which blasts country and *ranchero* music all day long. They have excellent *carne a la plancha*, fish, shrimp, lobster, pork, and beef dishes.

INFORMATION AND SERVICES

Supermercado Monter has a surprisingly full repertoire of canned and dry goods, fresh foods, and basic housewares. On the north end of town, **Minisuper Membreño** (next to the cafetín of the same name) has a decent selection of foodstuffs.

Both banks in town have **ATMs. Bancentro** (a block south of the Alcaldía) and **BanPro** (across from Claro, tel. 505/2792-2211, Mon.-Fri. 8am-4:30pm, Sat. 8am-noon) sometimes have long lines.

For Internet, **Cyber Saballos** (half a block north of the stadium) has the best connection, newest computers, and air-conditioning. A great alternative to the rundown municipal **Hospital Nuevo Amanecer** (1 block from the bus terminal, tel. 505/2792-2259) is U.S.-trained **Dr. Humberto Lacayo** (next to the Policlínica).

GETTING THERE
Air

La Costeña (Bilwi tel. 505/2792-2282 or 505/2792-1640, www.lacostena.com.ni) offers a flight from Managua (90 minutes, $148 round-trip). There are three scheduled daily flights to and from Managua. Flights leave three times weekly from Bluefields (1 hour, $97). Always confirm flights beforehand. Reservations or advanced ticket purchases are recommended. If you need to make changes to flight reservations, it is best to do so at the local office.

Land

You are a brave soul indeed! Two daily buses (9am and 1pm) make the arduous 24-hour journey from Managua through Nicaragua's muddy interior. The municipal bus terminal in Bilwi is located on the western edge of town. At the time of research it was under construction, and buses were leaving from

the Miskito Cays

nearby Madensa. Overloading the buses is a consistent problem. Expect to pay $4-8 extra for your luggage. Bilwi buses leave Managua's Mayoreo terminal, or you can piece the trip together from Jinotega's north terminal on a bus bound for Waslala; from there, board a second bus to Siuna, and then another to Bilwi. There's an alternate road from Matagalpa to Siuna by way of Río Blanco and Mulukuku. Both roads are largely impassable during the wet season. It's not for everyone, but this route offers a close look at the heart of Nicaragua.

Boat

The freighter **Captain D** (tel. 505/8850-2767 or 505/8902-6846, transportemaritimonormand@gmail.com) does a quasi-weekly run from Big Corn Island (12 hours overnight, $33). Call for their schedule. They only make the trip when they have enough freight.

GETTING AROUND

Bilwi has no bus system, though the mayor's office is trying to put a couple of local city buses in place. In the meantime, Bilwi has an astounding number of taxis (many of which are pirate cabs without plates, but you can use them, too). The price is fixed ($0.50 pp) to go anywhere in town. Locals recommend taking a trusted taxi at night. The city center is easily walkable during the day; use a cab after 7pm. **Puerto Cabezas Rental & Transport** (tel. 505/8513-6979) rents cars, motorcycles, and trucks with drivers. Bikes ($5/day) are available.

MISKITO COMMUNITIES

It's possible to travel by boat north or south along the coast to visit Miskito communities near Bilwi, though you should have a basic command of Miskito to travel on your own, both to avoid suspicion and to be able to communicate. Northbound boats leave from the shore to the right of the pier (down the stairs right of the dock).

Tuapí (17 kilometers north of Bilwi) has a popular swimming hole called **Brakira** on the banks of the eponymous river. There are no restaurants at the *balneario*. Buses leave daily for Tuapí from Bilwi (30 minutes, $1.15). If you don't have a vehicle, you'll have to stay the night in the community. The bus to Bilwi leaves first thing in the morning. You can also contract a taxi from the city ($12), and then pay by the hour ($5) for them to wait for you.

A bit farther north, the community in **Krukira** built their home along the edge of

Catch boats to nearby Miskito communities from Bilwi.

the lake of the same name, which offers excellent opportunities for swimming and fishing. They have an organized tourism association, with homestays available. It's a two-hour bus ride from Bilwi ($1.35). Hire a boat from Krukira to take you three kilometers out to sea to visit the river sandbanks that make up the **Malvinas Cays** (30 minutes). If you can get there, the **Laguna de Phara** offers swimming and sandboarding from the town of the same name at its northern tip. **Karatá** (17 kilometers south of Bilwi) is an easy day trip. Take a guided wildlife tour through the streams of the Río Wawa.

Someday, travelers will have interesting adventures in the gorgeous beachfront community of **Sandy Bay** (2 hours north of Bilwi) and the sandy white islets of the **Miskito Cays** (2 hours across the open sea from Sandy Bay). However, both locations are known rendezvous points for drug runners. Luckily, drug-related violence has diminished due to increased efforts by the Nicaraguan authorities, and there are now communities in Sandy Bay equipped to receive tourists.

★ Tours to the Miskito Communities

The best way to visit local indigenous communities is with **AMICA** (Asociación de Mujeres Indígenas de la Costa Atlántica, 1 block south of the baseball stadium, tel. 505/2792-2219, asociacionamica@yahoo.es), an organization that promotes the empowerment of women along the northern Atlantic coast. AMICA gives training in gender development, reproductive health, leadership, and AIDS, plus the laws that affect indigenous women. They can set you up with trips to the Miskito communities of Haulover, Wawa Bar, Karatá, Sandy Bay, Pahra, and Tuapí with homestays, nature tours, and dance or cultural presentations. Accommodations aren't as rustic as you'd think. They include box spring mattresses and towels. Prices depend on transport costs; renting a boat adds considerably to the cost (about $4 pp per night, meals $4). It's crucial to call at least three days ahead.

Norton Britton (tel. 505/8630-9906 or 505/8450-8504, elvinkind@yahoo.com) can arrange day trips to the mainland Miskito communities of Tuapí and Boom Serpi, sailboat tours, and lobster dives. He loves to talk about Nicaragua, knows where absolutely everything is, and speaks English, Spanish, Miskito, and Creole.

North American Cody Clare has spent over 10 years exploring this corner of Nicaragua. His tour company **Adventure Nica** (tel. 505/8513-6979, www.adventurenica.com) arranges day or overnight trips to nearby Miskito communities, as well as sailing adventures, rafting, fishing charters, and biking expeditions. Sign up for workshops taught by locals covering everything from natural medicine to Tunu artisanry, cooking, and language classes.

Waspám and the Río Coco

★ WASPÁM

Waspám, in the far northern reaches of the Miskito pine savanna and at the edge of the mightiest river in Nicaragua, is the gateway, principal port, and economic heart of the Miskito communities that line the banks of the Río Coco. Waspám is not expecting travelers. You will find no package tours here, no one hawking T-shirts, real estate, or their new bed-and-breakfast. Rather, you will be immersed in a very traditional community that retains a strong cultural identity despite growing mestizo influence, and that is prepared to show you exactly what it is, not what it expects you are expecting.

The Miskito people live largely off the river, fishing for small freshwater species, and off their small, neatly tended fields. Their version

Health and Safety Concerns in the Río Coco Region

Due to its low, wet geography, the Río Coco area is particularly prone to **malaria** and **dengue fever** outbreaks. All travelers should ensure they're taking a prophylaxis to prevent malaria, as well as standard precautions to prevent being bitten by mosquitoes, i.e., keep your skin covered, try to stay indoors around 5pm, and use repellent and a mosquito net.

At the same time the Río Coco is venerated by local communities, it is also the public toilet for most of the communities that line its shores. Don't be surprised to see someone scooping a bucket of river water out for cooking just downstream of someone defecating. Although the **water** is usually treated with chlorine, pay extra attention to the **food** and **beverages** you ingest, and especially all water and water-based drinks. Treat all water with iodine pills or a portable water filter before drinking. That goes double any time you are downstream of Waspám. If you are not carrying bottled water from Managua, it is recommended that you use a good water filter. While it is possible to purchase bottled water in Waspám, the supply is not always guaranteed, so don't rely on it.

The Río Coco was a heavily mined area in the 1980s. Though the **land mines** have largely been cleared away, known mined areas still exist and have been cordoned off with ribbon or wire. Ask the locals before you go wandering too far from the road or riverbank.

Finally, the entire Atlantic coast is experiencing the effect of **drug trafficking** from Colombia, and the Río Coco area provides particularly good hiding spots. The delta at Cabo Gracias a Dios is a known point of entry for small smugglers who take advantage of the lack of police vigilance there. In 2014, flights to Waspám were cancelled due to the mysterious disappearance of one of La Costeña's aircrafts. *Narcos* generally leave travelers alone, but don't wander too far off the beaten path in this region. Expect police to thoroughly inspect bags at every dock and airport in the area.

---

of the tortilla is a thick, wheat-flour cake that is fried in coconut oil. Starch, including tubers like *quiquisque* (taro) and yucca, makes up the rest of the diet along the Río Coco. *Rondón* and *gallo pinto* are cooked in coconut milk. Wild game also finds its way onto the menu; don't be surprised to find boar, deer, and armadillo.

The Miskito people are reserved but friendly. Once you've broken the ice, you'll find them helpful and inquisitive. They're also more conservative than other Nicaraguans. Most Miskito people speak Spanish as a second language and practically no English at all. Foreigners who speak languages other than Spanish or Miskito will inevitably be called Miriki (American). Even Nicaraguans from the Pacific region are considered foreigners.

The chance to visit this frontier—and it is truly frontier—to travel amongst the Miskito people, and to feel the spiritual power of the mighty Río Coco should not be missed.

Accommodations and Food

Accommodations are frequently basic but reasonable (you might want to bring your own mosquito net).

At **Las Cabañas** ($4-14 d) the cost varies depending on how much comfort you'd like. At the top end, the rooms even have cable TV. ★ **Hotelito El Piloto** (north end of the main street, 2 minutes from Wangki, tel. 505/8642-4405, $25 s, $35 d) has air-conditioned single rooms with private bathrooms and a kitchen area with meals available.

In the main house of **La Estancia de Rose** (across from the airport, tel. 505/8944-2335, $16 d with fan, $21 with a/c) all the rooms have private bathrooms and 24-hour electricity. Three meals are available, as well as Internet and satellite TV. Rose has the town's

Waspám and the Río Coco

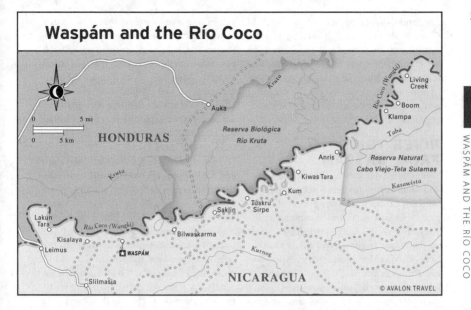

© AVALON TRAVEL

only Internet connection, adjacent to the *hospedaje.*

There are several small eateries in town, most serving rice and beans accompanied by a hunk of meat, sometimes fish. You can ensure fish or shrimp for dinner by arranging beforehand with the restaurant that you intend to eat at later that day. Vegetables are scarce and any salad usually consists of cabbage and some tomatoes in vinegar. Eggs are usually available. Ask to try some *wabul*, a thick, warm, green banana drink, which has many variations. Coconut bread can usually be found at the market during the evening, when it's still warm from the oven, or in the early morning. **Papta Watía** (between the dock and the church, $3-6) is currently the best meal in town, though other places appear sporadically and then disappear after a few months in business.

Information and Services

There is a local, underequipped **police station** in town and a health clinic with very basic services. The Catholic church has a private **clinic** with slightly better service and

more supplies. In case of an emergency, go to the convent and tell the nuns. One of the attending doctors speaks good English.

Getting There and Away

La Costeña (tel. 505/8738-4387, www.lacostena.com.ni) pilots radio ahead to have someone shoo the cattle away. Midday flights leave Managua Tuesday, Thursday, and Saturday. The flight (90 minutes, $103 one-way, $160 round-trip) passes over some of the most exotic scenery in Nicaragua.

Land transportation to Waspám can be arranged in Bilwi. The grueling bus trip takes 5 hours when the road is in good condition and it isn't raining; in the rainy season it can take as long as 12 hours. Two or three daily Waspám-bound buses ($10) leave Bilwi at the crack of dawn; get there early for the 6am bus. The following day, the same buses leave Waspám at the crack of dawn bound for Bilwi. Because all the buses leave their respective starting points in the morning, day trips are impossible.

A truck—a lumbering, diesel-belching IFA—leaves Bilwi every morning between

5am and 6am. Many opt to travel with El Chino Kung Fu, a local character with a decent pickup truck who makes regular trips between Waspám and Bilwi. Ask around and try to form a group to share the costs. Bear in mind that hitchhiking runs the danger of being an unknowing accomplice to transporting narcotics.

RIVER TRIPS FROM WASPÁM

Waspám is your gateway to the Río Coco, and small boats—fiberglass *pangas* and dugout *batu* canoes—are your means of transport. One local volunteer recommends the *panga* trip to San Carlos, which has a simple *hospedaje*. In the upriver villages located between Waspám and Leimus, visitors are not common and facilities are somewhere between limited and nonexistent. Don't plan on staying overnight or finding food for sale.

Nothing is easy or cheap, by the standards of travelers accustomed to the prices of the Pacific side. In general, expect to pay $50-100 per person per day for boat transportation along the Río Coco, which includes the boat, the gasoline, and the boatman. The dream adventure is a 550-kilometer voyage all the way up to Wiwilí, the upstream port town. El Bailarín ($1,000 pp round-trip) makes the trip from time to time.

Two tributaries to the Río Coco, the Yahuk and the Waspuk, are both home to waterfalls the locals say are beautiful places to visit but make for long trips. To visit the Yahuk, for example, you'd have to hire a boat for two days. The first day, you can motor up the Río Coco to the Yahuk and continue upstream to the falls, then spend the night in San Carlos, and return the following day. The Waspuk falls are reportedly a site of religious significance to the Miskito people. The trip is just upwards of 130 kilometers in each direction.

The Mining Triangle

Throughout the mining triangle (the term refers to the towns of Siuna, Bonanza, and Rosita), roads, power supply, and water systems are unreliable, and the towns are filled with drunks and cowboys. There are cheap places to stay and eat in all three towns, and Bonanza has a working Canadian-owned gold mine and a dozen casinos. Each town has a handful of natural attractions nearby and local guides to get you there. The Bosawás reserve, to the north, is one of the largest expanses of wilderness in Central America.

SIUNA

In the heart of the mining triangle, Siuna (pop. 12,000) is the best point of entry for the Bosawás Biosphere Reserve. It is home to a growing number of Mayangna Indians who have gradually migrated from the Atlantic coast and the Río Coco.

Accommodations and Food

Hotel Siu (Barrio Sol de Libertad, from the police station, 1 block west and 1 block south, tel. 505/2794-2028 or 505/2794-2093, $20 d with fan, $23 with a/c) has nice rooms and tasty meals. **Los Chinitos** (Barrio Luis Delgadillo, tel. 505/2794-2121, $16 d with fan, $20 with a/c), with a range of 15 rooms, is clean and well recommended. It has a nice wooden deck and lounging area.

Las Praderas (Barrio Campo Viejo, near URACCAN, $6-10) is recommended for dining. Or, rub elbows with the cowboys over steaks at **El Machin** (tel. 505/8840-8193).

Beer joints are everywhere. Locals prefer **El Secreto** (on the landing strip in the center of town), a gritty disco that seems to be full all weekend. Eat at the *fritanga* right outside.

A Few Miskito Phrases

The Miskito language doesn't use the vowel sounds "e" (as in bread) or "o" (as in boat), which makes it a flowing, rhythmic language of "a," "i," and "u." Here are some phrases you might come across during your travels in the northeast:

ENGLISH	MISKITO
Hello	Naksa
Goodbye	Aisabi
What is your name?	Ninam dia?
How are you?	Nahki sma?
Fine	Pain
Bad	Saura
Sick	Siknis
Thank you	Tingki pali
Food	Plun
Toilet	Tailit
Water	Li
Dirty	Taski
Clean	Klin
Meat	Wina
Chicken	Kalila
Rice and beans	Rais n bins
Fish	Inska
Small boat	Duri
Lagoon	Kabu
River	Awala
Birds	Natnawira nani
Parrot	Rahwaa

Getting There

La Costeña (www.lacostena.com.ni) runs separate flights to all three towns from Managua that leave every morning. The flight to **Bonanza** (tel. 505/2794-0023, 90 minutes, $96 one-way, $148 round-trip) leaves first, followed by a plane to **Siuna** (tel. 505/2794-2017, 90 minutes, $83 one-way, $127 round-trip), and then **Rosita** (tel. 505/2794-1015, 1 hour, $96 one-way, $148 round-trip). Bilwi-bound buses will drop you in Siuna or Rosita ($12) halfway through the journey from Managua.

★ BOSAWÁS BIOSPHERE RESERVE

Located 350 kilometers north of Managua, the 730,000 hectares of land collectively known as Bosawás are located within the municipalities of Waspám, Bonanza, Siuna, El Cuá-Bocay, Wiwilí, and Waslala. Although inhabited by some 40,000 widely dispersed people (more than half of whom are Mayangna and Miskito), most of Bosawás remains unexplored, unmapped, and untamed. Its name is derived from the region's three most salient features: the Río Bocay (BO), Cerro Saslaya (SA), and the Río Waspuk (WAS).

It's the largest uninterrupted tract of primary rainforest north of the Amazon. Besides unparalleled stretches of cloud forest, Bosawás contains tropical humid forest, rainforest, and a wealth of disparate ecosystems that vary in altitude from 30 meters above sea level at the mouth of the Waspuk River to the 1,650-meter peak of Cerro Saslaya. Bosawás is a Central American treasure, an immense genetic reserve of species that have vanished elsewhere in Mesoamerica, including jaguars, rare small mammals, 12 kinds of poisonous snakes, and many bird species, including the gorgeous scarlet macaw and 34 boreal migratory species.

Bosawás was designated a protected reserve in 1997, but where there is no money, there is little enforcement and few rangers. There are many more desperately poor who continue to make a living from this ancient land. In many cases, this translates into slash-and-burn clearing of the forests and the continual push of the agricultural frontier, mostly for subsistence. The 1.8 million acres of protected area was declared a part of the Nature Conservancy's international Parks in Peril program in 2001.

Visiting the Reserve

To do anything in Bosawás, you *must* receive permission (free). In Siuna, talk to the **Bosawás Office** (at central park near the stadium, not far from Hotelito Los Chinitos, tel.

505/2794-2036) who will help arrange a guide. There is also a park office in Bonanza (Barrio Marcos Antonio Samarriba, tel. 505/2794-0109), located in the MARENA office, that can help you find local trails and guides. The Bonanza **INTUR** (next to Casa Materna in the mayor's office, tel. 505/8665-9534, Mon.-Fri. 8am-noon and 1pm-5pm) delegate can also help you get in touch with the Bosawás Offices. **Guides** ($15-25/day plus food) are both obligatory and absolutely necessary. You may be convinced to hire two guides for your trip, a recommended safety and comfort precaution.

Unless you have months to explore the reserve, you'll have to pick and choose from various possible destinations. Get off the bus at Casa Roja (1.5 hours from Siuna) to stage an ascent of Cerro Saslaya (4-5 days); or continue to Santa Rosita (2.5-hour bus ride) for a two-hour hike to the river or trailhead to Cerro El Torro (4-5 days). Waslala is a 4-5 hour ride from Siuna and home to the original tomb of Carlos Fonseca (his remains were moved to Managua after the revolution's victory).

Be advised: Any trip in Bosawás is a serious backcountry undertaking and should not be attempted without proper supplies, some wilderness experience, a tolerance for dampness and discomfort, and a basic survival instinct. You should already have supplies like water bottles, a mosquito net, and some kind of pump or purifying tablets for water (start your hike with at least three liters; a fresh source is available in the park), a brimmed hat, sunscreen, sturdy shoes, and a medical kit. Additional supplies that can be purchased in Siuna or Bonanza include rubber boots (for snakes and knee-level mud), four yards of heavy black plastic for a roof in the jungle, a piece of plastic or waterproof cover for your backpack, a machete, a hammock, extra rope, and food.

Take a local bus to Rosa Grande, then walk or rent a horse ($5/day) to Rancho Alegre. From there, the journey is a challenging one-hour hike through the community of Rancho Alegre to a series of waterfalls at Salto Labu. Another one-hour hike up a steep path leads to Mirador, a lookout and an incredible view of an absolutely stunning waterfall, before you reach the primary forest on the path into Bosawás.

Background

The Landscape

The largest and lowest Central American country, Nicaragua is a nation of geographical superlatives. Located at the elbow where the Central American isthmus bends and then plummets southward to Panamá, Nicaragua is almost dead center between North and South America and is approximately the size of Greece or New York State.

GEOGRAPHY

Nicaragua's nickname, "The Land of Lakes and Volcanoes," evokes its primary geographical features: two great lakes and a chain of impressive and active volcanoes. Nicaragua's water and volcanic resources have had an enormous effect on its human history, from the day the first Nahuatl people settled on the forested shores of Lake Cocibolca (Lake Nicaragua) to the first Spanish settlements along the lakes to the plans to build a trans-isthmus canal.

Convergence of the plates ensures crustal instability, which manifests itself in frequent volcanic and earthquake activity in all of Central America, and especially in Nicaragua. Usually, earthquakes are so small they go unnoticed. In April 2014, consistent earthquakes over the course of a week led to serious damage in many homes in Nagarote, as well as permanent damage to several structures in Managua, including the large amphitheater in La Plaza de la Fe that once dominated Managua's waterfront.

Volcanoes

Nicaragua has about 40 volcanoes, a half dozen of which are usually active at any time. Running parallel to the Pacific shore, Nicaragua's volcanoes are a part of the Ring of Fire that encompasses most of the western coast of the Americas, the Aleutian Islands of Alaska, Japan, and Indonesia. The Maribio (Nahuatl for the "giant men") and Dirian volcano ranges stretch nearly 300 kilometers from Concepción and Maderas in the middle of Lake Cocibolca to Cosigüina, which juts into the Gulf of Fonseca.

The first volcanic event in recorded history was a major eruption of Volcán Masaya in the early 1500s. The lava formed the present-day lagoon at the base of the mountain. Another great lava flow occurred in 1772, leaving a black, barren path still visible today where the Carretera Masaya highway crosses it. In 1609, Spanish settlers abandoned the city of León when Momotombo erupted. In January 1835, Volcán Cosigüina violently blew its top, hurling ash as far away as Jamaica and Mexico, covering the area for 250 kilometers around the volcano in ash and burning pumice and forcing the entire peninsula into three days of darkness. All this volcanic activity is responsible for the exceptional fertility of Nicaragua's soils, most notably the agricultural plains around Chinandega and León.

Volcán Masaya is the most easily accessed of Nicaragua's volcanoes and boasts a paved road leading right to the lip of the crater. Volcán Masaya is actually formed of three craters, the largest of which, Santiago, is the only crater in the Americas that contains a visible pool of incandescent liquid lava in its center. The visibility of this lava fluctuates on a 30-year cycle.

Climbing a few Nicaraguan giants is a great way to experience Central America. **San Cristóbal** is the highest peak, at 1,745 meters. A smaller peak adjacent to San Cristóbal, **Volcán Casita** still bears the immense scar of the landslide that buried thousands in an

---

Previous: *nacatamales* heating over firewood; soccer game on Ometepe.

avalanche of rock and mud during Hurricane Mitch and trembled briefly again in January 2002. Isla de Ometepe's twin cones are popular for hiking and easily accessible. No matter where you hike, always hire a guide, as several foreigners have gotten lost and perished while peak bagging.

Momotombo, San Cristóbal, and **Telica** are the most active peaks and are prone to emit plumes of poisonous gases, smoke, and occasionally lava. La Isla de Ometepe's **Volcán Concepción** (1,610 meters) last blew its top in 2009 and 2012. The other half of Ometepe (Nahuatl for "two peaks") is **Volcán Maderas** (1,394 meters), which sleeps, its crater drowned in a deep lagoon that feeds a thriving jungle.

Volcán Telica, just north of León, erupts approximately every five years, while gas vents at its base churn out boiling mud and sulfur. Neighboring **Cerro Negro** is one of the youngest volcanoes on the planet: It protruded through a farmer's field in the middle of the 1800s and has since grown in size, steadily and violently, to a height of 400 meters. Cerro Negro's last three eruptions have been increasingly powerful, culminating in 1992 when it belched up a cloud of burning gases and ash seven kilometers high, burying León under 15 centimeters of ash and dust. Eight thousand inhabitants were evacuated as the weight of the ash caused several homes to collapse. Volcán Momotombo's (Nahuatl for "great burning peak") perfect conical peak is visible from great distances across the Pacific plains, as far away as Matagalpa. Momotombo is responsible for approximately 10 percent of Nicaragua's electricity via a geothermal plant located at its base. It hasn't erupted since 1905, but Momotombo remains a monster whose menace is taken quite seriously. In April 2000 it rumbled long enough to get Managua's attention, then quieted back down.

A popular day trip from Granada is the cloud forest park and coffee plantations of **Volcán Mombacho** (1,345 meters), a dormant volcano whose explosion and self-destruction formed the archipelago of *isletas* in

Lake Cocibolca. Mombacho took its modern shape in 1570 when a major avalanche on the south slope opened and exposed the crater, burying an indigenous village of 400 inhabitants in the process.

Lakes and Lagoons

Two lakes, Cocibolca (Lake Nicaragua) and Xolotlán (Lake Managua), dominate Nicaragua's geography, occupying together nearly 10 percent of the country's surface area. **Lake Xolotlán** is broad (1,025 square kilometers) and shallow, with an average depth of seven meters. It is at its deepest (26 meters) near the island of Momotombito. Lake Xolotlán is, for the most part, biologically dead, after a century of untreated human waste and extensive dumping of industrial wastes, including benzene and mercury, during the 1970s. The tremendous opportunities for tourism, recreation, and potable water that a clean lake would facilitate have led to an ambitious plan to detoxify Xolotlán. Backed by loans from Japan and the World Bank, the project has begun treating Managua's sewage and, gradually, cleansing the lake in water treatment plants on the lakeshore. See the result for yourself on a booze cruise from Managua's Malecón.

Lake Cocibolca, the larger of Nicaragua's two lakes, is one of Nicaragua's greatest natural treasures. At 8,264 square kilometers and 160 kilometers long along its axis, Lake Cocibolca is nearly as big as the island of Puerto Rico and lies 31 meters above sea level. It's also deep (up to 60 meters in some places) and relatively clean. The prevailing winds, which blow from the east across the farmlands of Chontales, make the eastern part of Cocibolca calm and the western half choppy and rough. A massive pipe system carries drinking water from Cocibolca to surrounding towns. In 2014 plans for an interoceanic canal were announced; the planned route would involve dredging a large section of Lake Cocibolca and is expected to have disastrous environmental impacts.

Nearly a dozen stunning lagoons mark

the maws of ancient volcanic craters. Near Managua is **la Loma de Tiscapa** lagoon. West of Managua, the picturesque twin craters of **Xiloá** and **Apoyeque** form the Chiltepe peninsula. Near Masaya, the 200-meter-deep **Laguna de Apoyo** was formed sometime in the Quaternary period (1.6 MYA) by what is thought to be the most violent volcanic event in Nicaragua's prehistory. Not far away is **Laguna de Masaya,** at the base of the volcano of the same name. There are other gorgeous lagoons in the craters of the Maderas and Consigüina volcanoes, which flank Volcán Momotombo to the south and north, respectively.

Rivers

To the original Spanish settlers in Granada, the Río San Juan was the elusive "drain" of Lake Cocibolca. Since then, the possibility of traveling up the Río San Juan, across Lake Cocibolca, and then by land to the Pacific Ocean has made the San Juan the most historically important river in Nicaragua. In the years of the gold rush, thousands of prospectors navigated up the Río San Juan en route to California. Some made the return trip laden with riches, others with nothing. These days, several sets of rapids and decades of sedimentation reduce its navigability, exacerbated by shifts in the riverbed from occasional earthquakes. The river is regularly dredged to allow boat traffic to pass.

Formed by the confluence of three major rivers—the Siquia, Mico, and Rama—the **Río Escondido** is the principal link in the transportation corridor from Managua to Bluefields and the Atlantic coast. Produce and merchandise (and busloads of travelers) reach El Rama and then proceed down the Escondido. The Escondido and its tributaries are important to the cattle industry in Chontales, but massive deforestation along its banks have unleashed dangerous floods that frequently put the river port of El Rama under water.

The 680-kilometer-long **Río Coco** is the longest river in Central America, fed by headwaters in Nicaragua and Honduras. Also known as the Río Segovia or its indigenous name Wanki, the Coco traverses terrain that varies from several minor canyons to vast stretches of virgin forest. The indigenous Miskito people, for whom the river bears great spiritual significance, live in small communities along its shores.

The **Estero Real** (Royal Estuary), at 137 kilometers in length, is the most consequential body of water on the Pacific coast and is one of Nicaragua's best places to spot waterfowl. It drains most of northwestern Nicaragua through extensive mangroves and wetlands to the Gulf of Fonseca and is the nucleus of extensive shrimp-farming operations.

CLIMATE

Nicaragua's tropical climate ranges 27-32°C (81-90°F) during the rainy season, and 30-35°C (86-95°F) in the dry season. It varies remarkably by region: In the mountains of Matagalpa and Jinotega, the temperature can be 10°C cooler, while in León and Matagalpa, they can be 10°C warmer. *Invierno* (winter, or rainy season) lasts approximately May-October, and *verano* (summer, or dry season) lasts November-April. Rain during these months may mean just a quick shower each afternoon, or a deluge that lasts for days. As you travel east toward the Atlantic coast or down the Río San Juan, the rainy season grows longer and wetter until the dry season only lasts the month of April.

ENVIRONMENTAL ISSUES
Deforestation

Nicaragua's primordial environmental concern is the rapid loss of forests—at the rate of 150,000 hectares per year. The great majority of country-dwellers cook on firewood, so population expansion into previously unsettled lands has boded poorly for forests. Population pressure and the swelling cattle industry have pushed the agricultural frontier inward from both the Atlantic and Pacific sides of the country, reducing Nicaragua's forests by 4.6 million hectares from 1950 to 1995. From 1990 to 2010, forest cover was reduced by 21 percent. On the Atlantic coast, much of the hardwood logging is happening at the hands of U.S., Canadian, and Asian companies that have negotiated lucrative timber concessions with Nicaragua's successive cash-strapped governments. Nearly half of the timber cut in Nicaragua is illegally logged.

Nueva Segovian pine forests are under further ecological pressure from pine bark beetles, which bore into the trees to feed on resin. At the start of each rainy season, young beetles disperse and fly longer distances. The infestation can spread up to 20 meters per day. That's a full kilometer in just under two months.

Deforestation exposes fragile tropical soils to rainfall, leading to erosion, contamination and elimination of water sources, and outright microclimate changes. In much of Nicaragua, within one human generation, once-perennial rivers and streams now flow only sporadically, if at all. On the Pacific coast, decades of chemical-intensive agriculture and wind erosion have caused the loss of once-rich volcanic soils. In general, the entire Pacific, central, and northern regions of the country are at immediate risk of sustained soil erosion. Efforts are underway to attack the problem from all sides, from environmental education of children to active replanting of hillsides, to the introduction of less-destructive agricultural techniques.

National Parks and Reserves

Nicaragua's complex system of parks and reserves encompasses more than two million hectares. The Sistema Nacional de Areas Protegidas (SINAP) is made up of 76 parks, reserves, and refuges classified as "protected" by the Ministerio del Ambiente y los Recursos Naturales (Ministry of the Environment and Natural Resources, or MARENA). Of these, many are privately owned land, which strains enforcement of their protected status. That, combined with MARENA's paltry resource

base and budget, has led to the decentralization of park management. Since 2001, MARENA has been experimenting with the co-management model in six natural reserves, handing natural-resource management responsibilities over to local NGOs who work with the communities within the areas to create sustainable alternatives to natural resource use and ecotourism infrastructure. While co-management has been successful in some areas, the great majority of protected lands in Nicaragua remain unmanaged, unguarded, and completely undeveloped for tourism. They are sometimes referred to as "paper parks," existing only in legislation and studies. The Río Estero Real, a wetlands preserve in the northwest corner of the country, is one of those, where half of the "protected" territory has been granted to private shrimp farmers who have eliminated most of the mangrove swamps and lagoons where shrimp once bred naturally, replacing them with artificial breeding pools.

Remoteness and neglect provide meager protection to some regions. More frequently Nicaragua's richest treasures succumb to foreign and national cattle, logging, and mining interests. *Campesino* (country folk) populations given little incentive or education to better manage the land are equally destructive. Worst of all are the cases where the government "protects" a territory where people have been living traditionally for generations. They are suddenly expected to drastically alter their fishing, hunting, and planting patterns to protect a "park" that is their homeland. For example, the Mayangna and Miskito people were not consulted during the planning of the Bosawás Biosphere Reserve. Consequently, they have fought against new regulations that interfere with their traditional lifestyle.

Conversely, Fundación Cocibolca, managing La Flor, has staffed the reserve with local residents and turned to them for input on how to run it. Tourism can go a long way toward bolstering local incentive to protect—rather than consume—the natural world.

Plants and Animals

Part of a biological corridor that for millions of years has allowed plant and animal species from two continents to mingle, Nicaragua boasts an extraordinary blend of flora and fauna.

PLANTS

Of the world's known 250,000 species of flowering plants, an estimated 15,000-17,000 are found in Central America. Nicaragua is home to 9,000 species of vascular plants, many of medicinal value. But outside a few protected areas, conservation efforts are half-hearted or underfunded, and even protected areas are under intense pressure from the agricultural frontier and the scattered human settlements grandfathered within the confines of the reserves.

The *madroño (Calycophyllum candidissimum)* is Nicaragua's national tree. The hills south of Sébaco form the southern limit of the pine family found on the continent; south of Nicaragua, the pines are out-competed by other species. At the turn of the millennium, Nicaragua's forest area measured 5.5 million

hectares, the majority of which is broadleaf forest, followed by pine *(Pinus caribea* and *P. oocarpa)*. At altitudes greater than 1,200 meters, the forests also include the conifers *P. maximinoi* and *P. tecunumanii*. A full 2.5 million hectares of forest are classified as commercial timber forest. Though often privately owned, the Nicaraguan government regulates exploitation of forest products (and not infrequently simply sells the forests for its own profit).

Principal Ecosystems

Nicaragua's varied topography and uneven rainfall distribution, not to mention the presence of tropical reefs, volcanoes, and volcanic crater lakes, result in a phenomenal diversity of terrain and ecosystems. You can burn your feet on an active volcano's peak and cool your heels in ocean surf the same day. Nicaragua's higher peaks are isolated ecosystems in their own right and home to several endangered as well as endemic species. The streams, rivers, and two very different coastlines furnish myriad other distinct ecosystems. In general,

tiny orchid in Los Guatuzos

This tree's conical spikes store water.

the land is comprised of the following ecological zones:

Pacific Dry Forest: The lowlands of the Pacific coast, specifically the broad, flat strip that borders the Pacific Ocean from sea level to approximately 800 meters in altitude, are a rain-stressed region dominated by thorny, rubbery species. The region typically receives less than 2,000 millimeters of rain per year. Both trees and non-cactuslike plants in this ecosystem shed their leaves in the middle of the dry season, and burst into flower in April or May.

Upland Pine Forest: With the exception of the slopes of several Pacific mountains, namely San Cristóbal and Las Casitas in Chinandega and Güisisíl in Matagalpa, the majority of Nicaragua's pine forests are found in the north near Jalapa and Ocotal. Pines particularly thrive on poor, acidic soils, which erode easily if the area is logged.

Lower Mountainous Broadleaf Forest: Nicaragua's higher peaks are cloud covered for most of the year and home to a cool, moist

biosphere, rich in flora and fauna. Most of these areas are the more remote peaks of Matagalpa and Jinotega, like Kilambé, Peñas Blancas, Saslaya, and Musún. It's easier to enjoy this ecosystem on the beautiful and easily visited peaks of Volcán Mombacho near Granada, and Volcán Maderas on Ometepe.

Caribbean Rainy Zone: The Atlantic coast receives rain throughout nearly 10 months of the year and the humidity hovers around 90 percent year-round. Most of the Atlantic coast is covered with tropical forest or even lowland rainforest, with trees that often reach 30 or 40 meters. In the north along the Río Coco are the remains of Nicaragua's last extensive pine forests *(Pinus caribaea)*, presently subject to intensive logging by national and international concessions.

ANIMALS

Nicaragua is home to a great deal of exotic wildlife, much of which, unfortunately, you'll only see for sale on the sides of the highways and at intersections in Managua, where merchants peddle toucans, reptiles, ocelots, parrots, and macaws. This is a considerable, largely unchecked problem. Of the animals that are captured for sale or export in Nicaragua, 80 percent die before reaching their final destination. Viewing fauna in their natural habitat involves being still, looking, and listening. Most critters are shy and many are nocturnal. To date, 1,804 vertebrate species, including 21 species endemic to Nicaragua, and 14,000 invertebrate species have been defined. However, Nicaragua remains the least-studied country in the region. Excursions into the relatively unexplored reserves of the north and northeast will surely uncover previously undiscovered species.

Mammals

One-hundred seventy-six mammal species (including sea life) are known to exist in Nicaragua, more than half of which are bats or small mammals. Of the at least three endemic mammal species, two are associated with the Caribbean town of El Rama: the **Rama** squirrel *(Sciurus richmondi),* considered the tropical world's most endangered squirrel, and the **Rama rice mouse** *(Oryzomis dimidiatus).*

Nicaragua is also home to six big cat species. All six are listed as endangered, most seriously of all the **jaguar** and **puma,** both of which require vast amounts of wild hunting territory. In the Pacific region, isolated communities on the higher slopes of some forested volcanoes like Mombacho may remain, but they have not been seen. In the Atlantic region, small communities of cats survive in the dense forests of the southeast side of the Bosawás reserve. These species are unstudied and untracked, and are presumably preyed upon by local communities. The smaller feline species like **ocelots** and *tigrillos* have fared better. Though they are largely trapped in the central forests, the latter at least makes a decent living preying on farming community chickens.

There are three kinds of monkeys in Nicaragua: the **mantled howler monkey** *(Alouata palliata),* known popularly as the *mono congo;* the **Central American spider monkey** *(Ateles geoffroyii);* and the **white-faced capuchin** *(Cebus capucinus).* Of the

monkeys, the howler monkey is the most common: 1,000 individuals roam the slopes of Mombacho alone. You can also find them on Ometepe and the mountains of Matagalpa, particularly Selva Negra. Howler monkeys can project their throaty, haunting cries to distances as great as several kilometers. They eat fruits and leaves and spend most of their time in high tree branches. The threatened white-faced capuchin lives in the forests in southeastern Nicaragua and parts of the Atlantic coast. The spider monkey has nearly been eliminated and is the most threatened of the three.

The **Baird's tapir** is present in very small numbers in eastern Nicaragua. Several communities of this three-toed ungulate inhabit Bosawás, but this species is threatened with extinction. The **agouti paca** (a large, forest-dwelling rodent known in Nicaragua as the painted rabbit), the **white-tailed deer** *(Odocoileus virginianus),* and the **collared peccary** *(Tayassu tajacu),* a stocky piglike creature with coarse, spiky fur, though abundant, are under much pressure from hunters throughout northeastern Nicaragua. You may still see an agouti or peccary east of Jinotega if you're lucky.

Take a tour to discover local wildlife, including monkeys, in Los Guatuzos.

turquoise-browed motmot, also known as the *guardabarranco*

Aquatic Life

A wide variety of both saltwater and freshwater species of fish take advantage of the two large lakes, two ocean coastlines, and numerous isolated crater lakes. Among Nicaragua's many **saltwater species** are flat needlefish *(Ablennes hians)*, wahoo *(Acanthocybium solandri)*, three kinds of sole, spotted eagle rays *(Aetobatus narinari)*, the Gill's sand lance *(Ammodytoides gilli)*, two kinds of moray *(Anarchias sp.)*, croakers *(Bairdiella sp.)*, triggerfish *(Balistes sp.)*, hogfish *(Bodianus sp.)*, eight kinds of perch *(Diplectrum sp.)*, sea bass *(Diplectrum sp.)*, and a dozen kinds of shark, including blacktip *(Carcharias limbatus)*, great white *(C. carcharias)*, silky *(C. falciformis)*, and spinner *(C. brevipinna)*.

Among the **freshwater species** are needlefish *(Strongylura sp.)*, grunts *(Pomadasys sp.)*, introduced tilapia *(Oreochromis aureus)*, catfish *(Hexanematichthys sp.)*, mojarra *(Eucinostomus sp.)*, and snook *(Centropomus sp.)*. Some species of cichlid *(Amphilophus*

sp.) found nowhere else in the world swim in Nicaragua's varied crater lakes.

At least 58 different types of **marine corals** have been identified in the Atlantic, specifically in the Miskito Cays, Corn Island, and the Pearl Cays. Studied for the first time in 1977 and 1978, the shallow reefs of the Pearl Cays contain the best coral formations in the nation, but are now threatened by the enormous sediment load discharged by the Río Grande de Matagalpa.

The **manatee** *(Trichechus manatus)* is an important species currently protected by international statutes. You may see it at the mouth of the Río San Juan and in the coastal lagoons, notably in Bluefields Bay. In 1993, the **freshwater dolphin** *(Sotalia fluviatilis)* was first spotted in Nicaragua and since then has been occasionally sighted in Laguna de Wounta, despite conjecture that this species' northern range was Panamá.

Birds

Thousands of bird species migrate through the Central American biosphere corridor. To date, 676 species of birds in 56 families have been observed here, the more exotic of which live in the mountains of the north and east, and along the Atlantic shore. Nicaragua has no endemic bird species, but hosts 87 percent of all known bird species. The most exotic species known to reside in Nicaragua is also its most elusive, the **quetzal** *(Pharomacrus mocinno)*, known to inhabit highlands in Bosawás, Jinotega, and Matagalpa, especially along the slopes of Mt. Kilambé, and in Miraflor in Estelí.

Nicaragua's elegant and colorful national bird is the turquoise-browed motmot, also known as the ***guardabarranco*** *(Momotus momota)*. The Guardian of the Stream (as its Spanish name translates) can be found catching small insects in urban gardens in the capital. It is distinguished by its long, odd-shaped, iridescent tail, which it carefully preens to catch the eye of the opposite sex. The ***urraca*** is a bigger, meaner version of the North American blue jay, with a dangly black crest on the top of its head. It's one of the larger of the common birds in Nicaragua and scolds humans from the treetops. Though the *urraca* are everywhere, a particularly sizeable population patrols the slopes of Ometepe's twin volcanoes and Las Isletas by Granada. Also in Las Isletas, look for the brightly colored **oropendolas** *(Psarocolius wagleri)* that hang their elaborate, suspended bag-nests from the treetops around the lakeshore.

Reptiles

Of the 172 reptile species in Nicaragua, nearly half are North American, found in Nicaragua at the southern limit of their habitat. Fifteen species are found only in Central America and another five are endemic to Nicaragua.

You'll see a lot of the common **Asian House Gecko** *(Hemidactylus frenatus)* on walls and windows, especially around lights, where they wait to catch bugs. They're often referred to as *perrozompopos*, especially in Managua.

Nicaragua's several species of marine turtles are all in danger of extinction. The **Paslama turtle** *(Lepidochelys olivacea)* in the Pacific and the **Carey turtle** *(Eretmochelys imbricata)* and **Green turtle** *(Chelonia mydas)* in the Atlantic are protected, and

much effort has gone into setting aside habitat for them. However, the struggle against those who'd like to harvest their eggs, meat, and shells is fierce. There are approximately 20 beaches in the Pacific whose conditions permit the nesting of these turtle species, most of which play host to only occasional nesting events. But two beaches, Chacocente and La Flor on the Pacific coast, are the nesting grounds of the Paslama turtle and experience massive annual egg-laying events between July and January (primarily during the first and third quarters of the moon). In them, 57,000 and 100,000 turtles crawl up on the moist sand at night to lay eggs. Only 1 out of 100 hatchlings makes it to adulthood. Armed guards on these beaches try to make sure the youngsters make it to the sea instead of the soup.

Alligators, crocodiles *(Crocodilus acutus)*, **caimans** *(Caiman crocodilus)*, and the **Ñoca turtle** *(Trachemys scripta)* are frequently seen along the Río San Juan and some larger rivers of Jinotega. The ***garrobo*** is a bush lizard the size of a small house cat you're more likely to see suspended by its tail on the side of the road than in the wild. Poor *campesino* children hunt and sell them to passing motorists who make an aphrodisiac

Amphibians inhabit Nicaragua's forests and riversides.

soup from the meat. Similarly, the *cusuco* (*Dasypus novemincinctus*) is a type of armadillo with plated sides and sharp-clawed feet, commonly found in drier areas of the countryside.

Amphibians

Sixty-four known species of amphibians, four of which are endemic, live in Nicaragua's humid forests and riversides. They include the **Mombacho salamander** (*Bolitoglossa mombachoensis*), the **miadis frog,** the **Cerro Saslaya frog** (*Plectrohyla sp.*), and the **Saslaya salamander** (*Nolitron sp.*).

Insects

Each of Nicaragua's different ecosystems has a distinct insect population. Estimates of the total number of species reach as high as 250,000, only 1 percent of which have been identified. Notable species to seek out are several gigantic species of **beetles,** including *Dynastes hercules* (found in cloud forests); several species of brilliant green and golden **Plusiotis** (found in Cerro Saslaya and Cerro Kilambé); the iridescent blue butterfly *Morpho peleides,* common all over the country, and its less common cousin, *M. amathonte,* found at altitudes of 300-700 meters, especially in the forests of Bosawás. Nocturnal moths like the **Rothschildia, Eacles,** and others are common. There is an increasing number of *mariposarios* (butterfly farms) in Nicaragua, notably in Los Guatuzos, Papaturro, El Castillo (Río San Juan), and San Ramón (Matagalpa).

History

PRE-COLONIAL YEARS

A Caribbean coastal people known as *Los Concheros* (the shell collectors) are the first evidence of human settlement on Nicaraguan soil 8,000 years ago. Two thousand years later humans living on the southern shores of Lake Managua left their footprints in drying mud in an archaeological site called *Las Huellas de Acahualinca.* Agriculture began around 5,000 years ago with the cultivation of corn, and pottery making followed 2,000 years later.

Sometime in the 13th century, the Chorotega and Nicarao people, under pressure from the aggressive Aztecs in Mexico, fled south through the Central American isthmus, led by a vision of a land dominated by a great lake. The Chorotegas settled on the shores of Lake Cocibolca and around the volcanic craters of Masaya and Apoyo, and the Nicaraos settled farther south.

COLONIALISM (1519-1821)

In July 1502, Christopher Columbus (Cristóbal Colón in Spanish) skirted Nicaragua's Mosquito Coast, then continued on to South America. Seventeen years later, the conquistador Pedro Arias Dávila returned under orders from the Spanish crown to explore the land bridge of Nicaragua. Indigenous leaders Nicarao and Diriangén engaged them in a brief battle. But regardless, Francisco Hernández de Córdoba arrived soon after to establish Spain's first settlements in the new land. Córdoba settled Granada alongside the Chorotega communities on the banks of Lake Cocibolca, and, forging farther inland and up the Tipitapa River, the settlement of León on the western shores of Lake Xolotlán. Nicaragua remained a part of Spain's overseas possessions for the next 300 years under the governance of the colonial capital in Guatemala.

INDEPENDENCE, WILLIAM WALKER, AND THE U.S. MARINES (1821-1937)

Central America won its independence from Spain in 1821, and for a short time remained

U.S. Intervention in Nicaragua

In President Teddy Roosevelt's addition to the Monroe Doctrine of regional dominance, he proclaimed that the United States, by virtue of its status as a "civilized nation," had the right to stop "chronic wrongdoing" throughout the Western Hemisphere. Subsequently, the so-called Roosevelt Corollary was used to justify troop deployment to Latin America 32 times between the end of the Spanish-American War and the years of the Great Depression. President William Howard Taft provided further rationalization for aggressively dominating Latin America with his Dollar Diplomacy, an unabashed strategy to advance and protect U.S. businesses in other countries. Nicaragua, which had been host to U.S. fruit, mining, and transportation interests since the 1850s, was a frequent recipient of such foreign policy.

U.S. Marines landed at least seven times during the aforementioned period, and spent a total of 21 years occupying Nicaragua. Official reasons for these visits included "pacification of Nicaragua," "prevention of rebellion," and, of course, "protection of U.S. interests and property." It would be unfair to call these visits uninvited, since nearly all were ostensibly serving the purpose of one or more Nicaraguan oligarchs, usually of the Conservative Party.

The following is a more detailed list of gringo interventions.

1853: Washington sends U.S. Navy commander George H. Hollins to Greytown to extract an apology from local British officials for having insulted U.S. diplomat Solon Borland. Those responsible were nowhere to be found, so, reports a U.S. Marine Corps historical website, "Hollins' only alternative was to bombard the town, and this he tried to do in the most humane manner possible." Hollins allowed 24 hours for evacuation, then commenced firing. "At 0900 on 13 July, 177 shells plowed into Greytown. That afternoon a landing party of Marines and seamen completed the destruction of the town." Humanely, of course.

1853-1856: U.S. citizen William Walker usurps power and declares himself president of Nicaragua. He is briefly recognized by Washington before the other Central American nations briefly unite, drive him out, and eventually execute him by firing squad.

1894: The U.S. Marines under Lieutenant Franklin J. Moses have a month long occupation of Bluefields.

1896: In May, when fighting near Corinto "endangers American holdings," 15 Marines, under First Sergeant Frederick W. M. Poppe, and 19 seamen land in Corinto and stand guard in a "show of force."

1898: As President Zelaya extends his tenure for still another term, the local U.S. consular agent requests the U.S.S. *Alert*, at anchor in the harbor of Bluefields, to stand by in case of an attack on the city. On the morning of February 7, the U.S. flag on shore rises "union downward" over the consulate, signaling a force of 14 Marines and 19 seamen to land; they withdraw the following day.

1899: Another display of force lands, this time with a Colt automatic gun "to prevent both rebels and government troops from destroying American property."

1910: Marines and Navy vessels concentrate in Nicaraguan waters and land in Bluefields and Corinto on May 19 "to guard American property."

1912: Nicaraguan president Adolfo Díaz requests the support of U.S. forces. The United States complies when the U.S.S. *Annapolis* arrives in Corinto, deploying a contingent of naval officers to Managua on August 4. Three companies of marine infantry also land and are transported to Managua by train.

1927-1933: President Coolidge sends Marines to find Sandino and "gun the bandit down." They fail.

1981-1990: The CIA runs a secret command operation directing and financing Contra forces in their attempt to topple the Sandinista government. U.S operatives carry out supply and intelligence activities, train commanders and soldiers, plant harbor mines, and sabotage Sandinista holdings.

All citations from "Marine Corps Historical Reference Series, The United States Marines in Nicaragua," by Bernard C. Nalty, Historical Branch, G-3 Division, Headquarters, U.S. Marine Corps, Washington, D.C.

united as the five provinces of the Central American Federation. The belief that Europe would act militarily to return the former colonies to Spain forced the United States to issue the Monroe Doctrine in 1823, declaring the New World off limits to further European colonization and interference, paving the way for two centuries of political domination in Latin America. The Central American Federation was short-lived, however: When Nicaragua withdrew from the federation in 1838, the remaining states opted to become individual republics as well and the federation dissolved.

Newly independent Nicaragua was anarchic for years, dominated by the independent, feuding city-states of León and Granada until 1845 when a national government was finally agreed upon (the political rivalries endure to this day). In the early 19th century, export of cacao, indigo, and cattle allowed the landed and merchant classes to accumulate considerable wealth at the expense of the Native Americans and landless class. A nascent liberal class grew in León inspired by the French and American revolutions that sought more equal distribution of wealth.

Nicaragua's unique geography has inspired multiple plans for a transcontinental-canal over the years. During the California gold rush (1849-1856), prospectors transited Nicaragua courtesy of steamship baron and businessman Cornelius Vanderbilt's Pacific Steamship Company, then operating in Panamá. Travelers bound for California sailed up the Río San Juan and across Lake Cocibolca to the small port at San Jorge. There, they were taken by horse cart 18 kilometers across the narrow isthmus through Rivas to the bay of San Juan del Sur. Ships waiting in the harbor then carried the travelers north along the Pacific coastline to California. Vanderbilt dredged the channel of the Río San Juan and built roads, railroads, and docks on both coasts to accommodate the traffic. At about that time, the Leóneses, embroiled in a bitter battle with the Conservatives of Granada, enlisted the help of William Walker, an American filibuster

(and proponent of Manifest Destiny) who eventually installed himself as president of Nicaragua, razed the city of Granada, and caused a whole lot of trouble.

Though the relative peace of the 30-year Conservative period fostered many advances in infrastructure and technology, including the Granada-Corinto train and the telegraph, Nicaragua remained several decades behind its neighbors in coffee exportation. The economy mostly stagnated. The bourgeoisie became restless and rebelled, installing Liberal General José Santos Zelaya as president. Zelaya was a fierce nationalist who reclaimed the Atlantic region at gunpoint from its British occupants (the two administrative units of the Atlantic coast bore Zelaya's name until the 1990s). Zelaya furthermore rejected Washington's proposals to build a cross-isthmus canal through Nicaraguan territory while courting Great Britain to finance the construction of a transcontinental railway.

The United States, which since 1904 had been building the Panama Canal, felt threatened by the nationalist leader and his railway proposal and in 1909, sent the U.S. Marines to secure Zelaya's ouster. The U.S. intervention reestablished the Conservatives in power until 1912, when Liberal and nationalist Benjamin Zeledón led another rebellion. This time the U.S. Marine occupation happened on a much larger scale: 2,700 marines landed at Corinto and took immediate control of the railways, ports, and major cities.

Nicaragua became subject to the United States financially at about this time, as U.S. financial institutions began to quietly acquire coffee-export businesses and railway and steamship companies, easing Nicaragua into a credit noose. Under the watchful eye of the U.S. Marines, governmental control was handed over to the Conservatives, whom Washington thought would more faithfully represent U.S. business interests. But the Liberals staged 10 uprisings between 1913 and 1924, all of which the U.S. military quelled.

In 1924, Conservative President Bartolomé Martínez instituted a novel form of government: a power-sharing arrangement between the Liberals and the Conservatives at the local level. The United States withdrew Marines in 1925 but they were back within the year. No sooner had power sharing begun than ambitious Conservative Emilio Chamorro staged a coup d'état, seized power, and sparked the Constitutional War. The United States stepped in to prevent the imminent takeover by the Liberals, but because the Conservatives had discredited themselves, the United States was unable to simply hand the power back to them. The deal they worked out was known as the Espino Negro Pact (named after the town where it was signed; Spanish for "Black Thorn"). It was a crucial moment for the Liberals. One of their generals, Augusto C. Sandino, was opposed to the pact, and fled with his men to the northern mountains to start a guerrilla war in opposition of the continued presence of the United States in Nicaragua. The leader of the Constitutional Army was forced to declare, "All my men surrender except one."

Unaccustomed to guerilla warfare, the U.S. military tried unsuccessfully to flush Sandino from the mountains despite drastic measures like the aerial bombing of Ocotal. In 1933, Washington tried a new approach. Withdrawing U.S. troops from Nicaragua, the United States formed a new military unit called the National Guard and placed young Anastasio Somoza García at its head.

During the presidency of Juan Bautista Sacasa, Sandino enjoyed overwhelming support in Nicaragua's northern mountains, as he was perceived to have successfully accomplished both the repatriation of both U.S. armed forces and the removal of Conservative oligarchy from power. But he represented a major threat to Somoza's political and military ambitions. In February of 1934, President Sacasa invited him to Managua to negotiate an agreement. When Sandino left the presidential palace that night, several National Guard members ambushed and assassinated him on the streets of Managua. The National Guard immediately swept the northern countryside

subsequently, destroying cooperatives, returning lands to their previous owners, and hunting down, exiling, imprisoning, or killing Sandino's supporters.

AUGUSTO CÉSAR SANDINO (1893-1934)

The term Sandinista is easily associated with Nicaragua. Less well known is the story of the man, who, through his fight against imperialism, became a legend in Nicaragua and the world, and is recognized today by the mere rendering of his famous broadbrimmed hat.

Augusto C. Sandino was born in Niquinohomo (Nahuatl for "valley of warriors"), the bastard son of a wealthy, landed judge and one of his servant women. But while the judge lived well in town, Sandino's family was so poor they often resorted to stealing crops to eat. Sandino grew disgusted at Nicaraguan society, which engendered such inequity, and questioned both civil society and the Catholic Church, which he believed was guilty of reinforcing the aristocracy. At the age of 17, Sandino witnessed the U.S. Marine invasion of Nicaragua to prop up Adolfo Díaz's failing Conservative presidency. When they crushed a rebellion led by General Benjamin Zeledón, their parading of Zeledón's dead body through the streets of Masaya affected Sandino deeply. Nine years later, Sandino fled to Mexico where he was inspired by Tampico laborers struggling to unionize in spite of resistance from the U.S.-owned oil companies. Sandino returned to Nicaragua with a new sense of purpose and a strong self-identity shaped by anarchy, socialism, and armed conflict.

He became a renegade general from the Liberals and set up his camp in the mountains outside San Rafael del Norte, Jinotega, where he became one of the first to practice guerrilla warfare, staging effective hit-and-run raids against U.S. Marine installations in Ocotal and the north. Sandino's men, who grew to number nearly 1,800 by 1933, attacked some mining and lumber companies

Sandino is commonly depicted with his distinctive hat.

ranchers and businessmen to support them. He also fought in support of the exploited timber, banana plantation, and mine workers. Contrary to FSLN doctrine, Sandino was no communist. Rather, Sandino's crusade was often against the bourgeois Nicaraguan Conservatives. His ideology was a mix of his own peculiar leftism with a curious indigenous mysticism. He changed his middle name from Calderón to César in honor of the Roman emperor, claimed he could give orders to his troops using silent mental communication, and predicted Nicaragua would be the site of Armageddon, where "armies of angels would do battle alongside more temporal troops."

During the Great Depression, the Marines eventually left Nicaragua, and the future president of Nicaragua, Anastasio Somoza García, had Sandino assassinated in February 1934. Sandino's body was never found. To this day, Sandino remains a hero to Nicaraguans and the world's leftist community. He spearheaded a movement that fought for drastic social and political change and sought to make up for centuries of class discontent that continues today.

with enough force to drive them away from the Atlantic coast.

Sandino and his troops were brutal: they sometimes killed prisoners of war or slit the throats of the dead and pulled the tongue out and down through the gash, like a necktie. The U.S. military struggled diligently but fruitlessly for seven years to flush Sandino out of the hills. In the words of one U.S. Army lieutenant, "Sandino poses as the George Washington of Nicaragua but he is only a cutthroat and a bandit, preying upon foreigners and the law-abiding citizens of his country." But in Sandino's advantage was a profound knowledge of the land, vast popular support, the willingness to live poor, and an uncanny ability to vanish into thin air.

While Sandino's struggle was ostensibly to force the U.S. military and business interests out of Nicaragua, he represented much more than brute nationalism. In the Segovias, where Sandino enjoyed massive popular support, he formed agricultural cooperatives of landless peasants, imposing taxes on wealthy

THE SOMOZA ERA (1937-1979)

General Anastasio Somoza García overpowered Sacasa in 1937. His enormously wealthy and powerful family dynasty would permanently reorient and dominate Nicaraguan politics for the subsequent 42 years. Nicaraguans and foreigners to this day refer to the nearly continuous succession of three Somoza presidents as one all-powerful "Somoza." The Somozas were wily politicians with a near-genius for using existing political conflicts to their personal advantage. They were also expert practitioners of a favorite trick of Latin American dictators, *continuismo,* in which a puppet leader would be elected but resign shortly afterward, handing the power back to the Somozas. Five such "presidents" were elected during the 42-year reign of the Somozas, not one of which lasted longer than three years. The Somozas maintained a strong foothold in the national economy by manipulating government licensing requirements and importing duty-free goods with the complicity of the National Guard. The Somoza family extracted personal income from public utilities and the financial sector, monopolized the cotton industry when it surged in the 1950s and, later, meat, shrimp, and lobster export in the 1960s and 1970s. They owned the nation's prime food-processing industries; sugar refining; cement production; the cardboard, tobacco, and recording industries; and sea and air transport. In fact, by the late 1970s, the Somoza family owned just about everything in Nicaragua worth owning.

Born in San Marcos, Carazo, and educated in Philadelphia, Anastasio Somoza García ascended rapidly through the military. The Roosevelt administration overlooked his greed, questionable politics, and strong-handed military tactics in exchange for a Central American ally. FDR reportedly said of the dictator, "He may be a son of a bitch, but he's our son of a bitch." World War II was an economic windfall for Nicaragua and for Somoza's industries, which exported raw material. But just in case, Somoza declared war on Germany and Japan as a pretext for confiscating the valuable German-owned coffee land. Somoza García's administration oversaw construction of the Chinandega-Puerto Morazán railway, Managua's city water system and International Airport, and the Pan-American Highway. Popular frustration at his heavy-handedness grew until 1956 when, at a celebratory ball in the Social Club of León, poet, political idealist, and frustrated nationalist Rigoberto López Pérez shot him. (Every year on the anniversary of the assassination, flowers are placed at Pérez's monument in the University Rotunda in Managua.)

Anastasio's son Luís Somoza Debayle, a.k.a. Tacho, took the reins, overseeing the construction of the hydropower plant and reservoir of Lake Apanás in Jinotega; the improved port facilities at Corinto; the highway from San Benito to El Rama, which helped unite the Atlantic and Pacific coasts; and the nation's first social security system (INSS). In 1963, Tacho lost in popular elections to the Liberal Renée Schick, and died of a heart attack four years later.

The third of the Somozas was the most avaricious and cruel. As "Tachito," a 1964 graduate of the West Point Military Academy, rose to power, the nascent Sandinista (FSLN) movement was gaining attention in the north through attacks and kidnappings. Over the next decade, they would goad Tachito into becoming the most bloodthirsty president the nation had ever seen. The devastating earthquake of December 1972 provided Tachito a unique opportunity: Appointing himself head of the Emergency Committee, he did little more to rebuild the country than funnel aid money into his own bank accounts. Meanwhile the National Guard terrorized survivors. He was "reelected" in 1974, but Tachito's increasingly flagrant human rights violations including the assassination of journalist Pedro Joaquín Chamorro, and his increasingly violent responses to FSLN attacks earned him international opprobrium. When the FSLN finally ousted him on July 16, 1979, he fled to Miami, and then to Paraguay, where on September 17, 1980, he was assassinated with an anti-tank rocket.

THE SANDINISTA REVOLUTION (1962-1979)

Guerrilla groups opposed to the Somoza dynasty and inspired by Fidel Castro began training in clandestine camps in the northern mountains of Nicaragua in the early 1950s and coalesced a decade later when Carlos Fonseca Amador, Silvio Mayorga, and Tomás Borge formed the **Frente Sandinista de Liberación Nacional (FSLN).** Carlos Fonseca's ideas, an inspired combination of Marxism (which he'd experienced firsthand in a trip to Moscow) and the nationalist, anti-imperialist beliefs of Augusto Sandino formed their ideological framework: Sandinismo.

Early Sandinista insurrections in Río Coco

and Bocay (1963) and Pancasán (1967) were easily crushed but legitimized the FSLN. Somoza's embezzlement of relief funds after the 1972 earthquake was the final straw for most Nicaraguans. As trade unions, student organizations, and private and religious organizations all threw their weight behind the Sandinista insurgency, Tachito grew more brutal and outraged. In January 1978, Pedro Joaquín Chamorro, editor of La Prensa and a relentless critic of Somoza, was gunned down in Managua. One month later, the largely indigenous population of the Masaya neighborhood of Monimbó protested for five days until the National Guard responded by massacring hundreds. By May 1979, the guerrillas were ready for the final insurrection, which would last 52 days.

Combat erupted simultaneously around Chinandega, León, and Chichigalpa in the Pacific, and in the mining triangle in the northeast. At the same time, Sandinista troops began pressing north from the border with Costa Rica. They entered León, capturing the city after a two-day battle. The rest of the nation began a massive general labor strike. On June 8, 1979, Sandinista soldiers and supporters began marching from Carazo, just south of Managua, into the capital itself. The National Guard responded by shelling Managua. Most of the fighting in Managua took place in the lower-middle-class neighborhoods of Bello Horizonte and El Dorado, where extensive networks of concrete drainage ditches made easy battle trenches. The people tore up the concrete paving stones of the streets and used them to erect barricades. The world watched, appalled, as Somoza's aircraft indiscriminately strafed the capital.

The FSLN captured Matagalpa on July 2, 1979, and the strategic town of Sébaco the day after. The Estelí military barracks—the last and most important one after Managua—fell on July 16. Finally, with complete control of the north, FSLN forces surrounded the capital. Trapped by the Sandinistas and abandoned by the United States, Somoza fled Nicaragua in the predawn hours of July 17. July 19, 1979 is

still referred to as "el triunfo" and is celebrated every year across the country.

THE FSLN GOVERNMENT (1979-1991)

The exuberance of military victory quickly faded as the new leaders struggled to convert revolutionary fervor into support for the new nation they wanted to build. They were starting from scratch: Somoza had run Nicaragua as his own personal farm, and overthrowing him had implied dismantling the national economy. The sweeping reforms of the Sandinista revolution therefore made Nicaragua a real-time social experiment. The entire world looked on with anticipation and anxiety.

Land reform proceeded immediately. The Sandinistas confiscated two million acres of Somoza's holdings and distributed it to the landless for farming. Though this was true social revolution, the clearing and planting of previously unexploited hillsides resulted in massive deforestation and erosion. Worse, the Sandinista elite kept the most profitable lands for themselves, a hypocrisy that did not go unnoticed.

A massive literacy campaign saw thousands of volunteers—typically zealous university students—teaching reading, writing, and basic math skills to the illiterate majority. The literacy rate soared to nearly 90 percent, and the campaign received international recognition. The Cuban-inspired mix of education and revolutionary propaganda meant many campesinos' first reading lessons taught revolutionary dogma, and math exercises frequently involved counting items like rifles and tanks. Nonetheless, the literacy campaign encouraged young idealists to explore and take pride in their own country and culture, and reinforced Nicaragua's nationalism.

THE CONTRA WAR (1980-1991)

In their zeal to "defend the revolution at all costs," Sandinista leaders ran into opposition from all sides: from the business community (headed by the business organization COSEP and future president Enrique Bolaños); from Somoza's former cronies; from the former members of the National Guard, many of whom regrouped outside of Nicaragua and became the nucleus of the Contras; and lastly, from the United States government under President Reagan, which was downright hostile to Sandinista socialism. The Contras remain one of the most powerful, divisive, and enigmatic elements of Nicaragua's recent history. They owe their name to the Sandinista leaders who christened them *contra-revolucionarios*. The Contras preferred to call themselves La Resistencia.

As the first *campesinos* picked up arms and slipped across the northern border into Honduras, they encountered former members of Somoza's National Guard, professional military personnel who longed for their former positions of power and prestige. Though they received some early training and organizational help from Argentine military advisers, the Contras weren't an organized force per se until late in the game. The only thing that united the various Contra groups was the feeling that the Sandinista Revolution had been a step in the wrong direction. That included U.S. President Ronald Reagan, who, in March 1986, said, "I guess in a way they are counterrevolutionary, and God bless them for being that way. And I guess that makes them Contras, and so it makes me a Contra, too." The U.S. government played a critical part in the financing and arming of the Contras, in violation of its own laws and without the knowledge of the public.

The Sandinistas openly turned to Cuba and the Soviet Union for support in addition to supporting El Salvador's FMLN, a similar revolutionary group. These policies led the United States to impose an economic embargo in 1985. Some Nicaraguans supported the U.S. government intervention. To moderate Nicaraguans, the FSLN had simply imposed themselves as a new elite.

Regardless, in 1984 the Sandinistas easily won an election that international observers declared fair and transparent while the economy spiraled and the military conflict grew bloodier. Washington continued to fund the Contras, and Cuba and the Soviet Union continued to fund the Sandinistas, in a proxy war that made Nicaragua a geopolitical pawn.

Though the Sandinista military committed its share of atrocities, the Contras' propensity for brutality and terror is well documented and undeniable. Militarily, they were best at short, sharp raids and random ambushes of military and civilian vehicles and seeding terror in the hillsides. Their tactics were barbaric: Reagan's "Freedom Fighters" regularly disemboweled victims (including children), chopped their limbs off, and tore bones out of bodies, which they shook at the victims' family members. Columns of hungry Contra troops didn't think twice about taking at gunpoint anything they needed from local *campesinos*, from cattle to liquor to boots. Many young women and girls were raped and killed, sometimes by decapitation. Young boys and men were routinely castrated and mutilated before being killed.

The Contras commonly targeted suspected Sandinista sympathizers, including government workers in nonmilitary organizations. Often, those victims who escaped death at the hands of the Contras were forced into the mountains at gunpoint to become soldiers. Intent on derailing the Sandinista economy by preventing the harvest, Contras frequently burned the installations of agricultural cooperatives and massacred anyone who stayed to defend them.

The Contra War and U.S. embargo hastened economic collapse and inflation soared. By 1985, export earnings were half the pre-Revolution figures, and much of the confiscated agricultural land remained unproductive in cooperatives. The business class recoiled in fear of further expropriation, and skilled laborers fled the country. In order to combat the Contras, the Sandinistas increased military spending and sent much of the country's productive labor force into battle. Austerity measures didn't earn the Sandinista government many friends either, as previously common goods, like toothpaste and rice, were parsimoniously rationed and shoddy Eastern-bloc goods replaced imports of better quality. Finally, to counter the increasingly violent Contra attacks in Matagalpa, Jinotega, and much of the east, the Sandinistas instituted a much-despised obligatory draft, forcing Nicaraguans to defend—with their sons' lives—a revolution in which they were rapidly losing faith. *Servicio militar patriótico* (patriotic military service), or SMP, was parodied by young men as *"Seremos muertos pronto"* (soon we will be dead).

At the close of the 1980s, both the Contras and the Sandinista government were physically and economically exhausted. The collapse of the Soviet Union left the Sandinistas without a sponsor, while the Contras had little real hope of a military victory. The Iran-Contra scandal in the United States exposed the illegal mechanisms President Reagan's team was employing to fund their Contra "Freedom Fighters" and torpedoed the Contras' funding source. The moment was propitious for Costa Rican president Oscar Arías to propose a peace initiative. In 1987, five Central American presidents attended talks at Esquipulas, Guatemala, and emerged with a radical peace accord. The Sandinistas organized elections in 1990 to show the world that their government was committed to democratic principles and to give Nicaraguans the chance to reaffirm their support for the FSLN. The Bush family economically supported the campaign of opposition candidate Violeta Chamorro (spouse of Somoza-assassinated journalist Joaquín Chamorro), and made the message clear: her election would end both the war and the embargo. Tired of fighting, the Nicaraguan people voted the FSLN out of office. The Revolution had ended. The Sandinistas remain the only revolutionary party that gained power through war to turn over their power through democratic means.

If Nicaragua was going to revert to capitalism, the Sandinista elite wanted to ensure they got their share. On their way out the

door, the Sandinistas signed over hundreds of millions of dollars of state property to themselves in a hypocritical disgrace now known as the Piñata. FSLN party heads privatized many state companies under anonymous cooperatives and passed a series of decrees ensuring they would retain some power. Thus, the new bourgeoisie of former bourgeoisie-haters was born.

THE NEOLIBERAL PERIOD (1991-2006)

Violeta Barrios de Chamorro became president with a coalition of Sandinista opposition groups called the Unión Nacional Opositora (UNO). Her charisma and leadership led the nation through a period of reconciliation and rebuilding. She reestablished diplomatic and economic ties with the rest of the world, ended the draft, reestablished the army and the police under civil control, privatized public industries, and disarmed the Contras. To help them re-assimilate into the agrarian workforce, they were offered 1,600 square kilometers of land, including much of the Río San Juan area and some parts of Jinotega and Matagalpa. Failure to live up to some of these land promises set the stage for further unrest in the 21st century. The international donor community pardoned much of Nicaragua's debt, but did little else to help. Once the proxy war ended, it seemed as though the world had lost interest in Nicaragua.

The elections of 1996, run without the massive international funding that characterized previous elections, were rife with abnormalities, near-riots, and chronic disorder: Polling places opened hours late, bags of discarded ballots were found afterward in the houses of officials, and the communication network failed. Not surprisingly, in the aftermath, all sides had reason to accuse the others of vote rigging and fraud. Even so, Nicaraguans turned out in record numbers and elected Managua's slippery mayor, Arnoldo Alemán.

Arnoldo Alemán was a political conservative and hard-core capitalist lawyer with a sworn aversion to all things Sandinista and a professed admiration for the Somozas. Alemán oversaw the continued growth of the economy, boosted the development of *zonas francas* (free trade zones) and the construction of *maquiladoras* (export clothing assembly plants). Politics returned to the back room, where endless scandals of kickbacks, insider deals, and frenzied pocket-filling embarrassed and infuriated the nation. His personal fortune soared from $20,000 when he took office as mayor of Managua, to $250 million, when he was voted out in 2001. But as he came under increased political and popular pressure for corruption, he and Daniel Ortega engineered the infamous **El Pacto.** The agreement provided them both diplomatic immunity and a lifetime seat in the Assembly, and divided up the government's most important roles between the FSLN and PLC, including the Supreme Court and the Consejo Supremo Electoral (which runs elections). Other political parties were excluded from the power sharing arrangement. Together, Nicaragua's top two *caudillos* (political strongmen) had eviscerated Nicaraguan democracy and divided the spoils.

Enrique Geyer Bolaños, Arnoldo Alemán's nondescript vice-president and former head of COSEP (the Nicaraguan private industry association) won the 2001 election for the PLC party on an anticorruption platform that resonated with Nicaraguans appalled with Alemán's avarice and duplicity. Upon entering office, Bolaños moved quickly to bring indictments against high-ranking PLC officials, including Alemán himself. Alemán was found guilty of corruption and money laundering, and sentenced in December 2003 to 20 years in prison. This was the first time in recent Latin American history that an overtly corrupt leader had been convicted and punished. But Alemán continued to wield considerable political influence even from house arrest, and the majority of the PLC turned against Bolaños in retribution for biting the hand that fed him. Congress, evenly divided between PLC and FSLN members, mostly opposed Bolaños's legislation, and the

PLC mounted a vindictive effort to convict him of corruption himself. Ironically, Enrique Bolaños had better political support from the outside world than he did from his own political party. He relinquished his mandate in 2006 having accomplished little of value despite the best of intentions.

THE RETURN OF ORTEGA (2006-PRESENT)

The Pact strengthened Ortega's hand, and through the Sandinistas in the National Assembly he methodically weakened and divided the political opposition. Mayoral elections in 2004 went overwhelmingly to the Sandinista party. Alemán, under house arrest, could do little to counter him, and in late 2004 Ortega's and Alemán's people again conspired to change the criteria under which one could become president: The threshold for victory was lowered from 45 percent to 35 percent and the mandatory margin over the second candidate was set at 5 percent, both criteria skillfully tailored to Ortega's proven electoral capacity. The FSLN party was by then largely only Daniel supporters or "Orteguistas," the old guard of the Revolution having been blocked in an FSLN primary, while breakaway Sandinistas' new party, the Movimiento Renovador Sandinista (MRS) lost its chance when its popular candidate, Herty Lewites, was felled by a mysterious heart attack while campaigning. Ortega, ever the opportunist, embraced the Catholic Church by supporting a total abortion ban, assured the private sector and Brettons Woods institutions that he had no intention of returning to a policy of land confiscation, and that he would support free enterprise and a capitalist economy. He married his longtime partner Rosario Murillo and "atoned for the sins committed during the FSLN in the 1980s." In November 2006, Nicaraguans turned out in record numbers to vote and were stunned to discover Daniel Ortega had won the presidency with only 38 percent of the vote.

Ortega kept his promise to respect private

enterprise, but he worked vigorously to ensure his return to power would be permanent. Despite rhetoric about the continuation of the 1979 Revolution, there was nothing revolutionary about Ortega's mandate. His administration relentlessly pursued political foes and solidified FSLN control of the courts, the National Assembly, and attempted the same with the police and military to lesser effect. State agents ransacked the offices of a leading investigative journalist, Carlos Fernando Chamorro (son of the former president and slain newspaper man) and a women's NGO. He sent agents to confiscate the computers of 15 other organizations, including Oxfam, under suspicion of money laundering and "subversion," a provocative accusation of supporting opposition political parties. Masked gangs attacked both major newspapers in November 2009, launching mortars and rockets at the building. Meanwhile, youth spray-painted "Viva Daniel" from one end of Managua to the other.

Sandinista "supporters" were required to register with their local Consejo Popular Ciudadano (Community Citizen Committee, CPC) and receive a membership card. Noncardholders found life close to impossible, as suddenly doors were closed to them. Cardholders were permitted to skip certain college exams, non-cardholders could not; cardholders got chosen for scholarships, non-cardholders did not; cardholders got discounted food at the markets, non-cardholders did not. After the damage of the 2014 earthquakes, relief materials were not distributed to non-cardholders in Nagarote. Government workers have been subjected to intimidating and illegal workplace recruitment campaigns by the Sandinista party, facing the threat of dismissal if they refuse to accept the party card.

Within the same strategy, the CPCs aligned themselves with disaffected youth to ensure opposition protestors were unable to assemble in public places. With thinly veiled threats of "the Sandinistas control the streets," popular protests were quickly put down over 30 times

in 2008 alone by stone-throwing Sandinista "supporters"—little more than paid mobs. In June 2013, police stood by while students and senior citizens were beaten during a protest demanding minimum state pensions be distributed to the elderly.

Ortega strengthened diplomatic ties with Libya's Mohammar Qhadaffi, Iran's Mahmoud Ahmadinejad, Venezuela's Hugo Chávez, and Cuba's Fidel Castro. Nicaragua was the only nation to recognize the two republics Russia liberated from Georgia (South Ossetia and Abkhazia), and the abortion ban claimed its first female victims, starting with an 18-year-old who was denied the right to terminate a pregnancy that had developed life-threatening medical complications. Both she and the five-month-old fetus perished.

In 2008, municipal elections for regional officials were overtly sabotaged to engineer a victory for Orteguistas in the National Assembly. It drew the immediate ire of the international community, who withdrew financial support for development projects. Between the United States and the member states of the European Union, over $300 million in funding was suspended. Ortega responded by threatening to send a trillion dollar bill to the European Union to compensate for the ravages of colonialism, and Hugo Chávez offered to substitute the $300 million, which he never did. But Ortega's obstinate march toward dictatorship continued. Supreme Court justices loyal to Ortega met over a weekend in August 2009 and ruled that presidential term limits were a violation of Daniel Ortega's constitutional rights. Despite blustering by the opposition members of the National Assembly, Ortega insisted, "this decision is stone; it cannot be altered." The Sandinistas approved a constitutional reform in 2013, without requesting the legally mandated popular vote of Nicaraguans. The reform abolishes the cap on an individual's presidential terms, and incorporates the interoceanic canal, a project approved without free and prior consent of the indigenous communities it will impact. An increasingly skeptical populace is gauging whether they are ready to accept Ortega as their newest leader-for-life.

Meanwhile, in the mountains north of Jinotega, a group of disaffected militants calling itself the Fuerza Democratica Nicaragüense (FDN) emerged in late 2009.

"We oppose the second dictatorship of Daniel Ortega," they announced, and angry, disaffected Nicaraguans are gradually joining and supporting them. To date, no military action has been attributed to them, but analysts speculate it will just be a matter of time. Sound familiar?

Government and Economy

GOVERNMENT

It seems Nicaraguan politicians' sole purpose for governing is to gerrymander the system sufficiently to ensure their indefinite power and/or enrichment. But talk to any Nicaraguan and you will find Nicaraguan politics are infinitely subtle and the battlefield is constantly being redrawn.

The Republic of Nicaragua is a constitutional democracy. The two autonomous regions of the Atlantic coast are governed somewhat separately and choose their leaders through elections independently of the national government.

Branches of Government

Nicaragua's government is divided into four branches. The **executive branch** consists of the president and vice president. The **judicial branch** includes the Supreme Court, subordinate appeals courts, district courts, and local courts, plus separate labor and administrative tribunals. The Supreme Court oversees the entire judicial system and consists of 12 justices elected by the National Assembly for seven-year terms. Though the judicial system is relatively ineffective and plagued by party interests and manipulation by the wealthy elite, it does have some points in its favor, including an approach that attempts to reduce crowding in jails by having the aggressor and the aggrieved meet to strike a deal. For minor offenses, this is effective. There is no capital punishment in Nicaragua, the maximum sentence being 30 years (though

the abominable conditions of Nicaraguan prisons makes one wonder if the sentence isn't equally harsh).

The **legislative branch** consists of the Asamblea Nacional (National Assembly), a chamber in which 90 *diputados* (deputies) representing Nicaragua's different geographical regions vote on policy. The *diputados* are elected from party lists provided by the major political parties, though defeated presidential candidates that earn a minimum requirement of votes automatically become lifetime members. By law, former presidents are also guaranteed a seat.

The fourth branch of government is unique to Nicaragua: The **Consejo Supremo Nacional** runs the elections and oversees the campaign period. Politicized since the Pact of 2000, the body is rampantly abused to further the interests of Arnoldo Alemán and Daniel Ortega.

Prior to his election in 2006, Ortega attempted repeatedly to implement a parliamentary system that would weaken the executive and permit a sort of power sharing favorable to the Sandinistas, without success. Upon regaining the presidency, he immediately instituted direct or participatory governance through **Consejos Populares Ciudadanos (CPCs)**. Though they ostensibly reach down to permit the poor a more direct engagement with the government, in practice they undermine the other layers of government and facilitate rabble-rousing by Nicaragua's populist and belligerent president.

Elections

The president and *diputados* are elected every five years. The president could not run for consecutive terms until 2009, when Ortega had a Supreme Court justice overrule that decision (to the dismay of many). The **Consejo Supremo Electoral** (Supreme Electoral Council, or CSE) consists of seven magistrates elected by the National Assembly for five-year terms. The CSE has the responsibility of organizing, running, and declaring the winners of elections, referendums, and plebiscites. However, electoral reforms put in place in 2000 allowed the FSLN and the PLC the new ability to name political appointees to the Council, politicizing the CSE to the extreme. The international community decried the fact that the entire process of recognizing new political parties, declaring candidates, and managing the mechanics of holding elections could be so easily subverted to ensure that the two strongest parties—the PLC and the FSLN—divide the spoils of government between themselves. These "reforms" have led to a perceived reduction in the transparency of the Nicaraguan government as a whole.

Nearly every Nicaraguan presidential candidate (with the exception of Doña Violeta) has been, at one time or another, jailed by a previous administration. Tachito jailed Ortega, and Ortega in turn jailed at one point or another both Arnoldo Alemán and Enrique Bolaños.

The Constitution

The present constitution, written in 1987 by the FSLN administration, has been amended seven times. In 1995, it was amended to balance the distribution of power more evenly between the legislative and executive branches. The National Assembly's ability to veto was bolstered and the president's ability to veto reduced. It was revised in 2000 to increase the power of the Supreme Court and the comptroller-general's office, and in 2013 to do away with mandated presidential term limits.

Though there is no official government

censorship of journalists, journalists and photographers report harassment, interference, and threats of violence, and Ortega has not hesitated to send the police through offices of newspapers and NGOs that don't fully toe the party line. The Nicaraguan constitution prohibits discrimination by birth, nationality, political belief, race, gender, language, religion, opinion, national origin, or economic or social condition. Nicaraguans are permitted to form labor unions. Nearly half of the workforce, including much of the agricultural labor, is unionized. However, unions who criticize the Sandinista administration put their political legitimacy (and their personal safety) in danger.

Political Parties

Nicaraguan politicians change from one political party to another as necessary to suit their own ambitions, while smaller parties coalesce into alliances that later fracture into new arrangements. Infighting and division have been an integral part of the Nicaraguan political scene since the 1800s' Liberal-Conservative split. No other major political party came onto the scene until the FSLN took power in the 1980s. By 1990, no fewer than 20 political parties had risen in opposition to the FSLN. Doña Violeta's UNO coalition was formed from 14 of them. In the 1996 election, 35 parties participated either on their own or as one of five coalitions. In 2000, new legislation made more stringent the requirements for a political party to participate in elections. While the exclusionary tactics diminished the previous election's free-for-all, skeptics believe the purpose of the law was to deny newcomers a piece of the pie.

Five parties participated in the presidential election of 2006: the FSLN; the PLC; and three new ones: a liberal alliance by the name of ALN-PC, a Sandinista splinter party called the MRS (Movimiento Renovador Sandinista) headed by Managua's well-loved mayor Herte Lewites, and the tiny AC party (Alternativa para Cambio) under ex-Contra rebel Eden

Pastora. In 2011, the participating parties were the FSLN; Alemán representing the PLC; Bolaños's APRE; the ALN-PC; and the Independent Liberal Party representing the UNE alliance (Nicaraguan Unity for Hope) and Ortega's closest competition.

ECONOMY

Two successive governments have had to jump-start the Nicaraguan economy from a standstill: the Sandinistas, who picked up the shattered remains upon ousting Tachito; and Doña Violeta, who had to recover from the war and a decade of economic embargo. Her administration made dramatic progress, reducing the foreign debt by more than half, slashing inflation from 13,500 percent to 12 percent, and privatizing hundreds of state-run businesses. The new economy began to expand in 1994 and grew at 4 percent until 2006, weathering several major catastrophes, including Hurricane Mitch in 1998.

Nevertheless, Nicaragua remains the second poorest nation in the Western hemisphere with a per capita gross domestic product of $1,337 and its external debt ratio nearly twice the gross national product. Unemployment is pervasive. More than half of the adult urban population scrapes by in the informal sector (selling water at the roadside, for example), and population growth will likely keep it that way. High demand for jobs means employers can essentially ignore the minimum-wage requirement, especially in the countryside, where agricultural laborers typically earn as little as $1 a day. Nearly 600,000 people face severe malnutrition.

Nicaragua's economy is based almost entirely on agricultural export of primary material, plus recently, tourism and several nontraditional exports like sesame, onions, melons, and fruit. Export earnings are currently $381 million. Their main trade partners include the United States, other Central American countries, Venezuela, and the European Union.

Debt, the HIPC, and Foreign Aid

For years, Nicaragua has been one of the most highly indebted nations of the world. When Somoza fled the country, he took the capital reserves of the banks with him, leaving behind $1.6 billion of debt. The Sandinistas, through a combination of gross economic mismanagement, extensive borrowing (primarily from Eastern bloc nations), the U.S. economic embargo, and high defense expenditures augmented the national debt by a factor of 10, nearly half of which was in arrears. By 1994, Nicaragua had the highest ratio of debt to GDP in the world, a challenge every successive administration has had to deal with. Germany, Russia, and Mexico were the first nations to forgive Nicaraguan debt entirely.

Propitious to Nicaragua's future economic growth was its inclusion in the **Highly Indebted Poor Countries** (HIPC) debt relief initiative in 2000. Inclusion in the initiative means Nicaragua will be exonerated from the majority of its international debt upon compliance with an International Monetary Fund (IMF) and World Bank program, but that program mandates several austerity measures, debt restructuring, and the opening of its economy to foreign markets. More hotly contested is the mandated privatization of public utilities, including the telephone system (privatized in 2002) and municipal water distribution. City water systems have not yet been privatized and the issue is extremely controversial with those who consider water a human right rather than a commodity. The electrical grid was auctioned to the sole bidder (notorious Spanish company Unión Fenosa) in 2000. The company enjoyed a monopoly of the industry, charging outrageous prices and consistently overbilling clients. In 2013, Fenosa sold its shares to the Spanish companies TSK and Melfosur, who have not lowered rates. Central to the HIPC initiative is Nicaragua's continued effort toward macroeconomic adjustment and structural

¿Pura Vida? Nicaragua's Rocky Relationship with Costa Rica

Costa Rica is a wealthier, more politically stable country than Nicaragua. To keep it that way, the Costa Rican economy is wholly dependent on low-cost Nicaraguan laborers for harvesting their sugarcane and coffee and filling the ranks of the construction workforce in urban centers. In an effort to control immigration, Costa Rican officials conduct regular roundups of illegal aliens, returning as many as 150 to Nicaragua daily. If you travel south into Costa Rica, expect patrols to stop and search your bus several times for undocumented travelers. Some estimates put the number of Nicaraguans living in Costa Rica at more than a million, but with the constant flux and large percentage of undocumented Nicas, no one knows for sure.

The tense relationship between these incongruous Central American neighbors loosely parallels the relationship between the United States and Mexico. Namely, a massive flood of immigrants crosses the border (pushed by neoliberal trade policies) into a more prosperous and stable nation and is subsequently accused of driving down wages, taking all the jobs, and straining social services without paying taxes. As Nicas are darker skinned and easy to distinguish, they're easy to scapegoat. Ask most Ticos (as Costa Ricans call themselves) about the issue and you'll likely get an earful of racist comments about Nicaraguans being "lazy, no-good, poor, and dirty." Nicaraguans, for their part, generally mistrust Ticos and don't appreciate their arrogance.

Costa Rica continues to press for a resolution to Nicaraguan immigration issues. Too much blustery rhetoric from Managua regarding other issues, like the sovereignty of the Río San Juan, may tempt the Ticos to crack down even more on illegal immigrants, something Managua would very much like to avoid. Even today, Nicaraguan immigrants have reported irregular and inhumane incarceration by Tico authorities, often for weeks at a time without formal charges (and sometimes without daylight, toilets, and food).

Rhetoric aside, the two neighbors desperately need each other. Perhaps pragmatism will win out over politics in the end.

and social policy reforms, particularly basic health and education, both of which remain publicly owned.

DR-CAFTA

The **Dominican Republic-Central American Free Trade Agreement** was ratified in 2005 and resembles the similar North American Free Trade Agreement (NAFTA). The agreement generated much debate and more than a few anxious farmers. According to macroeconomic figures, Nicaragua has benefited from DR-CAFTA more than any other Central American country. Under the agreement, Nicaraguan exports to the United States are up 71 percent. Foreign Direct Investment has increased an average of 7.3 percent a year, and the average annual growth rate in the number of export-oriented foreign-owned factories (*maquilas*) operating

in Nicaragua's "Free Trade Zones" (referred to locally as "*zonas francas*") grew from 6.7 to 9.8 percent.

The United States agreed to import a greater quantity of Nicaraguan goods—notably beef and sugar—while permitting Nicaragua to protect domestic farmers from most American foodstuffs. Quotas were raised for most Nicaraguan exports and they are scheduled to increase further over time, giving Nicaraguan farmers a better opportunity to export their crops. But the country's biggest win was for the textile industry. Nicaragua negotiated the right to import cloth from Asia, assemble clothing, and sell it duty-free in the United States. This attracted numerous investors, and therefore jobs to the country. However, Nicaragua supplies few of the products or labor for these factories (U.S. machinery is a significant national import) and offers huge tax breaks to foreign investors. U.S. cotton producers won the concession that by 2010 half of the fabric Nicaragua imports from other countries must come from the U.S., which is more costly.

The United States negotiated the right to export yellow corn for chicken feed, rice, and powdered milk, among other things. Nicaraguan farmers produce white (not yellow) corn, and cattle ranchers are anxious about the effect corn and milk imports will have on their livelihood. U.S. rice exporters were granted significant subsidies and a quota (to be reached by 2024) that will allow them to dominate the majority of Nicaragua's rice market.

Opponents of CAFTA bring up other concerns. For one, CAFTA promotes the Washington consensus export-economy model, where Nicaragua exports cash crops and imports basic foodstuffs. With little leverage in the marketplace, that increases Nicaragua's vulnerability to prices. The textile provisions certainly promote job creation, but what kind of jobs are they? The Nicaraguan government does not have the capacity to protect its workers (and investors are less attracted to countries with strict labor laws), so folks working in the free trade zones (mostly women) are subject to abuse and are not permitted to freely form unions. Finally, studies of CAFTA's predecessor, NAFTA, have failed to show a notable improvement in the lives of the Mexicans it claims to affect. Rather, it has been directly connected to rising levels of migration, as small business owners are forced out of business, unable to compete with both national and foreign industry giants.

Agriculture

Nicaragua is, above all, an agricultural nation. A third of its gross domestic product is agriculture-based, and agriculture represents the fastest growing economic sector, at 20 percent growth per year. However, much of the new land put into agricultural production is opened at the expense of the forests, the indiscriminate harvesting of which has a negative effect on the environment and water supply. Agriculture employs 28 percent of the workforce. Outside of the small, upscale producers who export to international markets, the majority of Nicaraguan agriculture is for domestic consumption, and much of that is subsistence farming. Drought years often require importing of basic grains. Primary exports include coffee, beef, sugar, tobacco, fruits, vegetables, shrimp, and lobster.

Subsistence farmers typically grow white corn and red beans. The cultural choice of red beans over black beans presents additional challenges to farmers, as red beans are more susceptible to drought (and less nutritious) than black or soybeans.

The Sébaco Valley is an agriculturally productive area and the primary source of wet rice for local consumption. It's also widely planted with onions. Extensive irrigation of rice plantations caused the water table in the Sébaco Valley to drop more than three meters in the 1990s. Jinotega's cool climate is a major source of fruit and vegetable production, including cabbage, peppers, onions, melons, watermelons, squash, and tomatoes.

Coffee

There's no underestimating the importance of coffee to the Nicaraguan economy. Coffee contributes an average of $140 million per year to the economy, includes more than 40,000 farms, and employs more than 250,000 people. That is 10-20 percent of the agricultural workforce. Nearly all coffee farmers are small-scale farmers or micro-producers. Nicaragua exports its beans primarily to North America, Europe, and Japan to the tune of 1 million 100-pound sacks every year. These beans are roasted and ground (usually abroad) to produce 11 billion pounds of java. Over half of Nicaragua's coffee comes from Jinotega. Because most Nicaragua growers produce full-bodied arabica beans under the shade of diverse trees at altitudes of 900 meters and higher, the quality of its crop is recognized the world over. Furthermore,

Nicaragua's coffee industry has been recognized for its attention to social justice and the environment.

Unfortunately, the fungus known as coffee rust *(Hemileia vastatrix)* has been contributing to massive crop loss. The fungus has gotten out of control in recent years as global temperatures rise (coffee rust can't survive in temperatures less than $10^\circ C$). Unless climate change slows, it will only get worse. A new species of the coffee plant is supposedly immune to coffee rust and is being experimentally planted in the RACS.

THE FUTURE OF COFFEE

Discerning North American and European java swillers have created an enormous demand for a superior cup of coffee and they are willing to pay extra for it. The future of sustainable coffee production, many agree, is in family-run cooperatives in which small-scale farmers, rather than a single, rich hacienda owner, control their product. At present, over half of Nicaraguan coffee is grown by small-scale *campesino* producers working as members of cooperatives in the country's northlands. As much as 80 percent of their coffee can be marketed as specialty coffee for the Fair Trade and organic markets, making

these growers less vulnerable to the extreme price oscillations of conventional coffee.

Nicaragua has a number of other advantages over other coffee-producing nations in the region. Nearly 95 percent of Nicaraguan coffee is grown under a forest canopy that provides shade for coffee bushes and, at the same time, habitat for migratory birds. This can earn a grower a "Bird Friendly" sticker, which, like organic certification, gains a significantly higher market price. Coffee families and their communities also benefit enormously from the Fair Trade certification program (www.transfairusa.org), in which participating companies must comply with strict economic, social, and environmental criteria, guaranteeing producers a fair price. The small-scale farmers who represent most of the certified-organic producers and those linked to Fair Trade markets recently formed **Cafenica** (www.web.cafenica.net), an association of small-scale coffee farming co-ops, to represent their interests at the national and international level. Finally, a number of coffee growers, especially those who own their own land, have diversified their income with non-coffee crops and activities, including several awesome ecotourism projects.

BACKGROUND GOVERNMENT AND ECONOMY

coffee drying along the highway between Sébaco and Matagalpa

Industry

Industrial production in Nicaragua reached its zenith in 1978 under Anastasio Somoza, who encouraged industrial expansion in Managua at the expense of the environment, especially Lake Xolotlán. Investment policies of the time exonerated industries from the need to worry about environmental protection. Industry—even agro-industry—has been underdeveloped in the years following the Revolution. There is a small amount of production for domestic and regional markets, including cement processing, petroleum refining, and some production of plastic goods. Another aspect of Nicaragua's export industry is the steadily increasing number of *zonas francas* (free trade zones) near Managua, Sébaco, Masaya, and Granada, where tens of thousands of Nicaraguans are employed in foreign-owned sweatshops.

Tourism

At present, tourism represents the third largest source of foreign exchange, and the so-called "industry without smokestacks" is widely hoped to be a panacea to Nicaragua's economic ills. The government agency in charge of tourism development and marketing is El Instituto Nicaragüense de Turismo, better known as **INTUR** (www.intur.gob.ni). Public Law 306 provides a 10-year tax break to newly constructed tourist facilities that meet certain criteria. Since the mid-1990s, investment in tourism has skyrocketed, notably in

Managua, Granada, and San Juan del Sur. The total number of visitors to Nicaragua has increased from more than 800,000 in 2005, to over one million in 2010. In 2014, tourism generated over $445 billion.

ECOTOURISM

The warm and fuzzy "eco" prefix has been used and abused all over the world, and, unfortunately, Nicaragua is no exception. Alternative tourism goes by many other names as well: "sustainable," "responsible," "ethical," "rural," or "fair trade" tourism, to name a few.

The concept of protected areas and national parks is relatively new in Nicaragua and is, in some places, viewed with skepticism, especially by *campesinos* who live near (or even within) these areas and have always used the forests to supplement their paltry incomes. MARENA, the government ministry charged with protecting Nicaragua's vast system of parks and refuges, has scant resources to prevent such activities. But money from nature-loving visitors can help create alternative source of income, as foreigners who come to see the local waterfall or coffee cooperative need to eat breakfast, hire a guide, or rent a horse. I've pointed out community-sponsored tourism efforts, namely in Granada, Isla de Ometepe, Matagalpa, and the Miraflor region of Estelí. Here, existing cooperatives arrange homestay opportunities that involve volunteer work, Spanish language class, alternative agriculture, and trips to local sites.

People and Culture

POPULATION

Nicaragua's population is fast approaching six million, a third of whom live in Managua. Nicaragua is both the least populous Central American nation and the fastest growing, at just over 3 percent annually. At this rate, the country's strained resources will have to support 9-12 million people by the year 2030. In

addition, well over a million Nicaraguans live outside of the country, particularly in Costa Rica (679,000) and the United States (500,000), as well as Mexico and other Central American nations. Many families depend heavily on remittances from their relatives abroad. In 2011, remittances totaled over $9 million.

ETHNIC GROUPS

Most of the population is a blend of Spanish, Native American, and sometimes other European stock. Indigenous blood runs most strongly in the northeast, where the Spanish had less influence, and on the mid-Atlantic coast, where English and African influences were dominant. In the Pacific region, the indigenous population thinned from 800,000 when the Spanish arrived to less than 60,000 after a couple centuries of conquistador policy (i.e., war, slavery, genocide, and diseases). The native peoples of the northeast, including Matagalpa and Jinotega, were less affected, and thus retain larger indigenous populations today.

Mestizos

The term mestizo refers to any mixture of Spanish and indigenous blood and describes the majority of Nicaraguan citizens, whose Spanish colonial ancestors began intermingling with the locals about as soon as they got off the boat. A second wave of *mestizaje* (mixing) occurred in the 1860s-1890s, during the wave of rubber and banana production along the Atlantic coast, and again in the 1950s as Pacific farmers moved eastward in search of new agricultural lands at the expense of the Sumu-Ulúa and Miskito peoples. Mestizo Nicaraguans sometimes use the racist term *"indio"* as a derogatory label for anyone with Native American features (high cheekbones, straight black hair, short eyelashes, and dark brown skin) or someone who is ignorant.

Creoles

After decimating the indigenous peoples of the New World, the Spanish realized they lacked laborers; so they imported African slaves to their colonies in the Americas. Beginning in 1562, English slave traders, and later Dutch, Spanish, and others, supplied the colonies with human cargo. Along the Atlantic coast of Nicaragua, African slaves intermingled with Miskitos, giving birth to the Zambo (or Sambo) people. They also bred with the Spanish and English, forming the Creoles, primarily found today in Bluefields and San Juan del Norte. Creoles speak a form of English that still bears traces of 19th-century Queen's English, as well as Caribbean and Spanish traits. Their culture includes distinct African elements, including the belief in a form of African witchcraft called *obeah* or *sontín*, the latter from the English "something" or "something special."

Miskitos

Modern-day Miskitos are really a mixture of several races, and include traces of English and African blood. The Native American Bawihka people, whose territory extended from the Río Coco (Wangki) at Cabo Gracias a Dios south to Prinzapolka, mixed with the African-slave refugees of a Portuguese ship that wrecked on the Miskito Cays in 1642. They later mixed with the English during their long occupation of the Atlantic coast. Over the centuries, the word "Miskito" has been written many other ways, including "Mosquito," "Mosca," and "Mískitu." The name derives not from the insect but from the Spanish word *mosquete* (musket), a firearm the British provided the locals to ensure a tactical advantage over their neighbors.

The Miskitos' warlike nature and superior firepower helped them subdue 20 other Native American tribes along the Atlantic coast of Central America. They were valuable allies to the English, who used them in raids against inland Spanish settlements, and crowned their "kings" in an Anglican church in Belize City. The Miskitos also absorbed the Prinsu tribe (located along the Bambana and Prinzapolka Rivers) and the Kukra tribe.

Today the Miskitos inhabit much of the Atlantic coast of Nicaragua, from Bluefields northward and all along the Río Coco, which they consider their spiritual home. There are additional Miskito settlements on both Corn Islands, but their two principal centers are Bilwi (Puerto Cabezas) and Waspám. Their language, Miskito, is the old indigenous

Popular Nicaraguan Sayings

Nicaraguans in general, and *campesinos* in particular, love to speak using *refranes* (sayings or refrains). They're an easy way to make a point, and both the way they are phrased and the points they make say much about the *campesinos'* way of thinking. If you learn a refrain or two and throw one out once in a while in casual conversation, you will be sure to earn broad smiles.

Hay más tiempo que vida. There is more time than life. (There's no need to rush things.)

Él que a buen árbol se arrima, buena sombra le cobija. He who gets close to a good tree will be covered by good shade. (He who seeks protection will find it.)

Perro que ladra no muerde. Dogs who bark don't bite.

No hay peor sordo que él que no quiere escuchar. There's no deaf person worse than he who doesn't want to hear.

A cada chancho le llega su sábado. Every pig gets his Saturday. (Everyone eventually gets what he deserves.)

Quien da pan a un perro ajeno, pierde el pan y pierde el perro. If you give bread to someone else's dog, you'll lose the bread and lose the dog.

Él que madruga come pechuga, él que tarda, come albarda. He who gets up early eats the best piece of chicken, he who gets up late eats the saddle.

Él que no llora no mama. He who does not cry does not suckle. (If you don't complain, you'll never get any attention.)

Él que anda con lobos, aullar aprende. He who walks with wolves, learns to howl. (A warning about the company you keep.)

Barriga llena, corazón contento. Full belly, happy heart. (Lean back and use this one after a big meal.)

Él que tiene más galillo, traga más pinol. He who has a bigger throat, drinks more *pinol*. (Being aggressive will get you farther.)

Tawira language enriched with English and African vocabulary.

The Kukra

The Kukra people were assimilated by the Miskitos over the last two centuries and no longer exist as a tribe. Of unknown but reportedly cannibalistic Caribbean origin, they once inhabited Bluefields, the Corn Islands, and the area around Pearl Lagoon. Today, the only trace of them is the name of the small Pearl Lagoon community of Kukra Hill.

The Garífuna

The Garífuna, as a distinct culture, are relative newcomers to the world. Their history began on the Lesser Antillean island of San Vicente (Saint Vincent), which in the 1700s had become a refuge for escaped slaves from the sugar plantations of the Caribbean, including Jamaica. These displaced Africans were accepted by the native Carib (Arawak)

islanders, with whom they freely intermingled. As the French and English settled the island, the Garífunas (as they had become known) established a worldwide reputation as expert canoe navigators and fierce warriors, resisting the newcomers. The English finally got the upper hand in the conflict after tricking and killing the Garífuna leader, and in 1797, they forcefully evacuated the Garífunas from San Vicente to the Honduran Bay Island of Roatán. From there, many of the Garífunas migrated to the mainland communities of Trujillo, Honduras and Dangriga, Belize. Today, they exist up and down most of the Central American Caribbean coast, with a small but distinct presence in Nicaragua, primarily around Pearl Lagoon. Orinoco (originally Urunugu) is the largest settlement of Garífunas in Nicaragua, established in 1912 by the Garífuna John Sambola. The communities of San Vicente and Justo Point are both Garífuna as well. During the 1980s, the

Contra War forced many Garífunas out of their communities and into Bluefields, Puerto Limón (Costa Rica), and Honduras.

The Mayangna

The Mayangna are a combination of several Ulúa tribes, including the Twahka, Panamka, and Ulwa, who once settled the Kurinwas, Siquia, Mico, Rama, and Grande Rivers of the Atlantic coast. Mayangna tradition has it that in the 9th and 10th centuries they were the inhabitants of a territory that extended from the Atlantic coast and Río Coco to the Pacific, but they were forced off the Atlantic coastal lands by the more aggressive and warring Miskito and out of the Pacific by the Nahuatls, Maribios, and Chorotegas. The Mayangna are now centered around the mining triangle and the massive forest reserve of Bosawás.

The Rama

The Rama are the least numerous indigenous people in Nicaragua, numbering only several hundred. Their language is distinct from Miskito and Mayangna and is closely related to the ancient tribal languages of Native American tribes of Panamá and Colombia. Today, only several dozen people can still speak Rama. Anthropologists are scrambling to document what they can of the language before it disappears entirely. The Rama people inhabit the pleasant bay island of Rama Cay in the Bay of Bluefields, where they fish and collect oysters. They also grow grains and traditional crops on small plots of land on the mainland of Bluefields Bay and along the Kukra River. The Rama people are reserved and keep mostly to their traditional ways, even using traditional tools and implements. They are excellent navigators and fishers.

CULTURE

Nicaraguans are generally open, talkative, and hospitable. In most areas of the country, Nicaraguans are accustomed to seeing foreigners, but they are still curious and not very discreet. Expect blunt questions about your age, marital status, and your opinions about Nicaragua. The reaction is nearly always one of curiosity, hospitality, and friendliness.

Despite their directness, Nicaraguans are prone to circuitous, indirect behavior associated with the cultural concept of "saving face." When asked something they don't know, people often invent an answer so that neither party is embarrassed. Be warned, this is especially true about directions and distances. Many Nicaraguan city dwellers are, in fact, recently immigrated *campesinos,* and they often bring their country ways and livestock with them to the city.

Anti-U.S. sentiment, in my experience, is rare since Nicaraguans are particularly adept at distinguishing between a nation's people and its government's policy. In addition, because most Nicaraguan families adore cable TV and have at least one relative sending money back from Miami, Houston, or Los Angeles, many are quite fond of the United States. The word "gringo" is used most often as a descriptive, casual term for anyone who comes from north of the Mexican border. In rare cases, it is meant as an insult (in which case, it will likely be accompanied by a swear word). Likewise for *chele, chela,* and their diminutives, *chelito* and *chelita,* all of which mean pale or light-skinned, and are in no way disrespectful. In fact, many cries of, *"¡Oye, chele!"* ("Hey, whitey!") are used as much for light-skinned Nicaraguans as for foreigners.

Family

The Nicaraguan family is the most basic and strongest support structure of society. Rural women have an average of 4-6 children, and families of a dozen aren't uncommon. Urban couples, particularly in Managua, typically have no more than three or four children. Extended families—cousins, in-laws, aunts, and uncles—are all kept in close contact and relied upon during hard times. Families live close together, often in small quarters, and the North American and European concepts of independence and solitude are not well understood. Nicaraguans' traditional dependence on large family structures mandates that they take care of stragglers. If, for example, you were stranded in a strange country town in the pouring rain, it would not be unlikely for someone to invite you into their home for coffee or a bed.

Clothing and Neatness

Nicaraguans place a great deal of importance on cleanliness. Even the poorest *campesino* with threadbare and patched clothing takes great care to tuck his shirt in and keep his clothes clean and wrinkle-free. Nicaraguans only wear shorts for playing sports or lounging around the house. Nicaraguan women dress the spectrum from long, conservative dresses to bright, tight, and revealing outfits, though this is less common in rural communities. Unshaven *internacionalistas* wearing stained shorts, ripped T-shirts, and dreads stand out like sore thumbs, even without their trademark bulky backpacks. A little effort into your wardrobe and hygiene will go a long way.

a homemade Catholic altar

Etiquette and Terms of Address

While Costa Ricans tend to gravitate toward the formal *usted* form of address among themselves, Nicaraguans prefer the friendly *vos* (second person) form with each other, although *tú* is widely understood. For travelers, it's best to use *usted* until you've really gotten to know someone. The terms *don* for men and *doña* for women are used far more commonly in Nicaragua than elsewhere in Latin America, and indicate a higher level of respect or affection, particularly for the elderly, the important, or the wealthy. Practitioners of certain careers sometimes drop their names entirely and go by their profession. That is, it's not uncommon to be presented to someone everyone calls simply *"la doctora," "el ingeniero,"* or *"la abogada."*

It's customary to kiss women on the cheek when greeting, but women will provide the signal whether that's appropriate by turning their cheek toward you. (This is less common in the countryside.) Men will offer you their hands for a limp handshake. When someone new enters the room, rise from your seat to greet them, and when you're ready to end a conversation or leave the room, a friendly *"con permiso"* will pave the way to the door.

Concept of Time

Nicaraguan life goes according to *la hora Nica* (Nica Time), which means a meeting scheduled in Managua for 2:30pm might not start until 3pm, or an hour later in the countryside. Foreign travelers accustomed to *la hora gringa,* in which everything starts and stops exactly when planned, will spend their days in Nicaragua endlessly frustrated (and consistently early for meetings).

RELIGION

The Republic of Nicaragua officially endorses no religion, though more than half of Nicaraguans call themselves Catholic. Over a hundred evangelical Protestant sects comprise about 30 percent of the population. Evangelicals have increased their presence significantly over the last couple of decades (especially in rural areas) with persistent door-to-door campaigns. Beginning in the early 1970s and continuing through the Revolution, Nicaragua created its own version of liberation theology, a school of Christianity and bourgeois thought that equated Jesus's teachings with Marxism. The degree to which biblical parables were equated to the Marxist struggle varied, and the most radical versions placed Sandino as Jesus or Moses, Somoza as the Pharaoh, and the Nicaraguan masses as the Israelites searching for their promised land through revolutionary struggle.

A tiny percentage of Nicaraguans are descendents of one of several Jewish families that found refuge here during World War II. Some of them still identify themselves as Jewish, but there is no real practicing community. Most Nicaraguans, especially in the countryside, have little concept of Judaism as a modern religion, relating the word *judío* only to the ancient race of *hebreos* in the Old Testament. Many Nicaraguans connect Israel to the Old Testament. You'll notice a surprising number of Israeli flags. In 2008, the construction of a mosque in Managua raised eyebrows in the diplomatic community, who feared increasing Iranian influence. It was instead the work of the growing Lebanese community, present in Nicaragua for a century but only now numerous enough to consider building their own place of worship.

LANGUAGE

Spanish is the official language of Nicaragua, though indigenous languages are respected and even used officially in certain areas of the Atlantic coast. Ninety-six percent of Nicaraguans speak Spanish as their first language, 3 percent speak indigenous languages (Miskito, Mayangna, and Rama), and 1 percent speak languages of African origin (Creole and Garífuna). To hear pure Miskito, travel north from Bluefields or visit Puerto Cabezas, where English is often preferred to Spanish. In some villages along the Río Coco Spanish is completely unknown.

Nicaraguan Spanish is spoken rapidly

and liquidly, the words flowing smoothly together and eating each other's tails. Central Americans enjoy making fun of how their Latin neighbors talk, and the Honduran nickname for Nicaraguans, *mucos* (bulls whose horns have been chopped off), is a reference to the Nicaraguans' habit of chopping the "s" off the ends of spoken words. And then there are the vulgarities. Even a simple vegetable name can cause a room to break out in wild laughter if said in the right tone and context. Be careful using dirty words. The degree to which most *vulgaridades* are considered offensive varies depending on the gender of your company, their age, your relationship with them, and other factors.

Body Language

Watch locals interact, and see if you can spot any of the following gestures in action—then try some out yourself.

Probably the single most practical gesture is a rapid side-to-side wagging of the index finger. It means "no," and increases in strength as you increase the intensity of the wagging and the amount of hand and arm you use in the motion. In some cases, a verbal "no" in the absence of the **Finger Wag** is disregarded as not serious enough. Use this one liberally with pushy vendors, beggars, and would-be Romeos.

To pull off the **Nicaraguan Wrist Snap,** join the tips of your thumb and middle finger and let your index finger dangle loosely. Then with a series of rapid wrist flicks, repeatedly let your index finger slap against the middle one, exactly as you would do with a round tin of tobacco dip. The resulting snapping noise serves to either emphasize whatever it is you're saying, refer to how hard you've been working, or, when combined with a nod and a smile, infer something like, "Damn, that's good!"

You can ask, "What?" (or "What do you want?") with a quick **Nose Scrunch,** occasionally performed with a subtle upward chin tilt. Use the **Lip Point** rather than your finger to indicate something by puckering up as if for a kiss and aiming where you want. Or, if you

A Few *Nicaraguanismos*

The textbook Spanish you learned back home will be understood without trouble, but Nicaraguans take pride in the fact that their version of the old-country Castilian is decidedly unique. When you try to look up some of the new words you're hearing and realize they're not in the dictionary, you'll see what I mean. Nicaraguan Spanish uses some old, proper Spanish no longer used in the Old World, and has assimilated pre-Columbian words from Nahuatl and Chorotega tongues (especially local plant and animal names). Still other words are pure onomatopoeia. Those interested in pursuing the topic should seek out Joaquim Rabella and Chantal Pallais's *Vocabulario Popular Nicaragüense*, available in some bookstores in Managua. Here's an incomplete sampling (with the Castilian in parentheses when possible).

arrecho: extremely angry *(enfurecido)*
bacanal: party *(fiesta)*
bicha: beer *(cerveza)*
bochinche: a fistfight among several people
boludo: lazy, unmotivated *(haragán)*
bullaranga: loud noises, ruckus *(tumulto, alboroto)*
cachimbo: a whole lot *(un montón)*
chapa: earring *(arete)*
chigüin: little kid *(bebé)*
chinela: sandal *(sandalia)*
chingaste: the granular residue of a drink like coffee *(poso, residuo)*
chunche: any small, nameless object *(cosita)*
chusmón: mediocre
cipote: child *(niño o niña)*
curutaca: diarrhea *(diarrea)*
deacachimba: awesome, cool *(genial)*
encachimbarse: to get angry *(enojarse)*
guaro: general term for booze or alcoholic beverages

are listening to a friend's dumb story, point to the speaker with your lips while looking at everyone else to imply, "This guy's crazy or drunk."

The gesture North Americans would normally use to shoo something away—the outstretched, waving, down-turned hand—means just the opposite in Nicaragua, where the **Downward Wave** (occasionally combined with the whole arm for emphasis) means "Come here." This one is a favorite with drunks in the park who love to talk at foreigners. The North American "come here," that is, the upturned and beckoning index finger, is a vulgar, possibly offensive gesture. Speaking of vulgar, a closed fist atop a rigid forearm indicates the male sex organ, and an upturned, slightly cupped hand with the fingertips pressed together into a point is its

female counterpart. Here's one more for the road: Make a fist, lock your elbow into the side of your body, and move your hand up and down; combined with a dramatic grimace, the **Plunger Pump** tells the whole world you have diarrhea.

THE ARTS
Literature
As anyone here will tell you, every Nicaraguan is a poet at heart. "Nicaragua," wrote the poet Pablo Neruda, "where the highest song of the tongue is raised." José Miguel Oviedo called the writing of Nicaragua, "the richest and most tragic national literary tradition on the continent." Most start the story of Nicaraguan literature with the groundbreaking words of Rubén Darío. It continues with the vanguardists of the 1950s and 1960s, the subsequent

hamaquear: to rock something rhythmically *(mecer rítmicamente)*
jaño/jaña: boyfriend/girlfriend *(novio/novia)*
maje: person, informal, similar to "dude" in the U.S. *(persona, tipo)*
moclín: perverted old man
ñaña: excrement *(excremento)*
panzona: big bellied, implies pregnant *(embarazada)*
pinche: cheap *(tacaño)*
pipilacha: small airplane *(avioneta)*
salvaje: awesome; literally, "savage;" fun response to *"¿Como estás?"*
timba: big belly *(barriga)*
tuani: cool *(genial, chévere)*
yeyo: rip-off *(engaño, embaucamiento)*

EXCLAMATIONS

¡Ahuevo!: Right on! or expressing obligation (Tomorrow I have to wake up early, *ahuevo*. Short for *"a juevos."*)
¡A la puchica!: Wow!
¡Chocho!: Woah! Crazy!
Dalepué: OK, I agree, let's do that.
hijueputa: extremely common salutation or reference to a friend, pronounced huway-POO-tah and used liberally. From the vulgar *hijo de puta* ("son of a whore") which, when said slowly, is an insult.
¿Ideay? (eedee-EYE?): What was that all about? What do you mean?
¡Qué barbaridad!: What a barbarity! How rude! What a shame!
¡Sí hombre!: Yeah man!
Tranquilo como Camilo: Chillin' like Dylan; fun response to *"¿Como estás?"*
Va pué: OK then; see you; I agree; or whatever (short for *va pués*)

generation of revolutionary poets and novelists, and the current wave of soul-searchers.

Poet and author Gioconda Belli was called one of the 100 most important poets of the 20th century. Her work deals with the themes of feminism, mystical realism, and history, all mixed with a breath of sensuality. Her books *Wiwilí, Sofía de los Presagios*, and *El País Bajo Mi Piel* (The Country Under My Skin) are widely acclaimed.

The writing of Ricardo Pasos Marciacq reflects not only his appreciation for the long and tumultuous history of Nicaragua but for the richness of its society. His books *Maria Manuela Piel de Luna* and *El Burdel de las Pedrarias* are modern classics. The former evokes the years when British-armed Miskitos were wreaking havoc on the Spanish settlements of the Pacific.

Rubén Darío is loved throughout the world of Latin American literature and is considered the father of modernism in Spanish literature. A few of the many other books by Nicaraguan writers worth reading if you have the facility of the language include *El Nicaragüense* by Pablo Antonio Cuadra, *Nicaragua, Teatro de lo Grandioso* by Carlos A. Bravo, and *El Estrecho Dudoso* by Ernesto Cardenal.

Dance and Theater

Nicaragua's traditional folk dances are often mixed with a form of theater, like a play in a parade. Several dance institutions in Managua teach folk classics alongside modern dance and ballet, and sponsor frequent performances. The presence of dance schools outside the capital is on the rise, which means fortunate travelers have a good chance of seeing a presentation outside of Managua, especially in Masaya, Diriamba, Matagalpa, León, and Granada.

Nicaraguans love to dance. Period. And there is no occasion (except maybe a funeral) at which it is inappropriate to pump up the music and take to your feet. The ultra suave, loose-hipped movements associated with merengue, salsa, *cumbia,* and reggae are most commonly seen at discos, street parties, or in living rooms around the nation. The Palo de Mayo is a popular modern Caribbean dance form featuring flamboyant costumes, vibrating chests, and not-so-subtle sexual simulations. When you see mothers rocking their babies to loud Latin rhythms, and two-year-old girls receiving hip-gyrating lessons, you'll understand why Nicaraguans are able to move so much more fluidly on the dance floor than you are.

Visual Arts

A number of Nicaraguan sculptors and painters have work displayed at galleries in Managua, Granada, León, and other places. Though the primitivist painters of Solentiname have gotten the lion's share of the press, there is much more to be seen. In Managua, there are frequent expos of art, often accompanied by buffets or musical performances.

Music

Expect to find loud, blaring radios in most restaurants, bars, vehicles, and homes. It may seem strange at first to find yourself listening to fast, pulsing merengue beats at six in the morning on a rural chicken bus (or in your hotel lobby at midnight) when the only people listening are sitting calmly in their seats or rocking chairs. Realize, however, that this behavior is seen as a way to inject *alegría* (happiness) into the environment, or alternately, to get rid of the sadness that some Nicaraguans associate with silence.

Radio mixes are eclectic, featuring the latest Dominican merengues, Mexican and Miami pop, cheesy *románticas,* plus a bizarre U.S. mélange of Backstreet Boys ("Los

Back," for those in the know), Air Supply, and Guns N' Roses. Another wildly popular genre is the *ranchera,* which comes in the form of either polka beats or slow, drippy, lost-love, mariachi tearjerkers, performed by one of a handful of super-celebrity Mexican crooners. Old, rootsy, U.S. country music is extremely popular on the Atlantic coast, and in northern Nicaragua, Kenny Rogers (pronounced "Royers") is recognized as the undisputed king of "La Música Country."

Managua is host to a small, exciting scene of young local bands and solo musicians, most of whom are direct descendants of the generation of musicians that brought Nicaraguan folk music to the world. Their acts range from quiet acoustic solo sets to the head-banging throaty screams of a couple of angry, politically-minded metal bands. You can hear a lot of them at **El Caramanchel** in Managua.

Live music is also found at most *fiestas patronales,* performed by one of several Nicaraguan commercial party bands whose sets imitate the radio mixes of the day. Among the most popular bands is Los Mokuanes (named after the enchanted mountain and its resident witch in La Trinidad, Estelí), which has been around in one form or another for more than three decades. During the war, they were conscripted by the government to don fatigues and perform at army bases throughout the country. Other favorite bands are Macolla and, representing the Palo de Mayo side of things, Sir Anthony and his Dimensión Costeño.

BASEBALL

A hundred years of North American and Cuban influence has engendered a nation of baseball *(el béisbol)* fanatics. Throughout Nicaragua, few pueblos lack a ball field, even if the kids put together games with homemade bats and balls of wound twine and tape. The casual traveler is more often than not welcome to join. A plethora of municipal leagues, town leagues, little leagues, competitions between universities, and even between government ministries make up the bulk of the national sport. Nicaragua's pro league seems to be constantly in flux, often due to funding problems. At last check, only four teams were competing in the top division: Managua (El Boer), Masaya (San Fernando), the León Lions, and Chinandega Tigers. These teams play with professional ringers from the United States who come to Nicaragua to stay in shape during their off-season. The other division consists of ball clubs from Estelí, Granada (Los Tiburones, or the Sharks), Matagalpa, and Rivas. The **Federación Nicaragüense de Beisból Asociado** (www.feniba.org) has an office in the national stadium in Managua.

There are several concurrent seasons. The pros play November-February, and the minors start around January. Playoff games and a seven-game championship series are played in the spring. The games and the fans are serious, but the series' charm is its humility. Here, baseball is a pastime, not a mega-marketed seven-figure-salary circus. Not that Nicaraguan players don't dream of making it big in "The Show" like their major league colleagues, Vicente Padilla, Marvin Bernard, and Everth Cabrera, whose every move is followed passionately in the Nicaraguan sports pages.

Essentials

Transportation

GETTING THERE AND AWAY

Air

American Airlines (tel. 505/2263-1045) has daily flights via Miami, **United Airlines** (tel. 505/2263-1030) via Houston, and **Delta Airlines** (tel. 505/2233-9943) via Atlanta. The Salvadoran airline **TACA** (tel. 505/2266-3136, www.taca.com) has daily flights from Los Angeles and Miami with a brief stopover in San Salvador. This is typically a less expensive flight, but the cheapest possible flight is from Fort Lauderdale, Florida, on **Spirit Airlines** (tel. 505/2233-2884). Panama-based **Copa Airlines** (tel. 505/2233-1624, www.copaair.com) has daily flights across the region with continuing flights to the U.S. and South America. Costa Rican airline **Nature Air** (tel. 505/2276-9199, www.natureair.com) offers flights to San José on Monday, Wednesday, Friday, and Sunday. National airline **La Costeña** (tel. 505/2298-5360, www.lacostena.com.ni) has direct flights from Tegucigalpa, Honduras, every day but Sunday.

From the airport **Augusto C. Sandino** (tel. 505/2233-1624), you can change money, arrange rental cars, stop by the INTUR desk for hotel recommendations, and even buy or rent a cell phone. Skycaps will help you with your luggage (about $2). Don't use the services of anyone not sporting a skycap uniform. The airport taxi collective always has drivers waiting out front.

Land

The three northern border posts are (from west to east): Guasaule, Chinandega; El Espino, Somoto; and Las Manos, Somoto. Travelers who entered the region via Guatemala, Honduras, or El Salvador can enter Nicaragua without getting additional visas thanks to Nicaragua's participation in the CA-4 Border Control Agreement of 2006. Under the agreement, your initial entry visa is valid for the whole region for up to 90 days and can be extended once with little hassle.

On the southern border, Peñas Blancas is the principal corridor on the Pan-American Highway leading to Costa Rica, and no such agreement exists. You'll need a stamp if arriving from Costa Rica. You can also enter Nicaragua in the south from Los Chiles, Costa Rica, a trip that involves a lovely boat ride to San Carlos at the head of the Río San Juan.

Detailed border-crossing instructions are provided in the corresponding regional chapters of this book. Every overland crossing involves two steps: exiting the first country and entering the second. If you forget to get the second stamp in your passport, you will regret it.

DRIVING ACROSS THE BORDER

If you are driving your own vehicle, the process to enter Nicaragua is lengthier, but usually not difficult. You must present the vehicle's title, as well as your own driver's license and passport. You will be given a temporary 30-day permit ($10) to drive in Nicaragua. Should you lose the permit, you will be fined $100. Alamo Rent a Car shares cars between Costa Rica and Nicaragua, permitting you to pick up in one country and drop off in another.

INTERNATIONAL BUS

A half-dozen long-haul bus companies run between Managua and other Central American capitals. Several have affiliate offices in other Nicaraguan cities, like Rivas and León.

ESSENTIALS
TRANSPORTATION

Previous: ferry on Lake Nicaragua with one of Ometepe's volcanoes in the background; street scene in front of Granada's cathedral.

A ride from Managua to San José, Costa Rica takes 10 hours ($29 each way). To Tegucigalpa, Honduras it can take 8-10 hours ($25 each way), depending on the line at immigration. **Tica Bus** (two blocks east of the *antiguo* Cine Dorado, tel. 505/2298-5500, www.ticabus.com) is the oldest and best-established Central American international bus company, with three daily departures to San José, as well as service to the rest of Central America with connections all the way to southern Mexico. Many of their stations (including Managua) have hotels attached for those travelers leaving early in the morning. Nearby in Boloñia, **Del Sol Bus** (tel. 505/2222-7785, www.busesdelsol.com) provides transport between Nicaragua, Guatemala, and El Salvador. **Central Line** (from the former Cine Cabrera, 2.5 blocks east, on 27 de Mayo Ave., tel. 505/2254-5431, www.transportescentralline.com) has one route between Managua and San José. Recently re-opened **Nica Bus** (tel. 505/2222-2276 or 505/2222-6746, nicabusinternacionalsa@gmail.com) provides service between Costa Rica and Managua. For travelers heading north, **King Quality** (at the end of Calle 27 de Mayo, Avenida Bolívar, on the west side of Plaza Inter, tel. 505/2222-3065 or 505/2228-1454, www.platinumcentroamerica.com) is the priciest option, with double-decker buses complete with onboard Wi-Fi. **Transnica** (from the Rotonda Metrocentro, 300 meters north, 25 meters east, tel. 505/2277-2104 or 505/2270-3133, www.transnica.com) offers transport between Nicaragua, Costa Rica, and Honduras.

Many of these companies collect passports and immigration fees from travelers at the border crossings that will permit it, taking care of the paperwork for you.

GETTING AROUND
Air
La Costeña (tel. 505/2298-5360, www.lacostena.com.ni, reservacion@lacostena.com.ni) is Nicaragua's sole domestic airline. Its humble fleet of small craft fly between Managua and the Atlantic coast (Mining Triangle, Puerto Cabezas, Waspám, Bluefields, Corn Island), Ometepe, San Carlos, and San Juan del Norte, as well as a new international route to Tegucigalpa, Honduras. Seats are limited on the 12-passenger twin-prop Cessna Grand Caravans (they have one 40-passenger Short 360 aircraft as well), and cost about $80 one-way, $160 round-trip. It is almost imperative that you reserve your flight before arriving in Nicaragua. This has been difficult in the past, but La Costeña's new online booking system will help matters. If your schedule is flexible, save yourself $18 in online fees by booking at the airport.

Bus
Nicaragua's intercity bus system is made up primarily of retired U.S. yellow school buses, each one lovingly customized with stickers, paint, sound systems, and plastic streamers. Modern, air-conditioned coaches are increasingly joining the lineup for popular express routes. Bus coverage is excellent, though the ride is bumpy, crowded, and often slow. Each major population center has one or two bus hubs, with regular and express service to nearby cities and to Managua, plus rural routes to the surrounding communities. If you've got the time, riding the Nicaraguan bus network will provide endless memories and probably make you a couple of friends, as there's little else to do on the ride but chat.

Local buses, called *ordinarios* or *ruteados,* stop for anyone standing by the roadside and flapping their hand. *Expresos* are more expensive and make fewer stops; they are also often better quality vehicles and are well worth the extra 25 percent you will pay for a ticket. In addition, *expresos* usually work on a reserved/numbered seat basis. Before you settle into town it's worth spending a couple more minutes at the bus station to make your onward reservations, if possible.

To points west and south from Managua, there is an especially large number of express microbuses (minivans or *interlocales*) that leave every 20 minutes (or whenever they fill up).

On the *ruteados,* you'll board the bus, find a seat, and then wait for the *ayudante* (driver's helper) to come around and collect your *pasaje* (fare). Ask a fellow traveler how much the ride should cost just to be sure, though my experience is that the *ayudantes* are typically honest. The *ayudante* will write the amount owed to you on your ticket if he doesn't have exact change, returning later in the trip to pay you. Most buses have overhead racks inside where you can stow your bags. Less desirable, but common, is for the *ayudante* to insist you put your backpack on the roof or in some cargo space in the back of the bus. It is safer to keep your stuff on your lap or at least within sight, but I've never had a problem stowing bags out of sight.

Taxi

Taxis are a great way to get around and are well worth the extra money if you want to save time. In Managua, they're essential, as walking between destinations is usually out of the question. In every city except Managua, urban taxis operate on a fixed zone rate, usually under $1 within the central city area. In the capital, however, you are expected to bargain out a rate before sitting down. In all cases,

avoid taxis where the driver is traveling with a friend, and pay attention to where you're going.

Shuttle Services

This is a relatively new option in Nicaragua, a direct response to travelers in Granada and León who would rather not negotiate taxi fees or muck around with the chicken buses. You'll board a new minivan filled with other tourists willing to spend $15-20 to be whisked between the pueblos, beach towns, and ferry docks. Most offer airport service as well.

Start with **Adelante Express** (tel. 505/8850-6070 or 2568-2083, www.adelanteexpress.com), based in San Juan del Sur, which offers full service shuttles and transport all over Nicaragua. Their online reservation system is easy to use and 24-hour advance reservations are required. **Paxeos** (tel. 505/2552-8291 or 505/8465-1090, www.paxeos.com) is another reliable shuttle service, based in Granada, specializing in personal airport pickups at any time of night (and they have an online booking service). You can check with tour operators, especially **Tierra Tours** (www.tierratour.com), who offers shuttles and airport transfers. You'll find a convenient price list on their website.

ESSENTIALS
TRANSPORTATION

Retired yellow school buses make up a large part of Nicaragua's public transportation.

Driving

RENTING A CAR

While it seems convenient to zip out of the airport in a rented car, the hassle of driving and the risk of making sure the car doesn't get stolen or damaged are not to be underestimated. If you are traveling with a lot of luggage, children, or surfboards, it's a no-brainer. But be aware that if you have just a little bit more time, you can get around extremely easily in taxis, shuttles, and public buses.

All the major car rental agencies have set up shop at the Managua airport, and you can arrange a car through most hotels costing $50 or higher. Be sure to reserve in advance: **Alamo** (tel. 505/2277-1117, www.alamonicaragua.com), **Avis** (tel. 505/2233-3011, www.avis.com.ni), **Budget** (tel. 505/2255-9000, U.S. tel. 786/955-9000, www.budget.com.ni), **Hertz** (tel. 505/2233-1237, www.hertz.com.ni), **National** (tel. 505/2270-8492 or U.S 877/862-8227, www.nationalnicaragua.com), **Thrifty** (tel. 505/2255-7981, www.thrifty.com.ni). Most of these companies have offices elsewhere in the city, and in major tourist hubs across the country.

Plan on spending $40-50 per day, $300 a week during the high season for the smallest four-seater "econobox," or $75 a day, $450 a week for a pickup truck, plus insurance costs and gasoline, which is well over $4 per gallon.

VEHICULAR SAFETY

The most dangerous thing you will do in Nicaragua is travel on its highways. Outside the cities, roads are poorly lit, narrow, lacking shoulders, and are often full of potholes, unannounced speed bumps, and fallen rocks. Even in Managua, expect to find ox carts and abandoned vehicles in the lanes, and hungry dogs and grazing horses wandering the streets. Because there are no shoulders for taxis to use when boarding passengers, they stop in the right lane and let traffic swerve around them. The fact that beer and rum are sold at most gas stations should give you an idea of how many drivers are intoxicated, especially late at night.

When possible, avoid traveling during peak rush hours in cities, and after dark anywhere. Plan your route before entering a city, as you will not have the luxury of reading a map while you navigate traffic. That goes double for Managua, where choosing the wrong lane can be disastrous. Motorcycles are especially dangerous, as many drivers are unlicensed and choose to beat rush hour by squeezing between stopped cars. Look twice before changing lanes.

TRAFFIC ACCIDENTS AND GETTING PULLED OVER

Nicaragua's police force is poorly paid and not averse to a little pocket money. Foreign drivers without diplomatic plates are frequent targets for document checks, but if you commit a *mala maniobra* (moving violation, literally "bad move") in their presence, you'd better have your papers ready. Crooked cops will confiscate your license and threaten to hold it hostage until you come in the following week to pay the fine, unless, of course, you'd rather take care of the issue right then, hint hint, wink wink.

If you are involved in a vehicular accident, *do not* move your vehicle from the scene of the crime until authorized by a police officer, even if it is blocking traffic. Nicaraguan police will try to understand how the accident occurred based on what they see at the site. Drivers who move their vehicle at the scene of the accident are legally liable for the incident. Any driver in Nicaragua that causes injuries to another person will be taken into immediate custody, regardless of insurance and circumstances, and remain there until the courts reach a decision—sometimes weeks later—or until the injured party signs a waiver releasing the driver of liability. To avoid a lengthy court proceeding and horrifying jail stay, it may be worth your while to plead guilty and pay a fine (which historically does not exceed $1,000, even in the case of a death). But call your embassy and get a lawyer immediately.

Motorcycles and Bicycles

If you intend to ride a motorcycle or bicycle in Nicaragua, be sure to bring a helmet, an item largely ignored by Nicaraguans, many of whom manage to fit a family of four on one bike. If biking, keep your eyes on the road; the entrances to Matagalpa and Granada have unmarked speed bumps.

Biking Central America is a breathtaking experience but puts you at risk in a couple of ways, though thru-bikers report that Nicaragua is neither better nor worse than the rest of Central America. Small shoulders at roadside and the occasional bottle-throwing idiot careening by in a fast car are par for the course. Travelers have reported some harassment and even robbery of bikers in the stretch between San Juan del Sur and the Costa Rican border.

Boats

In several regions of Nicaragua—notably Solentiname, Río San Juan, Río Coco, and the entire Atlantic coast—a boat will be your only means of transportation. Here, rising gasoline prices determine the fare, which will be more expensive than you expect. Locals get around in public water taxis called *colectivos* that help cut costs. Any water-bordering community will likely have small boats the owners use for fishing or transport. Ask for a *canoa, panga,* or *botecita,* and see what shows up. Dugout canoes are common throughout the country, and you can ask to rent one along the Río San Juan and other areas. For recreation, there are a handful of sailboats that can take you out in San Juan del Sur, and some boat-based tour companies out of Granada and León. **Ibis Exchange** (www.ibis-kayaking.com) offers paddle trips in the Estero Padre Ramos in expedition ocean kayaks.

Visas and Officialdom

PASSPORTS AND VISAS

Every traveler to Nicaragua must have a passport valid for at least six months following the date of entry. A visa is required only for citizens of the following countries: Afghanistan, Albania, Bosnia-Herzegovina, Colombia, Cuba, Haiti, India, Iran, Iraq, Jordan, Lebanon, Libya, Nepal, Pakistan, People's Republic of China, People's Republic of Korea, Somalia, Sri Lanka, Vietnam, and Yugoslavia. Everyone else is automatically given a tourist visa ($10) at the airport or land border, good for three months. Technically, you must have an onward/return ticket, and evidence of sufficient funds; in practice, this is never checked.

Renewing a visa has gotten easier in the new tourist-friendly Nicaragua. In Managua at the Metrocentro shopping mall, there's an **Immigration branch office** (tel. 505/2244-3989 x284-287, Mon.-Fri. 10am-6pm,

Sat.-Sun. 10am-1pm) that will process your request for an extension. You'll pay $0.19 for the form, and must present photocopies of your passport's information page as well as the page with your visa. A 30-day tourist visa extension is $10. If you've overstayed your current visa, you will pay an additional $1 for each day over the limit. Many travelers in San Juan del Sur prefer to just take a bus over the Costa Rican border, and return the same day on a fresh, new tourist visa. Furthermore, Nicaragua entered into the CA-4 Border Control Agreement permitting travelers to travel among Nicaragua, Guatemala, Honduras, and El Salvador without getting additional visas: Your initial entry visa is valid for the whole region for up to 90 days and can be extended once.

Anything more serious than a basic tourist visa extension requires a trip to the main **Office of Immigration** (Dirección General de Migración y Extranjería, 1.5 blocks north of the *semáforos* Tenderí, tel. 505/2222-7538, www.migob.gob.ni, Mon.-Fri. 8am-5pm). Show up at least four days before it expires with your passport, current visa, and $25.

CUSTOMS

Tourists are invariably ignored by customs officials, who have their eyes peeled for wealthy Nicas returning from shopping binges in Miami. Should they go through your luggage, you can expect to be taxed for carrying items you obviously don't intend to use yourself, including electronics, jewelry, and perfume. To save yourself trouble, avoid carrying more of anything valuable (such as a laptop) than a traveler would typically need. Surfers, that goes for your boards, too. If it looks like you're importing sales stock, you will be stopped and hassled.

EMBASSIES AND CONSULATES

All diplomatic missions in Nicaragua are located in Managua, mostly along Carretera Masaya and Carretera Sur. The city of Chinandega hosts consulates from El Salvador, Honduras, and Costa Rica.

Americans living or traveling in Nicaragua can register with the **U.S. Embassy** (Kilometer 5.5, Carretera Sur, Managua, tel. 505/2252-7100, nicaragua. usembassy.gov, Mon.-Fri. 7:30am-4:15pm) at the main international travel page of the U.S. State Department (www.travel.state. gov). Registering is not a legal requirement but is encouraged by the embassy so that they can send you updated travel and security advisories regarding Nicaragua. These advisories, and the warning messages on the embassy website, are invariably on the conservative side as far as risk assessment. In case of emergency call 505/2252-7104 during business hours, and after hours request to speak with the Embassy Duty Officer (505/2252-7171 or 505/8768-7171).

The **Canadian Embassy** (in Bolonia on Calle El Nogal, 2 blocks down from "Los Pipitos," tel. 505/2268-0433 or 505/2268-3323, mngua@international.gc.ca, Mon.-Thurs. 8am-noon and 12:30pm-4pm, Fri. 7:30am-1pm) in Managua is actually an outpost of their main embassy in San José, Costa Rica. For emergencies involving Canadian citizens, call the emergency consular service in Ottawa collect at 613/996-8885.

Embassies or consulates for the following countries can be found at these locations: **Costa Rica** (Reparto San Juan, from Hotel Seminole 2 blocks north, half a block west, tel. 505/2270-7464; there is also a consulate in Chinandega), **El Salvador** (Las Colinas, Ave. El Campo Pasaje Los Cerros no. 142, tel. 505/2276-0712 or 505/2276-2134), and **Honduras** (Carretera Masaya Km 12, 100 meters toward Cainsa, tel. 505/2279-8231). The **British Embassy** (from the Hospital Militar, 1 block north, 10 meters west, tel. 505/2254-5454 x127) in Costa Rica has an honorary consulate in Managua. The **Australian Consulate** (from Optica Nicaraguense 4 blocks west, tel. 505/2266-1925) is a branch of their Mexican embassy.

Conduct and Customs

HOLIDAYS AND FESTIVALS

Like the rest of Latin America, every town and city has its own patron saint whom the residents honor each year with a party that lasts 1-3 weeks. These *fiestas patronales* combine religious fervor with the consumption of alcohol in biblical proportions. Most celebrations include Virgin and Saint parades, special masses, fireworks, cockfighting, rodeos, concerts, gambling, dances, and show-horse parades *(hípicos)*. Many towns have additional celebrations of specific events in their history.

Semana Santa (Holy Week) is the biggest celebration of the year, occurring during the week leading up to Easter Sunday. The weeklong vacation sends most city folk to the beach for sun and debauchery; many shops close their doors. In popular beach areas like San Juan del Sur, expect hiked prices and few vacancies. In other areas, you may also encounter altered bus schedules and other travel annoyances.

Expect all public offices to be closed on the following days: **January 1** (New Year's Day), **late March/early April** (Semana Santa, including Holy Thursday, Good Friday, and Easter), **May 1** (Labor Day), **May 30** (Mother's Day), **July 19** (National Liberation Day), **September 14** (Battle of San Jacinto), **September 15** (Independence Day), **November 2** (Día de los Muertes, All Souls' Day), **December 8** (La Purísima, Immaculate Conception), **December 25** (Christmas Day).

Remember that Nicaraguan holidays are subject to decree, shutting the banks down without warning to suit some politician's inclination. The list that follows should help you catch (or avoid) *fiestas patronales*. Year-round weekly events include the following: Thursdays in Masaya are Jueves de Verbena, Fridays in Granada are Noches de Serenata, and Sundays in León are Tertulias Leónesas.

January
1: New Year's Day
Second week: Señor de los Milagros, Chinandega
15: Señor de Esquipulas, Rivas
18: *Fiestas Patronales,* El Sauce
20: San Sebastian, Carazo
Third Sunday: Señor de Esquipulas, El Sauce (León)
Third weekend: Viva León Festival, León
Third weekend: San Sebastían, Acoyapa (Chontales), Diriamba, Carazo (San Sebastián)
Last weekend: La Virgen de Candelaria, LaTrinidad (Estelí)

February
9-11: San Caralampio in Cinco Pinos Chinandega
15-22: Poetry Festival, Granada
22-24: Festival of Traditions, Masaya
24: King Pulanka, Puerto Cabezas

March
17: San Benito, León
19: San José de Buenos Aires, Rivas
Third weekend: Folklore, Gastronomy, and Handicraft Festival, Granada

April
Semana Santa
First week: Religious Ash Paintings in León
19-21: *Fiestas Patronales,* San Jorge (Rivas)

May
1: Labor Day
1: *Fiestas Patronales,* Jinotega
15: San Isidro Labrador, Condega (Estelí)
20: Tiangue, León
Third weekend: Palo de Mayo Festival, Bluefields
28: Carnaval de Nicaragua, Managua
30: Mother's Day

June

16: Virgen del Carmen, San Juan del Sur (Rivas)
16: Procession of the Virgen de los Pescadores, Río San Juan
24: St. John the Baptist, San Juan de Oriente (Carazo), San Juan del Sur (Rivas), San Juan de Jinotega (Jinotega)
29: St. Peter the Apostle, Diriá (Masaya)
Last Friday: El Repliegue Sandinista (Managua)

July

6: Corn Fair, Chinandega
Second Saturday: Carnaval, Somoto
15-25: *Fiestas Patronales,* Somoto
19: National Liberation Day
25: Santiago, Boaco, Jinotepe (Carazo)
26: St. Ana, Nandaime (Granada), Chinandega, Ometepe
25-27: Rosquillas Festival, Somoto

August

1-10: Santo Domingo (Noches Agostinas), Managua
10: St. Lorenzo, Somotillo (Chinandega)
14: Gritería Chiquita, León
14-15: *Fiestas Patronales,* Ocotal
15: The Assumption, Granada
15: The Assumption and Fiesta del Hijo Ausente, Juigalpa
Third weekend: Mariachis and Mazurcas Festival, Estelí

September

10: San Nicolás de Tolentino, La Paz Centro (León)
14: The Battle of San Jacinto
15: Independence Day
14 and 15: Fishing Fair, San Carlos (Río San Juan)
15: Patron Saint Festival of Villa Nueva, Chinandega
20: San Jerónimo, Masaya
24: La Merced, León, and Matagalpa
Fourth weekend: Polkas, Mazurcas, and Jamaquellos, Matagalpa; Festival of Corn, Jalapa

October

12: San Diego (Estelí)
Second weekend: Norteño Music Festival in Jinotega
24: San Rafael Arcángel, Pueblo Nuevo
Penultimate Sunday: Fiesta de los Agüisotes, Masaya
Last Sunday: Toro Venado, Masaya

November

2: All Souls' Day
3-5: Equestrian Rally in Ometepe
4: San Carlos Borromeo, San Carlos (Río San Juan)
9-11: Garífuna Heritage Day; Bluefields, Orinoco
12-18: San Diego de Alcalá, Altagracia (Ometepe)
Fourth Sunday: Folkloric Festival, Masaya

December

First Sunday: Procesión de San Jerónimo, Masaya
6: Lavada de La Plata, Virgen del Trono, El Viejo (Chinandega)
7: Purísimas (Immaculate Conception Celebrations) in Managua, Granada, Masaya, and León

FOOD AND DRINK

Nicaraguans enjoy good food and good times, and being too dainty while eating signals that you're not pleased with the meal. There are limits, so keep an eye on your dining companions for what's appropriate and what's not, but don't be afraid to enjoy what's on your plate. If you'd like to get a laugh out of your Nicaraguan hosts or waiters, after you've finished your plate, tell them, *"Barriga llena, corazón contenta"* ("Belly full, happy heart").

Corn Culture

Maíz (corn) is central to the Nicaraguan diet. Beans are just as critical a staple (and a nutritionally critical complement), but in Nicaragua, corn is prepared with more variety, taste, and frequency. Corn is prepared and consumed in more than a hundred different

nacatamales

ways. **Tortillas** are flat cakes of corn dough softened with water and cooked on a slightly rounded clay pan known as a *comal*. The only place you'll find flour tortillas is in a Mexican restaurant in Managua. Nica corn tortillas are thick, heavy, and (hopefully) hot off the woodstove. When the same dough is fortified with sugar and lard, then rolled into small lumps and boiled while wrapped in yellow corn husks, the result is a **tamal,** steaming heavy bowls of which market women balance on their heads and loudly vend in the streets. **Nacatamales,** a Nicaraguan classic, are similar but with meat, often spiced pork, and often potatoes in the middle. **Atol** is corn pudding, and **güirila** is a sweet tortilla of young corn, always served with a hunk of **cuajada** (soft, salty white cheese).

Elote is corn on the cob, which is especially tasty when roasted over open coals until the kernels are a little chewy. When harvested young, the ears of corn, called **chilotes,** are served in soup or with fresh cream. Corn is also oven-baked into hard,

molasses-sweetened cookie rings called **rosquillas**, flat cookies called **ojaldras,** and many other shapes. The same dough is also combined with cheese, lard, and spices to produce dozens more items, including **perrerreques, cosas de horno** (usually sweet corn cake), and **gofios.**

What do you wash it down with? More corn, of course. **Pinol,** drunk so frequently in Nicaragua the Nicaraguans proudly call themselves *pinoleros,* is toasted and ground corn meal mixed with water. **Pinolillo** is *pinol* mixed with cacao, pepper, and cloves; *tiste* is similar. **Pozol** is a ground cornmeal drink prepared from a variety of corn with a pinkish hue. The ultra-sweet, pink baggies of *chicha* are made from slightly fermented cornmeal (especially strong batches are called *chicha brava*). Then, of course, there is crystal clear, Nicaraguan corn tequila, or **cususa.**

Alcohol

It goes largely undisputed that Nicaragua makes the best **rum** in all of Central America. Flor de Caña is the highest caliber, of which the caramel-colored, 7-year Gran Reserva is only surpassed by the 12-year Centenario (which is twice as expensive). A media (half-liter) of seven-year, bucket of ice, bottle of Coke, and plate of limes (called a servicio completo) will set you back only $7 or so. Rum on the rocks with a squirt of Coca-Cola and a spurt of lime is called a Nica Libre. Reach for a clear plastic bottle of Caballito or Ron Plata, and take a giant step down in price and quality. Enormously popular in the countryside, "Rrrrron Plata!" is the proud sponsor of most baseball games and not a few bar brawls. Bottles are $5 or less. But wait, you can get drunk for even less! Most street corners and town parks are the backdrop for many a grimacing shot of Tayacán, or its homemade, corn-mash equivalent. Nicaraguans call it *cususa, guaro,* or *lija,* brought down from the hills by the moonshine man on his mule. It's sold by the gallon for about $4, often in a stained, sloshing, plastic container that used to contain

Nicaraguan Dining Terms

DESAYUNO	BREAKFAST
Huevos	Eggs
Enteros	Hardboiled
Revueltos	Scrambled
Volteados	Over-easy
Estrellados	Sunny-side up

ALMUERZO Y CENA	LUNCH AND DINNER
Carne/res	Beef
Desmenuzada	Shredded and stewed
A la plancha	Served on a hot plate
Churrasco	Grilled steak
Filete jalapeño	Steak in a creamy pepper sauce (not spicy)
Puerco/cerdo	Pork
Chuleta	Pork chop
Pollo	Chicken
Empanizado	Breaded
Frito	Fried
Al vino	Wine sauce
Rostizado	Rotisserie
Valenciano	A chicken, jam, and rice dish
Mariscos	Seafood
Pescado entero	The whole fish
Langosta al ajillo	Lobster in garlic sauce
Camarones al vapor	Steamed shrimp
Sopa de conchas	Conch soup
Huevos de Paslama	Endangered turtle eggs

some automobile product, and then resold in plastic baggie-size portions.

The national **beers**—Victoria and Toña—are both light-tasting pilsners. Expect to pay $1-2 a beer, depending on your environs. Recent additions to the beer selection are Premium and Brahva, largely indistinguishable, and the Victoria Frost, an ice-filtered beverage with slightly higher alcohol content. Towards the end of the year, Victoria sells a popular seasonal beer called Maestra. Brahva is the only alcoholic beverage whose production or distribution isn't controlled by the Pellas family, which produces every other beverage mentioned in this book. Two new exceptions are the new breweries Moropotente (based in Jinotepe, but sold nation-wide), and the gringo-owned Cervecería in San Juan del

Sur. Both make delicious microbrews. In response to these higher quality options, Victoria has begun marketing a new beer called Mytos, essentially an unfiltered version of Victoria Clássica with higher alcohol content.

ALCOHOLISM

Alcohol abuse is rampant in Nicaragua and increasingly acknowledged as a problem. Most towns have an Alcoholics Anonymous chapter, and many churches forbid their members to drink. Nevertheless, most otherwise religious holidays (including Sundays), in addition to all nonreligious events, serve as excuses to get falling-down drunk. Just about all men drink and are firm believers in the expression *"una es ninguna"* ("one is none"). In small towns, women are socially discouraged

PLATOS TRADICIONALES	**TRADITIONAL DISHES**
Baho	Plantain and beef stew
Nacatamales	Meat-filled corn *tamal*, wrapped and boiled in banana leaves
Indio viejo	Beef, veggie, and cornmeal mush
Caballo bayo	A sampler's plate of traditional dishes
Gallo pinto	Red beans and rice, generously doused in oil and salt
Cuajada	White, soft farmer's cheese
Leche agria	A sour cream-yogurt combo
Vigorón	Pork rinds with yucca and coleslaw, served on a banana leaf

BOCADILLAS	**APPETIZERS**
Tostones	Thick, fried, green plantains
Tajadas	Crunchy, thin strips of green plantain
Maduro	Ripe, sweet plantains fried in their own sugar
Ensalada	Shredded cabbage, sometimes with tomatoes and lime juice

BEBIDAS Y (RE)FRESCOS	**DRINKS AND FRUIT JUICES**
Tiste	Toasted cooked corn with cacao, pepper, and cloves
Pinol	Toasted, milled corn
Pinolillo	Pinol with pepper, cloves, and cacao
Horchata	Toasted and milled rice with spices
Chicha	Rough-milled corn with vanilla and banana flavors, sometimes fermented

POSTRES	**DESSERTS**
Flan	Flan
Sorbete	Sherbet
Helado	Ice cream

Toña is one of Nicaragua's national beers.

from drinking, though they sometimes do so in the privacy of their own homes or with close friends. Should you decide to partake in this part of the culture and find yourself drunk *(borracho, bolo, picado, hasta el culo),* be sure you have a decent understanding of your environment and feel good about your company.

Health and Safety

BEFORE YOU GO
Resources
Dirk G. Schroeder's *Staying Healthy in Asia, Africa, and Latin America,* a concise guide to preventative medicine in the Developing World, is small enough to fit in your pocket. Consult the "Mexico and Central America" page of the **U.S. Centers for Disease Control** (CDC, www.cdc.gov) website for up-to-date health advice. You can also contact the Nicaraguan embassy in your country.

Vaccinations
A certificate of vaccination against **yellow fever** is required for all travelers over one year of age and arriving from affected areas. It's also smart to make sure that your **tetanus, diphtheria, measles, mumps, rubella,** and **polio** vaccines are up-to-date. Protection against **hepatitis A** and **typhoid fever** is recommended for all travelers.

MEDICAL SERVICES
Medical care is in short supply outside of Managua, and even in the capital city, doctors in public hospitals are underpaid and overworked. Though there are many qualified medical professionals in Nicaragua, there are also many practicing doctors and medical staff who have less-than-adequate credentials. Use your best judgment, and be your own advocate. Private hospitals and clinics typically expect immediate payment for services rendered, but their rates are ridiculously cheaper than they are back home. Larger facilities accept credit cards; everyone else demands cash.

Government-run health clinics, called **Centros de Salud,** exist in most towns throughout the country, usually near the central plaza. They are free, even to you, but are often poorly supplied and inadequately staffed. The most modern hospital in the country is **Hospital Vivian Pellas** (tel. 505/2255-6900), a $23-million private institution seven kilometers south of Managua on the Carretera Masaya. For dental emergencies, or even just a check-up, seek out the bilingual services of **Dr. Esteban Bendaña McEwan** (300 meters south of the ENITEL Villa Fontana, tel. 505/2270-5021 or 505/8850-8981, estebanbm@hotmail.com). Dr. Bendaña is accustomed to dealing with foreign patients and his prices are reasonable. The U.S. Embassy website has a helpful list of doctors if you need something specific.

Natural Medicine
Many *campesinos* (country folk) have excellent practical knowledge of herbal remedies. Try crushed and boiled papaya seeds, oil of *apazote* (a small shrub), or coconut water to fend off intestinal parasites; *manzanilla* (chamomile) for stress or stomach discomfort; or *tamarindo* or papaya for constipation. A popular cold remedy involves hot tea mixed with two squeezed limes, *miel de jicote* (honey from the *jicote* bee), and a large shot of cheap rum, drunk right before you go to bed so you sweat out the fever as you sleep.

Medications and Prescriptions
Many modern medicines are sold in Nicaragua. Because of a struggling economy and plenty of competition, some pharmacies may sell you medicine without a prescription. For simple travelers' ailments, like stomach upsets, diarrhea, or analgesics, it's worth

A Guide to Nicaragua's Restrooms

TOILETS

Nicaragua boasts an enormous diversity of bathrooms, from various forms of the common *inodoro* (modern toilet, a.k.a. *el trono*) to the full range of dark, infested *letrinas* (outhouses). Despite so many options, many regions of Nicaragua suffer a shortage of actual toilet seats, so having to squat over a bare bowl is common. Because water supplies are sometimes sporadic, even in cities, you may have to employ a manual toilet flush. Mastering this move is important. (Leaving a toilet unflushed is considered very rude.) Use the plastic bucket sitting beside the toilet (or near the sink) and dump the water into the bowl, all at once, forcefully and from high up to ensure maximum swirlage.

In most mid-range and expensive hotels, you can probably safely flush your toilet paper, but the norm in Nicaragua is still to put used toilet paper in the waste basket next to the toilet so as not to clog the weak plumbing. It's never a bad idea to travel with a roll of toilet paper *(papel higiénico)* protected in a plastic bag. Otherwise, try the following phrase with your host: "*Fíjase que no hay papel en el baño*" ("Look, there's no toilet paper in the bathroom.")

SHOWERS

In the cooler parts of the country, namely Matagalpa and Jinotega, some hotels and *hospedajes* offer hot water by means of electric water-heating canisters attached to the end of the showerhead. Cold water passing through the coils is warmed before falling through the spout. The seemingly obvious drawback to the system is the presence of electric wires in and around a wet environment. While not necessarily the electric death traps they appear to be, they should be approached with caution. Before you step into the shower, check for frayed or exposed wires. Set the control knob to II and carefully turn the water on. Once you're wet and water is flowing through the apparatus, it's in your best interest not to mess with the heater again.

To save you many cold showers trying to figure out how the darned thing works, I'll let you in on the secret: If the water pressure is too low, the heater isn't triggered on, and the water will not be heated, but if the water pressure is too high, it will be forced through the nozzle before it's had sufficient contact with the coils, and the water will not be heated. Open the faucet to a moderate setting, and rub-a-dub-dub, you're taking a hot shower. When you've finished, turn the water off first and dry off, then turn the little knob back to Off.

going to the local pharmacy and asking what they recommend. Even relatively strong medications like codeine can be purchased over the counter (in fizzy tablet form).

Condoms are cheap and easy to find. Any corner pharmacy will have them, even in small towns of just a few thousand people. A three-pack of prophylactics costs less than $2. Female travelers taking contraceptives should know the chemical name for what they use, but you may not find exactly what you take at home, so it's best to bring plenty of your preferred brand. *Pastillas anticonceptivas* (birth control pills) are easily obtained without a prescription in pharmacies in Managua and in larger cities like

León, Granada, and Estelí, but other monthly methods (rings, patches, etc.) are uncommon. Emergency contraception *(anticonceptivo de emergencia)* can be purchased over the counter at any pharmacy.

STAYING HEALTHY

Your digestive system may take some time getting accustomed to the new food and microorganisms in the Nicaraguan diet. Wash or sanitize your hands often, eat food that is well cooked and still hot when served, and avoid dairy products if you're not sure whether they are pasteurized. Be wary of uncooked foods, including ceviche and salads. Use the finger wag to turn down food from street vendors and be aware that pork carries the extra danger of trichinosis, not to mention a diet of garbage (and worse) on which most country pigs are raised.

Prevent flies, which are transmitters of food-borne illness, from landing on your food, glass, or table setting. You'll notice Nicaraguans are meticulous about this. If you have to leave the table, cover your food with a napkin or have someone else wave their hand over it slowly. You can fold your drinking straw over and put the mouth end into the neck of the bottle to prevent flies from landing on it, and put napkins on top of the bottleneck and your glass, too. Have the waiter clear the table when you've finished with a dish. If it's really bad, ask the waiter to bring a fan over.

Sun Exposure

Nicaragua is located a scant 12 degrees of latitude north of the equator, so the sun's rays strike the Earth's surface at a more direct angle than in northern countries. The result is that you may burn faster than you are used to. Did I mention that you should drink lots of water? Ideally, do like most locals do, and stay out of the sun between 10am and 2pm. It's a great time to take a nap anyway. Use sunscreen of at least SPF 30 and wear a hat and pants. Should you overdo it in the sun, make sure to drink lots of fluids. Treat sunburns with aloe gel, or better yet, find a fresh *sábila* (aloe) plant to break open and rub over your skin.

Drinking the Water

While most Nicaraguan municipal water systems are well treated and safe (sometimes over-chlorinated), there is not much reason to take the chance, especially when purified, bottled water is widely available. But rather than contribute to the growing solid waste problem in Nicaragua, bring a single reusable plastic water bottle and refill it in your hotel lobby's five-gallon purified water dispensers. If you'll be spending time in rural Nicaragua, consider a small water filter or, alternately, use six drops of iodine (or three of bleach)

in a liter of water. This will kill every organism that needs to be killed, good if you're in a pinch but not something to do on a daily basis. Boiling water is also an effective means of purification.

Avoid ice cubes unless you're confident they were made with boiled or purified water (which they are in many restaurants). Canned and bottled drinks without ice, including beer, are safe, but should never be used as a substitute for water when trying to stay hydrated.

Oral Rehydration Salts

Probably the single most effective item in your medical kit is the packet of powdered salt and sugar known as *suero oral*. One packet of *suero* mixed with a liter of water, drunk in small sips, is the best immediate treatment for diarrhea, sun exposure, fever, infection, or hangovers. Rehydration salts replace the salts and minerals your body loses from sweating, vomiting, or urinating. Consuming enough *suero* and water is often the difference between being just a little sick and feeling really awful.

Sport drinks like Gatorade are superconcentrated *suero* mixtures and should be diluted at a ratio of three to one with water to make the most of the active ingredients. Gatorade is common in most gas stations and supermarkets, but *suero* packets ($0.50/packet) are more widely available and much cheaper, available at any drugstore or health clinic. It can be improvised even more cheaply, according to the following recipe: Mix one-half teaspoon of salt, one-half teaspoon baking soda, and four tablespoons of sugar in one quart of boiled or carbonated water. Drink a full glass after each time you use the bathroom. A few drops of lemon will make it more palatable.

DISEASES AND AILMENTS
Diarrhea and Dysentery

Many visitors to Nicaragua stay entirely regular throughout their trip. Some don't. Diarrhea is one symptom of amoebic (parasitic) and bacillic (bacterial) dysentery, both caused by some form of fecal-oral contamination. Often accompanied by nausea, vomiting, and a mild fever, dysentery is easily confused with other diseases, so don't try to self-diagnose. *Examenes de heces* (stool-sample examinations) can be performed at most clinics and hospitals and are your first step to getting better (cost is $5-10). Bacillic dysentery is treatable with antibiotics; amoebic is treated with one of a variety of drugs. Of these, Flagyl is the best known, but other non-FDA approved treatments like Tinedazol are commonly available, cheap, and effective. Do not drink alcohol with these drugs, but do eat something like yogurt or acidophilus pills to re-foliate your tummy.

Generally, simple cases of diarrhea in the absence of other symptoms are nothing more serious than "traveler's diarrhea." If you do get a case of Diriangén's Revenge, it's best to let it pass naturally. Constipating medicines like Imodium-AD are not recommended, as they keep the bacteria (or whatever is causing your intestinal distress) within your system. Save the Imodium for emergency situations like long bus rides. Most importantly, drink water! If the diarrhea persists for more than 48 hours, is bloody, or is accompanied by a fever, see a health professional immediately.

Malaria

Risk of malaria is higher in rural areas, especially those alongside rivers or marshes. But, malaria-infected mosquitoes breed anywhere stagnant pools of water (of any size, even in an empty bottle cap) are found, including urban settings. At times, western Nicaragua is declared malaria-free, at other times, the U.S. CDC recommends weekly prophylaxis of chloroquine, specifically Aralen-brand pills (500 mg for adults). Begin taking the pills two weeks before you arrive and continue taking them four weeks after leaving the country. A small percentage of people have negative reactions to chloroquine, including nightmares, rashes, or hair loss. Alternative treatments are

available, but the best method of all is to not get bitten.

The telltale symptoms include fever followed by chills, fever, and even nausea and vomiting on a 24 hours good/24 hours bad cycle. If you observe this pattern, seek medical attention immediately. They'll most likely take a blood test and if it tests positive, prescribe you a huge dose of chloroquine. Allow time to recover your strength.

Dengue Fever

Dengue ("bone-breaking") fever may be the only thing worse than malaria. The symptoms may include any or all of the following: sudden high fever, severe headache, muscle and back pain, nausea or vomiting, and a full-bodied skin rash, which may appear 3-4 days after the onset of the fever. Although the initial pain and fever may only last a few days, you may be out of commission for up to several weeks, possibly bedridden, depressed, and too weak to move. There is no vaccine, but dengue's effects can be successfully minimized with plenty of rest, acetaminophen (or Tylenol) for the fever and aches, and as much water and *suero* (salt packet) as you can manage. Dengue itself is undetectable in a blood test, but a low platelet *(plaquetas)* count indicates its presence. If you believe you have dengue, get a blood test as soon as possible to make sure it's not the rare hemorrhagic variety, which can be fatal if untreated.

Chikungunya

This mosquito-induced virus (pronounced "chik-en-gun-ye") is of African origin and has been spreading across the Caribbean since 2013. The same mosquitoes that transmit dengue fever and yellow fever cause Chikungunya. A mosquito that is exposed to a large number of people (in grocery stores, malls, churches, schools, and markets) is more likely to be a carrier of the infection. Its fatality rate is very low, and it's generally gone in a few days. Symptoms include an abrupt onset of fever/chills to 40°C (104°F) lasting 2-10 days; severe joint and tendon pain, usually in

Land Mines

Nicaragua has the ignominious honor of having had more land mines—more than 135,000 in place and another 136,000 stockpiled in the wilds of the northeast—than any other country in the Western Hemisphere. This is one of the most brutal and pernicious legacies of the conflicts of the 1980s, and the focus of a major de-mining cleanup effort by the Nicaraguan Army and the Organization of American States (OAS). In fact, no other country in the world is making a greater effort than Nicaragua to clear the land of mines.

The de-mining process, though ongoing, can largely be considered a success: 75 percent of installed antipersonnel mines have been located and destroyed, and more than 3.8 million square meters of minefield have returned to productive use. During the de-mining process, specially trained troops and dogs trained to sniff out explosives comb the territory. Weapons that are uncovered are detonated on-site. Stockpiles are transferred to and destroyed at one of two special detonating zones.

Currently, OAS troops are searching for and destroying land mines in four areas: outside of Matagalpa and Jinotega, outside of Murra (Nueva Segovia), and the lands around Jalapa (Nueva Segovia). Both Sandinista and Contra troops mined Nueva Segovia heavily, and, in 1998, Hurricane Mitch caused flooding and mudslides that washed many known minefields downstream, burying other sites under a layer of earth. Since 2002, OAS troops have been combing the Honduran border from Las Sabanas (Madriz, just south of Somoto) through Jalapa to Wamblán, Jinotega, a distance of nearly 150 kilometers. The department of Chinandega and the border with Costa Rica have been declared free of mines.

Antipersonnel explosives have crippled nearly 1,000 Nicaraguans and injured countless more (to this day, about 20 people per year). More frequent still are losses of cattle, which go unreported but are the subject of many a *campesino* story. An intensive education campaign aimed at the *campesinos* in the affected areas employs comic books with a story line discussing the danger of land mines and what to do if you suspect you've found one.

As a traveler, you should ask a lot of questions if you leave the beaten trail, particularly in the north: Nueva Segovia, Jinotega, Matagalpa, and Jalapa, as well as eastern parts of Boaco. Loose mines don't lie scattered randomly in the hillsides; they were placed at strategic locations, like radio towers, bridges, airstrips, and known Contra border crossings. The locals are your best sources of information. They'll be able to tell you if there were battles or heavy Contra presence in the area, if there are known minefields, and if the OAS teams have already passed through. In towns like El Cuá and Bocay, you'll find parcels of land in chest-high weeds even though the land on both sides is intensely farmed. Ask around, and look for the yellow Area Minada signs, then move on.

Numerous international organizations work both to clear minefields around the world, such as the UN-sponsored Adopt-a-Minefield program (www.landmines.org), and to ban the devices (www.icbl.org).

the small joints of the hands, wrists, feet, and ankles; headache; muscle pain; joint redness and swelling; nausea and vomiting; abdominal pain; flushed skin, followed by a pink-red rash when the fever breaks; sore throat; and red eyes and sensitivity to light. Diagnosis is confirmed by a blood test. There is currently no vaccine to protect against infection and no treatment. Get through it with plenty of fluids, bed rest, and acetaminophen as needed for pain.

HIV and AIDS

Although to date Nicaragua has been spared a major HIV outbreak, health professionals estimate that geography, cultural, political, and social factors mean an outbreak isn't far off. Exacerbating the spread of AIDS (SIDA in Spanish) is the promiscuous behavior of many married males, an active sex-worker trade, poor use of condoms, and growing drug trouble. AIDS is most prevalent in urban populations, mainly Managua and Chinandega, and is primarily transmitted sexually, rather than through needles or contaminated blood.

Travelers should avoid sexual contact with persons whose HIV status is unknown. If you intend to be sexually active, use a fresh latex condom for every sexual act and every orifice. Condoms are inexpensive and readily available in just about any local pharmacy. In Spanish, a condom is called *condón* or *preservativo.*

Other Diseases

Cholera is present in Nicaragua, with occasional outbreaks, especially in rural areas with contaminated water supplies. Vaccines are not required because they offer incomplete protection. You are better off watching what you put in your mouth. In case you contract cholera (the symptoms are profuse diarrhea the color of rice water accompanied by sharp intestinal cramps, vomiting, and body weakness), see a doctor immediately and drink your *suero* (salt packet). Cholera kills by dehydrating you.

Leptospirosis is caused by a bacteria found in water contaminated with the urine of infected animals. Symptoms include high fever and headache, chills, muscle aches, vomiting, and possibly jaundice. Humans become infected through contact with infected food, water, or soil. It is not known to spread from person to person and can be treated with antibiotics in its early stages.

Hepatitis B also lurks in Nicaragua. Avoid contact with bodily fluids or bodily waste. Get vaccinated if you anticipate close contact with the local population or plan to reside in Nicaragua for an extended period of time.

Most towns in Nicaragua, even rural ones, conduct a yearly **rabies** vaccination campaign for dogs, but you should still be careful. Get a rabies vaccination if you intend to spend a long time in Nicaragua. Should you be bitten, immediately cleanse the wound with lots of soap, and get immediate medical attention.

Tuberculosis is spread by sneezing or coughing, and the infected person may not know he or she is a carrier. If you are planning to spend more than four weeks in Nicaragua (or plan on spending time in a Nicaraguan jail), consider having a tuberculin skin test performed before and after visiting. Tuberculosis is a serious and possibly fatal disease but can be treated with several medications.

BITES AND STINGS
Mosquitoes

Mosquitoes (Nicas refer to them as *zancudos*) are most active during the rainy season (June-Nov.) and in areas near stagnant water. They are much more common in the lower, flatter regions of Nicaragua than they are in mountains, though they can thrive even in the highlands and major urban areas. The mosquito that carries malaria bites during the night and evening hours, and the dengue fever carrier is active during the day, from dawn to dusk.

Ensuring you don't get bitten is the best prophylaxis. Limit the amount of skin you expose. Long sleeves, pants, and socks will do more to prevent bites than the strongest chemical repellent. Mosquitoes are attracted to dark colors, so stick to lighter ones. Choose lodging accommodations with good screens. If this is not possible, use a fan to blow insects away from your body as you sleep. Avoid being outside or unprotected in the hour before sunset, when mosquito activity is heaviest, and use a *mosquitero* (mosquito net) tucked underneath your mattress when you sleep. Hanging-type mosquito nets are available in Nicaragua. Also, many *pulperías* sell *espirales* (mosquito coils), which burn slowly, releasing a mosquito-repelling smoke; they're cheap and convenient, but full of chemicals, so don't breathe in too much smoke.

Spiders, Scorpions, and Snakes

Arachnophobes, beware! The spiders of Nicaragua are dark, hairy, and occasionally capable of devouring small birds. Of note is the *pica-caballo,* a kind of tarantula whose name (meaning horse-biter) refers to the alleged power of its flesh-rotting venom to destroy a horse's hoof. Don't worry, though; spiders do not aggressively seek out people, and do way more good than harm by eating things like Chagas bugs. If you'd rather the spiders didn't share your personal space, shake out your bedclothes before going to sleep and check your shoes before putting your feet in them.

Scorpions *(alacranes)* are common in Nicaragua, especially in dark corners, beaches, and piles of wood. Big and black Nicaraguan scorpions look nasty, but their sting is no more harmful than that of a bee. Your lips and tongue may feel a little numb, but the venom is nothing compared to their smaller, translucent cousins in Mexico. For people who are prone to anaphylactic shock, it can be a more serious or life-threatening experience. In Nicaragua the Spanish word *escorpión* usually refers not to scorpions but to the harmless little geckos (also called *perrozompopos*) that scurry around walls eating small insects. In spite of what your *campesino* friends might insist, those little geckos are neither malevolent nor deadly and would never, as you will often hear, intentionally try to kill you by urinating on you.

There are 15 species of poisonous snakes in Nicaragua, but your chance of seeing one is extremely rare, unless you're going deep into the bush. In that case, walk softly and carry a big machete. Keep an eye out for 1 of 11 pit viper species (family *Viperidae*), especially the infamous fer-de-lance *(Bothrops asper)*, or *Barba amarilla*. The most aggressive and dangerous snake in Central America, the fer-de-lance is mostly confined to the humid central highlands and the Caribbean coast. Less common pit vipers, occasionally seen in western parts of the country, are the Ponzigua *(Porthidium ophryomegas)*; the Central American rattlesnake *(Crotalus durissus)*, known in Spanish as *cascabél;* and a relative of the copperhead, the Cantil, or Castellana, *(Agkistrodon bilineatus)*. In addition, there are four rarely seen species of the *Elapidae* family (three coral snakes and the pelagic sea snake). There are many coral mimics out there with various versions of the famous colored markings. The true coral (only one species of which is found on the west side of the country) has ring markings in only this order: red, yellow, black, yellow.

Chagas' Disease

The Chagas bug *(Trypanosoma cruzi)* is a large, recognizable insect, also called the kissing bug, assassin bug, and conenose. In

Spiders may look scary but generally aren't aggressive.

Spanish it's known as *chinche,* but this word is also used for many other types of beetle-like creatures. The Chagas bug bites its victim (usually on the face, close to the lips) and sucks its fill of blood, then defecates on the newly created wound. In Nicaragua, Chagas bugs are found mostly in poor *campesino* structures of crumbling adobe. The Chagas carries a disease of the same name, which manifests itself in 2 percent of its victims. The first symptoms include swollen glands and a fever that appear 1-2 weeks after the bite. The disease then goes into a 5- to 30-year remission phase. If and when it reappears, Chagas' disease causes the lining of the heart to swell, sometimes resulting in death. There is no cure.

CRIME

Nicaragua is considered one of the safer countries in Central America. Tourism-related crime like petty theft and scam artists (and the occasional robbery and assault) sometimes occur, usually at night and involving alcohol. There have also been some problems with carjacking by criminals posing as police. For the moment, Nicaragua has *mostly* escaped the gang violence that has plagued the cities of Guatemala, El Salvador, and Honduras.

Smugglers, mafiosos, dealers, and crackheads are found along the Atlantic coast, where drug-related crimes threaten local communities, although to a lesser extent in recent years. The Corn Islands have experienced several rapes, and San Juan del Sur experienced an extreme wave of violence in 2008 that included a kidnapping. In 2015, a woman was accosted while walking on an isolated road outside of town. In 2014 a tourist was raped and killed after walking some distance along the beach from the Montelimar resort. The Tipitapa-Masaya highway, formerly a convenient shortcut for going from the airport to Granada while avoiding Managua, is increasingly dangerous at night as it is the scene of fake "police inspections" that end up with foreign tourists being forced to go from ATM to ATM, withdrawing cash.

Before traveling, check official reports, including the U.S. State Department's warnings (www.travel.state.gov) and the travel forums at www.gotonicaragua.com. Managua is the city with the most crime. Big cities, like Estelí and Chinandega, have neighborhoods you should skip as well (ask at your hotel to get the most updated local info). Avoid traveling alone, especially in remote areas including beaches, at night or while intoxicated, and pay the extra dollar or two for a cab. No one should take a cab when the driver has a friend riding up front—complain loudly if he tries—and pay attention to your surroundings and where you are going. You are most at risk of pickpocketing (or hat/watch/bag snatching) in crowds and on public transport. Keep a low profile and leave flashy jewelry, watches, and expensive sunglasses at home. Keep your cash divided up and hidden in a money belt, sock, or your undergarments (take a cue from the many Nica women pulling *córdoba* bills out of their cleavage).

Immediately report crimes to the local police department (dial 118), at a minimum because your insurance company back home will require an official police report before reimbursing you. Nicaraguan police have good intentions but few resources. Don't be surprised if you are asked to help fill up a vehicle with gas. This is annoying but not uncommon, and chipping in for $20 of gas will help get the job done. While police corruption does exist (Nicaraguan police earn very little), the Nicaraguan police force is notably more honest and helpful than in some Central American nations, and has gotten more professional during the Ortega administration.

Illegal Drugs

Nicaragua is part of the underground highway that transports cocaine and heroin from South America to North America and, as such, is under a lot of pressure from the United States to crack down on drug traffickers. Drug-related crime has recently been decreasing on the Atlantic coast, particularly in

Bluefields and Puerto Cabezas. All travelers in Nicaragua are subject to local drug-possession and use laws, which include stiff fines and prison sentences of up to 30 years.

Marijuana thrives in Nicaragua's climate and conditions. It is known locally as *la mota, el monte,* or, in one remote Matagalpa valley, *pim-pirim-pím.* It is officially prohibited despite popular usage, and the current laws allow harsh penalties for possession of even tiny quantities. Canine and bag searches at airports, docks along the Atlantic coast, and at the Honduran and Costa Rican border crossings are the norm. You may be offered pot at some point during your trip, especially on the Atlantic coast and in San Juan del Sur. The proposal may be a harmless invitation, or it may be from a hustler or stool pigeon who is about to rip you off or get you arrested. Use the same common sense you would anywhere in the world.

Prostitution

Though illegal, *puterías* (whorehouses), thinly disguised as "beauty salons" or "massage parlors," operate with virtual impunity. Every strip club in Managua has a bank of rooms behind the stage, some with an actual cashier stationed at the door. Then there are the commercial sex workers on Carretera Masaya, and the nation's numerous auto-hotels, which rent rooms by the hour. The situation is nowhere near as developed as the sex tourism industries of places like Thailand and Costa Rica, but it is undeniable that foreigners have

contributed in no small way to Nicaragua's sex economy. Travelers considering indulging should think seriously about the social impacts that result from perpetuating this institution, and should start by reading the section on AIDS in this chapter.

BEGGING

It is generally assumed that foreigners with the leisure time to travel to Nicaragua are wealthy. Expect poor children and adults to occasionally ask you for spare change, usually by either a single outstretched index finger or a cupped hand, both accompanied with an insistent, *"Chele, deme un peso"* ("Whitey, give me a coin") or *"deme un dolar."* Beggars generally aren't aggressive. Another poignant sight, encountered at sidewalk restaurants, are hungry children watching eagerly as you finish your meal. Your leftovers will not go to waste here. In many cities, including Granada, many children and adolescents asking for money are *huelepegas* (glue sniffers), identified by glazed eyes, unkempt appearances, and sometimes a jar of glue tucked under a dirty shirt. Do not give them money (it will only go to buy them more Resistol), but feel free to give them some attention and a little food. In general, giving money to beggars, especially in tourist centers, perpetuates dependency, bad habits, and children skipping school (sometimes at their parents' request) to ply tourists for money. There are many other ways to direct your good intentions.

Travel Tips

WHAT TO PACK

Everything you bring to Nicaragua should be sturdy and ideally **water-resistant,** especially if you intend to visit the Atlantic coast or Río San Juan, where you'll inevitably find yourself in a boat. Be prepared for rain during the wet season. Choose a **small, strong bag** not so large you'll be uncomfortable carrying

it for long distances or riding with it on your lap in the bus, and secure its zippers with small padlocks. If you're planning to stay in a midrange or upscale hotel for the duration of your trip, your bag is of less concern, but do take a small **daypack** or shoulder bag for your daily walkabouts.

Pick clothes that are **light and**

breathable in the heat. If your plans include Matagalpa, Jinotega, or Estelí, you may appreciate something a bit warmer, like a flannel shirt and warm socks. For sun protection, bring a **shade hat** that covers the back of your neck. Having a neat and clean personal appearance is important to all Latin Americans, and being well groomed will open a lot more doors. In the countryside, Nicaraguan men typically don't wear shorts, unless they are at the beach or at home. **Jeans** travel well, but you will probably find them hot in places like León and Chinandega; **khakis** are lighter and dry faster. Roads are rough, even in cities, so good **walking shoes** will ease your trip considerably. Lightweight hiking boots or sturdy sneakers are sufficient. Take a pair of **shower sandals** with you, or buy a pair of rubber *chinelas* anywhere in Nicaragua for about $2.

Bring a small **first-aid kit,** plastic bags, and Ziplocs for protections from both rain and boat travel, and a cheap set of **ear plugs** for the occasional early-morning rooster or *chichera* band. A lightweight, breathable **raincoat** and/or small **umbrella** are a good idea. A small **flashlight** is indispensable for walking at night on uneven streets, and an **alarm clock** will facilitate catching early-morning buses. If you wear glasses, bring along a little repair kit. Bring a pocket **Spanish dictionary** and **phrasebook.** Photos of home and your family are a great way to connect with your Nica hosts and friends. A simple **compass** is helpful, as directions in this book typically refer to compass directions (finding the hotel 3 blocks north of the park is a lot easier if you know which direction north is).

Make a photocopy of the pages in your passport that have your photo and information. When you get the passport stamped in the airport, it's a good idea to make a photocopy of that page as well after you get situated in your first hotel, and store the copies somewhere other than with your passport. This will facilitate things greatly if your passport gets lost or stolen. Consider taking a copy of your health and medical evacuation insurance policy.

MONEY
Currency

Nicaragua's currency is the *córdoba,* also referred to as a *peso.* It is divided into 100 *centavos* or 10 *reales.* Between wars and the embargo, inflation ran to 30,000 percent in the 1980s. These days the *córdoba* is essentially stable, but to offset inflation, it is being steadily devalued at the rate of approximately US$0.37 every six months. The exchange rate is currently hovering around 26 *córdobas* to 1 dollar, making for simple calculations. Find the actual rates at the Central Bank of Nicaragua's website (www. bcn.gob.ni).

The **U.S. dollar** is also an official currency and the only foreign currency you can hope to exchange (although many communities along the Río San Juan also use Costa Rican *colones*). Exchange your Costa Rican or Honduran currency on the border before entering. While it's easier to travel using *córdobas,* virtually all merchants now take dollars and give you the bank rate (which means you too need to know what the bank rate is, just to be sure) as change. They usually have trouble breaking anything bigger than a $20 bill. Make sure your dollars are good quality; tattered bills may be refused.

ATMs

ATMs (*cajeros automáticos*) litter all major cities and bigger gas stations, though you won't find them outside of the cities. They dispense both *córdoba* (unfortunately, often in the larger, C$500 denominations) and U.S. dollars, and take cards from the Cirrus and Star networks, plus most Visa and MasterCards. You will pay a bank fee for each withdrawal, but it's worth it. You cannot rely on just one card, as some establishments will accept Visa but not MasterCard, or vice versa. Stash photocopies of the front and back of your cards somewhere safe, in case they are stolen, and inform your credit card companies you will be traveling in Nicaragua so they don't block your card when they receive foreign charges.

Traveler's Checks

Traveler's checks are nearly impossible to change in banks and at exceedingly bad rates. Traveler's checks for currencies other than U.S. dollars will not be cashed. You will need to show your passport to cash traveler's checks, and be sure that your signature matches your previous one or you'll convert your precious dollars into a worthless piece of paper. Some banks actually demand to see your original receipts (the ones you are supposed to keep physically separate from the checks!). If you get stuck, every Nicaraguan city has a branch of Western Union, permitting family back home to wire you money, for a steep fee (up to 25 percent).

Bank Hours

Unless noted otherwise in this book, all bank hours are Monday-Friday 8:30am-4:30pm and Saturday 8:30am-noon. Nicaraguans receive their pay on the 15th and 30th or 31st of every month (*días de pago* are the best nights to go out dancing in Managua and beyond). On those days, expect the lines at the bank to be extra long.

Your Travel Budget

Nicaragua remains a budget travel destination, with generally cheaper prices than nearby Costa Rica and Belize. You can comfortably exist in Nicaragua on $50 per day, or half of that by eating the way the locals do and forgoing the jalapeño steak and beer. Those interested in stretching their money to the maximum should eat at *fritangas* (street-side barbecues and fry-fests) and market stalls, take the slow bus, and stay at the simplest *hospedajes*. In Granada, León, and Managua, you can now choose to pay $50-150 for a room, so budget accordingly if you prefer extra comforts (like air-conditioning, security, and cleanliness).

Sales Tax and Tipping

Nicaragua's **sales tax** (referred to as IVA) is 15 percent, the highest in Central America. It is automatically applied to the bill at nicer restaurants, fancy hotels, and upscale shops in major cities and should be clearly indicated on your receipt. Elsewhere, sales tax is casually dismissed. Some restaurants may not bring you a bill at all, preferring to just tell you the price. This saves you paying the tax. If you splurge on a fancy dinner (more than $6-10), expect to pay 25 percent of your bill for tax and tip. Prices in this book usually do not include the IVA. If a hotel does not charge you this tax, they (and you) are breaking the law.

Tipping is not common among Nicaraguans, but it is generally expected in touristy restaurants. In better restaurants, a 10-15 percent *propina* (tip) may be automatically added on to your bill. You are under no obligation to pay it if it is unmerited. Skycaps at the International Airport in Managua will jostle to carry your luggage out to a taxi for about $2. Taxi drivers and bartenders are rarely tipped and don't expect to be unless they are exceptionally friendly or go out of their way for you. If you accept the offer of children trying to carry your bags, find you a hotel, or anything else, you have entered into an unspoken agreement to give them a few *córdobas* (5-20 *córdobas* or $1 or less).

Bargaining

Looking for a good deal is a sport in Nicaragua, and is expected with most outdoor market vendors and taxi drivers. But be warned: Bargaining in Nicaragua is *al suave!* Aggressive, prolonged haggling is not cool, won't affect the price, and may leave ill feelings. Remember these guidelines when bargaining:

- Bargaining is friendly, or at least courteous. Keep your temper under wraps and always smile.

- After you are given the initial price, act surprised and use one of the following phrases: *"¿Cuánto es lo menos?"* ("What is your lowest price?") or *"¿Nada menos?"* ("Nothing less?")

• Go back and forth a maximum of two or three times. Then either agree or walk away. Remember that some Nicaraguans, to save face, may lose a profit.

• Once you make a deal, it's done. If you think you've been ripped off, remember the $2 you got overcharged is still less than you'd pay for a latte back home.

• Bargain hard with taxi drivers in Managua, but agree on a price *before* you enter the cab.

COMMUNICATIONS
Phones and Cell Phones

The national phone company Empresa Nicaragüense de Telecomunicaciones (ENITEL) has been absorbed into telecommunications giant **Claro** (tel. 505/2278-3131, www.claro.com.ni). A 24-hour Claro customer service operator is available by dialing 121. You can purchase phone cards that work in Claro and Publitel pay phones, located in any town bigger than Estelí. Also check in copy shops, Internet providers, and post offices. Many local cybercafes offer VOIP calls; of note is the **Llamadas Heladas** chain, present in at least 29 locations.

In 2009, Nicaragua switched from a 7-digit to an 8-digit phone number system. All land lines earned an additional "2" at the beginning, and all cell phones took on an additional "8." If you see a number with only seven digits, follow this formula.

CELL PHONES

Nicaragua's two networks are **Claro** and **Movistar.** Claro has better coverage nationwide (even in Waspám!) but calls are more expensive. Cheaper Movistar works best in city centers but drops out while you're on the road. Calls between networks are a bit more expensive than calls within networks, hardly enough to worry about, but enough for many Nicas to carry two cell phones.

Getting your own cell phone for travel is easy and inexpensive. You can rent a cell phone from a booth in the airport in the luggage pick-up area (open during daylight business hours only), but it may make more sense to purchase a nearly disposable cell phone *(chiclero)*, available in Claro and Movistar outlets and at most gas stations for around $20. You can also put a local SIM card in your own dual-band cell phone (Nicaragua operates on the 800 and 900 Mhz frequencies). It's easy to get a chip for either of Nicaragua's two competing cell phone networks.

There are little booths all over the nation that offer *"recargas"* of minutes. Many other stores can recharge your phone as well. Just give them your money and your cell number and they'll dial it in; you'll get an SMS within 60 seconds confirming the added time. C$300 is probably enough for a week's worth of travel.

IMPORTANT NUMBERS

• **Information:** 113
• **To place a collect-call within Nicaragua:** 110
• **International operator:** 116
• **Police:** 118
• **Firefighters:** 115 and 120
• **Red Cross:** 128

INTERNATIONAL CALLS

Cybercafes throughout the nation offer Internet calling, and **Llamadas Heladas** specializes in VOIP-based, cheap international calls. Connection quality can be dodgy, but with rates at $6 per hour to call the United States, Canada, or Europe, this is a great way to quickly get in touch back home. You can also call home on skype.com or other broadband services, especially if you have a laptop, since many hotels now offer Wi-Fi in your room.

Internet

Internet cafés exist throughout the nation, and even in smaller towns you'll find several *cybers* (pronounced SEE-bear). Prices start at $1 per hour. Free Wi-Fi connections are spreading quickly across Nicaraguan restaurants, hotels, and cafés. These free networks are often riddled with security threats, so use them to check your email, not your bank account.

Mail

The national postal system, called **Correos de Nicaragua,** is effective and reliable. Every city has at least one post office, often near the central plaza and adjacent to the telephone service. *Correos* are open standard business hours (with some variations), almost always close during lunch, and are open until noon on Saturday.

WEIGHTS AND MEASURES

Nicaragua is in **standard time zone GMT-6.** Daylight saving time is not observed. But no matter what your watch says, you're always on Nica time (everything starts a little late and meeting times are considered approximate).

Nicaragua uses the same **electrical** standards as the United States and Canada: 110V, 60 Hz. The shape of the electrical socket is the same as well. Laptop users should bring a portable surge protector, as the electrical current in Nicaragua is highly variable, and spikes, brownouts, and outages are commonplace.

Distances are almost exclusively in kilometers, although for smaller lengths, you'll occasionally hear feet, inches, yards, and the colonial Spanish *vara* (about a meter). The most commonly used land-area term is the *manzana,* another old measure, equal to 1.74 acres. **Weights** and **volumes** are a mix of metric and non-metric: Buy your gasoline in liters, your beans in pounds, and so on.

TOUR OPERATORS

Nicaragua's range of independent tour companies offer trips from afternoon city tours to week-long expeditions to the farthest reaches of the country, the logistics of which would be nearly impossible for the solo traveler. You can

pay for exclusive personal guides and drivers, or visit Nicaragua as part of a group. Doing so decreases your independence, but provides added security and freedom from making plans. In general, all-inclusive nine-day tours cost $1,000-2,000. Following are the most reliable outfitters we've found:

Explore Nicaragua Tours (U.S. tel. 800/800-1132, www.explorenicaragua.com) has many years of experience leading individual and group tours and staying at top properties; included in your price are a personal cell phone and bottled water.

Green Pathways (tel. 505/8917-8832, www.greenpathways.com) offers customized tours and packages with a sustainable focus with themes like yoga and wellness, surfing, adventure, romance, and golf. They also offer day-trips from the city of León.

Matagalpa Tours (tel. 505/2772-0108 or 505/2647-4680, www.matagalpatours.com) is a guide service, travel agent, and backcountry outfitter run by Dutch expat Arjen. Packages include kayaking and rafting expeditions, Bosawás camping treks, coffee plantation tours, and community tourism. You can also try white-water rafting. Arjen has hiked and camped throughout the Nicaraguan countryside and has even drawn a number of trail maps.

Nicaragua Adventures (tel. 505/8883-7161, www.nica-adventures.com) is a full-service, professional Granada-based outfit with services including tailor-made package tours and private transportation. They can also help book your La Costeña flight within the country.

Solentiname Tours (tel. 505/2270-9981, www.solentinametours.com), with offices in Managua and San Carlos, specializes in bird-watching, nature tours, and the Río San Juan region.

Tierra Tours (www.tierratour.com), with offices in Granada and León, has a long menu of volcano or history tours, countrywide all-inclusive packages, international bus tickets, and domestic flight booking.

Tours Nicaragua (tel. 505/2265-3095,

www.ToursNicaragua.com) offers private, fully guided trips using the best hotels in each locale. Their expert guides include working biologists, national museum archaeologists, and historians. Customize your trip by asking to meet with current political figures, artists, or ex-combatants from both sides of the Contra War.

Vapues Tours (tel. 505/2270-1936, www. vapues.com), with offices around the country, offers a huge range of reasonably priced trips, plus shuttle services between cities. They have some unique community tourism connections and lots of experience with groups and packages.

Alternative Tour Operators and Camping Trips

Read regional chapters for information on local, specialist tour guides and unique trip offerings (León is particularly rich in this department). There are also a few small companies operating across the country:

Eco Camp Expeditions (tel. 505/2311-1828, www.ecocampexpeditions.blogspot.com, geraldpavn@gmail.com), a locally owned and operated agency, specializes in overnight camping trips that take people to often-missed hidden locations. They offer multiday expeditions to volcanoes, beaches, lagoons, and organic farms. Prices are reasonable ($35-80 per day; guide, food, camping gear, and transportation included).

¡Un Buen Viaje! (tel. 505/8959-7097, www. ToursToNicaragua.com), a unique grassroots tour company started by former Peace Corps volunteer Jessica Schugel, gives opportunities to visit homes and communities.

Roadmonkey Adventure Philanthropy (www.roadmonkey.net) expeditions combine physically challenging adventures with sustainable, custom-designed volunteer projects in which travelers work with Nicaraguan communities in need.

Wildland Adventures (tel. 800/345-4453, www.wildland.com) offers family-oriented and experiential trips, with many knowledgeable Nica guides on their staff.

Reality Tours and Learning Delegations

Global Exchange (www.globalexchange. org) offers Reality Tours in Nicaragua. These educational trips explore various social justice issues, including the fair-trade coffee economy, monitoring elections, and learning about labor rights in free trade zones.

Witness for Peace (www.witnessforpeace.org) is a grassroots organization that documents the impact of U.S. policy in Nicaragua and other Latin American countries. Based in Managua, Witness for Peace has maintained a permanent presence in this Central American country since 1983. They offer a range of delegations combining international education with the struggle for peace, economic justice, and sustainable development.

VOLUNTEERING

Nicaragua's poverty and history of social experimentation have long attracted altruistic volunteers. Shortly after 1979, hordes of *"Sandalistas"* poured in from around the world to participate in the Sandinista Revolution. They picked coffee, taught in schools, wrote poetry and editorials of solidarity, put themselves in the line of fire, and protested in front of the U.S. Embassy. Today, *internacionalistas* volunteer with organizations (both faith-based and secular) throughout the country, assisting with construction, education, translation, agriculture, and general solidarity. Check www.volunteerabroad. com for the most updated listing of available assignments, or inquire about opportunities with the following organizations:

Habitat for Humanity (www.habitat.org) is active building homes throughout Nicaragua. **American Jewish World Service** (www.ajws.com) runs the Jewish Volunteer Corps, providing support for professionals looking to volunteer in Nicaragua and other countries. If your social circle wants to participate in a Nicaraguan work trip, **Bridges to Community** (U.S. tel. 914/923-2200, www.bridgestocommunity.

org) will help plan a trip, find a project, and facilitate logistics to connect you with small Nicaraguan communities where your communication, construction, and environmental skills will be put to good use. **Seeds of Learning** (www.seedsoflearning.org) is a group based in El Salvador, Ciudad Dario, Nicaragua, and northern California. They accept groups of 13 or more to volunteer with a community, help construct a school, and share in Nicaraguan culture. Your fee covers living expenses and building materials.

STUDY ABROAD

There are a few possibilities for spending a summer, semester, or extended internship in Nicaragua. Programs range from biological fieldwork at remote research stations to language training and social justice programs. Find additional listings at www.studyabroad.com.

School for International Training (U.S. tel. 802/257-7751, www.sit.edu) has been running a dynamic semester program entitled "Youth Culture, Literacy, and Media" in Managua for years. Ausberg College's **Center for Global Education** (U.S. tel. 612/330-1159, www.augsburg.edu, globaled@augsburg.edu) places students in Guatemala, Costa Rica, and Nicaragua during their semester abroad. On La Isla de Ometepe, near the village of San Ramón, **Estación Biológica de Ometepe** is a biological field station frequented by student groups and researchers from all over the world. At the **Mariposa Eco-Hotel and Spanish School** (www.spanishschool-nica.com), owner Paulette Goudge, PhD, offers a three-month course in the "Politics of Development."

SPANISH LANGUAGE SCHOOLS

Nicaragua has a growing network of independent Spanish schools, and an increasing number of visitors to the country choose to combine their travels with a few days, weeks, or even months of language study. Those listed here stand out for their reputation and experience. Most schools follow the same

basic structure, mixing language instruction with cultural immersion: 2-4 hours of class in the morning, community service activities or field trips in the afternoon, and optional homestays with Nicaraguan families.

There are quality schools across the country. Choosing one is as much a question of your geographical preference as anything else. If possible, it's a good idea to come down and personally look into a few options before making a long-term commitment. Get a feel for the teachers (ask about their experience and credentials), the professionalism of the business, and the lesson plan. Do not trust everything you see on the websites.

Always confirm prices before booking. In general, expect to pay around $150-300 per week, depending on the quality of services offered. This usually includes room, board, instruction, and sometimes tours. Schools in the northern regions are generally cheaper. You can create your own language tour by studying at several schools, using your class schedule and family homestays as a way to travel throughout Nicaragua.

Managua

Viva Spanish School (tel. 505/8877-7179 or 505/2270-2339, www.vivaspanishschool.com, vivaspanish@btinternet.com, $90 for 10 hrs/week, $175 for 20 hrs/week) offers intensive classes to students of all ages and backgrounds, catering mainly to NGO members, embassy employees, and missionary workers. The school is located in the heart of Managua, just a couple of blocks from Plaza Metrocentro. They offer semi-intensive (10 hrs/week) and intensive programs (20 hrs/week). Homestays and other lodging options are available. Advanced and specialized classes are available as well as online classes and home-office classes.

Granada

Granada's status as ground zero for the Nicaragua tourism scene makes it a natural choice for many students who love the city's aesthetic as much as its bar scene. **Casa**

Xalteva (across from the church by the same name, tel. 505/2552-2436, www.casaxalteva. com, $125/week) offers a week package, with a stress on volunteer activities. It's highly recommended by former students, has a quiet location, and is part of a small group home for boys, which is supported by your tuition.

Roger Ramirez's **One-on-One Spanish Tutoring Academy** (on the Calle Calzada, 4 blocks west of the central park, tel. 505/5749-7785, www.spanish1on1.net, $110/week) offers 20 hours of instruction per week, which includes various instructors and five afternoon activities (city tour, salsa lesson, field trips, etc.), plus an end-of-week dinner celebration. Homestays are an additional $130 paid directly to the family. They also offer classes via Skype ($15/hour).

Los Pueblos Blancos and Carazo

Tucked into the forest off the road to the village of San Juan de la Concepción (also known as La Concha, 12 kilometers west of Ticuantepe, under an hour from Managua), **Mariposa Eco-Hotel and Spanish School** (tel. 505/8669-9455, www.spanishschoolnica. com, $400/week) offers language classes in an isolated-feeling setting that is only an hour from Managua or Granada. Enjoy views of Volcán Masaya, horseback riding, hiking trails, and a library. Mariposa's all-inclusive Spanish school packages include homestays or lodging in their eco-hotel.

Laguna de Apoyo

If you prefer to avoid the bustle and nightlife of the city, the **Estación Biológica** (www.gaianicaragua.org, apoyo@gaianicaragua.org, $200/week) is a Spanish school in a purely natural setting. The lakeside lodge is in the crater of an ancient volcano. The spot is incredible, only an hour from Managua, less to Granada, yet still tucked away in its own green world. Lodging and food are excellent (homestays are possible too), and the organization is not-for-profit. One week includes classes, activities, and room and board in

their lodge. Next door, **Peace Project** (www. thepeaceprojectnicaragua.org) offers Spanish classes and volunteer opportunities to travelers in a friendly environment.

San Juan del Sur

Latin American Spanish School (tel. 505/2568-2158, www.nicaspanish.org, spanishschoollss@yahoo.com) is a good option, run by a half dozen entrepreneurial and professional Nicaraguan Spanish instructors with significant experience teaching foreigners. They offer a basic 20-hour instruction and activity package ($125), or $250 a week for lodging with private bath and three meals a day, plus homestay and volunteer activities.

Across from the BDF bank, in the Lago Azul restaurant (right on the beach!), the **San Juan del Sur Spanish School** (tel. 505/8372-4666, www.sjdsspanish.com, sjdsspanish@yahoo.com, $260/week) has all-inclusive packages. The teachers are experienced and friendly. Homestays include private bathroom. They also have opened a sister school in Ometepe.

León

Vapues Tours (tel. 505/2315-4099, www.vapues.com, $195/week) recently began offering an intensive, full-immersion Spanish course: 20 hours of one-on-one class (over five days), includes room and board. There are new schools all the time in León. Check the **Casa de Cultura** class schedule or the bulletin board at the **Vía Vía Hospedaje** for private tutors and lessons. Managua's **Viva Spanish School** (tel. 505/8877-7179 or 505/2270-2339, www.vivaspanishschool.com, vivaspanish@btinternet.com) also offers classes in León.

La Isla Foundation (from Movistar, half a block south, tel. 505/2311-3101, www.laislafoundation.org, laislafoundation@gmail.com) is a nonprofit organization that offers both English classes to local residents and Spanish immersion courses to international travelers and students in León. Beginner, intermediate, and advanced classes plus opportunities for tours and work exchanges are available.

Estelí

You'll find a cool climate and a number of natural excursions available at these schools in Estelí, all of which have been around since the 1990s. **Spanish School Horizonte Nica** (3 blocks form the northwest side of the Red Cross, tel. 505/2713-4117, www.horizospanishschool.com, info_spanishorizonte@yahoo.com, $220/week) has one of the longest track records in town and proffers the lofty vision of "promoting peace and social justice for those living in poverty, those struggling against class, race, and gender prejudices, and those fighting for political freedom." It donates part of your weekly fee to local organizations and has an afternoon activity program that includes visits to local cooperatives and community-development programs. Price includes 20 hours of intensive study, afternoon activities, and homestay. Service projects are sometimes available.

Centro Cultural Juventus (from the southwest corner of the central plaza, 2 blocks west, tel. 505/2713-3756 or 505/8923-6283, walter_delgado_2007@yahoo.com, $100 for 20 hrs/week, $35/week dorm, $60/night private room) is a *tranquilo* little compound with dorm facilities, nice rooms, a shared kitchen, and a breezy café with cappuccino and fruit shakes. Various language professors are on hand to tailor your Spanish curriculum. The private rooms are lovely and modern.

Spanish School Nicaragua (www.spanishnicaragua.com, $210/week) offers afternoon activities, including trips to local Estelí attractions. Price includes class and homestay.

Matagalpa

This is a remarkable mountain city in which to spend a few weeks, attending **Spanish School Colibrí** (tel. 505/2772-0108, www.colibrispanishschool.com, $278-397/week), which is run collectively by a group of eight local women. Price includes instruction and homestay. As it shares its building with Matagalpa Tours, you'll have immediate access to a range of day trips and backcountry hiking expeditions in the surrounding mountains. The school is conveniently located next door to one of the country's most *suave* cafés, El Artesano.

TRAVELING WITH CHILDREN

Nicaraguans love children, and traveling with children can open doors and form new connections. That said, your children will have to endure the same lack of creature comforts, change in diet, and long bumpy bus rides you do. Disposable diapers are expensive but readily available in supermarkets, as are powdered milk/formula, pacifiers *(pacificadores* or *chupetas)*, and bottles *(pachas)*. Ask your doctor and consult the CDC about malaria prophylaxis for your child. Perhaps the most important thing to pack is strong sun protection and disinfectant hand soap or foam. Travel with a stroller is half useful and half annoying, as Nicaragua's sandy and cobbled streets frequently require bigger-wheeled strollers that are hard to pack and carry around. Make sure your rental car company can provide a car seat for you, or you will be required to bring one (highly recommended, considering the danger of Nicaraguan road travel).

WOMEN TRAVELERS

In Nicaragua, as in most of Latin America (and many parts of the U.S.), women are "admired" through street harassment by males of all ages and walks of life. Walking down the street, women can expect to hear a chorus of catcalls *("piropos")* and whistles, often accompanied with an *"Adiossss, amor."* Generally speaking, these guys don't see this act as violent, and will not do more than hurl "compliments" in various stages of rudeness. It is rare (though not unheard of) that someone will approach you or accost you physically. That said, you define your own personal space. If someone makes you feel uncomfortable, tell them loudly to back off. (Some helpful phrases include, *grosero,* meaning "rude," *desgraciado,* meaning "jerk," and ¡qué *barbaridad!* "What stupidity!") Since most women ignore these commentators, it *will* be a surprise. The

Nicaraguan feminist movement has done much work focused on ending *piropos*. If you feel safe, a witty retort won't go amiss. If you'd rather avoid dealing with it altogether, walking with a man seems to lessen the amount of unwanted attention.

Physical harassment, assault, and rape are less common in Nicaragua than elsewhere in Central America, but they do occur, sometimes to travelers. Be careful about walking around alone in isolated places (including beaches), especially at night. For more, download a copy of "Her Own Way: Advice for the Woman Traveller" at the Canadian Consular Affairs website (www.voyage.gc.ca). Find good advice and tips at www.journeywoman.com.

Tampons can be difficult to find, as most Nicaraguan women use pads *(toallas sanitarias)* due to custom and social stigma. Most pharmacies and *pulperías* carry pads, usually called "Kotex," regardless of the actual brand name. Try the supermarket if you're in a pinch, but you won't often find more than one or two brands available.

GAY AND LESBIAN TRAVELERS

As of March 2008, consensual gay sex is no longer a criminal act in Nicaragua, though the Catholic Church still forbids it and homophobia is rampant throughout Latin America. Even so, Nica society is generally tolerant of homosexuality. The gay or lesbian traveler should not feel threatened in Nicaragua provided they maintain a modicum of discretion and choose their situations wisely. Managua and Granada have a few openly gay clubs and gay-friendly hotels. Elsewhere same-sex couples may find local gay communities that will help orient them to tolerant clubs and bars.

ACCESS FOR TRAVELERS WITH DISABILITIES

Travelers with disabilities should contact **Accessible Nicaragua** (www.craiggrimes.com, craig@craiggrimes.com,) before coming. Founder Craig Grimes, a disabled

traveler himself, is somewhat of the authority on the matter. Wheelchair-bound travelers to Nicaragua have reported that the two most important things to consider bringing are toilet seat extenders and suction cups, and note that Nicaraguans will quite helpfully offer to help you up and down curbs as necessary. Nicaragua's *descapacitados* (disabled) get around with much difficulty because of ruined sidewalks, dirt roads, aggressive crowds, and open manholes. While Nicaraguans agree people with disabilities have equal rights, no attempt is made to accommodate them, and the foreign traveler with limited mobility will certainly struggle, but will no doubt find ways to get by.

RACE

While plenty of Nicaraguans will tell you there is no racism here, minority groups often report discrimination. A few years ago, when the dark-skinned daughter of a diplomat was refused entry to a popular Managua nightclub for wearing her hair in braids, the issue received national news coverage. This treatment of the black community continues. Businesses reserve the right to refuse admission to potential customers, and racial profiling and mistreatment by police and immigration officials is not unheard of. Hold businesses accountable for poor or hostile customer service by using consumer-reviewed travel websites or other social networking tools.

Travelers of color often experience having their nationality questioned, North American or European being synonymous with white for many Nicaraguans. Black travelers who've been mistaken for Nicas have reported being addressed as maids, drug dealers, or prostitutes. Hip-hop-loving folks who don't understand the connotations of the N-word in U.S. culture may use it freely with blacks they identify as North American.

As in many Latin American countries, Nicaraguans label others by their physical characteristics: height, weight, race, and gender identity, among other things. You may be called *gordo/a* ("fat"), *negro/a* ("black"), or *chele/a* ("white") without any offense intended. People of Asian descent might be referred to as *chino* or *chinita* ("Chinese"). There's not a lot of social consciousness about racism. If you're up to it, starting conversations is a great way to practice your Spanish.

Tourist Information

The **Instituto Nicaragüense de Turismo** (INTUR, 1 block west and 1 block north of the Crowne Plaza Hotel, tel. 505/2254-5191, www.intur.gob.ni, Mon.-Fri. 8:30am-5pm) has a sometimes-useful kiosk in the airport arrival area (just before you claim your baggage). Most regional offices can help arrange tours with local operators. Also visit their tourist-directed site (www.visitnicaragua. us). One helpful online resource is www.vianica.com. **Anda Ya!** (www.andayanicaragua.com) is a free Spanish language booklet packed with helpful contacts and listings in Granada, San Juan del Sur, León, Managua, and Estelí.

MAPS

The longtime champion map of Nicaragua is published by **International Travel Map** (ITM, www.itmb.com), scaled at 1:750,000, colored to show relief, and with good road and river detail. It's found in many bookstores and travel shops, but not in Nicaragua. A new favorite is produced by German cartographers **Mapas NaTurismo** (www.mapas-naturismo.com, salsa_klaus@yahoo.de). Their water resistant 1:500,000 country map features detailed tourist attractions and natural reserves better than any other. It also has a few

handy inserts, including Isla de Ometepe at 1:200,000. Samples are available on their site. They go for about $7 at www.omnimap.com or www.gotrekkers.com. The **Nelles Central America** map (1:1,750,000) offers a quality overview of the region (plus more detail on Costa Rica) and is good if you are traveling the whole area and don't intend to venture too far off the beaten track.

INETER, the Nicaraguan Institute of Territorial Studies, produces the only complete series of 1:50,000 maps (or topo quads) of Nicaragua, now available online. These are the most detailed topographical maps of Nicaragua that exist. They can be purchased from the **INETER office** (across from Hospital Solidaridad in Managua tel. 505/2249-3890, www.ineter.gob.ni, Mon.-Fri. 8am-4:30pm, $3/map) in Managua (and occasionally at regional offices).

Tactical Pilotage Charts (TPC K-25B and TPC K-25C) cover northern and southern Nicaragua, respectively, at 1:500,000 scale. Designed for pilots, these maps have good representation of topography and are useful if you do any adventuring in the eastern parts of the country (far easier than carrying a stack of topo maps). Many smaller towns are shown but only with their major roads.

Resources

Glossary

alcaldía: mayor's office
arroyo: stream or gully
artesanía: crafts
ayudante: "helper" —the guy on the bus who collects your fee after you find a seat
barrio: neighborhood
beneficio: coffee mill
bombero: firefighter
bravo: rough, strong, wild
cabo: cape
cafetín: light-food eatery
calle: street
cama matrimonial: "marriage bed" -- motels and hotels use this term to refer to a double, queen, or king-size bed; a bed meant for two people.
camión: truck
campesino: country folk
campo: countryside
carretera: highway, road
cayo: cay
centro de salud: public MINSA-run health clinic; there is one in most towns
centro recreativo: public recreation center
cerro: hill or mountain
cerveza, cervecita: beer
chele, chela: gringo, whitey
chinelas: rubber flip-flops
ciudad: city
colectivo: a shared taxi or passenger boat
colonia: neighborhood
comedor: cheap lunch counter
comida corriente: plate of the day
complejo: complex (of buildings)
cooperativa: cooperative
cordillera: mountain range

córdoba: Nicaraguan currency
corriente: standard, base
coyote: illegal-immigrant smuggler; or profit-cutting middleman
cuajada: white, homemade, salty cheese
departamentos: subsection of Nicaragua, akin to states or counties
empalme: intersection of two roads
entrada: entrance
estero: estuary or marsh
expreso: express bus
farmacia: pharmacy, drugstore
fiestas patronales: Saint's Day parties held annually in every town and city
fresco: natural fruit drink
fritanga: street-side barbecue and fry-fest
gallo pinto: national mix of rice 'n beans
gancho: gap in a fence
gaseosa: carbonated beverage
gringo: North American, or any foreigner
guaro: booze
guitarra: guitar
guitarrón: mariachi bass guitar
hospedaje: hostel, budget hotel
iglesia: church
isla: island
laguna: lake
lancha: small passenger boat
lanchero: *lancha* driver
malecón: waterfront
manzana: besides an apple, this is also a measure of land equal to 100 square *varas*, or 1.74 acres
mar: sea or ocean
mariachi: Mexican country/polka music
mercado: market

mesa/meseta: geographical plateau
mosquitero: mosquito net
muelle: dock, wharf
museo: museum
ordinario: local bus (also *ruteado*)
panga: small passenger boat
panguero: *panga* driver
pinche: stingy, cheap
playa: beach
pueblo: small town or village
pulpería: corner store
puro: cigar
quintal: 100-pound sack
rancheras: Mexican drinking songs
rancho: thatch-roofed restaurant or hut
rato: a short period of time
reserva: reserve or preserve
río: river
sala: living room
salida: exit, road out of town
salon: large living room, gallery
salto: waterfall
sierra: mountain range
suave: soft, easy, quiet
tope: a dead-end, or T intersection
tranquilo: mellow
urbano: public urban bus
vara: colonial unit of distance equal to roughly one meter
volcán: volcano

ABBREVIATIONS
ENEL: Empresa Nicaragüense de Electricidad (electric company)

ENITEL: Empresa Nicaragüense de Telecomunicaciónes (telephone company)
FSLN: Frente Sandinista de Liberación Nacional (Sandinista party)
IFA: (EEH-fa) East German troop transport, used commonly in Nicaraguan public transportation system; it probably stands for something in German, but in Nicaragua, it means *imposible frenar a tiempo* (impossible to brake on time).
INETER: Instituto Nicaragüense de Estudios Territoriales (government geography/geology institute)
MARENA: Ministerio del Ambiente y los Recursos Naturales (Ministry of Natural Resources and the Environment), administers Nicaragua's protected areas
MYA: Million Years Ago
NGO: Nongovernmental Organization
PCV: Peace Corps Volunteer
PLC: Partido Liberal Constitucionalista, the conservative anti-Sandinista party
SINAP: Sistema Nacional de Areas Protegidas (National System of Protected Areas)
UCA: Universidad de Centroamerica
UN: United Nations
UNAN: Universidad Nacional Autónoma de Nicaragua
USAID: United States Agency for International Development, channels congressionally approved foreign aid

Spanish Phrasebook

PRONUNCIATION GUIDE
Spanish pronunciation is much more regular than that of English, but there are still occasional variations.

Consonants
c as "c" in "cat," before "a," "o," or "u"; like "s" before "e" or "i"

d as "d" in "dog," except between vowels, then like "th" in "that"
g before "e" or "i," like the "ch" in Scottish "loch"; elsewhere like "g" in "get"
h always silent
j like the English "h" in "hotel," but stronger
ll like the "y" in "yellow"
ñ like the "ni" in "onion"

r always pronounced as strong "r"
rr trilled "r"
v similar to the "b" in "boy" (not as English "v")
y similar to English, but with a slight "j" sound. When standing alone, it's pronounced like the "e" in "me."
Z like "s" in "same"
b, f, k, l, m, n, p, q, s, t, w, x as in English

Vowels

a as in "father," but shorter
e as in "hen"
I as in "machine"
o as in "phone"
u usually as in "rule"; when it follows a "q," the "u" is silent; when it follows an "h" or "g," it's pronounced like "w," except when it comes between "g" and "e" or "i," when it's also silent (unless it has an umlaut, when it is again pronounced as English "w")

Stress

Native English speakers frequently make errors of pronunciation by ignoring stress. All Spanish vowels a, e, i, o, and u carry accents that determine which syllable of a word gets emphasis. Often, stress seems unnatural to nonnative speakers. The surname Chávez, for instance, is stressed on the first syllable but failure to observe this rule may mean that native speakers may not understand you.

USEFUL WORDS AND PHRASES

Nicaraguans and other Spanish-speaking people consider formalities important. Whenever approaching anyone for information or some other reason, do not forget the appropriate salutation good morning, good evening, etc. Standing alone, the greeting *hola* (hello) can sound brusque.

Hello. *Hola.*
Good morning. *Buenos días.*
Good afternoon. *Buenas tardes.*
Good evening. *Buenas noches.*

How are you? *¿Cómo está?*
Fine. *Muy bien.*
And you? *¿Y usted?*
Awesome! *De acachimba!*
So-so. *Más o menos.*
Thank you. *Gracias.*
Thank you very much. *Muchas gracias.*
You're very kind. *Muy amable.*
You're welcome. *De nada ("It's nothing").*
yes *sí*
no *no*
I don't know. *No sé.*
It's fine; okay *Está bien.*
Good; okay *Bueno.*
please *por favor*
Pleased to meet you. *Mucho gusto.*
Excuse me (physical) *Perdóneme.*
Excuse me (speech) *Discúlpeme.*
I'm sorry. *Lo siento.*
Goodbye. *Adiós.*
See you later. *Hasta luego ("Until later").*
more *más*
less *menos*
better *mejor*
much, a lot *mucho*
a shot of strong liquor *un cachimvaso*
very drunk *hasta el culo*
a little *un poco*
large *grande*
small *pequeño, chico*
quick, fast *rápido*
slowly *despacio*
bad *malo*
difficult *difícil*
easy *fácil*
He/She/It is gone; as in "She left" or "he's gone." *Ya se fue.*
I don't speak Spanish well. *No hablo bien el español.*
I don't understand. *No entiendo ni papas.*
How do you say...in Spanish? *¿Cómo se dice...en español?*
Do you understand English? *¿Entiende el inglés?*
Is English spoken here? (Does anyone here speak English?) *¿Se habla inglés aquí?*

TERMS OF ADDRESS

When in doubt, use the formal *usted* (you) as a form of address. If you wish to dispense with formality and feel that the desire is mutual, you can say, *"Me puedes tutear"* ("You can call me 'tu'").

I *yo*
you (formal) *usted*
you (familiar) *vos*
you (familiar) *tú*
he/him *él*
she/her *ella*
we/us *nosotros*
you (plural) *ustedes*
they/them (all males or mixed gender) *ellos*
they/them (all females) *ellas*
Mr., sir *Señor or Don*
Mrs., madam *Señora or Doña*
Miss, young lady *Señorita*
wife *esposa*
husband *marido or esposo*
friend *amigo (male), amiga (female)*
sweetheart *novio (male), novia (female)*
son, daughter *hijo, hija*
brother, sister *hermano, hermana*
father, mother *padre, madre*
grandfather, grandmother *abuelo, abuela*

GETTING AROUND

Where is...? *¿Dónde está...?*
How far is it to...? *¿A cuanto está...?*
from...to... *de...a...*
highway *la carretera*
road *el camino*
street *la calle*
block *l a cuadra*
kilometer *kilómetro*
north *norte*
south *sur*
west *oeste; poniente*
east *este; oriente*
straight ahead *al derecho; adelante*
to the right *a la derecha*
to the left *a la izquierda*

ACCOMMODATIONS

Is there a room? *¿Hay cuarto?*
May I (we) see it? *¿Puedo (podemos) verlo?*
What is the rate? *¿Cuál es el precio?*
Is that your best rate? *¿Es su mejor precio?*
Is there something cheaper? *¿Hay algo más económico?*
single room *un sencillo*
double room *un doble*
room for a couple *matrimonial*
key *llave*
with private bath *con baño*
with shared bath *con baño general; con baño compartido*
hot water *agua caliente*
cold water *agua fría*
shower *ducha*
electric shower *ducha eléctrica*
towel *toalla*
soap *jabón*
toilet paper *papel higiénico*
air-conditioning *aire acondicionado*
fan *abanico; ventilador*
blanket *frazada; manta*
sheets *sábanas*

PUBLIC TRANSPORT

bus stop *la parada*
bus termina *l terminal de buses*
airport *el aeropuerto*
launch *lancha; tiburonera*
dock *muelle*
I want a ticket to... *Quiero un pasaje a...*
I want to get off at... *Quiero bajar en...*
Here, please. *Aquí, por favor.*
Where is this bus going? *¿Adónde va este autobús?*
round-trip *ida y vuelta*
What do I owe? *¿Cuánto le debo?*

FOOD

menu *la carta, el menú*
glass *taza*
fork *tenedor*
knife *cuchillo*
spoon *cuchara*
napkin *servilleta*
soft drink *agua fresca*

coffee *café*
cream *crema*
tea *té*
sugar *azúcar*
drinking water *agua pura, agua potable*
bottled carbonated water *agua mineral con gas*
bottled uncarbonated water *agua sin gas*
beer *cerveza*
wine *vino*
milk *leche*
juice *jugo*
eggs *huevos*
bread *pan*
watermelon *sandía*
banana *banano*
plantain *plátano*
apple *manzana*
orange *naranja*
meat (without) *carne (sin)*
beef *carne de res*
chicken *pollo; gallina*
fish *pescado*
shellfish *mariscos*
shrimp *camarones*
fried *frito*
roasted *asado*
barbecued *a la parrilla*
breakfast *desayuno*
lunch *almuerzo*
dinner (often eaten in late afternoon) *comida*
dinner, or a late-night snack *cena*
the check, or bill *la cuenta*

MAKING PURCHASES

I need... *Necesito...*
I want... *Deseo... or Quiero...*
I would like...(more polite) *Quisiera...*
How much does it cost? *¿Cuánto cuesta?*
What's the exchange rate? *¿Cuál es el tipo de cambio?*
May I see...? *¿Puedo ver...?*
This one *ésta/ésto*
expensive *caro*
cheap *barato*
cheaper *más barato*

too much *demasiado*

HEALTH

Help me please. *Ayúdeme por favor.*
I am ill *Estoy enfermo.*
pain *dolor*
fever *fiebre*
stomachache *dolor de estómago*
vomiting *vomitar*
diarrhea *diarrea or curutaca*
drugstore *farmacia*
medicine *medicina*
pill, tablet *pastilla*
birth-control pills *pastillas anticonceptivas*
condom *condón; preservativo*

NUMBERS

0 *cero*
1 *uno (masculine)*
1 *una (feminine)*
2 *dos*
3 *tres*
4 *cuatro*
5 *cinco*
6 *seis*
7 *siete*
8 *ocho*
9 *nueve*
10 *diez*
11 *once*
12 *doce*
13 *trece*
14 *catorce*
15 *quince*
16 *dieciseis*
17 *diecisiete*
18 *dieciocho*
19 *diecinueve*
20 *veinte*
21 *veintiuno*
30 *treinta*
40 *cuarenta*
50 *cincuenta*
60 *sesenta*
70 *setenta*
80 *ochenta*
90 *noventa*
100 *cien*

101 *ciento y uno*
200 *doscientos*
1,000 *mil*
10,000 *diez mil*
1,000,000 *un millón*

TIME

While Nicaraguans mostly use the 12-hour clock, in some instances, usually associated with plane or bus schedules, they may use the 24-hour military clock. Under the 24-hour clock, for example, *las nueve de la noche* (9pm) would be *las 21 horas* (2100 hours).

What time is it? *¿Qué hora es?*
It's one o'clock *Es la una.*
It's two o'clock *Son las dos.*
At two o'clock *A las dos.*
It's ten to three *Son las tres menos diez.*
It's ten past three *Son las tres y diez.*
It's three fifteen *Son las tres y cuarto.*
It's two forty-five *Son las tres menos cuarto.*
It's two thirty *Son las dos y media.*
It's six in the morning *Son las seis de la mañana.*

It's six in the evening *Son las seis de la tarde.*
It's ten in the evening *Son las diez de la noche.*
today *hoy*
tomorrow *mañana*
morning *la mañana*
tomorrow morning *mañana por la mañana*
yesterday *ayer*
week *la semana*
month *mes*
year *año*
last night *anoche*
the next day *el día siguiente*

DAYS OF THE WEEK

Sunday *domingo*
Monday *lunes*
Tuesday *martes*
Wednesday *miércoles*
Thursday *jueves*
Friday *viernes*
Saturday *sábado*

Suggested Reading and Viewing

FICTION AND POETRY

Belli, Gioconda and March, Kathleen (Translator). *The Inhabited Woman*. Madison, WI: The University of Wisconsin Press, 2004. A sheltered young woman is inhabited by the spirit of an indigenous woman warrior who propels her to join a revolutionary movement against a violent dictator.

Morelli, Marco, ed. *Rubén's Orphans*. New Hyde Park, NY: Painted Rooster Press, 2001. An anthology of contemporary Nicaraguan poets, with English translations.

Sirias, Silvio. *Bernardo and the Virgin*. Chicago, IL: Northwestern University Press, 2005. *Bernardo*'s real-life texture and ingenious use of voices and characters portrays

a thick slice of Nicaragua's past and present while recounting the true story of the Virgin Mary's appearances to a *campesino* in Cuapa.

Sirias, Silvio. *Meet Me Under the Ceiba*. Houston, TX: Arte Publico Press, 2009. Sirias's second novel is also set in small-town Nicaragua and continues the vibrant cultural portrait he began in *Bernardo*. It is based on a 1998 hate-crime murder in La Curva and addresses many issues, including homophobia and gay rights in Latin America.

NONFICTION

Babb, Florence. *After Revolution: Mapping Gender and Cultural Politics in Neoliberal Nicaragua*. Austin, TX: University of Texas

Press, 2001. Professor of Anthropology and Women's Studies at the University of Iowa, Babb has published scores of academic papers on Nicaragua, mainly on issues of gender and sexuality.

Barrios de Chamorro, Violeta. *Dreams of the Heart.* New York, NY: Simon & Schuster, 1996. A very human history of Nicaragua from the Somoza years through Doña Violeta's electoral triumph in 1990.

Belli, Gioconda. *The Country Under My Skin: A Memoir of Love and War.* New York, NY: Anchor Books, 2003. This phenomenal book provides a close-up look at various stages of *la lucha* (the struggle), written by one of the country's premier living poets.

Cabezas, Omar. *Fire from the Mountain (La Montaña es Algo Más que una Grán Estapa Verde).* Phoenix, AZ: Crown, 1985. A ribald, vernacular account of what it's like to be a guerrilla soldier in the mountains of Nicaragua. This is one of the few books about the early stages of the Revolution.

Cardenal, Ernesto; Walsh, Donald D. (translator). *The Gospel in Solentiname.* Maryknoll, NY: Orbis Books, 1979. Transcripts of the masses given by Cardenal on Solentiname that helped spawn the *Misa Campesina* and liberation theology movements.

Chomsky, Noam. *Turning the Tide: U.S. Intervention in Central America and the Struggle for Peace.* Cambridge, MA: South End Press, 1985. Succinctly and powerfully shows how U.S. Central American policies implement broader U.S. economic, military, and social aims, with Nicaragua and El Salvador as examples.

Dando-Collins, Stephen. *Tycoon's War: How Cornelius Vanderbilt Invaded a Country to Overthrow America's Most Famous Military Adventurer.* Philadelphia, PA: Da Capo Press, 2008. This account of one

of Nicaragua's most fascinating historical periods (the mid-19th century) is painstakingly researched and told in an exciting narrative. Dando-Collins weaves the stories of Vanderbilt and William Walker with a striking degree of detail.

Dickey, Christopher. *With the Contras.* New York, NY: Simon & Schuster, 1985. Dickey was the *Washington Post* correspondent in Honduras and gives an exciting account of his experience with the secret Contra army.

Hobson Herlihy, Laura. *The Mermaid and the Lobster Diver: Gender, Sexuality, and Money on the Miskito Coast.* Albuquerque, NM: University of New Mexico Press, 2012. Hobson discusses the lucrative and life-threatening profession of many Miskito men on the Caribbean coast, and the "mermaid sickness" (decompression sickness) they claim befalls those who take too many lobsters. These men must also confront what the Miskito call the "sexual magic" of human women on land. Interspersed with short stories, songs, and incantations, she demonstrates the archetypes of femininity and masculinity within Miskito society, highlighting the power associated with women's sexuality.

Kinzer, Stephen. *Blood of Brothers: Life and War in Nicaragua.* New York, NY: G. P. Putnam's Sons, 1991. Kinzer, the *New York Times* Managua bureau chief during the war, sensed that Nicaragua was "a country with more to tell the world than it had been able to articulate, a country with a message both political and spiritual."

Lancaster, Roger N. *Life Is Hard: Machismo, Danger, and the Intimacy of Power in Nicaragua.* Berkeley, CA: University of California Press, 1992. This ethnography addresses the effect of current events on the Nicaraguan individual and family. It is intimate and offers details about Nicaraguan life that one can only get living with the people.

Lancaster pays attention to often-neglected issues like homosexuality, domestic violence, broken families, and the roots of machismo.

Marriot, Edward. *Savage Shore: Life and Death with Nicaragua's Last Shark Hunters.* New York, NY: Owl Books, 2001. A curious and descriptive journey up the Río San Juan and beyond.

Pastor, Robert. *Not Condemned To Repetition: The United States and Nicaragua.* Boulder, CO: Westview Press, 2002. Robert Pastor was a U.S. policymaker in the period leading up to and following the Sandinista Revolution of 1979. A decade later, he organized the International Mission led by Jimmy Carter that mediated the first free election in Nicaragua's history. This updated edition covers the events of the democratic transition of the 1990s and extracts lessons to be learned from the past.

Randall, Margaret. *Risking a Somersault in the Air: Conversations with Nicaraguan Writers.* San Francisco, CA: Solidarity Publications, 1984. A fascinating series of interviews with Nicaraguan authors and poets, most of whom were part of the FSLN revolution and government.

Randall, Margaret. *Sandino's Daughters: Testimonies of Nicaraguan Women in Struggle.* Point Roberts, WA: New Star Books, 1981. Explores the role of feminism in the Sandinista Revolution, via a series of interviews with participants.

Rushdie, Salman. *The Jaguar Smile.* New York, NY: Viking, 1987. Representing the pro-Sandinista Nicaragua Solidarity Campaign in London, Rushdie takes readers on a poetic, passionate jaunt through Nicaragua as part of a government cultural campaign. He offers a careful (if short) examination of their policies.

Volz, Eric. *Gringo Nightmare: A Young American Framed for Murder in Nicaragua.* New York, NY: St. Martin's Press, 2010. It is definitely every traveler's worst nightmare to end up in a filthy foreign prison, but Volz's case goes way beyond his cramped cell, and it is also much greater than the volatile social conditions in San Juan del Sur that helped lead to his arrest. This is a harrowing tale by any account.

Walker, Thomas W. and Wade, Christine J. *Nicaragua: Living in the Shadow of the Eagle.* Boulder, CO: Westview, 2011. Documents how the historical and ongoing interventions by the United States—the "eagle" to the north—continue to shape Nicaraguan political, economic, and cultural life.

Zimmerman, Matilde. *Sandinista: Carlos Fonseca and the Nicaraguan Revolution.* Durham, NC: Duke University Press, 2001. This is the first English-language biography of the legendary leader of the FSLN and arguably the most important and influential figure of the post-1959 revolutionary generation in Latin America.

PHOTOGRAPHY

Dix, Paul and Fitzpatrick, Pamela. *Nicaragua: Surviving the Legacy of U.S. Policy.* Just Sharing Press, 2011. Photographer Paul Dix worked in Nicaragua with Witness for Peace during the Contra War documenting the impact of U.S. foreign policy on the citizens of Nicaragua. In 2002 he returned with his co-author to find 100 individuals photographed by Dix in the 1980s. It is an impressive visual comparison of Nicaragua then and now as told through the testimonies of 30 people they were able to find (in English and Spanish).

LANGUAGE

Rabella, Joaquim and Pallais, C. *Vocabulario Popular Nicaragüense.* Managua: Hispamer, 2004. A wonderful dictionary celebrating

Nicaraguan Spanish, complete with regional usages, sayings, and a plethora of profanities. It is available (hopefully) in the UCA bookstores in Managua.

FILMS

Carla's Song, a 1996 drama by Ken Loach, stars Robert Carlyle and Oyanka Cabezas. Set in 1987, Scottish bus driver George meets Carla, a Nicaraguan exile living a precarious, profoundly sad life in Glasgow. George takes her back to her village in northern Nicaragua to find out what has happened to her family, boyfriend, and country. Notable for its real and gritty location shots in both Scotland and Nicaragua.

My Village, My Lobster (www.thelobsterfilm. com) is a documentary about the perils of lobster diving on Nicaragua's Caribbean coast.

Walker, a bold 1987 anachronistic biography of the infamous soldier-of-fortune from Tennessee, starring Ed Harris. Filmmaker Alex Cox wanted to show that "nothing had changed in the 140-odd years between William Walker's genocidal campaign and that of Oliver North and his goons." Critics mostly panned the film but confirmed Nicaphiles will surely get a kick out of the familiar scenery.

The World Stopped Watching, a 2003 Canadian film by Peter Raymont and Harold Crooks, was shot in 56 mm film. Nicaragua dropped from the spotlight after the end of the Contra War. This documentary, shot in late 2002 and early 2003, picks up the pieces of what happened next. Essentially, this is a sequel to *The World is Watching*, a critically acclaimed documentary from the 1980s, involving many of the same characters.

Internet Resources

NICARAGUA PORTALS

Go to Nicaragua
www.GoToNicaragua.com
Chat with fellow Nica travelers and expats, ask travel questions, post travelogues, read the latest Nicaragua headlines, and check for updates.

The Latin American Network
www.lanic.utexas.edu/la/ca/nicaragua
The Latin American Network Information Center boasts a ton of Nica-sites, including many academic links.

The Nicaragua Network
www.nicanet.org
For more than 25 years, The Nicaragua Network, a coalition of U.S.-based nonprofits (many of them regional sister city organizations), has been committed to social and economic justice for the people of Nicaragua.

The Nicaragua Dispatch
www.nicaraguadispatch.com
The only English-language newspaper in Nicaragua produced by Tim Rogers, a U.S. journalist with 14 years experience reporting from Central America.

OFFICIAL

U.S. Embassy
nicaragua.usembassy.gov
The U.S. embassy page in Nicaragua.

U.S. State Department
www.travel.state.gov
U.S. State Department fact sheet for travelers, including security overviews.

Government of Canada
www.voyage.gc.ca
The Canadian fact sheet for travelers,

including security overviews. The Canadian government has never really been politically involved in Nicaragua, so its travel warnings provide a good reality check for what you read at the U.S. State Department's site.

TRAVEL AND TOURISM

Hecho Magazine
www.hechomagazine.com
Culture and arts magazine in Managua with current event listings in Spanish.

INTUR
www.intur.gob.ni
Nicaraguan government tourism agency.

Nicaragua Guide
www.nicaragua-guide.com
A thorough, diverse traveler portal run by expats living in Granada.

MARENA
www.marena.gob.ni
The Nicaraguan Natural Resources Ministry provides information on visiting specific parks and reserves.

ViaNica.com
www.vianica.com
An independent and informative overview of travel destinations throughout Nicaragua. They even maintain updated Nicaragua bus schedules!

Nicaraguan Institute of Travel
http://visitnicaragua.us/
Nicaraguan government tourism agency and its English-language promotion site.

Xolo
www.xolo.com.ni
A Spanish-language Nica-run portal focusing on the arts, plus links to many recommended hotels and restaurants.

Index

List of Maps

Photo Credits

Acknowledgments

This book came together with the help of many, many people. Cyndi Malasky, Marcelo Gutiérrez, Brooke Denmark, and Carlos Barrera were all instrumental in their contributions of research, photographs, and general Nica knowledge. Beyond that, their friendship and support were invaluable to me. Thanks to José Davíd Barrera for his limitless support of my work on this book as well as his excellent photography skills. Thank you Flor Velásquez and Daniel Hochbaum for your beautiful photos. I'd also like to thank Josh Berman for supporting my research on the 6th edition. I wish I had the space thank all of the individuals who helped me in every region of the country. You know who you are, and I'm grateful to each of you. I'll be forever appreciative that I had the opportunity to come to Central America to work with Witness for Peace in 2012. Thanks to all the wonderful friends and colleagues I've made over the past years who have taught me about Nicaragua. I hope I did justice to this country I've come to love.

Also Available

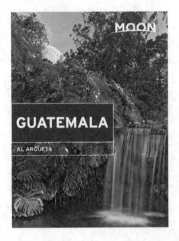

MAP SYMBOLS

≡≡≡	Expressway	○	City/Town	✈	Airport	⛳	Golf Course
═══	Primary Road	◉	State Capital	✈	Airfield	🅿	Parking Area
───	Secondary Road	⊛	National Capital	▲	Mountain	⛩	Archaeological Site
─ ─ ─	Unpaved Road	★	Point of Interest	✛	Unique Natural Feature	⛪	Church
───	Feature Trail	•	Accommodation		Waterfall	⛽	Gas Station
- - -	Other Trail	▼	Restaurant/Bar		Park		Glacier
⋯⋯	Ferry	■	Other Location	🚩	Trailhead		Mangrove
═══	Pedestrian Walkway						Reef
▪▪▪	Stairs	▲	Campground		Skiing Area		Swamp

CONVERSION TABLES

$^{\circ}C = (^{\circ}F - 32) / 1.8$

$^{\circ}F = (^{\circ}C \times 1.8) + 32$

1 inch = 2.54 centimeters (cm)
1 foot = 0.304 meters (m)
1 yard = 0.914 meters
1 mile = 1.6093 kilometers (km)
1 km = 0.6214 miles
1 fathom = 1.8288 m
1 chain = 20.1168 m
1 furlong = 201.168 m
1 acre = 0.4047 hectares
1 sq km = 100 hectares
1 sq mile = 2.59 square km
1 ounce = 28.35 grams
1 pound = 0.4536 kilograms
1 short ton = 0.90718 metric ton
1 short ton = 2,000 pounds
1 long ton = 1.016 metric tons
1 long ton = 2,240 pounds
1 metric ton = 1,000 kilograms
1 quart = 0.94635 liters
1 US gallon = 3.7854 liters
1 Imperial gallon = 4.5459 liters
1 nautical mile = 1.852 km

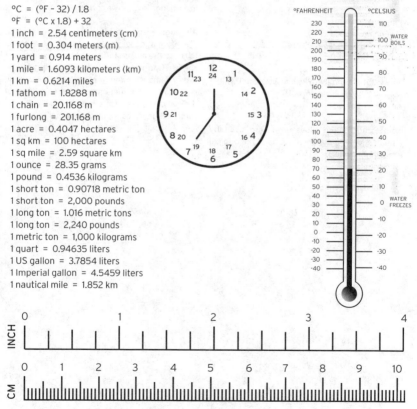

MOON NICARAGUA
Avalon Travel
a member of the Perseus Books Group
1700 Fourth Street
Berkeley, CA 94710, USA
www.moon.com

Editor: Nikki Ioakimedes
Series Manager: Kathryn Ettinger
Copy Editor: Naomi Adler Dancis
Graphics and Production Coordinator:
  Lucie Ericksen
Cover Design: Faceout Studios, Charles Brock
Moon Logo: Tim McGrath
Map Editor: Kat Bennett
Cartographer: Brian Shotwell
Indexer: Greg Jewett

ISBN-13: 978-1-61238-863-2
ISSN: 1539-1019

Printing History
1st Edition — 2003
6th Edition — December 2015
5 4 3 2 1

Text © 2015 by Elizabeth Perkins & Avalon Travel.
Maps © 2015 by Avalon Travel.
All rights reserved.

Some photos and illustrations are used by
  permission and are the property of the original
  copyright owners.

Front cover photo: Iglesia de la Recoleccion, León ©
  Rob Francis/robertharding.com
Back cover photo: The Cascada Blanca waterfall near
  the city of Matagalpa © Nicolas De Corte/123RF

Printed in Canada by Friesens.